THE BOOK COVER:
An image of star-core-zeus from the database of NASA's space-telescope Wide-field Infrared Survey Explorer (WISE)

THE AUTHOR, Dr. Rupert D. Holms, has a PhD in molecular biology from the University of Edinburgh. His thesis was focused on gene-editing by site-directed-mutagenesis. Later he invented a new peptide pharmaceutical technology for the modulation of cell signaling, immune enhancement, and tissue regeneration. The novel technology was developed in Russia into a pharmaceutical product called Gepon, which has been successfully used in the treatment of various infections and ulcers of the gut. Dr. Holms also studied astronomy at University College London (part-time) during his research for this book. Dr. Holms is the founder and chairman of Nearmedic Group, a leading pharmaceutical company in Russia. He lives in London, Moscow, and Cyprus.

Star Core Zeus

Star Core Zeus

THE EVIDENCE FOR OUR BINARY STAR SYSTEM

● ● ●

Part Two of the Star-Core Trilogy

Rupert D. Holms
Primrose Hill, London

"How often have I said to you?
When you have eliminated the impossible,
Whatever remains, however improbable,
Must be the truth?"

—Sherlock Holmes
Baker Street, London

Illustrations
Rupert Holms

ISBN-13: 9781545579961
ISBN-10: 1545579962

Contents

Preface

● ● ●

LONG AGO THE ANCIENT GREEKS used the name "Zeus" for their most powerful sky-god. It is a very old tradition that can be traced back thousands of years to archaic Indian and Aryan sky-watchers. When Zeus crossed the high heavens, he controlled all the planets. Zeus set the positions of the horizons and stars, he made the day, the night, and the year. He made the moon, the mountains, and the seas, and sometimes he brought fire and flood to Earth. Zeus was the origin of everything.

The first book of the Star-Core Trilogy, *Cataclysms & Renewals*, revealed the myths of Zeus and related sky-gods, which were echoes of a common tradition around the world that there was another powerful but hidden object in our solar-system. *Cataclysms & Renewals* presented a detailed analysis of ancient astro-mythology and archeo-astronomy, demonstrating that there must be a cold massive star-core orbiting with our solar-system: star-core-zeus.

The Sun and star-core-zeus are the components of a binary-star-system. In contrast to the eight planets, star-core-zeus travels in a very-eccentric and steeply-inclined orbit. It flies away from the solar-system in the direction of Sirius, traveling five hundred times the distance of Earth from the Sun. Star-core-zeus then falls back toward the center of gravity of our binary system and loops around the Sun.

Star-core-zeus and the Sun orbit their common center of gravity, every four thousand years. As star-core-zeus commences another orbit, it flies-by our Earth, and its powerful gravity induces tidal forces that violently disturb our planet. Star-core-zeus re-orientates our planet in space, modifies its orbital radius, and changes its orbital eccentricity. It also routinely displaces the rotation axis of Earth and its geographic poles.

The orbiting star-core and the wobbly Earth are the cause of a regular cycle of natural climate changes. Climate history research has confirmed that there have been distinct climatic-ages, not only over the millions and millions of years of geological time but in cycles of change on the scale of hundreds of thousands and tens of thousands and thousands of years. These changes to Earth's climate have been induced by star-core-zeus, which regularly relocates the climatic-belts of our planet, causing the distinct ages of the world.

Star-core-zeus has been perturbing and sculpting our planet since it was formed. Its irresistible gravity has been regularly raising and lowering sea-levels to drown or expose land. On rare occasions star-core-zeus came so close to Earth that it pulled up whole mountain ranges and opened great gashes across our planet, which we now call rift-valleys and ocean-trenches.

On one terrible occasion, the force applied by star-core-zeus was so great that it ripped-off fifty percent of the crust of the Earth and simultaneously gouged out the ocean basins. Pangaea, the remains of the old planetary surface of Earth, was shattered into huge fragments, which we now call the continents.

During this terrible disaster, land was crumpled, mountain ranges were pulled up from the plains, the atmosphere was poisoned, volcanoes spewed lava, and hot liquid basalt flooded from deep fractures. The awesome catastrophe exterminated almost everything alive on Earth at the time. The cataclysmic event was called the Great Permian Extinction, and it marked the end of the Paleozoic geological era.

The archaic "super-continent" Pangaea was not a continent at all; it was the cracked hemispherical remains of the original surface, half of the Earth's old crust. We still teach that continental-drift is caused by the slow continuous motion of plate-tectonics: this book shows that it was the tidal forces of star-core-zeus that periodically lifted and dragged the continents across the surface of the Earth.

This book *Star Core Zeus* also explores the enigmas of our solar-system and our mysterious Moon. By the autumn of 2013, all lunar formation models had been refuted by new data. The Royal Society in London called a special meeting to answer a simple question: "How was our moon formed?"

The answer is "with the help of star-core-zeus." About two-hundred-and-fifty million years ago, star-core-zeus almost collided with us. As it flew past our planet at only four-hundred-thousand kilometers, it was traveling at very high velocity. Its irresistible gravity ripped the moon out of mother-earth, and it was during this violent caesarean birth that Pangaea was shattered.

There are a number of puzzles about our planetary system, which have become deeper with the recent discoveries of exo-planetary systems orbiting other stars. New explanations described in this book *Star Core Zeus* regarding the anomalies of Venus, Neptune, and The Kuiper Belt lead us to star-core-zeus. Some peculiar motions of our solar-system shall be described, which are a warning that we are already feeling the force of star-core-zeus.

This book *Star Core Zeus* details a new hypothesis about how the Sun and planets came into being. The Sun's former companion star was a large magnetic star of about ten solar-masses, and its matter was the origin of the planets. Four-point-six billion years ago, it exploded in an ultra-violent supernova explosion. When it blew-up, the companion star was about the same distance from the Sun as Venus. Although this local supernova explosion disrupted our former close-binary star-system, star-core-zeus remained in orbit. We are still located in the center of its great blast bubble, which is now many thousands of light-years across.

The planets were formed from the supernova explosion debris of the obliterated companion star. Vast nickel-iron fragments from the shattered core of this large star attracted other matter and started the rapid accretion of the planets. The rapidity of planet formation has been revealed by the discovery in meteorites and interplanetary dust of the decayed remains of very short-lived radioactive isotopes.[1]

When the hot magnetic star-core was first exposed, it was very hot and radiated UV-light. However, it was enveloped in vast clouds of debris blown-off from the dead companion star, which were rich in carbon, oxygen, nitrogen, and hydrogen. The supernova explosion not only made all the chemical elements and isotopes that formed Earth and the other planets; it was responsible for extra-terrestrial chemistry and molecular biology.

The radiation from the young star-core included great jets of circular-polarized UV-light that emerged from its magnetized rotation poles. This energy beam catalyzed polymer chemistry in the cloud of supernova debris. It specifically enhanced the synthesis of left-handed amino-acid polymers and other macromolecules, which became the pre-fabricated starting-material of supernova-life on Earth. This new theory of the origin of life is described in Appendix A and Appendix B of this book.

The massive star-core is coming: it is already on its way back to the Sun. Astronomers are currently hunting for the great perturber of the Kuiper-Belt objects at the outer edge of our solar-system, but they do not yet understand its real nature. The precise details of the location and flight path of this massive object are described in this book *Star Core Zeus*.

Astro-mythology described in my previous book *Cataclysms & Renewals* warned of global-warming and climate-change, a few centuries before the arrival of star-core-zeus. It is not only Earth that is suffering global-warming; Mars and Neptune and its moon Triton are also experiencing climate-change, due to the influence of star-core-zeus on the whole solar-system.

Recently, a wide range of new technologies have become available both on Earth and on satellites, which are capable of detecting star-core-zeus. Their data will be accessible online, so watch out for the arrival of star-core-zeus on the virtual telescope sites on the Internet and be the first to make a confirmed observation.

All these concepts and ideas, and the relevant evidence from the climate sciences, geology, astronomy and biology, shall be discussed in the following chapters of this book *Star Core Zeus*.

CHAPTER 1

The Four-Thousand-Year Cataclysm Cycle

● ● ●

Introduction

IN MY PREVIOUS BOOK *CATACLYSMS & Renewals*, which investigated ancient astro-mythology, I arrived at the hypothesis that our solar-system is part of a binary-star-system with the remains of a former companion star of the Sun, which blew up in a supernova explosion four-point-six billion years ago.[2]

This cold massive star-core still orbits the Sun every four thousand years in a very eccentric and highly inclined orbit. Soon after its perihelion, the star-core dives down through the ecliptic plane close to the orbit of Earth, and powerful tidal forces shake our planet.[3] A prediction from this hypothesis is that star-core-zeus has caused cataclysms and climate-changes every four thousand years.

Over the previous fifty years, a huge quantity of climate-history data has been accumulated, mainly as a result of increased research funding due to fears that global-warming is being caused by man-made carbon-dioxide pollution.[4] However, when the ancient ice-cores from the deep-drilling of the ice-caps around the world were analyzed, scientists were very surprised by the results.[5, 6, 7] Rather than the expected very slow natural climate changes, followed by sudden global-warming caused by industrial gases, the ice-core data from the Arctic and the Antarctic showed that the weather has been fluctuating wildly for hundreds-of-thousands of years.

Over the previous million years, our climate "crashed" repeatedly. The rip-saw-tooth pattern in the graphs of the climate history data provides compelling evidence that a periodic catastrophic process has been at work. It is quite obvious that there is a natural cycle of abrupt and cataclysmic climate-change, but its cause is an enigma.

THE CLIMATE CHANGE RIP-SAW

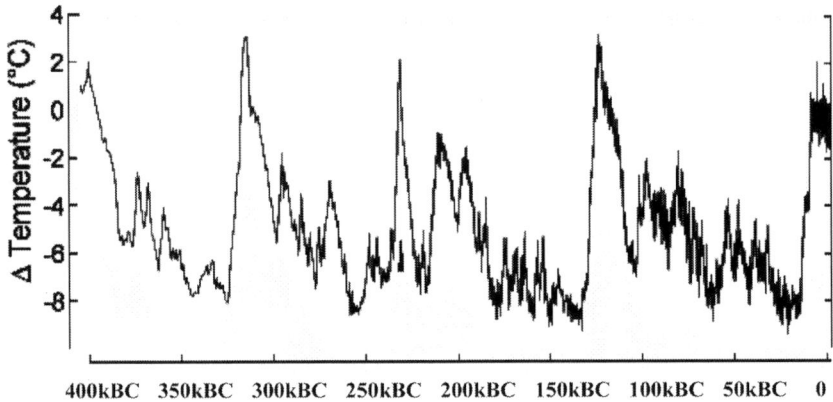

Temperature-change in degrees Celsius, versus BC-AD time-scale (k=1000s), derived from deuterium content of the ice, versus depth/band-count in the Vostok Ice Core. Data Source: Petit, J. R., et al., "Climate and atmospheric history of the past 420,000 years from the Vostok ice core, Antarctica." *Nature* 399 (1999): 429-436.

Our culture is obsessed with industrial carbon-dioxide contamination of the atmosphere. It is supposed to be causing global warming of about one degree per century.[8] However, the cause-and-effect relationship is actually backward: ocean-warming leads to increases in carbon-dioxide concentrations in our atmosphere.

In addition, the original hypothesis that atmospheric-warming is due to an enhanced greenhouse-effect caused by a high atmospheric-carbon-dioxide-concentration was based on a misunderstanding about the process that heats the planet Venus. Recent data from space probes to Venus has shown that the idea of a runaway-greenhouse-effect is wrong. The truth is that our real influence on the climate is tiny, in comparison to the power of the natural cataclysmic weather-cycles that affect our planet.

High-altitude near-polar drill-sites in Greenland and Antarctica have yielded nearly three kilometer-deep cores of ancient ice, containing an archive recording ancient climates up to eight-hundred-thousand years old. This data, combined with drill-cores into ocean-floors and lake-beds around the world, has shown that something suddenly heats the atmosphere and forces violent changes in the weather on a regular basis.

Oxygen-isotope data revealed a complex series of alternating peaks and troughs of warm and cold atmospheric temperatures. Extreme variability in all parameters, including isotopes, atmospheric gases, and dust, were recorded in ice-cores from the Arctic and the Antarctic.[9, 10, 11]

Mountain glaciers, ocean-floor cores, and lake-bottom cores told the same story of a sequence of cataclysms that had triggered extraordinary climate fluctuations and complex cycles of global climate change.[12, 13, 14, 15, 16]

According to the Committee on Abrupt Climate Change, National Research Council, the climate record for the past one-hundred-thousand years clearly indicates that the climate system has undergone periodic and often extreme shifts, sometimes in less than a decade. The trigger of abrupt climate change has not been established.[17]

Climate Cycles within Climate Cycles

Ice-cores revealed a remarkable series of climate cycles within climate cycles.[18, 19] In addition, the cores revealed a distinct series of global climate-cataclysms, stretching far back into the mists of time. The typical rip-saw-tooth patterns in the graphs of the climate history data recorded an abrupt change followed by a slow recovery, providing compelling evidence that a periodic catastrophic process was at work. The ice-core data and other sources showed that these cataclysms had happened very quickly, probably in only a few days.[20, 21, 22, 23]

There is an obvious one-hundred-and-twenty thousand year cycle that corresponds to a cycle of extremely cold poles. These extremely cold conditions were interrupted by warmer periods about forty thousand years long, similar to the present global climate. In addition, our weather-systems also wobble on a millennial scale.[24, 25, 26] The oscillations appeared to be due to external forcing, but the cause of this cycle of global warming, cataclysm, and the sudden climate reversal remained an enigma.[27, 28]

Carbon-dioxide Did Not Cause Global Warming

The most startling discovery was that the heating of the atmosphere over the last half million years was certainly not triggered by high atmospheric carbon-dioxide levels. Increases in carbon-dioxide concentrations in the atmosphere *lagged behind* the heating of the oceans.

Data on oxygen-isotope-ratios and carbon-dioxide concentrations in the Vostok ice-core from Antarctica clearly showed a series of cataclysms that led to ocean and atmospheric heating, then subsequent increases in atmospheric carbon-dioxide concentrations, with a delay of about ten years.[29, 30, 31, 32]

The explanation for this observation was simple. Carbon-dioxide is less soluble in warmer water, so when the oceans warmed up, more carbon-dioxide escaped into the atmosphere. It was the heating of the oceans that caused more carbon-dioxide in the atmosphere, not the other way around.[33, 34]

Some of the increase in atmospheric carbon-dioxide could be attributed to the disruption of the Earth's crust during each cataclysm. Abrupt increases in sea-floor volcanic-activity occurred during each cataclysm, which contributed to subsequent abrupt increases of atmospheric carbon-dioxide.[35]

The simple conclusion was that the periodic changes in ocean temperature every four-thousand, forty-thousand, and one-hundred-and-twenty thousand years had caused the subsequent fluctuations in the atmospheric carbon-dioxide levels. It was obvious from all this data that increases in the concentration of atmospheric carbon-dioxide was not the cause of this cycle of global-warming and catastrophe.

Insolation (the Intensity of Sunlight) and Global-Warming

The variation in the intensity of sunlight at the surface of the Earth (known as insolation) has had important effects on the history of Earth's climate.[36, 37, 38, 39] However, for many years climate scientists tried to prove that the significant changes of insolation that had been detected were due to a combination of slow regular changes in Earth's orbital eccentricity, the slow precession of Earth's rotation axis, and slow changes in the tilt-angle of Earth's rotation axis.[40, 41, 42, 43]

In order to squeeze the climate data into this astronomical theory, an invalid assumption was made that there was a regular one-hundred-thousand year-long glacial cycle.[44] This is not true: the actual data shows the previous two cold-cycles were one hundred-*and-twenty*-thousand years long.[45]

The big problem with this astronomical cycle theory was that it predicted very slow natural climate changes, not the abrupt changes recorded in the data, which were totally out of proportion and out of phase with the small theoretical effects of precession and changing axial tilt of the Earth.

In contrast, variation in the radiation output of the Sun has had profound effects on insolation and the climate of Earth. Solar energy is generated by proton-fusion in the core of the Sun, but most of the energy remains trapped. The slow release of electro-magnetic energy from the core is controlled by magnetism.[46] The internal magnetic fields regulate the amount of hot plasma that reaches the surface by convection and the radiation output of the Sun.[47]

Although the surface of the Sun radiates at six thousand degrees, the corona above the Sun's surface is heated by magnetism up to one million degrees Kelvin. The total heat output of the Sun is influenced by a poorly understood coupling between the solar-magnetic-field and the interplanetary-magnetic-field.[48]

Later in this book, we shall learn how fly-bys of star-core-zeus through the inner solar-system, not only varied the heat output of the Sun but also altered the average orbital radius of the Earth, and the combination of these factors caused profound global climate change.

Cumulative Errors in Dating Climate Change Events

Cumulative errors in ice-core dating methods prevent exact measurement of the periodicity of recurring cataclysmic events and obscure the fundamental millennial-scale harmonic-period of the cataclysm-cycle. The depth of an ice-sample, or the layer-count of ice below the surface, is only a rough estimate of age.[49, 50, 51, 52] The ice-thickness-per-year also varies along the ice-cores, according to average climate conditions in the year the snow fell and the depth of the ice that formed from this snow.

The accuracy of ice-core dating decreases by roughly one percent for every thousand years from the present, so cumulative errors generate a scatter of dates between different studies for the same abrupt climate-change events.[53, 54] However, fixing the exact dates for the catastrophic events has been achieved by carbon-14 dating of organic material in drill-cores from ocean-floors and lake-bottom sediments or samples from glacial moraines.[55, 56]

Carbon-14 is generated by a continuous bombardment of high-energy particles from space, which hit the atoms of the upper atmosphere. This results in the secondary-emission of high-energy-neutrons, which collide with nitrogen atoms and convert them to carbon-14. The newly formed carbon-14 isotope then reacts with oxygen to form carbon-14-monoxide and then carbon-14-dioxide. However, almost all the carbon-dioxide of the atmosphere is made of carbon-12.

Generally, living plants and the animals that eat them contain a similar ratio of carbon-14 to carbon-12 as the atmosphere, but only while they are alive. After death, the carbon-14 in the organic remains radioactively decays with a half-life of about six thousand years. The changing ratio of carbon-14 to carbon-12 in organic remains provides an estimate of how many years have elapsed since the material was alive.

The carbon-14 dating method has been used to obtain the ages of samples up to about fifty-thousand years old. However, to obtain accurate results, the carbon-14 isotope dating has to be calibrated by dendrochronology, using tree-ring samples from ancient timbers, whose ages have been established. Standard samples of ancient wood are assayed to provide standard carbon-14 to carbon-12 ratios for various ages.

However, the actual production rate of carbon-14 in the upper atmosphere has fluctuated, giving rise to carbon-14 anomalies.[57, 58, 59] Carbon-14 production-rates shows significant changes four thousand, eight thousand, and twelve thousand years ago.[60, 61, 62]

The Fundamental Four-Thousand-Year Climate Cycle

To overcome the problem of ice-core dating errors, the average periodicity of the fundamental climate cycle was estimated using a simple graphical meta-analysis of sequences of recent abrupt climate events, which are described in different studies.[63, 64, 65, 66, 67, 68, 69, 70, 71]

An example of this type of analysis shows the frequency of abrupt climate events, which converges on approximately four thousand years. In addition, in 2004 members of the North GRIP team analyzed twenty-five temperature spikes in the ice-core oxygen-isotope records from Greenland, which correlated to a series of recurring global climate cataclysms.[72] During the hundred-thousand year period, between 110,000 BC and 10,000 BC, there had been twenty-five such cataclysms, an average of one every four thousand years.

Isotope and Chemical Cataclysm Markers

The nitrogen-15 isotope provided the clearest signal in ice-cores for a four-thousand-year cataclysm cycle. The ice-cores revealed that nitrogen-15 abundance peaked during the previous four climate catastrophes in 13,600 BC, 9600 BC, 5600 BC, and 1628 BC.[73, 74]

The mystery was the origin of this sudden increase in the atmospheric concentration of the nitrogen-15 isotope: the isotope is usually produced in a supernova explosion of a large star, in high energy nuclear impacts between nitrogen-14 and either hydrogen or helium.[75]

Titanium is another marker for the four-thousand-year periodicity. It too is usually produced in the core of large stars, prior to a supernova. Two cores from Lake Malawi showed that Africa had a heavy fallout of titanium-rich dust in significant concentration-spikes that corresponded to the cataclysms of 9600 BC, 5600 BC, and 1600 BC.[76] High concentrations of the same titanium dust were also detected in the ice-cores from

^{15}N-ASSOCIATED 4000 YEAR CLIMATE CYCLE

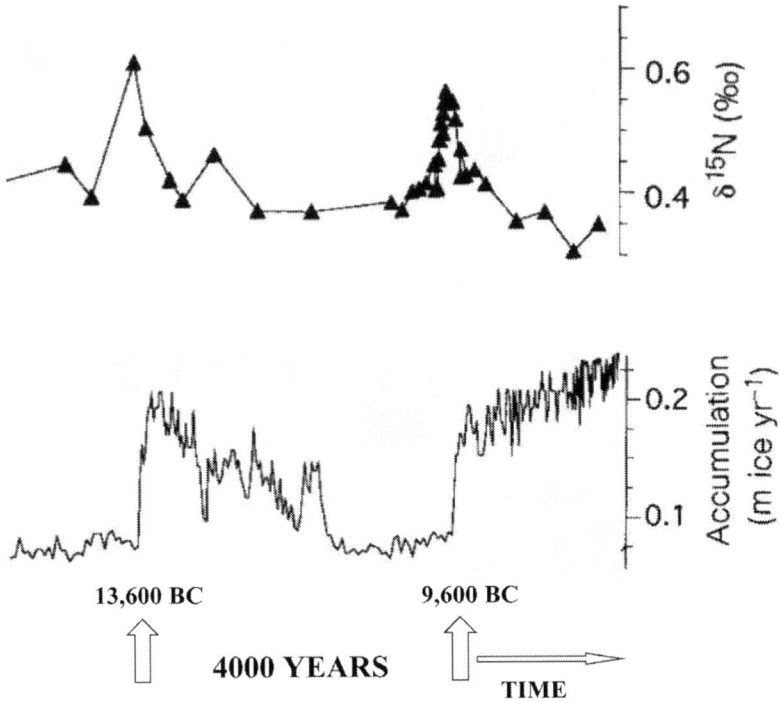

Ice accumulation in metres per year correlates to global atmospheric temperature and the abrupt climate changes are marked by ^{15}N spikes.

Date source: Severinghaus, J.P., et al ., "Timing of abrupt climate change at the end of the Younger Dryas interval from thermally fractionated gases in polar ice" *Nature* 391 (1998): 142 figure 2

Mount Kilimanjaro.[77] The Caribbean sediment core from the Cariaco basin, off the coast of Venezuela, had dark bands rich in titanium, which corresponded to cataclysmic conditions.[78]

Iridium and helium-3 also occurred in concentrated bands in the ice-cores corresponding to the time of disaster, with notable peaks twelve thousand, eight thousand, and four thousand years ago.[79, 80] The analysis of cosmic dust in Antarctic ice showed peaks three-times, background of helium-3 marking three of the five recent climate crashes.[81]

Nitrogen-15, titanium, iridium, and helium-3 are all common in supernova explosion debris. This evidence links the climate cataclysms to an extra-terrestrial perpetrator.

Supporting evidence came from a forensic investigation of the Clovis massacre at Gainey, Michigan, United States, which occurred during the 9600 BC cataclysm. In the destruction-horizon that contained charcoal and charred bones, a sharp peak of radioactivity was discovered, which was twenty times the level of background-radiation.

There was also a smaller radioactive peak (twice-background) in another horizon in the upper layers of the Clovis sites. The second signal corresponded to a destructive event about eight thousand years ago, presumably in 5600 BC. The radioactivity at the Clovis sites also correlated with unusual concentrations of alien uranium and thorium isotopes.[82]

The sampling also revealed the radioactivity was associated with two layers that had high concentrations of magnetic grains. There was a dense peak of magnetic grains corresponding to the Clovis destruction level twelve thousand years ago, and there was another concentration of magnetic grains about half the density, corresponding to a cataclysm about four thousand years later.

The Detailed Profile of Climate Cataclysm

Each climate cataclysm commenced with sudden and rapid atmospheric heating, which caused a sudden jump in global temperatures: an abrupt increase between ten and twenty degrees Celsius. Climate cataclysm was also characterized by a brief fall-out of ash, followed by colder sea and air temperatures over the following hundred years.[83, 84] Each cataclysm was followed by freezing conditions, which evolved into a period of slow recovery. Within the last few hundred thousand years, whole environments have been repeatedly reconfigured by these cataclysms.

The cataclysmic upheavals became known as *Dansgaard/Oescher* events, or "D-O" events.[85, 86] Despite the obvious pattern of cataclysmic D-O events in different studies, there have been serious problems in measuring the exact dates to determine frequencies and correlations.[87] In the previous twenty-thousand years since the last-glacial-maximum (known as the LGM), the climate was punctuated by four severe D-O events, each separated by a stable period of approximately four thousand years.

Ancient-pollen-analysis provided information on the paleo-botany and the weather of Europe in the Late Pleistocene epoch. Every four thousand years, a stable climate was punctuated by a hiatus, followed by a period of intense cold, and marked by a general dying of plants, with the exception of hardy frost-adapted species.

The dates of mass extinctions of large mammals also correspond to the dates of each D-O. For example, the D-O of 9600 BC, better known as the "End-Ice-Age" event, was a particularly violent catastrophe, which caused the well-known Late Pleistocene megafauna extinctions. Mammoths, mastodons, and, at least, thirty other species of large land mammals were totally wiped-out in North America and Eurasia.[88]

Thousands of miles to the south, a similar repeating pattern was recorded in sediment-cores from the lake-beds in Africa: environmental cataclysms were recorded every four thousand years.[89] They commenced with a two to three century period of atmospheric warming and drought, which resulted in up to eighty-meter drops in the lake-levels, which heralded the coming of an apocalypse.

A lake-sediment study in the *Ziway-Shalla* basin in southern Ethiopia showed a series of major climate upheavals in Africa around 13,600 BC, 9600 BC, 5600 BC, and around 1600 BC, which correlated with the ice-core D-O events.[90]

These abrupt heating events also coincided with a sharp spike-up in atmospheric-dust concentrations every four thousand years, as revealed by the dust-bands in the ice-cores recovered from the southern ice field of Mount Kilimanjaro, East Africa. This study showed that at the terminations of a few centuries of global warming and drought, there were sudden heating events and massive atmospheric dust storms. These catastrophes also occurred around 13,600 BC, 9600 BC, 5600 BC, and 1628 BC. The dust spike in 1628 BC was particularly intense and towered above background dust levels.[91]

Radiation and Forest Fires Every Four Thousand Years
In the ice-cores, concentrated bands of ammonium-ions, nitrate-ions, and nitrous-oxide occurred together, which corresponded to cataclysms around 13,600 BC, 9600 BC, 5600 BC, and 1600 BC.

The high concentrations of ammonium-ions were identified to be the result of the incineration of forests on a global scale. One study revealed a sharp ammonium-ion inferno-peak of twenty-eight parts-per-billion that occurred four-thousand years ago; another sharp ammonium inferno peak of twenty-five parts-per-billion that occurred eight thousand years ago; and a huge ammonium spike of sixty-three parts-per-billion, corresponding to forests ablaze all over the world, that occurred at the end of the Pleistocene, twelve thousand years ago.[92, 93]

Ash bands from these global fires were also found in North-Atlantic sediment cores.[94] The notable concentration peaks of nitrate-ions and nitrous-oxide in the ice-cores had been produced by chemical reactions of atmospheric nitrogen with oxygen, activated by high energy radiation of unknown origin.[95]

Cycles of Death and Decay
The relative abundance of plant pollen versus fungal-spores has been used as a technique to determine the ratio of growing plants to death and decay, during particular climate events. Strata-sequences from excavation trenches at Clovis occupation sites in North America, from the end of the Pleistocene, revealed three concentration peaks of fungal-spores, around four thousand years apart. There were high concentrations of spores roughly around 13,600 BC, a large peak around 9600 BC (corresponding to the Clovis destruction layer), and a peak one-tenth of the size in a later strata that probably corresponded to the 5600 BC event.[96]

A Glacier Re-advance Cycle of Four Thousand Years.
In the extreme cold that occurred immediately after each cataclysm, glaciers re-advanced down mountain-valleys pushing the debris of the disasters in front of them. This material formed heaped embankments known as push-moraines, at the position of the maximum advance of the

snout of a glacier. When the weather warmed up again, the moraines were left behind by the melting ice.

When research teams investigated the material in these moraines, they discovered ancient pollens and other remains of different types of plants, which had been trashed and burnt. The samples were carbon-14 dated, and a series of dates for the maximum re-advances of glaciers across South America showed a four-thousand-year periodicity.

It was discovered that the glaciers had repeatedly retreated and then re-advanced at the same time, down the southern hemisphere mountain valleys in both Chile and New Zealand, every four thousand years. A series of these moraines recorded that cataclysms had occurred in the Late Pleistocene around 33,000 BC, 28,000 BC, 25,000 BC, 21,000 BC, 17,600 BC, 13,600 BC, and 9600 BC.[97]

The four-thousand-year cataclysm-cycle was also revealed in Antarctica. Abrupt deglaciations in McMurdo Sound and in the western Ross Sea occurred after the Last Glacial Maximum twenty thousand years ago and then during cataclysms about sixteen thousand years ago, twelve thousand years ago, eight thousand years ago, and four thousand years ago.[98]

Abrupt Changes in Sea-Temperature

Abrupt sea-surface-temperature changes, inferred from the oxygen-isotope-ratios in plankton-microfossils from sediment-cores, showed sea-surface temperature in the Atlantic, Mediterranean, Red Sea, and Indian Ocean, which also varied with the same four-thousand-year pattern.[99, 100] A Pacific Ocean sediment-core drilled at Chatham Rise (east of New Zealand) showed sea-surface temperature abruptly jumped ten-to-fourteen degrees Celsius during the cataclysm of 9600 BC.[101]

About eight-thousand years ago, the sea-surface was chilled by a large deluge of fresh water into the oceans around the world, an event which corresponded to the mythical great-flood.[102] Climate scientists usually refer to this cataclysm as the 8200 BP event, estimating its date by ice-core annual-band-counting.[103] However, more accurate carbon-14 data from Black Sea sediments showed the great-flood occurred around 5600 BC (between 7600 and 7700 BP$_{1950}$).[104]

Evidence for the same huge flood was also found in British Columbia, Canada on the other side of the planet, in sediments from Eleanor Lake.[105, 106] A sediment core from the Gardar Drift, south of Iceland, also recorded the same event, confirming that the great-flood was a global disaster.[107]

Around 1600 BC, there was another abrupt hiatus in sea-surface temperature. There was a plus-one degree heat-spike, followed by a sharp minus-three degree fall, and then a plus-one degree rise to the present stable sea-surface temperature.[108]

Generally, over the previous twenty thousand years, there have been cataclysmic changes in sea-surface-temperature every four thousand years, which correlated with a stepwise rise in sea-levels around the world.

Abrupt Sea-Level Change Every Four-Thousand Years

There is a mystery about the coastal margins of the oceans: drowned tree-stumps and other terrestrial organic material have been found deep underwater. In addition, land plant remains have been found in drill-cores, buried under deep layers of marine sediments.

A cycle of changes in sea-level, with a periodicity of one hundred-and-twenty-thousand years, is well established by different studies, in which mean sea level oscillated from present sea-level down to minus-one-hundred-and-twenty meters below current sea-level. The cause is an enigma.[109]

Many studies from different parts of the world have revealed that over the previous twenty-thousand years, there were periods of relative sea-level stability, punctuated by rapid rises in sea-level. The correlation between the series of jumps in sea-level in different locations showed that global sea-levels rose up and up in great steps, caused by a series of catastrophic floods. This process is referred to by climate scientists as episodic-sea-level-rise.[110, 111, 112, 113, 114]

Coral-reefs flourish in shallow sun-lit sea-water. However, the sea-level jumps caused the abrupt drowning of ancient reefs in deep water, which killed the coral. Layers of ancient coral-reefs around Barbados, Tahiti, and New Guinea, which formed during the previous twenty thousand years, were dated by the uranium-thorium isotope method and revealed a four-thousand year periodicity in reef-drowning.[115, 116]

A detailed study of the Red Sea showed a long-term sea-level cycle of one-hundred-and-twenty-thousand years, with abrupt jumps in sea-level every four-thousand years.[117] In another study, forty-eight dated shoreline samples from around the world were plotted as a graph of sea-level-versus-age and a "staircase" of jumps in sea-level every four-thousand years was revealed.[118]

Sea-level data should be presented as bar-charts with error-bars, but it is often misrepresented by average-curves that smooth-out these abrupt changes. However, a survey of recent sea-level studies from around the world reveals a very clear pattern of stepwise sea-level jumps.

Between twenty-four and twenty-thousand years ago during the Last Glacial Maximum, the sea-level was approximately one-hundred-and-twenty meters lower, so vast tracts of dry land were exposed around the world, which are now drowned continental-shelves.[119, 120]

The data from various studies in the Bonaparte Gulf off the north coast of Australia, and on the Sunda Shelf in Southeast Asia, showed a distinct sea-level jump around 17,600 BC.[121] Land was inundated by ten-to-forty meters of sea-water. Data from a study in an archaic mud-filled river channel on the Northern Ireland coast of the Irish Sea also showed the same sea-level jump, showing this was a global flood.[122]

There is evidence of a sudden fresh-water flood into the oceans around 13,600 BC, which caused a sea-level jump of between fifteen-to-thirty meters.[123, 124] This event is generally referred to as Melt-Water-Pulse 1A and thought to coincide with a catastrophic heating event that occurred immediately prior to the *Oldest Dryas* chill, which is conventionally dated to around fifteen-thousand years ago.[125] Elevations and ages of the drowned Acropora Palmata reefs from the Caribbean-Atlantic region supported the evidence for this catastrophic sea-level rise.[126] Another rapid flooding of the Sunda Shelf in Southeast Asia also occurred at this time.[127]

In 9600 BC there was a sudden and extraordinary heating of the oceans that corresponded to apocalyptic conditions on land. The rapid heating of the sea-water initially caused an abrupt ten-meter-drop in sea-level. It was then followed by an abrupt fifty-meter-rise in sea-level, a net gain of forty meters.[128, 129]

An enigma for climate scientists was that following both the 13,600 BC and 9600 BC cataclysms, sea levels continued to rise during the re-freezing conditions of the *Oldest Dryas* and *Younger Dryas*, while ice was also accumulating on land and glaciers were re-advancing.[130] The source of all the extra water is a mystery, but it could have been delivered from space.

The sea-level jumped again in 5600 BC, across the planet from the Atlantic to the South China Sea.[131, 132, 133] The simultaneous formation of large river-deltas across the globe occurred during this sudden sea-level rise.[134] Radiocarbon dating has shown that thirty-six river-deltas, including the Mississippi delta, the Nile delta, the Rhine delta, and Yangtze delta, all formed about eight thousand years ago.[135, 136, 137, 138, 139]

Four thousand years later around 1600 BC, data from places as far away as the coast of southern California and the southern tip of India revealed that the sea-level suddenly jumped by a few meters.[140, 141]

Every four-thousand years, massive additions of fresh water were poured abruptly into the oceans, causing low salinity and sudden death of plankton.[142] Data from cores drilled in the Atlantic Ocean on the Bermuda Rise and a core drilled in the western-Pacific off Indonesia both showed similar abrupt changes in salinity.[143, 144] A Caribbean sediment core from the Cariaco basin, off the coast of Venezuela, confirmed large and abrupt shifts in ocean conditions that had occurred every four-thousand years.[145]

Averaging data from different locations shows that mean-sea-level rapidly rose about twenty meters around 13,600 BC, then jumped forty meters around 9600 BC, jumped again another ten meters around 5600 BC, and finally rose a further few meters around 1600 BC.

Sea Level Changes and Drowning of Land

These abrupt changes in sea-levels led to sudden shifts in the location of coastlines. Vast areas of land were lost forever to the sea around 17,600 BC, 13,600 BC, and 9600 BC, and further territories became drowned continental shelf around 5600 BC.

However, drawing accurate global maps of sea-depth and coastlines in different eras is still problematic.[146] Ancient shorelines are not only found in deep water. Sometimes they are raised-beaches with wave-cut terraces on dry-land, high above present sea-level. In northern regions, it is generally accepted that raised-beaches are the result of the elevation of land, caused by a geological process known as isostatic-adjustment, after massive ice-sheets have melted away.

However, raised-beaches nearer to the equator such as those found in Bermuda, the Bahamas, and East Timor in tropical Southeast Asia, which can be up to a thousand meters above sea-level, are examples of a process of crustal-elevation, which is not understood. However, despite these mapping problems, there is a general picture of the lands lost to the sea around the globe.

For example, twenty thousand years ago, off the north coast of mainland Australia, was the great land of Sahul. It stretched all the way from the northern coast of Australia to New Guinea but is now drowned under the Arafura Sea. It also extended west toward the island of Timor, but this part of the lost territory was inundated by the Timor Sea. The original shoreline of Sahul is now one-hundred-and-forty meters below sea-level, due to both sea-level-rise and land-subsidence.

Beyond this ancient coastline the seabed rapidly descends into the Timor Trough. However, at the time of the Last Glacial Maximum, it used to be possible to island-hop by canoe, northwest from Timor to Bali and arrive at another vast but now drowned land called "Sunda."

The Sunda continental-shelf is the southeast extension of the continental-shelf of Southeast Asia. However, twenty thousand years ago, the Malay Peninsula, Sumatra, Borneo, Java, Madura, Bali, and their surrounding smaller islands were the hills and mountains of a continental region.

The ancient lowlands of Sunda are now drowned under seawater, which varies between twenty and fifty meters deep. The topology of this ancient land was mapped with sonar and was revealed to have a complex system of river valleys, carved by the tributaries and main channels of three great rivers: the long vanished River Malacca, River Siam, and River Sunda.

The first drowning was a huge flood around 17,600 BC, which inundated the land of Sahul north of Australia and part of the great land of Sunda. Following the cataclysm of 13,600 BC, there was another rapid flooding of more of Sunda. An immense area of dry land covering about two-million square-kilometers disappeared into the sea. This catastrophic flood completely inundated the archaic lands that had once connected Malaysia, Singapore, the Indonesian archipelago, and Vietnam. The catastrophic flood added at least sixteen meters to the sea level, which only finally stabilized about a thousand years later.[147]

Twenty thousand years ago, during the Late Pleistocene, the land of Beringia was a dry low-lying territory, connecting eastern-Siberia to Alaska. Twelve-thousand years ago, the Bering Straits suddenly appeared and this extensive area of forested low-land was drowned in a catastrophic subsidence and sudden rise in sea-level.

South from the Bering Straits, off the eastern shoreline of the present Kamchatka peninsula and all along the far east coastline of Asia, there was a sharp rise in sea-level. In addition, there was a spectacular collapse of the continental shelf and some areas of land dropped two kilometers to the ocean floor. As the land disappeared below the waves, hill-tops and mountains formed arcs of new islands, most notably the islands of Japan.[148]

In the Late Pleistocene, there was also another extensive tract of dry land on the northern continental shelf of Eurasia, named by geologists as "Fennoscandia," which extended north of Siberia and stretched west to Scandinavia. When this land was also drowned suddenly in the cataclysm of 9600 BC, the highlands of this ancient land were transformed into the New Siberian Islands, Novaya Zemlya, Franz Joseph Land, and Spitsbergen.

On the old hill-tops that formed these new islands, vast mounds of muck and bone were dumped by great tidal-waves that had destroyed the north-Siberian forests. Animal carcasses and trees had been violently ripped apart, as they were washed off the Eurasian continent. The heaps of muck from this convulsion were carbon-14 dated to the cataclysmic end of the Pleistocene, just under twelve-thousand years ago.[149]

Appalachia was an ancient land south of Greenland, which once connected Iceland to Scandinavia. Appalachia was also drowned about twelve-thousand years ago and now forms part of the continental shelf. Huge quantities of sand, gravel, and mud from the former valleys of this sunken land were found on the sea floor, in deposits up to a mile thick.[150] In addition, in the ocean depths between Greenland and Norway, evidence was uncovered of a subsidence of continental-shelf rock, which had tumbled almost three kilometers into the abyss, to the deep floor of the North Atlantic.[151, 152, 153, 154]

Fossil evidence of land-animals of the Pleistocene epoch has been dredged up from the bottom of the sea in this region. The species were common to both Greenland and north-west Europe, showing that dry land had once connected these regions in the Pleistocene epoch.[155, 156]

Twelve thousand years ago, Appalachia, Fennoscandia, and Beringia were a continuous area of forested continent that encircled the north polar region. It was ruptured and sank below the northern oceans during a series of terrible cataclysms.[157]

In the Pacific Ocean, off the west-coast of Canada, on the central continental shelf of British Columbia, land-plant remains still rooted in ancient soil were found in a sediment-core at a water depth of ninety-five meters. The core-layer of terrestrial material was overlain by shallow-marine sediments. Radiocarbon dates of woody root fragments recovered indicated that the site was suddenly flooded in the 9600 BC cataclysm. During the same rapid rise in sea-level, the fiords on the British Columbia mainland were also abruptly flooded.[158]

In the Indian Ocean, an extensive territory now called the Chacas-Laccadive Plateau was a large tongue of land that long ago stretched due south from the Indian sub-continent far out into the Indian Ocean.[159,

[160] It was submerged suddenly, approximately twelve-thousand years ago, together with other continental fragments, which once formed land around the Seychelles, Mauritius, the Adas Bank, the Laccadives, Maldives, Chagos Archipelago, and the Saya de Malha.[161, 162] Sri Lanka, on the southern tip of the Indian subcontinent, was also severed from India during this cataclysm.[163]

At the same time, the land of "Atlantis," which was located north of the Azores and west of the coasts of Portugal and France, was broken-up and drowned at the end of the Pleistocene. Atlantis was a triangular continental-platform, which in Permian times connected to France at the Bay of Biscay but was dragged away from Europe during the opening of the Atlantic over two-hundred-million years ago (described in a later chapter).

Abrupt Changes in Earth's Magnetic Field

About twelve-thousand years ago, at the sudden end of the Pleistocene epoch, there was an abrupt change in Earth's magnetic field. Some sediments revealed a sudden reversal in the magnetic polarity and that the magnetic field-strength had suddenly increased.

These reverse-magnetized-sediments were discovered near Gothenburg in Sweden, which dated to the end of the Pleistocene. A drill-core from Gothenburg recorded a one-hundred-and-eighty degree south-to-north flip in the geomagnetic pole, at the boundary between the Allerød warm-climate and the frosty younger-dryas climate.[164, 165, 166]

The sediments recorded that the Earth's magnetic field had increased five-times in strength, as if it had been pumped up by magnetic-induction from a powerful external field. There are other examples of similar reversed-magnetized rocks from this event in northern and central Europe, eastern Canada, the Gulf of Mexico, New Zealand, Japan, and Australia.[167]

There is also evidence of other disturbances to the magnetic field of the Earth, around eight thousand years ago and four thousand years ago.[168] However, these results remain controversial, and conventional geology only recognizes a full inversion of Earth's magnetic field about eight hundred thousand years ago.[169]

The Four Most Recent Cataclysms
The 13,600 BC Cataclysm

About sixteen thousand years ago, a cataclysm occurred that changed the global climate. It started with a heat-pulse, which was recorded in the ice-cores around 13,600 BC. It also corresponded to strange jumps in the atmospheric methane concentration.[170, 171] One explanation for the excess methane is the sudden exposure and sublimation of vast quantities of buried marine methane-hydrates, during a cataclysmic disruption of the continental-shelves.[172]

There followed a climatic period called the *Oldest Dryas*, a name derived from white dryas, a cold-tolerant eight-petal alpine-flower whose pollen was abundant in soils from that time. The century of winter coincided with the Heinrich-Event-1, a severe freeze in which summers never came and glaciers re-advanced, for example, in the Pyrenees.[173] The date of the *Oldest Dryas* is still not well defined, but its duration is agreed to have been less than two centuries.

For the next four millennia following the cataclysm, Greenland and most of North America north of the Great Lakes was an ice-covered polar waste. However, Europe and Asia had a temperate climate during this era, known as the Bølling-Allerød. There is general agreement from ninety different sources that the duration from the start of the Bølling-Allerød to the end of the *Younger Dryas* freeze around eleven thousand years ago was a duration of approximately four thousand years.[174]

The 9600 BC Cataclysm: End of the Ice-Age

The cataclysm that terminated the Pleistocene epoch in 9600 BC was the most severe recent climate-crash.[175] There appears to have been a devastating blast in which the atmosphere was suddenly heated by more than ten degrees Celsius. It developed into a multi-stage catastrophe of inferno, fallout, flood, death, and extinction.

All the forests of Europe were ruined in the terrible apocalypse. Enormous quantities of trashed vegetation were buried suddenly preserving leaves and berries, showing that the cataclysm occurred in the summer.[176] In Siberia, huge trees were ripped out of the ground, shredded, and converted into heaps of rotting vegetation.[177]

The cataclysm was marked in the Greenland-Ice-Sheet-Project-ice-core-two by an ice-band containing high-concentrations of methane, sulfuric-acid, and volcanic-ash.[178] At the same time, a massive volcanic fallout known as the Vedde Ash was deposited all over the Arctic region. However, there was so much sulfate in the ice that the source of the bulk of the sulfuric acid has remained an enigma.[179, 180]

Mammoths, mastodons, and other large Pleistocene animals were slaughtered and buried during the disaster. Enormous quantities of fossilized bones and tusks were discovered at many sites across Siberia, Europe, and North America.[181, 182] Clues to the nature of the killer were deposits of strange minerals associated with these end-Pleistocene bones.[183, 184, 185]

North America suddenly became a charred and rotting destruction zone covered in black-mat, a thick layer of ash and decomposing material. The terrible shroud was found draped over the bones of both extinct giant mammals and human remains. In Europe, a similar charred layer called the usselo-horizon marked a related massacre and also defined the end of the warm Allerød climatic era.[186, 187]

The oxygen-18 and calcium-ion profiles from three ice-cores (NGRIP, GRIP, and GISP2) revealed a massive excess calcium-carbonate dust, which fell together with very heavy snow at the poles.[188] The remains of this dense dust can still be seen in the cloudiness of all the ice-core samples from this time. The source of this pure calcium-carbonate remains unknown.[189] All over Africa, an alien titanium-rich dust fell and formed distinct layers in the sediments cored in Lake Malawi.[190] The same dust layers were detected in glacier cores drilled at the top of Mount Kilimanjaro.[191]

In the GRIP ice-core from Greenland, the cataclysm was marked by a strange concentration peak of iridium and platinum that was three-times the background.[192] High concentrations of alien-isotopes, such as helium-3, carbon-14, aluminum-26, and beryllium-10, spiked together in one massive abundance peak.[193] Furthermore, cores from the floor of the Arabian Sea revealed two ocean sediment strata that were approximately twelve thousand years old and eight thousand years old, which also contained relatively high elevations of alien helium-3.[194]

There was darkness, freezing weather, snow, and ice for about a century, before the recovery at the dawn of a new age of our world. This century of extreme cold was named the "Younger Dryas." It got its strange name from the re-appearance of abundant amounts of pollen from the arctic-flower known as white dryas. "Younger" was added to the name of the flower, because a century of extreme cold had occurred approximately four thousand years earlier, after the end of the previous age of our world.[195, 196]

The duration of the Younger Dryas freeze itself is often over-stated due to extraordinary dating errors. An unusually large amount of snow fell as a direct result of the cataclysm, disrupting the continuity of the ice-layers, and this created a large error in ice-core dating.[197]

Many publications allocate over a thousand years, rather than a hundred years, to this period of eternal winter. The confusion was also caused by irradiation of the upper atmosphere, which caused increased Carbon-14 production.[198]

There are no reliable non-ice-core markers for the start of the Younger Dryas.[199] Generally, carbon-14 dates for organic material associated with the cataclysm cluster around the end of the Younger Dryas, as would be expected if the ice-core data was over estimating duration of the extremely cold weather.[200] However, there is still uncertainty over the date of the 9600 BC cataclysm, and some authors push back the date of the disaster by over a thousand years to 10,800 BC.[201, 202, 203]

Europe and Siberia suffered severe cold, and these chill conditions effected the whole planet.[204] Many southern hemisphere glaciers re-advanced at this time including The Franz Josef glacier in New Zealand.[205] There is related evidence of the Younger Dryas freeze on the outlet glaciers of the Southern Patagonian Icefield at the southern tip of South America.[206, 207]

There is general agreement that the Younger Dryas ended around 9500 BC. At the end of this strange century of winter, there was a very rapid clearing of dust from the atmosphere.[208] The abrupt transition was visible as a boundary between cloudy-dusty ice at the end of the Pleistocene with more recent transparent ice at the start of the Holocene.[209] As the climate abruptly warmed up, the amount of snowfall over the summit of Greenland doubled.[210] The atmospheric temperature continued to warm until it stabilized at a new level, the higher global temperature of our Holocene epoch.

The 5600 BC Cataclysm: Deluge and Flood

In the Early Holocene, the average sea level was approximately fifty meters below the present sea level, and the land area of our planet was up to ten percent greater than today. Approximately eight thousand years ago, another cataclysm commenced abruptly with a sudden heating event that rapidly drove up global air temperatures by at least two degrees Celsius. Data from equatorial East Africa, Antarctica, and Greenland show that the whole planet was heated, and large areas of the Antarctic and Arctic Sea ice melted.[211, 212]

As before, the precise date of this cataclysm is disputed, but it occurred approximately eight thousand years ago, around 5600 BC. Evidence of the great flood was precisely recorded in a layer of freshwater sediment, below marine layers in the Black Sea. Organic material in this layer was accurately dated using multiple core samples and carbon-14 analysis to around 5600 BC (7600 BP).[213]

However, inaccurate dates derived from counting ice bands in ice-cores erroneously placed this mid-Holocene cataclysm between 6050 BC to 6250 BC (8000 BP to 8200 BP) and the great flood is often named the "8200 BP event" in the scientific literature.

At the start of this cataclysm, Sweden was buckled by awesome gravitational tidal forces that made a standing wave of rock called the Parvie Fault. It is one-hundred-and-fifty kilometers long and is also dated to 5600 BC by the age of disturbed surface deposits of peat.[214] The rocks of

Scandinavia were also exposed to a powerful external magnetic field at this time, which caused significant magnetic anomalies.[215]

There was a tectonic disaster off the west coast of Norway around 5600 BC.[216] Part of the continental shelf off Norway, called the Storegga-Great-Edge, was ruptured along a three-hundred-kilometer front. Two enormous slabs of continental bedrock, ten by thirty kilometers across, were broken away and thrown into the abyss with such incredible momentum; they traveled an amazing two hundred kilometers across the ocean floor before they finally came to rest.[217]

In the Antarctic, ice-cores at Byrd Station and at Camp Century showed a dark ash band that coincided with high acidity and a big jump in electrical conductivity. This was followed by a sharp drop in oxygen-18 isotope levels, indicating a severe chill.[218]

Chemical analysis of the ice-layer corresponding to the flood showed there was a huge concentration spike of nitrate, from radiation-driven chemical reactions between oxygen and nitrogen. A big concentration spike of ammonium ions at the same location in the ice-cores recorded continent-wide forest fires.

The destruction of the forests was the cause of the scarcity of ancient timber in Europe that dated to the time of this disaster.[219] Data from an ocean drill core collected off eastern Greenland showed there was a dramatic influx of alien magnetic dust at the same time as the deluge.[220, 221]

A vast flood of freshwater also washed out of Hudson bay at this time.[222, 223] Huge quantities of freshwater were also dumped into the North Atlantic, causing the sea-level to rise and flood continental margins around the world.[224] In the great flood, land was drowned under the sea, and ancient coastlands disappeared under new or expanded seas, all around the world.[225] Around North America, the sea-level permanently rose more than ten meters, and large areas of coastal territory, particularly around Florida, vanished under the waves.

Large areas of Europe became drowned continental shelf and new seas.[226] The Baltic Sea, North Sea, English Channel, Black Sea, and Persian Gulf all suddenly appeared in this disaster. Before 5600 BC, the United Kingdom was not a group of islands but a western region of the

European continental landmass. At this time a pleasant, green lowland connected Britain to continental Europe.

Around eight thousand years ago, a giant wave hit Scotland. Four-meter-high heaps of sediment were dumped on its newly formed east coast, which buried organic remains of plants that were dated to 5600 BC.[227, 228] On that day a flood-wave traveling at over thirty-five meters per second roared south and drowned Dogger-land under the North Sea.[229] Huge flood waves then divided the British Isles from Europe in a violent geological Brexit in which the English Channel was formed.[230]

As this awesome torrent of water excavated the English Channel, the violence of the flood surge created the White Cliffs of Dover.[231, 232] Eight thousand years ago, there was also an abrupt rise in the water level of the Thames Estuary by twenty meters.[233]

The 5600 BC flood affected the whole Mediterranean region, and large areas of land were drowned. Part of Mount Etna collapsed, causing marine landslides. Huge piles of flood debris were discovered twenty kilometers off the coast of Sicily under the Mediterranean Sea. The organic material was C14-dated to eight thousand years ago.[234]

The Black Sea became a salt-water sea in 5600 BC, revealed by carbon-14 dating of a thick layer of rotten organic material and fresh-water mollusk shells below the marine sediments.[235] The Persian Gulf, a very shallow sea with an average depth of around fifty meters, also only formed around 5600 BC.[236, 237]

As the deluge hit North America, lakes across the continent burst their banks and overflowed.[238] In Nebraska, the flood deposited massive amounts of sand, burying trashed plants that eventually turned into peat. The rotten material was dated to approximately 5600 BC.[239]

A powerful volcanic explosion occurred, which was over forty times more violent than the 1980-eruption of Mount Saint Helens. Mount Mazama, part of the Cascade volcanic-arc in Oregon, blew-up and formed a vast crater. Carbon dating of organic material, along with the ash from Mount Mazama's eruption dated the event to around 5600 BC. When the crater basin filled up with water, it formed the famous circular lake in Crater Lake National Park.[240]

Around Singapore, drowned organic remains, including peat and mangrove roots, revealed that a sudden twenty-meter-rise in the sea-level occurred around 5600 BC.[241] In the Pacific Ocean, there was an abrupt jump in sea-level, which killed the coral. The final top terminal growth level dated by carbon-14 analysis marked the time of death precisely in 5600 BC.[242, 243]

After the great flood, there was an abrupt chill and a sudden cooling of the oceans, and the snow accumulation rate dropped by ten percent.[244] The oxygen-18 isotope records from Greenland ice-cores showed a minus-five to minus-eight degree Celsius drop in air temperature over central Greenland at this time.[245, 246, 247] Even the sea temperature in the Mediterranean dropped three degrees Celsius.[248]

All over the world, these freezing conditions persisted for half a century before the global climate recovered.[249] This two-generation period of chill, with its dry and dusty fallout, was about half the severity of the Younger Dryas freeze, which had occurred four thousand years earlier following the previous cataclysm.[250]

Generally, the 5600 BC cataclysm forced a total change in the global climatic patterns, which had persisted in the previous four thousand years.[251, 252, 253, 254]

The 1628 BC Cataclysm of Fire

In 1628 BC, there was an earth-shaking cataclysm in which fire fell from the sky. Whole cultures were devastated, cities were depopulated and lands were laid waste. Agriculture ceased and societies collapsed in Greece, Egypt, the Levant, Mesopotamia, Central Asia, Pakistan, India, and China.

At first scientists attributed the destruction in the Mediterranean region to the eruption of Thera, a large volcano on the Aegean island of Santorini. Initial radiocarbon dating analysis of an olive tree buried beneath a lava flow from Thera indicated that an explosive eruption had occurred in 1628 BC. However, it was soon discovered that the chaos and climate change had been on a global scale.[255, 256, 257, 258]

The following volcanoes are known to have erupted around 1628 BC: Etna in Italy; Vesuvius, Italy; Campi Flegrei, Italy; Hekla, Southern

Iceland; Thera-Santorini, Greece; Aso Kyushu, Japan; Kaimondake volcano, Kagoshima Prefecture, Japan; Avachinsky, Kamchatka Peninsula, Russia; Shiveluch, Kamchatka Peninsula, Russia; Taranaki, New Zealand; Okataina, New Zealand; Aniakchak, Alaska Peninsula; Veniaminof, Alaska Peninsula; Hayes, Southwestern Alaska; St. Helens, Washington, United States.

The great eruption at Mount Aniakchak, Alaska, blasted tiny shards of volcanic glass into the sky, and these were detected in far-off Greenland.[259] There was a massive sulfate concentration spike and acidity peak at 1628 BC in the Arctic Greenland Dye 3 ice-core.[260] In the Antarctic Mizuho core, oxygen isotope data recorded sharp heating together with a very large spike of volcanic dust.[261]

A carbon-14 production anomaly in the atmosphere at the time of the catastrophe caused a hiatus in atmospheric carbon-14 background levels and caused difficulties with accurate carbon-14 dating.[262]

However, the date of the global disaster has been precisely established by tree-ring dating of frost damage of bristlecone pines in North America, stunted growth of oak trees in Ireland and fir trees in Sweden, and even floods in China to the northern hemisphere spring of 1628 BC.[263, 264, 265, 266, 267, 268, 269, 270]

The 1628 BC climate catastrophe was also recorded in high-altitude ice-cores in South America. At Sajama in Bolivia, significant concentration spikes were identified of sulfate, nitrate, chloride, and fallout dust, from the 1628 BC cataclysm.[271]

In Africa there was a heavy fallout of dust that was recorded in an ice-layer in the ice-core drilled at the top of Mount Kilimanjaro.[272] Lake Victoria suffered huge waves and violent sediment mixing.[273] A sediment core from the Gulf of Oman recorded the cataclysmic heating event and a heavy fallout of dust containing strontium-87, tephra, and calcium-carbonate.[274, 275]

The sea-level abruptly rose in the Atlantic, and vast areas of low-lying forest were drowned forever off the west-coast of the British Isles.[276] There was a rapid two-meter rise in water level in the Thames Estuary, which caused the sea-coast to move farther inland toward the future site of London.[277] The River Thames in central London also switched from a freshwater system to a tidal river.[278]

Both the Atlantic and Pacific coasts of North America were hit by violent storms as the sea-level rose by over two meters to reach its present level.[279] Offshore from Effingham Inlet on Vancouver Island, Canada, sediment-cores drilled in the North American West Coast continental shelf showed that four thousand years ago the gentle sedimentation in the Pacific Ocean was violently disrupted by chaotic ocean currents and huge waves.[280] Around the coasts of Southeast-Asia, the sea-level suddenly rose by up to five meters around Singapore and in the Strait of Malacca.[281]

Simultaneously, massive rock falls of sea-cliffs south of Sydney in Australia trapped and preserved datable organic debris. This evidence was mirrored by discoveries in a sea cave at Valla, on the North Coast of New South Wales. The data suggested that a very big tsunami struck the Australian coast at the same time as ancient coastlands of Crete were drowned under the Mediterranean.[282, 283]

The climatic system of the whole planet was shifted into a new pattern by the Cataclysm of Fire.[284, 285] Territories were abandoned by civilizations in north-west India and Pakistan. All across China, there was a collapse of farming, depopulation, and evidence of civilization just disappearing.[286]

Conclusion

Allowing for errors in determining exact dates, the results of all these studies converge on an average periodicity of cataclysm every four-thousand years, with resonances at forty-thousand years and one-hundred-and-twenty thousand years.

There is a large amount of evidence for the most recent cataclysms, which occurred approximately sixteen-thousand, twelve-thousand, eight-thousand, and four-thousand years ago. The correlations between different sources of data for each cataclysm show that these events were global.

The details of the four most recent cataclysmic events also displayed a similar pattern: they all commenced with a period of global-warming and drought. A few hundred years later there was sudden and extreme heating, recorded by organic trash of burnt plants and changes in oxygen-isotope ratios. They were followed by a century or two of extreme cold, coinciding with colder sea-surface temperatures and the re-advance of glaciers. Finally, the climate recovered with a rise in temperature to a new equilibrium level.

The astro-mythology already published in my previous book *Cataclysms & Renewals,* and more scientific evidence to be presented here, point to the same conclusion: our planet has been subjected to a periodic cycle of cataclysms, driven by the return of star-core-zeus. Each cataclysm brought an end to an age of the world and triggered the dawning of a new age in which the global climate was quite different.

The distinct climatic-ages of our world, which were induced by fly-bys of star-core-zeus, are the subject of the next chapter.

C H A P T E R   2

Distinct Climatic Ages

● ● ●

THE EVIDENCE PRESENTED IN THE previous chapter shows that there is a cycle of global cataclysms, which has caused abrupt climate-change, every four thousand years.

Since the Last Glacial Maximum twenty-thousand years ago, the cycle of global cataclysms has initiated five distinct climatic-ages. The five Ages of the World, described in the myths of ancient human civilizations, which I detailed in my previous book *Cataclysms & Renewals*, correspond to these five climatic-ages.[287]

For easy reference, the five climatic-ages shall be referred to in this chapter as the first, second, third, fourth, and fifth-ages. The first-age started in 17,600 BC (soon after the Last Glacial Maximum). The second-age started in 13,600 BC and finished in 9600 BC at the sudden end of the Ice-Age (corresponding to the end of the Late-Pleistocene epoch). The present warm epoch commenced with the third-age (the Early-Holocene); the fourth-age started in 5600 BC (the Mid-Holocene); and finally our fifth-age started in 1628 BC (the Late-Holocene), which includes the present times.[288]

Studies of Regional Climate Change

Studies of climate-history based on data from ice-cores and ocean-floor-cores provided information about the past climatic-conditions of the whole planet. However, it was the regional studies that brought to life the archaic climates of the different parts of the world.[289]

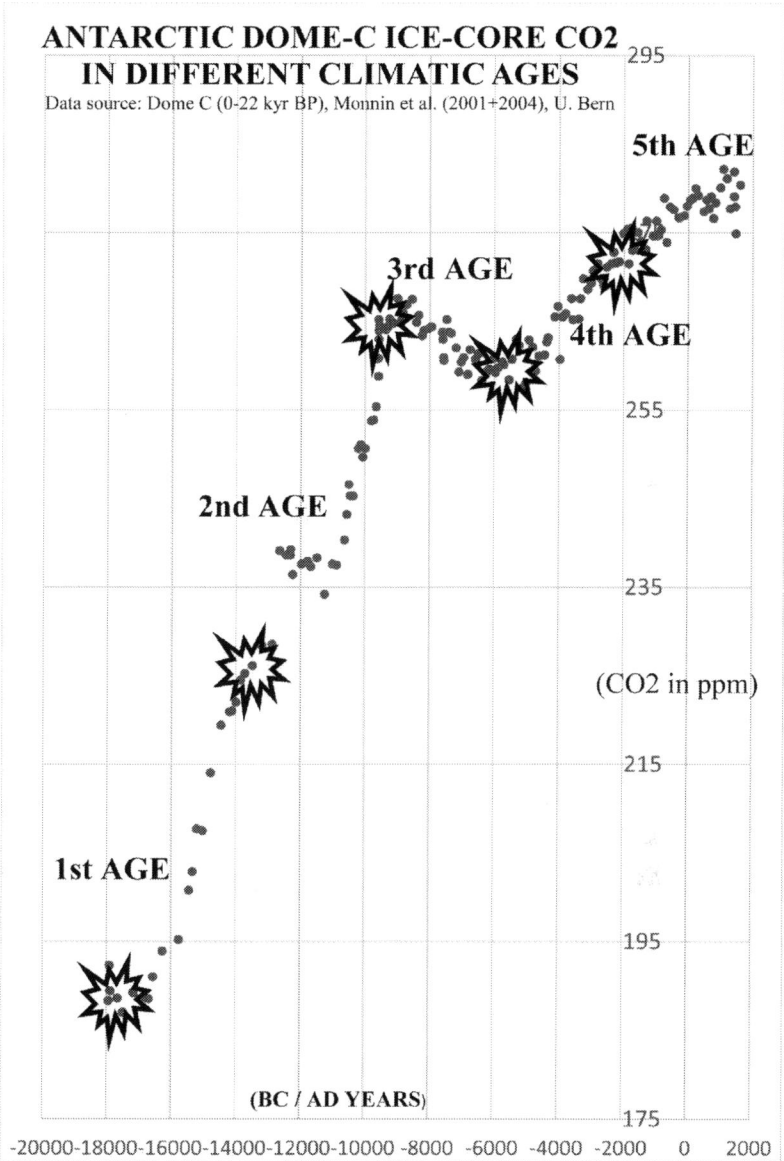

ANTARCTIC DOME-C ICE-CORE CO2 IN DIFFERENT CLIMATIC AGES
Data source: Dome C (0-22 kyr BP), Monnin et al. (2001+2004), U. Bern

A range of techniques were used to determine local climatic conditions: deep trenches were cut in ancient soils and peat, and the plant material, pollen, and the remains of temperature-sensitive insect-populations were analyzed. Pollen and beetle remains in ancient soils were used to construct geographic pictures of regional summer-winter temperature ranges. Drill-cores were pushed deep into lake sediments, and the chemical, physical, and biological characteristics of the extracted material provided insight into the ancient weather of the region.

The field-studies demonstrated that five climatic-ages have occurred over the previous twenty-thousand years but revealed distinct regional differences. In addition, abrupt changes in ancient regional climates were also uncovered, which were sometimes marked by datable layers of volcanic ash or burnt plant remains.

Some of the regional climate history results were very surprising. Rain-forests were not a permanent feature of either South America or Africa—the Amazon rain-forest and the Congo rain-forest were less than twelve thousand years old.[290, 291, 292, 293] Ten thousand years ago, the Sahara-region was not a desert; it was very wet and replete with broadleaf forests, lush green parkland, lakes, and rivers.[294] The Nile delta was not a permanent feature either: it suddenly appeared only eight-thousand years ago.[295, 296]

The Climatic-Ages of Europe

During the first-age, in the geological epoch that was once referred to as the Ice-Age, Europe was a region of climatic extremes, but there was no evidence of any thick and permanent ice-sheet.[297]

In northwest Europe of the first-age, open birch woods and forests grew across the northern plains from the Netherlands to Germany. This ancient climate in Germany was colder than present: summer temperatures did not exceed plus-fifteen degrees Celsius, and the winters were very cold with minus-twenty degree frosts.

Cores from the highland lakes in Lago Grande di Montichio in Italy and Lake Ionnina in Greece produced pollen records that revealed an unexpected picture of the climate changes, which had occurred in southern Europe during the past hundred-thousand years.[298, 299] In total contrast to Germany: only a thousand kilometers further south, the Balkans were so warm that hyena populations thrived.[300] There was a strangely steep north-to-south temperature-gradient across the whole of Europe at this time.[301]

In the second-age, European rainfall increased, and northern Europe became much warmer. Dense oak forest cloaked the Atlantic coastal regions of Europe of Portugal and France, onto the Netherlands and Scotland.[302, 303] Britain was just the western extension of Europe at this time and heavily forested. Birch and conifer woodland covered central-Europe, Germany, and extended to Russia.[304, 305, 306] Trees even grew in northern Scandinavia, further evidence that there were no ice-sheets covering Europe in this era either.[307]

The third-age commenced with the Younger Dryas freeze at the start of the Holocene epoch. However, after this very cold century, the dense clouds broke up and the weather in Europe became much warmer and wetter.[308] Distinct seasonality commenced and warm summers supported the spread of oak forests eastward all over Central Europe.[309] A mixture of open parkland and dense forest was common throughout southern Europe.[310]

At the beginning of the fourth-age, the British Isles appeared suddenly, cut off from Europe by a raging flood that carved the North Sea and English Channel in 5600 BC. During the fourth-age, Europe became even warmer and wetter, as increased rainfall stimulated the spread of dense oak and beech forests all across Europe.[311]

The Cataclysm-of-Fire destroyed many forests and heralded the cooler temperate climates of the fifth-age, which are now typical for western and central-Europe. A lake-core from Greece, which recorded one-hundred-and-thirty thousand years of climate history, confirmed this cataclysmic forest destruction and climate change.[312]

The Climatic-Ages of Iceland

Lake sediment studies from Iceland supported the changing pattern of the weather between the climatic-ages. Iceland was cold in the first-age but became abruptly warmer at the beginning of the second-age: its inland ice sheet suddenly disappeared. There was also a steep north-to-south temperature gradient in Iceland in the first-age and second-age.[313, 314]

At the beginning of the third-age, equivalent to the start of the Holocene epoch, Iceland suddenly warmed and its highland glaciers also melted. After the climate hiatus and chill around 5600 BC, its average climate became three degrees Celsius warmer than present, allowing forests and parkland to blanket Iceland. At the beginning of our fifth-age, the climate suddenly switched back to colder temperatures and the glaciers re-advanced from the highlands.

The Climatic-Ages of Siberia

Analysis of fossil pollen, ancient timber, and buried animal bones in Siberia also recorded a series of distinct climatic-ages.[315] Analysis of the northern limits of ancient forests in north-western Siberia, which lay buried under arctic tundra, revealed the local temperature of northern Siberia in previous climatic-ages.[316, 317]

The results showed that in the first-age, northern Siberia had a more temperate climate.[318] In the second-age Siberian summers were warmer than today but winter was colder.[319] By the third-age and fourth-age, Siberia was generally much warmer than today, and the forests grew much further north than the present limit for trees at latitude-seventy-degrees-north.[320] The unusually good growing conditions in fourth-age Siberia led to very strong summer growth. On average, trees lived for five hundred years and grew to vast sizes.

There was a cataclysmic destruction of forests around 1628 BC, followed by five years without summer. In our colder fifth-age, only sparse tundra plants replaced the grand forests. All that remained of the ancient forests of the previous age were huge trunks of broken trees buried under frozen muck.

The Climatic-Ages of Central Asia

Long ago Central Asia had a huge inland sea, which expanded and contracted in different climatic-ages, due to extreme changes in rainfall. This ancient sea was originally called the Vourukasha Sea in Aryan mythology but was later named the Khvalynian Sea by Russian climatologists.[321, 322]

In the first-age, the level of this land-locked saltwater sea was about thirty meters above the present level of the Caspian Sea and extended right across Central Asia from the Caspian basin, eastward to Lake Balkhash in south-eastern Kazakhstan.[323] The surrounding lands received regular rains, so grasslands and forests thrived in territory that is now desert.

In the second-age, there was a sudden increase in the rainfall and the volume of rainfall on the Himalayas was similar to the tropical downpours at the present equator. The huge quantity of water that flowed along the major rivers of Central Asia swelled the Vourukasha Sea to its maximum extent and depth. Its water level rose more than twenty meters above its level in the first-age, equivalent to fifty meters above the present level of the Caspian Sea.

The climate over central Asia was abruptly altered at the transition between the Pleistocene and Holocene epochs. During the third-age, the run-off rainwater from the Asian mountain ranges was much lower, and the Vourukasha Sea shrank.[324] After the Flood Cataclysm, the rains returned suddenly in the fourth-age, causing the water level in the Caspian basin to rise back to twenty meters above its present level. An extensive drainage network of streams, rivers, and lakes developed across Central Asia at this time. The River Amu Darya widened its ancient channels and carried huge volumes of water into the Caspian basin.

In our fifth-age the rains failed, and the Vourukasha Sea evaporated to such an extent that all that remained of it was the Caspian Sea and Aral Sea, and the formerly fertile planes surrounding it were transformed into desert.

The Climatic-Ages of China and Southeast Asia

China and Southeast Asia also experienced abrupt climate changes since the last glacial maximum.[325, 326, 327] At the start of the first-age, soon after the last-glacial-maximum, the climate in China was colder and drier than today. The north-western deserts were about thirty percent bigger than in our age.[328] The mean annual temperature was ten-degrees Celsius lower in the North and was six-degrees lower in the South.[329]

After a cataclysm and chill that corresponded to the Older Dryas climatic era of Europe, there was a substantial increase in rainfall, which was revealed during the analysis of cave stalagmites in China at Sanbao Hulu and Dongge.[330] A tropical climate quickly developed in the second-age, and dense tropical rain-forest extended across southern China, particularly in Yunnan.[331, 332, 333, 334] Higher rainfall in northern Southeast Asia supported dense forests, but, in contrast, the second-age in Borneo was cool, the rainfall was modest, and only subtropical open forest grew there.[335, 336]

At the Pleistocene-Holocene transition, there was a cataclysm and then extreme chill, followed by an abrupt shift in the climatic patterns. In the third-age, the temperature was generally four degrees Celsius higher than today.[337] The general rise of sea level caused a huge loss of land, which now lay drowned beyond the new eastern coastline of China.[338]

Glaciers retreated and in some cases disappeared in north-eastern China. The permafrost zone was relocated much farther northward of its current limit. The area of desert and loess-dust-bowl was greatly reduced. The highest lake levels of all the recent ages were recorded in this era. Conifer forest grew much further north than at present, and areas now dominated by steppe-grasses were covered in broad-leaved forests.[339] Generally, forests migrated about two degrees of latitude northward during this warm age of China.[340]

After the Great Flood, fourth-age China was colder than the previous age, but the climate was still warmer than present. Deserts expanded in the northeast, and conditions in the south were more temperate[341]

After the Cataclysm of Fire four thousand years ago, sea surface temperatures in the East China Sea dropped by about five degrees Celsius.[342] In fifth-age China, the climate became colder with less rain in the north.[343] Generally, the weather of China shifted into a new climatic pattern, which oscillated between a hot and dry season and a cold and humid season.[344]

The Climatic-Ages of India

India also had distinct climatic periods, both in the north and in the south of the subcontinent.[345, 346] A surprising feature was that after the

Last Glacial Maximum, in the first-age there was a steep north-to-south temperature gradient across the Indian subcontinent, like that discovered in Europe and Iceland. In this age, the Himalayas were colder than present, and glaciers advanced down the valleys.[347, 348] However, central India had an equatorial climate and rain-forest jungle flourished.[349]

In the second-age, the Himalayas were much warmer and wetter. The glaciers melted, and there was warm torrential rain in the highlands. However, the weather in central India switched to a subtropical climate and had a lower volume of rain than in the previous age.

During the third-age, although precipitation in the Himalayas was lower than the previous age, monsoon rainfall increased to twice current levels over central-India. The substantial rainfall caused lakes to fill to their maximum extent. Although India had a subtropical climate, at the end of the climatic-age, there was global-warming and a severe drought in the few centuries prior to the flood-cataclysm of 5600 BC.[350] During this hiatus, there was significant rain-water erosion and sediment transport all across the Indian subcontinent.

However, at the commencement of the fourth-age, the monsoon rainfall stabilized at a new lower level, and the climate of central India was drier than the previous age. The Indian rainforest retreated to refuges in the highlands of the Western Ghats, one of the world's eight hottest hotspots of biological diversity.[351] The weather was still warmer and wetter than present, providing an ideal climate for the emergence of agriculture in northwest India and Pakistan.

The Cataclysm-of-Fire induced an abrupt climate change in India. In the northwest, the rains failed, lush agricultural land was transformed into arid desert, and a cool, dry climate developed over the Himalayas. In central India of our fifth-age, the typical monsoon climate became established, but it produced much less rain than in the previous two climatic-ages.

The Climatic-Ages of Arabia

Recent surveys of Arabia revealed startling results: this desert-land was once covered with huge river-systems and lakes.[352] Analysis of the ancient lake deposits deep in the Arabian deserts revealed the strange climate history of the region.

THE LOST RIVERS OF GREEN ARABIA

Based on: (1) Crassard R, et al., 'Beyond the Levant: First Evidence of a Pre-Pottery Neolithic Incursion into the Nefud Desert, Saudi Arabia.' *PLoS ONE* 8 (7) (2013): e68061. doi:10.1371/journal.pone. (2) Edge, H.S., *Arabian Deserts: Nature Origin and Evolution* (New York NY Springer 2006) (3) "Asiae Nova Descriptio": a hand-coloured map of Asia (19 x 15 inches) made by Abraham Ortelius in Antwerp in 1570, from archaic source maps which still marked some of the lost lakes and rivers of Arabia.

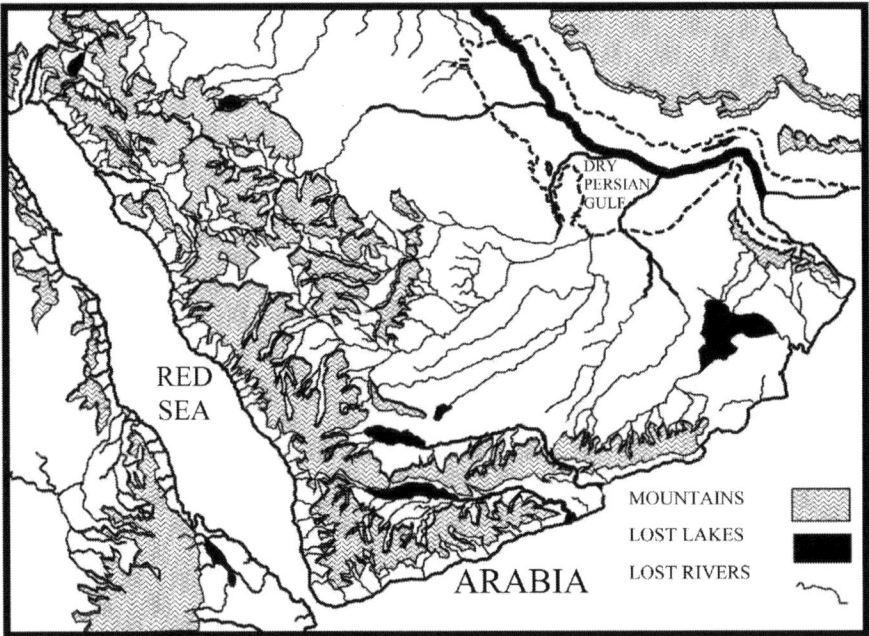

After the Last Glacial Maximum, the climate of the first-age in Arabia was hot and dry like today. However, there was a sudden change in the weather around 13,600 BC. In complete contrast, the climate of second-age Arabia was humid and equatorial. Heavy rainfall caused the formation of extensive river systems. Depressions turned into lakes and grew to cover more than four percent of the land area of Arabia.[353]

The climate of third-age Arabia had less rain than the previous age, but its wet climate still supported extensive forests.[354] Ten thousand years ago the Arabian environment resembled that of present day Europe. Arabia was a green land of meadows, lakes, and rivers, rich in plants and animal life.[355]

The climate of fourth-age Arabia was drier and hotter, and savannah grassland replaced the ancient forests. Actual desert conditions only arrived in Arabia with the fifth-age.[356] At the beginning of our fifth age, the region suddenly became desiccated and desolate, the ancient rivers and lakes rapidly dried out, and they were soon buried beneath the wind-blown dust and sand.

The Climatic-Ages of Africa

Africa also had a related and distinct pattern of climatic-ages, punctuated by cataclysms every four thousand years.[357, 358, 359] In first-age Africa, the Sahara was a vast grassland, not a desert.[360] The Congo basin was much drier than present and five degrees Celsius cooler. Soil samples from the Congo of this era revealed the pollen of a savannah grassland, which long ago covered this region. Tropical jungle did not exist yet in the Congo basin; true rain-forest only grew along a stretch of the west coast of central Africa, from Ghana to Cameroon.

By the second-age, the pattern of climatic-belts across the African continent had changed. Morocco and the Western Sahara became exceptionally wet and green. From the Atlas mountains on the Atlantic coast to the Ahaggar Massif of southern Algeria, there was a zone of very high rainfall.

Extraordinary tropical rains fell in the Sudan and Arabia. This equatorial climate extended eastward over Iran and on to the Himalayas. However, south of this equatorial zone, from south of West Africa near Mali to southern Ethiopia, there was desert.[361]

In second-age Africa, the Blue Nile from Lake Tana in Ethiopia provided much less water than present. The White Nile was almost dry, due to the drought conditions further south. The Nile delta did not exist at this time, and the sea-level was a hundred meters lower. The Nile River raged northward over rapids into a deep canyon, which ran another fifty kilometers farther north of the present North African coast, across dry continental-shelf, before draining into a shallower Mediterranean Sea.

In Africa of the second age, only the northwest coast of the Congo basin around Cameroon was hot and wet enough to support tropical rain-forest. Studies at fifty-eight lake basins in Africa showed that in the second-age, lakes were small because the central and southern half of the African continent was much drier.[362]

At the beginning of the third-age, the climate in Africa suddenly became hotter and more humid, an era climatologists refer to as the African Humid Period.[363, 364, 365] The sudden increase in rain volumes led to a dramatic increase in the extent of lakes and wetlands in northern Africa. Grasses and shrubs invaded regions that are now desert, creating the "Green Sahara." [366] As heavy rains continuously washed the continent, the Sahara became forested.[367, 368] The highlands of the central Sahara were transformed into a vast rain catchment area and were the source of many rivers. Vast underground reservoirs under the Sahara were filled up with huge volumes of fresh water at this time.

In this climatic-era, both the White Nile and Blue Nile conveyed heavy sediment loads and flooded regularly. Rivers also flowed along the wadis of Egypt and drained into the lower Nile. The soft rocks of the wadis were rapidly eroded, and swamps developed in the wider channels. Around the tributaries of the Nile, hippos and crocodiles became common, even in the central Sahara region. Many new rivers drained off Africa into both the Mediterranean and Red Sea.

In Central Africa, the Magadi-Natron basin on the Tanzania-Kenya border collected huge amounts of rainwater and filled to become fifty meters deep, forming a sixteen hundred square kilometer lake. The surface area of Lake Chad to the south of the Sahara grew to twenty-five times larger than today.[369] A sediment core from the Gulf of Guinea confirmed intense precipitation and high volumes of river discharge from West Africa.[370] At the end of the third-age, a harsh drought commenced, and the land dried rapidly in a few centuries.[371, 372]

After the Cataclysm-of-Flood, an abrupt climate change at the start of the fourth-age led to the African climate becoming much drier.[373, 374, 375] The Sahara Desert started to form as rain and river run-off declined substantially.[376, 377, 378] The Nile became a wide placid river that braided into multiple channels, as it passed through the newly formed Nile delta.

The North African coast still received more rain than today but significantly less than the previous age. North Africa generally became much drier and dustier. A core from Lake Yoa in northern Chad showed the vegetation cover changed to more drought-tolerant species. In these dry conditions, the swamp-forest that existed in the West African Sahel (south of the Sahara) in the previous age quickly perished.[379]

After the Cataclysm-of-Fire, fifth-age Africa developed the climate patterns we recognize in present times. The Sahara became harsh desert and rain-forest expanded in the Congo basin.[380] The climate became cooler and much drier around Mount Kenya and Mount Kilimanjaro in central Africa. In the southern half of Africa, rainfall declined and lake levels fell as evaporation exceeded water input. Further south the Kalahari expanded to become a larger desert.

The Climatic-Ages of North America

In North America, the weather in the northern latitudes showed similar distinct changes during the different climatic-ages.[381,382] For example, studies of ancient pollen from cores drilled on the west coast of Alaska and in the Great Lakes region showed that this northern region of the United States had distinct weather patterns in each climatic-age.[383, 384]

In the first-age in North America, only tundra grasses grew in Alaska, and the northern region was icy and dry. However, there was open forest and parklands in the Great Lakes region, which developed into full forest-cover further to the south.

Pollen studies from the Great Lakes region produced surprising results: there was no evidence of ice sheets or even tundra vegetation. During the so-called Ice-Age, the pine forests extended north beyond their modern ranges. The data showed plant communities in North America had continuity throughout the Late Pleistocene and into the

Holocene. However, the types of vegetation dominant at different times provided clear evidence for the five climatic-eras.

Further south, there was a huge lake in the State of Utah, which climatologists have named Lake Bonneville. It was over three-hundred meters deep and covered over fifty-thousand square-kilometers. It was really an inland sea.[385, 386]

The second-age in North America commenced after the 13,600 BC cataclysm, which had triggered an abrupt switch in the climate. The second-age was so warm in Alaska that birch forests grew in the summer, but much more snow fell in the winter.[387, 388] In contrast, a great ice-cap covered the Hudson bay region and extended south almost as far as the Great Lakes. The inland sea had shrunk, but there were still extensive lakes in Utah and in surrounding states further south. The American southwest received substantial rainfall, and in the second-age it was green with shrubs and trees.

After the 9600 BC cataclysm and the Younger Dryas freeze at the start of the third-age, the climate switched again. Alaska heated up so much that it developed a warm and wet climate similar to present-day Western Europe. Plants proliferated rapidly, total pollen increased significantly, and warm-temperate trees such as poplars became established. This was a very odd climate for a polar region.

Around the Great Lakes and all across northern states of the United States, there was rapid development of dense hardwood forests. The trees dominated the land for four thousand years until there was a huge destruction of forests during the 5600 BC Flood Cataclysm.

During the fourth-age, Alaska became cooler and forests of cold-tolerant alder replaced the birch trees and poplar trees of the previous age. The 1628 BC cataclysm triggered another abrupt climate-change: the cold tundra climate we now associate with Alaska was only established at the start of our fifth-age.

These three distinct climatic-ages were also recorded in a sediment core from Eleanor Lake in British Columbia, western Canada.[389] The cores also recorded bands of volcanic tephra, which marked the abrupt climate-change during the 5600 BC and 1628 BC cataclysms.

Generally, in fifth-age North America, the land became drier, and the central and southwestern regions became semi-desert. All that remained of the ancient huge body of water that once flooded the middle of North America was the Great Salt Lake in Utah, which was now only a fraction of the size of the original Lake Bonneville.

The Climatic-Ages of South America

In South America, there were also distinct climatic-ages.[390] El Nino, the ocean current off the west coast of South America that controls the weather, changed in each climatic-age. In the first-age, El Nino was much weaker than present.[391] In contrast, El Nino suddenly increased in intensity after the 13,600 BC cataclysm and drove different weather patterns in the second-age.[392, 393, 394]

On the south coast of Peru, the town of Quebrada Jaguay is one of the oldest known fishing settlements in the world. Carbon-14 analysis showed that it dated back to 11,000 BC, at the end of the second-age. An investigation of the ancient environments around Quebrada Jaguay showed that either desert or jungle had alternately surrounded this site in the different climatic-ages. The changes in local climate also correlated with big fluctuations of El Nino.[395] Heaps of fossil mollusk shells near the fishing huts also yielded a twelve thousand year climate history of the region.[396]

In the third-age, the sea surface temperature off the coast of Peru was much colder, and the tropical waters were much further north. Between twelve thousand and eight thousand years ago, there was almost no El Nino and the climate of South America was quite different.[397] An ocean-floor core from the Cariaco basin, offshore of Venezuela, showed very substantial river volume run-off from the northern coast of South America during this wetter era.[398]

After an abrupt period of cold in South America caused by the flood of 5600 BC, El Nino was absent in the following fourth-age.[399, 400, 401] The El Nino ocean current re-commenced at the start of our fifth-age. Today the tropical Pacific climate oscillates with a periodicity of five years, in phase with the appearance of the warm El Nino ocean water.[402]

Evidence for these climate-change patterns was also found on the Altiplano, the high plateau in the northern Andes on the border of Peru and Bolivia. There is good evidence that long ago the Altiplano was the floor of an ancient ocean, which had been elevated high above the clouds to become the world's largest and highest salt-flat.[403]

All that remained of the sea was Lake Titicaca, which contained fresh-water animals and plants that had adapted from marine life. A deep-water core from Lake Titicaca revealed huge differences in lake levels and distinct climatic-ages.[404] In the second-age, Lake Titicaca was much bigger, filled by the high volume run-off from heavy rainfall in the region.

The most startling result from the data was that a tropical climate appeared suddenly on the Altiplano at the beginning of the second-age and then disappeared suddenly at the beginning of the third-age.[405]

Andean glaciers also recorded extraordinary climate change. Studies of the Ritacuba Negro glacier showed that in the second-age, the glaciers in the northern Andes expanded and Ecuador and Colombia were much colder than the tropical conditions there today.[406] In direct contrast, in the second-age Greenland was much warmer, in an era climatologists refer to as the Bølling-Allerød climatic period.

The last major re-advance of glaciers in the northern Andes corresponded to the 9600 BC cataclysm and the Younger Dryas chill. In South America, data clearly showed the freeze persisted for only a hundred years. At the end of the century of winter, a much warmer climate rapidly developed in the southern hemisphere and glaciers in both the northern Andes and southern Andes retreated simultaneously.

In Northern Chile, the highland desert region of Atacama also contained evidence of these remarkable climate-changes. The Atacama Desert is located at four-thousand-five-hundred meters above sea-level, and between twenty and twenty-five degrees of latitude south of the current equator.

However, this area had also undergone abrupt switches in climate between different climatic-ages. What is today a cool desiccated barren waste-land was once so hot and wet that it supported rain-forest.

All evidence suggests that Atacama was located at the equator in the second-age.[407]

Climate studies in the Amazon basin also revealed related stunning results. Multiple studies showed the famous Amazon rain-forest zone was not permanent and had not always straddled the present position of the equator.

A sediment core from the Serra Sul dos Carajás swamp in southeastern Amazonia recorded over seventy thousand years of climate history. The core was investigated for ancient pollens, fern spores, ash, sediments, and minerals. Substantial shifts between climatic-ages were revealed, in which the region switched from tropical-forests to savanna. The species composition changed dramatically, and even a sequence of cataclysmic infernos was discovered.[408]

A study of the inland-area along the Piranhas River, in the state of Piranha, Brazil, showed that in the first-age the region was about five degrees colder than present, and the Amazon-basin was covered in dry savannah grasses, not rain-forest. In the second-age the Amazon-basin became even cooler and was a wind-swept grassland.[409]

The mystery is that in the first-age and second-age, rainforest was only found in a small refuge located to the southwest of the Amazon basin. This discovery indicated that in the second age, in the late-Pleistocene climatic period, equatorial climatic conditions in South America existed far to the south of the river Amazon.

Amazonia suffered abrupt climate-change and a century of chill after the 9600 BC cataclysm. The region then quickly recovered and developed a hot and wet climate at the start of the third-age. From the beginning of the Holocene climatic period twelve thousand years ago, tropical forest progressively expanded in the stable hot and humid conditions. There was also a remarkable increase in seasonality in the weather patterns of South America from this time.

At the beginning of the fourth-age, after the flood of 5600 BC, there was another sudden shift in the climate. A strange regional contrast in the weather conditions suddenly appeared between north-Amazonia and south-Amazonia.

In north-Amazonia, the land rapidly got cooler, the weather became even more seasonal, and rainfall declined substantially; northern Amazonia developed a stable, dry, and warm climate, typical of the weather in latitudes much further north in present times. In response to this abrupt climate change and the significant down-shift in temperature and rainfall, the rain-forest declined in northern Amazonia.

In contrast, south-Amazonia became hotter and wetter but less seasonal. The predominance of this hot, humid climate was revealed in the substantial increase in the relative abundance of tree ferns and palms. The center of high density rainforest had shifted southward in the fourth-age.[410]

For a few centuries prior to the Cataclysm-of-Fire, Amazonia suffered a drought. Then just under four thousand years ago, the Cataclysm-of-Fire shook the globe. After the weather systems around the world stabilized at the start of the fifth-age, present-day climatic conditions appeared, and Amazonia developed the tropical rain-forest we now associate with the region. In the southern extremes of Amazonia, the climate abruptly changed from equatorial to the modern seasonal climate patterns, typical of that region today.

In Patagonia, at the southern tip of South America, there was a related sequence of distinct climatic ages.[411, 412] Tierra del Fuego switched from cold and dry tundra in the first-age to warm and wet woodlands in the second-age, which persisted in the third-age and fourth-age. In our fifth-age the climate turned back to wet and cold.[413]

Other studies confirmed there were different but related climate histories in the different latitude bands of South America. For example, in the second-age, maximum rainfall occurred to the north, whereas the middle and southern latitudes of South America were drier and cooler. As a result of the 9600 BC cataclysm, there was a massive ash fall-out offshore of the Pacific coast of Patagonia, and glaciers advanced east of the Andes. Then in the third-age, the northern regions dried out, and maximum rainfall shifted to the mid-latitudes, while southern South America remained dry.[414, 415]

The Climatic-Ages of Antarctica

The abrupt climate changes in South America correlated with abrupt climate changes in Antarctica, where various ice-cores revealed sudden switches in the local weather, the most recent being the WAIS-Divide ice-core project.[416, 417]

Generally, over the previous twenty thousand years, there have been sudden changes in iceberg-flux from the Antarctic ice-sheets, which corresponded to the different weather conditions on the southern continent in each climatic-age.[418]

The Antarctica ice-cores showed that the severest cold had occurred before the Last Glacial Maximum of the Northern Hemisphere, twenty thousand years ago. During the first-age, between twenty-thousand and sixteen-thousand years ago, climatologists were surprised to discover that Antarctica near the South Pole actually got warmer. At the same time, Greenland near the North Pole got colder. The cause of this simultaneous warming of the Antarctic and cooling of the Arctic is still debated.[419, 420]

In the first-age, sea-ice retreated around Antarctica as the southern continent warmed up. There was a substantial decrease in the extent of sea-ice and an increase in iceberg-production off West-Antarctica, the region of the southern continent closest to South America.

Ice-cores drilled in the high-altitude Antarctic ice-fields revealed an oxygen-isotope spike, indicating that abrupt atmospheric heating had occurred in the 13,600 BC cataclysm, just prior to the start of the second-age. This climate-disruption also correlated with heavy snow-falls and substantial ice-accumulation in Antarctica.

At the start of the second-age, the average climate in Antarctica got a bit colder. However, the detailed analysis of the climate records from various high altitude ice-cores, recovered from different locations on the Southern Continent, revealed an enigma.[421, 422, 423] Substantial differences had appeared suddenly between the local climates of East-Antarctica and West-Antarctica, which are still inexplicable for climatologists.

The conclusion from the ice-core data was that the two major features of Antarctica: the western-ice-sheet and eastern-ice-sheet had very different climate histories in the second-age, even though they were both close to the South Pole.

In the second-age, East-Antarctica, which faces Australia got colder. In contrast, West-Antarctica, which is closer to South America, got warmer. Iceberg production off West-Antarctica increased and remained high during this warmer period. Generally, the warming of West-Antarctica corresponded to the warming of Greenland in the second-age and the general sea-level rise world-wide. This milder climate remained stable until about twelve-thousand years ago.[424, 425, 426]

The 9600 BC cataclysm in Antarctica was marked by a double-peak of very heavy snow fall, which dramatically increased ice accumulation over a very short period of time. This end-Pleistocene upheaval confused the dating methods: it is not clear if the two peaks are part of one cataclysmic process or were separated by a few hundred years.

After the abrupt increase in temperature in 9600 BC, the weather systems recovered at the beginning of the Holocene epoch (the start of the third-age). Antarctica warmed up and significant melting occurred.

In West-Antarctica the atmospheric temperature continued to rise in the third-age, as revealed by a study of the Pine Island Glacier, which melted and left behind a datable sub-ice shelf ridge. At the same time, there was an abrupt increase in iceberg production from the West Antarctica ice-sheet.

A sediment-core recovered from the bottom of Lake Terrasovoje revealed the lowland climate-history of East Antarctica, during the Early Holocene.[427] The basal sediments of the Terrasovoje core recorded the ice melted suddenly at the beginning of the third-age in a rapid thaw, which formed an ancient lake.

Atmospheric warming at the end of the third-age was revealed by the rapid thinning of the Pine Island Glacier in West-Antarctica, which occurred in less than a century. The Terrasovoje core in East-Antarctica also recorded a brief but significant heating at the end of the third-age, immediately prior to the Cataclysm-of-Flood.[428] After the upheaval at the beginning of the fourth-age, the global weather systems stabilized, and West-Antarctica got colder and iceberg-production declined.

The present generally colder climate in Antarctica only appeared suddenly about four thousand years ago, at the beginning of our fifth-age.[429] In the early fifth-age, the temperature in West-Antarctica fell. In contrast, the Vostok ice-core revealed that East-Antarctica warmed up a little.

Conclusion and Interpretation

Generally, the local climate history data from different regions around the world supported the concept that huge natural changes in the regional climates of our planet have occurred every four thousand years.

Before claims for man-made climate-change can be established, the natural climate-change process must be quantified and understood. The climate-changes in the prior one hundred years are insignificant when compared to the dramatic natural climate-changes during the Late Pleistocene and Holocene epochs. In the previous twenty-thousand years; ice-fields, deserts, grasslands, temperate-forests, and rain-forests were all violently re-arranged across the surface of our planet.

In the next chapter, an astonishing discovery shall be revealed, which makes sense of the patch-work puzzle of regional climates that once existed in different climatic-ages of the world.

CHAPTER 3

Shifting Climatic Belts

● ● ●

THE REGIONAL CLIMATE DATA DESCRIBED in the previous chapter, covering the previous twenty thousand years, were used to assemble a picture of the climatic-belts across the globe in each age of the world.[430] The results and implications were astounding.

The World of the First-Age

The big mystery of the first-age was the lack of evidence for seasonal differences in climate across most of our planet. Another mystery was our planet had an unusually steep temperature-gradient from the poles toward the equator.

For example, there was a strangely steep cold-to-hot temperature gradient between northern Europe to southern Europe of the first-age. Northern Europe in the first-age had winters like the present climate in central Russia, while southern France and Italy were hot and dry, and palm trees grew on the Mediterranean coast.

Desert conditions in southern France were confirmed by desert sand dunes and the bones of the desert-adapted Saiga antelope, dating to this time. The Levant at the eastern end of the Mediterranean also had a very hot climate with low rainfall, which only supported dry savannah and dispersed woodland. This narrow desert belt extended eastward, crossing Uzbekistan, the Tarim basin, and Gobi Desert, as far as the Manchurian plain of northern China.

In contrast, northern Siberia had a temperate climate; it received generous rainfall and was densely forested with deciduous trees. Ocean levels were about one hundred and ten meters lower than today, so land now lost continued out on the present continental shelf, far to the north of the present Arctic Ocean coasts. These ancient forests of far-northern Siberia now lie drowned under the Arctic Ocean, and there is nothing but small hardy plants and permafrost on the current northern coast of Siberia. This forested lowland called Beringia connected Siberia to Alaska. In the first-age, it was possible for herds of grazing animals and hunters to walk from Russia to North America.

The warm and wet climate band curved through Afghanistan and the Himalayan mountain chain. Central Asia had a subtropical climate that supported grasslands, forests, and lakes. Big rivers flowing north filled the Vourukasha Sea that drowned the Caspian and Aral basins and flooded Central Asia. Further south, central India supported equatorial rainforest.

There is still a refuge of the first-age India equatorial rainforest near the border of Gujarat and Maharashtra, south of the Tapti River. Another fragment of the original extensive forest still flourishes at the northern end of the Western Ghats or Sahyadri, a mountain range that runs parallel to the western coast of the Indian peninsula. The ancient rain forest is a UNESCO World Heritage Site that has over ten thousand species of plants and over a thousand different vertebrate species.

Africa in the first-age was also quite different from today. The Sahara climate was wetter and supported savanna. In contrast to the present arid climate, the northwest highlands of the Sahara toward the Atlas Mountains were wet. The region had a parkland and forest ecology that supported large herds of grazing animals.[431]

Only a narrow diagonal belt of semi-desert extended across Africa, and desert conditions could only be found in central Niger. Another startling discovery was the lack of jungle in the Congo basin. Only a narrow strip of rainforest grew along the coast from Ghana to Cameroon. In southern Africa, a second narrow desert belt crossed the continent, the remnants of which are still visible as the ancient linear dunes of Botswana.

A diagonal desert belt stretched across Eurasia of the first-age. In first-age East Asia, the Yellow Sea, the East China Sea, and the Korean

Strait did not exist. Japan was not an island but was part of continental Asia. From the highlands of Japan, across the present seafloor to southern China, temperate oak forest flourished south of the desert strip. There is plenty of fossil evidence that mammoths came to the main Japanese island of Hokkaido from Siberia, and animals could migrate between southwest Japan and the Korean Peninsula.[432] Jungles thrived across Cambodia and Vietnam, while in contrast in Southeast Asia, there was little rain, and river volumes were much lower in a region that straddles today's equator.

In the first-age, the climate of northern America was very cold, and a thick ice cap was centered on the Queen Elizabeth Islands off the north coast of Canada, presently the edge of the Arctic Circle. In the first-age, Alaska was deep frozen, and north of Montreal there were ice fields, dry tundra, and polar desert.[433]

There was a steep north-to-south temperature gradient in first-age North America too. The climate warmed rapidly southward and south of the Great Lakes; the territory was covered with river valleys cloaked in thick forest.

In place of the grasslands of the prairies, there were dense spruce forests in the mid-west. Further to the east and south in North America, the forests became denser. Even the currently arid southwestern states of North America supported dense forests. In the southeast, there was a huge territory of oak forests, which extended offshore of Florida into the Gulf of Mexico and around the Bahamas, due to much lower sea-levels.

The climate of South America was much drier and cooler than present. The north-eastern region of South America was a large desert, which got drier toward the Caribbean coast of Venezuela. A remarkable fact is that the huge Amazon rain-forest did not exist in the first-age. For thousands of years most of the Amazon basin was semi-dry savannah, and only small areas of rainforest occurred in the far southwest corner of the Amazon basin, near the Bolivian border.

Ecuador and the high salt flats of the northern Andes were much drier than today and suffered desert conditions. The climate around Lima in Peru was equatorial, while Northern Chile was desert, and farther south of Santiago, there was temperate beech forest and grass. In the first-age, another belt of sandy desert existed in northwest Argentina. The far south of Patagonia around Tierra del Fuego was very much colder than present, and there was sparse tundra vegetation, as if it was much closer to the south-pole.

All this data provided clues to the big picture of what had really happened to our planet.

The World of the Second-Age

In Europe of the second-age, a strange diagonal desert-belt extended from northern Algeria across southern Italy, Greece, the Balkans, and Asia. There was a very low total pollen-count in Greece and Italy, confirming near-desert conditions. However, this climate-belt was at a steeper angle than the climate-belt of the previous first-age and significantly angled to present latitude lines. In the second-age, semi-desert scrub land covered southern France and northern Italy and extended as far as Kazakhstan.

In sharp contrast, the Near East to the south of this belt received regular rainfall and the climate was generally warm. In Turkey, Lebanon, and Syria, there were lush grasslands supporting abundant game, while oak and pistachio forests covered the hills. Further south, Arabia had a hot and wet equatorial climate.

The climatic-belts in Africa had shifted from the previous first-age and now lay diagonally across the continent from southwest to northeast. The African climatic-belts were quite different from the horizontal equatorial and subtropical climatic stripes we observe today.

In the second-age, much of the Sahara was a green well-watered territory, supporting small trees and grasses. Between sixteen and twelve thousand years ago, there was an equatorial-belt running southwest-to-northeast, across the continent from Cameroon to the Nubian Desert in northeast Sudan, which was much wetter at this time.

Further south of this enigmatic equatorial strip, desert conditions existed near the present equator, particularly in east central Africa. The region around Mount Kenya was also hot and dry. It was a big mystery to climatologists why large areas of land we associate with tropical forest, such as the Congo basin, were semi-desert in this age. Arid conditions on the east side of Africa were so severe that the White Nile almost dried out.

In contrast, the upland catchment area of the Blue Nile further north was subtropical and very heavy rainfall fed the great river. The ocean level in the second-age was sixty meters higher than the previous first-age but still fifty meters below present ocean level.

Another enigma was that Arabia had anomalously high rainfall. Equatorial rain-forests and rivers covered a territory synonymous with desert. These ancient rivers have been detected in infra-red satellite surveys, now buried deep under the desert-sands. In southern Africa, the Kalahari (a desert region today) was also wetter and supported lush parklands.

The climate in Central Asia in the second-age was generally much wetter and warmer than in the first-age. Rainfall had increased significantly over the Pamir and Himalayan mountains as if they were close to the equator. However, as a result of a shift in climatic-belts, the former desert belt that had crossed Asia in the first-age was wetter and was invaded by shrubs and woodland. Even though the rivers flowing from the slopes of the Tien Shan mountains were full, there was much less rain over the northern Central Asian plains, which suffered semi-desert conditions.

In contrast in the second-age, southern Siberia had open woodlands of birch and conifers extending far to the east. At this time, the northern Japanese island of Hokkaido was still connected to continental Asia and was covered in dense larch forest. Northern Siberia was a temperate region of dense forests growing far out on a northern land, which is now drowned under the Arctic Ocean.

In the second-age, much higher rainfall in northern Southeast Asia supported dense forests. However, there was something very odd about the orientation of our planet in this age: Sumatra, which currently straddles the equator, was over four degrees colder than present and lacked jungle, but at the same time, a dense tropical rain-forest extended across southern China.

Stalagmites and stalactites from caves in South Korea recorded a very wet period.[434] Climate scientists call these cave deposits speleothems, which form from dissolved water-eroded limestone in dripping-water in caves. Speleothem is usually calcium-carbonate in the form of calcite or calcium sulfate in the form of gypsum. In contrast, the rainforest of central India of the previous age retreated to the western coastal highlands of the subcontinent.

Between the first-age and second-age, the North American ice cap had been shifted further south to cover Hudson bay. The northern limit of this ice cap was the Queen Elizabeth Islands, the center of the ice-cap in the previous age. The circular region of thick ice extended across Canada to ice cliffs north of the Great Lakes and Chicago. In contrast, shrubs grew and insect populations expanded in northern Alaska that was warmer than in the first-age.

Southward of the Hudson bay ice cap, there was still a steep temperature gradient, and generally North America was warm and received regular rainfall. In the second-age, the continent was covered with ancient river courses, which are now dry and buried. Thick deciduous forest covered much of the lowland, while spruce and pine woodland blanketed the hills and mountain slopes. Large populations of mastodon and mammoth roamed the whole continent.

South America was about five degrees cooler in the second-age. Ecuador had semi-desert conditions, while in northern Peru the rain was regular and heavy. Lake Titicaca was much larger than today, the water-level was seventy meters higher, and the region around Lake Titicaca had a wet-temperate climate with heavy rain.

In the second-age, the equatorial zone of South America was about two thousand kilometers south of its present position and was oddly compressed. It was located in northern Chile, which had a hot-wet equatorial climate that supported dense tropical rain-forest, but it only grew there for about four thousand years.

In the second age, southern South America became much warmer. In addition, a steep temperature gradient was revealed in the climate data from South America of this age: the boundary of the temperate zone was about a thousand kilometers closer to the equatorial zone. In addition, there was an odd lack of evidence for seasonality in South America in the first-age and second-age.

SHIFTS OF THE EQUATOR IN EACH AGE OF THE WORLD
RELOCATED THE AMAZON RAINFOREST

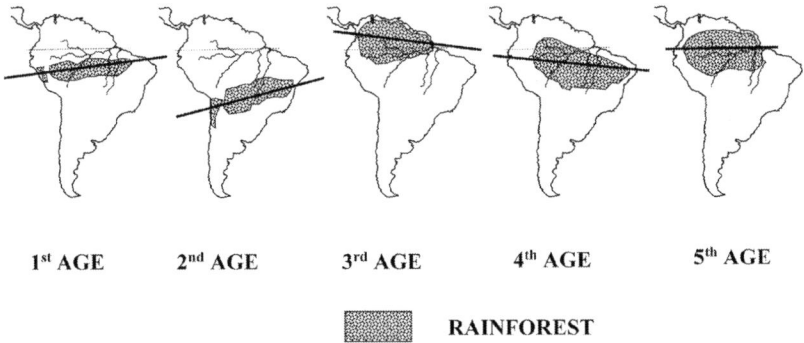

| 1ˢᵗ AGE | 2ⁿᵈ AGE | 3ʳᵈ AGE | 4ᵗʰ AGE | 5ᵗʰ AGE |

RAINFOREST

An abrupt climate change occurred in Tierra del Fuego on the southern tip of South America, across the Southern Ocean from West Antarctica. The environment switched from the cold and dry tundra of the first-age to warm and wet woodlands in the second age.[435]

This abrupt climate change correlated with an extraordinary difference in climate that also opened up across Antarctica in the second-age. West-Antarctica, the side of Antarctica closer to South America, got warmer, while in contrast East-Antarctica, which faces Australia, got much colder. It seemed as if the South Pole had been shifted toward Australia.

The World of the Third-Age

Between the second-age and third-age, there was a huge shift in the pattern of the climatic-belts across our planet.[436] During the 9600 BC cataclysm, the diagonal climate-stripes across the globe of the previous age vanished. In the new pattern of the third-age, the climatic-belts crossed

Africa parallel to the present equator, but all the belts were shifted about a thousand kilometers to the south of their present boundaries.[437]

At the beginning of the third-age, the start of the Holocene climatic period, the seasonal changes across the planet had also been dramatically amplified, particularly in the summer. There was also a general increase in total heating of the planet surface; this resulted in such warm summers that even inside the Arctic Circle, most of the ice-fields on land melted away and sea-ice was substantially reduced. Although the climate of the Holocene was more stable than the previous Late Pleistocene, there was still substantial variability.[438]

The 9600 BC cataclysm destroyed the great Russian forests that long ago stretched northward deep into the Arctic. Their remains were deep-frozen, during the bitterly cold century of the Younger Dryas. However, after the heavy cloud cover broke up, the higher insolation led to a much warmer climate during the third-age. Regrowth of dense forests occurred in northern Siberia, beyond the present northern limit for forest, as the trees exploited the warmer arctic region.

The strange belt of desert that had crossed Europe and Asia of the second-age had abruptly disappeared. In third-age Europe, warm winters and hot wet summers supported thick oak forests. Southern Europe became much warmer and wetter too. Pollen recovered from sediment cores drilled into lake bottoms in both Italy and Greece, demonstrated that the local climates in the third-age supported dense forest of oak, hornbeam, and ash.

Another oddity was that typical northern European trees started growing all around the Mediterranean region, not only on Crete but even on the north coast of Africa. The north coast of Africa from Algeria to Israel during this warm and wet period seemed to have had a climate similar to Europe of the present day.

The highlands and mountains on the east coast of the Mediterranean received unusually high rainfall. Across Turkey, northern Syria, and northern Iraq, forests progressively colonized the land. Thick cedar and pistachio forest grew in Lebanon and Palestine. The Lebanon and anti-Lebanon mountains were the source of many rivers that crossed a lush and green Syria. Inland beyond the Mediterranean coastal mountains, there were verdant hills and water-eroded river valleys, not the desert of today.

At the start of the third-age, across the whole of Africa there was a substantial increase in temperature and rain. The higher rainfall supported a web of river systems across North Africa from the Atlantic coast to the Red Sea. The Sahara was a vast territory of green grasslands and open woodland, with rivers and lakes scattered across the whole territory.[439] In the central Saharan highlands, woodlands flourished in this very wet climate, which persisted for the next four thousand years.

In the third-age, the Nile River ran in a deep gorge, channeling raging torrents of run-off water from wet northern Africa. The great river delivered huge volumes of freshwater into the eastern Mediterranean. Southern Ethiopia was subtropical, and the rainfall had more than doubled in volume, compared to the previous age. As a result of the larger volumes of rainwater runoff, the water levels in the lakes were fifty percent higher.

In east-central Africa, around Mount Kenya and around Mount Kilimanjaro, it was hot and wet. Rainfall was at least twice what it is today in East Africa, and lakes rose to maximum levels. Dense tropical forest blanketed the hills around Lake Tanganyika, as if this was the location of the equator in this age of the world.

In West Africa, rivers and lake levels also rose rapidly, and the River Niger showed a sudden burst of flood activity. Rain-forest increased in density along the southern side of the Congo basin and expanded eastward toward Tanzania.

The climate of southern Africa also shifted: the annual rainfall was lower than the previous second-age and the climate became warm and dry. The Kalahari region switched from lush grass parkland to dry savannah.

In the third-age, Arabia was drier than the previous age and no longer had an equatorial climate, but the territory still had sufficient rain to support rolling grasslands, forests, and many rivers. Sediment cores drilled in the bottom of the northern Red Sea confirmed there was still a huge fresh water run-off from this strange rain-washed Arabia.[440]

At the beginning of the third-age, there was also a shift in the climatic-belts across Asia. Central Asia supported forest and pastures in what are now the dry Karakum and Kyzylkum deserts. Heavy rainfall on the Pamirs and Himalaya mountain ranges filled the rivers carrying huge volumes of water, both to the north and to the south.

In contrast, the weather in China transformed into a northern temperate climate and became rapidly cooler and much dryer. The equatorial conditions in southern China of the previous age vanished, as the tropical zone had moved southward.

In contrast, in East Asia there was an increase in temperature and humidity, and flooding resulted in a rapid expansion of mangrove forests.[441, 442] In Southeast Asia, temperature and humidity increased substantially to extreme tropical conditions. In the third-age, there were dense equatorial rainforests forming a belt from Sumatra, through Borneo to New Guinea, further to the south of the present equator.

The third-age in North America commenced after a slow recovery from the lethal 9600 BC cataclysm. Mass extinctions wiped out most of the large mammals in both North and South America. When the third-age commenced thirty-five genera including mammoth, mastodon, camel, horse, and ground sloth, which had all proliferated in the second-age, had vanished from North and South America. The most remarkable change was the sudden disappearance of the huge ice cap in Hudson bay, which had dominated the continent in the previous age.

Polar conditions disappeared from North America, and the climate stabilized to a new level that was warmer and wetter than present. Large lake systems replaced the ice-sheet in de-glaciated Canada. Conifers colonized the northern territory, and southern Canada was taken over by dense forests of spruce trees.

With the new warmer climate, the prairie zone extended hundreds of kilometers further to the north. Forests and prairie grasslands colonized the Midwest. Generally temperate forests dominated the territory further south, and the mix of tree species shifted from oak and ash to larch and birch. The climate in the southwest of North America was more humid, supporting open forest, where today is desert waste.

In third-age South America, there were equatorial conditions in Columbia, to the north of the present equatorial zone in Ecuador. River systems expanded rapidly in the Amazon basin, and rain-forest colonized the land as far as the mouths of the Amazon River. The high salt flats of Peru and Bolivia in the northern Andes became sub-tropical. Lake Titicaca overflowed and ancient lake-shore settlement sites were drowned. There were no El Nino cycles in this age of the world.

In the Pampa region of Argentina, the semi-dry climate of the second-age switched suddenly to a warmer and more humid climate supporting a wide range of plants. In Patagonia and Tierra del Fuego in the south, the region was cooler and drier than in the second-age, and savannah vegetation claimed the territory.

Generally Antarctica warmed in the third-age and remained warmer until the start of the fifth-age.[443] However, there were still climatic differences between West Antarctica and East Antarctica, as if the South Pole had been shifted closer to South America.

A sediment-core recovered from the bottom of Lake Terrasovoje, East Antarctica, revealed that during the Early Holocene, after a rapid thaw, an ancient lake was sufficiently ice-free for a three meter layered deposit of algal-microbial mats interspersed with moss. This seasonally ice-free lake, which was green in the southern hemisphere summer, persisted in East Antarctica until the end of the third-age, eight thousand years ago.[444]

The World of the Fourth-Age

At the cataclysmic start of the fourth-age, there was a break in the pollen record in Europe at 5600 BC, showing vast areas of forest had been destroyed suddenly. Studies of the sea floor show that eight thousand years ago, a massive underwater landslide happened off the coast of Norway; huge waves struck the Shetlands and then raged down the east coast of Scotland. The Great Flood ripped across the territory connecting the United kingdom and Europe, drowning the land under the North Sea and English Channel.

The North Sea, English Channel, Baltic Sea, and Black Sea all appeared suddenly at this time. The climate of Europe abruptly shifted to a new pattern. Forests spread into northern Scandinavia and northern Scotland.[445] Switzerland developed a warm wet climate, and there was no evidence of winter ice on alpine lakes or any alpine feeder glaciers.

In the Mediterranean region, when the forests recovered in the early fourth-age, a different mix of species of trees grew compared to the previous age. In Italy, there was a sharp drop in the density of forest, and the oak trees were replaced by Alder. In Greece and Cyprus, evergreen trees and shrubs became dominant. These drought-tolerant trees replaced the earlier rain-watered deciduous forests of ash and oak. In contrast, Mesopotamia and Persia of the fourth-age were wetter and greener than the arid conditions of those lands today.

In fourth-age Africa, a new climate developed that was drier than the previous age, though still wetter than our present age. In the Sahara, the forests had been destroyed, and the dominant vegetation was savannah grasses.

Similarly, in East Africa forests were replaced by savannah and parkland. Around Mount Kenya and Mount Kilimanjaro, wet and warm conditions prevailed. Rain-forest trees grew rapidly and spread northward in the Congo, and the rain-forest reached its maximum territorial extent in central Africa in the fourth-age.

In contrast, the volume of rainfall in Arabia dropped at the start of the fourth-age. However, the territory still supported shrub and savannah, in areas that are only harsh sandy desert today. The atmospheric temperature in this region also increased to a higher average level. Salinity of the Red Sea steadily increased, due to increased evaporation and the sharp decrease in the run-off of fresh water from Arabia.

In Central Asia, an unusually warm, wet temperate climate developed, known as the Neo-Caspian. Half a meter of rainfall each year and the average July temperature was a pleasant twenty-three degrees Celsius. This weather supported lush plant growth, even as far east as the Tarim basin, which is now a harsh desert region on the border with China.

At the start of the fourth-age, Siberian winters were mild, and in eastern Siberia birch forests advanced north into the Tundra.[446] Summers in northern Finland were about two degrees Celsius warmer than present.[447] Warmer winters on the island of Spitsbergen north of Norway kept it ice-free and sedimentation increased in its lakes.[448, 449]

Like the United Kingdom, Japan was cut off completely from its nearby continent during the Great Flood of 5600 BC. Warm temperate forests spread across China and Japan. The new temperate wet climate in China, northern India, and Pakistan, allowed the development of intensive agriculture.

At the start of the fourth-age, northern Greenland developed a polar climate. The climate in Canada shifted to cold and damper conditions. In contrast, most of North America became much hotter and drier, compared to the previous age. In central North America, there was drought, plants died, and sand dunes replaced parkland.[450, 451] In the prairies, grasslands replaced the forests of the third-age. In what is now the southern states of the United States, the lakes and rivers dried out, and old waterways became choked with sand as deserts expanded.

In South America, during the 5600 BC cataclysm, there was a massive destruction of the forests. In the fourth-age that followed, the climate of South America was much drier. When forests grew back, they were much less dense than in the previous age. An El Nino ocean current cycle along the Pacific coast of South America commenced at the beginning of the fourth-age, but coral records showed that the sea water off Peru was warmer than today.

On the coastal territory straddling southern Peru and northern Chile, a new arid climate transformed the territory into desert. In the ultra-dry conditions, human settlement collapsed, and the region became a wasteland for the next four thousand years.

The climate in the Andes also became hotter and drier. After the rains ceased to fall on the high plateau, the lake-levels dropped exposing former lake-bottoms. Even the vast Lake Titicaca almost dried out completely in the fourth-age: its water level fell eighty-five meters. Freshwater planktons disappeared and were replaced by salt tolerant species.

At the start of the fourth-age, at the southern tip of the South American continent, the climate down-shifted to wetter and colder weather. West-Antarctica also got colder at the beginning of the fourth-age.

The World of the Fifth-Age

Ecosystems were destroyed all around the world in the Cataclysm-of-Fire of 1628 BC. Only at the beginning of our current fifth-age, did the climate patterns we recognize today become established. In Europe, the Alps became significantly colder and alpine glacial conditions commenced. Siberia became suddenly colder at the start of the fifth-age, and the island of Spitsbergen off the north coast of Norway got so much colder that glaciers grew rapidly.[452]

In Greece, the climate became much drier. Only low-density forest grew back and typical drought-tolerant Mediterranean plant species dominated. As Italy became cooler and drier, beech trees became common, but the total forest density declined.[453]

As the rains failed in the Near East, the lands beyond the mountains at the eastern end of the Mediterranean were gripped by desert conditions. Whole river systems vanished from Syria and only their dry river beds remain crossing the region. Arabia and the Sahara also became the harsh uninhabitable desert regions we recognize today.

In Africa, there was generally less rain, and the climate to the south of the Sahara became drier than in the previous age. The larger central African rain-forest, which had expanded in the fourth-age, retreated west and concentrated in the Congo basin, leaving the land to the east with semi-deciduous trees and open parkland.

Across Asia the current climate zones were established. Arid desert replaced large areas of land previously favorable to agriculture in Central Asia, as rainfall dropped to near zero and average annual temperatures doubled. From the middle of the second millennium BC, agriculture was only possible on irrigated land, mainly around the lower Amu-Darya River. The extreme desiccation caused the rapid formation of the Karakum and Kyzylkum deserts, which replaced once-green lands.

The fertile growing lands of the Indus valley of Pakistan also abruptly dried out and were replaced by the Thar Desert. The Saraswati River system of northwest India vanished, causing the collapse of the city-based civilization that had once flourished in that region. China also experienced the collapse of urban culture in the northwest as drought forced people to migrate southeast, toward the river-valleys and coasts.

In North America, the climate shifted to its present conditions; cool wet conifer forest in Canada, prairie in the center, and hot dry desert in the Southwest. In South America, after huge fires destroyed large areas of forest in the 1628 BC cataclysm, the present climatic-belts became established.[454]

The South American climate became regulated by a powerful El Nino ocean current off the Pacific coast and the characteristic stripes in lake sediment cores appeared, recording the regular changes in the ocean currents and weather. On the southern coastal region of Peru, the climate switched from harsh desert to temperate grassland, and shrubs began to grow as the weather became warmer and wetter.

On the Altiplano in the high Andes, the weather suddenly became much wetter. Deep water cores from Lake Titicaca and high altitude ice cores from Sajama in Bolivia showed that the lakes re-filled with fresh water. In Northern Chile, the rains suddenly returned and the climate improved. The climate in Tierra del Fuego on the southern tip of South America became wet and cold. Only hardy frost-tolerant scrub plants survived in the region.

In our fifth-age, the climates of East-Antarctica and West-Antarctica changed to the relatively uniform cold climate of present Antarctica. These conditions are usually explained to be the result of concentric isotherms surrounding the South Pole, which is currently located near the middle of the Southern Continent.

Conclusion

There is a very significant pattern in this huge trawl of data. It is obvious from the description in the previous two chapters, that the climate history of every region had distinct climatic-ages, which arrived suddenly during terrible cataclysms and lasted around four thousand years.

The annual seasons were not a permanent feature of the weather system of our planet either. During the first-age and second-age, the Earth had remarkably little seasonality and it was generally colder, with extremely cold polar zones. In these two ages, our planet also displayed sharp north-south transitions from cold to temperate climates.

However, there is a deeper message. During each age, the climatic-belts of the Tropic of Cancer, the equator, and the Tropic of Capricorn had different orientations and extents, compared to today. The regional climate data in different eras suggested that the geographic poles of our planet had been moved.

BETWEEN 2nd AGE AND 3rd AGE OF THE WORLD,
THE POLES AND EQUATOR SHIFTED, THE AXIAL TILT INCREASED
AND THE TROPICS WIDENED

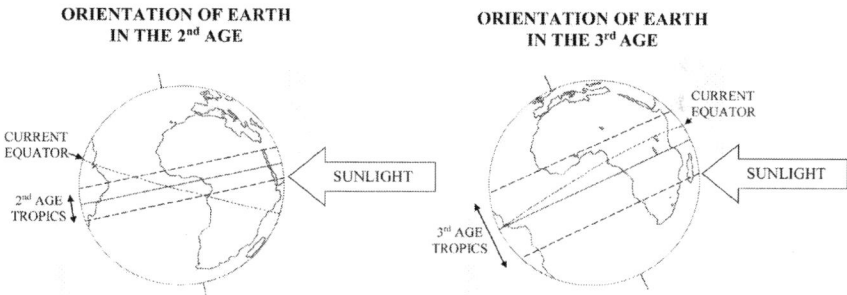

A revolutionary synthesis of all this information shall be presented in the next chapter.

CHAPTER 4

Abrupt Axial and Orbital Shifts of Earth

● ● ●

THE COMPLEX RESULTS OF CLIMATE-HISTORY research can be explained by a simple but extraordinary theory. In each age of our world, the remarkable changes in the global climate, and the strange shifts in the Earth's climatic-belts, were caused by fly-bys of star-core-zeus.

Every four thousand years, as star-core-zeus returned to the Sun, it dived at high velocity through the inner solar-system. As it passed close to Earth, its gravitational and electromagnetic fields caused our planet to rock-and-roll. Our planet was even dragged into slightly different orbits around the Sun by this massive celestial body.

Those seemingly immoveable reference points—the north-pole, the equator, and the south-pole—have been repeatedly forced to change location, resulting in shifts in the positions of the climatic-belts. The angle between the rotation axis of the Earth and its orbital plane around the Sun has also been changed: this altered the amount of seasonality between one climatic-age and the next.

The average orbital radius of our planet around the Sun was also altered, which changed the insolation: the total amount of solar heating our planet received. In addition, my previous book, *Cataclysms & Renewals*, described how the change in orbital radius altered the number of days-per-year.

Pole and Equator Shift

A sudden shift in the location of the north-pole, the equator, and the south-pole is the simplest explanation for the abrupt relocation of the climatic-belts across the globe, from one climatic-age to the next.

The climate data collected from the ice-core sites in Greenland and Antarctica, combined with other coring data from around the world, suggests that the ice-caps at the Arctic and Antarctic had been relocated on a number of occasions. Both poles of the rotation axis seem to have been shifted across the surface of our planet from their current positions, by up to five-thousand kilometers.

POLE SHIFT & EQUATOR SHIFT
BETWEEN THE WORLD AGES

1st Age: -17600-13600BC. (1)

2nd Age: -13600-9600BC. (2)

3rd Age: -9600-5600BC. (3)

4th Age:-5600-1600BC. (4)

5th Age: -1600BC-PRESENT.

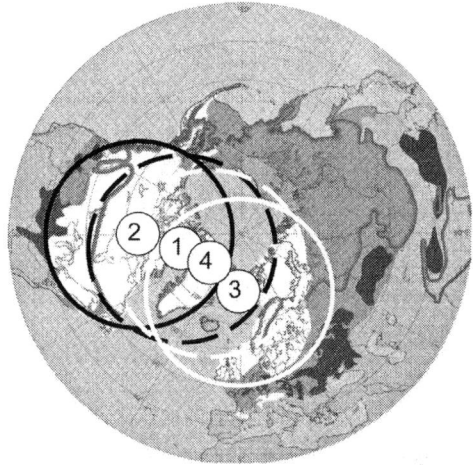

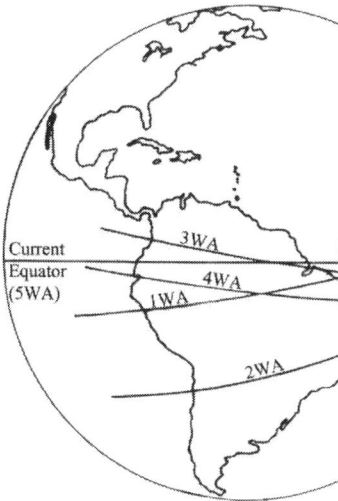

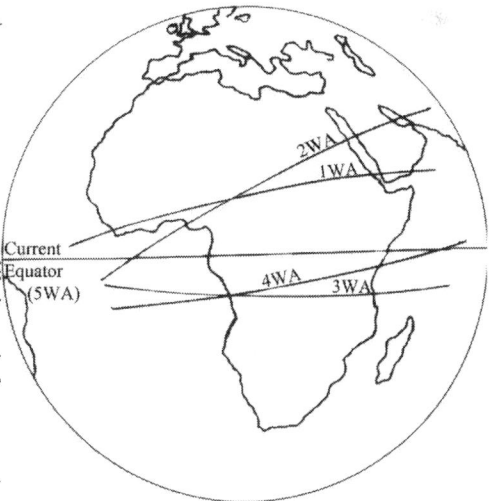

These pole-shifts resulted in relocation of the equator and all the associated climatic-belts, in each age of the world. This idea is simple to demonstrate using a globe removed from its axial mount: shifting the north-pole by fifteen degrees across the Arctic Ocean automatically rotates the equator by fifteen degrees, and hence shifts all the climatic-belts by the same angle.

The possibility of recent pole-shifts has only been seriously considered by a few scientists. One of the best reviews on the subject was a scientific paper by Warlow, in which he demonstrated by mathematical models that the Earth was quite sensitive to pole shifts by tumbling. He reviewed evidence that the formation of huge crustal fractures in the Earth were closely connected to magnetic pole reversal and extinctions of animals. He believed these events could have been induced by violent changes in the Earth's rotation, caused by close-encounters with a massive astronomical object.[455, 456, 457]

First-Age Poles

Between 17,600 BC and 13,600 BC, north-pole-1 of the first-age was fifteen degrees away from the present North Pole. This north-pole-1 was located in the western Queen Elizabeth Islands, off the northern coast of Canada (Latitude 76° N, Longitude 120° W). In this age of the world, Alaska was very cold and dry, because it lay only five to fifteen degrees away from north-pole-1.[458] Alaska's present location between sixty-degree-north-latitude and seventy-degrees-north-latitude is between twenty and thirty degrees away from the present North Pole.

The equator-1 of the first-age passed through central Peru and Brazil to the south of the Amazon basin; then crossed the Atlantic Ocean and cut through Africa via Liberia, Nigeria, Chad, and Sudan; and then crossed on through Yemen in Arabia, central India, South Vietnam, and the southern Philippines. The previous two chapters detailed that all these regions had had a hot and wet equatorial climate in the first-age.

Second-Age Poles

At the beginning of the second-age, the north pole had been shifted from Queen Elizabeth Islands in northern Canada, to a new position in Hudson bay (Latitude 60° N, Longitude 90° W). The Laurentide ice sheet grew from a new spreading center located at north-pole-2 in Hudson bay. Glacial ice flowed north as far as Queen Elizabeth Islands, the location of the previous north-pole-1.

However, the ice-core sites in the highlands of central Greenland remained cold because they were still at approximately the same distance from north-pole-1 and north-pole-2, so no warm-period appeared in the northern ice core data covering the second-age. In this age of the world, Alaska was also between twenty and thirty degrees away from this north-pole-2, so it had a cold and damp climate similar to the present.

In contrast, in the second-age, the island of Spitsbergen off the north coast of Norway in the Arctic Ocean was much warmer than today.[459] Remains of temperate plant species found buried on the island suggests that in the second-age Spitsbergen was located at a latitude much further south, much further away from north-pole-2 than it is from the present North Pole.[460]

During the second-age, the Arctic coast of Siberia was also ice-free. Northern Siberia had a temperate climate and supported meadows and forests. This was confirmed by stomach content preserved in the carcasses of mammoths, which were discovered buried in the perma-frost of northern Siberia. They had been abruptly killed and flash-frozen during the cataclysm of 9600 BC. The remains of temperate summer meadow vegetation including flowers could still be identified.

The second-age poles were thirty degrees from their present positions, so equator-2 was also rotated by thirty degrees relative to its present orientation. Equator-2 crossed the Pacific Ocean near Easter Island and then passed through South America via central Chile, northern Argentina, and southern Brazil. It ran across the South Atlantic and reached the African coast at Cameroon. Equator-2 then bisected Sudan and Saudi Arabia, crossed southern Iran and Pakistan, and then passed along the southern wall of the Himalayas and on through southern China, which supported an equatorial rainforest in this age.

As a result of a huge shift of climatic-belts: there was harsh desert in Mali and Liberia, but tropical rain reached northward to the Red

Sea and Arabia. The climate of the present western Mediterranean was shifted south into the Atlas Mountains of Morocco. This orientation of equator-2 put Turkey, Cyprus, Greece, and Italy in a desert belt. In contrast, Spain (the Iberian Peninsula) retained a mild climate in both the first-age and second-age.

A shift of the Earth's poles was the only reasonable explanation for a curious set of regional climate changes in South America.[461] For the four millennia of the first-age, Chile had a temperate climate that supported beech trees and grass. The environment was destroyed in the cataclysm of 13,600 BC, and there followed a brief period of extreme cold recorded by the advance and retreat of glaciers.

Then suddenly at the start of the second-age, tropical rain-forests colonized central Chile and persisted until the climate cataclysm of 9600 BC. While Chile supported steaming jungle, the temperature of the tropical waters off Barbados were four degrees Celsius colder than today.[462] At the same time, a thick ice cap accumulated over Hudson bay in Canada.

These co-ordinated changes of climate across the globe could be simply explained by a shift of equator-2 into Chile during the second-age. The location of equator-2 in Chile, thirty degrees south of the present equator in Ecuador, automatically meant that north-pole-2 must have been thirty degrees south of the location of our present North Pole and located in Hudson bay.

Simple geometry also dictated that south-pole-2 must have been located off the east coast of Antarctica facing Australia, which explained the enigmatic warming of West-Antarctica relative to East Antarctica in the second-age.[463]

Third-Age Poles

The 9600 BC cataclysm that ended the second-age also terminated a very long cold period in the global climate that had persisted for one hundred and twenty thousand years.[464, 465] Something strange happened at this time, because while Greenland, Europe, and Siberia were suddenly frozen for at least a century, the North American ice-cap centered on Hudson bay explosively melted and promptly disappeared.

Temperatures jumped almost instantly by sixteen degrees Celsius at the ice-core drill sites located near the North Pole and the South Pole. Simultaneously, there were huge changes in the climatic system of the world. The average global temperature was maintained at much higher levels in the third-age and fourth-age (the early and mid-Holocene), a duration of approximately eight thousand years.

In contrast to this general rise in global temperature, the peaks of the Rocky Mountains in North America, the Altiplano of the Andes in South America, and the high mountain crags of the Pamirs and Himalayas of Asia, all suddenly got much colder. There is some evidence, which shall be covered later in this book, that unusual tectonic activity during the cataclysm of 9600 BC caused an abrupt rise in the elevation of mountain chains all around the world.

After the 9600 BC cataclysm, north-pole-3 was relocated close to the island of Spitsbergen (Latitude 85° N, Longitude 30° E) off the north coast of Norway. Spitsbergen and northern Norway suffered a century of severe cold at the beginning of the third-age during the Younger Dryas freeze, but after the cloud cover dissipated, more intense solar radiation warmed up the whole planet.

This natural global warming in the third-age was so intense that even though the island of Spitsbergen was very close to north-pole-3 in the third-age, its glaciers melted away.[466] Alaska became warm and wet as a result of the pole-shift and increased insolation in the third-age.[467] During this age, Alaska was located more than thirty degrees from the north-pole-3, so it developed a climate similar to modern France. The favorable growing conditions stimulated a rapid proliferation of insect life, plants, and even poplar trees.[468]

It appears that the major global-warming after the 9600 BC cataclysm was due to not only a shift of the poles and equator but also due to a small reduction in the radius of the orbit of Earth around the Sun.

This increased insolation, the average annual amount of solar energy arriving at the surface of Earth.

Fourth-Age Poles

After the 5600 BC flood-cataclysm, the new north-pole-4 was located on the north coast of Greenland (Latitude 82° N, Longitude 60° W), which became much colder in the fourth-age. However, this did not significantly affect the average temperature over the whole Arctic region.

However, the new location of north-pole-4 pulled the subtropical desert belt into the southern Sahara region. At the start of the fourth-age, the climate and ecology in the rest of the Sahara was transformed from wet lush parkland into semi-dry grass savannah.

In the fourth-age, the equator-4 crossed Africa from northern Angola to southern Tanzania, which was about five degrees south of the present equator. This resulted in desert conditions in much of the Congo basin. Mean lake-levels decreased in central Africa due to increased global temperature, faster evaporation, and less rainfall. The higher intensity of solar radiation, due to a slightly smaller orbital radius of our planet, gave rise to generally higher global temperatures.

Fifth-Age Poles

In the 1628 BC cataclysm, the geographic poles were shifted to their present positions. Equatorial rain-forest only arrived in the Congo and the Amazon basin four thousand years ago, due to the change in orientation of our planet. At the same time, the Sahara region became much drier, resulting in the harsh desert conditions we know today. Generally, between the fourth-age and our fifth-age, the average global temperatures fell by about two degrees Celsius. It appears that Earth had been shoved about one to two percent further from the Sun, decreasing annual average insolation and increasing the number of days per year by a similar percent.

Pole Shift and Sea Level change

If the Earth was a perfect sphere, shifting the geographic poles would have little effect on local sea-level. However, Earth is slightly flattened at the poles and slightly fatter at the equator. The radius of the Earth at the poles is about twenty kilometers less than the radius at the equator. This geometry dictates that pole-shifts directly affect local sea-level.[469]

When the poles shifted suddenly, the water rapidly rushed into the lowest basins in a matter of days, but the rocks took centuries to adjust to the change in orientation of the rotation axis. Consider this extreme example: if Greenland was suddenly shifted to the equator by a seventy degree pole shift, even the highest land in Greenland would be drowned kilometers-deep underwater.

Sudden pole-shifts must have caused dramatic differential changes in sea-level around the globe. Land moving away from the equator rose relative to the new local sea-level, whereas land moving toward the equator sank relative to the new local sea-level.

The most dramatic shift in polar latitude was between the second-age and third-age, when the poles moved twenty degrees during the cataclysm of 9600 BC. Europe was simultaneously shifted twenty degrees north, away from the new equator-3, while North America was shifted by the same amount toward the new equator-3.

This twenty degree pole-shift caused extreme sea-level changes midway between the poles and the equator-3: large areas of continental shelf disappeared into the sea. There is one famous result of this effect: the sudden drowning of ancient lands that had existed around the peaks of the Mid-Atlantic Ridge.

Atlantis disappeared suddenly under the rapidly rising Atlantic Ocean in 9600 BC. Plato said that the land of Atlantis was once located in the middle of the Atlantic Ocean beyond the Straits of Gibraltar (Pillars of Hercules), but it was drowned in a single day, nine thousand years before the time of Solon (which was 9600 BC). Once written-off as just an ancient fable, the drowning of Atlantis in the context of this model was a real phenomenon.

In addition in the second-age, Easter Island was located on equator-2. The twenty degree pole-shift before the start of the third-age resulted in a sudden fall in local sea-levels in the South Pacific. This revealed many new lands, large tracts of new territory, around Easter Island, the Marquis Islands, and the shallower regions of the East Pacific Rise. This new territory gave rise to the legends of Hiva or Khiva told by the Polynesians of the South Pacific and the Hopi Indians of Arizona.

During the Great Flood of 5600 BC, the legendary land of Hiva was inundated but is still recalled in the names of the Marquis Islands; Nuka Hiva, Fatu Hiva, and Hiva Oa were long ago its former mountain-tops. At the start of the fourth-age, north-pole-4 was moved five degrees from Spitsbergen to the north coast of Greenland. This caused the Middle East to move toward the equator-4 by five degrees, which resulted in land being lost to the sea.

As the land of the Middle East sank relative to local sea level, very high pressures were applied to the sub-surface aquifers, which resulted in huge fountains of water bursting-up through the ground. This was described in ancient myths of the Great Flood as "the breaking open of the fountains of the deep," which were described in my previous book *Cataclysms & Renewals*. The wide dry river valley of the lower Euphrates suddenly flooded at this time to become the Persian Gulf.

During the Cataclysm of Fire in 1628 BC, the old north-pole-4 shifted from the north coast of Greenland to its present location in the middle of the Arctic Ocean. As a result of this pole-shift, the Middle East moved north by two-point-five degrees. This latitude shift was confirmed by ancient astronomical observations, which gave the position of Babylon around 1900 BC, two-point-five degrees of latitude further south, than the position given by more recent ancient astronomical observations also made in Babylon about a thousand years later, which corresponded with present geography.[470]

EQUATOR & POLES IN EACH AGE OF THE WORLD

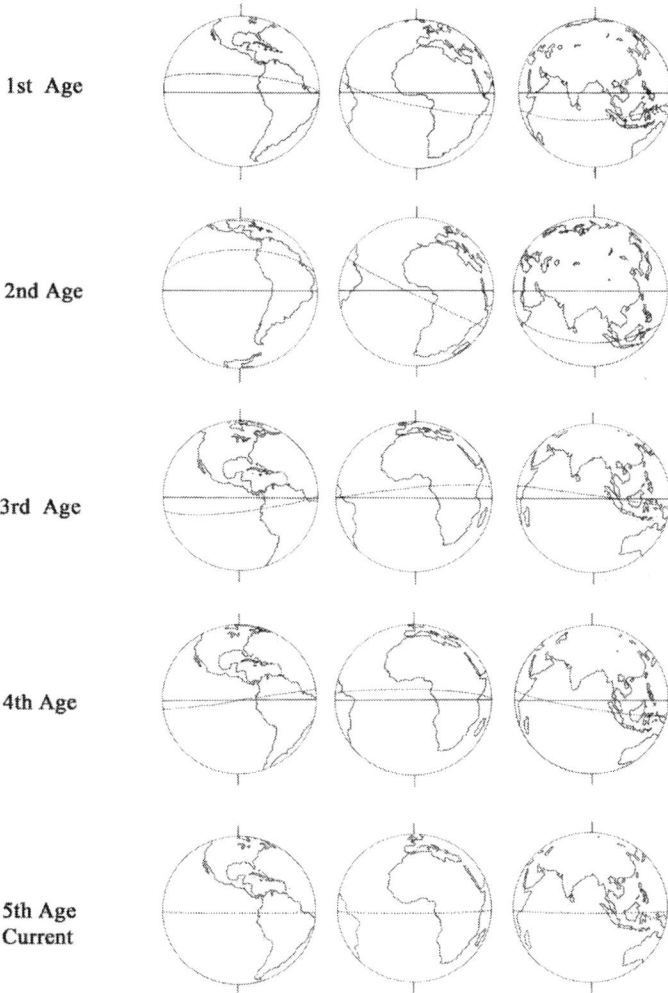

1st Age

2nd Age

3rd Age

4th Age

5th Age
Current

Changes of Axial-Tilt of Earth and Changes of Seasonality

The climate history data also revealed that intensity of global-seasonality and the regions of the globe experiencing seasonality changed from one age of the world to the next.

The origin of seasonality can be understood by simple observations at night. Looking due north and up at the starry-sky in the northern hemisphere from dusk to dawn, the constellation of Ursa Major—the Great Bear constellation of stars, which contains the seven bright stars of the Plow (Big Dipper)—seems to revolve around a fixed position in the night-sky. The location of this pivot in the sky, also known as the north celestial pole, is marked by a small dim star, known as the North Pole Star (Polaris).

In addition, every night of the year the location of the pivot in the sky seems to stay the same. The North Pole Star in the northern sky remains the apparent location of the pivot of the other stars. However, the north celestial pole around which the stars appear to rotate is an illusion; it is our planet that is rotating around its rotation axis, which remains in a fixed orientation relative to the distant stars throughout the year, as the Earth orbits around the Sun.

Seasonality is the result of our planet traveling around the Sun, with its rotation axis in a fixed orientation, angled to the plane of its orbit. As the Earth revolves around the Sun in one year, its rotation axis maintains its fixed orientation, mainly due to the gyroscopic forces of our massive rotating planet. However, the rotation axis of Earth is not fixed at a right-angle to the orbital plane of Earth, so the amount of solar-energy warming different regions of our planet varies throughout the year.

The relative geometry and the motion of the Earth around the Sun creates local summer, autumn, winter, and spring. The seasonal weather change at a particular location on Earth is due to the changing angle of incident solar-energy hitting the surface, the amount of atmospheric filtering of the solar-energy, and the relative duration of day and night.

The range of variation of the seasons during one year is controlled by the extent of the tilt of the Earth's rotation axis, away from the right-angle to the orbital plane of the Earth around the Sun. This angle is known as the axial-tilt and is currently twenty-three-point-five degrees.

The angle of the axial-tilt of the Earth determines the area of our planet's surface, which is outside the tropics, and is subject to seasonality. The zone of the tropics covers two belts of territory on either side of the equator, bounded by latitude-lines called the Tropic of Cancer to the north and the Tropic of Capricorn to the south. The two latitude-lines of Cancer and Capricorn are located at a latitude-angle of

THE SEASONS, THE FIXED ORIENTATION OF EARTH & ITS ELLIPTICAL ORBIT AROUND THE SUN

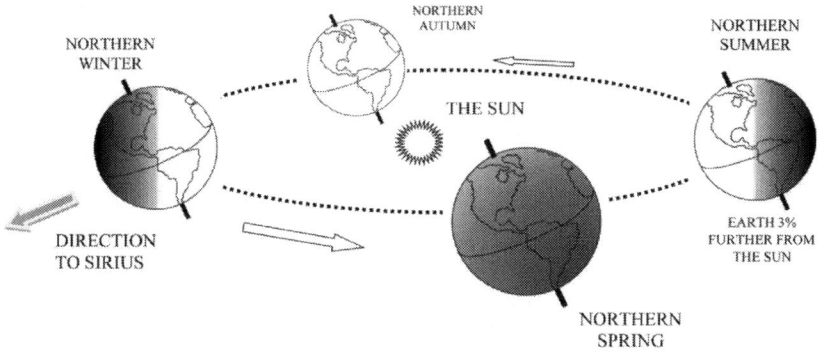

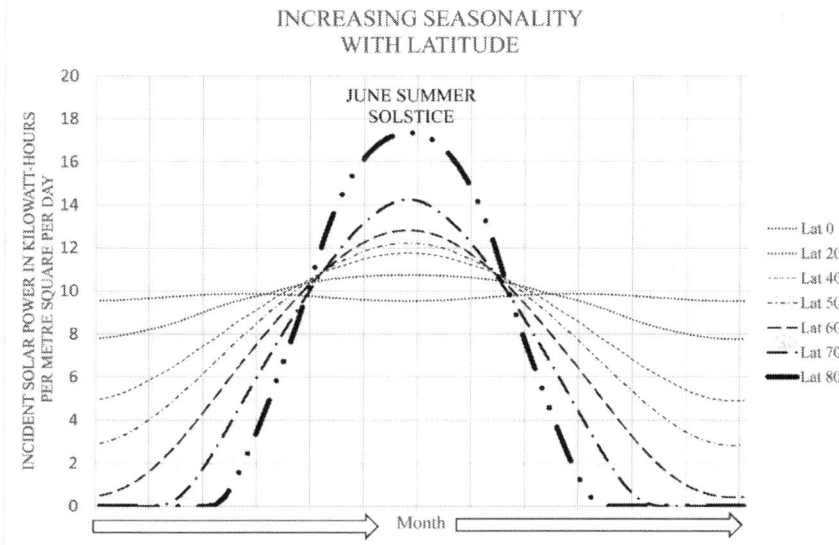

twenty-three-point-five degrees either side of the equator. Simple geometry determines that the latitude-angle is the same angle as the axial-tilt of our planet.[471]

Within the zone of the tropics, there is very little seasonality, because the duration of daylight and the temperature throughout the year is fairly constant. For example, in modern times, Nairobi on the equator has no seasonal variation in temperature, and even Addis Ababa ten degrees north of the Equator within the Tropic of Cancer has no obvious seasons and only a two degree Celsius variation in temperature between January and June.

In contrast outside the tropics, the duration of daylight and the temperature throughout the year varies significantly, inducing seasonal variations in climate. For example, Cyprus located thirty-five degrees north of the equator has definite seasons and up to a thirty degree Celsius variation in temperature from January to June.

Increasing the axial-tilt of the Earth not only increases the intensity of seasonality; it also reduces the extent of the climatic-belts of the globe beyond the tropics that experience seasons. In addition, increases in the axial-tilt *decreases* the temperature gradient between the poles and the equator.

In contrast, reducing the axial-tilt of the earth reduces the intensity of the seasonality and also reduces the zone of the tropics. In addition, decreases in the axial-tilt *increases* the temperature gradient between the poles and equator.

If there was no axial-tilt, the rotation axis of the Earth would be perpendicular to its orbital plane. The result would be no seasons and almost no solar-energy would heat the poles. The solar-heating at the equator would be at a maximum, so the temperature gradient between the poles and equator of Earth would also be at a maximum. Keep these ideas in mind when we consider the climate history data.

Sudden Changes in Seasonality between the Climatic-Ages

Local changes in seasonality between different climatic-ages have been found in a large number of climate history studies.[472, 473, 474] Globally, there was an abrupt and obvious increase in seasonality between the Pleistocene and Holocene climatic periods.

Changes of seasonality are recorded in wood from ancient forests that grew in the temperate regions, at higher latitudes of the Earth. Trees grow more rapidly in the summer months, and logs cut from old tree trunks reveal visible seasonal growth rings. Tree ring width and "cambium contrast" clearly record the intensity of the seasonal cycle between summer and winter in each year, at the location where the tree had grown. Conversely, the trees from the tropics display no rings, because there are no seasons in the tropics, so there is no seasonal growth variation.

The variation of seasonality between the climatic-ages was also confirmed by studying the variations in temperature-sensitive beetle populations. For example, beetle populations in ancient soils spanning the last twenty-two thousand years in the United Kingdom were intensively investigated and produced a very precise picture of past local seasonality there.[475]

Very significant variations in seasonality and summer-to-winter temperature changes were discovered from these beetle studies. The United Kingdom was cold in the first-age, with average summer temperatures of five-degrees-Celsius, with a summer-to-winter temperature difference of fifteen-degrees-Celsius. In the second-age, average summer temperatures in the United kingdom rose to ten-degrees-Celsius, but the summer-to-winter temperature difference dropped to nine-degrees-Celsius.

Summer temperatures then jumped to sixteen-degrees-Celsius in the third-age, and seasonal temperature variation also jumped to twenty-degrees-Celsius. Summer temperatures reached a peak of eighteen-degrees-Celsius in the fourth-age, but seasonal temperature variation declined to fifteen-degrees-Celsius. In our present fifth-age, summer temperatures declined to around fourteen-degrees-Celsius, and the summer-to-winter temperature difference decreased to ten-degrees-Celsius.

This variation of the seasons in the United Kingdom was mainly caused by changes in axial-tilt of the Earth and changes in paleo-latitude due to geographic shifts of the poles. The large change in seasonality in the United kingdom at the beginning of the third-age was partly due to the north-pole being relocated to Spitsbergen.

Combining this type of data with other climate history studies, a general picture of sudden changes in the seasonality of our planet emerges. In the first-age, the poles were cold, there was a large temperature gradient from north-pole-1 to equator-1 and south-pole-1 to equator-1, but the belts of the tropics were narrow. This can be interpreted as a result of a smaller axial-tilt in the first-age. However, the lack of good tree-ring data from the first-age means this is a preliminary conclusion.

In the second-age, north-pole-2 and south-pole-2 became colder and the temperature gradient to equator-2 was larger. The belt of the tropics in Africa and South America was only about five-degrees either side of equator-2. In Europe in the second-age, the temperature gradient was very steep, with average winter temperatures of minus-twenty-five-degrees-Celsius at latitude-fifty-five-degrees-north, for example, in northern Poland. This compared to plus-five-degrees-Celsius near the Mediterranean coast.[476] This type of data suggests the axial-tilt of the Earth was only about five degrees in the second-age.

This small axial-tilt explained the strangely sharp north-to-south climate transition in North America during the second-age. There was a thick polar ice cap north of the Great Lakes; yet just to the south of the ice cliffs, lush forests grew supporting herds of large mammals and Paleo-Indian hunting camps. Ancient tree trunks from Europe in the second-age also contained growth-rings that were difficult to observe, suggesting there was much less seasonal variation than today.[477]

In contrast, trees from Europe and North America in the third-age had much wider rings, meaning much stronger seasonal growth, which implied larger seasonal changes than today. In fact, the seasonality in the third-age was the largest of the past twenty thousand years.

The extreme seasons of the third-age can be explained by an axial-tilt that was greater than the present twenty-three-point-five degrees.[478] In the third-age, there was also a higher average temperature at north-pole-3 and south-pole-3 and a shallower temperature gradient to equator-3.

Greenland warmed rapidly as an increased axial angle brought longer and warmer summers to the Arctic.[479] A rise of summer radiation from very low levels was unmistakable in the ice core record. Ice accumulation per year increased steadily as the warm oceans produced more moisture, which precipitated as snow.

The Changing Orbital Parameters of Planet Earth

The climate history data also seemed to have been affected by sudden shifts in the orbital parameters of the Earth, from one climatic-age to the next. The higher summer temperatures in the third-age and fourth-age were probably due to the Earth being on average slightly closer to the Sun, in addition to the usual variation in orbital radius throughout the year. Evidence is accumulating that variations in Earth's orbit and spin vector are a primary cause of sharp changes in insolation and climate as far back as the Cretaceous Period.[480, 481]

The current distance between the Earth and the Sun varies by three percent during the year, because the orbit of the Earth is an ellipse, not a perfect circle. The point where the Earth is closest to the Sun (perihelion) occurs on January 2 during the northern hemisphere winter. The effect reduces seasonality in the northern hemisphere and simultaneously intensifies seasonality in the southern hemisphere.

Climatologists accept changes to the orbit of the Earth can affect the climate and cause ice-ages.[482] In 1842, a French mathematician called Adhemar was one of the first to propose this astronomical theory, claiming there was a regular rhythm of climate-change driven by slow changes in the orientation of the Earth's axis of rotation, relative to changes in the shape and orientation of the elliptical orbit of the Earth around the Sun.[483]

However, climatology dogma of the previous century held that the Earth had experienced consistently colder temperatures in ice-ages because of slow differential precession of the perihelion of Earth's orbit combined with slow precession of the axial orientation of our planet.[484]

This idea was originally developed by Milankovitch, but his model had a fatal flaw. This type of slow astronomical process could only produce very cold winters at one pole at a time. This process could not induce simultaneous cold at both poles to induce the global cooling required for an ice-age.

In addition, climate studies over the previous fifty years have shown that the old idea of long global ice-ages, which produced continent-sized ice-sheets, was simply wrong. The ice core data from both the Arctic and Antarctic clearly showed that although the whole planet had been chilled or warmed in different epochs, there was no evidence of enormous ice-sheets covering most of the land.[485] Generally, there have been four-thousand-year-long oscillations in local climate patterns, during forty-thousand and one-hundred-and-twenty-thousand-year-long epochs of warmer or colder global temperatures.[486]

The best explanation for the general heating or cooling of the climate of the whole planet is that the average orbital radius of Earth changed. Not only did the shape of our orbit change, but our planet traveled at slightly different average distances from the Sun.

There is growing evidence that changes in the global climate over the past eight hundred thousand years are due to abrupt shifts in orbital parameters, and the familiar rip-saw tooth graph can be explained by these type of perturbations.[487]

For example, during the hundred-and-twenty thousand years of the Pleistocene epoch before the cataclysm of 9600 BC, the Arctic and Antarctic polar regions were on average ten-degrees colder than today.

Changes in solar-heating per-square-meter of Earth's surface are known to climatologists as a change of insolation. The amount of insolation, the solar energy received by the Earth, appears to oscillate between two states that causes the alternating cycle of one-hundred-and-twenty-thousand year-long cold periods separated by forty-thousand year-long warm periods. The hundred and twenty thousand year-long colder epochs appear to be when the Earth was on average slightly further from the Sun. The forty-thousand yearlong warmer epochs appear to be when the Earth was on average slightly closer to the Sun.

The heating up of the whole Earth at the beginning of the third-age can be explained by the average orbital radius of the Earth around the Sun, being about one percent smaller than today. In the fourth-age, our planet even warmed-up relative to the third-age: an example is the fourth-age climate of central Asia and northwest Siberia between 5600 BC and 1628 BC, which were much warmer than in the preceding third-age climate. The average orbital radius of Earth in the fourth-age was probably about one-point-five percent smaller than today.

Such a smaller average orbital radius would result in fewer days per year. If the average orbital radius was one-point-five percent smaller than now, this would result in only 360 days per year in the fourth-age that ended in 1628 BC. My previous book *Cataclysms & Renewals* presented the astonishing evidence that before the cataclysm of 1628 BC, ancient calendars recorded a year of only 360 days rather than the 365.25 days we count in our calendars.

Star-Core-Zeus and the Wobbly Earth

In these first four chapters of this book *Star-Core-Zeus*, I have presented detailed evidence for the reality of a natural regular cycle of climatic-ages every four thousand years. I conclude that they were caused by cataclysmic events, which triggered a combination of abrupt changes: in the location of the poles and equator of our planet; in the orientation of Earth's rotation axis in space; and in the average orbital radius of our planet around the Sun.

Although the idea of a cycle of cataclysms may still be challenged, there is no doubt about the reality of the 9600 BC cataclysm, which marks the boundary between the Pleistocene and our Holocene climate epochs, and its cause remains an enigma.

A German rocket scientist with the excellent name Otto Muck presented an early hypothesis to explain the cataclysm: he suggested the cause of the Pleistocene extinction was an asteroid-impact in the North Atlantic.[488] He even identified a possible impact site: a deep pit on the Atlantic Ocean floor at the bottom of the western slopes of the Mid-Atlantic Ridge.[489]

Later Allan and Delair speculated that the cause of the cataclysm was an ancient asymmetric supernova explosion in the Vela star system, which had shot the remains of a hyper-massive star-core in our direction. Their idea was that this hyper-dense object had traveled at high-velocity for thousands of years across forty-five light years of space, before flying through the inner solar-system very close to Earth.[490] More recently, Richard Firestone and colleagues proposed that a huge blast-wave from a distant supernova irradiated the inner solar-system at the termination of the Pleistocene epoch.[491, 492, 493]

However, they all missed the importance of the cycle of cataclysms and renewals in the climate history data. The 9600 BC cataclysm that ended the Pleistocene epoch was not an isolated event; it was part of a regular pattern of cataclysms, which have been re-occurring every four thousand years.

I propose that the regular periodicity of cataclysms and climatic-ages are consistent with the Sun being part of a binary-star-system with star-core-zeus. The idea is that the Sun and star-core-zeus orbit around their common center of mass in highly eccentric, elliptical binary orbits, which briefly bring them very close together every four thousand years. As star-core-zeus passes Earth at high velocity, its steep and deep gravity well transiently induces huge tidal-forces, which shakes and sometimes tumbles our planet.

Tidal-forces increase rapidly with decreasing separation between two massive bodies. While gravity increases in proportion to the square of the decreasing distance, gravitational-tidal-force increases in proportion to the cube of the decreasing separation.[494] Each brief high-velocity fly-by of Earth by star-core-zeus rapidly resulted in a new axial angle, a new location of the poles and a new orbital radius for our planet.

In the next chapter, I shall consider the gravity of star-core-zeus as a possible solution to another unsolved problem: the origin of the mountain ranges that span our globe.

CHAPTER 5

Making Mountain Ranges

● ● ●

THE ORIGIN OF THE FORCES responsible for mountain ranges is still an enigma, because the evidence seems to show that mountain-ranges have formed from great slabs of rock, which were lifted off the crust of the Earth.[495]

All geologists agree that enormous natural forces are necessary for mountain-building, but the majority still assume mountains were formed over very long periods of time, by powerful local forces from *within* the Earth.[496, 497] However, a large number of geological field studies confirmed that mountain-building is not a slow continuous local process: they revealed that mountain-building is an episodic, synchronous, abrupt, and global process.

There is currently no plausible explanation for how these large-scale deformations of the crust of our planet have occurred. Generally, the dogma of plate-tectonics is evoked to explain away the mystery, without providing any clear description of the origin of the forces that resulted in the simultaneous up-thrusting of mountain ranges all over the planet.

The credibility of all plate-tectonic explanations is undermined by field studies that show the very short geological time-frame for mountain-building. Some mountain ranges were formed in less than a million years, while plate-tectonic explanations require over a hundred million years to grow a mountain. In addition, geologists who specialize in the study of mountains have concluded that many mountains have formed in places where no plate-tectonic explanation makes any sense.

There is abundant evidence of vertical lifting of great areas of crustal rock by an unexplained force. In some cases, such as in the Himalayas and the European Alps, crustal rocks have been mysteriously dragged skyward and then dropped back on to the ground, on top of much younger strata. These elevated plateaus have been then fractured, disrupted, and finally eroded into the familiar shapes of mountains. Generally, the field evidence refutes the concept that individual mountains, mountain chains, or table lands had been pushed up by a terrestrial folding mechanism or by a force originating from inside the Earth.

Extra-Terrestrial Forces Make Mountains

The formation of mountains is associated with cataclysm. Most of the familiar mountain ranges spanning the globe today appeared suddenly at the time of the Permian mass extinction, two-hundred-and-fifty million years ago.

Alfred Wegener, the German founder of continental drift theory, proposed that at the end of the Permian period, all the continents were joined together into one supercontinent called Pangaea. Wegener proposed that during the Permian mass extinction, the supercontinent suffered catastrophic tidal stresses from the powerful gravitational field of a massive extra-terrestrial object (which shall be discussed in more detail in the next chapter). The lifting, buckling, and fracturing of the surface of Earth not only led to the formation of the present continents, it also caused the formation of the great mountain ranges of Earth.[498, 499]

There is also strong evidence for the sudden appearance of some mountain ranges in the Pleistocene epoch, within the previous two-million years. There is even surprising evidence of the peaks of mountain ranges abruptly increasing in altitude in the last twelve-thousand years, during cataclysms in the Holocene epoch.

Paul Lowman, a planetary geologist of the NASA Goddard Space Flight Center, revealed the unexpected results of gravity mapping mountains from satellites orbiting Earth. They showed that mountain ranges did not add concentrations of mass to the crust; they compensated for a deficiency of mass below them or around them, as if they had been dragged out of the ground.[500]

MOUNTAIN RANGES: TIDAL EARTH-WAVES

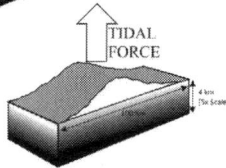

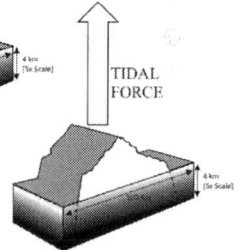

The mountain ranges which span the globe, were pulled out of the ground by powerful tidal-forces from above, just like ocean-waves. They were neither squeezed out by local horizontal plate-tectonics motion, nor pushed up by local mantle plumes from below.

TIDAL EARTH WAVES

THE MOUNTAINS OF
CENTRAL TURKEY
RESEMBLE OCEAN-WAVES

TIDAL FORCE

TIDAL FORCE

MOUNTAIN RANGES
OF THE WORLD

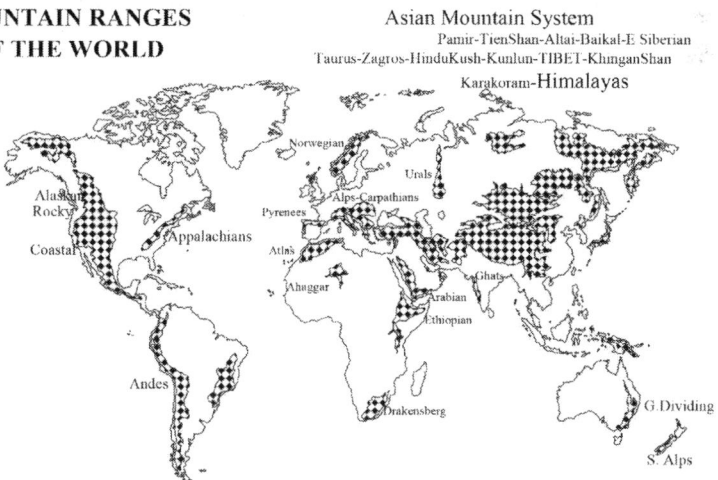

Asian Mountain System
Pamir-TienShan-Altai-Baikal-E Siberian
Taurus-Zagros-HinduKush-Kunlun-TIBET-KhinganShan
Karakoram-Himalayas

David Allan and Bernard Delair (two British geologists) compiled compelling evidence that mountains had probably been created by extra-terrestrial tidal forces and that many of the great mountain ranges only acquired their familiar forms within the previous twelve thousand years.[501] Some mountains even grew in height just eight thousand years ago, and there were a few examples of elevations as recently as four thousand years ago. Their evidence is so relevant to the subject of this book that much of their research is summarized here in this chapter.

Growth of the Mountain Ranges of Asia

Very recent folding of mountains in many parts of the Asian landmass was recognized during surveys in the early twentieth century.[502] Studies of mountain ranges in China confirmed that huge uplifts of the Earth's crust had occurred only twelve-thousand years ago, at the termination of the Pleistocene.[503]

Around 9600 BC, all the Asian mountain ranges rose to their present altitudes. The Pamirs, the Hindu-Kush, Karakoram, Kailas, Himalayas, Kunlun, Altai, and Tien Shan ranges, all grew skyward simultaneously during the cataclysm that terminated the ice-age.[504] Incredible forces were responsible for this end-Pleistocene mountain-building.

To the north of the Himalayas and the Tibetan plateau, unusually craggy young ranges border the western Gobi Desert, which stretches from the Russian Altai Mountains to the Chinese Tien Shan range. The general topology of the great Gobi basin is also a recent feature, which formed at the same time as the uplift of the Trans-Baikal mountain ranges.[505]

More than twelve thousand years ago, the Gobi basin was filled with a huge inland sea, which was one thousand one hundred kilometers wide. It stretched from the Tien Shan and Pamir ranges in the west to the Chinese Great Khingan Shan range in the east, a total distance of over three thousand two hundred kilometers. At the time this inland sea existed, the entire basin lay about a kilometer lower than it does today.

The volume of this archaic sea was immense; almost half the volume of the Mediterranean. In ancient Chinese mythology, the sea that used to occupy the Gobi basin was known as Han Hai, meaning Great

Sea. There was abundant field evidence that in one terrible catastrophe twelve-thousand years ago, the Han Hai was abruptly uplifted together with the mountains immediately to the south.

The retaining walls of this sea were breached, and an awesome flood swept north across Siberia. The huge volume of water formed irresistible torrents that carried away the forests and animals. This huge flood of water eventually drained into the Arctic Ocean, dumping the plant and animal remains on Asia's arctic continental shelf.

As the upheaval ripped through the mountainous region of northern China, huge lava outpourings occurred on the Great Khingan Shan range, and vast basaltic flows gushed in the Sikhote-Alin range.[506] Simultaneously, the ranges in Yunnan Province and the Bayan Kara Shan range in western China were upheaved some two kilometers, while the high peak of the Minya Konka was uplifted about one kilometer. At the same time, the Tibetan Plateau was elevated to three kilometers.[507] All of these uplifts occurred during the 9600 BC cataclysm, at the transition between the Pleistocene and the Holocene epochs.[508, 509]

Meanwhile on the south side of the Himalayas, lake and river deposits of the Kashmir valley in northern India, known as the Karewa series, were folded, tilted, and dragged up to a height of two kilometers. The tilting and elevation of the Potwar and Salt ranges occurred during the same cataclysm.[510] Terraces cut by new rivers revealed the remains of twelve-thousand year-old Pleistocene plants and mega-fauna bones to a depth of about one kilometer.

The violence of these Earth-shattering events was demonstrated by over-thrusting, which had lifted and dumped older rocks upon newer formations. The Kohistan plateau in northeast Pakistan, at the edge of the mountain chain that becomes the Himalayan plateau, is an example of the incredible forces involved in mountain building.[511] A continental platform of rock was dumped on top of another platform, forming a sandwich of two continental surfaces on top of each other.

Kohistan rocks have an unusually high concentration of a primitive lead isotope, similar to the lead isotope content of chondrite meteorites, which is up to forty times higher than the primitive lead content of volcanic eruptions. The isotope evidence shows that the Kohistan plateau is made from ancient rocks, which formed near the foundations of the crust fifty kilometers underground. They had been ripped out of the crust and then dropped back onto the ground.

There are other examples of huge masses of much older Himalayan rocks dumped on top of younger Pleistocene gravel and alluvia.[512] In Kashmir, shallow marine sedimentary rock-beds were dragged-up by more than one and a half kilometers. Some of the sedimentary beds even contained Late-Paleolithic stone tools, dropped by ancient peoples, who were killed during the apocalypse that ended the Pleistocene.[513]

An extraordinary uplift also occurred at the same time in the Pir Panjal mountains in Kashmir. The last stage of this uplift resulted in peaks also rising about two kilometers. Again, late-Paleolithic stone tools of former inhabitants of a lowland region were discovered buried on the very highest peaks of these new mountains.

Not only were the central Himalayas affected by this gigantic crustal uplift, but detailed studies of the Nanga-Parbat massif in the western Himalayas revealed the same up-rise had coincided with the start of the Younger Dryas climate freeze, which occurred immediately after the 9600 BC cataclysm.[514]

Similar powerful forces generated the mountains in northern India. The large scale crustal movements lifted rain-water catchment-zones and changed river systems. For example, the course and gradient of the Narbada River was altered and the precipitous water-falls at Jabalpur were formed in this era.[515]

The Ganges trough formed as a huge and deep tectonic fracture, one-thousand-nine-hundred kilometers long and four-hundred kilometers wide. Although the mighty river Ganges was later channeled along this feature, it is not a river valley.

The scale of this vast fracture indicated the colossal power of the forces that had produced it. The Ganges trough is choked by Pleistocene debris of enormous thickness that had been washed into the trough by floods of awesome magnitude.[516] Gravity surveys have indicated that these in-filling deposits are two kilometers deep.[517]

At the same time in Southeast Asia, there were similar extreme changes in the elevations of hills and mountains and abrupt re-organization of the water drainage patterns.[518] These topological changes extended from Burma to northern Thailand, Laos, parts of Vietnam, and Malaysia.

Cataclysmic Mountain Building in Africa

During the end-Pleistocene cataclysm twelve thousand years ago, gross ruptures of rock-strata and sea-level changes occurred all around the world. Related violent events happened in Africa: the Anti-Atlas Mountains used to extend out into the Atlantic Ocean as far as the Canary Islands. This former westerly prolongation of Africa was suddenly drowned in 9600 BC.[519, 520] The north-west African continental shelf off-shore from Morocco was flooded at the same time as the triangular continental fragment of Atlantis disappeared under the waves of the mid-Atlantic, west of France and Portugal.

During the same cataclysm, the central hills of the Sahara variously called "Ahaggar" or "Hoggar" were abruptly upheaved to become higher land.[521] Coincidental with these uplifts, huge crustal movements across Africa changed the elevation of vast regions of the continent. Lakes and inland seas were emptied, while simultaneously existing rivers were enlarged and new rivers formed.

In Nigeria, there are straight parallel crustal fractures that were formed at the end of the Pleistocene by powerful tidal-stresses. The North-South cracks penetrate deep into the crust and are hundreds of miles long. At the end of the Pleistocene, huge tectonic disturbances also created new and raw ruptures in the Great Rift Valley of East Africa, which had originally formed about two-hundred-and-fifty million years earlier, at the end of the Permian period.[522, 523]

The Great Rift Valley was part of a huge crack that traversed the African continent for over sixty-five-thousand kilometers, curving on a north-to-south course from the Near East to southern Africa.[524, 525] Nearly all the sub-fractures associated with this huge crack showed geologically youthful features, which corresponded to the recent upheaval and movement at the end of the Pleistocene.

The large scale rifting in Africa occurred simultaneously with the elevation of mountain ranges in America and fracturing in the Pacific and around Australia.[526, 527, 528]

Cataclysmic Mountain Building in the Americas

Similar dramatic changes in continental topology occurred abruptly in the Americas twelve thousand years ago. On the west coast of North America, the whole of the western Cordilleras of the Rocky Mountains suddenly rose to higher elevations.[529]

Professor Daly, who was head of the Department of Geology at Harvard University for thirty years up to 1942, reported extraordinary evidence of mountains dragged out of the ground and dropped. For example, Chief Mountain in Montana was picked up as one vast chunk of rock, slammed down upon much younger strata on the Great Plains, and then dragged eastward for a further ten miles.[530] At the same time, unimaginable forces had dragged Glacier National Park in Montana and the Rocky Mountains up to the Yellowhead Pass in Alberta, in an eastward direction.[531] In the Cascade Mountains, Sierra Nevada in Oregon, and in eastern California, cataclysmic strata-contortion and two-kilometer crustal uplift occurred, twelve thousand years ago.[532, 533]

The Coastal Ranges of Southern California made from jumbled slabs of marine sediments up to one mile thick were dumped there at the end of the Pleistocene. These young formations were uplifted and deformed over a quarter of a mile above the sea level, creating a series of terraces on the westward slope of the range facing the Pacific Ocean.[534]

Similar uplifting of mountain ranges occurred in South America. The Andes of South America, the longest continuous range on Earth, is an ancient mountain range that was formed at the end of the Permian period. However, the jagged and fresh-looking peaks only acquired their present sharp relief at the end of the Pleistocene epoch, during an inexplicable process.[535]

Field studies confirmed that parts of the Andes have recently emerged from the Pacific Ocean, and the Altiplano basin experienced an abrupt jump in altitude.[536] On the high plateau of the Altiplano, there are sea-salt deserts with ocean sea-shells, estimated to be less than twenty thousand years old. In this region there are a group of remarkable lakes, the largest being Lake Titicaca.[537] The lakes support creatures recently adapted to fresh water but closely related to sea-life in the Pacific Ocean, four thousand meters below.[538]

The elevations of the Andes occurred suddenly, attended by intense volcanism in which several of the cones attained enormous heights.[539] The Andean uplift was so immense that some mountain passes in Peru and Bolivia rose to almost four kilometers.

Elevation of Mountains around the World

At the close of the Pleistocene, mountain ranges all around the world were uplifted simultaneously. Most of the mountains of Asia, Africa, and the Americas were elevated to their present height in the Earth-shaking cataclysm at the end of the ice-age. There is also field evidence for simultaneous uplifts in the Alps of Western Europe and the mountains of Scandinavia.

Before the end of the Pleistocene, the Alps were little more than a chain of high hills, not more than six hundred meters high.[540] The sharp and relatively un-eroded summits of three of the highest Alpine peaks— Monte Blanc, Monte Rosa, and the Matterhorn—were abruptly dragged up recently to stand at about five kilometers above sea level.

At the same time, the surface rocks of the northern Alps of Switzerland had been pulled northward up to five hundred kilometers. Much of the material that formed the Alps somehow flew from northern Italy.[541, 542] Massive over-thrusting of older rocks upon younger strata in the Alps has been studied. Gigantic slabs of rock over a kilometer thick, hundreds of kilometers long and tens of kilometers wide, had been lifted and then dropped on top of layers of the younger rocks. The scale of the enormous uplift required forces cosmic in magnitude.

This jumbling of geological strata has been observed throughout the Alpine region, with over-thrusting on a grand scale in the Jura Mountains and Glarus Mountains.[543, 544] Incredible examples of strata-inversion were discovered around the Roggenstock, Monch, Jungfrau,

Silbern, and Glarnisch peaks. Whole mountains had been picked up, turned upside down, and dropped back to the ground.[545] Trillions of tons of rock had been lifted into the air, rolled and dumped on top of surface-strata, crushing and obliterating everything underneath. The total force required to move a mountain in this manner is hard to contemplate.[546]

In Scandinavia, dramatic crustal-cracking also occurred during the 9600 BC cataclysm. The final uplift of the Norwegian mountains, the formation of deep fractures between them, and the drowning of the vast fissures, which became the fiords, occurred only twelve thousand years ago.[547]

The idea that the slow grinding action of glacial ice had carved out fiords has been refuted by detailed field studies of the well-developed fiord systems of Greenland, the Hebrides, and Scandinavia.[548, 549] Some fiords are open at both ends and higher ground is non-existent: they could not have been dug out by a glacier creeping down a gradient.[550, 551] Fiords are deep cracks in the Earth's crust that extend across the sea floor, some at depths where they could never have been accessed by glaciers even at times of the lowest sea-levels. There are related giant cracks across the deep oceans of the planet.

In central Westland, New Zealand, similar large crustal dislocations occurred at the end of the Pleistocene. Studies of the great fault in the Southern-Alps on South-Island New-Zealand revealed awesome forces had raised a huge mass of rock up an astounding eighteen kilometers from the bottom of the ocean and then dumped it on land, turning the deep sea-floor rock into a mountain.[552, 553]

Land Pulled Skyward

The geological evidence from all around the world demonstrated massive amounts of displaced rocks and fractures that were caused by the crust of our planet being pulled toward the sky.[554, 555, 556, 557]

The evidence for land pulled skyward can be found everywhere. In the Arctic, highlands elevated at the end of the Pleistocene occur all over the region.[558] In Europe, there are published examples of elevation of land in the British Isles, Norway, The Alps, Carpathian Mountains, Ural Mountains, and Gibraltar. In the North American region, obvious and enigmatic elevation of land can be seen in the Rocky Mountains, the Coastal Ranges, the Cascade Mountains, Sierra Nevada, St Lawrence Valley, the Atlantic coast, and Bermuda.

In the Central American region, there is evidence of elevation of land in Florida, the Gulf of Mexico, Nicaragua, Guatemala, Costa Rica, and many parts of the Caribbean. In South America, there is clear evidence of elevation of land in the Andes Mountain Range, Colombia, Ecuador, Peru (Lake Titicaca), Bolivia, Chile, and Guyana.

In the Western Pacific region: elevation of land occurred in Indonesia, in New Hebrides, and also in Australia around Adelaide, the Blue Mountains, and Eastern Highlands. In New Zealand and the South Antarctic Peninsula, there are other published reports of abrupt recent elevations.

The most significant elevation in Asia was in the continuous belt of mountains from Iran to China.[559] Elevations also occurred in Burma, Thailand, Malaysia, Laos, and Vietnam. Although there was a general fifty meter rise in sea-level at the end of the Pleistocene, there is evidence of elevation of beaches along the Malayan coast, and in the Philippines and Indonesia, connected to general land elevation and mountain building.[560, 561, 562, 563, 564]

Earth's Crumpled and Buckled Crust

The mountain ranges span half the planet from Europe and north Africa, across Asia to the far east. Other mountain ranges stretch almost half the planet from northern Alaska through the United States and southward as the Andes. There is an abundance of evidence from all over the world that mountains are the result of extra-terrestrial forces acting on the whole planet.

Movements of the fracture systems, faulting of the ocean floor and submergence of the continental shelves, together with simultaneous mountain-building, have occurred repeatedly.[565, 566, 567, 568, 569] The deep trenches and troughs in the oceans of the world connect with the mountain ranges on land and form part of a global pattern. Investigations under the oceans of the world point to geologically recent catastrophic changes. Many of the deep-sea trenches contain only small amounts of recent in-filling sediments, and the walls of many fractures show little evidence of erosion.[570, 571]

Even though the evidence is on a global scale, generally geologists only examine local areas and ignore the big picture. The data clearly shows evidence of repeated and gigantic crustal convulsions of our planet. Taken together, these inter-related patterns of mountain belts and ocean troughs of the Earth are evidence of external forces that acted on the crust of our planet.[572, 573] However, geologists still try to explain away the formation of mountains as the result of internal forces that drive very gradual plate tectonic processes or due to the effect of local mantle plumes rising from deep in the hot interior.[574, 575]

The Maker of Mountains

The related features of the great mountain systems and the vast ocean-floor cracks of the world support the hypothesis that mountains are made by tidal distortion of the whole planet. There is also a strong correlation between the four-thousand-year cycle of climate catastrophes, the shifting of climatic-belts, the lifting of mountain ranges, and the fracturing of the ocean floor. The maker of mountains must be a massive stellar body, whose gravity can induce overwhelming tidal forces.

There is even an accepted example from elsewhere in the solar-system in which powerful tidal forces induced by a massive extra-terrestrial body have made mountains and fractures. The innermost of the four Galilean moons of Jupiter called "Io" has mini-mountain ranges, which are up to seventeen kilometers high and extend for a few hundred kilometers. More than a hundred mountains have been identified on Io together with strange rugged plateaus. Io's mountain ranges are tilted and broken crustal blocks with peaks and steep scarps, which resemble small versions of terrestrial mountain chains.

The mountains on Io are not volcanic in origin. As Io orbits the massive planet Jupiter in an eccentric ellipse, this inner moon suffers changing gravitational tidal stresses from the powerful gravity of planet Jupiter. The mountains on the surface of Io are formed rapidly by ruptures in its crust, which relieve the stresses caused by Jupiter's gravity.[576]

THE TIDAL MOUNTAINS
OF JUPITER'S MOON 'IO'

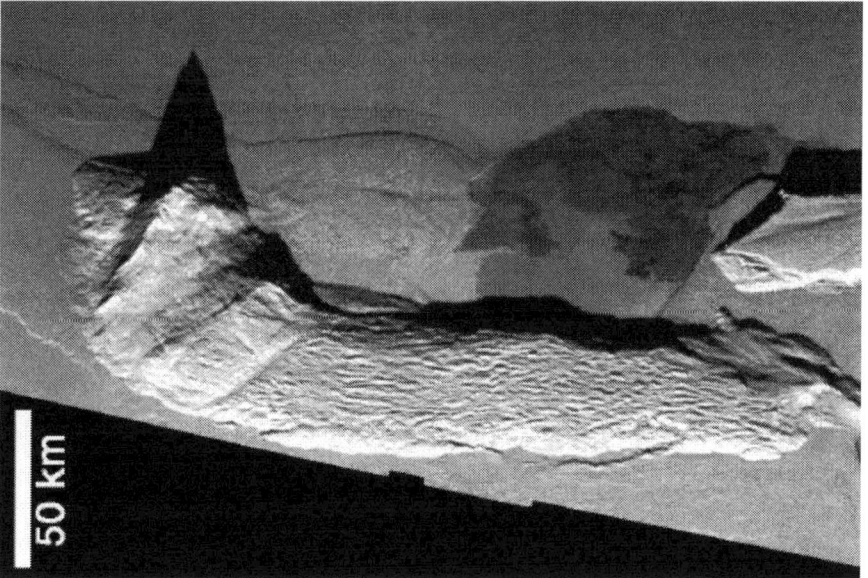

50 km

The mountains of Venus are another example of extra-terrestrial mountain chains that are not due to plate-tectonics or volcanism.[577] The mountains of Venus, which resemble the mountains of Io and Earth, also seemed to have been formed by intense tidal forces. My previous book *Cataclysms & Renewals* described the strange recent history of Venus and the story of its earlier eccentric orbit around star-core-zeus, prior to its capture by the Sun at the end of the Pleistocene.

The powerful gravity of star-core-zeus created the global system of mountains and faults on Earth. Each time star-core-zeus flew through the inner solar-system, its powerful gravity rolled and crumpled our planet. Only a super-massive and dense supernova remnant could apply such extreme tidal forces to rupture the Earth's surface like this.

The tremendous forces applied to Earth by star-core-zeus not only made the mountain ranges. At the end of the Permian period, two-hundred-and fifty-two million years ago, star-core-zeus passed so close to the Earth that it broke the crust of our planet into enormous slabs, which we now call continents. These awesome events shall be described in the following chapters.

CHAPTER 6

"Super-Continent" Pangaea and Drag

● ● ●

WE LIVE ON A STRANGE planet: half the surface is made of continental platforms of granite rock and half the surface is made of ocean floor of basalt rock. However, the sea drowns forty-two percent of the continental platforms, so only twenty-nine percent of our planet is land and seventy-one percent is sea.

The current theory of plate-tectonics assumes the huge continental platforms slowly drift across the surface of the Earth like icebergs floating on the surface of the sea. There is something very wrong with plate-tectonics theory: the global jigsaw puzzle of the continental lands and the ocean basins still hold a great secret.

Continental Drift

The fit between the shape of the Atlantic coasts of South America and Africa had been noted a number of times, before Alfred Wegener first presented his new hypothesis on continental drift at the Geological Society of Frankfurt am Main in 1912. At the meeting, he revealed his map of all the continents assembled into one extended super-continent, which he named Pangaea, meaning "all-Earth."

Wegener's model of Pangaea re-connected locations of fossils of extinct plant and animal species, geological features, and climatic-belts of the Carboniferous and Permian periods of the Paleozoic era.[578, 579] About a quarter-of-a-billion years ago, half of our planet was one huge continental plateau made of ancient layers of thick granite-like rocks.

In addition, ancient glacial features revealed that at the time of Pangaea, the Permian south-pole was in the interior of the supercontinent on territory that would become Botswana.[580, 581, 582] Pangaea was located in the Permian southern-hemisphere and was supposed to have been surrounded by a huge ocean.

Wegener believed the whole of the northern hemisphere was covered by one huge Permian Pacific Ocean, centered on the old Permian north-pole, which was located at the Hawaiian hot-spot. It was thought that during the Permian period, sea-water filled this deep continuous basin and drowned continental shelves so that it covered seventy percent of our planet.

According to Wegener, the topology of Earth was very odd at the time of Pangaea. The two hemispheres of our planet had distinctly different rock surfaces: granite land and basalt ocean-floor, vertically separated by at least five kilometers. Wegener was unable to explain why the Earth should be so asymmetric at the end of the Permian period.

Wegener went on to propose that Pangaea was violently broken-up during the mass-extinction of life at the termination of the Permian period, which also marked the end of the whole Paleozoic era. He had no explanation for the origin of the incredible forces that had smashed the huge super-continent into continent-sized fragments.

However, there was no doubt that at the very end of the Permian period, Pangaea had been shattered into pieces in one terrible event, which had caused massive volcanic activity and vast floods of boiling liquid basalt. At the same time, the crust was crumpled into mountain ranges, and there was a devastating change in the atmosphere.

Wegener believed that immediately after the great Permian extinction two-hundred-and-fifty-two million years ago, all the continents started to drift away from each other. For millions and millions of years after the terrible cataclysm, during the early Triassic and in later geological periods, the continents continued to drift very slowly apart, until they reached their present configuration.

Wegener proposed that extra-terrestrial tidal forces applied by a massive object, combined with centrifugal-forces related to Earth-rotation, had pulled the continents apart. He hypothesized that continental drift was driven by a combination of buoyancy forces, shifting the continents away from the poles of our planet, and the extra-terrestrial tidal forces, lifting and pulling the continents across the surface of the planet in a westerly direction; while the Earth rotated eastward.

The geological establishment ignored the details of Wegener's new model but attacked his central concept of continental-drift. They demanded an explanation for the huge forces required to break-up the super-continent and then shift rigid continents through the solid crust of Earth. No known solar-system body was massive enough or had got close enough to Earth to have applied such huge forces. Over the following decades, Wegener's ideas were ridiculed, and he died in 1930 without his revolutionary theory being verified.

Discoveries in the 1960s of seabed spreading-zones in the mid-Atlantic and the global mid-ocean ridge system revived interest in Wegener's ideas. Paleo-magnetic orientations of ancient rocks on land, geomagnetic-field-reversals recorded in alternating stripes of magnetized rock across the sea-floor, together with new data on the young age of all ocean-floor sediments combined to support Wegener's concept of continental-drift.[583, 584] Geologists began to reluctantly accept that the continents may have moved, but they still refused to consider Wegener's model of extra-terrestrial tidal-forces driving continental-drift.

However, there was no known terrestrial force or mechanism that could have broken Pangaea into continents, then pulled them apart and moved them thousands of kilometers across the surface of our planet. Sir Harold Jeffreys, FRS, Professor of Geophysics at University of Cambridge, who is credited with the discovery of the internal structure of the Earth, summed up the situation at the time; "no force even remotely strong enough to move the continents across the Earth's surface is evident."[585]

The Flawed Theory of Plate Tectonics Emerged.
By the end of the 1960s, the unproven and flawed modern explanation for continental-drift emerged.[586] According to this new model, the

continents are supposed to sit on top of huge but invisible slabs of rock called tectonic-plates, which are supposed to float like icebergs, on a semi-liquid rock below called the asthenosphere.

The ridiculous notion is that rigid and inter-locked tectonic plates of rock, tens of kilometers thick, continuously move around the surface of the planet with ease, powered only by the heat from the interior of the Earth. Plate tectonics theory avoids any reference to non-terrestrial forces.

In denial of basic physics, the unbelievable suggestion is that the continents are continuously pushed and pulled around the planet. The driving force to push the continents is supposed to be generated by hot liquid magma plumes, rising from the interior of the Earth, forcing hot basaltic magma between the tectonic plates at great cracks in the middle of ocean basins, called spreading centers.[587] All tectonic-models ignore Professor Jeffreys' calculations of the enormous forces required to nudge a whole continent, which is surrounded by solid rock with no space to maneuver.

The other impossible proposal is that a driving force to pull the continents is provided by cold solid rock at the edges of the tectonic-plates, falling continuously under gravity down into deep ocean trenches. This small mass of falling material, in a process called subduction, is supposed to pull whole continents across the surface of our planet. However, when models of the subduction of the crust into the mantle are run on super-computers, they only work if they are programmed with fake pseudo-plasticity and impossibly ultra-low-viscosity.[588]

The standard model of plate tectonics also assumes the deep faults in the Earth's crust, marking the active tectonic plate-boundaries. However, many seismically active faults are far from theoretical plate-boundaries, and most of the theoretical plate-boundaries are totally inactive. Rather than admit sea-floor spreading cannot be detected, a special category of fake ultra-slow-spreading ridges has been created.[589] This is not theory; this is fantasy: there is no evidence for any of it.

In the standard model, the Pacific tectonic plate is assumed to be fixed, and all the continents are assumed to move relative to it, at an average velocity of eight-centimeters per-year. At that rate, in the twenty-five million years since the beginning of the Miocene geological epoch, Africa should have moved two thousand kilometers relative to the mantle. This tectonic motion of Africa has never been observed: hotspot analysis of active volcanoes has shown that Africa did not move at all during the whole Miocene.[590]

The general mechanism of plate-tectonics is that the heat of the Earth caused continents to gradually separate from Pangaea and drift continuously, until they achieved the present configuration. In fifty years since sea-floor spreading was proposed in 1966, plate-tectonic-theory predicts that all the continents should have moved about four meters: this motion has never been detected either.[591] The theory is wrong: it is no better than a fairy tale.

Plate-Tectonics before Pangaea?

The new plate-tectonic modification to Wegener's drift-theory also relegated the supercontinent Pangaea to a temporary chance close-packing of randomly drifting continents. Conventional plate-tectonics proposes that the super-continent of Pangaea was formed by a chance temporary gathering of continental plates, which occurred in the early Permian period.

Advocates of plate-tectonics make extraordinary claims for drifting continents, hundreds-of-millions-of-years before Pangaea. However, there is no evidence for any jig-saw puzzle of pre-Pangaea continental margins. Despite this fact, plate-tectonic enthusiasts continue to hypothesize more and more complex arrangements, based on very speculative interpretations of paleo magnetic data. In fact, most of the paleomagnetic orientations of ancient rocks are better explained by uplifts and tilts of old rock platforms, rather than by the horizontal displacement of whole continents.

Some of the new proposals for pre-Pangaea arrangements actually contradict geological field data. For example, plate-tectonics theory claims that the Ural Mountains were the junction between the formerly separate Siberian and European continental platforms. However, abundant field data refutes the concept: this region has been continuous crust since at least Precambrian times, six-hundred-million years ago. Pre-Pangaea models show the east of Asia facing an ocean, whereas field evidence from Japan has shown there was a continental landmass to the east of the Japanese Islands, which suddenly disappeared at the end of the Permian period.[592]

The Young Ocean Basins Mystery

There is no evidence of any ocean basins before Pangaea, and the geological process that created the ocean basins is a big mystery.

The oldest continental rocks are eighteen-times older than the oldest ocean floor. The continental crust is up to four-point-five billion years old, based on analysis of archaic zircons in ancient rocks.[593, 594] Continental rock is made of lower-density granites and is on average up to fifty kilometers thick. It covers about half of the Earth, at an average elevation, which is five kilometers higher than the floor of the oceans. Continental rock is also crumpled by mountain ranges.

In contrast, the relatively flat ocean floor crust covers about fifty percent of the surface of the Earth. It is made of younger rocks such as higher-density basalt and gabbro, with an average thickness between six and ten kilometers. There is only a very thin layer of sediments on top of the oceanic crust.

No ocean floor has ever been found that is over two hundred and fifty million years old. The oldest known oceanic-sedimentary-rock was recovered from Hole-801C in the Pigafetta basin in the western Pacific Ocean, near the Mariana Islands, where Jurassic-age rocks and sediments about one-hundred-and-seventy million years old were recovered.[595, 596] Sediments of nearly identical age have also been found at the Deep Sea Drilling Project Hole 534A, located on the Blake-Bahama basin in the central Atlantic Ocean.[597]

Some Early Triassic sediments have been claimed for the floor of the Mediterranean Sea, but they are certainly less than two-hundred-and-fifty million years old. There are no known examples of sedimentary rock strata on oceanic crust that are older than the beginning of the

Mesozoic era. The thick layer of sediment that should have been deposited on the ocean floor in the Paleozoic era, is missing.

The logical interpretation for the difference in the age of the sea floor and the land is that a cataclysmic rupture of the whole planet removed all the older rock from the ocean basins. However, some tectonic theorists try to explain away the young ocean basins by speculating the lighter crustal rocks of the Earth spontaneously sank into the denser and heavier interior rocks of the planet, in defiance of the physics of buoyancy.[598, 599]

Other plate-tectonic theorists say that in the previous two-hundred-and-fifty million years, the subduction zones in the Pacific Ocean swallowed-up all the older ocean-floor rock, amounting to almost fifty percent of our planet's surface, so no old ocean-floor remained.

It is not credible to claim that wandering continents, which only cover half our planet's surface, randomly swallowed up the other half of our planet's surface, without even crossing the Pacific Ocean basin. There is certainly no evidence for this fantasy.

No Evidence of an Asthenosphere

According to plate-tectonics-theory, the asthenosphere is a semi-fluid layer of rock, between the crust and the mantle, located between fifty kilometers and two-hundred kilometers below the surface of Earth. The outer crust of the Earth, called the lithosphere, is supposed to float on this asthenosphere like freely-moving sea-ice.

There is no evidence for a molten or semi-liquid asthenosphere required by plate tectonics theory. The internal structure of Earth has been deduced from the behavior of seismic earthquake-waves, but no semi-liquid asthenosphere has ever been detected. Seismic and related studies reveal that the crust and mantle of the Earth is solid.

On land, the crust consists of old continental granites, metamorphic rocks, and sedimentary rocks, with an average thickness of around thirty-five kilometers and can be up to one hundred kilometers thick in places. At the base of the crust, below both the continents and the oceans, is a seismic discontinuity known as the Moho. This is a boundary between the crustal rock, where the seismic velocity is around six kilometers-per-second, and the denser ultra-mafic rocks of the mantle, where the seismic velocity is around eight kilometers-per-second. The total mantle is a layer of solid rock about three thousand kilometers thick, with density increasing with depth. It is definitely rigid: it consists mainly of peridotite, an iron-magnesium-rich silicate rock.

Earthquakes produce two types of seismic wave: pressure-waves (P-waves) and sheer-waves (S-waves). Pressure-waves are waves of compression in the direction of propagation. Sheer-waves vibrate transversely, meaning they wobble at right-angles to the direction of propagation. Molten or semi-liquid areas within the Earth's interior stop sheer-waves because their transverse-motion cannot be transmitted in a fluid, while pressure-waves can continue but at lower velocity.

Both the pressure-waves and sheer-waves from earthquakes are propagated through the crust and upper mantle of the Earth, proving it is solid. The behavior of seismic waves from surface earthquakes demonstrate that there is no liquid or semi-liquid asthenosphere below the crust.

P-waves and S-waves are produced by earthquakes in the crust, but P-waves travel through solid-rock faster than S-waves. Both P-waves and S-waves travel slightly slower when they pass through the solid upper-mantle layer of rocks. At depths greater than six hundred kilometers beneath Earth's surface, the wave velocity increases again. P-waves can pass right through both the mantle and the core, but they are slowed and refracted at the mantle-core boundary. This zone of the outer-core is made of an ultra-hot high-pressure semi-liquid rock, which occurs at a depth of about three thousand kilometers.

In contrast, S-waves hitting the mantle-core boundary are absorbed, because S-waves are not propagated in semi-liquid rock. This semi-liquid rock of the outer core produces a shadow-zone on certain parts of the Earth's surface, where S-waves produced by earthquakes are not detected. The size of this shadow-zone has been used to deduce the size of the core, which is calculated to have a radius of about three thousand five hundred kilometers.

In contrast, S-waves generated by earthquakes in the crust have been demonstrated to pass right through the upper-mantle, demonstrating there is no semi-liquid rock in this region of the Earth's interior and leading to a simple conclusion: there is no asthenosphere.

No Evidence of Mantle Plumes Moving Continents

Tectonic theory predicts hot mantle rising in convection plumes from the interior of Earth, continuously pushing continents apart by widening tectonic-plate boundaries at the mid-ocean ridges, thus causing sea-floor spreading. The behavior of sheer-waves from earthquakes refutes the existence of hot liquid mantle plumes clustering at the tectonic-plate boundaries.

Only a few plumes have been found close to any ocean ridge system.[600] For example, in the Atlantic there are only three major plumes: one under Iceland and two off the coast of Africa.[601] However, a recent study showed that some mantle-plumes cluster in the middle of the Pacific Ocean near the Hawaiian Sea-mounts, the location of the old Permian north-pole.[602]

Mid-Ocean Ridges Do Not Push Continents

No one has ever demonstrated shifting continents moved by either ridge-push at sea-floor spreading faults or by subduction-pull into ocean trenches.

According to tectonic-theory, eruptions of basalt at the mid-ocean-ridges are supposed to be pushing the continents apart. However, coring of ridge system rock shows no evidence of any powerful high pressure eruptions. The complex nature of the rock types suggests liquid rock has sporadically bled up through existing faults, but it is not continuously pushing the continents apart.[603]

The amount of volcanism at the mid-ocean ridges required by the plate-tectonic theory to drive sea-floor spreading is simply not observed. Hydro-acoustic monitoring at the East Pacific Rise, the northern Mid-Atlantic Ridge, and the Juan de Fuca Ridge revealed very few eruptions.[604, 605, 606]

In contrast, the structure of the sea-floor of the mid-ocean-ridges is a record of a series of abrupt cataclysmic events, which split the sea-floor on a number of occasions. Parallel to deep faults in the ocean crust are a sequence of ridges a few hundred meters high, spaced from one to ten kilometers apart. The cliff-like fault-scarps that face the deep crustal fractures suggest the sea floor was lifted by gravitational tidal forces during each event.

Similar topology was revealed at both the Australian-Antarctic Ridge and East Pacific Rise, refuting tectonic-theory which proposes a very slow continuous seafloor-spreading process. There is no evidence of continuous lava production driving continental drift at these locations.[607]

Impossible Plate Motion from Ocean Rift to Trough

Even the principles of plate-tectonic theory are contradictory. The supposed plate-spreading rifts at the mid-ocean ridges are three times longer than plate subduction troughs: the simple geometry of continental motion across the surface of a sphere is impossible.

Plate tectonic theory also gives no theoretical explanation for the concentration of the so-called subduction-troughs around the edge of the Pacific Ocean, while the supposed plate spreading-rifts are generally in the middle of all the other ocean basins.[608]

Space Research Challenges Plate Tectonics

Dr. Irwin Shapiro, head of the Harvard-Smithsonian Center for Astrophysics, one of the pioneers of continental-drift measurement using satellites and VLBI, stated in 1983 "there has never been direct observation of such motions." [609] Since that time over thirty years ago, the evidence from space research has not supported plate-tectonic theory. Generally, the new data supports a model in which the super-continent was broken catastrophically and then pulled apart in jerks, rather than continuously.

We now know from remote-sensing satellites that the model of a mosaic of twelve discrete and rigid tectonic plates forming the crust of Earth does not reflect reality. We also know from the ongoing exploration of Mercury, Venus, and Mars, which are essentially similar to Earth in composition and structure, that there is no evidence of plate-tectonics on these planets.[610]

No Direct Measurement of Continuous Drift

In 1984, *New Scientist* published an article, "Continental Drift: The Final Proof."[611] That New Scientist announcement over thirty years ago was more than over-optimistic. Since that time no scientific paper has ever been published, which details conclusive measurements in support of a continuous process of seafloor spreading and continental drift.

Generally, published velocities of plate motion are based on assumptions and estimates, calculated from the distance of particular magnetic anomalies from an assumed spreading center and then applying circular-reasoning based on the assumption that plate-tectonics exists.

Accurate measurements using the Very Long Baseline Interferometry (VLBI) astronomy network, between base stations located in different countries, can show distance variation between two points across our planet, with an accuracy of about one centimeter.

However, this data combined with information that has been collected using GPS satellites shows random deformation of our planet. The movements are made up of some lateral thermal distortion, together with the rising and falling of the Earth's crust. No continuous coordinated motion of the continents in the directions predicted by plate-tectonics theory has ever been detected.

In fact, the distance changes that have been detected are contradictory. For example, the inter-island distances in the Pacific seem to be constant, but distance changes between base-stations on other parts of the planet are consistent with crustal deformation, but not continental drift.

Across the Pacific the relative motions between different points do not add up and contradict each other. However, on average they do show the Pacific is expanding, while in contrast plate-tectonic theory predicts the Pacific is contracting.

No motion can be detected between North America and Australia. In contrast, the data seems to show Huahine Island near Tahiti moving away from North America at four centimeters per year and Tahiti moving toward Australia at seven centimeters per year. Therefore, a net motion of North America to Australia should be three centimeters per year. This contradictory result can be explained by Tahiti sinking and North America rising.

It has been demonstrated that continental rock in the western United States and also around Japan is not rigid. Satellite laser ranging results, also known as space geodesy, show the whole North American continent is expanding.[612, 613]

Western Europe seems to be moving toward the northwest and away from Siberia, refuting the rigidity of the Eurasian-Plate. In contrast, southern Eurasia is contracting. This type of data generally supports a model of the continents thermally expanding and contracting, not moving around the surface of the Earth on separate solid plates.

More recently, combining data from satellite laser ranging (SLR), very long baseline interferometry (VLBI), and the Global Positioning System (GPS) has yielded an even more confusing picture of the motions of the surface of our planet.[614] Reference positions certainly move but not in the directions or speeds consistent with plate tectonic theory. Generally, these random motions refute plate tectonic prediction of large rigid continents in concerted continuous motion.[615]

However, rather than discard a thoroughly refuted theory, the new data is disregarded, and up to a hundred new plates have been created to hide inconvenient results. Even terrestrial reference frames have been changed to make these random movements appear to fit conventional theory.

Tidal Forces, Continental Drag, and Climate Change

A strange correlation between extra-terrestrial tidal forces, climate change, and abrupt shifts in the positions of the continents has been uncovered.[616]

A remarkable discovery was made that recent mid-ocean ridge eruptions have occurred primarily during two-weekly neap-tides and during the first six months of the year, after the closest approach of the Earth to the Sun. The data suggests that fault-rupture is sensitive to the effect of tidal forces of the Sun and Moon on the Earth and occurs at times of maximum extensional stress.[617]

Another remarkable discovery was that the formation of sea-floor ridges at spreading zones on either side of mid ocean fault lines seems to show the same periodicity as glacial cycles. This was first observed beneath the Southern Ocean at the Australian-Antarctic ridge between

Tasmania, South Island New Zealand, and Antarctica. The bathymetry data of ridges running parallel to faults corresponds to gravitational tidal forcing, with harmonics at twenty-thousand, forty-thousand, and one hundred-and-twenty-thousand years.[618]

Clear examples of sudden increases in underwater eruptions and magnetic anomalies, corresponding to climate cataclysms during the Pleistocene, were discovered in well-dated sedimentary records from the East Pacific Rise.[619] There are significant activity peaks around one-hundred-and-thirty-two thousand years ago, corresponding to the peak of the one-hundred-and-twenty-thousand year climate-cycle and another peak of eruption activity about twelve-thousand years-ago, during the 9600 BC cataclysm.

In addition, the age of the ridges at the Australian-Antarctic boundary corresponds to dates of abrupt changes in sea-level and mirrors the periodicities of climate-change of twenty-thousand, forty-thousand, and one-hundred-and-twenty thousand years, recorded in the ice-core-data.

All this data is telling us something very important: continental drift and tectonic theory are wrong. The accumulating evidence supports abrupt and cataclysmic separation of thick slabs of continental rock, in great jerks and surges, caused by immensely powerful extra-terrestrial tidal-forces.

Mistakes in the Tectonic Model of Pangaea

Although Wegener's brilliant new idea of Pangaea was basically correct, his model of Pangaea did not achieve the correct arrangement of all the continents. The fit between South America and Africa was obvious, but the poor fit of other continents gives the impression of a broken bowl, which had been glued back together with misplaced fragments. A better arrangement is possible, and the solution to this three-dimensional jigsaw puzzle revealed the real origin of Pangaea.

As explained earlier, Wegener already had a problem with Spain and Portugal (the Iberian Peninsula), because the continental shelf extending under the Atlantic Ocean west of Iberia is geologically dissimilar from the east-coast of America.

To solve the problem, Wegener modeled Pangaea with a Central Pangean Mountain Range: the northern Appalachian Mountains of North America running through Newfoundland and extending from-southwest-to-northeast to join the Scottish Highlands.

Wegener assumed Iberia had continuity with a piece of sunken continent in the mid-Atlantic. A piece of drowned land had once occupied the Bay of Biscay off the coast of western France and had also extended to the south along the coast of Portugal. The remains of this large triangular continental fragment are on the Atlantic ocean floor east of the Mid-Atlantic Ridge, between thirty-eight-degrees-north-latitude and forty-eight-degrees-north-latitude.[620, 621]

This missing territory was Plato's lost Atlantis. At a location named Bald Mountain, an eighty cubic kilometer block of Paleozoic continental rock was identified. Dredging the ocean floor in the region produced granite and other terrestrial rocks.[622] Continental rocks containing trilobite fossils, dating to the lower Paleozoic from the Carboniferous to Permian periods, were dredged from the underwater uplands and mountain ranges, covering a large area to the north-east of the Azores.

In addition, eighty-million year old Cretaceous sedimentary rocks typical of Western Europe were also found in cores drilled in the same area of the mid-Atlantic.[623] This part of the mid-Atlantic region was dry land in the time of the dinosaurs and probably remained above sea-level until about twelve thousand years ago. In contrast, the bottom of the Atlantic south of the Azores, in an area of ocean floor erroneously called the "Atlantis Massif," is made of mainly basalt and gabbro and was drowned in the Triassic.[624]

In the 1960s, an arbitrary modification to Wegener's model of Pangaea was made when plate-tectonics was adopted. Although it was never expressly stated, the change seems to have been made to cover-up the potential embarrassment of the evidence in support of the Atlantis legend. In order to "disappear" the drowned triangular continental fragment north of the Azores, which Wegener had used to fill the gap in the north Atlantic between Europe and America, the orientation of the whole of Eurasia was changed.

In the new arrangement of tectonic-Pangaea, Iberia was stuck next to Newfoundland, and Eurasia was rotated by almost ninety degrees to fill in the Bay of Biscay and the gap in the Atlantic left by sunken Atlantis. This doesn't make sense: the geology of Newfoundland matches the submerged continental platform around Rockall and northwest Scotland, but there is no geological continuity between Portugal and the continental shelf of Newfoundland.[625, 626, 627]

NEW MODEL OF PANGAEA

OLD TECTONIC MODEL OF PANGAEA

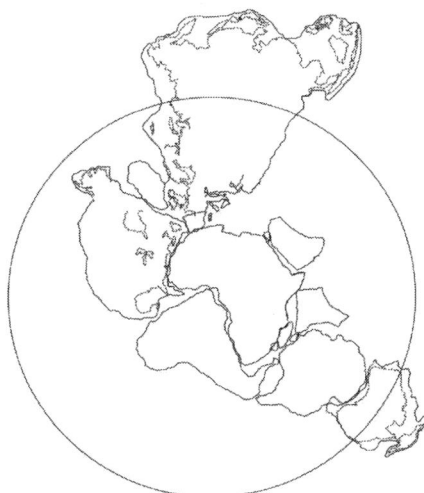

STAR-CORE-ZEUS MODEL OF PANGAEA

Rockall (from the Norse words "sea-mountain") is a very small island in the North Atlantic, located approximately five hundred kilometers off the west-coast of Scotland. Rockall is made of continental granite, similar to the rocks found on the Isle of Skye. Strontium-87 isotope analysis shows that the granite of Rockall is a Precambrian crustal rock, which is at least one billion years old.[628]

The big mistake caused by a ninety degree rotation of Eurasia relative to the North African coast was the artificial creation of a vast fantasy ocean named "the Tethys Sea" to the south of Siberia and the Himalayas, separating India and Australia far away from Asia. In addition, Australia was placed next to Antarctica but totally separated from India.

There is no evidence that the Tethys Sea ever existed. No Late-Paleozoic ocean floor rock of the Tethys Sea has ever been found, and there are no examples of the Mesozoic ocean sediments, which should have accumulated. In 2000, David Pratt identified a long list of published data that conflicted with tectonic theory and the existing model of Pangaea and the Tethys Sea.[629, 630]

The isolation of India, thousands of miles away from Asia, across the fantasy Tethys Sea, was refuted by abundant fossil evidence for the continuity of Mesozoic animal life in India and Asia for over two hundred million years. There is also compelling geological evidence that India has always been connected to Asia.

According to plate-tectonic theory, India had crashed into Asia from the south. However, the strata from the supposed collision zone, on the south side of the Himalayas, shows no north-south compression. In contrast, deep faults and other geological evidence pointed to the movement of the Tibetan plateau from west-to-east, not south-to-north.

The very existence of the Tethys Sea is refuted by the fossilized plant remains found in New Guinea and Indonesia, which is a mixture of Cathaysian flora from China and Glossopteris tree-like ferns from Australia. China, Southeast Asia, and Australia have always been one land mass and have never been separated by a wide ocean. Plate-tectonic dogma also asserts that there are two subduction zones that closed the non-existent Tethys Sea: they have never been found.

The Caribbean is also a huge problem for plate-tectonic models because it does not fit the dogma. The Caribbean region is made up of a number of huge and deep crater-like basins, underlain by shattered and drowned continental rock, which was dry land at the end of the Permian period, two-hundred-and-fifty-two million years ago. The evidence for the cataclysmic origin of the Caribbean gave rise to its geological name: the Caribbean Large Igneous Province (CLIP), but the cataclysmic process that formed it has remained a mystery.[631]

On the other side of the Atlantic, the Senegal basin and Cape Verde Islands, off the west coast of Africa, are also underlain by drowned continental crust, which are possibly the remains of half a huge impact crater. This enormous semi-circular structure is offshore from a smaller crater discovered in Senegal at Velingara, which has been confirmed as an asteroid-impact site.[632]

A New Model of Pangaea

Millions of air-travelers flying to and from the United States look at drowned Atlantis every day without a second thought. On modern aircraft, computer generated global navigation maps are displayed on screens in the cabin. From a range of satellite data inputs, they provide detailed outlines and topology of not only the land but also the continental shelves, underwater uplands, and other drowned land masses.

Wegener's match between the continental shelves across the South Atlantic is unmistakable on these displays. However, the correct fit of North America and the Mediterranean regions is still a puzzle. It is fascinating to see how the drowned uplands on the east side of the Mid-Atlantic Ridge to the north of the Azores fit so perfectly into Portugal and the Bay of Biscay off the west coast of France.

Staring at these patterns on another long flight across the Atlantic, I was snapped out of my train of thought, by the familiar coastline of southern Spain. It suddenly struck me: if Eurasia was shifted eastward, then southern Spain plus Sicily fitted almost exactly into the Gulf of Sidra (Sirte), cut into the north coast of Africa. In a second, I conceived a new close-packed model of Pangaea.

Back in London I tracked down a group at University College London who provided me with accurate satellite maps, printed according to the spherical geometry of our Earth.[633] My plan was to construct precise globes based on current satellite data and re-assemble the ancient surface of our shattered planet.

The objective of the new model was to find an arrangement of present day continents and sunken land masses, which minimized migration of Pangaea-fragments to their present positions as the continents and eliminated the more obvious contradictions of current plate-tectonic models.

To establish proof of principle, I assembled a number of crude planetary models using the materials at hand. With the aid of a hot-air drier, the continental slabs were formed from clear plastic sheet and melted onto commercial globes, as I experimented with the puzzle.

I assumed the global fault line system dated from the time of the shattering of Pangaea, which had occurred during the Permian extinction two-hundred-and-fifty-two million years ago. Using trial and error, the best arrangement and fit of the continental slabs was established, which allowed the re-formation of an almost perfect hemisphere of the old surface of our planet.

I then moved on to a high resolution construction: the final model of Earth at the time of Pangaea was assembled from printed gores of five degrees of longitude, from a combined database of satellite altimetry and bathymetry.

The continents and drowned land were assembled around the western half of Africa as a fixed reference point, which has been shown by hotspot analysis to be a fixed part of the crust.[634] Europe plus Asia was then moved east, and southern Spain plus Sicily were fitted into the Gulf of Sirte off the northern coast of Libya, matching up similar rock strata. Strike-slip-faults from the Gulf of Cadiz along the floor of the Mediterranean that fitted Spain into Libya also supported this revolutionary construction of Pangaea.[635, 636]

The land to the east of the Great Rift Valley running through Africa was moved southeast in a giant curve along other known strike-slip fault lines. Afar-Large-Igneous-Province is evidence of this massive disruption of Africa, which straddles the Ethiopian rift and continues south all the way along the Great Rift Valley to southern Africa.

Turkey was moved northward to fill in the Black Sea basin, and then Egypt, Italy and the Balkans were merged together, which resulted in the closing of most of the Mediterranean. Iran, Afghanistan, and India were moved west as one block of crust to fill the remaining Mediterranean basin. This automatically generated a huge and continuous mountain chain stretching from the Atlas Mountains in North Africa to mountains of the Middle East, which connected on to the Himalayas and mountain ranges of East Asia.

Wegener's original fit of South America to Africa was maintained. Sunken Atlantis in the mid-Atlantic was also added back to connect North America to Europe, fitting the Bay of Biscay and the coast of Portugal like a key fits a lock. To the north of Atlantis, the Rockall-Plateau was fitted in as another piece of the puzzle closing the gap between Newfoundland, Greenland, and Scotland.

Rockall is the tip of a great mountain in the north Atlantic, which is only twenty-four meters wide at its base and a little over twenty meters in height above sea level. The mountain sits on submerged highlands, known as the drowned Rockall Island, which is on average two hundred meters below sea-level. These mountains sit on top of a slab of continental platform called the Rockall-Plateau, which is about a thousand meters below the surface. The whole sunken land is the same size and shape as southern England (from Kent to Cornwall) and extends southwestward off the northwest coast of Ireland.

The most significant feature of this new model was that both the hypothetical Tethys Sea and the erroneous separation of India from Asia were eliminated. Africa, Arabia, and India were grouped along known Permian faults and made into one. This resulted in sufficient space to pack in Australia and Antarctica.

The mysterious undersea rifting that formed the South China sea, which separates Asia from the Philippines and Borneo, was reversed. Generally, drowned continental plateaus such as the East Pacific Rise are omitted from plate-tectonic models.[637] When submerged land from around the world was added back to the model, it fitted into the new bowl of Pangaea perfectly.

The single landmass connecting western-Alaska to eastern-Siberia was moved transversely along known faults to connect northern Russia, Greenland, and Canada. The remains of this huge crustal relocation are the Alpha-Mendeleev Ridge and Lomonosov Ridge under the Arctic Ocean.[638]

The Caribbean sunken land was modeled as a zone of large impact craters, with Cuba defining the northern half of a huge crater, which was brought into register with the southern half of the same crater, now located off the coast of Senegal, Africa. The Caribbean crater zone was probably formed during the Permian catastrophe by relatively low velocity impacts of continental slabs crashing back to Earth after being temporarily lifted into the air by intense gravitational tidal forces, which shall be described in a later chapter.

In order to display the detailed three-dimensional model in two dimensions, the models of the present configuration and Permian configuration of the continents were accurately photographed. The digital photographs were then traced using the position of Greenwich at the end of the Permian period, as the reference for longitude and latitude. The result was a bowl shaped super-continent, which minimized known geological and climatic anomalies.

By superimposing the present positions of the continents on the model of Pangaea, it was obvious how the shattered Pangaea fragments had moved away from each other in a co-ordinated fashion, along the fault lines that span the whole planet. The amount of displacement increased with distance from the impact zone offshore of Senegal in Africa. However, the long and totally artificial journey of India across the globe, shown in conventional plate-tectonic models, was eliminated.

A curious result of the model building was the association of large oil fields with Permian faults. The model predicted the large oil fields on the western continental shelf of India, which have recently been discovered. At the end of the Paleozoic era, the Indian oil fields were adjacent to the oil fields of the Persian Gulf and Iraq.

SHATTERED PANGAEA
Three views of the shattering of Pangaea
Single arrows ●—→ mark the direction & distance to the present location of the
fragments (double ●—→←—● arrows show tidal distortion & mountain formation)

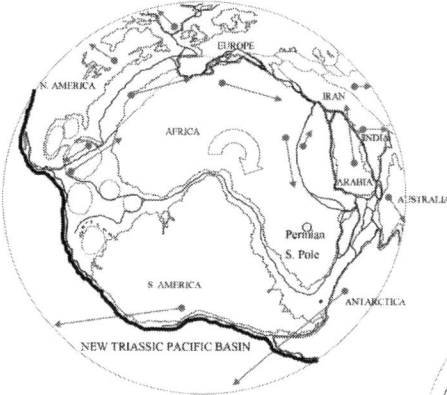

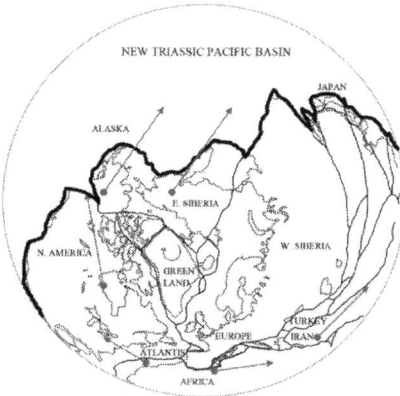

Pangaea was half the old surface of Earth
I realized that if the continental fragments could be reassembled with
such a perfect fit into a hemispherical bowl of rock, then they had to be
the shattered remnants of half the former surface of our planet. A more
significant conclusion was that if Pangaea was half of the old surface of
our planet, then Pangaea never existed as a super-continent surrounded

by a vast Permian Pacific Ocean basin. Before the end-Permian extinction a quarter of a billion years ago, the original Paleozoic surface of the Earth was comprised of crustal rocks equivalent to two Pangaeas!

Before the end-Permian extinction, the Paleozoic crust covered the whole planet and was mostly drowned by one vast global ocean, no more than five hundred meters deep. Pangaea was mostly shallow global-sea-floor, and its hills and mountains were originally clusters of small islands.

These Paleozoic islands, protruding from the ancient sea surface, were populated by terrestrial plants and animals, after life first emerged from the original shallow global ocean. This concept of the ancient Earth is supported by the extensive evidence of fossils of Paleozoic marine organisms now found buried on land but never on the ocean floor.

If Pangaea was the fractured remains of half the ancient surface of the Earth, then star-core-zeus must have got so close to Earth during the end-Permian mass extinction that its intense gravity ripped-off the other half of the crust of our planet, like peeling the skin off a ripe orange.

I have calculated that a shell of crust about eighty-six kilometers thick was removed from half of the surface of Earth. The destiny of this huge mass of Earth's crust shall be discussed in a later chapter.

After this violent removal of half of Earth's crust by star-core-zeus, one hemisphere of our planet was left as one vast wound of hot liquid basalt. After the planet achieved isostatic equilibrium and the boiling rock cooled, the vast hole became the Triassic Pacific basin, surrounded by a fractured and broken Pangaea. This radical proposal fits all the evidence.

Tidal Forces and Continental Drag

It is well understood that the gravity of the Sun and the Moon can lift tidal bulges in the ocean-water to produce the ocean-tides. During each close fly-by of star-core-zeus after the Permian cataclysm, gravitational tidal forces produced enormous tides, which induced episodic continental-drag and the stepwise movement of the continental fragments across the surface of our planet.

Repeated applications of gravitational tidal forces of star-core-zeus lifted, distorted, buckled, ripped, and dragged the continental fragments of Pangaea. Mountains were raised out of the ground, and sometimes rocks were even pulled completely off the surface. Huge chains of mountains and great faults were formed.[639]

Every four thousand years, for millions of years, the massive continents were dragged away from each other, step by step in this tidally-induced lifting, pulling, and rotating, during close encounters with star-core-zeus. Each abrupt shift in the continental slabs coincided with elevations of mountain ranges, massive environmental destruction, and partial extinctions of life forms. Some sort of binary-orbital-resonance seems to dictate closer fly-bys of star-core-zeus every one-hundred-and-twenty-thousand years, which drove the basic rip-saw-tooth climate change pattern.

The Journey of the Continents

As the continental fragments were separated after the Permian Annihilation, a big rift opened up that became the Mediterranean basin. As the north continental margin of Africa was rotated relative to southern Europe; Spain moved toward Morocco.

Italy was split from the Balkans, and the Adriatic Sea was created in the process. Turkey was dragged out of the Black Sea basin, and Arabia was pulled away from the west-coast of India. At the same time, Australia and Antarctica were dragged away from the east-coast of the Indian subcontinent. However, during this separation of the continental fragments, the Indian subcontinent remained attached to Asia.

North America and South America were dragged west as two separate continents, divided by the Caribbean impact zone. Star-core-zeus discontinuously shifted the pieces of shattered Pangaea, until the continents reached the final positions we observe today, where the land and oceans are distributed fairly evenly around the globe.

Star-core-zeus has a powerful magnetic field: during very close encounters, it induced a pole-reversal of the Earth's magnetic field. As star-core-zeus passed over the Earth, regions of basaltic rock near deep fault lines rapidly melted due to the heat generated by the intense tidal stress. Later as these rocks slowly cooled and re-set, they contained a record of the orientation of the newly reversed magnetic field of the Earth.

Repeated fly-bys of star-core-zeus were responsible for creating the series of parallel stripes of reverse-magnetized basalt rock on the ocean floors on either side of the major fault lines, such as the Mid-Atlantic Ridge. These stripes of reversed-magnetized rock are a record of the discontinuous process of continental-drag and the direct effect of magnetic star-core-zeus.

The Original Crust

This new model of Pangaea and continental-drag reveals that the continents are the remains of the original crustal surface of our planet. However, the geology establishment still promotes invalid explanations for the formation of continents and asserts that basalt must be the remains of the original surface of Earth.

Geologists still claim the continents were formed by some process similar to the formation of the volcanic islands in the Pacific, in which huge numbers of such islands were merged by some sort of plate tectonic process, which forced them to cluster into larger land masses. This fanciful process called terrane accretion and suturing is refuted by field studies.

The volcanic islands in the Pacific are not made of granite-like continental rocks. In addition, the so-called terranes within continents are made of gneissic-granite rocks, with no evidence of any volcanic processes or any boundaries made of ocean basalt rock.

Isotope analysis shows that continental-granites are not produced by any continuous extraction process from the mantle rock: the continents are the remains of the original global crust and have been in existence since the formation of Earth. Examples of archaic crustal structures are the Precambrian shield rocks in Canada, Greenland, and southern

Africa. The thick slabs of ancient rock found in Canada have been isotopically dated to more than four billion years old.

Deep analysis using lithoprobe-technology in Canada has shown the continental platforms are deep structures of archaic granitic rocks.[640] The greater the depth, the more archaic and more horizontal the strata. More than twenty kilometers underground, there are horizontal layers of intermediate granulite rocks metamorphosed by the high pressure and temperature. Generally, the continents are made of granitic rocks forty to fifty kilometers thick, sitting on the white foundation rocks of anorthosite, at the interface with the inner hot basaltic mantle rock.[641]

There is also geological evidence of the effect of powerful tidal forces billions of years before the Permian period. In this archaic crustal rock, there are deep fractures called dykes and lineaments, associated with granite-greenstone terrains. Greenstone is quite different from ocean floor basalt: it is a metamorphic rock produced by transforming granites at high temperature and pressure.

The dykes cut through all exposed Precambrian shields and are evidence of archaic cataclysmic events that cracked the Earth's crust on a number of occasions, during the early life of our planet. Some of these deep fractures did bleed hot liquid basalt rock long ago. This is evidence of metamorphic cycles driven by cyclic tidal forces, which stressed our planet repeatedly since its formation.

An example is the Isua Supracrustal Sequence in southwest Greenland, which records four extreme metamorphic events during a period of two billion years. The Sudbury Structure in Ontario, Canada, also revealed that catastrophic metamorphic events had occurred on a similar time scale. In southern Africa, there is also evidence of eleven archaic cataclysmic events.

A cycle of cataclysms resulting in the heating and deformation of the old crust of our planet seems to have occurred with a periodicity of approximately fifty-two million years. This cycle also harmonizes with the frequency of mass-killings of living species in the history of our planet every twenty-six million years.[642] This data indicates close fly-bys with star-core-zeus have been occurring since the formation of Earth.

Conclusion

The super-continent of Pangaea was the remains of the old surface of the Earth, after star-core-zeus had ripped off half of the Earth's crust, at the end of the Permian period.

Before Pangaea there were no continents, only the old intact crust of our planet, so continental-drift was impossible. After the end-Permian cataclysm, Pangaea was the shattered remnants of the old crust, which had been broken into continental fragments. In the previous two-hundred-and-fifty-two million years, the continents have been periodically lifted and dragged across the globe in great jerks every four-thousand years by extra-terrestrial tidal forces induced by star-core-zeus.

In the next chapter, we shall take a closer look at one of the consequences of the cataclysmic destruction of Pangaea: the great Permian extinction of life on Earth.

CHAPTER 7

The Destruction of Pangaea and the Great Permian Extinction

● ● ●

THE PERMIAN DESTRUCTION STRATUM WAS originally identified around the city of Perm in Russia in 1845 by Sir Roderick Murchison, a Scottish geologist. Later radiometric dating established that the Permian period commenced around three hundred million years ago but ended suddenly in a terrible cataclysm forty-six million years later, two-hundred-and-fifty-two million years before our time.

THE PERMIAN EXTINCTION EVENT
The apocalypse at the end of the Permian Period destroyed almost everything alive at the time and around 95% of the fossil species recorded in the Permian disappeared from the geological record.

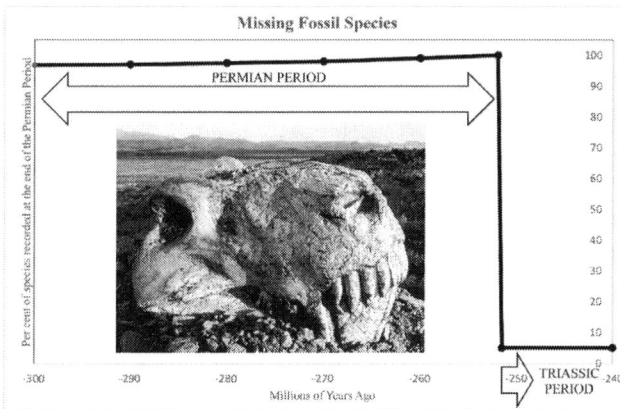

The very top layer of the youngest Permian rocks is comprised of iron-rich red-beds and mudstones, which had been laid down by incredibly powerful floods. This destruction layer contains masses of fossils of ancient amphibians, reptiles, and small surface-water creatures, which had all been exterminated in an instant and then abruptly buried. Entombed in the similar red-beds of Texas and New Mexico is more evidence of mega-death of shallow-water marine life-forms, which occurred at the very end of the Permian period.[643, 644]

Paleozoic Life before the Disaster

The Permian extinction event marked the sudden end of the three hundred million year-long era of the Paleozoic life, which had first appeared on Earth around five-hundred-and-fifty million years ago. The Paleozoic era was divided into five long periods of geological time preceding the Permian: the Cambrian, Ordovician, Silurian, Devonian, and Carboniferous. These geological periods were originally characterized by the different types of fossils dug out of rocks from different regions of the United Kingdom.

In the Paleozoic era, land was only a large number of islands and islets, surrounded by shallow seas that flooded the old crust of Earth. The first vertebrate animals crawled onto land in the Late Devonian period, three-hundred-and-seventy-five-million years ago. By the end of the Permian period, both the shallow seas and the islands were teaming with diverse forms of life.

No Deep Paleozoic Ocean Basins

At the bottom of the shallow Permian seas, a layer of marine-limestone formed by sedimentation (called zechstein in Europe). The mystery is that this type of rock is now only found on land and never on the bottom of the sea.

An even bigger mystery is that after two-hundred years of fossil collecting, not a single Paleozoic deep-water species of animal or plant has been found. Not one fossil of a deep-sea bathypelagic species, which live in one to four kilometer deep water, nor any fossil of a bottom-living abyssopelagic species, which live in four to six kilometer deep water, has ever been discovered. Before the start of the Mesozoic Era, it seems that there were no deep-water marine species adapted to life below three hundred meters of water.

In contrast, one hundred million years later, descendants of some shallow-water species from the Permian period had evolved into new forms adapted to life in deep oceans. The problem of the missing Paleozoic deep-marine fossils is so embarrassing that the subject is either not discussed or dismissed with the unbelievable assertion that all the deep marine sediments from before the Triassic no longer exist.

The incredible proposition is that the whole ocean floor of the vast Permian Pacific Ocean, which was supposed to predate the Permian-Triassic boundary and which was supposed to cover half of the planet, has simply vanished. The excuse is that the hypothetical Paleozoic ocean-floor had been completely swallowed down subduction trenches and magically covered-up under moving tectonic plates so that not one single fragment of it survives.

The real reason for the total absence of ocean-floor rocks more than two-hundred-and-fifty-million years-old and the total lack of evidence for fossils of deep-ocean-species pre-dating the Permian extinction is simple: there were no deep ocean basins in the Paleozoic era of our planet. The incredible conclusion is that the deep ocean basins only appeared on planet Earth at the start of the Mesozoic Era.

Shallow Paleozoic Seas

During the Permian period, more than a quarter-of-a-billion years ago, seawater drowned three-quarters of the present continental platforms. North America, Europe, and the United Kingdom were partly flooded, and most of the present land area was under shallow seas with an average depth of about a hundred meters.[645, 646] These Permian seas covered most of the surface of our planet: only scattered regions of higher land pushed up through the sea surface to form islands.

The Permian period was the time of the crinoids: echinoderms that were attached to the bottom of the shallow seas by long storks. They lived by filter-feeding on microscopic plants and animals in the illuminated sub-surface waters. The ecological range of the crinoids was from a few meters below the sea-surface to only a few hundred meters under water. For over two hundred million years, these crinoids, together with bivalve shell-fish called brachiopods and branching twig-like colonial bryozoans, dominated the shallow oceans of the Earth.

Prelude to the Permian Extinction

Some Permian rock formations have been studied intensively, because they contain a detail record of the end-Permian cataclysm. The marine Permian rocks around Perm in the Ural Mountains in Russia and marine Permian rocks in West Texas in the United States recorded similar stories of the disaster at sea. The fossil-beds in the marine Permian rocks south of the Yangtze River, between Shanghai and Nanjing in China, are so complete that they have become the reference point for the detailed analysis of the catastrophic events at the Permian-Triassic boundary. In addition, the terrestrial Permian rocks in southern Africa recorded the destruction of terrestrial life forms on land.

There were actually two disasters at the end of the Permian period: a lesser cataclysm followed by a violent annihilation and separated by may be as little as a few thousand years. The smaller earlier event caused sea-level to drop and the seas to retreat rapidly so that organisms attached to the newly exposed coastal margins were killed. Evidence of this retreat of the seas has been found both in the West Texas former shallow-sea-basin and in the rocks from Zechstein Sea floor, which once covered Europe. This event correlated with a mysterious abundance-spike in the carbon-12 isotope (discussed in the next chapter).

There was no build-up of ice on land, so the big mystery was where did all the sea water go? It was as if a huge volume of seawater had simply been sucked off the planet.

However, this awesome event was only an insignificant prelude to the planet-wide annihilation that followed, probably only four thousand years later. The importance of this evidence of two Permian catastrophes is because it suggests a cyclical catastrophic process was at work, as opposed to the great Permian mass-extinction being the result of a one-off apocalyptic asteroid impact.

The Permian Annihilation

The main planet-wide cataclysm about a quarter-of-a-billion years ago caused destruction on an awesome scale and was responsible for the great Permian mass-extinction. In the geological record, the Permian-Triassic boundary is a global tombstone marking the mega-death and extermination of almost everything alive at the time. Uranium-lead and potassium-argon analysis of end-Permian marine rocks at Meishan in China accurately dated the main destruction event to two-hundred-and-fifty-one-point-five million years ago.

The dating of volcanic ash beds above and below the Permian extinction layer confirmed the wipe-out of life at the end of the Permian period was abrupt. Within the error of geological dating methods, the catastrophe could have occurred in as short a period of time as one day.

During the terrible end-Permian event, volcanoes erupted all over the world, and hot liquid basalt flooded the area from western-Siberia to Lake Baikal. The crust was buckled, and huge chains of new mountains suddenly appeared all over the planet, including the Atlas, Alps, Zagros, Urals, Himalayas, and Andes.

There was a lethal drop in atmospheric oxygen levels and a huge dump of extra-terrestrial iron-pyrite (FeS_2) and iron-sulfide (FeS), which remained in an unoxidized state in marine chert sedimentary rocks that marked the Permian-Triassic boundary.[647] Such rocks were recovered from all around the edges of the Pacific Ocean, for example, off the coasts of both Canada and Japan and on the coast of Arabia.

Shredding of the Permian Forests

All over the world the forests just disappeared; even tree roots were yanked from the ground. In Bowen basin in Australia, the plant material from forests had been ripped to shreds and dumped in mounds the size of hills and then buried under a layer of sand and gravel. The Karoo Desert of South Africa, which stretches from Cape Town to

Johannesburg, contained compelling evidence of the destruction of all land plants and animals of the late Permian period. All over the world, forests were torn down, land was stripped of its surface layers, and the debris was mixed and entombed. Eighty-two percent of all vertebrate species of the Permian period became extinct at the Permian-Triassic boundary.

Raging Floods

In southern Africa, the Permian landscape was water-blasted and transformed by the annihilation. What had once been a lush wet-land of meandering rivers suddenly became a region of raging floods that scoured-out braided-river-systems. Criss-crossed straight channels were rapidly carved by a huge deluge of fast moving flood water and debris, which cut deep into the land surface. These abrasive rapids were a global phenomenon: vast floods raged across the land-surface, while sand and gravel filled-in existing river-channels. Evidence of these braided-river systems can be found in Australia, Europe, and the Urals in Russia, which had all appeared suddenly and ripped through the land at the Permian-Triassic boundary.

Decay and Fungus

Immediately following the world-wide destruction of living things in the Permian-annihilation, masses of rotting plant and animal remains were broken down by opportunistic fungi. On land, all that remained of Permian life were hill-sized mounds of rotting pulp and flesh, still recorded today as a thin but dense layer of organic matter and fungal spores.

In the late Permian period, fossil pollens from plants were abundant and fungal spores were almost non-existent. However, in the Permian destruction layer, pollen vanished, and fungal spores represented almost all of the pollen-sized particles.[648] The sudden disappearance of all types of pollen confirmed that almost all the plants on the planet had been killed in the disaster.

The drained floors of the shallow Permian seas were abruptly transformed into vast stinking tips of dead marine plants and animals, a feast for terrestrial fungi. Direct evidence of the sudden draining of the shallow seas and the extermination of marine life was discovered in rocks in the Southern Alps and in Israel, which recorded the marine Permian extinction. The seabed suddenly became land and terrestrial fungi feasted on the noisome heaps of rotting marine debris and produced a huge abundance of terrestrial fungal spores, which formed a distinct and dense layer.

One curiosity was the evidence of the heavy concentrations of fungal spores predominantly on the eastern side of Pangaea. It appeared that huge flood waves had traveled from west-to-east in a line running from Antarctica to the Urals, stripping organic remains off the continental land, which was then dumped as hill-sized-mounds of decaying dead matter in the Far East.

Graveyards of Coal

The dumps of the trashed Permian Glossopteris forests abruptly turned into graveyards of coal. Thick coal layers at the Permian-Triassic boundary are found all over the world.[649] Similar layers of coal have been found at the Permian destruction level in Antarctica, Australia, India, Russia, and China.[650] The buried plant matter was chemically transformed to coal in environment enigmatically rich in kerogen, hydrogen, sulfur, iron-pyrite, and iron-sulfide. Permian coals also contain huge quantities of carbon macromolecules known as kerogens, which are identical to the insoluble material found in carbonaceous chondrite meteorites. Permian coals are also very acidic with high concentrations of sulfuric acid, formed from the hydrolysis of vast amounts of hydrogen-sulfide gas.

These coal beds mark the sudden end of permian plant species, which populated our planet. The forests of Glossopteris trees, which used to grow all over Pangaea during the Permian period, completely disappeared in the following Mesozoic era.

Earth Scarred and Bleeding

The Siberian Traps were an awesome monument to the scale of the Permian apocalypse.[651] An enormous area of territory was drowned under a huge volume of very hot liquid basaltic rock. The hot basalt spread out over an area of seven-million square-kilometers, forming a continuous layer from one-hundred meters up to six kilometers deep. This igneous province was a huge magma clot and probably comprised of four million cubic kilometers of basaltic rock. While still super-hot liquid, the basalt filled up ancient valleys and drowned hills, forming a smooth undulating surface like an ocean of rock, which cooled and hardened to seal the archaic Permian period land-surface below.[652]

The incredible floods of hot liquid basalt had welled-up and poured out of abruptly-formed deep-fractures, which had cracked all the way down through the crust to the mantle of Earth. A vast region of Russia was ruptured and bled boiling liquid basalt from at least four major locations. The explosive nature of these eruptions was shown in the diamond-rich Kimberlite Pipes preserved in Taymir region in northern Siberia.

The composition of the rock showed that the ultra-hot-flow of basaltic material had come from deep in the Earth's mantle. The flood-basalt was chemically different from the silica-lava produced by volcanoes, which spew from magma chambers within the upper-crust. The liquid basalt material was so ultra-hot that it had gushed out of the deep upper-mantle like super-heated water.

Uranium-lead dating of zircon crystals in the basalt produced a close scatter of dates averaging around the time of the Permian extinction. For example, samples from a volcanic intrusion at Norilsk, which occurred immediately after the Siberian traps formed, gave an age of two-hundred-and-fifty-one-point-one million years ago. Averages of the radiometric dating of the isotopes in different samples of the material in the Siberian traps generally produced an age of two-hundred-and-fifty-two million years old.

These dates that clustered around the Permian-annihilation were very similar to radiometric dating of the volcanic ash beds on the east coast of China, discovered at Meishan near Shanghai. Large areas in southwestern China had also been flooded with hot liquid basalt from deep fissures.[653, 654]

This data suggested that a sudden shattering of the planet had simultaneously caused gushing-bleeds of liquid basalt and eruptions of volcanoes all over the globe. These eruptions are on a scale beyond comprehension; the largest known volcanic eruption produced only twelve cubic kilometers of material. Even the Deccan-Traps rupture in India, triggered by the asteroid impact that killed the dinosaurs, was only one thousandth of the volume of the Siberian flood-basalt bleed.

Another strange fact is that the flood-basalt of the Siberian Traps is the oldest example of the flood-basalt phenomenon on Earth. There are no older examples prior to two-hundred-and-fifty-two million years ago.

The Permian cataclysm that caused the formation of the Siberian Traps also shattered the super-continent Pangaea into continental-sized fragments. However, the strange location of the deep Siberian faults that had bled so much liquid basalt is another mystery. Current plate tectonic theory cannot explain how these four deep ruptures formed, because they are in the middle of an ancient continental platform.

One explanation for the location of the deep Siberian fissures is that they were at the re-focal point of antipodal impact waves. This mechanism has been established as the cause of the Deccan Traps flood-basalt eruption in India, sixty-five million years ago. The Chicxulub dinosaur-killing asteroid-impact in the Gulf of Mexico sent shock waves across the globe, which focused on the opposite side of the planet, causing a local rupture in the crust in the deccan region of India. Additional evidence has been discovered at a depth of seven kilometers below the Indian continental shelf offshore of Mumbai. The lower crust has a rupture five hundred kilometers across and more than twelve kilometers deep.[655]

The Siberian ruptures may have been induced in a similar way when rings of impact-waves triggered by the massive impacts that formed the Caribbean basin rippled across the planet to converge in a destructive focus in central Siberia.

Death in the Shallow Seas

The Permian extinction struck all types of marine organisms but was particularly lethal to species attached to the bottom of the shallow seas. Sedentary shallow-water filter-feeders, such as crinoids, brachiopods, ammonoids and lacy-bryozoans, were all wiped out. All reef attached organisms suddenly perished as the water rushed away, and only mobile varieties survived.

Where the Permian disaster struck at Meishan in China, the catastrophe resulted in the sudden extermination of two-hundred-and-sixty-five species in ninety-three genera. Worldwide, eighty-two percent of all marine-genera and half of all marine-families were wiped out in an instant.

This type of killing correlated with a sudden draining of the seas off the continental platforms, leaving the seabed-attached species high-and-dry. For example, the shallow sea that once filled the West Texas basin and the Zechstein Sea that covered Europe simply vanished.

The Triassic Pacific Basin

During the Permian period, up to three quarters of the continents were under shallow seas. During the Permian cataclysm, the sea-level suddenly and mysteriously dropped by at least three-hundred meters, turning shallow sea into dry-land. After the terrible catastrophe, less than ten percent of continental platforms were underwater, but there was no build-up of ice on land to account for the missing water. No equivalent disappearance of water has ever been known on our planet at any other time in geological history.

A fantastic solution to the problem of the missing ocean water two-hundred-and-fifty-two million years ago is that it all drained away into the newly-formed Triassic Pacific basin, which had suddenly appeared during the Permian annihilation. The basin was initially a vast cauldron of hot liquid upper mantle rock—the hole remaining after half of the Earth's crust had been ripped off the planet.

The seas that used to cover the Permian planet-surface cascaded off newly-formed continental-shelf-precipices. Sea-water dropped as an awesome waterfall on a scale that defies imagination, roaring off cliffs which were up to eighty-kilometers high. The water boiled off the burning hot basin of liquid basalt until it eventually quenched and cooled the rock to form ocean-floor basalt.

Some evidence for the sudden creation of the Triassic Pacific basin in this manner comes from an unusual source: studies of an isotope called strontium-87. It is known that small amounts of strontium-87 are released when hot basaltic magmas from ruptures in the ocean floor come into contact with seawater. Two-hundred-and-fifty-million years ago, there was a massive release of Strontium-87, forming a huge abundance-spike, which marked the end-Permian catastrophe in the geological column.[656, 657, 658]

Such a huge Strontium-87 release has never been repeated at any other time in the geological history of our planet. The huge amount of Strontium-87 suggested that half of the surface of the Earth was one huge bubbling cauldron of hot basaltic magma, which was then quenched with a volume of water equivalent to all the oceans of the world.

At first the seawater boiled away, driving the dissolved oxygen into the burning atmosphere. The huge clouds of steam generated violent storm systems that raged across the land. It took decades for our wounded planet to achieve thermal equilibrium.

As the huge cascades of water roared off the edges of the continental platforms, titanic rapids eroded deep channels across the continental margins and dug out vast waterways that ran far out across the newly solidified floor of the Triassic Pacific basin. Where the wild torrents of water slowed, sediments were dumped as alluvial fans, which formed all around the fresh edges of the basin.

The remains of the old Permian southern-hemisphere of Earth had been broken into vast fragments separated by ninety-kilometer deep chasms. Vertiginous cliffs traced the familiar outlines of the present continents: the fractured table-land was Pangaea.

Over the following millions of years, Pangaea slowly sank while the bottom of the vast Triassic Pacific Ocean basin slowly rose, until isostatic equilibrium was achieved when the two surfaces stabilized at a vertical separation of approximately five kilometers.

Conclusion

The Permian cataclysm left our planet bleeding hot magma, with a poisoned atmosphere and almost all life-forms dead. Smashed continental fragments and the new deep Triassic Ocean basin were all formed violently by the same cataclysm, which caused the mass extinction of life. In the next chapter, we shall consider the evidence that convicts star-core-zeus as the extra-terrestrial killer.

CHAPTER 8

Death from Space and the End of an Era

● ● ●

THE NATURE OF THE EXTRA-TERRESTRIAL object that caused the Permian mega-massacre is still debated. The geological strata that record the death from space at the end of the Permian period contain no evidence of iridium or shocked quartz, the sign of a violent impact of a massive asteroid. However, there are concentrations of strange materials usually associated with type-two supernova explosions and hyper-condensed stellar remnants.

Supernova Fullerenes

The dark, thin layer in the Permian-Triassic boundary strata that corresponds to the Permian cataclysm contains high concentrations of fullerenes, which are completely absent above and below this destruction layer.[659, 660] Fullerenes are large macro-molecular balls of carbon atoms, formed from a cage-like aromatic carbon mesh of sixty to two hundred carbon atoms. This layer of fullerenes is like a fingerprint, connecting a massive supernova-remnant to the Permian annihilation.

Fullerenes are usually synthesized from hot carbon gas in ultra-violet-light-driven chemical-reactions, within the dust clouds produced by type-two supernova explosions of large stars. The spectra of fullerenes can be detected easily, because they give rise to near-infrared absorption features that redden starlight. Fullerenes are abundant in the supernova dust found near our solar-system and probably make up one percent of all interstellar carbon dust. Fullerenes can often be detected in dense dust clouds, which surround neutron-stars.

Analysis of the Permian annihilation material revealed there were high concentrations of alien helium and argon trapped inside the molecular carbon balls. Fullerenes recovered at the Permian-Triassic destruction layer at Meishan in China, at Graphite Peak in Antarctica, and at sites in Japan, all had significant amounts of alien helium-3 trapped inside their spherical carbon cages.[661]

Helium-3 is evidence that the Permian annihilation fullerenes had not formed on Earth. Helium-3 is rare on Earth but common in interplanetary dust, the remains of the early solar nebula that had formed from supernova explosion debris.[662] However, the big mystery is how such a huge quantity of this ancient extra-terrestrial supernova dust got deposited precisely in the Permian destruction layer.

In my previous book *Cataclysms & Renewals*, I described how a fullerene-rich cloud of dust, which surrounds star-core-zeus, changed the color of the light arriving from the bright star Sirius from white to red, during the period of the classical-Greeks and Romans.[663] The evidence suggests that during the Permian annihilation, the Earth actually flew through the middle of this fullerene-rich cloud surrounding star-core-zeus.

Other Alien Fingerprints

A fragment of the Permian land surface was identified in the United Kingdom on a cliff-face at Littleham Cove near Exeter in Devon. In the Budleigh-Salterton-pebble-beds that mark the point of the Permian annihilation, spherical nodules of supernova debris up to thirty centimeters in diameter were recovered.

These nodules are rich in heavy rare-earth-elements and are also radioactive. They contain an abundance of the typical nucleo-synthetic products of type-two supernova explosions: vanadium, uranium, nickel, copper, cobalt, chromium, and arsenic. The composition of these nodules also closely resembles the KREEP-rocks from the surface of the Moon, which were collected during the Apollo missions.[664]

At other locations in the United Kingdom, such as Heysham in Lancashire, there are related remnants of the Permian-Triassic boundary, where extra-terrestrial nodules, rich in uranium, iron-pyrite, and bitumen-like hydrocarbons, have been found. Similar nodules have been found associated with red iron-oxide sandstones in distinct layers from the Devonian Period up to the point of the Permian annihilation.[665]

There was also a strange increase in the concentration of nitrogen-15, an isotope produced in supernova explosions, at the Permian-Triassic boundary. In addition, there was an abundance of strontium-87 (mentioned earlier), which had been produced by massive reactions between hot liquid basalt and sea-water. Permian-Triassic boundary rocks with these markers have been found in the dolomites of Italy, in Pakistan, in South China, and even in Spitsbergen in the Arctic Circle.

At some locations, the Permian-Triassic destruction strata contains extra-terrestrial grit rich in organic carbon-macro-molecules and hydrated silicate minerals, which closely resembles the material of carbonaceous chondrite meteorites. In the Permian-Triassic destruction layer at Graphite Peak in Antarctica, there were tiny extra-terrestrial nickel-iron spheres. This shiny metallic material must have rained down when the atmosphere lacked oxygen, because they were preserved in a non-oxidized state.

Supporting evidence for the lack of oxygen in the atmosphere at the time is an unusual green mineral known as berthierine found in the earliest Triassic fossil soils. Berthierine could only have formed if there was no oxygen in the atmosphere.

There are significant amounts of other extra-terrestrial materials in the Permian destruction layer. At Graphite Peak in Antarctica, other grains containing iron-nickel-phosphorus-sulfur materials, iron-pyrite, and other rare iron-sulfide compounds were isolated from Permian-Triassic boundary rocks.

In a number of locations around the world, the rocks from the Permian-Triassic boundary contain high concentrations of iron-sulfide and iron-pyrite. In these minerals, the iron is in its reduced ferric ionic-form, which could only occur if the iron had not been exposed to oxygen.

Generally, there is a huge sulfur-abundance anomaly in the Permian destruction layer around the world, which remains an enigma. Analysis of biomarkers at the Permian-Triassic boundary also indicated the over-growth of green sulfur-bacteria, which confirmed the strange low-oxygen, high-sulfur poisoned atmosphere at the time of the disaster.[666]

Extra-terrestrial iron-pyrite, iron-sulfide, phospho-compounds, and hydrocarbon-macro-molecules had been dumped by star-core-zeus at the Permian-Triassic boundary. This is a significant clue to the origin of life on Earth four-point-five billion years ago, which shall be described in detail in Appendix A and Appendix B of this book.

The End-Permian Carbon-12 Anomaly

At the Permian-Triassic boundary, there was a strange abundance peak of carbon-12 (C^{12}, the lighter isotope of carbon) and relative to carbon-13 (C^{13}, the heavier isotope of carbon), which has been detected all over the world, in samples from New Zealand, Armenia, China, Greenland, British Colombia, and Japan.[667]

The origin of the carbon isotope balance in the environment is known. During photosynthesis, plants select for lighter C^{12} carbon-dioxide at the expense of the heavier C^{13} version. As a result, plants preferentially accumulate the lighter C^{12} carbon isotope into their organic molecules. Animals that eat these plant-products also carry a similar amount of C^{12} as the plants.

In addition, C^{12} carbon-dioxide is also preferentially taken up from seawater by photosynthetic plankton. The C^{12}-to-C^{13} ratio of plankton is preserved in their carbonaceous shells, and C^{13} is concentrated in the ocean water. Generally, materials from non-living sources tend to have a higher proportion of C^{13}.

In the Permian-Triassic boundary around the world, there is a remarkably high concentration of the lighter C^{12} isotope of carbon, which is difficult to explain. Even if a massive quantity of carbon was generated by burning all the terrestrial plants and animals, in which all their C^{12} was added to the carbon-dioxide in the atmosphere, the amount of C^{12} theoretically released is still insufficient to explain the Permian C^{12}-anomaly.

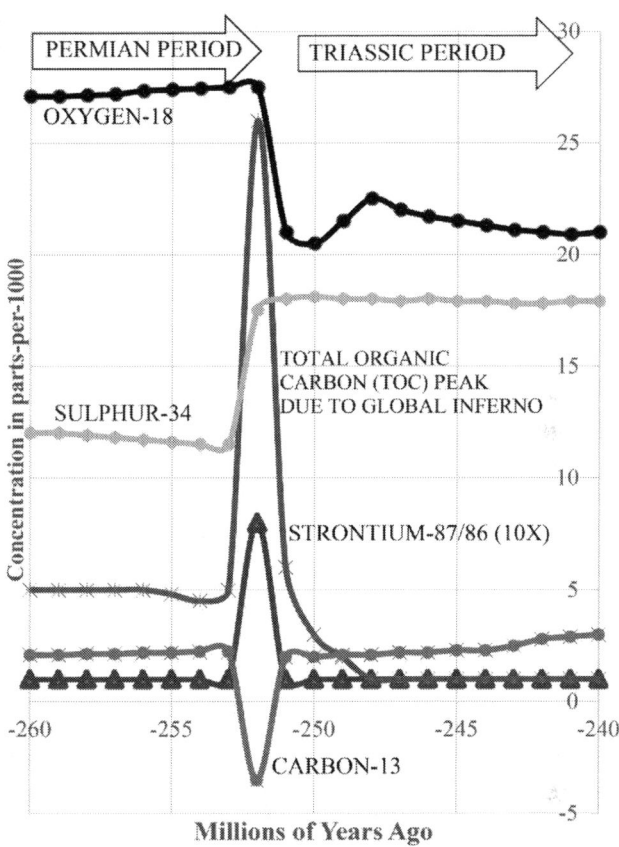

ABRUPT ISOTOPE CHANGE WITH THE PERMIAN EXTINCTION

Dudas, F., et al., "A conodont-based revision of the 87Sr/86Sr seawater curve across the Permian-Triassic boundary" *Palaeogeography Palaeoclimatology Palaeocology* 470 (2017): 40-53
Payne, J., "Large Perturbations of the Carbon Cycle During Recovery from the End-Permian Extinction" *Science* 305 (2004): 506-507
Holser, W., et al, "Catastrophic chemical events in the history of the ocean, *Nature*, 267, (1977) 403-408,
Kani, T., et al., "The Paleozoic minimum of 87Sr/86Sr ratio in the Capitanian (Permian) mid-oceanic carbonates: A critical turning pointin the Late Paleozoic," *Journal of Asian Earth Sciences* 32 (2008) 22–33

A Methane Hydrate Explosion

The C^{12}-anomaly can be explained by the explosive release of the buried methane hydrates from the beds of the shallow Permian seas. Methane hydrates found below the sea-floor have an unusually high carbon-12 to carbon-13 ratio.

Methane hydrate is the waste product of a huge population of ancient microbes that live underground and digest carbon macro-molecules from geological hydrocarbon deposits. These methanogenic-archaean-microbes preferentially metabolize carbon-12 by hydrogen-reduction of carbon-carbon double-bonds. The Carbon-13 abundance of their waste methane is very low, with a C^{13}/C^{12} ratio of 1/95, compared to crude oil and meteoric hydrocarbon, with a C^{13}/C^{12} ratio of 1/92.

The methane eventually migrates up through sediments of the crust and into the sea-bottom forming a blue-ice on contact with water, called methane-clathrate. Under the high pressure and low temperature of deep water, methane-clathrate is a stable ice made of a combination of four methane molecules and twenty-three water molecules.

However, methane-clathrate is less dense than water, so it will float to the surface and explosively sublime if exposed. During the Permian annihilation, probably a million cubic miles of methane-clathrate was shaken from the Permian sea-beds.

Global Fire-Storm

There is good evidence for a sharp spike in global temperatures during the Permian annihilation. Huge volumes of methane probably mixed with oxygen in the atmosphere and developed into an explosive mixture. The evidence suggests there was enough methane to burn almost all the oxygen in the atmosphere in one awesome world-wide firestorm, which produced huge quantities of C^{12}-rich carbon-dioxide and water.

After the Permian fire-storm had burnt itself out, oxygen levels in the oceans rapidly dropped to very low levels. All rocks deposited at the time of the Permian-Triassic boundary revealed strong evidence of oxygen depletion. The only shell fish to survive the Permian catastrophe were claraia and lingula, which can survive extremely low oxygen concentrations in seawater.

Black chert sediments found in Japan and British Colombia confirmed that the sea-water became anoxic. Chert is a micro-crystalline silica rock produced from the ocean fall-out of siliceous microfossils. Normally, iron in the microfossils reacts with oxygen in seawater to produce brick-red ferric-compounds. Brick-red chert was common in the rocks of the shallow seas of the Late-Permian period and again later on the continental shelves of the Mid-Triassic period. However, at the boundary that marks the Permian annihilation, there is a layer of sulfur-rich black chert and sooty carbon-rich clay stone, both demonstrating the lack of oxygen in the atmosphere and also a strange extra-terrestrial fall-out.

Dumping of Extra-Terrestrial Calcium Carbonate Dust

There is a mysterious layer of almost pure calcium-carbonate (chalk) on top of the Permian annihilation horizon and its origin is hard to explain. Some sort of massive calcium-carbonate precipitation from sea-water occurred suddenly during the Permian annihilation, but the origin of the material and the process that occurred is not understood.[668]

One example of this strange phenomenon is the Lalongdong Reef, a late-Permian reef, now lying on its side in a field to the north of the city of Chongqing, China. When the reef had been a living Permian colony of coral, it had suddenly been buried under pure inorganic calcium carbonate, which formed a cap of rock about one meter thick. This carbonate cap rock was later slowly buried by Triassic shales.

A similar one meter thick layer of inorganic calcium carbonate material was found capping late-Permian rocks at Abadeh in central Iran, and there were other examples in Japan. The dolomites in Italy, which are made of related calcium magnesium carbonate, were also produced suddenly during the Permian disaster.

The chalks dumped at the Permian-Triassic boundary contain a strangely large proportion of carbon-13.[669, 670] The ratio of C^{13}-to-C^{12} for Permian calcium carbonate rocks is 1/89. In contrast, the ratio of C^{13}-to-C^{12} for atmospheric carbon-dioxide is 1/90; the ratio for terrestrial plants and marine algae is 1/91.[671, 672]

It is known that the carbonates in all carbonaceous-chondrite-meteorites also have a high Carbon-13 content. The carbonate rock-particles in CI-carbonaceous-chondrite-meteorites have the highest ratio of C^{13}-to-C^{12}, at around 1/85.[673, 674, 675] The origin of the large amount of Carbon-13 in the Permian calcium carbonate precipitates is hard to explain but points to an extra-terrestrial source.

The CI-carbonaceous-chondrite meteorites are unusual because they lack glassy chondrules and show evidence of extensive aqueous alteration. CI-carbonaceous-chondrite-meteorites seem to be the remains of the debris of the Sun's partner star that was blasted into the Sun during the formation of the solar-system, because the non-volatile elemental content of CI meteorites exactly matches the photospheric abundances of elements in the Sun.[676, 677]

Rocks Ripped Off Earth

Another mystery is that the whole rock strata carrying the actual fossil record of the Late-Permian period is missing from below the Permian-Triassic boundary in most parts of the world. It seems that rocks of the late-Permian period were torn off our planet by awesome cosmic forces during the cataclysm.

There is a mysterious gap between mid-Permian rocks in Texas and Triassic rocks in Utah. Mid-Permian limestone was found at the rim of the Grand Canyon in Arizona, in the Guadalupe Mountains of Texas and the Sangre de Cristo Mountains near Santa Fe. However, it was weird that directly above this stratum was a covering of thousands of square miles of rock from the start of the Triassic. The transition layer of Permian rock, equivalent to more than twenty million years of deposition and rock formation, had simply vanished.

The same transition layer of rock was missing in many other parts of the world. In Western Europe, the end-Permian cataclysm was so destructive that much of the Permian strata had totally vanished. For example, a walk through geological time along the sea-cliffs from Devon to Dorset in the United Kingdom reveals most of the surface rocks of the Late Permian period are missing. The same gap in the geological record occurs in Greece and Sicily, where the geological column jumps from a layer of mid-Permian rock to a layer of rock from the start of the Triassic.

There is abundant evidence that during the Permian annihilation, the upper surface of the continental rocks had been removed in an awesomely violent process. However, this missing layer of Permian rocks was dwarfed by the missing half of the whole crust of the Earth, which had suddenly vanished from the enormous Triassic Pacific basin. Between the end of the Permian and the start of the Triassic, half of the Earth's crust seems to have been pulled off our planet and dragged-off into space.

The Early Triassic Aftermath

The massive destruction of the Permian annihilation was followed by a permanent change in the global climate. Earth was cloaked in thick dense clouds, and the atmosphere had only very low levels of oxygen. Sunlight was blocked out for hundreds of years, and there was a global freeze.

The shallow Triassic ocean, which covered more than half the planet, turned into sea-ice. Above the multi-kilometer-high cliffs, on the fractured plateau of the old crust of Pangaea, all the land was covered in snow. The Earth was a strangely asymmetrical world with a deeply fractured landmass on one hemisphere and a deep ocean basin, only partly filled with frozen shallow sea-water, covering the other hemisphere. Trillions of tons of carbon-dioxide had also been dissolved in the oceans, so the sea-water was sharply acidic.[678]

The Barren Triassic Desert

After the dust settled out of the atmosphere, the poisoned air cleared, the clouds dissipated, and enough sunlight again penetrated to the surface to warm up the Earth. However, at the beginning of the Triassic period, the whole planet was generally much colder than in the earlier Permian period. It was as if the Earth had been dragged into a new orbit slightly further away from the Sun.

There is little evidence of life in the early Triassic period. Europe was a desert land, revealed by a layer of rock that covers the continent called Buntsandstein, a type of sandstone formed from fused desert sand.

A harsh dry desert also covered the area around Perm in central Russia, which had been under a shallow sea in the Permian period.

After the Permian mega-death, only the tiniest fraction of a percent of the populations of individual species survived and most of the Permian period vertebrates had been killed off. The annihilation had been so lethal that even whole species of insects had disappeared. Pollen analysis showed only hardy weeds such as quillwort grew during the first few million years of the early-Triassic.

However, huge mushroom-shaped rocks called 'stromatolites', built by structured communities of marine micro-organisms thrived in the anoxic and toxic environment of the early-Triassic. These complex cities of micro-organisms, which colonized the shallow edges of the new empty ocean of the early-Triassic, were a throw-back to the deep past of life on Earth, billions of years earlier.

The few surviving Permian species began to reproduce from tiny populations of lucky individuals, but it took a very long time to repopulate the planet. A hundred-million years passed, before the number of families of plants and animals around the world recovered to pre-extinction levels.[679]

Filling the Triassic Ocean Basin from Space

The origin of the ocean water that mysteriously appeared in the early-Triassic is another big geological mystery. For a hundred million years after the end-Permian cataclysm, sea water was twice as salty as today.[680] However, during the Triassic, there were stepwise rises in sea-level, which progressively filled up the new Pacific Ocean basin and led to a reduction in the ocean salt concentration.

The problem with sequential rises in sea level was that they required the melting of multi-kilometer thick ice sheets, but there was no known source of melting glacial ice in the Triassic deserts to account for all the water appearing in the ocean. A solution to this conundrum may be that water was being added back to our planet, from a ring of water and ice surrounding star-core-zeus.

Conclusion

The cause of the Permian annihilation, the most destructive event in the history of our planet, is still a great mystery, but the evidence points to star-core-zeus. In the next three chapters, a synthesis of reliable data is presented to tell a fantastic story: during the Permian annihilation, star-core-zeus pulled the Earth's crust out of the Triassic Pacific basin to make our mysterious Moon.

CHAPTER 9

Our Mysterious Moon

● ● ●

Moon Formation Theories

OSMOND FISHER, AN ENGLISH GEOPHYSICIST, who published *The Physics of the Earth's Crust* in AD 1881, suggested the Moon had been pulled out of the crust by tidal forces caused by a large astronomical mass, which had passed near to Earth. He believed that the Pacific Ocean basin was the remains of a huge hole from where the material of the Moon had been scooped out. If the old crust which used to fill the Triassic-Pacific-basin became the Moon, then super-continent Pangaea was certainly the remains of the old surface of the Earth.

In our era, approximately half of the five-hundred-and-ten-million square kilometer surface of the Earth is continental crustal rock. However, forty-two percent of this granite crust is drowned under the sea. The volume of the Moon is about twenty-two billion cubic kilometers, so if half the crust was pulled off the Earth to make the Moon, then the shell of rock removed would had to have to been about eighty-six kilometers thick.

Toward the end of the nineteenth century, Professor George Darwin (son of Charles Darwin) was working at Cambridge University, studying the effect of tidal forces on planets and the evolution of the Sun-Earth-Moon system. He was the first scientist to attempt to explain the origin of the Moon using a mathematical model. He proposed that tidal forces had pulled out the Moon from a rapidly rotating and molten young Earth.[681]

These highly intelligent and imaginative men were quite right that there was an important connection between the continents, tidal forces, and the Moon. However, the absence of any evidence of a massive astronomical body, which had passed close enough to cause the separation of the Moon from the Earth, led to these inspired guesses being discredited and ridiculed.

However, scientists continued to wonder why the Earth's crust had two distinct surfaces: old continental platforms of granite and deep ocean basins made of young basalt, which dominated one side of the planet. Professor Reginald Daly, a Canadian geologist and head of the Department of Geology at Harvard University for thirty years until 1942, proposed that the Moon had been thrown out of the Earth during an impact, and it had taken more than half the crust with it. Daly believed that Wegener's continental drift was linked to the rebalancing of the planet after the birth of the Moon.[682]

By the early twentieth century, alternative Moon formation models had been proposed. Either the Moon had co-accreted from the same material that condensed to become Earth, or the Moon was the result of a lucky capture by Earth of an adjacent dwarf-planet. However, after the co-accretion-model was shown to be unworkable and the capture-model was discredited as extremely unlikely, Ralph Baldwin, a leading lunar specialist of the twentieth century, stated, "No existing theory of the origin of the Moon gives a satisfactory explanation of the Earth-Moon system."[683]

Toward the end of the twentieth century, it was hoped that the manned Apollo spacecraft missions to the Moon would answer all the questions and prove how the Moon was formed. Unfortunately, the data from the Apollo missions and later unmanned probes to the Moon only deepened the mystery.

Analysis of the lunar rock brought back by Apollo spacecraft showed that the Moon was made of Earth-like rocks, so the capture-model for the origin of the Moon was eliminated and the giant-impact model gained more acceptance.[684, 685]

The idea was that around four-point-five billion years ago, a Mars-sized planet named Theia made a tangential impact with a large rocky planet, which was the precursor of Earth.[686, 687] The explosive collision sprayed off hot liquid rock and vapor into space, which eventually condensed and solidified to form the Moon.[688, 689] The large rocky planet was re-melted during the impact, due to the conversion of kinetic energy into heat, but it eventually cooled to become the Earth.[690] Even though the giant-impact model became high-fashion by the end of the twentieth century, it was deeply flawed.[691, 692]

The Age of the Moon

Most of the Apollo spacecraft landed in the Procellarum region of the Moon, a relatively flat plain on the near-side containing the dark maria. When the Apollo astronauts started to dig out lunar soil samples from the surface of the Moon, below a thin layer of fine dust, they found a firm light subsurface soil called regolith.

It comprised of a complex mixture of sand and grit from meteoric debris plus some genuine Moon-rock fragments, which had fused together in the form of breccias. The mixed-breccias of small fused particles of rock contained an unusually high abundance of potassium (K), rare earth elements (REE), and phosphorus (P), so were named KREEP rocks.[693]

At the Apollo landing sites, this lunar regolith was packed on top of the Moon's native crustal rocks, which were assumed to be about three to five meters below the surface at the landing sites. Most of the rocks collected on the Apollo missions and returned to Earth were lunar regolith samples picked up from the surface, not genuine lunar bedrock.

The main method used to date the Moon-rocks was based on measuring rubidium-to-strontium ratios. Rubidium-87 decayed into strontium-87 with a half-life of forty-nine billion years. The original amount of strontium-87 in the Moon-rock was unknown, but it was possible to calculate the age using the ratios of the daughter-isotopes.

The lunar sub-surface regolith had isotopic ratios that suggested it was approximately four-point-five billion years old. As this lunar soil comprised of a mixture of mainly meteoric material and some native

Moon-rock, it was no surprise that lunar regolith dated to about the same age as the meteorites.

Based on the age of the components of regolith, the conventionally accepted estimate for the age of the Moon is four-point-five billion years.[694, 695, 696] However, this age estimate does not date the actual formation of the Moon, as shall become clear over the next few chapters.

Earth-Like Moon-Rocks

During the early Apollo missions, some light colored lunar rock particles were discovered mixed in the regolith. Analysis revealed a coarse-grained igneous rock—about ninety-five percent plagioclase feldspar—which was contaminated with small amounts of pyroxene, olivine, and iron oxides. These particles turned out to be fragments of an abundant type of continental Si-Al granite found on Earth.

This discovery of unmodified Earth-rock on the Moon was a great surprise. These white rock particles indicated that the Moon contained Earth-like rocks. In contrast, the giant-impact hypothesis had predicted that if Earth-rock was present on the Moon, it should have been melted and metamorphosed by ultra-high temperatures of the proposed giant inter-planetary collision.

These perfect particles showed that the Moon had never been completely molten, so they alone refuted the reality of a giant impact. This was only the beginning of the enigma of the Moon: the more we learned, the deeper the mystery became.

Moon-Rock Is the Same as Earth-Rock

The rocks returned to Earth during the Apollo missions revealed a surprising result: the isotopic compositions of nearly all elements are the same on Earth and on the Moon.[697] There was no evidence of any alien material from the imagined Mars-size impactor called Theia.[698]

In fact, the light colored rocks of the Moon's crust in the lunar highlands resembled the rocks that formed the foundations of the continental platforms on Earth. The rocks recovered from the lunar maria resembled basaltic rock found on the Earth's ocean floor.

It has now been confirmed that the rocks of Earth and the Moon are chemically, elementally, and isotopically identical. For every isotopic system analyzed, Earth and Moon-rocks are the same, but unlike every other object in the solar-system.[699, 700]

The Earth and Moon have the same isotopic compositions for chromium, silicon, titanium, and tungsten, whereas the isotope abundances vary between Earth, meteors, asteroids, and Mars. Earth and Moon have almost identical oxygen isotope compositions (the ratio between oxygen-16, oxygen-17, and oxygen-18), whereas there are large differences in oxygen composition between Earth-rocks, Mars-meteors, and asteroid-Vesta.[701] Even the isotopic composition of the noble gas xenon, discovered trapped in Moon-rocks, is also identical to the isotopic composition of xenon trapped in Earth-rock.[702]

This diverse set of data cannot be explained by current impact models of the Moon's origin but is a major clue to the truth about the Moon's formation.[703]

The Deep Mantle Manufacture of Earth-Rock

Basaltic Earth-rocks were believed to have been formed four-point-five billion years ago in an ultra-hot magma-ocean when our planet was still molten.

Under these primitive conditions of high temperature and pressure, basaltic rocks concentrated at an average depth of about three-hundred kilometers. Special rocks such as olivine were formed, which is a silicon-magnesium-iron containing basalt (a Si-Ma basalt). It is still a geological mystery how olivine got back up to the surface of our planet to become the common rock on Earth's ocean floors.

It is an even greater mystery that olivine is found in the dark maria on the near-side of the Moon. These Moon-rocks could only have formed in a similar process, three hundred kilometers inside Earth. There is no evidence of such a hot deep magma-ocean on the Moon.

Lunar-sample-number-15405 is a particular problem. It is a green rock containing glass beads of pure olivine, which was collected on the surface of the Moon during the Apollo 15 mission. This pure green glass olivine was shown to have been produced under very high pressure, at a depth of probably a thousand kilometers, near the bottom of the melt of the magma-ocean of the young Earth.

It was impossible for this rock to have been synthesized on the Moon, because the deep hot liquid magma-ocean required for its formation never existed on the Moon. Even if pure olivine had been produced a thousand kilometers deep inside the Moon, it is impossible to explain how it returned to the surface. In addition, Theia, the hypothesized impactor, was not massive enough to reproduce these conditions, which had occurred inside the young Earth.

The Siderophile Elements

Siderophile elements such as Tungsten are iron-loving elements, which readily combine with hot liquid iron. Highly-siderophile-elements associate very quickly with hot liquid iron, and examples are rhenium, osmium, iridium, ruthenium, rhodium, palladium, platinum, and gold.

During the accretion phase of Earth formation four-point-six billion years ago, our planet was a ball of hot churning material. Hot dense liquid iron quickly sank to the core of Earth, taking highly-siderophile-elements with it, as our planet formed. Only trace amounts of these materials remained in the scum that floated on top of the planetary-melt, which hardened to become the crustal rocks of Earth.

In primordial chondritic meteors, which represent the type of material from which the Earth formed, the highly-siderophile-elements are found in approximately the same ratio as the ratio in terrestrial rocks, but the concentration is two-hundred times higher.

In contrast, Moon-rocks and Earth-rocks contain almost the same abundances of siderophiles, so they went through the same depletion process. This is more evidence that the Moon-rocks and Earth-rocks were formed the same way, and the Moon was once part of Earth.

A particular puzzle is the tungsten isotope ratios: the tungsten-182 to tungsten-184 isotope ratio is the same in Moon-rock and Earth-rock. The origin of this ratio is known: radioactive hafnium-182 decays into tungsten-182 in nine million years, and during Earth-formation hafnium remained in the silicate mantle and crust, whereas tungsten preferentially partitioned into the metal-melt of the young earth and sank into the core.

Even though the Moon has no iron core at all, the Moon's tungsten ratio is exactly the same as the Earth's. It is impossible that the tungsten-182 to tungsten-184 ratio was copied on another planet and then this material was dumped on the Moon later, because of large differences in the growth of various planets, their mantles, and their cores. The tungsten isotope data is very strong evidence the Moon is built from material which came from Earth.[704, 705, 706]

In addition, the tungsten-hafnium isotope ratios demonstrate that thirty million years after the birth of the solar-system, Earth already had a solid crust. Samples of Earth's mantle and crust surviving from the primary planetary formation period refutes any later giant-impact, which would have re-melted the Earth.[707, 708]

Related results come from the analysis of the neodymium-142 to neodymium-144 ratio in crustal Earth-rock and Moon-rock. Accurate analysis of the neodymium isotope ratio shows that all lunar and all terrestrial samples are essentially identical.[709]

The Moon never had an iron core and was never fully molten, so the only way for the Moon-rocks to have been fractionated and depleted of siderophiles was by being produced on Earth. The isotope-identity leads to only one conclusion: the Moon was born out of Earth.

Moon-Rock: Cooked Earth-Rock

Although the Moon-rocks are very similar to related types of Earth-rocks, there is also evidence that they had been modified slightly by a brief low-pressure heating-process. Analysis of the chemical make-up of Moon-rock revealed consistently lower concentrations of certain volatile elements compared to Earth-rock.[710]

Moon-rocks are relatively depleted in lower melting point elements such as sodium, potassium, copper, and zinc, which are volatile in the temperature range between six hundred and thirteen hundred degrees Kelvin. The Moon-rocks are more depleted in bismuth and lead, which are volatile above six hundred degrees Kelvin. The lunar rock samples seemed to be terrestrial rocks that had at some time in the past been cooked for a short time to roughly a thousand degrees Kelvin in a vacuum, but they had not been melted.

A small elevation in the abundance of oxidized iron was also detected in basaltic Moon-rock.[711] This could be explained by hot Earth-mantle rock being exposed to oxygen in the Earth's atmosphere before it was dumped in the maria of the Moon.

Lunar Rocks Magnetized on Earth

In 1998, the NASA spacecraft Lunar Prospector revealed a complex jumble of randomly orientated magnetized rocks on the far-side of the Moon and weak local magnetic fields associated with the near-side maria. The problem is that the Moon does not generate its own magnetic field, and there is no evidence that it ever had a magnetic field. In addition, if the Moon had really formed from a molten globe after a giant impact, the heat at its formation should have erased any remnant magnetism, so there should be no random surface magnetic fields at all.

The paleomagnetism in Moon-rock was discovered to be surprisingly intense, evidence that the rocks had been exposed to a magnetic field essentially identical to that of Earth. The only reasonable conclusion is that magnetism in Moon-rock was produced by a field external to the Moon, and it was most likely the rocks had originally been magnetized on Earth, over four billion years ago.[712]

Supernova debris on the Moon

Another enigma was the discovery that breccias on the Moon have a two-to-six-times relative-enrichment of high atomic-weight and high melting-point elements such as barium, uranium, thorium, and titanium. In addition, the Procellarum region containing the maria has high surface concentrations of heat-producing radioactive elements uranium and thorium.[713] All these heavy elements are produced in supernova explosions of large stars.

It is a surprising fact that the same proportions of heavy elements found in this lunar material were also detected in destruction layers on

Earth, which were associated with both the Permian mass extinction two-hundred-and-fifty million years ago and the Pleistocene extinction at the end of the ice-age, only twelve thousand years ago.

In addition, data from Lunar Prospector's chemical maps of 1998 showed a zone of elevated radioactivity centered on Mare Imbrium. This new data created a problem, because the radioactivity indicated the impactor comprised of heavy elements usually associated with super-nova debris, not meteoric or asteroidal material.

The Enigma of an Asymmetric Moon

Early observations of the Moon revealed the lack of symmetry of the Moon.[714, 715, 716] Data collected in the late twentieth century by the Apollo missions, the later Clementine Space Orbiter, and Lunar Prospector missions clearly demonstrated that the Moon is oddly asymmetric.

Scientists were astonished when the precise shape and internal structure of the Moon was established. The Moon, like the Earth at the time of the super-continent Pangaea, has two distinct surfaces. Apollo and later spacecraft confirmed that the Moon is roughly pear-shaped, a distorted tri-axial ellipsoid, with its fatter near-side bottom facing Earth and its smaller more conical far-side pointing away from us.

The surprising discovery made by both Russian and American spacecraft was that the Moon's whole center of mass is displaced one kilometer toward the near-side face of the Moon.[717] The Moon is so irregular that it has two principal axes: a gravity axis and a topology axis, which are angled thirty-four degrees to each other.[718] Only the near-side hemisphere of the Moon is ever seen from Earth, because the Moon behaves like a loaded-dice, continuously rolling its heavier near-side toward the center of gravity of the Earth-Moon system.[719, 720]

The Moon is not the symmetrical sphere with concentric layers of rock, predicted by the giant-impact hypothesis. There is also no evidence of volcanic activity, no evidence of a hot magma interior, and no evidence of an iron-core. This picture of a very asymmetric cold solid Moon refutes the majority of the Moon formation models, including the fashionable giant-impact hypothesis.

The Apollo-12 Passive Seismic Experiment to probe the interior structure of the Moon added to the mystery. At the end of the Apollo-12 mission, the lunar module was launched to crash into the surface of the Moon. The shock waves from the impact built up to a peak in eight minutes, and the whole Moon vibrated for an hour. The experiment was repeated with Apollo-13, and even more dramatic results were obtained: the Moon resonated like a bell. The pattern of seismic returns suggested disorganized layers of solid crustal rocks, separated by strange cavities.

The conclusion of all this evidence is that the Moon had never been molten. The distorted shape and offset center of gravity meant the Moon must have formed from very large slabs of solid rock, which had randomly clumped together under gravity.

The Maria and Mascons Mystery

During the mapping of the Moon from lunar orbit in 1966 and 1967, in the search for flat potential landing sites for Apollo spacecraft, a new enigma emerged. There were strange mass concentrations under the lunar surface, which were named mascons. These odd areas of higher gravity were only located on the near-side of the Moon and centered under the dark lunar maria, which are the large dark approximately circular zones visible from Earth.

The motion of the spacecraft suggested the dark maria were made of much denser rock than the lighter highland rocks of the lunar surface. These dark basalt maria, which cluster on the near-side of the Moon but are absent on the far-side of the Moon, remain very hard to explain by any conventional theory.

There are eight of these huge dark zones on the near-side of the Moon but none on the far-side. The maria are depressions with depths of four kilometers and are full of solidified pools of hard dark basaltic rock, each more than three-hundred kilometers in diameter. In contrast, the shores of the maria are made of light-colored feldspar rocks, typical of the far-side of the Moon.[721, 722]

The maria on the near-side are not impact structures. An example of an impact crater is Mare-Orientalis located on the far-side of the

Moon. This crater is a huge deep bowl-shaped hole in the white rock, surrounded by concentric rings of frozen shock waves and radial rays of ejecta. This big crater had probably been formed by a high-speed impact of a lump of hard rock two-hundred kilometers across. On the far-side of the Moon, there is also a dense patchwork of small high-speed impact-craters, probably formed by smaller objects colliding with the lunar surface at about fifteen kilometers-per-second.[723]

The geological characteristics of the maria are quite different from impact craters: they have an irregular shape, no shock wave features, and no evidence of ejecta. However, despite the visual evidence to the contrary, some planetary scientists initially suggested that the dark maria on the near-side were impact craters too.

One model for the mares-and-mascons suggested high speed impacts of fifty-kilometer-asteroids into a thin lunar crust, which had caused a basaltic-lava bleed from the mantle of the Moon. These models predicted impact-temperatures of more than fifteen-hundred Kelvin. However, the chemistry of the mare-rock-samples brought back by the Apollo spacecraft refuted the hypothesis: the data showed the maria had never been heated to such a high temperature.[724, 725]

Other results from the chemical analysis of the dark maria-rock were even more startling. The mare basalt from the Moon was identical to ocean floor rock and upper mantle rocks on Earth. Elemental analysis showed the lunar marias had exactly the same abundance of iron, nickel, cobalt, tungsten, phosphorous, copper, gallium, sulfur, and selenium, as found in Earth-basalt.

More detailed analytical work confirmed that the maria are made from exactly the same materials as the basaltic rock floors of the ocean basins of Earth. The chemistry of the lunar basalt is actually identical to a type of ocean floor rock found on Earth, known as tholeiitic basalt. This type of rock could only have formed under the conditions of high pressure, metallic-iron phase-segregation, fractionation, and partition, which had occurred on Earth, soon after the formation of our planet.

In addition, terrestrial-pyroxine—an iron-magnesium silicate—and terrestrial-ilmenite—a dark heavy iron-titanium oxide—were also identified in the maria rock samples. These two types of rock are also produced under the extreme conditions very deep in a hot mantle. They could only have formed inside the young Earth and certainly not on the Moon.

The strongest evidence that the basaltic Moon-rock of the maria came from the Earth was the ratio of the three isotopes of oxygen. The O^{16}-O^{17}-O^{18} ratio of the Moon basalts from the maria and terrestrial basalts from the ocean floor are identical. In contrast, the oxygen isotope ratio of meteoric material is very different.[726]

The only difference between the Moon basalt and the Earth basalt is that Moon basalt is depleted of some volatile elements. This suggested the material in the maria had been briefly heated up to no more than one thousand degrees kelvin in a vacuum.

Another conundrum is the age of the basalt from the maria: decay-series isotope-ratios gives a range of dates around three-point-seven billion years old.[727] The problem is that the maria basalts are eight hundred million years younger than the lighter rocks from the lunar highlands.

To explain away this anomaly of two different ages for the Moon, Wasserburg suggested a "late heavy bombardment" had pummeled the Moon after it had already formed. However, there is no evidence of similar cratering on Earth three-point-seven billion years ago, and the origin of the impactors that were supposed to have bombarded the Moon three-point-seven billion years ago has never been provided. Despite the lack of data, this explanation has become dogma, even though a late-heavy-bombardment is not a valid explanation for the maria, which are not impact craters.

The difference in age between the rocks of the maria and lunar highlands can be explained by a terrestrial process. It is likely that Earth's upper-mantle solidified eight-hundred-million years after the outer crustal rocks of Earth. The maria are made of basalt rock from Earth's upper mantle, which solidified three-point-seven billion years ago. Vast slabs of this material impacted the lunar surface at relatively low velocity, during the formation of the Moon.

The Enigmatic Far-Side Highlands

In 1998, the Lunar Prospector confirmed that the far-side of the Moon was topologically, geologically, and chemically very different from the near-side. The far-side of the Moon is covered in heavily cratered uplands and mountains, made of lower-density white rocks, on top of a thick crust. The crust on the far-side is one hundred kilometers thick, compared to the near-side crust, which is only sixty kilometers thick.

On the Apollo 15 mission to the edge of the lunar highlands, a survey of the area around Mount Hadley yielded some very strange results. Near the Apollo 15 landing site was an ancient dry river bed that meandered for about fifty kilometers, which has never been explained.

ODD EARTH-LIKE RIVER BEDS AND CLIFFS OF LAYERED ROCK ON THE MOON

Apollo 15 was launched from NASA Kennedy Space Center on July 26, 1971, and after a flight time of 104 hours, the lunar module Falcon arrived its landing site on the Moon by a dry river bed. Hadley Delta behind Falcon rises approximately 4000 meters above the plain and the base of the mountain is approximately 5 kilometers away. During a stay of 67 hours on the Moon, the crew explored the lunar surface for over 18 hours. They discovered Silver Spur, a multi-layer structure that resembled beach cliffs on Earth and could only have formed by sedimentation underwater.

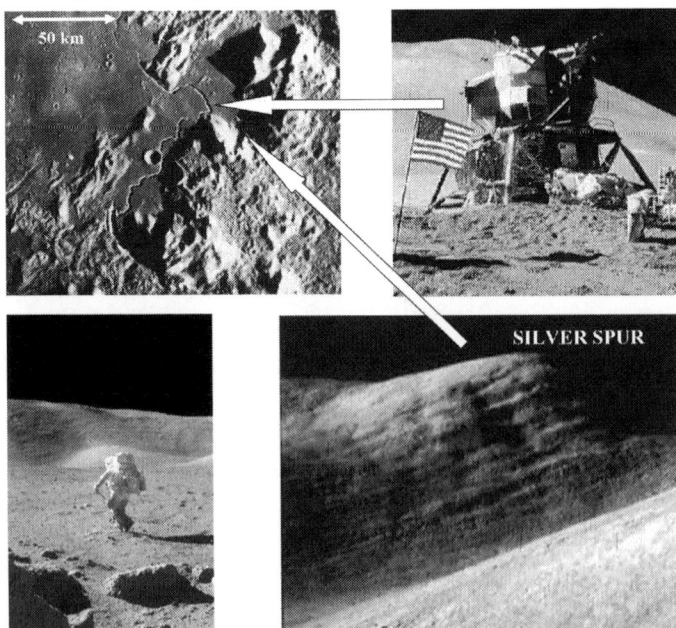

The astronauts discovered anomalous cliff-faces with a layered structure inclined to the horizontal that looked remarkably like huge cliffs of terrestrial sedimentary rock. An example was a stratified eight hundred meters high cliff face called Silver Spur, which was photographed on the Apollo 15 mission. Similar examples on the west face of Mount Hadley were also investigated.[728]

These odd cliff-faces were impossible to explain: they were stratified just like beach-cliffs of marine sedimentary rock on Earth. In addition, related subsurface layering was detected by radar on the Apollo 17 flight.[729] A process that could produce such layered rock strata on the Moon was unknown: sedimentation required an ocean of water.

The most startling discovery was that the rocks of the lunar highlands of the far-side of the Moon were also identical to Earth-rocks. Samples of the light colored rock from the lunar highlands were demonstrated to be almost identical to light crustal rocks common in terrestrial continental platforms. They were extraordinarily similar to light colored plagioclase feldspars, a family of Earth-rock that includes granite. These distinctive silicate rocks are known to have been manufactured by chemical fractionation in the mantle of the hot young Earth.

The Lunar Prospector also reported that while the near-side was dry, the rocks on the far-side of the Moon, particularly toward the lunar-poles, had a high water content. The data was inexplicable: these rocks must have originally solidified in the presence of liquid water.

The inescapable conclusion was that the mountains of the Moon were made from a huge mass of the Earth's crust, just as Osmond Fisher and Reginald Daly had predicted.

The Paradox of the Old and Young Moon

Old controversies have provided new ideas to help to solve the riddle of the Moon data. The paradox of the conflicting evidence supporting both an old and a young Moon is particularly important.

When the Apollo astronauts landed on the Moon and stepped off the ladder of the Eagle Lunar Module for the first time in July 1969, their footprints revealed a layer of dust about one centimeter deep.[730] They were very relieved.

Before the first Moon landing, NASA teams had been very concerned about the danger of their spacecraft sinking into deep dust deposits.[731,] [732, 733] The Moon has no atmosphere or liquid water, so there is no wind or water erosion to remove the dust that should have accumulated over billions of years.

They were very surprised when the unmanned Surveyor-1 spacecraft touched down on the Moon in 1966 and revealed an anomalous lack of dust on the surface. If the Moon really was four-point-five billion years old, then various calculations showed that the steady fallout of fine solar-system dust over billions of years should have accumulated as a layer at least one meter deep, which should have uniformly buried the whole lunar surface.

Solar system bodies dated to be four-point-six billion years old do have such deep layers of dust. For example, in 1998, the Mars Observer spacecraft found that Phobos, the red planet's larger moon, is coated with the expected one-meter-deep dust-layer.[734] In addition, the NEAR-Shoemaker spacecraft discovered that asteroid 433-Eros has a similar thick blanket of dust all over it.[735]

In contrast, when the Apollo astronauts landed on the Moon, they discovered only a thin covering of fine solar-system dust. Depending on the location, this dust layer averaged about four to five centimeters deep. The depth of dust on the Moon was not meters deep: there was simply twenty-times less dust than expected.

Models based on meteoric accumulation rates, derived from the measured influx of meteoric material on Earth and compared to lunar-dust depth; suggested the surface of the Moon was much younger than the four-point-five billion years, derived from radiometric dating of rock particles.[736] The actual depth of lunar-dust gave the surface of the Moon, an age of two-hundred-and-fifty million years, the same age as the Permian mass extinction and the birth of Pangaea!

The solution to the Moon formation enigma will become apparent after more astonishing lunar secrets are exposed in the next chapter.

CHAPTER 10

Lunar Secrets Exposed

● ● ●

The Anorthosite Enigma of the Moon

THE WHITE NATIVE LUNAR ROCK discovered by Apollo astronauts, mentioned in the previous chapter, was given the name lunar-anorthosite because it is almost identical to a type of continental rock of the same name found on Earth.[737] Terrestrial anorthosite is a light colored igneous rock with coarse grain and large crystals, which had cooled slowly and crystallized in the under-surface of the crust, during the formation of our planet.

The oldest samples of lunar-anorthosite were discovered in the lunar highlands. The rock was collected on the Apollo 16 mission to the Lunar Apennine Mountains and dated back to four-point-five billion years ago. Lunar anorthosite is essentially identical to archaic proterozoic-anorthosite, found in erratic out-crops on the Earth's surface.

In 1998 Lunar Prospector showed that the far-side of the Moon is very rich in anorthosite. It has now been established by data from the SELENE spacecraft that anorthosite makes up almost all of the thick lunar crust.[738] It is a huge mystery that the Moon is made of a specific type of rock that crystallized deep in Earth's crust, and it shows no evidence that it has been re-melted.

The Origin of the Earth's Crust

The formation of Earth was triggered by the accretion of large chunks of iron and nickel. These asteroid-sized lumps of metal also contained other heavier elements, including short-half-life highly radioactive isotopes, which came from our local supernova. These heavy metal bodies rapidly merged and melted to form the core of our planet, four-point-six billion years ago.

ANORTHOSITE ON THE EARTH AND MOON

Anorthosite was produced on the lower surface of the crust, during the formation of Earth. However, anorthosite massifs are also found scattered in a mysterious drop-zone across the surface of our planet, from the time of the end of Pangaea.

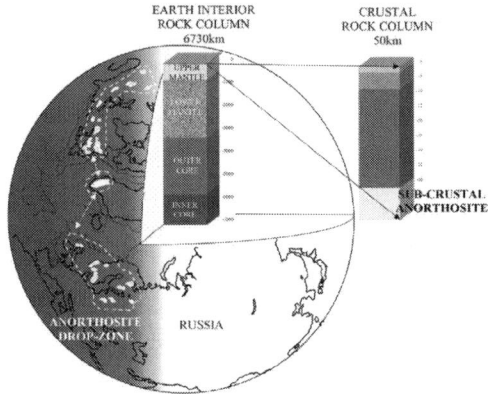

The Selene space-craft showed that the upper crust of the Moon is made from almost pure plagioclase anorthosite rock (White). [Ohtake, M., et al "The global distribution of pure anorthosite on the Moon" *Nature* **461**, (2009) 236-240]. In addition, the Clementine space craft revealed the Moon has iron-rich basaltic rock (Dark) pooled on top of the anorthosite in the near-side maria and in a strange square shaped depression on the far-side.
[http://www.lpi.usra.edu/lunar/missions/clementine/images/]

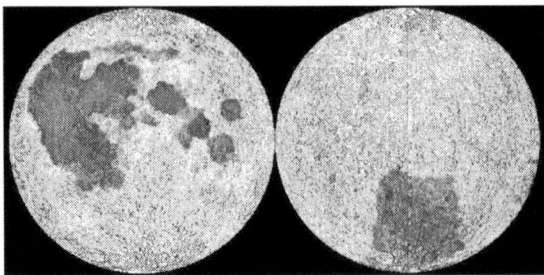

The heavy core of our planet continued to be bombarded from space with metals, hydrocarbons, water, and silicate rock particles. The early meteorites that formed the mantle were rich in supernova debris and contained titanium, chromium, nickel, molybdenum, and ruthenium, which had a high affinity for molten nickel iron. Earth's outer crust was formed by less dense enstatite chondrites, which are rich in silicates, hydrocarbon, iron-sulfide, and iron-pyrite but have lower concentrations of oxygen.[739, 740]

The rocky downpour also included space-gravel comprising of anorthite-granite: the calcium-plagioclase-feldspar, which is the starting material for anorthosite rock. Anorthite, hydrocarbons, and the remains of supernova-produced aluminum-26 were discovered together in the Allende meteorite.[741] Anorthite has been found in other chondritic meteorites and even in Comet Wild-2.

As more material collided with the growing Earth, the heat generated from the kinetic energy of impact and the rapid decay of radioactive-isotopes created a hot churning ball of molten metal and liquid rock. Huge quantities of meteoric material and water continued to rain down on the hot liquid young Earth, turning its surface into a hot steaming magma ocean.

Lower density solid rock particles floated and separated out of the hot liquid mantle rock, while heavier metals sank to the core. The crust of Earth probably solidified in under thirty million years and certainly less than one-hundred-million years after planet-formation. This first-differentiation-stage produced a solid crust of feldspar-like rocks, sitting on top of a semi-liquid mantle of denser rocks.

In this extreme environment, four-point-five billion years ago, anorthite from meteorites was heat-processed on Earth in the wet-magma-melt to become anorthosite rock. A hot slow melting-crystallization and remelting-recrystallization process at the interface between the outer molten mantle and the inner granite crust eventually manufactured huge masses of white anorthosite rock.

The anorthosite solidified permanently more than four billion years ago to become the solid white rock foundations of the Earth's crust. The upper mantle remained molten, probably until about three-point-seven billion years ago. No new anorthosite is being produced on Earth in our geological era, because our planet is now too cool. The ambient temperature at the base of the Earth's crust is currently in the range from

five-hundred to nine-hundred degrees Celsius, which is not hot enough
to re-melt anorthosite.

The Terrestrial Geology of Anorthosite

Anorthosite rock originally formed as a twenty-kilometer thick layer on
the inner surface of the crust of the Earth, about thirty to fifty kilometers underground, lying directly on top of the hot upper mantle layer. It
has been estimated that about sixty percent of the mass of Earth's crust
is anorthosite, and it forms the foundations of all the continents. These
primordial crustal-foundation rocks are rich in silicon and aluminum, so
they are classified as Si-Al rocks.

The lower crust differs substantially in its mechanical properties and
chemical composition, from the outer-mantle below. Approximately fifty
kilometers underground, the top of the mantle is defined by seismology
as the Moho layer, where a sudden increase in seismic velocity occurs.
Mantle-rocks are denser and have a high iron and magnesium content.
The mantle extends about four hundred kilometers deeper into the Earth.

The Anorthosite Enigma of the Earth

There is a terrestrial-geology enigma known as the anorthosite problem. The mystery is why a huge mass of ancient sub-crustal rock is found
scattered all over the surface of the Earth: it is inexplicable how it all got
up there. For example, an ancient mountain range made of anorthosite
is located between New York and Montreal, which has been dated to the
end of the Permian period, two-hundred-and-fifty million years ago (its
age is significant).

In addition, outcrops of surface-exposed anorthosite seemed to be
randomly scattered across the northern-hemisphere of Earth. It has been
difficult to explain how a perfect cross section of the foundations of the
continents, from fifty kilometers below ground, could have been delivered
up to the surface of the planet and then dumped on top of younger rocks.

Anorthosite appears in island-sized lumps called massifs, which extend
for thousands of square kilometers and also in huge chunks called plutons,
which are ten to fifty square kilometers in size. Massifs and plutons of

anorthosite are scattered in thousands of outcrops from the southwestern United States, to the Appalachian Mountains in Eastern United States, to eastern and northern Canada, to southwestern Greenland, and on to Harris in Scotland, Norway, Sweden, and Eastern Europe.

Anorthosite massifs and plutons are often found on top of a layer of denser but isotopically associated mangeritic rocks. These mangeritic rocks originally separated from upper-mantle-derived basaltic melts, underneath the anorthosite layer, after the anorthosite had fractionated, cooled, and solidified.[742] Surface anorthosite is never found associated with ultramafic rocks or basaltic magmas. There is no evidence that these enigmatic lumps of anorthosite had welled-up through deep fissures as a hot magma or lava and then solidified.

On the contrary, all the evidence seems to suggest the fantastic conclusion that solid anorthosite dropped from the sky. For example, the anorthosite pluton in the inner Sogn-Voss area in western Norway forms a thick block ten-by-twenty kilometers wide and two kilometers thick. It lies on the surface surrounded by heavily crushed, cracked, and faulted rock, as if it crash-landed there.[743] Although the rock itself is billions of years old, it seems to have been dumped two hundred and fifty million years ago. Under the anorthosite massif, there are much younger quartzites, schists, and phyllites.

Scattered around the main massif of anorthosite are five satellite plutons. A pluton in the Naeroydal Valley has been extensively investigated: the lower surface of the pluton is bowl-shaped and the anorthosite has been strangely transmuted by very high temperatures at the boundary zone, where it is metamorphosed into a white acid-insoluble anorthosite.

All this data suggests this huge pluton of anorthosite had been dropped on Earth from space, suffering severe heating on its lower surface, during high velocity re-entry into Earth's atmosphere, before impacting. Generally, it seems that all the surface deposits of anorthosite found in Europe and North America are foundation crustal rocks, which have been heated during atmospheric re-entry, before they crashed to the ground.

In addition, when the continents are reassembled into the supercontinent Pangaea, all the plutons and massifs of anorthosite form a single continuous drop-zone, as if they were originally a straight line of debris dumped across the globe from space.

An additional unsolved mystery is that when the Soviet spacecraft Vega-2 landed on Venus in 1985, light colored chunks of anorthosite were observed scattered on the basalt-lava surface of Venus, which seemed to be identical to the rock of the lunar highlands. This anorthosite was probably the remains of lunar building materials, which had been captured by the gravity of Venus and crashed onto its surface.

Water on the Moon

Most theories of Moon formation, developed in the twentieth century, assumed the Moon had always lacked water, and it is an ultra-dry world. This idea was proven wrong by multiple detections of water in the lunar surface rocks and mixed lunar-meteoric regolith, by recent robot-probes to the Moon. The primary crust of the Moon contains significant amounts of water.

The composition of lunar-anorthosite is a related paradox: it also has mysteriously high water content. Plagioclase grains in lunar anorthosite obtained in the Apollo missions revealed that the water content of the magma that had produced them was about one-point-four percent water by weight.[744] This lunar magmatic water was discovered to have an isotopic composition that is indistinguishable from water in terrestrial anorthosite and also meteoric-carbonaceous-chondrites.[745]

A water-rich rock called apatite is also present on the Moon. Direct measurement of water in samples of apatite from the Moon shows this rock is three-to-five percent water.[746] It appears that the identical apatite rocks from Earth and the Moon were made under identical wet conditions.

Water also played a key role in the original production of lunar-basalt, which also solidified from a wet magma. Lunar olivine crystals were made in a magma that was three-to-five percent water with volatile contents very similar to primitive terrestrial mid-ocean ridge basalt rock.[747, 748]

Water was first detected by NASA's Lunar Prospector mission to the Moon from 1998 to 1999. The instruments measured low-energy neutrons, a proxy signal that indicated hydrogen in water within one meter of the surface. In 2009 NASA's Lunar-Crater-Observation-and-Sensing-Satellite (known as LCROSS) slammed into a permanently-shadowed crater on the Moon, and the plume of material ejected was surprisingly rich in water-ice.[749]

The Moon also has permanent ice-caps, but the lunar ice-caps have been displaced over five degrees away from the present rotation axis poles, at both the north pole and south pole of the Moon.[750]

The presence of water in the primary lunar crustal rocks demonstrates that the Moon-rocks were formed in a prolonged crystallization on the surface of a magma-ocean saturated with water, conditions identical to the young Earth. The only reasonable conclusion is that the Moon is made of slabs of solid rock, which originally formed in a wet-magma on Earth.

This data totally eliminates the fashionable giant-impact-hypothesis as an explanation for Moon formation: the detected hydration of the lunar rocks would never have survived the extreme heating, resulting from a giant impact.

ICE-CAPS ON THE MOON AND POLE-SHIFT
Not only has water been discovered on the Moon, images of the lunar ice-caps taken by NASA Lunar Prospector space-craft, record a recent 5.5 degree lunar pole-shift. [Science 374 (2015):1398]

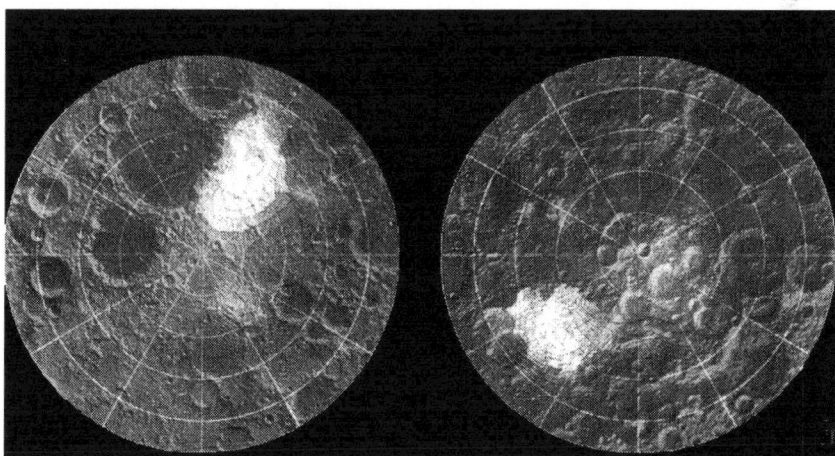

Weird Structures in the Moon

Two Gravity-Recovery-and-Interior-Laboratory (GRAIL) spacecraft were launched in late 2011 to study the detailed structure of the lunar crust. Data from the two GRAIL spacecraft, which orbited around the Moon on the same orbit in 2012, made a fine structure map of the interior of the Moon's crust.[751]

As the two spacecraft flew over areas of greater and lesser gravity, they moved slightly toward or away from each other. The changes in their relative velocity were translated into a high-resolution map of the Moon's gravitational field.

The data showed that the Moon did not solidify from molten rock: it was a fractured and faulted pile of solid rocks, which were porous and contained significant gaps.[752, 753] All models that assumed the Moon had formed from hot liquid rock solidifying to make a spherically symmetrical Moon were wrong.

The GRAIL spacecraft also made a startling discovery: there is a vast square-shaped fault structure in the surface of the Moon, which resembles a huge trapdoor in the lunar surface. The "trapdoor" is an incredible two-thousand-six-hundred kilometers wide. It is located in the Procellarum region, the plane that contains all the lunar maria and covers most of the near-side of the Moon.

The discovery of the trapdoor was made during analysis of anomalies in the free-air gravity field, corrected for surface mass topography and gravity gradients. The very deep sub-surface faults were revealed to be huge rift-gaps, forming the vast door-frame of negative gravity gradients. The trapdoor shape stunned the scientist when it first appeared in the mapping output. "The rectangular pattern of gravity anomalies was completely unexpected," said Jeff Andrews-Hanna (a GRAIL co-investigator) in 2014.[754]

The science team was expecting circular or elliptical impact features, not near-right-angle corners. The trapdoor is not associated with any impact features, and its origin is a huge mystery: it is certainly not an impact crater.[755] In addition, on exactly the opposite side of the Moon to the trapdoor, the Clementine spacecraft mapped a huge square patch of the rocky surface, also two-thousand-six hundred-kilometers across, which has a strangely high iron content, called the South Pole Aitken Terrane.

THE TRAP-DOOR ON THE MOON

The two GRAIL spacecraft discovered enigmatic square-shaped deep-faults in the Moon, framing the maria on the near-side, exactly opposite to the strange square-shaped iron-rich depression in the far-side, discovered by the Clementine space-craft. [Andrews-Hanna, J., et al., "Structure and evolution of the lunar Procellarum region as revealed by GRAIL gravity data," Nature 514 (2014) 68-71]

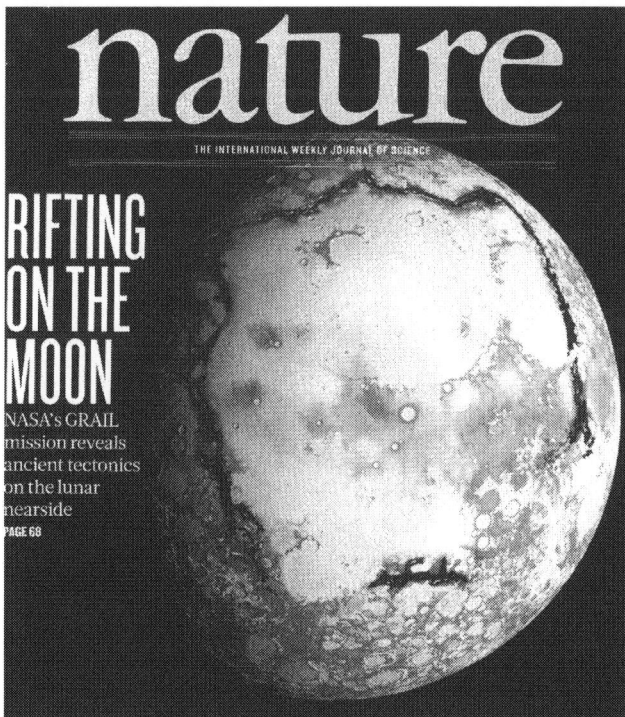

Generally, the origin of the Moon's large-scale irregular topology remains an enigma. The Moon is made of rock identical to terrestrial continental crust on the far-side and terrestrial ocean floor rock on the near-side. The moon is not a sphere: it has a complex shape comprising of a frozen in tidal-rotation-bulge, combined with large scale irregular features. This data totally contradicts all models, which require the Moon to be a hot rotating fluid body at formation.

A Deep Basin in the Lunar South Pole

The origin of a very deep basin discovered on the far-side, adjacent to the Aiken Crater near the South Pole of the Moon, corresponding to the square iron-rich terrane, is another enigma. This huge flat-bottomed depression is an irregular hole, which lacks lava or concentric shock features. It is certainly not an impact crater; it was created at the time the Moon originally formed.

When this extremely deep basin was first discovered, the depth of the hole was not obvious, because it is not visible from Earth. However, the Clementine topographic survey of the Moon showed that this strange hole was twelve kilometers deep, with a flat bottom two-thousand-five-hundred kilometers across. It resembled a small steep-sided ocean-basin on Earth.

The flat lowland at middle of the mysterious basin lies almost exactly on the opposite side of the Moon from the trapdoor, which frames the main concentrations of basalt-filled maria on the near-side. The origin of this strange basin shall become clear in the next chapter.

The Giant-Impact Model Is Refuted

Detailed information on the composition and structure of the Moon collected over the last twenty years has fully refuted the giant-impact model.[756] The composition of the Moon is almost identical to the crust and upper mantle of Earth. Moon-rock displays almost identical bulk chemical, elemental, and isotopic compositions to Earth-rock.[757, 758, 759]

Elements that would normally dissolve in hot liquid iron, called highly-siderophile-elements, are also found in almost identical proportions in Earth and Moon crustal rocks.[760] NASA's Lunar Reconnaissance Orbiter measurements, which demonstrated the refractory metallic elements with high condensation temperatures, are also essentially the same on Earth and the Moon. The chromium, titanium, tungsten, and silicon isotope compositions of the Moon and Earth are all indistinguishable.[761]

All silicate lunar rocks recovered on the Apollo missions share identical oxygen isotope compositions with Earth-rocks, which are quite different to meteorites and Mars.[762]

However, the volatile elements in lunar rock show that the Moon is made of Earth crustal rocks that never melted.[763] If the Moon had really formed after a giant-impact, from a mixture of molten and vaporized magma, all volatile elements and certainly all the water would have been lost. However, there is water in lunar rocks.[764]

There is also no evidence of any contaminating material from the supposed impactor, which should be in the lunar crust, if the giant-impact model is correct.[765] All the evidence shows that the Moon is literally "a chip off the old block" of Earth.[766] The giant impact theory is dead, but the planetary science community does not have an alternative model for Moon formation to replace it.[767, 768] Supporters of the giant-impact model still propose hopeful fantasies to keep their hypothesis on life-support.

Some improbable proposals were based on mixed models, such as Earth spinning at a near-break-up angular velocity before a glancing impact. Some scientists have even suggested the impactor was either a totally identical "Mirror-Earth" or made of pure ice. Another fantasy model for the birth of the Moon proposed a massive atomic-fission-explosion in Earth's core, which blew part of the crust into space. In September 2013, the Royal Society in London called a special scientific meeting to discuss the crisis that nobody had a viable model for Moon formation.[769, 770]

Conclusion

All current Moon formation theories have been refuted by new data and the search for the truth about the formation of the Moon is ongoing. Evidence that the Moon formed only two-hundred-and-fifty million years ago from solid rock derived from Earth, the mysterious deep basin near the south-pole, and the trapdoor on the opposite side of the Moon hold the key to understanding the Moon formation process. A revolutionary new mechanism for the formation of the Moon shall be unveiled in the next chapter.

CHAPTER 11

The Caesarean Birth of the Moon

● ● ●

THE PROFOUND DISCOVERY THAT THE Moon is made of Earth-rock supports a revolutionary new model of Moon formation: the birth of the Moon from mother-Earth by Caesarean-section. The Moon was ripped out of the surface crust of the Earth by star-core-zeus, during the end-Permian cataclysm, leaving behind the Triassic-Pacific-Ocean basin. This new Caesarean Moon Birth model can explain all the enigmatic discoveries relating to our Moon, which were detailed in the previous two chapters.

The Planet-Rupturing Fly-By

Star-core-zeus is an ultra-cool black-dwarf, weighing about ten percent of the mass of the Sun but compressed into a sphere two-to-three times the size of Earth. At the end of the Permian period two-hundred-and-fifty million years ago, the Earth passed too close to the flight-path of star-core-zeus and was exposed to its intense gravity.

Earth was approaching their orbital intersection in late May, as star-core-zeus looped around the Sun at its perihelion and started to drop from celestial north. Just as Earth was crossing the orbital intersection at the end of June, star-core-zeus plunged through the ecliptic plane at ultra-high velocity, almost adjacent to Earth.

The closing velocity of star-core-zeus with Earth was fifty kilometers-per-second, a speed approximately equivalent to one-hundred-and-eighty-thousand kilometers per hour. Star-core-zeus approached so rapidly and its gravity field was so intense that the native gravity at the surface of Earth was quickly neutralized.

As the super-massive body approached Earth at high-velocity, our planet suffered catastrophic tidal stresses. The super-dense star-core was small enough to zoom past the Earth without colliding, but it induced a nearly fatal transient gravitational field. As it got within one million kilometers away from our planet, Earth started to disintegrate. At the point of closest approach, star-core-zeus was only four-hundred-thousand kilometers away from Earth, and our planet was ruptured.

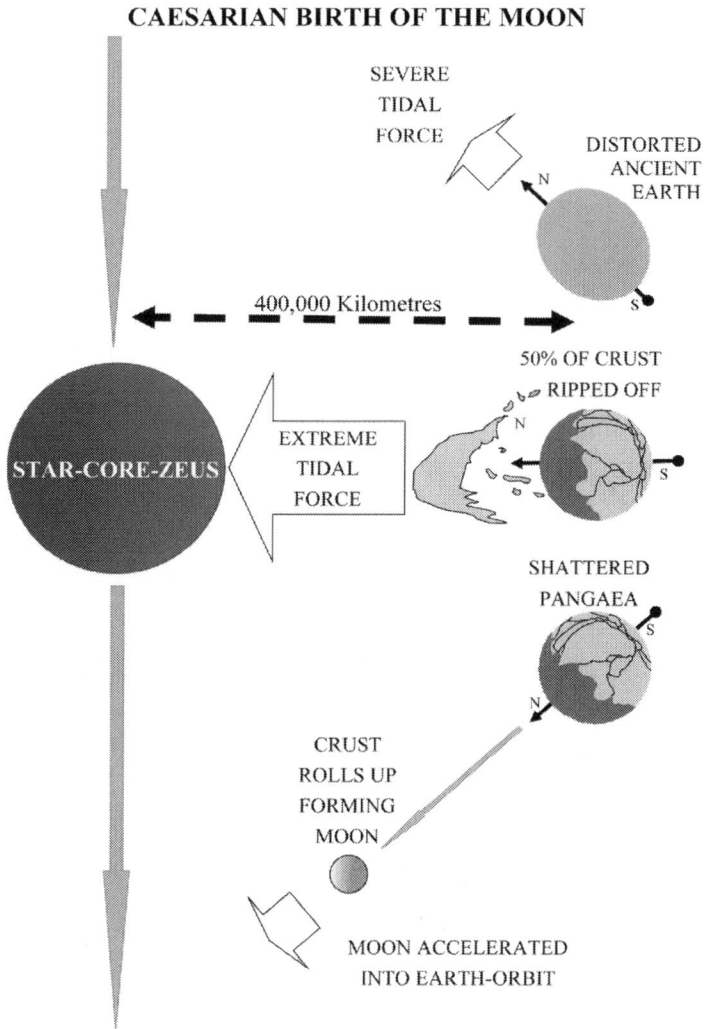

CAESARIAN BIRTH OF THE MOON

SEVERE
TIDAL
FORCE

DISTORTED
ANCIENT
EARTH

N

400,000 Kilometres

S

50% OF CRUST
RIPPED OFF

N

STAR-CORE-ZEUS

EXTREME
TIDAL
FORCE

S

SHATTERED
PANGAEA

S

N

CRUST
ROLLS UP
FORMING
MOON

MOON ACCELERATED
INTO EARTH-ORBIT

The alien gravity from star-core-zeus induced massive tidal bulges in the ancient Permian crust of the Earth, making our planet egg-shaped. As the whole northern hemisphere of our planet bulged out toward star-core-zeus, an equivalent bulge developed in the southern hemisphere too.

Southern Africa is still in the form of an enigmatic dome, which dates from the end of the Permian period. Tillites, the remains of Permian glaciers, are evidence that the location of the south-pole at the end of the Permian was centered around twenty degrees south-latitude in Botswana.

The Permian south pole should have been flattened relative to an equatorial bulge in the planet at that time, like our current North-Pole and South-Pole are flattened relative to the equator. However, southern Africa was bulged outward as our planet was exposed to the extreme tidal stresses of the close fly-by.[771, 772]

This strange dome in the Earth's crust is on the exact opposite side of the planet to the current position of the huge volcanic hot-spot region near Hawaii, which is the remains of the center of the rupture from where the Moon took off from Earth and which was also the position of the Permian north pole, located around twenty degrees north-latitude.

Peeling off the Crust of Planet Earth

When star-core-zeus was less than one million kilometers from Earth, the net gravity at the surface of our planet dropped to zero, and the solid rocky crust cracked right across the globe. Fissures up to ten thousand kilometers long and eighty kilometers deep fragmented the crust. These deep fractures formed the shape of the familiar outlines of the continental margins we recognize today.

As star-core-zeus got even closer, gravity reversed at the surface of Earth, causing rocks to become weightless and float into the air. Whole mountain ranges then started to grow out of the ground. The closest-approach was the same distance as the current Moon-Earth separation. As star-core-zeus flew overhead at an ultra-high relative velocity, it induced such powerful negative gravity that large areas of the crust started to fall-off.

Star-core-zeus removed half the crust from Earth, like shelling a hard-boiled egg. At the temporary center of gravity of the Earth and star-core, hot liquid mantle rock was scooped out to form a deep hole in the Earth, making a zone of volcanism in the North Pacific Ocean, which is still marked by the Hawaiian sea-mounts and is still very active.

Fifty-kilometer-thick shells of the crustal-rock, the size of a continent, took-off into the sky as Earth's crust was pealed-off. They were followed by up to forty kilometer thick chunks of semi-molten upper-mantle basalt. The density of the Moon is the same as the average density of the Earth's crust and upper mantle.

Separated from the underlying deep mantle-rock, these huge masses of crustal-rock started to accelerate toward star-core-zeus. The brief but massive gravitational pulse applied to Earth by star-core-zeus completely removed the old northern-hemisphere-surface of our planet.

The total separation of half of the crust from the remains of the Earth was probably achieved in about five hours. This was the time it took for star-core-zeus to travel approximately one-million kilometers at fifty kilometers-per-second. As the shells of the crustal-rock were pulled off the planet, they turned inside-out exposing the white foundation-layer of anorthosite, now visible on the surface of the Moon. These curled shells of broken crustal rock began to roll-up like sushi, under self-gravity.

Most of the Permian southern-hemisphere crust was left behind on Earth as shattered fragments, together with the denser inner-mantle and iron-core. Pangaea was not just a chance arrangement of drifting continents that had clumped together; "Pan-Gaea" really was the remains of "All-Earth," the shattered remnants of the old planet surface.

The Journey of the Moon

The crustal-rocks of Earth were initially accelerated very rapidly by the intense gravity of star-core-zeus to the current lunar-orbital-velocity.

However, as the huge mass of material was accelerating, the force of the external gravity field was declining rapidly, because star-core-zeus was flying away from Earth at a much higher velocity. The pull of the powerful gravity field of star-core-zeus was only a temporary impulse.

When a spacecraft takes-off from Earth to go to the Moon, the first step is to reach a parking orbit above Earth. This requires a rocket thrust to accelerate the spacecraft to about ten kilometers-per-second to overcome the gravity of Earth. Most rockets are launched nearly vertically for a few kilometers and then progressively flatten-out their trajectory at an altitude of approximately two hundred kilometers. The horizontal orbital speed at that altitude is approximately eight kilometers-per-second, equivalent to approximately thirty-thousand kilometers-per-hour.

Orbital-velocity is the velocity needed to balance the pull of gravity and the momentum of the satellite at a particular distance from Earth. To completely escape Earth's gravity and fly off into space, a rocket must accelerate to escape-velocity, equivalent to eleven kilometers-per-second at the surface of Earth, which in practice means above forty-thousand kilometers-per-hour. This is the minimum speed an object without propulsion must travel to be able to totally escape from the gravity of Earth.[773] However, to get to the Moon, a spacecraft only needs a velocity of ten kilometers-per-second combined with the tug of the Moon's gravity.

In the case of the new-born Moon, Earth-gravity had been temporally neutralized. Lumps of crust and upper mantle, equivalent to about one-point-five percent of the mass of our planet, were launched from the surface. The gravity of star-core-zeus tugged on the crust and provided a radial acceleration up to one kilometer-per-second, which was combined with the tangential rotation velocity of the surface (about half a kilometer-per-second) and which flung the crust and upper mantle into space.

The near-miss encounter between Earth and star-core-zeus was so rapid and the inertia of the crustal rocks so huge that the Earth's crust never had enough time to accelerate sufficiently to match the one-hundred-and-eighty thousand kilometers-per-hour (fifty kilometers-per-second) speed of star-core-zeus. As star-core-zeus receded at high velocity, its gravitational influence rapidly diminished, so it released the remnants of Earth's crust and mantle from its grip.

At the unusually low launch velocity, it took about four days for the material of the new-born Moon to travel from Earth out to its present location. By the time star-core-zeus had disappeared completely from the scene, the newly formed Moon had achieved a stable orbit, which was slightly closer to Earth than its present orbit. The initial orbit was an ellipse that passed over the old Permian north and south pole.

The Moon currently orbits the Earth in an elliptical orbit, at an average altitude of three-hundred-and-eighty thousand kilometers, traveling around the Earth between latitude-twenty-eight-degrees-north to latitude-twenty-eight-degrees-south. The Moon still passes above the Hawaiian hot-spot from where it originally emerged.

Angular Momentum of the Moon

The Moon contains five-sixths of the Earth-Moon system's angular momentum, which was provided by star-core-zeus as it tugged the new-born-Moon into orbit. The Moon has such a high angular momentum that it cannot be explained by any of the other Moon formation models, with the exception of the giant-impact model.

The angular momentum of the Earth-Moon system is certainly too high for the co-accretion model or the capture model. Darwin's fission model fails, because the total angular momentum in the Earth-Moon system is insufficient by a factor of three, for a rapidly rotating Earth to fling the Moon into orbit on its own.

After star-core-zeus had disappeared, the new-born Moon orbited slightly faster than its present orbital velocity and was about ten thousand kilometers closer to Earth. Earth-Moon tidal forces caused the Moon to recede and also slightly shifted the plane of the Moon's orbit toward the plane of the ecliptic. The original orbit of the Moon can be derived by back-extrapolation of the Moon's current orbital parameters over the previous two-hundred-and-fifty million years (but not the four-point-five billion years used in other models).

Moon Formed from Continent-Size Crust Shells

As star-core-zeus departed, the mass of Earth crust and upper mantle in orbit crumpled up together. Huge solid shells of continental rock up to fifty kilometers thick and lumps of hot semi-liquid upper mantle rock up to forty kilometers thick collapsed into each other under mutual gravitational attraction.

The Moon was formed from a collection of solid pieces of Earth crust and upper mantle. The Moon's density of about three thousand-three-hundred kilograms per meter cubed is similar to a mixture of granite and basalt but is much less dense than the Earth's inner mantle and iron core. The total mass of this material is only one-point-two percent of the total mass of the Earth.

The average diameter of the Moon is three thousand five hundred kilometers, about twenty-seven percent of the Earth, but the volume of the Moon is only about two percent of the Earth. The volume of the Moon is roughly equivalent to the volume of rock that can be generated by lifting off the surface rocks from half of the Earth's crust, down to an average depth of eighty-six kilometers. In addition to upper crustal granites, up to forty kilometers of soft upper mantle-rock was pulled off our planet too.

During the collisions of the Earth-rock, as the Moon crushed itself into an imperfect sphere, kinetic energy was converted to heat, which raised the average temperature of the fragments of terrestrial crust to one thousand kelvin (about seven hundred degrees Celsius). This heating process explains the differences in volatile elements between Earth-rock and Moon-rock.

The distribution of material within the newly born Moon was asymmetric. A thick layer of lighter crustal-rock that had been pulled off Earth accumulated on the conical far-side of the Moon. The complex magnetic field patterns discovered on the surface of the Moon, particularly on the far-side highlands, were generated from slabs of solid magnetized Earth-rock being randomly crushed and packed together.

The heavier basaltic mantle material was concentrated more on the fat-bottom near-side, under the influence of the Earth's gravitational field. This made the near-side surface of the Moon, geologically different from the far-side that faced out into space. The final result was our asymmetric Moon, with mainly continental rock from the old surface of the Earth on the far-side and terrestrial basaltic magmas similar to ocean floor material on the near-side.

The lunar maria arose from low-speed impacts of vast lumps of hot semi-liquid basalt, which had been torn from the outer mantle of the Earth. This non-homogenous hot basaltic rock partially melted on impact and re-solidified as lunar maria, with the denser material forming mascons under the center of each maria of the near-side. These huge chunks were big enough and dense enough to punch four kilometers into the outer-layers of the newly formed Moon.

The final result was our large asymmetrical Moon made of anorthosite, with the familiar structures of the maria made of upper-mantle basalt. The mysterious Aitken Hole and the trapdoor fractures were created as continent-size chunks of surface Earth-rock were irregularly rolled up and stacked together under their own gravity, during the formation of the Moon.

The far-side of the Moon suffered much more cratering than the near-side because rock that had been pulled further out into space crashed back mainly onto the far-side of the Moon, once the effect of the gravitational field of star-core-zeus had diminished. For some time after the departure of star-core-zeus, debris that had been dragged further away from Earth cascaded back onto the far-side of the Moon, resulting in the heavy cratering, which has been erroneously attributed to a "late-heavy-bombardment."

The Ruptured Earth

When star-core-zeus tore off the Permian northern hemisphere in the catastrophic near-miss, the huge Triassic Pacific Ocean basin was formed, initially with a very deep hole in the middle, which is still marked by the Hawaii seamounts in the present Pacific Ocean. The old crust of the Earth that had been left behind was the old heavily fractured Permian southern hemisphere, which became known as the supercontinent Pangaea.

The resumption of normal gravity around Earth meant that some crustal fragments, which had not collided and crumpled together under self-gravity to form the Moon, started crashing back to the surface of Earth. Some chunks of crustal debris fell back and impacted on the edge of Pangaea to form the huge Caribbean crater zone. Some crustal rock also crashed back to Earth and splashed-down into the Triassic Pacific Ocean basin, giving rise to the underwater masses of continental rock found around Easter Island and the East Pacific Rise. Anorthosite rock was also dumped across the fractured continental surface of the Earth.

The Permian annihilation caused an abrupt reversal of the polarity of the magnetic field of the Earth. The Permian-Triassic magnetic-field-reversal was recorded in the vast flood of hot liquid basalt, which solidified all over Siberia. It appears that the very close encounter between Earth and the immensely powerful magnetic-field of star-core-zeus was responsible.

Magnetic reversals of Earth's magnetic field occurred more frequently from the Triassic period, approximately one every four hundred thousand years. This is equivalent to one magnetic reversal for every hundred star-core orbits.[774]

Age of Lunar Rock and Date of Moon Formation

The lunar highlands on the far-side are made of the four-point-five billion year old terrestrial anorthosite. The lunar maria on the near-side of the Moon are made of three-point-seven billion year old terrestrial basalt from the upper mantle. The younger date for the basalt is probably due to the upper mantle of Earth becoming solid about eight hundred million years later than the crust.

Moon-rock radio-metrically dates as billions of years old, simply because the Moon is composed of old Earth-rock and regolith (a mixed breccia of mainly meteoric origin). The lunar basalt and lunar highland rock were never fully re-melted after leaving Earth, so their age corresponds to the date of their formation on Earth and not from the date of formation of the Moon.

In contrast, the date of Moon formation coincides with the date of the Permian mass extinction, two-hundred-and-fifty-two million years ago. This is the same as the age of the oldest ocean floor of Earth and the age of the Triassic Pacific Ocean basin.

Dust accumulation data also supports the date of formation of the Moon as approximately two-hundred-and-fifty million years ago. On the Earth, the mysterious difference in age between ocean basalts, which are never more than two-hundred-and-fifty-million years-old, and continental granites, which are up to the four-point-four billion-years old, is also explained by the Caesarean Moon Birth model.

Conclusion

All the evidence points to the same explanation: a high-velocity near-miss of Earth by star-core-zeus induced intense tidal forces, which ripped off almost half of the Earth's surface, to form the Moon. All the rock, which is now on the Moon, originally came from the Triassic Pacific Ocean basin, and ocean basins never existed prior to the Permian annihilation two-hundred-and-fifty million years ago.

The Caesarean Moon Birth model also leads to a profound prediction: in the not too distant future, astronauts will dig up Permian fossils on the Moon. The first samples of these fossils will probably be collected from twelve kilometers below the lunar-surface, from the floor of that mysterious basin on the far-side, near the south-pole of the Moon.

Only a supernova remnant of high mass, small size, high density, and intense gravity could pull out the Moon without colliding with our planet. In the next section, we shall investigate further extraordinary anomalies of our solar-system, in our continuing quest to track down star-core-zeus.

CHAPTER 12

How Did Our Solar-System Form?

● ● ●

IT IS NOT JUST MOON formation theory that is currently in crisis; new data has also invalidated our current model for the origin of our solar-system.

The solar-nebular-model, which was developed through the nineteenth and the twentieth centuries, described a rotating disc of dust and gas that collapsed to form the Sun and planets. It has been the standard explanation for generations of astronomers, but new data on the isotopes, elements, molecules, dust, meteors, and planets of our solar-system has refuted this model.[775]

In the next seven chapters, a competing model for the origin of our solar-system, which includes a massive star-core orbiting with our Sun, shall be considered in light of the recent discoveries of thousands of strange exo-planetary systems orbiting other host stars and the growing collection of anomalous data about our solar-system.

Our Solar-System

Our solar-system is defined as the Sun, with eight planets revolving around it. The Sun is ninety-nine-point-nine percent of the mass of the solar-system and about half of the tiny remainder is Jupiter. The other seven planets including Earth represents less than a two-hundredth of the total mass of the solar-system.

The perimeter of the solar-system is usually defined by the orbit of the outermost giant planet Neptune, which is about thirty times further out than the Earth from the Sun. The standard of measurement on the scale of our solar-system is the Astronomical Unit (AU), the average distance from the Earth to the Sun.[776] Using this system of units, Neptune is said to orbit 30 AU from the Sun.

The eight planets of the solar-system comprise of the four inner smaller rocky planets—Mercury, Venus, Earth, and Mars—and the four outer giant planets—Jupiter, Saturn, Uranus, and Neptune. In addition, between the orbits of Mars and Jupiter, there is an asteroid-belt, a ring of rocks that range from the size of pebbles to mountains, but its total mass is extremely small—less than five percent of the mass of the Moon.

Following its discovery in 1930, Pluto became known as the ninth planet. However, it stopped being recognized as a planet, after Eris was discovered in 2006. Eris is more massive than Pluto but travels in a highly inclined and very eccentric elliptical orbit, as far out as 97 AU from the Sun. Eris, Pluto, and related objects have been relegated to a new category of trans-Neptune-objects, which orbit beyond 30 AU.

Within this group of trans-Neptune-objects, there are a large number of small icy Kuiper Belt objects, which orbit out to 48 AU, and this group includes Pluto. Beyond this region, the outer edge of the solar-system has been swept clear, and there are almost no objects at 50 AU.

Beyond this frontier are the scattered-disc-objects, which have strange highly eccentric and steeply inclined orbits. The scattered-disc-objects appear to have been disturbed by some massive object, which is hiding out in the space, beyond the Kuiper belt.

All the planets travel around the Sun in the same direction, close to the surface of an imaginary solar-system-disc, the average orbital plane of the planets. If viewed from a hypothetical position above the solar-north-pole, all the planets revolve in an anti-clockwise direction. The Sun also turns in the same anti-clockwise direction.

Most of the planets also rotate in the same anti-clockwise direction, but there are exceptions to this general pattern. Venus rotates slowly in the opposite direction, and Uranus, the second outermost planet, has a rotation axis that lies almost in the plane of the solar-system-disc, as if long ago it was knocked-over by some massive object.

Problems with the Solar Nebular Model

The solar-nebular-model for the formation of the solar-system was originally proposed by Pierre-Simon Laplace over two hundred years ago. It was based on the simple assumption that our Sun and planets formed at the same time, from a cloud of dust and gas.

In summary, the idea is that four-point-six billion years ago, an interstellar cloud of gas and dust collapsed under gravity into a rotating disc, which further condensed to simultaneously form the Sun and planets. However, despite decades of work, computer simulations of the solar-nebular-model cannot reproduce the mass and orbital distribution of the planets and other objects in the solar-system.[777, 778, 779].

In addition, the solar-nebular-model has serious problems explaining many features of our solar-system: from the collapse of the original dust cloud to the initiation of planet formation, the final accretion of Uranus and Neptune, the co-ordinated motion of the planets, the distribution of angular momentum, as well as the relative distribution of chemical elements and isotopes between the Sun and the planets.

The original solar-nebular-model simply assumed the spontaneous formation of a large disc-like cloud of gas and dust, which was already rotating around one axis, without explaining how it originally formed. The model ignored the basic properties of low pressure gases and dust in a vacuum, which do not spontaneously condense into solids by gravity alone, even at low temperatures.

A patch had to be applied to the solar-nebular-model to solve the condensation-problem. A revised version of the model had to have the high-pressure shock-wave of a neighboring supernova to trigger the initial condensation steps of the solar nebula, before the formation of the solar-system was possible.

Another patch had to be applied to cause clumping of matter under near-zero-gravity conditions, introducing either magnetic fields or electrostatic attraction, prior to condensation of a fine sand that accreted to become the building material of the planets.

However, the solar-nebular-model still cannot explain the distribution of the planets on the basis of gravity alone. If a revolving disc of dense dust and gas had really collapsed to become the Sun and planets, then the larger planets would be expected to accrete closer to the Sun, like many exo-planetary systems orbiting other stars.

The solar-nebular-model also predicts a rapidly rotating Sun, whose rotation axis should be perpendicular to the solar-system-disc. It was a surprise to discover the equator of the Sun is angled at seven degrees to the solar-system-disc, and the Sun is rotating very slowly.

It is simply not possible to predict the orbits of the planets nor their common direction of rotation or the orientation of the Sun, from the conventional solar-nebular-model.

In addition, the solar-nebular-model cannot explain the distribution of angular momentum arising from massive planets orbiting at large distances from the Sun. Almost all the angular momentum of the solar-system is carried by the four giant planets; Jupiter, Saturn, Uranus, and Neptune. The Sun at the middle only contains half-a-percent of the total angular momentum of the whole solar-system.

The angular-momentum-per-unit-mass of each planet is up to one hundred thousand times greater than that of the Sun. In addition, the value of the angular-momentum-per-unit-mass for each planet increases in a smooth curve, with respect to its distance from the Sun.

All this data points to the same conclusion; the Sun and planets started as two independent dynamic systems, which had separate origins. At the birth of the solar-system, the matter which formed the planets was captured by a pre-existing Sun, in a process similar to that proposed by Prof Michael Wolfson in his solar-system-capture-theory.[780]

The Sun Compared to Binary-star-systems

The Sun's luminosity is class-V and its spectral-type is class-G2. The Sun is odd because most G-V stars are usually found in binary or multiple star systems, rather than alone.[781, 782] In fact, binary-star-systems are very common, and the majority of stars were born as part of binary or multiple star systems.[783]

Short-orbital-period binary systems in our local area of space have been the easiest to identify, and longer-period binary systems are continually being discovered. In the sixteen light years volume of space around Earth, forty-three stars are in multiple systems, compared to only twenty-seven single stars.[784]

When astronomers started to study the age of the stars, they made a surprising discovery about binary systems. Different infrared surveys designated to detect companion stars found that binary-star-systems were twice as common among young stars, compared to older main sequence stars. The proportion of binaries decreased with the age of the stars, because binary systems were unstable and one of the stars usually blew-up in a supernova explosion, after a few hundred million years.

There is evidence that SN1987A and SN1993J, two well-known Type-2 supernovas, were the result of a larger star in a binary system blowing up.[785, 786] There is also evidence that when supernova explosions occurred in binary systems, the remnant star-core of the former companion-star remained in orbit. More than twenty star-systems have been observed in which the visible star was being perturbed by a cool and dark star-core.[787] A Type-1c supernova has also actually been observed in a binary system.[788] There is plenty of evidence (described later), that a supernova explosion blew-up a large star near the Sun, just prior to the birth of our solar-system.

Sir Fred Hoyle and the Binary Star Model

This book reassesses an alternative model for the formation of the solar-system from a binary-star-system, because it provides a better explanation for all the current data. In 1950, Sir Fred Hoyle proposed that billions of years ago, before the planets existed, the Sun had already formed as part of a binary-star-system with a much larger companion-star. After a few hundred-million years, this companion-star blew-up as a supernova, and the planets formed from the debris of this explosion.[789]

BINARY SOLAR SYSTEM

~ 5 billion years ago: Companion-Star and the Sun orbited the Centre of Gravity of the Binary System (Barycentre)

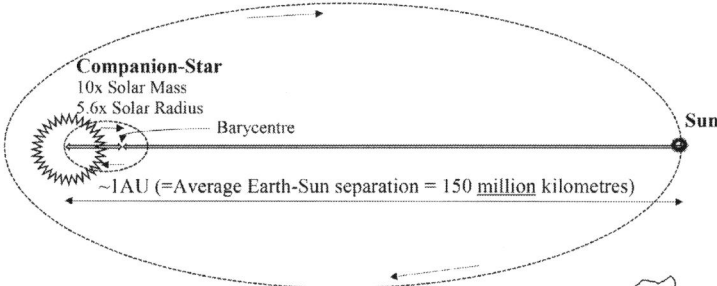

Companion-Star
10x Solar Mass
5.6x Solar Radius
Barycentre
Sun
~1AU (=Average Earth-Sun separation = 150 <u>million</u> kilometres)

~ 4.6 billion years ago: SUPERNOVA!
[Change of Scale 1000X]

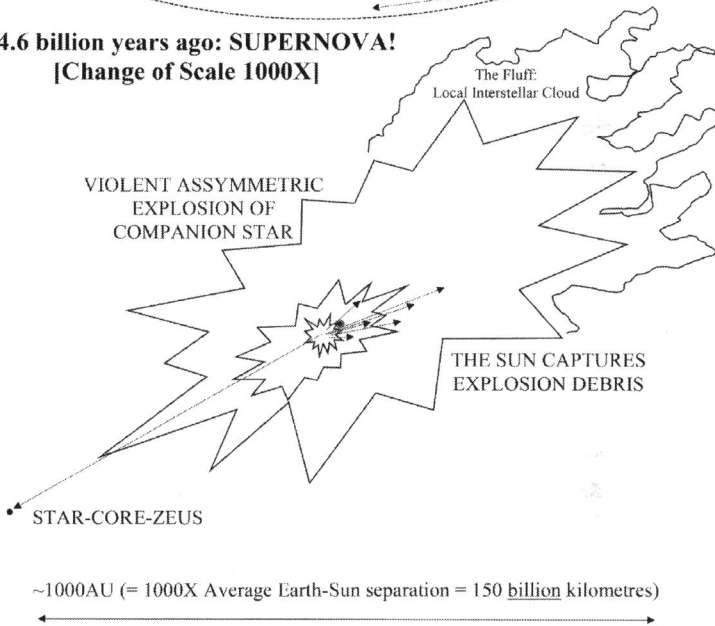

The Fluff:
Local Interstellar Cloud

VIOLENT ASSYMMETRIC
EXPLOSION OF
COMPANION STAR

THE SUN CAPTURES
EXPLOSION DEBRIS

STAR-CORE-ZEUS

~1000AU (= 1000X Average Earth-Sun separation = 150 <u>billion</u> kilometres)

The Birth of the Proto-Sun and Companion Star

According to Hoyle, about five billion years ago, non-identical twin stars were born in a dense nebula of hydrogen and helium gas. A weak turbulence in the nursery cloud caused the stars to orbit around each other, and as they condensed, they moved closer together. The Sun and its larger twin continued to accumulate more and more gas. However, the heavier companion-star sucked in gas much more rapidly, so it grew much faster, until it was between eight and ten times bigger than the Sun.

The companion-star continued to suck in more of the hydrogen and helium from the nursery cloud, until its interior reached a critical temperature and pressure, which triggered nuclear fusion reactions. The shock of the ignition of nuclear fusion in the companion-star probably catalyzed stellar-ignition of the Sun.

By the time the young couple of stars were fully formed, the larger companion-star was much hotter than the Sun and its high-temperature nuclear fusion-reactions burnt up its hydrogen around a thousand times faster.

The Dance of the Companion Star and the Sun

The original solar-system comprised of the Sun and a large, rapidly rotating magnetic companion-star but no planets. The companion-star and the Sun danced together, orbiting around their "barycenter" (the binary center of gravity), in linked eccentric elliptical orbits. Their distance of closest approach was probably much less than the average distance of the Earth from the Sun.

Intense tidal-forces between the stars created by mutual gravitational attraction gave rise to tidal-bulges. During each perihelion close-encounter, at the distance of minimum separation between the pair of stars, the two stars were distorted into egg-shapes. The larger companion-star even sucked hydrogen from the Sun's surface. Evidence of such close-binary interaction is revealed in the accretion-nova-isotopes, detected in the dust of the solar-system, which shall be discussed in a following chapter.

Tidal-locking meant the direction of rotation and revolution of both stars was the same. Capture-theory suggests that the common anti-clockwise direction of revolution of the planets around the Sun was due to the companion-star and the Sun revolving around each other in the opposite clockwise direction.

The Short Life of the Companion-Star

The companion-star consumed most of its hydrogen fusion fuel in approximately one-hundred-million years. Starved of hydrogen, the heat generated by the companion-star could not keep pace with the heat radiated from its surface, so it began to shrink.

This caused the pressure and temperature in the core of the companion-star to increase. The temperature at the center of the companion-star eventually rose to the helium-flashpoint of one-hundred-million Kelvin. At this point, the companion-star commenced nuclear fusion reactions that turned helium into heavier elements. The heat generated by the new source of energy caused the companion-star to get hotter again and even bigger.

However, the companion-star ate through most of its helium in about one million years, so the fusion-reactions slowed once again. The companion-star started to cool and shrink, because once again the heat generated from the fusion-reactions could not replace the heat lost into space.

As the companion-star shrank again, its core-temperature increased rapidly. Eventually, new fusion reactions were triggered that fed on progressively heavier elemental fuel. The pressure and temperature increased in a steep gradient toward the center of the core of the companion-star, creating concentric layers of reaction-shells. Different elemental fusion reactions took place at different depths, with the heaviest elements fusing together toward the center of the star.

Near the end of the companion-star's relatively short life, the bulk of its core comprised of concentric layers of fusion-burning shells that contained all elements up to iron. The enormous gravity at the center squeezed iron until it was converted into inert ultra-hot electron-degenerate matter of a star-core.

Rapid Rotation and Supernova Ignition

The rate of rotation of the companion-star accelerated each time it cooled and shrank. The rapid rotation also directly affected the fusion reactions, causing incomplete burning and early switching of nuclear fuels. The faster the companion-star rotated, the more its large tidal-bulges were shifted beyond the line connecting the centers of mass of the two stars.

The relative position of the tidal-bulge of the companion-star to the Sun is important, because it ultimately determined the trajectory of star-core-zeus after the supernova explosion and even the direction of revolution of the planets around the Sun.

The nuclear-fusion reactions generated heat energy in the sequence of elemental nucleo-synthesis up to the formation of iron. However, the fusion of elements heavier than iron actually requires energy and absorbs heat. As the companion-star used up all its heavier but less efficient elemental fuels, again the heat generated in star-core-zeus could not match the radiative heat loss from the surface.

As fusion-burning declined for the final time, the companion-star rapidly cooled. It shrank because the falling heat-pressure could not resist the intense gravity. The core was squeezed into progressively smaller volumes, until the atoms were crushed to such an extent that the normal atomic boundaries were breached. Atomic nuclei were rammed together to form a super-dense central star-core of electron-degenerate-matter, which weighed about ten-percent of the mass of the Sun.

As the companion-star shrank in size, conservation of angular momentum meant it had to spin even more rapidly. In the end, the redistribution of angular momentum caused the companion-star to spin so fast that its layered fusion-reaction shells were exposed down to the outer core.

At ultra-high angular velocity, gravity could no longer hold the star together against the extreme centrifugal forces. The outer layers of the companion-star's core were ruptured, and the fusion-reaction zone was completely deprived of fuel, so all fusion reactions abruptly stopped.

Asymmetric Type-2 Supernova Explosion

The sudden shut-down of the fusion reactions caused catastrophic heat-loss and an instantaneous implosion under the intense stellar gravity. As the matter in the companion-star accelerated toward its center, the tidal bulges caused an uneven distribution of matter impacting onto the degenerate star-core.

The degenerate matter reached a critical density during the implosion, so the companion-star's core abruptly stopped shrinking. The outer-core-shells, which were still crashing down, suddenly bounced off its new rigid surface so that an enormous mass of material reversed direction and rebounded explosively outward, converting gravitational-potential-energy into heat. The asymmetrical shock front of the explosion, colliding with the outer layers of the star still falling inward, erupted as an ultra-violent asymmetric type-two supernova explosion.[790, 791]

Core-Collapse Synthesis

Normal fusion reactions in the companion-star had produced all the elements up to iron. However, only a supernova explosion could produce the very heavy elements, such as gold or uranium.

The vast amounts of gravitational-potential-energy, which was converted to intense heat, triggered photon-dissociation of the elements and a rapid series of heavy-element nuclear-fusion reactions. The combination of the heat surge and the fragmentation of the star-core resulted in a complex mixture of supernova products.

This awesome asymmetrical type-two supernova explosion blasted out the external convective layers of the companion-star as a huge explosion plume. The shock-front was made of ultra-hot protons, which was followed by masses of heavier elemental materials. The isotopic data of solar-system dust strongly suggests this supernova explosion detonated too early, before all hydrogen fuel had gone.

The result of the unique explosion conditions was the planetary building materials of our solar-system, which are a complex mixture of isotopes, ranging from the lightest atoms of hydrogen up to the very heaviest elements. The core of the companion-star shattered into different sized fragments of ultra-dense nickel-iron, some hundreds of kilometers in diameter. Chunks of this matter were scattered far out into space, and some became the seeds from which the planets grew.

The Capture of Planetary Building Materials by the Sun

Although new elements and isotopes erupted out in all directions, the position of the companion-star's tidal bulge meant that most of the supernova explosion-debris was blasted in the approximate direction of the Sun.

As the huge explosion-plume blasted past one side of the Sun, it resembled the exhaust of a vast rocket engine. The blast-wave hit one pole of the Sun, flipping its rotation axis up-side-down and making the Sun rotate in an anti-clockwise direction. About a ten-thousandth of the explosion debris was captured by the Sun to become the planetary building materials, but most of the explosion-plume flew on to eventually spread over light-years to become a hot inter-stellar dust cloud.

IMAGES OF OUR COMPANION STAR EXPLOSION

The remains of the companion star explosion have been detected by the ROSAT X-ray satellite, mapping the X-ray signals surrounding the solar system. The image is about six thousand light-years across and is centred on our Sun. It records linear scaling of X-ray surface brightness local to our solar system. Reference: Puspitarini, L., et al ., Astronomy & Astrophysics Volume 566, (2014) Article A13 12 pages. The X-ray map correlates with the explosion dust-debris map and hyper-ionisation trail of Star-Core-Zeus.

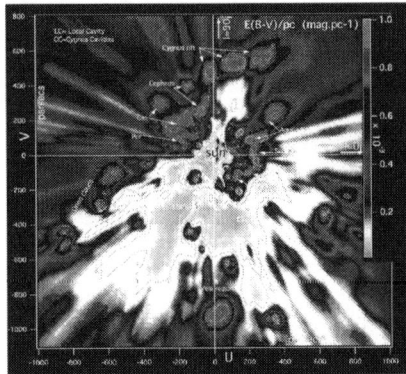

ZOOM IN ON X-RAY
MAP OF LOCAL SUPERNOVA

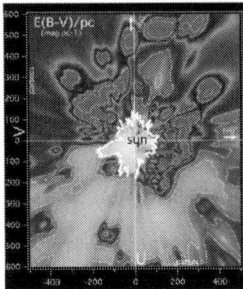

EXPLOSION DEBRIS MAP A&A 566, A13 (2014)

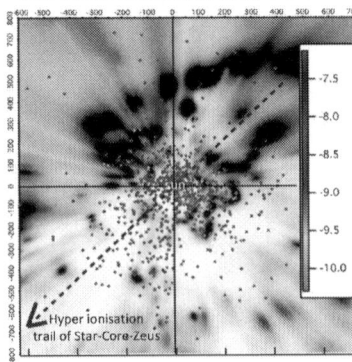

Conclusion

According to Hoyle's model, the planets of our solar-system were born from the supernova explosion debris of a former companion-star of the Sun. This binary-system-supernova model is superior to the solar-nebular-model in explaining the data on the solar-system and other exoplanetary systems. In the following chapters, evidence shall be presented of the supernova of the former companion-star, which occurred adjacent to the Sun, and the formation of planets from the matter of its explosion plume.

Hoyle assumed that after the supernova explosion, the core of the companion-star was blasted to escape-velocity and was lost in space billions of years ago as an invisible cold black-dwarf. On the contrary, evidence shall be presented in this book that star-core-zeus is still in orbit with the Sun.

CHAPTER 13

Our Local Supernova

● ● ●

THE COMPANION-STAR OF OUR SUN blew up in an enormous supernova explosion four-point-six billion years ago, just prior to the formation of the planets. The evidence is all around us.

The Solar-System in a Radio Bubble

When radio-astronomers started to map our galaxy, they made a surprising discovery: the space between the stars in our Milky Way is full of huge "radio-bubbles," on average around five-hundred light years across. The walls of these enormous bubbles are made of a compressed magnetized gas, which generates powerful synchrotron radiation at radio wavelengths.[792]

Inside the radio bubbles there is a much harder vacuum of hotter rarefied gas, which is the source of a soft X-ray background radiation.[793] The best explanation for these bubbles is that they are remnants of shock-fronts of ancient supernova explosions.

It was a great surprise when it was discovered that our solar-system sits in the center of a huge radio bubble.[794, 795] This is evidence that billions of years ago, there had been a huge supernova explosion, adjacent to the Sun.[796]

The local-bubble was crudely mapped with radio-telescopes as egg-shaped: an elongated ellipsoid bubble of ultra-low-density ultra-hot gas surrounded by a shell of denser dust and gas.[797] Our local-bubble is huge, approximately three-hundred light-years across and about a thousand light-years long.

The local-bubble is so big that it not only contains the Sun and planets but also many of the stars visible in the sky. The bright star Sirius about nine light-years away and other stars such as Vega, Altair, Arcturus, Fomalhaut, Alpha-Centauri, Procyon, the Hyades, and even the Pleiades are all located inside the shell of our local-bubble.

However, apart from the stars, the interstellar medium of the interior of our local-bubble is remarkably empty of matter. The density of the gas is only five percent of the average for the whole galaxy: it is a near perfect vacuum of fifty atoms-per-liter.

However, this rarefied, ionized and magnetized gas is ultra-hot, with a temperature of one-million degrees Kelvin. This ultra-hot local gas is known as the Local Inter-Stellar Medium or LISM. It is the source of the ubiquitous soft (quarter of a kilo-electron-volt) X-ray background-emission.[798, 799, 800, 801] The X-ray emitting LISM has structure, and its three-dimensional form has been mapped: it has an extraordinary cartoon-like explosion shape extending out three thousand light-years in all directions from the Sun.[802]

About a billion years ago, our local-bubble collided with shock-fronts of other ancient supernova explosions that had expanded from other directions. This process made radio-bubble-foam on a galactic scale. Our local-bubble appears to be a very old and relatively stable structure that is neither expanding nor contracting.

In contrast to the cavity, the shell of our local-bubble is not so hot: it has a temperature of less than one thousand degrees Kelvin. It is made of a denser neutral interstellar hydrogen gas, plus low concentrations of other elements and dust. Generally, the shell is thicker in the direction of the galactic plane, where galactic matter is generally denser. The ultra-hot ionized gas of the local-bubble impacting the neutral-gas shell is the source of the radio frequency radiation, which revealed the surface of our local-bubble.

The neutral hydrogen gas in the shell is also a very efficient absorber of ultra-violet light between wavelengths of seven and seventy-six nanometers. In contrast, the interior of the local-bubble surrounding our solar-system is a huge UV-transparent cavity.

This property of the shell meant that accurate mapping of the local-bubble was possible, along lines-of-sight to nearby stars. The UV-absorption-spectra of four-hundred-and-fifty stars, which already had reliable distance estimates, were measured by the NASA Extreme Ultraviolet EUVE satellite, to determine if they were inside or outside the local-bubble.

THE TUNNEL AXIS IN THE LOCAL BUBBLE
The hot tunnel was confirmed by the CHIPS spacecraft during its
Cosmic Hot Interstellar Plasma Spectrometer mission in 2003

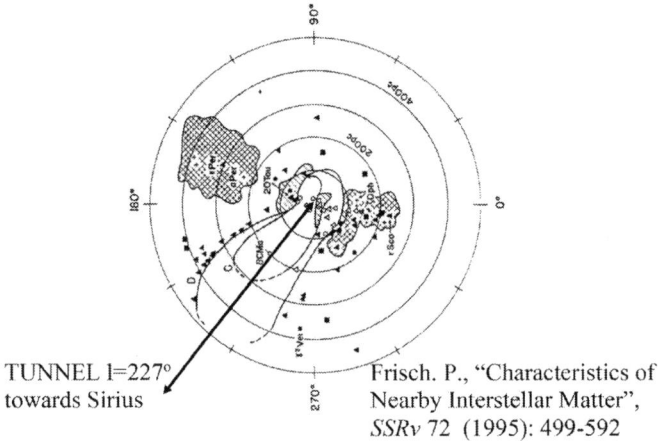

TUNNEL l=227°
towards Sirius

Frisch. P., "Characteristics of
Nearby Interstellar Matter",
SSRv 72 (1995): 499-592

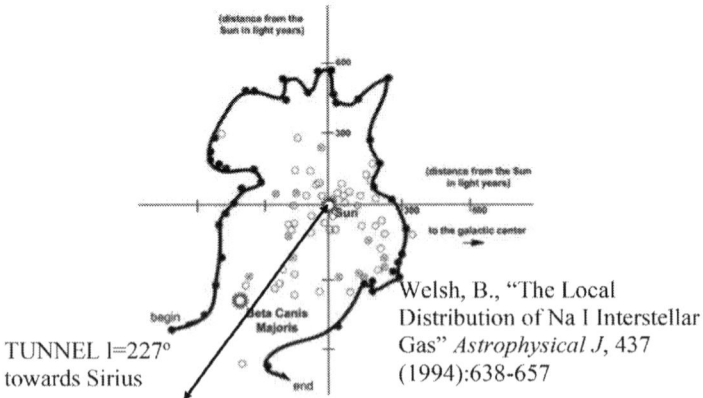

TUNNEL l=227°
towards Sirius

Welsh, B., "The Local
Distribution of Na I Interstellar
Gas" *Astrophysical J*, 437
(1994):638-657

In addition, there is an optical sodium-absorption signal coming from the shell, which is also absent within the cavity of the local-bubble.

The presence or absence of the Na-I sodium-adsorption-line, in the light from a thousand stars of known distance, was also measured.[803, 804] These types of studies produced information about the approximate distance to the shell in a particular direction, allowing the three-dimensional shape of the shell of our local-bubble to be mapped accurately.

Our solar-system sits at the very center of our local-bubble, surrounded by highly-ionized, very-rarefied, ultra-hot gas. The local-bubble seems to be the remnants of an ancient asymmetric supernova explosion that occurred next to the Sun, billions of years ago.

More studies using the accurate stellar distances generated by the Hipparcos satellite, combined with improved detector and grating technology carried by new satellites, enabled a wide range of high resolution UV absorption spectroscopy to be performed.[805] It was discovered the ultra-hot, ultra-low density gas in the local-bubble contained highly ionized carbon, nitrogen, oxygen, silicon, and iron from our companion-star.[806, 807, 808, 809]

The presence of "diffuse-interstellar-bands" in the UV spectra has also revealed dust containing fullerenes and polyaromatic hydrocarbon molecules, produced by post-supernova chemistry.[810] Recent work using infra-red dust detectors revealed the shape of the cavity immediately surrounding the Sun, also resembles a cartoon image of a huge explosion.[811] The old explosion shock front is extremely asymmetric and fragmented.

Long-ago, the ultra-hot gas of the supernova shock-wave blasted out vast holes through the interstellar medium of the galactic disc, both above and below us. A big hole that opens out into a funnel shape in the upper surface of the galactic disk was given the name "the chimney." [812, 813] Similar vents have been observed in other galaxies, where the pressure of ultra-hot ionized blasts from supernova explosions had been released.

The Hot Tunnel to Sirius

During the analysis of detailed three-dimensional maps of our local-bubble, a startling discovery was made. Corresponding to the axis of the stretched egg-shape of our local-bubble, there was evidence of a radially-focused blast-wave from the huge supernova that had blown up adjacent to our Sun. The axis of this ancient explosion was directed away from the Sun, along an imaginary straight-line toward the bright star Sirius.

This dominant feature of the local-bubble is known as "the Tunnel." [814] It is a linear feature of ultra-hot near-vacuum, containing only five neutral hydrogen atoms per liter. It is an incredible three-thousand light-years long.

Although the long axis of this straight tunnel from the Sun is directed toward the bright star Sirius about nine light-years away, it continues on another five hundred light-years to a star called Mirzam (beta Canis Major) and then extends for many light years beyond. [815] Both Sirius and Mirzam can be seen in the night-sky as adjacent stars in the constellation of Canis Major.

Star-light arriving from the direction of the end of the Tunnel far beyond Sirius has an anomalous absence of a Na-I line-width expansion. In this specific direction, the absorption column density is almost zero.

Long ago, the ancient supernova explosion that destroyed the companion star of the Sun fired an ultra-hot blast-wave beyond Sirius. It traveled on to punch a hole through the shell of our local-bubble at the end of the-tunnel, over a thousand light-years away from us.

In addition, the Tunnel extends in a straight line away from the Sun, in the exact opposite direction to Sirius, toward the bright star Cygnus. [816] In this direction, the Tunnel stretches away from the solar-system for a much shorter distance on cosmic scales of only sixty light years.

The Tunnel is not completely empty: the Cassini spacecraft detected a mysterious straight-trail of supernova dust, stretching away from the solar-system, along the center of the-tunnel toward Sirius. [817] The dust is concentrated toward ecliptic coordinates, seventy-nine degrees-longitude, minus-eight degrees-latitude, and is made of a mixture of silicon, carbon, oxygen, sodium, magnesium, potassium, calcium, iron, titanium, vanadium, manganese, and nickel, in similar ratios to the material found in chondrite meteorites, which are the building material of the planets. [818]

The Tunnel is like an enormous rifle barrel aimed at Sirius, which fired star-core-zeus away from the Sun like a massive bullet. [819] The data on the local-bubble and tunnel shows that the ancient asymmetric supernova explosion of our companion-star blasted star-core-zeus in exactly the same direction as had been predicted from the study of astro-mythology, described in my previous book *Cataclysms & Renewals*.

Age of the Local-Bubble

The age of the supernova explosion that formed our local-bubble remains controversial. In January 2003, NASA launched a satellite called the Cosmic Hot Interstellar Plasma Spectrometer (CHIPS) to study the local-bubble. According to Hurwitz, the chief mission scientist of CHIPS, "There's a great deal we don't know about the Bubble...like how old it is."

It has been very difficult to determine the absolute age of the local-bubble, because so far the dating methods have been limited to observing the rate of expansion of recent supernova shock-fronts and guessing how fast they stop growing. For example, the rapid deceleration of the shock front of Supernova 1987A suggested that radio bubbles approximately five hundred light years across are probably billions of years old.

The bubble surrounding the solar-system is huge, big enough to have blown up five-billion years ago. It has been estimated that the blast wave that punched out the linear Tunnel has already traveled more than three-thousand light years beyond Sirius. This is strong evidence that the powerful supernova explosion responsible for the Tunnel is billions of years old and probably as old as the solar-system.

However, some astrophysicists attribute the local-bubble to recent supernovae. They explain away the local-bubble, with the unlikely scenario of a series of recent local supernovae explosions only ten million years ago.[820, 821] One group even assumed twenty separate supernovae in neighboring stars of the Scorpius-Centaurus association.[822, 823]

The problem with these types of ideas is that there is no evidence for the supernova fall-out of these hypothetical explosions on Earth, nor are there any young hot supernova remnants local to our solar-system. For example, the closest known neutron star is in Corona Australis, more than two hundred light-years away from us.[824]

In addition, the lack of red-shifted clouds in the hole in the roof of the galactic disc, known as the-chimney, one thousand light years above us, shows the local-bubble had ceased to vent hot high pressure explosion gases, a very long time ago. Warm neutral cloud components referred to as galactic-rain are actually falling back into the-chimney and all around us, which is further evidence that the local-bubble is very ancient.[825, 826]

The reasonable conclusion is that our local-bubble is a multi-billion year old structure associated with the formation of the solar-system.

The Fluff: The Local Inter-Stellar Cloud

There is an elongated cloud of hot dust and gas, trailing away from our solar-system called "the Fluff."[827, 828] This cloud is in the form of a cone-shaped plume of material, which lies inside the local-bubble and the Tunnel.[829] The cloud stretches away from the solar-system toward the bright star Cygnus and the constellation of Hercules (which is the opposite direction to Sirius). The Fluff widens from a point of origin near the Sun, fanning out away from the solar-system, for up to thirty light-years, expanding from five to twenty-five light-years across.

The Fluff is as hot as the surface of the Sun, with a temperature around six thousand Kelvin. The Fluff contains gas at a density of about three hundred atoms per liter and also some dust. The elemental composition of dust in the Fluff resembles cometary dust and carbonaceous chondrites found in the solar-system.

The Fluff has an abundance of carbon (mainly in the form of diamond), plus hydrogen, helium, silicon, nitrogen, oxygen, sulfur, phosphorous, aluminum, magnesium, and iron, revealing its probable origin in the outer envelope of the companion-star. The Hubble Space Telescope detected a dense cloud of diamond dust in the Fluff and an abundance of nitrogen-diamond complexes, which absorb light in a wide waveband centered around 270 nano-meters.

The Fluff is a very ancient structure, now being blown back toward the solar-system by the stellar winds from young stars in a star-forming region of the Scorpius-Centaurus Association and the young expanding

Loop-1 Bubble, the shock front of a much more recent supernova explosion. The solar-system itself is slowly moving deeper into the Fluff, as it gradually catches-up with its own ancient explosion plume.

In addition, a ring-shaped feature of dense supernova material has recently been discovered surrounding our solar-system, which resembles the debris ring of supernova SN 1987A. This feature is additional evidence that our solar-system formed after a local supernova explosion.[830]

There is no doubt that the Fluff is a huge elongated cloud of dusty supernova explosion debris. It contains enough matter to make a ten-solar-mass-star and more than enough material to build the planets.[831] The Fluff is the remains of the asymmetric supernova explosion that destroyed our companion-star four-point-six billion years ago and that blasted debris past the Sun at the birth of our solar-system. It is also the remains of the recoil-blast of the supernova explosion that launched star-core-zeus into an extremely eccentric elliptical orbit.

One Supernova or Many?

In order to explain the abundance of both iron and oxygen in our solar-system and the unique isotope mixtures in star-dust and meteorites, which shall be described in the next chapter, recent versions of the solar-nebular-model assume three different supernova explosions to create the initial conditions for the formation of the solar-system.

This very improbable proposal is that two different types of supernova explosions (a type-one and a type-two) produced two different types of debris clouds, which eventually mingled together in our region of space. The reasoning is based on the facts that iron is the most abundant element produced in a type-one supernova, while oxygen is the most abundant element produced by a type-two supernova.[832, 833]

However, these improbable models then require a third local supernova to force these two randomly drifting clouds of different supernova materials to merge into a rotating nebular and condense to form the Sun and planets.[834] However, an investigation of the remnants of forty-five supernovae in the Large Magellanic Cloud, a satellite galaxy of the

Milky Way, found no evidence that supernova explosion shock-fronts trigger star-formation.[835]

This three supernova model is obviously wrong: it requires a very a rare set of initial conditions for planet formation. The abundance of exo-planets prove that a much more efficient planet formation process is at work, which is directly related to the life cycle of stars: one supernova is quite sufficient for planet-formation.

Conclusion

Studies of the local interstellar environment surrounding the Sun and the discoveries of the Bubble, the super-hot LISM, the Fluff, and the Tunnel prove that our former companion star of the Sun blew up in an asymmetric supernova explosion prior to the formation of the planets. Isotopic evidence of the former companion-star of the Sun is scattered all around our solar-system, and shall be described in the next chapter.

CHAPTER 14

Isotopic Evidence for Our Companion-Star

● ● ●

THE ELEMENTS THAT MAKE UP our solar-system have much to tell us about how it was formed. Even more information can be learned from the study of isotopes, particularly radioactive-isotopes and their decay products. Mixtures of isotopes, including the decay products of archaic radioactive elements, are locked in the solid matrix of interplanetary dust grains and meteorites. They are an archive of the composition of our solar-system at its formation.

The isotopes of each element found in the solar-system can be divided into three main groups: isotopes that were synthesized during the life-time of the companion-star, isotopes that were synthesized during the supernova that destroyed the companion-star, and daughter-isotopes that had formed by radioactive decay of unstable-isotopes, after the supernova.[836, 837, 838]

Carbon Isotopes of the Companion-Star

All the common carbon-12 (and rarer carbon-13) in our bodies was produced more than four-point-six billion years ago, in a fusion-furnace deep inside the companion-star.[839]

Generally, the carbon-13 isotope is produced as an intermediate in stellar nucleo-synthetic reactions based on hydrogen-fusion and in the core of large middle-aged stars, as part of the carbon-nitrogen-oxygen cycle (known as the CNO-cycle). At the end of the life of a large star, convection brings this carbon-13 to the stellar surface.

The carbon-12 isotope is made by helium-fusion in the deep reaction shells in older stars by the triple-alpha-process, which involves the nucleo-synthetic reactions based on helium-fusion. The great abundance of carbon-12 on Earth is probably the result of this type of nucleosynthesis in the later life of the ten-solar-mass companion-star.

NUCLEOSYNTHESIS IN THE CORE OF STARS

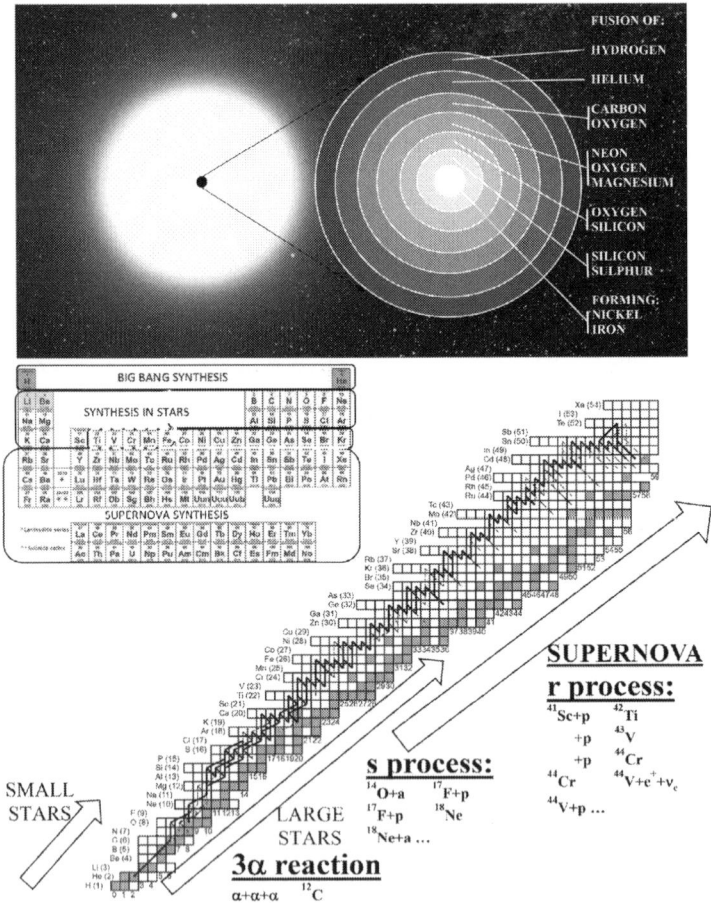

The supernova that destroyed the companion star ruptured its inner fusion zone and scattered huge quantities of carbon-12 and small amounts of carbon-13 in the form of graphite and silicon-carbide dust. Ninety-nine percent of dust grains in the solar-system were made during the life-time of the companion-star.[840] Earth and meteorites have a higher ratio of carbon-13-to-carbon-12 than the solar wind, evidence that the carbon in planets and meteorites did not come from the same matter that formed the Sun.[841]

Oxygen Isotopes of the Companion-Star

All the oxygen we breathe was made in the companion-star. Oxygen in air is mainly the oxygen-16 isotope, plus tiny amounts of oxygen-17 and oxygen-18.

The huge quantities of oxygen-16 isotope found in the solar-system were produced deep in the companion-star, by late-stage helium-fusion nucleo-synthesis. The oxygen-16 isotope was also manufactured by the slow *s*-process nucleo-synthesis, involving slow neutron-capture by low-mass-nuclei. Early-stage helium-fusion in the inner shells of the companion-star produced the oxygen-18. Accretion-nova reactions described below were responsible for most of the oxygen-17. The bulk of the oxygen isotopes found on Earth were probably blasted out when the supernova destroyed the companion-star.[842]

The oxygen-16:oxygen-17:oxygen-18 isotope ratio on Earth, Moon, and Mars are all essentially identical to each other, but different from the isotope ratio in the Sun.[843] This was revealed when the NASA spacecraft Genesis launched in AD 2001 collected particles ejected from the Sun and carried away by the solar wind.[844] When Genesis crash-landed back on Earth in the autumn of AD 2004, its solar-wind samples were found to have seven percent less oxygen-17 and oxygen-18 than expected, when compared to oxygen-16.[845, 846]

It was a surprise that the relative abundance of oxygen-16:oxygen-17:oxygen-18 from the Sun was different from Earth, Moon, and Mars. Dust particles also have thirteen times more oxygen-18 relative to oxygen-16 than the solar-wind and the Sun. The only reasonable conclusion is that the matter that built the Earth-Moon system and Mars was not the same as the matter in the Sun. This is more evidence that the matter of the planets came from the companion-star.

Accretion Nova Isotopes of the Old Binary-System

The accretion-nova-isotopes detected in the interplanetary dust of the solar-system provide direct evidence that long ago the Sun had been part of a close-binary star-system. The Sun and the companion-star probably orbited each other much closer than Venus. Prior to its violent death, the companion-star sucked in hydrogen from the Sun, which fuelled a special type of hydrogen-fusion process.

When the hydrogen gas pulled from the Sun arrived on the hot surface of the companion-star, it triggered accretion-nova explosions, powered by a nuclear fusion reaction known as the hot-CNO-cycle or explosive hydrogen burning.[847] The result was the synthesis of accretion-nova-isotopes.[848]

The mixtures of isotopes found in solar-system dust also suggests that the companion-star had an intense magnetic field and that stellar flares blasted these newly synthesized accretion-nova-isotopes away from the surface into space as a sooty dust. There is also evidence that toward the end of the life of the companion-star, churning convection-cells mixed the newly manufactured isotopes at its surface.

Oxygen-16 and oxygen-18, together with silicon, were also blown off the hot surface of the companion-star by magnetically-driven coronal mass ejections to produce dusty silicon-dioxide and silicates. The high silicon-30 to silicon-28 isotope ratio detected in solar-system dust can be attributed to large silicon-30 enrichments from the accretion nova explosions.[849] Generally, the isotope ratios detected in silicon-carbide dust grains correlate well with the products of accretion-nova nucleo-synthesis reactions on the surface of a ten solar mass companion-star.

There is only one atom of oxygen-17 for every three thousand atoms of oxygen-16 in solar-system dust and meteorites. This low abundance is consistent with a small proportion of the fresh hydrogen fuel sucked in from the Sun, being delivered by convection to the hotter helium reaction layers, deeper inside the companion-star.

BINARY ACCRETION SYNTHESIS

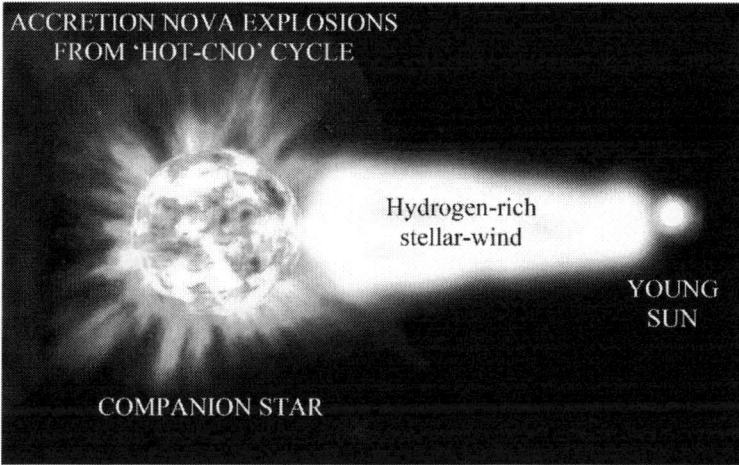

ACCRETION NOVA EXPLOSIONS
FROM 'HOT-CNO' CYCLE

Hydrogen-rich
stellar-wind

YOUNG
SUN

COMPANION STAR

HYDROGEN DRIVEN
'HOT-CNO' CYCLE

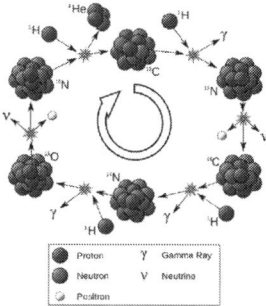

ACCRETION NOVA EXPLOSION
IN A BINARY STAR SYSTEM

Mróz, P., Warsaw University Astronomical Observatory.

The Abundance of Iron-56

There are huge quantities of iron-56 in nickel-iron meteorites and in the cores of the planets. It remains an enigma how the huge nickel-iron meteorites originally formed. The Hoba-West nickel-iron meteorite is a square block three meters across discovered in South Africa, and the nickel iron meteorite that punched out the huge and approximately square Meteor Crater in Arizona was calculated to have been fifty meters across.

Elements and isotopes up to the mass of nickel-56 were originally synthesized near the center of the companion-star, in the layered onion-like structure of its concentric fusion-reaction shells. Nickel-56 is a radioactive isotope with a short half-life that rapidly decays into cobalt-56 and then iron-56 in less than one year.[850]

In stars larger than eight solar-masses, the progressive nuclear fusion eventually leads to an accumulation of radioactive nickel-56 at the end of a series of energy-yielding fusion-reactions in the core. In the final hours of the companion-star's life, the fusion reactions shut down and the star rapidly cooled and started to collapse in on itself.

As the companion-star shrank, its angular momentum was conserved by its core spinning up to an ultra-high rotation-rate. The core started to disintegrate just before the main supernova implosion-explosion, which totally destroyed the companion-star. During this process, even more nickel-56 was abruptly produced, and huge lumps of nickel-56-rich core-fragments were thrown out into space. Some of this material was captured by the Sun and went on to form the metal cores of the planets.

Proton Bombardment in the Magnetic Companion-Star

The companion-star was a large rapidly-rotating magnetic-star. At its rotation axis, an ultra-powerful helical magnetic field collimated and accelerated protons to a significant percent of light-speed, creating bipolar axial jets. These ultra-high-energy protons bombarded other atomic nuclei to produce new *p*-process isotopes, in a process known as proton-spallation.

Almost instantly after manufacture, these *p*-process reaction products were blasted away from the companion-star along the axial-jets and spewed out as new solar-system dust.[851] The remains of radioactive beryllium-10 discovered in the SiC grains of solar-system dust and in the Murchison meteorite is evidence of this proton-spallation process.[852] The abundance of heavier elements clustered around the mass-number ninety, found in meteorites and solar-system dust, is further evidence of *p*-process nucleo-synthesis of our companion star.[853]

Nitrogen-14 and Nitrogen-15 Production

Almost all our atmospheric nitrogen is made of the nitrogen-14 isotope. The nitrogen in our atmosphere and the nitrogen in other solar-system objects seem to come from the same source, which is different to the matter that forms the Sun.

This nitrogen-14 was produced by hydrogen-fusion of carbon-13 in the so-called cold-CNO cycle (cold-carbon-nitrogen-oxygen-cycle) and in the deep reaction shells of the companion star. Over time, the companion-star accumulated huge quantities of nitrogen-14 in its core.[854] The enormous amounts of nitrogen-14 found in the solar-system was probably scattered into space during the supernova explosion, which destroyed our companion-star.

In contrast, nitrogen-15 was produced in two ways: accretion-nova nucleosynthesis on the surface of the companion-star and during the supernova explosion that destroyed it. Nitrogen-15 is produced explosively by proton-capture in a hot-CNO-cycle on the stellar surface of a large companion-star, fed with new hydrogen from a close-binary partner. This hot-CNO-cycle results in nitrogen-15 production by either proton-capture by nitrogen-14 followed by beta-decay or proton-capture via unstable oxygen-14.[855]

Nitrogen-15 is also produced by neutron capture in a supernova explosion. However, some models predict that Nitrogen-15 is only efficiently produced by a supernova if the progenitor star is very large, more than twenty-five times the mass of the Sun. The nitrogen-15 abundance detected in SiC-X grains in meteorites and space-dust suggests the likely source was accretion nova synthesis during the life of the close-binary partnership of the Sun and companion, rather than the supernova explosion of the companion-star.[856]

In contrast, the NASA Genesis spacecraft revealed the nitrogen-isotope-ratio produced by the Sun is quite different. The solar wind has about forty percent less nitrogen-15 than the abundance of nitrogen-15 in the atmospheres of Earth, Venus, and in Martian meteoric rocks.[857] The nitrogen on Earth probably originated from the inner regions of the companion-star, which erupted during the supernova explosion.

The nitrogen-15 to nitrogen-14 ratio also varies significantly between other solar-system objects. The amount of nitrogen-15 in Jupiter's atmosphere is about five percent higher than in the Sun.[858, 859] The atmosphere of Jupiter seems to be derived from the outer convective layer of the companion star.

In contrast, ancient titanium-nitrogen inclusions in chondrite meteorites have double the amount of nitrogen-15 compared to Earth and three times that of the Sun.[860, 861] Cometary dust has also been found to have similar high-levels of nitrogen-15.[862] Interplanetary dust particles have been found to contain organic macromolecules with high levels of nitrogen-15, more deuterium but less carbon-13 than Earth.[863, 864] In addition, the nitrogen-15 content of the meteoric amino-acids is also very high, and the smaller the amino-acid, the higher the nitrogen-15 content.[865] This is a clue to the origin of life, which shall be discussed in the Appendix A and Appendix B.

Some mysterious data links nitrogen-15 concentration peaks in ocean-cores and ice-cores on Earth to star-core-zeus related cataclysms (described in earlier chapters).[866, 867] For example, a Pacific Ocean core drilled off the coast of Alaska, showed abrupt ocean heating around 13,600 BC and around 9600 BC, which coincided with sudden increases of nitrogen-15 fall-out.[868] This data reveals that extra-terrestrial nitrogen-15 is still being regularly delivered to Earth by star-core-zeus, every four thousand years.

Violent Convection in the Companion Star

Generally, the isotopic ratios in the star-dust found in the solar-system can be accounted for by a combination of *s*-process nucleo-synthesis, which occurred during the life of the companion-star, and *r*-process supernova nucleo-synthesis.

The massive companion-star got very hot at the end of its short life. Its churning and boiling surface shed material as a dense stellar-wind of sooty-dust, just before the supernova detonation.[869] There is evidence of stormy convection at the end of the companion-star's life in the ratios of isotopes, which reveal significant mixing of different reaction-zones in its interior. The ratio of nitrogen-14:carbon-13:carbon-12 in the dust of the solar-system is evidence of the turbulent state of the companion-star before it blew-up.[870]

Nitrogen-14 and carbon-13 are important intermediate products of the CNO-cycle in fusion-reaction-shells deep in the star. However, violent convection must have brought them up to the surface. Some of the carbon-12 brought to the surface was destroyed by accretion nova explosions. This explosive hydrogen burning depleted carbon-12 and caused the lower carbon-12 to carbon-13 ratios, found in the silicon-carbide grains of solar-system dust.

Silicon-28 and titanium-44 were also synthesized in the deep oxygen-rich reaction shells near the core of the companion-star and then coughed up to the stellar surface and ejected as dust. Titanium-44 has a half-life of only sixty years, and daughter products of titanium-44 found in the silicon-carbide grains is further evidence of the violent convection that was occurring just before the supernova abruptly destroyed the companion-star. The carbon and nitrogen isotopic signatures in the solar-system dust-grains also provide evidence of this premature supernova detonation, when the companion-star still had significant amounts of hydrogen.[871]

Conclusion

The iron in the core of our planet and in our machines, the silicon in the rocks beneath our feet, the carbon in our bodies, and the oxygen and nitrogen we breathe were all made in the fusion-furnace of our companion star.

Then at the end of its life, the companion-star blew-up in a violent type-two-supernova-explosion. The isotopic evidence of the violent death of a star are all around us, like the finger-prints left at a crime-scene. This evidence shall be considered in the next chapter.

CHAPTER 15

Isotopic Evidence for Our Local Supernova

● ● ●

THE TRUTH ABOUT THE ORIGIN of the solar-system can be found in the complex mixtures of isotopes of the elements, which make up the materials of our solar-system. For example, the gold in our jewelry and uranium in our weapons can be traced back to the supernova explosion that destroyed the former companion-star of our Sun.

Some of the isotopes detected in star-dust and meteorites and in the rocks of the Earth, Moon, and Mars are obviously fractions of a type-two supernova explosion of a large star. The range of isotopes is consistent with an unstable rapidly-rotating magnetic star, ten times the mass of the Sun, which blew-up immediately before the accretion of the planets. In addition, the abundance of hydrogen and the range of elements with atomic-numbers between silicon and iron is evidence that the supernova explosion happened prematurely, before all the hydrogen fuel had been consumed.[872, 873]

Asymmetric Supernova Explosions

Asymmetry is required in most theoretical simulations of core-collapse supernova explosions.[874] There is a growing understanding that high rotation rates in large stars causes the reaction-core to be exposed at its poles, which triggers early detonation.[875, 876] In single-stars, high rotation rates of progenitor stars tend to produce bipolar-explosions along the rotation axis of the star.[877]

In binary-star-systems, tidal-forces induce an aspheric collapse of the iron core of the progenitor star. The asymmetric-shape of the blast that follows has its origin in asymmetries deep in the star. The significance of asymmetric supernova explosions is that they give rise to the ejection of relatively low-mass star-cores.

SUPERNOVA ISOTOPE SYNTHESIS

Much of the element abundance in the solar system is attributable to the supernova neutron-impact r-process. [Wallerstein, G., et al., "Synthesis of the elements in stars: forty years of progress"*Reviews of Modern Physics*, Vol. 69, No. 4, October 1997]

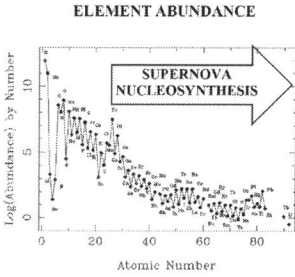

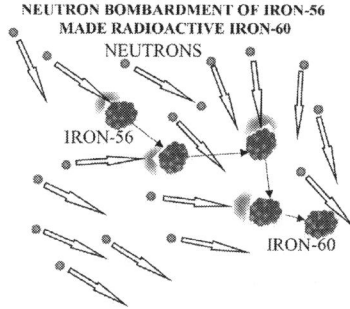

ELEMENT ABUNDANCE

NEUTRON BOMBARDMENT OF IRON-56
MADE RADIOACTIVE IRON-60

Decay products of short half-life radioactive isotopes found in meteorites, are evidence of a type two supernova explosion adjacent to the Sun, just before the formation of the solar system. Observations of Supernova 1987a has provided evidence of short-half life radioactive isotopes heating its explosion debris ring, fifty years after the main detonation.

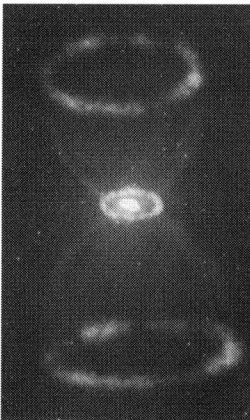

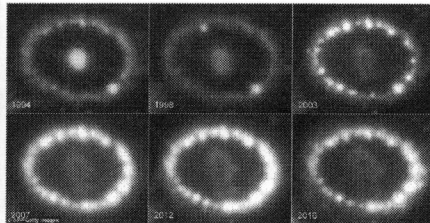

Studies of a number of supernova explosions in binary systems have shown that generally the blast waves are focused in one direction, resulting in a star-core blasting-off in the opposite direction. High space-velocities have been detected for most neutron-stars, showing they were all fired off in one direction by asymmetric-supernova-propellant.[878]

An example of this large-scale asymmetry and very high velocity material is the explosion remnant of supernova SN1987A, where most of the ejecta was blasted out in lobes. Hydrogen-rich explosion debris reveals early detonation and the asymmetric shock-fronts suggested perturbation by a binary partner.

There are heavy plumes of Nickle-56 isotope from its ruptured core, which are acting like rocket-propellant and traveling at four-thousand kilometers-per-second away from us. A star-core was kicked out of the explosion-center, which is traveling at high-velocity toward us.[879]

Another example is Cassiopeia A, located eleven thousand light-years from Earth. It blew up as a type-2b supernova and became visible about three hundred and forty years ago. X-ray emissions and three-dimensional maps of the isotopes produced by Cassiopeia A reveal iron in the shock-heated material and that the main shell rings seem to be reverse-shock heated cavities, created by explosion-plumes of highly radioactive Nickle-56.[880]

The debris of this supernova is expanding on average at about five-thousand kilometers-per-second, forming a spherical explosion shell about six light-years in radius. However, this explosion-bubble of expanding debris is decelerating rapidly.

The massive star-core of Cassiopeia A was first discovered in AD 1948 as a powerful radio-star, which is traveling at high velocity away from the center of the explosion.[881] It is highly magnetic and has powerful radio-jets, which are orientated almost perpendicular to its direction of travel. It is a hard X-ray source, which identifies it as a neutron-star.

Observations of Cassiopeia A have provided evidence of the convective instabilities and asymmetries of the original massive star, before the core-collapse supernova.[882] A large amount of radioactive Titanium-44 relative to Nickle-56 seems to be the fingerprint of an asymmetric supernova explosion. Titanium-44 is synthesized in the exploding star near the boundary between material falling back onto the collapsing star-core and debris ejected into the surrounding space.

Titanium-44 emits very hard X-rays when it radioactively decays, which were observed with the NuSTAR spacecraft launched in 2012, using its Nuclear Spectroscopic Telescope Array. The pattern of titanium-rich debris has provided information on the asymmetries of the supernova explosion.

The titanium-44 distribution suggests it was an imbalance in mass at the equator of the progenitor star that triggered the supernova explosion. This may have been caused by a partner-star in a former close-binary-star-system. An example of a similar event has been observed in another binary-star-system, in which a low-mass white-dwarf was shot out by an asymmetric-supernova-explosion.[883]

Cassiopeia-A was an asymmetric supernova explosion, with aspheric shock-front bubbles and high speed jets of debris. The majority of material was blasted in one direction, and a dense star-core is recoiling away in the other direction. The huge momentum of this massive star-core seems to have been powered by the expanding explosion bubble of reverse-shocked iron-56, which blasted away in the opposite direction from the star-core.

However, the mechanism is more complicated because there are also two powerful exhaust plumes rich in silicon and sulfur, expanding at ultra-high velocity in opposite directions, traveling at an incredible fifteen-thousand kilometers-per-second.[884]

The Magnetic Supernova Detonator

Generally, stars of more than eight solar masses, like our companion-star, tend to be highly magnetic when they form.[885] In fact, magnetic fields play an important role in all stages of stellar evolution.[886, 887]

It is now understood that gravity alone cannot trigger a supernova explosion. Dynamic instabilities and powerful magnetic fields acting on the core of the doomed star seem to be required.[888] Our companion-star was like a time-bomb, with its rapidly rotating electrically-charged plasma producing an intense magnetic field, which determined the moment of supernova ignition. One theory is that detonation of a supernova is caused by the helical magnetic field lines surrounding the rotation axis of the star.[889]

Powerful stellar magnetic fields are also responsible for highly asymmetric supernova blast waves.[890] Models of supernova explosions in magnetic stars predict two high-velocity jets of material moving in opposite polar directions, while the slower moving highly distorted ejecta from the equatorial regions contains most of the debris and often form rings.[891, 892]

Large magnetic stars in binary systems are even more unstable. An example of such a binary system is currently being observed at Nu-Carinae: the bigger magnetic-star is about ninety times the mass of the Sun and expected to blow-up soon. The two large stars orbit each other in eccentric ellipses, and the interaction between their magnetic fields produces wild fluctuations in radiation output.[893]

Supernova *r*-process Isotopes in the Solar-System

Elements of the periodic table from iron up to the heaviest atoms like gold and uranium were all synthesized in the supernova explosion of our companion-star. They were created in energy-consuming rapid-*r*-process nucleo-synthesis. The reaction is driven by high-energy neutrons crashing into low-to-middle mass atomic-nuclei produced during the life of the star.

The *r*-process-isotopes in the solar-system point to a type-two supernova, which blew up adjacent to the Sun, four-point-five-seven billion years ago. This explosion was the source of all short-lived nuclides with atomic masses greater than one-hundred-and-forty.[894, 895, 896]

During the supernova explosion that destroyed our massive companion-star, the energy-absorbing nucleo-synthetic *r*-process produced vast amounts of new elemental matter in minutes.[897] These ultra-rapid neutron-capture reactions produced a spectrum of elements from iron-56, up to heavy radioactive isotopes of polonium, thorium, uranium, and plutonium.

The huge abundance of the radioactive decay products of iron-60 in the solar-system provides strong evidence that a supernova explosion adjacent to our Sun triggered the formation of the solar-system.[898, 899, 900, 901] The iron-60 was originally produced in the early stage of our type-two supernova explosion by *r*-process nucleo-synthesis in which four high-energy neutrons rammed each iron-56 atom to produce enormous amounts of iron-60.[902, 903]

The extra neutrons make iron-60 unstable, so it radioactively decays with a half-life of two-point-six million years, by the ejection of an electron from a neutron to make a new proton, creating its daughter-product cobalt-60 in the process. Cobalt-60 is also unstable and radioactively decays with a half-life of five-point-three million years, ejecting an electron to become stable nickel-60.

All the oldest meteorites, the silicon-carbide SiC grains, and other types of star dust contain nickel-60 in tiny droplets of formerly molten nickel-iron metal. Nickel-60 is also found in the nickel-iron alloy of large metallic meteorites. This nickel-60 is the remains of short-lived radioactive iron-60, which had been produced in *r*-process nucleosynthesis during the supernova of our companion star.[904] The largest nickel-iron meteor is the Hoba West meteorite, discovered in South Africa. Hoba West is a massive sixty ton square slab of metal, three meters by three meters by one meter. The nickel-iron alloy is contaminated with supernova isotopes and decay products such as helium-3, aluminum-26, Nickel-59, and cobalt-60.[905]

Microscopic analysis of the location and amount of nickel-60 in the Semarkona and Chervony Kut meteorites, compared with the abundance of the stable iron isotopes, revealed that iron-60 must have formed suddenly in a single type-two supernova explosion, at exactly the same time as the solar-system building materials were formed.[906, 907] The nickel isotopes in samples of material from Earth, Mars, and asteroids support the hypothesis of a supernova explosion adjacent to the Sun, immediately before the formation of the planets.[908, 909]

In addition, the remains of iron-60 and its decay products found in the deep-ocean crust of Earth from the Indian Ocean, Atlantic, and Pacific not only confirms that Earth is built from the same supernova products but shows that regular deliveries of supernova materials to Earth have continued since the formation of our planet.[910, 911, 912]

Other Supernova Isotopes
The dust and meteorites of the solar-system contain mixtures of other isotopes derived from *r*-process nucleo-synthesis. Nano-diamonds in

the dust and meteorites of the solar-system contain an excess abundance of xenon-136 and unusual tellurium isotopic ratios, which could only have been made in rapid *r*-process nucleo-synthesis during a local type-two supernova explosion. The daughter products of short half-life manganese-53 and iodine-129 in meteoric material are more evidence of this type-2 supernova.

Collectively, the isotopes found in space-dust and meteorites support the hypothesis of a single supernova explosion, which destroyed a large magnetic rapidly-spinning star, located adjacent to the Sun, just before the formation of solar-system building-materials.

Mirror-Matched Isotope Mixtures

Further evidence for this single local supernova is an odd relationship called "mirror-matching," between the ratios of supernova-related elements and isotopes in different classes of meteorites. For example, samples from one class of meteorite have a deficiency of an isotope that is exactly balanced by an excess of the same isotope in another class of meteorite.

A good example is the mirror-matching between the Allende meteorite and Murchison meteorite. The Allende has an excess of isotopes produced by the *r*-process and *p*-process, such as barium, neodymium, and samarium, which are mirrored by deficits of the same isotopes in the Murchison meteorite.[913]

This mirror-matching is too precise to be due to chance alone: it is evidence of the fractionation of a single set of nucleo-synthetic reaction-products, in debris from a single local explosion.[914] Mirror-matched-isotopes provide additional strong evidence of the single supernova explosion, which occurred adjacent to the Sun, just before the planets formed.

Ancient Rocks and Very Short Half-Life Isotopes

The daughter products of very-short half-life radioactive isotopes are locked in rock-lattices of meteorites and certain archaic rocks on Earth.[915] They tell us that the supernova debris turned to stone extraordinarily rapidly.

The early formation of solid materials in the solar-system was recorded by the presence of xenon-129 in rocks. This isotope is the daughter product of radioactive iodine-129 produced in type two supernova explosions, which has a half-life of about sixteen-million years.

Large amounts of the daughter products of unstable beryllium-10, the radioactive isotope produced by the high-energy proton-bombardment *p*-process, in the radio-jets of the companion-star have been found in ancient calcium-aluminum-inclusions in meteorites. Beryllium-10 has a half-life of only one-point-four million years, so solid rock must have formed more rapidly than this to capture its daughter isotopes.[916]

The age of the earliest solid rock was pushed back even further by the evidence of the decay products of short-lived radioactive aluminum-26. Intense neutron-bombardment during the supernova explosion, which destroyed our companion-star, produced a huge amount of the radioactive isotope aluminum-26, which has a half-life of seven-hundred-and-thirty thousand years, and decays into stable magnesium-26.

Silicon-carbide SiC grains in meteorites contain highly elevated amounts of magnesium-26 relative to magnesium-24, indicating that they used to contain huge amounts of short-lived radioactive aluminum-26, which must have been trapped in the solid phase of SiC meteorites, less than one million years after they were formed.[917] The abundance of daughter products of aluminum-26 and the high ratio of aluminum-26 to aluminum-27 in meteorites shows these newly created radioactive isotopes had been rapidly trapped in solid rock particles.[918, 919]

A huge abundance of magnesium-26 derived from aluminum-26 was also discovered in the Allende meteorite.[920] In the Allende meteorite, fixed in the calcium-aluminum-inclusions, there is a ten percent excess of magnesium-26, the decay product of aluminum-26. These meteoric calcium-aluminum-inclusions are found in all carbonaceous chondrite meteorites and are four-point-five-seven billion years old, the oldest measured radiometric age for any solar-system material.[921] This aluminum-26 had been produced in a type two supernova and then rapidly trapped in solid rock, immediately before meteorite and planet formation.[922]

The wide range of other daughter products of unstable isotopes with ultra-short half-lives confirms the rapid solidification of the explosion debris of the companion-star. Another example is argon-36 derived from chlorine-36, which has a half-life of three-hundred-thousand years. The similar rapid condensation of solids after the supernova explosion was also recorded in the isotopes of xenon, krypton, and tellurium, which are fixed into the carbon lattice of nanodiamonds in meteorites and star dust.

Evidence of even more rapid formation of solid materials in the solar-system was also confirmed by potassium-41 in meteorites and dust. Potassium-41 is the daughter product of unstable calcium-41, produced by neutron bombardment of calcium-40 in the supernova r-process. Calcium-41 only has a half-life of one-hundred-thousand years, so this radioactive isotope was very rapidly trapped in solid rock.

The unstable titanium-44 isotope was produced during the final stages of s-process synthesis in the deep interior of the companion-star and also suddenly during r-process nucleosynthesis of the supernova explosion. Titanium oxide and titanium carbide in solar-system dust now contain only tiny amounts of radioactive titanium-44, but there is a huge excess of calcium-44, its daughter isotope. This is the result of in-situ decay of titanium-44, which has a half-life of only *fifty-nine* years, so excess calcium-44 is evidence of the extremely rapid solidification of the supernova explosion debris.

Finally, the discovery of the decay products of supernova-produced iodine-131, bromine-83, and antimony-125 in meteorites was extraordinary. These elements were fixed in the solid matter before the decay of the parent isotopes, a mere *three hours* after the supernova explosion.

One Local Supernova Explosion 4.568 billion Years Ago

Microscopic analysis of the isotopic ratios points to a single source for all the elements and isotopes in the dust, meteorites, and planets of our solar-system. Using a variety of radioactive isotope decay series, the date of the supernova that destroyed the companion-star of the Sun can be accurately determined.

As the data accumulated, the decay products of the unstable isotopes found together in both meteorites and in solar-system dust, all gave approximately the same date for a supernova explosion at the birth of our solar-system.[923, 924, 925] More recently, an exact date of this supernova has been obtained from the ratios of a range of decay products of a combination of unstable isotopes: calcium-41, aluminum-26, manganese-53, lead-107, hafnium-182, iodine-129, plutonium-244, and samarium-146, which are found together in both meteorites and solar-system dust. The supernova explosion of our companion-star occurred precisely, four-point-five-six-eight billion years ago.[926]

The next chapter reveals how the planets were born out of the portion of the supernova-debris, which had been captured by our Sun.

CHAPTER 16

From Supernova Debris to Planets

● ● ●

IN THE PREVIOUS CHAPTER, ISOTOPIC anomalies were described that prove the dust and meteorites in our solar-system were the product of one supernova explosion, which destroyed the large companion-star of the Sun. There is also physical and chemical evidence for this local supernova at the birth of our solar-system in the dust, meteorites, and planets.

Supernova Dust

The discredited solar-nebular-model assumed a cold cloudy nebula of icy-dust, which slowly stuck together at very low temperatures, long before the start of planet-accretion and ignition of the Sun. On the contrary, the glassy droplets inside the dust and meteorites of the solar-system record the intense heat of a supernova just before the planets formed.

All star-dust particles in the solar-system have a matrix of tiny glassy and metallic droplets.[927] The beads of once-molten rock are evidence of ultra-high temperature in which rock and even pure carbon was molten.[928] The silicon-carbide SiC-X grains contain silicon-nitride (Si_3N_4) glass, which has a melting point of two-thousand-two-hundred Kelvin.[929] Generally, the silicon-carbide SiC grains in the star-dust consist of isotope mixtures of silicon, carbon, nitrogen, and calcium, consistent with their origin in a local supernova explosion.[930]

Solar-system-dust also contains carbon in the form of glass, diamond, graphite, and fullerene, which had been formed at high temperatures and pressures. The carbon-glass in the dust had been produced at an extreme temperature of four thousand Kelvin, prior to sudden cooling.

Nano-diamonds are also abundant both in the interplanetary dust and the dust in comets.[931] The average carbon isotope ratio in the nano-diamonds is similar across the whole solar-system.[932] The nano-diamonds also contain isotopes of nitrogen and xenon that are rare on Earth but common in the energetic remnants of stars that blew-up as type-2 supernova explosions.[933] The silicon-nitride-glass, carbon-glass, and nano-diamonds are direct chemo-physical evidence of the high temperatures and pressures of our local supernova.

Other interplanetary-dust-particles contain organic macromolecules with unusually high levels of nitrogen-15. Interplanetary dust particles collected in Earth's upper atmosphere on average are about twelve percent carbon and have a range of isotopes related to chondrite meteorites, but they also have a large excess of deuterium and nitrogen-15, compared to the Sun.[934] This is evidence that all the carbon-rich dust came from the remains of the companion-star.

Meteorites Are Made of Supernova Debris

The mixtures of elements and isotopes in the stony-chondrite-meteorites reveal they rapidly solidified four-point-five-seven billion years ago, from the debris of a type-two supernova explosion adjacent to the Sun.[935, 936] The bulk of the chondrite-meteorites accreted from the portion of the cloud of explosion debris captured by the Sun, immediately before the formation of the planets.

The ultra-high rotation rate developed by the companion-star as it collapsed caused its core to fling off enormous lumps of hot liquid nickel-iron. These chunks of metal were blasted out during the supernova explosion to produce nickel-iron-meteorites, which soon accreted to form planet-cores.

In contrast, the stony-meteorites were formed from the supernova explosion-plume of vaporized materials, which cooled and condensed into droplets of glass, rock-grains, and dust. Collectively, these meteorites are so similar to rocks of Earth's crust that they are probably remnants of the material from which the original surface of the Earth formed.

The stony chondrite-meteorites contain melted glassy millimeter-to-centimeter-sized droplets of silicate and metallic materials, called chondrules.[937] These beads of formerly-molten rocks were fused together at high temperature, evidence of the high temperature post-supernova process, which occurred in our solar-system.[938]

The chondrules formed at over two-thousand Kelvin and then rapidly-cooled at a rate around five hundred Kelvin-per-hour. Star-dust particles can also be found heat-fused inside chondrite meteorites.[939] Mysterious magnetic fields have been detected in the olivine chondrules of the Semarkona meteorite, showing that a powerful magnetic field was associated with the supernova debris.[940]

Chondrite-meteorites also record evidence of a diverse range of reaction conditions after the companion-star blew up. Thermal metamorphism, shock metamorphism, and aqueous alteration all modified the material. There is evidence for a sea of dusty hot-water droplets orbiting the Sun after the supernova explosion, which formed the hydrous-silicates found in Earth-crustal rock and stony meteorites.

The chondrule material was later re-heated, re-melted, and metamorphosed, after it had clumped to form the chondrite meteorites. The probable heat-source was the decay of the short-lived radioactive isotopes from the supernova, trapped in the chondrite meteorites at their formation.

Local conditions in different regions of the explosion plume gave rise to the different bulk compositions of chondrite meteorites. The chemical-compositions and the proportions of different types of chondrules vary between chondrite groups. Chondrites are grouped into three principal classes, and then these classes are divided into numerous subgroups.

Generally, chondrite meteorites are fused concretions made mainly from carbon, silicon, oxygen, calcium, aluminum, and titanium. They have been compounded into very high-melting-point materials such as the ultra-hard corundum form of aluminum-oxide and perovskite, a calcium-sodium-iron-titanium-oxide. In addition, there is silicon-carbide, silicon-nitride, and diamond together with melilite, a high-melting-point mineral made of calcium-sodium-magnesium-iron-aluminum-silicon-oxide.

Chondrite meteorites also contain high-melting-point titanium-silicon complexes. An important but minor constituent of chondrite-meteorites are glassy-droplets called the calcium-aluminum-rich-inclusions, which were originally droplets of a very hot liquid, heated to a temperature around two-thousand-four-hundred Kelvin. These calcium-aluminum-rich-inclusions solidified when the temperature of the explosion debris dropped below fifteen-hundred Kelvin.[941]

Radiometric dating of daughter products of short-half-life isotopes in calcium-aluminum-rich-inclusions shows that they condensed very soon after the supernova explosion, about four-point-five-seven billion years ago. All calcium-aluminum-rich-inclusions have the same age allowing for measurement error, but their properties and abundances vary between chondrite-meteorite groups. Calcium-aluminum-rich-inclusions also show evidence of re-heating from the radioactive decay of short-half-life isotopes.

Chondrules and calcium-aluminum-rich-inclusions are surrounded by thin smooth rims and cemented together by a dark fine-grained matrix. In some cases, chondrules accreted their rims while they were still hot and plastic. Some of the carbon compounds in the dark matrix are in the form of insoluble graphite, diamond, and fullerene. About three percent of the carbon in chondrite meteorites is in the form of two-to-four-nanometer particles, made of high-melting-point carbon-glass and nano-diamond.[942]

Fullerenes found in meteorites encapsulate isotope mixtures of helium, xenon, and neon, consistent with their production in the local supernova explosion.[943] The nano-diamonds in chondrite meteorites also contain traces of xenon isotopes of supernova origin.[944] The fullerenes and nanodiamonds in carbonaceous chondrites must have formed simultaneously in a hot region of the explosion plume ejected from the local type-two supernova.[945].

The rims and matrix also contain highly volatile elements that escaped the highest temperatures in the explosion plume. The matrix and rims contain sodium, potassium, chlorine, and water. They also contain around two percent by weight organic carbon compounds, the bulk of which is macromolecular material. This matter was responsible for the origin of life, which shall be described in Appendix A and Appendix B.

The Anomalous Distribution of Chemical Elements

There is an anomalous distribution of chemical elements between the Sun and other material in the solar-system. The solar spectrum shows that by mass the Sun is seventy-one percent hydrogen, twenty-seven percent helium, and two percent other elements.[946] The full chemical composition of the Sun was determined from the line spectra of the solar corona. However, only sixty-seven of the chemical elements found on Earth were detected. It is an enigma why one-third of the elements found on Earth have never been detected in the solar atmosphere.

Light and volatile elements such as beryllium and boron, which are very common in the Earth's crust, are almost absent in the Sun. Even the volatile element lithium, which is abundant on Earth, is only present in tiny quantities in the solar atmosphere. In addition, there is no evidence that the missing elements are just trapped in the core of the Sun.

Planet Formation

It is an enigma that planets contain heavy elements that are never detected in the Sun. The gold and uranium in the crust of the Earth strongly suggest that the Earth was made of materials that came from the supernova explosion that destroyed our companion-star.

The supernova explosion ejected enormous lumps of molten nickel-iron, plus a hot dense cloud of supernova debris containing molten-rock droplets, dust, and gas. Some of the chunks of molten metal, which were thrown out of the shattered core of the companion-star, may even have been the size of small planets.

The tidal bulges caused by the attraction between the Sun and companion-star resulted in the blast of the supernova being directed toward the Sun. Some of the flying-debris passed close enough to the Sun to be captured by its gravitational field. The remaining material from the explosion plume blasted beyond the Sun to become the huge twenty-five light-year wide cloud of Fluff that stretches toward the bright star Cygnus.

The captured matter began revolving around the Sun in a doughnut-shaped cloud, forming a dense torus of debris centered around the orbits of Jupiter and Saturn, which was highly magnetized.[947] The supernova explosion of the companion-star provided this rapidly revolving torus of debris with a much higher angular momentum than the matter rotating in the Sun.

Although the collective cloud of captured material resembled a fat ring around the Sun, individual pieces of debris were in eccentric elliptical orbits. Some objects traveled in extreme orbits from aphelia beyond the orbit of Neptune to perihelia very close to the Sun. In two-dimensions, the dense torus of explosion debris can be visualized as a dense ring made up of a huge number of orbital paths, which can be drawn as a spirograph pattern of multiple ellipses.

The stellar explosion debris started to rapidly accrete from the hot cloud of debris onto massive molten lumps of metal. These enormous chunks of nickel-iron quickly accreted to form the massive cores of eight planets and stimulated the rapid accretion of more explosion debris. An example of the size of these lumps of metal is found at the Sudbury Structure in Ontario, Canada. A fifteen-kilometer-diameter lump of nickel-iron, rich in nickel-copper sulfide, impacted the old crust of Earth, more than two billion years ago.[948]

The iron cores of the four rocky inner-planets formed from lumps of nickel-iron from the ruptured core of the companion-star that had flown closer to the Sun. As the infant-planet-cores fed off the doughnut-cloud of debris, they grew rapidly. They maintained a common direction of revolution and rotation, due to the dynamics of the related trajectories of the nickel-iron lumps of explosion debris.

The mantle and crust of the rocky planets mainly consist of silicon, aluminum, magnesium, oxygen, sulfur, iron, nickel, and other chemical elements, which had all been manufactured during the life of the companion-star and then ejected into the explosion plume of the supernova. Isotopic evidence shows that the planets formed very rapidly, certainly in less than one-hundred-million years and probably immediately after the supernova explosion destroyed the companion star of the Sun.[949]

This material started to condense as a cloud of dust and hot stony-meteorites. The gravity of the nickel-iron cores quickly pulled down this rocky material to make primitive crust. The isotopic mixture of

THE FORMATION OF THE SOLAR SYSTEM

The common plane and 'anti-clockwise' direction of motion of all the planets is a characteristic feature of our Solar System. It was the result of the rapid 'clockwise' rotation and revolution of the Companion Star in our former binary system. Tidal bulges induced by the Sun's gravity were displaced by the rapid rotation. An asymmetric supernova explosion of the Companion Star, aligned to the tidal bulges, caused the bulk of the debris to blast out in one direction, forcing the dense inner star-core to recoil in the opposite direction. As material flew past the Sun, more of the heavier matter from the outer shells of the core, was pulled into orbits closer to the Sun and formed the inner rocky planets. The lighter gas and water vapour from the convective zone spread out on a larger radius. Outer core fragments which were flung further out from the Sun, eventually collected the material from the Companion Star's convective layer, to form the gas-giant and ice-giant planets.

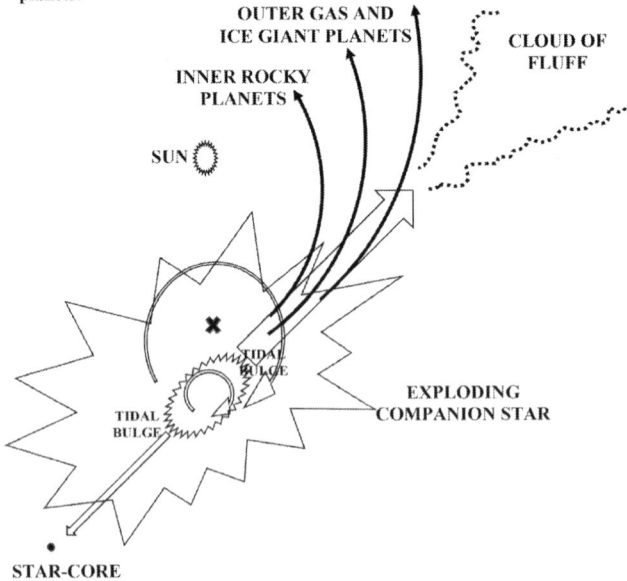

the material that accumulated on top of the metallic cores of Mercury, Venus, Earth, and Mars had originally formed in the outer-reaction shells surrounding the core of the companion-star. The lighter xenon isotope called xenon-124, from the convective region of the companion-star, has even been detected in archaic Precambrian crust of the Earth.[950]

The early-detonation of the companion-star meant it blew-up before all its hydrogen had been converted into heavier elements. The result was the large amount of hydrogen and oxygen in the solar-system, which is responsible for the abundance of water.

Further out in the torus of supernova debris surrounding the Sun, a collection of nickel-iron fragments, in total five-times the mass of Earth, formed the heavy cores of the gas giant planets Jupiter and Saturn. The cooling gaseous convective layer of the companion-star accumulated on these cores and rapidly grew into the gas-giants, as their gravity swept up the remaining material.

FORMATION OF THE PLANETS

As the supernova destroyed the Companion Star, debris was fired towards the Sun. The denser material was captured closer to the Sun, while lighter elements and gases were gathered into a huge toroidal cloud further out. The small dense rocky-planets formed from material blasted out of the outer core-shells, while low density gas-giants and ice-giants, formed from the convective layers of the Companion Star.

The planets accreted rapidly around the huge lumps of dense nickel-iron ejected from the shattered core of the Companion Star. An example is the massive Hoba-West nickel-iron meteorite discovered in South Africa (left) which is heavily contaminated with supernova isotopes [McCorkell et al, "Radioactive Isotopes in Hoba West and Other Iron Meteorites" Meteoritics 4 (1968):113-122]. The mantel and crust of Earth, and the other rocky planets, formed from concretions of explosion debris, similar to carbonaceous chondrite meteorites such as 'Allende' (right).

Generally, the giant planets accreted mainly lighter elements such as hydrogen, helium, carbon, nitrogen, and oxygen, which had been blasted out from the outer convective-region of the companion-star. Xenon-124 from the lighter convective zone of the companion-star has also been detected in the atmospheres of the outer giant planets.[951]

Even further out from the center of the new solar-system, the nickel-iron projectiles collected supernova explosion material rich in water vapor, which cooled rapidly, forming the ice giant-planets—Neptune and Uranus.

Sir Fred Hoyle's supernova-binary-model generally explains most of the known features of the solar-system, including the relative isotopic compositions of the planets, and also the separate isotopic composition of the hydrogen-rich Sun. Hoyle's model also provides a simple explanation for the distribution of angular momentum in the solar-system and the common direction of rotation and revolution of the eight planets.

In contrast, the solar-nebular-model cannot explain the angular momentum distribution in the solar-system. It also cannot explain how a huge rotating disc-shaped nebula, which concentrated most of its mass at its center, had built the planets from mixtures of isotopes, which are quite different from the isotopes in the Sun.

The solar-nebular-model also has serious problems building planets.[952] Starting from a diffuse nebula of planetary building material, computer simulations fail to create anything like our solar-system, unless initial conditions are applied that are totally inconsistent with the solar-nebular-model. For example, the only reliable way to produce Earth and Mars in a computer simulation is from a dense ring of rocks dumped near the present orbit of Earth.[953]

Other problems revealed by computer simulations are the difficulty in forming the gas giant planets—Jupiter and Saturn. The cores of Jupiter and Saturn have to be at least five Earth-masses, before they have enough gravity to accrete gas fast enough to form a gas-giant. The basic assumptions of the solar-nebular-model fail to produce gas-giants during the lifetime of the hypothetical nebular: the process is impossible starting from dust, an almost impossible from pebbles. The old solar-nebular-model also fails to explain the formation of Neptune and Uranus: they either require impossibly long growing times or an impossibly massive nebula.

According to the supernova-binary model proposed in this book, the planets formed around massive metallic bodies thrown out of the companion-star during a supernova explosion. In addition, during the accretion period, the growing planets had elongated elliptical orbits, stretched initially in the direction of the explosion plume, which progressively circularized.

To reach each perihelion fly-by of the Sun, the growing planetary bodies flew through a dense cloud of companion-star debris, which accelerated the accretion process. The intense bombardment of matter slamming onto their surfaces facing their direction of travel reduced their angular velocity. The resistive effect of traversing this dense cloud helped to circularized the orbits of the planets. In this hot environment near the Sun, the inner planets were stripped of most of their volatile elements. The gas giants and ice giants on different orbital tracks grew further out from the Sun.

Venus had a completely different history because soon after it formed as a new planet, it was captured by star-core-zeus. Venus was only recaptured by the Sun, twelve thousand years ago, and this story is described in my previous book *Cataclysms & Renewals*.

Formation of Earth

The original solid archaean crust of Earth was formed from fallout from a dense nebular of supernova explosion debris, onto the surface of a hot and massive nickel-iron body. Thin layers of sand-sized spherules discovered in ancient continental rocks are evidence of the dense early downpour of debris.[954]

Detrital-zircons dating back to at least four-point-four billion years ago, and the over four-billion-years-old continental-acasta-orthogeneiss rock, are the remains of the ancient rocky crust that formed the outer layer of the whole planet at this time.

The combination of large quantities of oxygen, silicon, and iron on Earth can be traced back to nucleo-synthesis deep in the companion-star.[955] However, the smaller quantities of heavy elements found in the crust of Earth were originally synthesized in the type-two supernova explosion, which destroyed the companion-star. The partitioning of isotopes in the crust is evidence that the rocks on Earth came from the matter made in the interior of the companion-star, and the planet formed very soon after the supernova explosion.

The xenon-131 to xenon-136 isotope ratio found in Earth's crust is the result of the decay of supernova produced plutonium-244, which has a half-life of eighty-one million years. Chromium-53 in continental rock is the remains of supernova produced radioactive manganese-53, which has a half-life of four million years.[956] Analysis of the in-situ chromium-53 in crustal rocks, the radioactive decay product of manganese-53, gives a date-of-birth of the Earth, very soon after the supernova explosion destroyed the companion-star, four-thousand-five-hundred-and-sixty-eight million years ago.[957]

Basalts derived from the Earth's upper mantle, as well as the gases in our present day atmosphere, contain excesses of xenon-129 from the radiogenic decay of the extinct parent Iodine-129, which has a half-life of sixteen million years. Earth must have formed rapidly before the complete decay of iodine-129 and Plutonium-244, their short-lived parent isotopes. Other data shows the first basalts were deposited onto the surface of Earth during initial planet formation. Some interplanetary-dust-particles of the inner solar-system are surprising: they are made of iron-rich olivine rock usually found in ocean-floor basalt.[958]

Evidence of Very Rapid Formation of Earth's Rocks

Samarium-146 is a radioactive isotope that was formed suddenly in the supernova explosion of the companion-star and has a short half-life of less than sixty-eight million years. Samarium-146 was almost immediately incorporated into our planet when it was still molten. Almost all the samarium-146 was partitioned into the molten basalt mantle, so the solid crust that floated to the top of the mantle-melt had very little samarium-146.

Very ancient "nuvvuagittuq" rock has been discovered at the northeastern edge of Hudson bay in Canada. The material was analyzed and found to have different proportions of neodymium-142 and other neodymium isotopes. These rocks formed at a time when there was still undecayed samarium-146 on Earth. This recent research has pushed back the date of formation of the oldest solid-rocks on Earth to four-point-four billion years ago.[959]

Other isotopic evidence of rapid planet formation comes from the unstable isotope hafnium-182, which decays to tungsten-182 with a half-life of only nine million years. During the first stage of planet formation, tungsten rapidly associated with molten-iron and combined with the young core of Earth, while hafnium remained on the surface silicate-slag that coated our molten planet. Using this dating method, iron cores of planets must have formed less than five-hundred-thousand years after the supernova that created the unstable isotope and other planet building materials.[960, 961]

Polonium-218 has been detected combined with rocky silicon dioxide debris, in the ejecta of violent supernova explosions of other stars.[962] This unstable isotope of polonium is produced by the gamma-process of nucleo-synthesis from oxygen-16, during the sudden implosive and explosive steps of a type-two supernova.

The in-situ daughter products of the unstable isotope polonium-218 in Earth-rock have been discovered in ancient granites. This is evidence for the extremely rapid formation of solid material that accreted to form the silicon-rich rocky crust, very soon after the supernova explosion that destroyed the companion-star.

Polonium-218 has a half-life of only *three minutes*, yet abundant micro-halos of polonium-218-daughter-products have been discovered in samples of archaean-rocks in the Canadian Shield, known to be more than four-point-four billion years old. These polonium halos show that the particles of rock, which later made up the bulk-granite, were solid just in minutes after the supernova nucleo-synthesis of polonium-218. This means the material of the granite crust of Earth first crystallized in space as a gritty dust in the explosion plume of the companion-star.

This data strongly suggests that the first crust of Earth formed from granite rock particles produced by a very rapid cooling of silicon-aluminum oxides, followed by rapid accretion on to a hot nickel-iron body ejected from the core of the companion-star.

Earth's Deuterium-Rich Water

Deuterium is heavy-hydrogen made of a proton plus a neutron. There is a mystery about the large abundance of deuterium in ocean water on Earth, because there is almost no deuterium in the Sun. This is strong evidence that the planets, meteorites, comets, and dust condensed from a material, which was different to the matter that had formed the Sun.

The theoretical yield of deuterium due to Big-Bang nucleosynthesis is about twenty-six deuterium-atoms-per-million-hydrogen-atoms. Experimental observations of the deuterium-to-hydrogen ratio in our local part of the galaxy, a few hundred light years from the Sun, have shown the theory is approximately correct.[963]

There is very little deuterium in the interior of the Sun or other main sequence stars, because deuterium is destroyed in the interiors of stars at a much faster rate than the proton-proton reaction that creates it.[964, 965]

The mystery is the origin of the huge amount of deuterium in ocean water and some other solar-system materials, which is much bigger than the big bang deuterium abundance. Ocean water on Earth has about one hundred and fifty-six deuterium-atoms-per-million-hydrogen-atoms. Comet 103P/Hartley was also found to have similar levels to Earth with around one hundred-and-sixty deuterium-atoms-per-million-hydrogen-atoms.

However, other comets in the inner solar-system have even higher levels of deuterium.[966] Comet Hale Bopp and Halley's Comet have been measured to contain around two-hundred deuterium-atoms-per-million-hydrogen-atoms. Meteoric compounds and interplanetary dust particles contain even more deuterium, about two-hundred to four-hundred deuterium-atoms-per-million-hydrogen-atoms.[967, 968] The Jupiter-family comet 67P/Churyumov-Gerasimenko was measured by the Rosetta space probe to have an even higher deuterium-abundance of five-hundred-and-thirty deuterium-atoms-per-million-hydrogen-atoms.[969]

In contrast, the abundance of deuterium in the atmosphere of Jupiter is much lower. It was directly measured by the Galileo space probe and found to be fifty deuterium-atoms-per-million-hydrogen-atoms.[970]

However, later observations with the Short Wavelength Spectrometer (SWS) on-board the Infrared Space Observatory (ISO) detected only twenty-two deuterium-atoms-per-million-hydrogen-atoms, near the local galactic abundance The Infrared Space Observatory (ISO) detected even less deuterium in the atmosphere of Saturn measuring seventeen deuterium-atoms-per-million-hydrogen-atoms.[971]

The large amount of deuterium in comet-water and ocean-water on Earth can be explained by the binary star-system origin of our solar-system. During the supernova explosion of the companion-star, its outer hydrogen envelope captured neutrons exploding out of the core. This created a temporary reaction-shell of deuterium production in the outer gaseous hydrogen envelope, before the companion-star was obliterated.[972] The deuterium-rich water then formed in the cooling explosion plume from oxygen and the deuterium-rich hydrogen.

Recent Accretion of Supernova Debris

There is plenty of evidence of ongoing delivery of supernova materials to Earth. There is strange supernova-derived material all over the ocean floor in the form of polymetallic-nodules, generally known as manganese-nodules, which range in size from that of a potato to a grapefruit. The nodules lie on top of the seabed sediment, often only partly buried, showing they were dumped in the oceans very recently.

Manganese-nodules vary greatly in abundance across the planet, but on average seventy percent of the sea floor is covered with them. In some regions the manganese-nodules cover the ocean floor at such high density that they are touching one another. The total amount of manganese-nodules on the sea floor has been estimated at more than five hundred billion tons. The highest concentrations have been found on the vast abyssal plains of the deep oceans, from four to six kilometers under the sea, concentrated particularly in the Pacific and Indian Oceans.

They not only occur at all depths of the sea, but they are also found in lakes. Similar strange manganese-nodules were discovered in Lake Michigan, suggesting the nodules were the remains of a bombardment from space, rather than the result of a terrestrial geo-chemical precipitation process occurring in deep ocean water.[973]

The most abundant metal in the nodules is manganese, followed by copper and nickel, plus small amounts of lithium. However, the nodules also contain significant amounts of supernova derived heavy elements: vanadium, titanium, cobalt, molybdenum, tungsten, arsenic, niobium, thorium, yttrium, bismuth, tellurium, thallium, and platinum, which are similar to the rare-earth-elements (REE) found on the surface of the Moon.

Manganese-nodules are also rich in the daughter products of the short-lived isotopes: iron-60, aluminum-26, and beryllium-10.[974] It seems that star-core-zeus is still making deliveries of supernova debris to Earth.

There is also a mystery about the surface abundance of platinum and gold, which are highly siderophile; a strong affinity for combining with molten iron. If all these materials arrived as the Earth formed, they should now be locked up in the core of our planet.

However, the high relative abundance of platinum and gold in crustal rocks at the surface suggests that they been delivered to Earth on a number of occasions, after the core and mantle had solidified below a shell of crustal rocks.[975] The abundance of platinum and gold on the surface of our planet supports the hypothesis that precious metals have been repeatedly delivered to Earth by star-core-zeus, as described in my previous book *Cataclysms & Renewals*.

Conclusion

The isotope data clearly demonstrates that the old solar-nebular-hypothesis is wrong: there was no time for different clouds of supernova material to drift together in our region of space, to mingle into a giant cloud and then form a rotating nebula, which eventually condensed as the Sun and planets.

The data on the distribution of elements and isotopes in the solar-system supports the new supernova-binary theory: a former companion-star was destroyed by a supernova, its explosion-debris was rapidly

captured by the Sun, and then huge lumps of nickel-iron from the ruptured companion star's core triggered fast planet-formation.

Star-core-zeus was blasted-away from the Sun during the supernova
explosion that provided the solar-system building materials. However,
strange enigmas about our solar-system provide evidence that star-core-
zeus is still in orbit and this evidence shall be considered in the next
chapter.

CHAPTER 17

Solar System Enigmas and Star-Core-Zeus

● ● ●

EVIDENCE THAT STAR-CORE-ZEUS PERIODICALLY PASSES through the inner solar-system is revealed by the enigmas of Venus, the strange distribution of uranium, evidence of tidal-heating of planets, the perturbations of the ice-giants, and the scattering of the outer Kuiper Belt objects.

Venus the Alien Planet

Venus is approximately the same size as Earth—a bit less massive and it orbits slightly closer to the Sun—so it was once thought to be our sister-planet. However, after analyzing the data from many space-craft missions and detailed observations from Earth, Venus is now known to be a very alien astronomical body.

Venus has a mysterious internal heat source that makes the surface so hot that it glows. However, the ultra-white clouds of Venus prevent almost all the sunlight from penetrating down to its surface. It is an enigma that Venus is so hot, because the so-called runaway-greenhouse-effect has been revealed as a fantasy, which shall be explained later in this chapter.[976, 977]

Red Hot Venus

Venus is anomalously hot and is pumping out heat from below its rocky surface. This geothermal heat boils the atmosphere of Venus and results in thermal radiation into space. The huge heat output of Venus was directly measured by the European Space Agency's *Venus Express* space-craft in 2007, which recorded that the night-side was radiating so much heat that it produced an eerie deep-red glow.[978] This intense heat output of Venus does not come from trapped solar energy.

The intensity of solar-energy incident on Venus is twice that of Earth, because the orbital radius of Venus around the Sun is only seventy-two percent of the orbital radius of Earth. However, Venus has a high albedo, meaning the planet is very effective at reflecting sunlight. Seventy-six percent of the sunlight incident on Venus is reflected back into space.

VENUS THE STRANGE PLANET

The ESA spacecraft Venus Express photographed the comet tail of Venus in 2007 (below left), and has recently recorded that the strange planet has a powerful electric field with a potential around 10 Volts. In 1991 NASA's Magellan spacecraft mapped the surface of Venus (below right), showing it was recently so hot its crust was molten.

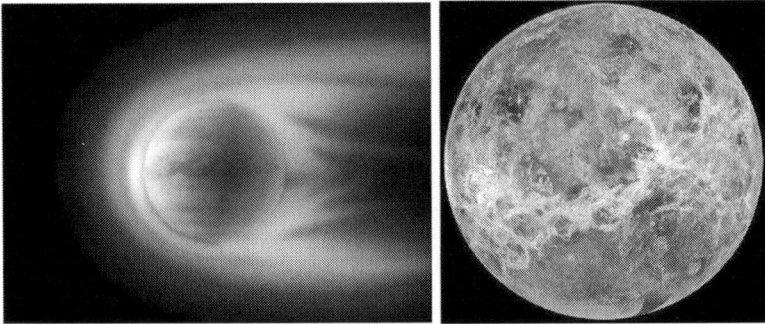

The night-side of Venus pumps out infra-red heat radiation from the surface, as shown by this 2.3 microns infrared image (below left) generated by Near Infrared Mapping Spectrometer aboard the Galileo spacecraft in 1990. There is no evidence of a heat-trap, nor atmospheric heating due to a 'runaway greenhouse effect' on Venus, as shown by the atmospheric temperature vs altitude chart based on Magellan data (below right), which records intense heat radiating from the interior of Venus.

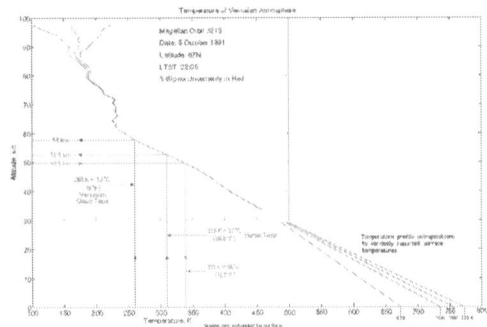

Its ultra-white cloud-tops are made of concentrated sulfuric-acid droplets, which efficiently reflect both heat and light photons without adsorption. Only two percent of the ultraviolet and visible light from the Sun reaches the surface of Venus. Solar heating of Venus is much less than that of the Earth, where clouds of water droplets efficiently absorb heat-photons. In fact, Venus receives approximately the same amount of net-heating from the Sun as chilly Mars.

Although no space-craft has yet made a direct measurement of the heat flux in the crust of Venus, the rocky surface of Venus radiates at least forty times more infrared heat radiation than the incident infrared it receives from the Sun. Solar heating of Venus is insignificant relative to the internal heat of Venus that emerges from within the planet.

However, Venus does not show much evidence of atomic fission-heating, the usual explanation for the high temperature of the interior of the Earth. The Venusian atmosphere has only seven percent of the argon-40 found on Earth, a noble gas isotope produced by potassium-40 radio-isotope decay in old crustal rocks, which slowly produces heat over billions of years. There is also only a small concentration of helium-4 in the Venusian-atmosphere, derived from alpha-particles produced by radioactive-decay of heavy-elements such as uranium.[979]

When the Soviet spacecraft Venera-8 landed on Venus, its gamma ray spectrometer confirmed that there were only low levels of uranium radioactivity at the surface of the planet.[980] This data eliminates fission-heating as a significant source of the heat on Venus, so its main heat-source remains an enigma.

Hot but Cooling Rapidly

Venus has been cooling steadily from incandescence. The red glow of Venus, known to astronomers as the "ashen-light of Venus," was recorded by the Jesuit priest Giovanni Riccioli of Bologna in AD 1643, and there are many earlier observations of red-hot Venus in ancient literature.

However, the mysterious red glow of Venus has become progressively dimmer over the four centuries since the Riccioli-observation. There are many observations of the dark-side of Venus from over a century ago, which still reported that it glowed a dull dark-red. Later observations reported the dark-side of Venus was a dim rusty-brown. In modern times, many astronomers have denied the existence of the ashen-light of Venus, because it has become very hard to observe at all.

However, recently the hot glow of Venus was directly confirmed by infrared detectors on Earth-based telescopes. The Anglo-Australian three-point-nine meter aperture telescope in New South Wales that was fitted with a near-infrared imaging spectrometer proved that the dark side of Venus is pumping out heat radiation, just below the red end of the visible light spectrum.[981]

These measurements not only proved that Venus is almost red-hot but also that the cloud layers are transparent to near-infrared heat. There is clear evidence that infrared from the interior of Venus radiates directly into space, and heat radiation from the surface is cooling down the planet.

The present surface temperature of Venus is around five hundred degrees Celsius, but it was much hotter only a few thousand years ago. The dull red-brown light coming from the dark side of Venus only a hundred years ago required a surface temperature of at least six-hundred degrees.

The visible red glow that was reported four hundred years ago required a surface temperature of at least eight hundred degrees Celsius. The Maya astronomers of the first millennium AD also said Venus produced a red light. A bright red light from Venus was observed by the Dogon in the first millennium BC and by Ancient Egyptians in the second millennium BC. Generally, most people can see red light emitted by rock heated to over a thousand degrees Celsius. These facts suggest that Venus has been cooling rapidly from an incandescent red-hot globe.

The Enigmatic Recent Surface of Venus

Radar mapping by space-craft confirmed that the surface of Venus is mainly a flat uniform landscape. Fifty percent of the area of the planet only deviates from the median altitude by less than five hundred meters.

There is no evidence of continents, ocean basins or plate tectonics. The basaltic crust of Venus is very thin, like the ocean-floor crust of Earth.

When the Soviet space-craft Venera-9 and Venera-10 landed, they found cracked plains of black basaltic rock formed from solidified floods of ultra-hot lava. At smaller scales, there were sharp and jagged unweathered rocks that had been exposed recently. The surface rocks of Venus probably formed only ten-thousand to twenty-thousand years ago, because there is little evidence of sand-blasting by the corrosive and gritty Venusian atmosphere.

In March 1981, Venera-13 and Venera-14 confirmed the nature of the baking volcanic landscape of Venus. The whole surface was made of hot liquid rock that had recently solidified. The on-board analyzer confirmed that most rocks were basalt with a high potassium content, while some of the rocks were fragile and resembled pumice. All the evidence indicated that Venus had a very young planetary surface.

Evidence of massive volcanism covers the whole surface of Venus. Large shallow domed-shaped features that were recent volcanoes are scattered everywhere, together with millions of small vents and domes, collective evidence of the very hot interior of Venus. However, the vents and fractures, which produced all this hot liquid rock, are no longer active, showing the planet is cooling rapidly.

It was also a surprise that attempts at hot-spot imaging from space to locate active volcanoes on Venus were unsuccessful. Some planetary scientists had claimed that bright patches observed in the atmosphere could be due to active volcanoes, but the infrared detectors did not support that interpretation.

When *Venus Express* activated its Monitoring-Camera coupled to an Imaging-Infrared-Spectrophotometer and pointed it at the surface of Venus, it failed to show any current volcanic eruptions. There is no direct evidence of any eruptions on Venus now, even though apocalyptic volcanic activity over the whole planet had happened very recently. These observations also support the idea that Venus was much hotter in its very recent geological past and is cooling down.

There are huge recent basaltic floods all over Venus, and the planet surface is coated with solidified lava. Some lava features show that not long ago there were rivers of ultra-hot lava, which were so fluid that they moved like water. Some stream-lined lava flows were the result of incredible flow-speeds; some over three-hundred kilometers-per-hour. Other lava flows extended up to five-hundred kilometers across the surface of Venus, before they cooled and solidified.

These low-viscosity lava-flows required a temperature of between one-thousand and two-thousand degrees Celsius. The lava floods suggest the ultra-hot lava must have remained in a very hot liquid state for a long time. However, despite the corrosive and abrasive atmosphere of Venus, all the volcanic features show little evidence of weathering: they must have occurred very recently. This is additional evidence of the very high temperature of Venus in the recent past, maybe only ten thousand years ago. All geological evidence supports the hypothesis that Venus had been heated to a very high temperature and has been cooling more recently.

There are also fractures and rifts of Venus, where the surface had been torn apart and ruptured by gigantic forces. Mountain ranges had formed where the surface was crumpled. The large scale topological features on Venus suggest the whole planet had been recently deformed and distorted by powerful tidal forces.

It was a big surprise that there were so few craters on Venus, compared to the Moon, Mercury, and Mars. In fact, less than a thousand craters can be confirmed for the whole surface of our sister-planet. This is not even enough data to make any statistically valid age-estimate for the surface of Venus.

However, various crude estimates based on crater-counting have been performed, and unreliable claims have been made that the surface of Venus is from one-hundred-million to five-hundred-million years old. In contrast, the geological features on the surface of Venus, which all lack evidence of erosion, suggest the current surface of the planet is around ten thousand years old.

A Powerful Electric Field but No Magnetic Field

Venus has a powerful ambipolar electric-field, which was recently detected by the ASPERA-4 electron-spectrometer aboard the ESA *Venus Express* space-craft. The electric field surrounding Venus is at least five times more powerful than Earth's and results in an electric-wind that ejects the Venusian atmosphere into space.[982] Velikovsky was the first to describe the strong planetary electric-field of Venus in his book *Worlds in Collision*. He also proposed that inter-planetary electrical discharges were the real phenomena behind the mythical thunder-bolts of Zeus.[983]

It is a mystery why Venus has no magnetic field, because it has an electric field and an iron-core that must be molten, because the planet is so hot. Many theorists expected convective motions of the molten iron-core of Venus to produce a strong magnetic field. However, as early as AD 1962, the magnetometer on-board Mariner-2 showed that Venus had no planetary magnetic field at all.

Some theorist explained away the lack of a magnetic field by assuming the interior of Venus must be too hot to produce any magnetic field. The lack of a magnetic field in surface rocks was also explained away with the assumption that they have recently been geothermally heated from the interior of the planet above the Curie temperature, where all magnetism is lost.

These ideas totally contradict greenhouse heating of Venus as a result of an atmospheric carbon-dioxide blanket, but this evidence from a separate scientific discipline has been ignored by climate scientists. In addition, the failure of "a convection-dynamo-system" inside Venus to produce a magnetic field even challenges our basic understanding of the origin of the magnetic field of Earth.

Venus is Phase-Locked to Earth

The rotation of Venus was discovered in AD 1966 by radar, in collaboration between Jodrell Bank in Manchester, United Kingdom, and a Russian installation on the Black Sea coast. It was a surprise to discover that the rotation of Venus is so slow; there is no rotation-induced equatorial bulge on Venus.

It was another surprise when the direction of rotation of Venus was found to be retrograde, meaning it is turning backward, compared to the common direction of rotation and revolution of the other planets in the solar-system. The axis of rotation has also been calculated to be almost perpendicular to its orbital plane, with an axial tilt of just three degrees.

The most startling discovery was that Venus is phase-locked to the Earth. When Venus is nearest to the Earth on its orbit, the same side of Venus always faces our planet. The two-hundred-and-forty-three Earth-day rotation period of Venus is almost identical to the resonance period of the Earth-Venus system that is also two-hundred-and-forty-three Earth days long.

Venus is a very symmetrical sphere because it has a thin crust and a molten interior. However, the rotation of Venus appears to have been slowed by tidal forces and synchronized. The phase-lock is impossible to explain without a catastrophic encounter between Earth and Venus. Phase-locking is also observed with the Moon, in which its near-side is always turned toward Earth, but this is due to mass-asymmetry and local tidal forces. The Venus-Earth phase-locking indicates the two planets were in very close proximity in the recent past.

The Venus phase-lock with Earth was probably the result of tidal-deformation and braking during the Venus-Earth fly-by that occurred during the Late Bronze Age Catastrophe of 1159 BC, which I described in my previous book *Cataclysms & Renewals*.

The Comet Tail of Venus

The spacecraft Pioneer-Venus made maps of the solar-wind of supersonic-protons that hit the upper atmosphere of Venus. The solar-wind is blasting-away atmospheric dust and gas of Venus into a long cometary tail. This dense tail of dust, molecules, atoms, and ions is carrying away the Venusian atmosphere at a rate of many tons-per-second. A circum-solar ring of dust at the orbit of Venus has also been discovered, which is being produced by the dissipating comet tail of our hot sister planet.[984]

A stunning picture of Venus was taken by the Venus-Express spacecraft in 2008, proving Venus still has a comet-like tail, as originally claimed by Velikovsky. The image captured its thick atmosphere trailing away in the solar wind, from the night side of the planet. There is also an unusual abundance of particles of iron-sulfide and red hematite in the comet tail streaming away from the planet, which is another clue to the origin of Venus.

The long tail of Venus stretches all the way to the orbit of the Earth. In the summer of 2004, Venus passed between the Earth and the Sun. During this transit of Venus on the eighth of June, a fine blood-red iron-rich dust from its tail fell as a red-rain. The red Venusian fallout was particularly visible on the white ice-sheet at the North Pole and was recorded by remote viewing cameras.[985]

The Anomalous Atmosphere of Venus

The atmosphere of Venus has an enigmatically large amount of deuterium, the heavy isotope of hydrogen.[986, 987] The deuterium-to-hydrogen ratio on Venus is five-thousand or more deuterium-atoms-per-million-hydrogen-atoms, up to one-hundred-times greater than on Earth or any other solar-system object.[988, 989, 990]

This is strong evidence of the alien origin of Venus, which I described in my book *Cataclysms & Renewals*. As recently as twelve thousand years ago, Venus was a satellite of star-core-zeus, and it probably collected its deuterium-rich atmosphere while passing through the gases and dust of the torus surrounding star-core-zeus.

The atmosphere of Venus is seventy-five times the density of the Earth's atmosphere. At the surface of Venus, the pressure of its atmosphere is approximately one-hundred-times that of Earth. The atmosphere of Venus is about ninety-six percent carbon-dioxide, three percent nitrogen, a small amount of sulfur dioxide, and an almost undetectable amount of water-vapor.[991, 992]

The tiny water content in the atmosphere declines with decreasing altitude from forty parts-per-million to twenty parts-per-million, and at the surface of Venus, the water content is only three parts-per-million. The logical conclusion is that the hot surface rocks of Venus react with water and strip it from the Venusian atmosphere. In comparison, Earth's atmosphere is ten-thousand parts-per-million water.

In the Venusian-atmosphere, there is an odd lack of carbon-monoxide and molecular-oxygen compared to carbon-dioxide. Solar radiation efficiently converts carbon-dioxide to carbon-monoxide, so the thick carbon-dioxide rich atmosphere may be evidence that Venus has only been exposed to solar radiation for about ten thousand years.

The high concentration of highly reactive sulfur-dioxide also shows Venus has a very young atmosphere, because sulfur-dioxide reacts rapidly with rock surfaces. High up in the atmosphere, the concentration of sulfur-dioxide is one hundred and fifty parts-per-million but decreases toward the surface to only twenty parts-per-million at an altitude of twelve kilometers. The sulfur-dioxide concentration drops to very low levels at the surface, where minerals strip out the gas. Highly reactive atomic sulfur is also present in the atmosphere, which also reacts with the surface rocks very quickly.

These facts show that the atmosphere of Venus was formed very recently. The hot atmosphere of Venus is not in thermal equilibrium either, and it is boiling off the hot surface. Various spacecraft have revealed that the Venusian atmosphere is undergoing rapid changes and is constantly being lost into space.

The atmosphere of Venus is far too hot to have received its heat from the Sun. During the long Venusian night, the cloud-tops on the darkside of Venus that face away from the Sun are actually much hotter than on the Sun-facing side of the planet.

The atmosphere is churning like a pan of boiling-water on a red-hot stove and generating huge convection systems. The atmosphere in contact with the hot surface of Venus conducts heat and then expands as it is heated to a temperature of over five-hundred degrees-Celsius. The hot lower density gases rise in huge thermals and the bubbling atmosphere of Venus is full of rapidly moving convection cells, which transport hot gas and dust from the super-heated surface up to the cold cloud-tops. The Mariner-10 spacecraft confirmed the exponentially decreasing temperature gradient from the glowing surface to the cloud-tops of Venus.

The structure of the whole Venusian atmosphere is weird: it is hotter at its poles and colder at its equator. In contrast, the atmosphere of Earth is heated by the Sun, so it is hotter at the equator and colder at the poles. The tiny tilt of Venus means that the Sun is almost permanently below the horizon at the poles, and there is almost no incident sunlight or summer-heating. However, the hot polar regions of Venus are heated by the glowing surface below.

On Venus, there is no evidence of north-south convection between the equator and the poles. In contrast on Earth, solar heating induces atmospheric circulation by way of huge cyclones and convections of rising and falling air. In our atmosphere, this process moves warm air from the equator, where air is heated more efficiently by the Sun, to the cooler polar regions.

The Venusian atmosphere rushes around the planet at ultra-high speed from east-to-west, faster than the planet rotates. These winds are powered by convection from the surface to travel around Venus at about one-hundred meters-per-second (three hundred and sixty kilometers per hour). The winds blow from east-to-west at all levels and are actually cooler at the equatorial region. The westward high speed "super-rotation" of the atmosphere means the cloud-tops of Venus circle the whole planet in only four Earth days, almost sixty times faster than the slow rotation of the solid body of the planet.

No Runaway-Greenhouse Effect

In the 1950s, infrared telescope measurements from Earth showed the average temperature of the atmosphere of Venus was around three-hundred degrees-Celsius, but this average is very misleading. The hot atmosphere of Venus is not due to solar heating.

However, in the mid 1950s, before the first spacecraft flights and prior to any reliable data on Venus, a young Carl Sagan made calculations for his doctoral thesis at the University of Chicago that the preliminary evidence of the hot atmosphere of Venus could be explained by a carbon-dioxide greenhouse-gas effect.

Carl Sagan assumed that Venus was hot because the Venusian atmosphere of Venus trapped heat much more efficiently than Earth. He proposed Venus was irradiated with ultra-violet and visible light from the Sun, which was then converted to heat in the atmosphere and at the surface. He believed that the high concentration of carbon-dioxide in the dense Venusian atmosphere, prevented heat in the form of infra-red, radiating and escaping back into space, thus causing extreme 'global-warming' of Venus. Sagan's conclusion was the very high temperature of Venus was due to a process, which he invented and named "the-runaway-greenhouse-effect."

At that time, Immanuel Velikovsky had just published his book *Worlds in Collision*, in which he explained that Venus was hot because it had recently been ejected from Jupiter. After this book became a best seller, members of the scientific establishment attempted to belittle Dr. Velikovsky's controversial proposal. During the propaganda campaign, Sagan was responsible for making his idea of "the-runaway-greenhouse-heating of Venus" an unchallenged dogma, which became the foundation of the current "greenhouse-gas-global-warming" dogma.[993]

Around ninety percent of the greenhouse effect that actually occurs on Earth is due to water-vapor in our atmosphere, not carbon-dioxide.[994, 995] Our wet-atmosphere is transparent to ultra-violet and visible light from the Sun but traps the heat that is re-radiated from the surface of the Earth. The result is that the humid atmosphere of Earth acts like a blanket that retains heat. The result of this greenhouse effect on Earth is that our planet is thirty-five degrees Celsius warmer than it would be without an atmosphere.

In contrast, the Venusian atmosphere is so dry that there is no water vapor to make an efficient insulating barrier that can stop heat escaping by infrared radiation. The lower levels of the atmosphere of Venus are being warmed by its hot surface, not the other way around. The surface of Venus is five hundred degrees Celsius and is transferring heat into its atmosphere by radiation, conduction, and convection.

From the 1960s to today, no evidence of runaway-greenhouse-heating has ever been found on Venus, despite the high concentration of carbon-dioxide in the Venusian atmosphere. In addition, Sagan's runaway-greenhouse-heating model required impossibly efficient insulation to raise the temperature of Venus over five-hundred degrees Celsius, above the temperature derived from net solar heating after the reflection by its white clouds.

Even as early as AD 1962, observations of the thermal output of Venus by Mariner-2 spacecraft traveling across the face of the planet revealed "limb darkening" at either edge of the planetary disc. This was evidence that the radiation from the Venusian atmosphere decreased from the hot rocks of the incandescent surface up to the cold cloud-tops.

When the Soviet spacecraft Venera-9 landed on Venus in 1975, the camera showed that most of the light that was reflected and scattered by the Venusian clouds was coming from its hot surface. This data proved that the heat was originating from the hot rocky surface of the planet, not from Sagan's runaway-greenhouse-heated atmosphere.

Despite the fact the Sun is twice as large in the sky on Venus compared to Earth, our sister planet receives less solar radiation than the Earth, because seventy-six percent is reflected away by its ultra-white clouds. Of the energy that does get into the Venusian atmosphere, only twelve percent of the total energy gets down to the ground. The combination of these two effects means that only two percent of incident radiation from the Sun reaches the surface of Venus. This was confirmed as early as AD 1978, with data from the Pioneer-Venus space-probe.

In contrast, fifty percent of the sunlight falling on Earth reaches the land and sea, where it is converted to heat and partly retained by the atmosphere. This greenhouse effect is mainly due to the atmospheric water vapor blocking infrared radiation back into space (carbon-dioxide only provides very poor insulation).

The thermodynamic process on Venus is quite different from the greenhouse effect on Earth. On Venus geothermal energy from the interior of the planet heats the surface rocks to scorching temperatures, which then pump out intense heat radiation. The whole planet emits a huge amount of radiation at thermal wavelengths into space, because the dry carbon-dioxide atmosphere is transparent to a wide spectrum of infrared radiation.

In addition, the upper atmosphere of Venus is not that hot. Pioneer-Venus showed that the outer atmosphere is very cold on the night-side of Venus and only heated up on the day-side by the Sun to plus-thirty degrees Celsius. In 2016, re-analysis of data from the *Venus Express* spacecraft showed the cloud-tops of Venus are ultra-cold, about minus-one-hundred-and-seventy degrees Celsius on the night-side and minus-one-hundred-and-sixty degrees Celsius at the poles. It is now obvious that the hot planet is heating its own atmosphere, not the other way around.

All the data on Venus collected in the previous fifty years, totally contradicts Sagan's idea that the atmosphere of Venus is causing global-warming of the planet by runaway-greenhouse-heating. The atmosphere is not heating the planet; the planet is heating the atmosphere. However, the fake runaway-greenhouse carbon-dioxide model for the Venusian atmosphere is still in use today to explain global-warming on Earth, and the idea has become such a sacred-truth, it is becoming a criminal offense to question it.

The Origin of Venus

A possible explanation for the mysteriously high temperature of Venus and the ancient observations of Venus as a comet is that only twelve thousand years ago Venus was a hot moon of star-core-zeus that was captured by the Sun.

The hypothesis is that Venus used to orbit star-core-zeus in a very eccentric elliptical orbit, so it was heated to high temperatures by extreme tidal-forces, which regularly deformed the planet. This process is simi-lar to the way the gravity of Jupiter distorts and heats its nearest moon Io. The remains of a series of floods of hot lava on the surface of Venus show some cyclical process used to heat the planet. Prior to capture by the Sun, Venus probably suffered repeated core-heating as a result of tidal-distortion during each peri-astron fly-by of star-core-zeus.

Supporting evidence for the early life of Venus in orbit around star-core-zeus is the abundance of argon-36 in its atmosphere. Venus must have been close to an alien source of this primordial noble-gas isotope, which is otherwise very rare in the inner solar-system. There is also a strange isotope ratio of argon-to-neon in the atmosphere of Venus, which does not match the Sun. In addition, the extraordinary abundance of deuterium is evidence of the alien origin of Venus.

All the available evidence supports the hypothesis described in my previous book *Cataclysms & Renewals*. Venus is a hot alien planet that was captured by the Sun from star-core-zeus. It first appeared in the sky as a red-hot dragon-comet, at the end of the Ice-Age in 9600 BC. The surface temperature and rate of heat loss from Venus is consistent with the planet cooling from incandescent temperatures over the last twelve-thousand years.

The Mystery of Earth's Hot Interior and Uranium

Like Venus, the Earth also radiates much more heat than it receives from the Sun. Measurements of heat-flow in deep mines shows there is heat-loss of about forty-seven terawatts at the Earth's surface, arising from a heat source inside our planet.

At the end of the nineteenth century, Lord Kelvin calculated primordial heat from the formation of our planet should have been radiated away in approximately two-hundred-million years. The usual explanation for the heat still coming out of our planet is that the Earth is a giant uranium-fueled atomic power-station. However, this is an incomplete explanation at best.

Analysis of the solar spectrum shows there is almost no uranium in the Sun. There are only tiny amounts of uranium in chondrite meteorites (an abundance of eight parts-per-billion) and nickel-iron meteorites have even lower levels of uranium.[996, 997] Ocean-floor-basalt on Earth, which is closely related to mantle rock, has even less uranium (an abundance of four parts-per-billion). In addition, it has also been calculated that there is almost no uranium in Earth's core, because uranium has a higher affinity for the types of molten rock that made the mantle rather than the molten nickel-iron that made the core. This data undermines the uranium-fission hypothesis as an explanation for the deep interior heating of our planet.

In contrast, there is a related mystery of the higher uranium abundance in the continental crust. There is geological evidence of a massive dump of uranium rich material on top of the crust of our planet soon after the formation of Earth. The granite landmass has an average uranium abundance of one-thousand-four-hundred parts-per-billion, and there are local concentrations of uranium in ancient granites up to fifty-thousand parts-per-billion. For example, some crustal rocks in Gabon, Africa, once contained so much uranium that they became a natural fission reactor. Uraninite mixed with iron-pyrite in fluvial placers of the Witwatersrand basin in South Africa is so abundant on the surface that it seems to have fallen from the sky.

There is also evidence of regular deliveries of uranium and other heavy metals in all geological epochs up to recent times. For example, a fragment of the quarter-of-a-billion year-old Permian land surface at Littleham Cove near Exeter in the United Kingdom contains nodules with an abundance of heavy metals typical of type-two supernova products, including uranium.[998] Uranium-rich nodules found at Heysham in Lancashire, resemble the manganese-nodules described earlier found all over the floor of the oceans, which also contain an abundance of uranium.

In addition, there is evidence of very recent delivery from space of uranium rich material. Ruins of twelve thousand-year-old Paleo-Indian Clovis settlements in North America were discovered coated with a strange fine yellow dust that was alien to the local geology. The yellow powder and the yellow stain turned out to be a radioactive potassium-uranium ore.

At one site, the yellow dust contained an incredibly high concentration of zero-point-three percent uranium (three million parts per billion). The radioactivity at the Clovis sites also correlated with unusual concentrations of supernova isotope mixtures of uranium and thorium.[999] A similar geological strata is the twelve thousand years old black-mat that marks the end of the ice-age in the United States, which contains uranium and other heavy metals in the same concentration ratio as the surface dust on the Moon.[1000]

When the Apollo missions brought back lunar surface soils from the near side of the moon, much of it was composed of potassium (K, mainly the potassium-40 isotope) and rare earth elements (REE) including radioactive thorium and uranium, plus phosphorous (P). Lunar surface rocks made of this mixture were given the name KREEP rocks. The Procellarum region of the Moon, which faces Earth and contains the maria, has high surface concentrations of KREEP, containing heat-producing radioactive uranium and thorium.[1001]

The Kaguya Gamma Ray Spectrometer recently identified uranium gamma ray lines from the Moon, allowing the generation of a lunar-global uranium-distribution map. The lunar surface has an average abundance of uranium around three hundred parts per billion, which is concentrated in some areas up to two-thousand parts-per-billion, with substantial variation on the far-side of the Moon.[1002] It is a mystery why the uranium-abundance on the surface of the Moon is similar to Earth crustal rocks but much higher than meteorites.

The uranium found in Earth's crust must have been produced by the supernova explosion of the companion-star, which was then delivered periodically throughout geological history, as a series of heavy-metal bombardments. Most of the uranium arrived on our planet as the granite crust of Earth formed, and lumps of uranium probably sank deep into the core, despite uranium's low affinity for molten iron. It appears that star-core-zeus has been regularly delivering uranium dust to both Earth and the Moon, since the formation of our planet.

Recent measurements of the neutrino-flux have reveal the scale of the radioactive decay of uranium isotopes inside the Earth. The results show that the heat generated by uranium radioactivity is only about twenty terawatts, and probably another four terawatts is produced by the radioactive decay of potassium-40.[1003, 1004, 1005] This shows that only half the heat flow up to Earth's surface has been accounted for as the result of radioactive-decay-heating deep inside our planet.

An explanation for the other half of the heat coming from the interior of Earth is still required. One possibility is that star-core-zeus regularly heats up our planet by gravitational tidal distortion and magnetic induction heating, in much the same way Venus was originally heated and 'Io' the Jovian-moon is still being heated today.

The Enigmatic Perturbations of the Ice-Giant Planets

Strange deviations of the orbit of the outer ice-giant planet Uranus were first discovered in AD 1781. Over the next seven years, while the planet traversed the constellation of Gemini, there was an enigmatic slowing in its angular velocity.

When the orbit of Uranus was calculated, taking into account the gravitational pull exerted by Saturn and Jupiter on Uranus, the discrepancies between theory and observation multiplied. The difference in the calculated and actual positions of Uranus suggested that a massive astronomical object was lurking further out from the Sun, exerting another force on Uranus.

In the mid-nineteenth century, two astronomers independently predicted the mass of the undiscovered planet: John Couch Adams expected a planet fifty-five times Earth's mass, while Urbain Le Verrier predicted a planet thirty-six times Earth's mass.

Astronomers at the Berlin Observatory discovered a new planet in AD 1846: it was the massive ice-giant planet Neptune orbiting 30 AU from the Sun. However, after astronomers tracked Neptune, they were surprised that the actual value of Neptune's mass was only seventeen-times Earth's mass: Neptune had only half the mass required to explain the significant gravitational perturbations of Uranus.

Less than half of the anomaly had been accounted for: there had to be something much more massive, much further out in the darkness beyond Neptune.

In addition, between AD 1781 and AD 1789, Neptune had been ahead of Uranus on its journey around the Sun, so it should have been pulling Uranus to accelerate: in contrast Uranus had been mysteriously slowing down. The only reasonable conclusion was that some other

PERTURBED URANUS & NEPTUNE

Something massive knocked Uranus over, causing its extreme axial tilt of 98 degrees (below left). Its South Pole (north rotation pole) points at Orionis-15, a star between Orion & Taurus located on the orbital track of Star-Core-Zeus. Neptune (below right) was discovered in 1846, at a position predicted from orbital perturbations of Uranus. Between 1860 and 1920 orbital perturbations of the position of Neptune were detected, suggesting a massive object is approaching the solar system from the approximate direction of Gemini (around 6-8 hours Right Ascension). Neptune has an orbital period of 165 years, so it has been on the other side of the Sun since that time.

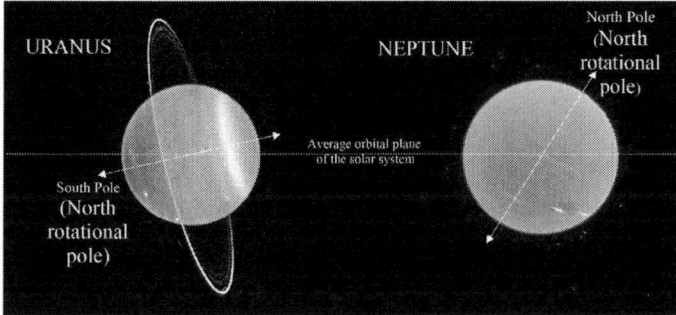

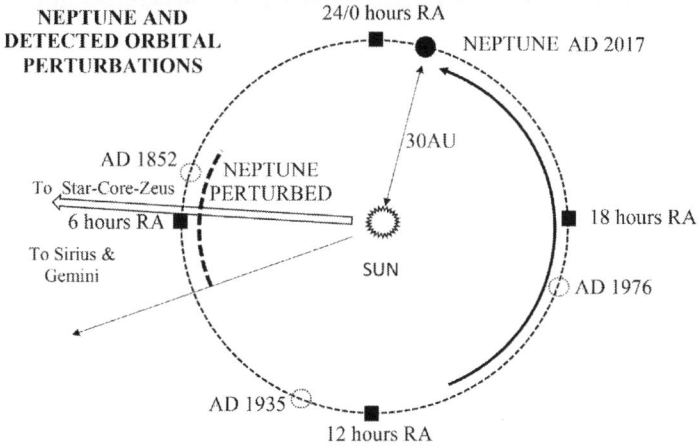

massive object much further out from the Sun was applying a powerful gravitational force on both of the outer ice-giant planets.

The perturbations of Uranus were recorded both in the radial and tangential direction, but they displayed a strangely complex pattern: the perturbations of Uranus seemed to be linked to its angular direction from the Sun. A powerful attractive force seemed to be pulling Uranus toward the general direction of the bright star Sirius and the constellations of Orion and Gemini.[1006] These complex deviations in the orbit of Uranus was evidence for a much larger perturbing mass, much further away from the Sun, located in the general direction of this triangle of the night sky.

When further irregularities in the orbit of Uranus had been noticed by AD 1906, the quest for a massive Planet-X commenced. The search beyond the orbit of Neptune was taken up by William Pickering and Percival Lowell, who had founded the Lowell Observatory in Flagstaff, Arizona.

Both astronomers were in agreement over the position for the huge perturbing mass: it must be hidden near Gemini. Their calculations were based on the deviations of Uranus from its expected orbit around the Sun, after taking into account the positions and gravitational pull of Saturn, Jupiter, and Neptune.

By AD 1909, both Lowell and Pickering had separately suggested several possible celestial coordinates for Planet-X. If the massive object was only a bit further out than the orbit of Neptune, then Lowell predicted the perturber was seven times Earth's mass, while Pickering predicted the perturber was two times Earth's mass.[1007] However, the same perturbation could also be due to something much more massive but located much further away from the Sun.

In AD 1915 Lowell published his predicted positions for a perturbing mass in the constellation of Gemini, but he died the following year. The Lowell Observatory continued his Gemini Project and systematically photographed the sky in an attempt to find his massive Planet-X.

Unknown to Lowell, his surveys had already captured two faint images of Pluto in AD 1915, but they were not recognized for what they were. Then in AD 1930, two photographs were taken that recorded a shift in position of a point of light near to the position predicted for the massive perturber in Gemini.

However, almost as soon as Pluto was discovered, astronomers understood there was a problem. The angular size of the big perturber should have been at least one arc minute, but telescopes of that era detected Pluto as a dimensionless point of dim light.

Crude estimates of the upper limits on the diameter of Pluto ranged around ten arc-seconds, based on the resolution-limit of ground based telescopes at the time. It was clear that Pluto did not match Lowell's prediction for a huge Planet-X and it was simply not massive enough to explain all the observed perturbations of both Uranus and Neptune.[1008]

In AD 1978, the discovery of Pluto's moon Charon finally allowed an accurate calculation of Pluto's mass. Pluto only had about a fifth of the mass of the Moon, so it was far too small to explain the large deviations in the orbits of the ice-giants Uranus and Neptune.

The mystery deepened a few years later. When measurements by the Voyager spacecraft passing Uranus and Neptune were analyzed, there was no evidence of any perturbations. Some astronomers confidently belittled the work of earlier experts and claimed there was no problem to answer.[1009] However, they ignored a critical piece of data: the ice-giants were on the opposite side of the Sun to Gemini at the time of the fly-by.

Other astronomers accepted the validity of the earlier observations, and after the low mass of Pluto was established, they continued to search for the massive Planet-X. Different astronomers tried to estimate the mass, position, and distance of the mystery object that had interfered with the orbits of the outer ice-giant planets.

One calculation of the mystery object's mass, distance, and position suggested an object of one Earth mass in a circular orbit fifty-five AU from the Sun, again in the direction of Gemini.[1010] Other models predicted a very much larger mass, much further out from the Sun.[1011] From the 1990s, data began to accumulate on long period comets which had been disturbed by a very large object far out from the Sun.[1012]

During over a century of observation, the perturbations of Uranus and Neptune consistently predicted a massive body in the region of sky defined by the constellation of Gemini, the constellation of Orion, and the bright star Sirius. The strange comet orbit clusters were also consistent with a massive object in this region of space. This near-stationary angular location was another important clue.

The perturbing mass could not be a low mass planet in a circular orbit beyond Neptune. It had to be a much more massive and distant body, approaching the Sun from an aphelion point located in the direction of Gemini-Sirius and traveling toward us on a highly eccentric elliptical orbit, over thousands of years.

However, many astronomers continued to dismiss the strange perturbations of Neptune and Uranus as experimental error. They failed to understand that for the last fifty years Saturn, Uranus, and Neptune have all been revolving on the opposite side of the Sun from the direction to Gemini-Sirius-Orion, so the anomaly has been less significant in recent decades.

A related enigma is that NASA's space-craft Pioneer-10 was flying into the tail of the heliosphere in the approximate direction of the gravity anomaly when its radio went dead only eighty AU from the Sun, and it was lost forever.

The Mysteries of the Kuiper Belt

Recently, a strange clustering of orbits of the distant scatter-disc-objects beyond the edge of the Kuiper Belt has been established, which supports the prediction of a massive object lurking far out beyond Neptune, again in the triangle of night-sky defined by Sirius and the constellations of Gemini and Orion.

The strange properties of the Kuiper Belt also challenge the conventional solar-nebular-hypothesis for the formation of our solar-system and provide more evidence for the existence of star-core-zeus. The Kuiper Belt is a torus-shaped region of the outer solar-system beyond the orbit of Neptune. It contains low-density icy bodies and some rocky objects, from the size of small asteroids up to dwarf planets, located between thirty AU and fifty AU, with the most densely populated zone lying between forty-two AU and forty-eight AU from the Sun.[1013]

Pluto is now a former-ninth-planet of our solar-system, after it was relegated to dwarf-planet status, when it was calculated to have a smaller mass than a Kuiper Belt object called Eris. The total mass of the Kuiper Belt objects based on the observed density of objects is estimated to be only four percent of an Earth mass.

KUIPER OBJECTS CUT-OFF AND SCATTERED

The Kuiper Belt of small icy bodies beyond Neptune, was expected to extend out, in a great disc dimishing in object-density with distance. However, some massive object has cut off the disc at 50AU from the Sun and scattered Kuiper objects into high eccentricity orbits, at steep inclinations to the average orbital plane of the planets. [Sheppard, S., & Trujillo, C., "New Extreme Trans-Neptunian Objects: Toward A Super-Earth In The Outer Solar System," *The Astronomical Journal* 152 (2016) 56 pages https://doi.org/10.3847/1538-3881/152/6/221]

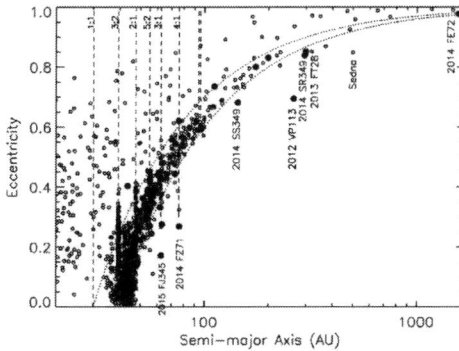

The orbital plane of many scattered objects coincides with the axis of the highly eccentric orbit of Star-Core-Zeus around the barycentre of our binary solar system.

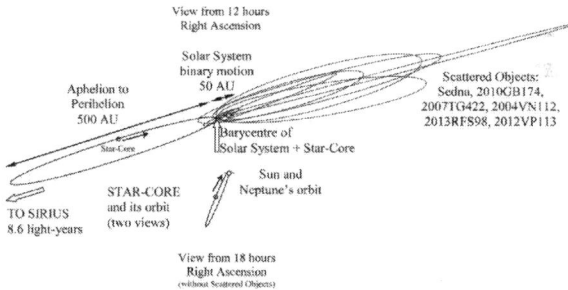

This is another challenge to the solar-nebular-hypothesis, which predicted the mass of the Kuiper Belt objects should be at least a thousand times greater. For example, the nebular density needed to accrete Kuiper Belt objects of more than a hundred kilometers in diameter requires a mass of material about thirty-times the mass of Earth. Estimations of the accretion conditions for Uranus and Neptune require an enormous amount of material in the outer-nebular. A solution to this paradox is that a massive object, such as star-core-zeus, long ago removed almost all the extra-mass from this outer region of the solar-system.

There is also evidence that a massive body has been directly interfering with the orbits of Kuiper Belt objects. The whole Kuiper Belt is inclined to the ecliptic plane of the solar-system by two degrees. The cloud of objects is quite extensive, spreading above and below the ecliptic plane of the solar-system by approximately thirty degrees, with some rare objects traveling up to ninety degrees. The mystery is what caused these objects to be thrown out of a simple disc arrangement.

The discovery that the Kuiper Belt is made up of two quite separate populations of objects was another surprise. There are a group of objects with nearly circular orbits, with orbital eccentricities of less than zero-point-one and relatively low orbital inclinations of less than ten degrees to the ecliptic plane of the solar-system. These dynamically-cold objects, representing approximately thirty-five percent of the Kuiper Belt population, occupy the zone near the plane of the solar-system, between forty-two AU to forty-five AU away from the Sun.

The dynamically-cold population with near-circular low-inclination orbits and perihelion distances larger than forty-two AU has extremely red surfaces.[1014] The source of the red color of these icy objects is unknown: it could be a red coating of iron-oxide or polycyclic-hydrocarbon compounds.

The second population is labeled dynamically-hot. This larger group of objects revolves in orbits inclined by more than thirty degrees to the ecliptic plane of the solar-system. These orbits occupy the zone of the Kuiper Belt between thirty-five AU to forty-seven AU away from the Sun and represent approximately sixty-five percent of the Kuiper Belt population.[1015] Another unexplained mystery about Kuiper Belt objects is the origin of the different colors of the two populations: the dynamically-hot objects are distinctly grey in color.

The behavior of some dynamically-hot Kuiper Belt objects is very odd. 2008KV42 and 2012DR30 have been thrown into strange eccentric and tilted orbits, which are almost at right angles to the plane of the solar-system. Other objects also have a large semi-major axis, with inclinations ranging between sixty degrees and one-hundred-and-fifty degrees.

Many objects only go up to the edge of the Kuiper Belt, its fifty AU frontier. In fact, the aphelions of many orbits of Kuiper Belt objects actually cluster there.[1016] There is no doubt that something huge is disrupting the orbits of low mass objects in the Kuiper Belt that venture more than fifty AU from the Sun. Very few objects have survived after straying into the blackness of space beyond the Kuiper Belt. Out beyond fifty AU, there is an almost total absence of objects orbiting in the plane of the solar-system disc. This effectively empty space was totally unexpected and what caused it remains an enigma.[1017]

Beyond this mysterious outer-edge of the solar-system disc, only a few objects are detected and all have been chaotically scattered by the gravity of a hidden mass. Cruttenden proposed that most of the objects beyond fifty AU from the Sun were long ago captured by some massive but hidden object, lurking further out in the darkness of space. He believes it is probably a cool dwarf-companion-star of the Sun.[1018]

I suggest that the combined gravity of star-core-zeus and the Sun have scattered or captured everything that stray into our barycenter, the center of gravity of our binary system. This barycenter can behave like the gravity-neutral Lagrange-point, which exists between Earth and the Sun, around which a satellite can orbit. The barycenter of our binary system is located fifty AU from the Sun when star-core-zeus is at aphelion. The inbound flight path of star-core-zeus also crosses the solar-system disc at fifty AU on its way to its closest approach to the Sun at perihelion.

The Enigmatic Scattered-Objects

The few objects that have been detected beyond the outer-edge of the Kuiper Belt have been flung into weird highly eccentric and inclined elliptical orbits, toward one part of the sky. These rare objects are known as the extended-scattered-disk-objects or simply scattered-objects.

A very curious feature of the scattered-objects is their perihelia start around seventy AU. It is very strange that there are no objects with a perihelion distance in the range from fifty AU to seventy AU, and generally nothing has been detected in this empty zone twenty-AU-wide, beyond the outer edge of the Kuiper Belt. These scattered-objects are only found more than twenty AU beyond the empty outer-edge of the Kuiper Belt, and some of these mountain-size objects travel more than one thousand AU away from the Sun.

In 2014, Trujillo and Sheppard suggested a super-massive perturber is hidden somewhere beyond the outer solar-system and is herding the scattered-objects.[1019] They simulated the effect of a super-massive object at two-hundred-and-fifty AU and found they could reproduce the clustering of orbital perihelia of the scattered-objects. The strangely aligned orbits of 2012VP113, Sedna, and ten other objects reveal the influence of a massive object hiding in the darkness, about two-hundred-and-fifty AU from the Sun, in the Sirius-Gemini-Orion triangle of the night-sky.[1020]

A scattered object called Niku, discovered in 2011 and tracked up to 2015, was revealed to be in a weird orbit, which is very highly inclined. It was a big surprise when the inclination of Niku's orbit to the ecliptic was calculated to be one-hundred-and-ten degrees: objects with inclinations greater than ninety degrees are by definition moving backward (retrograde) relative to the other planets. In other words, Niku's path projected on to the plane of the orbit of the Earth is in the opposite direction to the eight planets orbiting the Sun.[1021]

One other trans-Neptunian object has also been discovered with a retrograde orbit and with a nearly identical ascending node to Niku. 2008KV42, nick-named Drac after Count Dracula, has a path inclined one-hundred-and-three degrees relative to the ecliptic. Some massive object on a highly inclined and retrograde orbit must have kicked both Niku and Drac in to their related orbits.[1022] A significant coincidence is that the orbital inclination of star-core-zeus predicted from the observations of ancient astronomers and described in my previous book *Cataclysms & Renewals* is almost the same as the inclination of Niku and Drac.[1023]

The existence of the cut-off at the outer-edge of the Kuiper Belt beyond fifty AU, and the empty space up to seventy AU, reveals that either a massive object crosses this region of space on its orbital approach to the Sun or this is the location of a gravitationally neutral binary-system barycenter.

This concept generates two possible origins for the scattered-objects: either they are former Kuiper Belt objects disturbed by the perturbing mass or they are alien objects that have been delivered to our solar-system and captured by the Sun. New data also suggests the massive object that is disrupting the out Kuiper Belt, also penetrates deep into our solar-system.

Conclusion

Venus is an alien planet, the remains of a hot massive comet-like object, that recently arrived in the inner solar-system. Astronomy confirms the astro-mythology that Venus has been recently captured by the Sun from star-core-zeus.

Studies on the distribution of uranium in the solar-system, particularly surface deposits on Earth and the Moon and the mysterious additional heating of Earth, suggest our planet has had regular close encounters with star-core-zeus.

The long history of perturbations of both Uranus and Neptune combined with the more recent astronomical observations of the scattered outer Kuiper Belt objects indicates that star-core-zeus is approaching us from the triangle of night-sky defined by the bright star Sirius and the constellations of Gemini and Orion.

Twenty-first century astronomy is also providing a wealth of new information on exo-planetary systems orbiting other stars and how supernovas produce star-core remnants and drive planet-formation. In the next chapter, we shall assess information from these subjects to gain a better understanding of the relationship between star-core-zeus and our solar-system.

CHAPTER 18

Exo-Planets and White Dwarfs

● ● ●

THE PROPERTIES OF EXO-PLANETARY SYSTEMS orbiting other stars challenge the validity of the solar-nebular-model as an explanation for the formation of our solar-system. Studies of white-dwarfs, the hot star-core remains of other stars, help us to understand the nature of star-core-zeus.

Exo-Planets and Other Star-Systems

NASA's planet-hunting Kepler satellite has observed about two hundred thousand stars similar to the Sun and collected a wealth of data on exo-planets orbiting other stars. By the end of AD 2016, over three-thousand-six-hundred exo-planets had been characterized, orbiting around two thousand seven hundred host stars.[1024] Over five-thousand exo-planets are expected to be verified in the near future.

This database is far from complete: the results of planet-hunting are biased to detect planets with shorter orbital periods. Kepler is sensitive to planets transiting stars in under three years and less than twice the average Earth-Sun distance from the host-star. This limitation excludes planets similar to the outer giant-planets of our solar-system. For comparison, Neptune orbits the Sun every one-hundred-and-sixty-five years at thirty-times the average Earth-Sun distance.

Despite this limitation, the new data gives surprising results: generally the orbital-planes of exo-planets are not in the same plane as the host-star equator. Some exo-planets loop in trans-polar orbits around host stars, traveling above and below the stellar rotation poles. More than half of exo-planets have orbital planes angled more than fifteen degrees to the host star equator.

These exo-planetary-systems could not have formed from a simple rotating nebular of gas and dust.[1025] The statistics of exo-planets show that circular co-planar orbits like our solar-system are rare, and the conclusion is that no general theory exists to explain planetary system formation.[1026, 1027]

The discovery of the hot-Jupiters, massive gas-giant planets orbiting extremely close to other stars, with orbits misaligned to the stellar equator was also a great surprise. Many huge gas-giants, up to ten times bigger than Jupiter, have been discovered orbiting with radii from three AU to much less than the distance of Mercury to our Sun. Some of these huge balls of gas are cooking at three-thousand Kelvin. This should be impossible according to the old solar-nebular-model.

Many exo-planets trace extremely eccentric elliptical orbits. Exo-planetary orbits with thirty percent eccentricity and a wide range of inclinations are very common. Some exo-planets revolve around their host-stars in the opposite direction to the host star's rotation. The exo-planet evidence refutes the model that the formation of planetary-systems occurs by the gradual condensation of a simple rotating nebular disc and supports the hypothesis of the origin of planets in the debris from violent stellar explosions.

Stellar Metallicity, Supernova Debris, and Planets

Metallicity of a star is generally defined as the fraction of the mass of a star that is not hydrogen or helium. Stars with significant amounts of carbon, nitrogen, oxygen, sulfur, and other elements up to titanium and iron in their stellar atmospheres are considered to have significant metallicity.

However, the measurement of stellar metallicity is usually based on the spectroscopic analysis of the iron-content relative to the hydrogen content of the luminous outer atmosphere of a star. This abundance ratio called Fe/H is calculated as the logarithm of the star's iron abundance divided by the star's hydrogen abundance; less the logarithm of the Sun's iron abundance divided by the Sun's hydrogen abundance. By this definition, the Fe/H of the Sun is zero.

METALLICITY DISTRIBUTION OF LOCAL F-G-K TYPE STARS VERSUS PLANET-HOST STARS

The metallicity of the Sun (standard 0.0) is the same as the mean metallicity of the planet-host stars discovered so far. In contrast, the median of the metallicity distribution of the population of local F-G-K Sun-like stars is lower. In addition, Sun-like stars with a binary Companion Star have low mean metallicity. The conclusion is that stars from former binary systems, contaminated with iron-rich supernova debris, tend to host planets. Data: [www.exoplanet.eu], [Kordopatis, G., et al., "The rich are different: evidence from the RAVE survey for stellar radial migration" Mon Not R Astron Soc 447 (2015): 3526-3535. DOI: https://doi.org/10.1093/mnras/stu2726] and [Grether D., & Lineweaver, C., "The Metallicity of Stars with Close Companions" *The Astrophysical Journal*, 669 (2007): 1220-1234

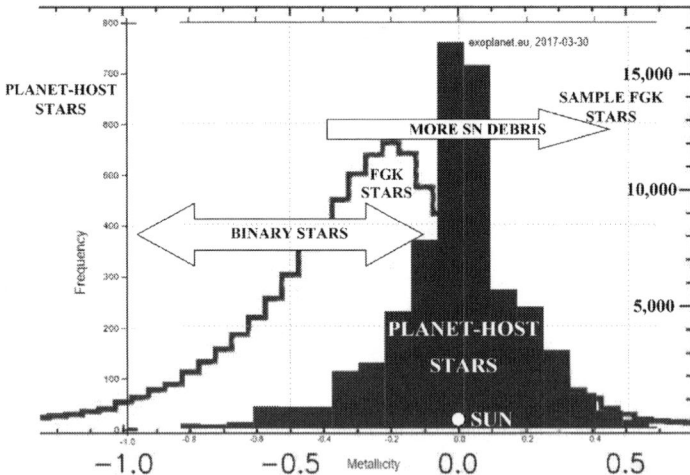

Any star with a higher metallicity than the Sun has a positive value for Fe/H. Conversely, any star with a lower metallicity than the Sun has a negative value for Fe/H. The scale is logarithmic, so stars with a value of plus-one have ten times the metallicity of the Sun. Conversely, stars with a value of minus-one have a tenth of the metallicity of the Sun. Fe/H can also be considered as a measure of the amount of contamination of a star's atmosphere with iron-rich supernova debris, relative to the Sun.

A local population of over four hundred and twenty thousand F G K stars have been analyzed, which are similar to our Sun. The median metallicity (Fe/H) of this population is half that of the Sun, and thousands of these stars have a metallicity less than ten percent of the Sun.[1028]

In contrast, the metallicity of the Sun is identical to the median metallicity (Fe/H) of the two-thousand-seven hundred stars that host planets.[1029] A study that correlated the abundances of elements heavier than hydrogen and helium, in more than four-hundred host-stars with more than six-hundred exo-planet candidates, allowed categories of different types of exo-planets to be grouped into different populations defined by host-star metallicity.[1030]

There is evidence that metal-rich stars had the metal contamination injected into them as supernova debris, at the same time as their exo-planets formed.[1031] NASA's Kepler spacecraft showed that exo-planets generally form around stars, which have been contaminated with supernova-debris. For example, the one-hundred-and-fifty-two stars with high metallicity that were inspected by Kepler had two-hundred-and-twenty-six planets.

The presence of adsorption lines for iron in the stellar atmosphere is a diagnostic marker for supernova debris contamination and the presence of planets: our solar-system fits this pattern perfectly.[1032] In contrast, the presence of planets cannot be predicted from the spectral classification of the stars.[1033]

The amount of iron in the Sun is unusually high for a typical G-type star.[1034] Our Sun must have collected debris from a local supernova to account for its unusually high abundance of iron relative to hydrogen, compared to the local population of stars. It has been found that host-stars contaminated with not only iron but also titanium, aluminum, magnesium, and silicon are much more likely to have planets.[1035]

There are strong correlations between host-star-metallicity and the presence of planets. Small rocky planets tend to orbit stars with metallicity very similar to the Sun. When the spectroscopic metallicities of stars hosting over two hundred small exo-planet candidates were studied, small rocky planets with orbits of less than four Earth-radii occurred around host stars with metallicity close to that of the Sun, whereas larger planets preferentially formed around stars with higher metallicities.[1036]

Generally, stars with very high metallicity are more likely to host giant-planets, and their presence can even be reliably predicted for the majority of stars with a metallicity of more than three percent.[1037] In addition, the closer the exo-planets orbit the host star, the higher the metallicity of the star.[1038]

The metallicity of the Sun is about a hundred times greater than in the majority of the medium G-class stars, which still exist in stable binary-star-systems. The metallicity of the local population of F G K type stars with a companion star in a close binary system also have much lower metallicity.[1039] Evidence is accumulating that binary-star-systems of Sun-like stars with no supernova-debris contamination are very unlikely to have planetary systems. In contrast, single Sun-like stars with more than two percent of the stellar matter being a cocktail of type-two supernova debris are very likely to have planets but no binary companion star.

In fact, the amount of iron in the Sun is very similar to the spectrum of Sun-like stars of former binary-star-systems, which have a dark star-core companion and host exo-planets. Generally, the atmospheres of these wobbling primary stars with an undetectable dark binary companion, which is probably a dark former star-core, contain unusually large amounts of heavy metals in their absorption spectra, which must have been generated by a local supernova.

The conclusion is that stars from former binary systems, which were contaminated with iron-rich supernova debris when their partner blew up, tend to host planets. These strong correlations mean that supernovas must be common in binary systems.

The pattern suggests there is a general mechanism for the formation of exo-planets from the debris of companion-stars of binary-star-systems, which blew up in supernova explosions. The additional conclusion is that the observed increase in metallicity of the host-star population comes from supernova explosion debris.

Binary-star-systems with Planets

Binary-star-systems with planets are very common: half of all the exo-planet host-stars discovered by Kepler were in binary-star-systems.[1040, 1041] Follow-up studies with Earth-based telescopes, such as the WIYN Telescope located on Kitt Peak in southern Arizona and the Gemini North Telescope located on Mauna Kea in Hawaii, confirmed the Kepler data that half of the stars that host exo-planets are binaries.[1042]

The presence of a second star, or star-core, does not prevent the existence of a stable planetary-system: for example, the binary-star-system Kepler-16b has one planet, and the binary-star-system Kepler-47 has two planets. Recently, an Earth-like planet has been found orbiting one star of a close-binary-star-system in which the two stars are only separated by fifteen astronomical units.[1043] Another study revealed that some planetary systems can even survive local supernova explosions.[1044]

The stability of planets in binary-star-systems has also been modeled using computer simulations. Binary-star-systems containing two stars of one solar mass each can have stable planetary systems. Models show that even if our Sun had a companion-star, which was of the same mass, our planetary system would be stable.

Harrington investigated the effect of a companion-star orbiting with the Sun in either a circular orbit or in an elliptical orbit with a fifty percent eccentricity. The computer simulations showed that such a companion-star in a circular orbit, which is more than five times the planetary distance from the Sun, is not a serious threat to the long-term stability of the solar-system.[1045, 1046, 1047]

Generally, the perturbations due to companion-stars are much weaker than the mutual-gravity-resonances of the planets of a star-system, which easily overcome any kozai instabilities.[1048] Generally, instabilities shown by nominal test masses do not match the real mutual gravity interactions of actual planets, which stabilize multi-planet systems.[1049] An example is the HK Tauri binary-star system in which two stars orbit each other at a distance of four-hundred AU: they have a stable protoplanetary disc that is angled about seventy degrees to the binary orbital plane.[1050] In addition, magnetic fields act to stabilize planetary systems.[1051]

The collective interactions of the planets of our solar-system have maintained its geometry and coherence for billions of years. For example, a two-dimensional model representing a theoretical Sun-Earth-Jupiter solar-system exposed to a fly-by of a rogue star was investigated to assess the minimum level of interaction between a passing star and the solar-system, which would be necessary to eject Earth from its orbit around the Sun.[1052]

The rogue star was modeled approaching the Sun in the orbital plane of the planets at a low velocity of forty kilometers-per-second, close to the orbital velocity of the Earth. Even assuming these extremely disruptive conditions, in which the gravity of the passing star had plenty of time to attract the planets, the solar-system model remained stable.

The model showed that under conditions very favorable for planet orbit disruption, even the increase of the orbital eccentricities of the outer planets was rare, while disruptive events such as escape or capture of planets from the inner solar-system was extremely unlikely.

An interesting result of these models was the prediction that in a binary system of the Sun and star-core-zeus, the Sun and planets should turn as one coordinated unit at the same angular rate, in a great orbit around the barycenter. This binary center of gravity for the whole solar-system is located fifty AU out from the Sun in the direction of Sirius-Gemini.

Binary-star-systems, White Dwarves, and Planet Formation

Our companion-star imploded in a supernova when its nuclear-fusion stopped, and the temperature of its core dropped so much that its heat-pressure could no longer prevent core-collapse. The massive weight of all the matter of the companion-star pressed on its core to such an extent that atoms were forced to merge. The extreme-gravity forced atoms to squeeze together to form degenerate-matter; a tight cluster of atomic nuclei surrounded by a sea of electrons.

However, the core suddenly stopped shrinking when it reached a critical high density, where a quantum-mechanical effect called the Pauli-exclusion-principle triggered a powerful electron-pressure that balanced the gravitational collapse. This remarkable Pauli-force that is independent of temperature prevented further shrinking of the core and resulted in a stable hot sphere of hyper-dense degenerate-matter.

However, during the collapse of the core of the companion-star, the matter had to spin faster and faster to conserve angular-momentum. In the process, the original larger core of the companion-star spun up to ultra-high rotation rates and shattered just before supernova detonation. Much of the former core was ejected into the surrounding space as enormous lumps of nickel-iron plus other heavy metals. Only the inner remains of the core of the companion-star was converted to a dense sphere of degenerate-matter, before being ejected by the asymmetric supernova explosion.

The remains of the core started life as a hot white-dwarf, a rapidly-spinning sphere of electron-degenerate matter about ten percent of the mass of the Sun.[1053] This enormous mass was squashed into a globe only two-to-three times the size of Earth.[1054, 1055, 1056]

An example of a star-core that continued to orbit its partner star after a type-two supernova explosion in a binary-star-system is SN 1993J.[1057] An example of a sun-like star with a white dwarf as its binary companion has also been observed by the Kepler space-telescope.[1058] Evidence is accumulating that very low mass white dwarfs tend to be produced in binary-star-systems, after one of the stars blows up.[1059]

Visible White-Dwarfs and Missing Black-Dwarfs

More than ninety-five percent of main-sequence stars end their lives after a terminal red-giant phase, leaving behind heavy white dwarfs between a half-solar and one-solar mass. Only a minority of the white dwarf population is produced by type-two core-collapse supernova explosions, usually when large rapidly-rotating magnetic stars blow-up. During the destruction of this type of star, the core shatters during the collapse phase, so not enough matter remains to form a neutron star and a very low mass white dwarf is formed.

Typical white-dwarfs take many billions of years to cool down. The detectable white-dwarf population local to our solar-system has an average mass of about seventy percent of the mass of the Sun and an effective temperature from six-thousand to twenty-thousand degrees Kelvin.[1060] The majority of white-dwarfs that have been detected in our galaxy are fifty to seventy percent of a solar mass.[1061] About thirty percent of white-dwarfs are found in binary-star-systems.[1062] These high-mass young white-dwarfs are easy to detect, simply because they are so hot and luminous.

Theoretical calculations show that high-mass white-dwarfs cool very slowly because of their huge heat capacity and small surface area. A one-solar mass white dwarf takes over five billion years to stop radiating light.[1063,] [1064] Lower mass white-dwarfs are dimmer and generally have temperatures below four thousand degrees Kelvin. Recent observations of cool white dwarfs of thirty to forty percent of a solar mass radiate one-micron-infrared with a blackbody radiation wavelength peak around one micrometer, which is equivalent to a surface temperature of three thousand Kelvin.[1065]

BLACK DWARF PHYSICS

Star-Core-Zeus is an old cold dark star-core fragment of the former Companion Star of the Sun. According to the physics of condensed stellar objects, it is likely to be about ten per cent of the mass of the Sun, compressed into a sphere 2-3 Earth diametres and currently at temperature of 130 Kelvin. Star-Core-Zeus should be detectable as a 22 micron Infra-red source.

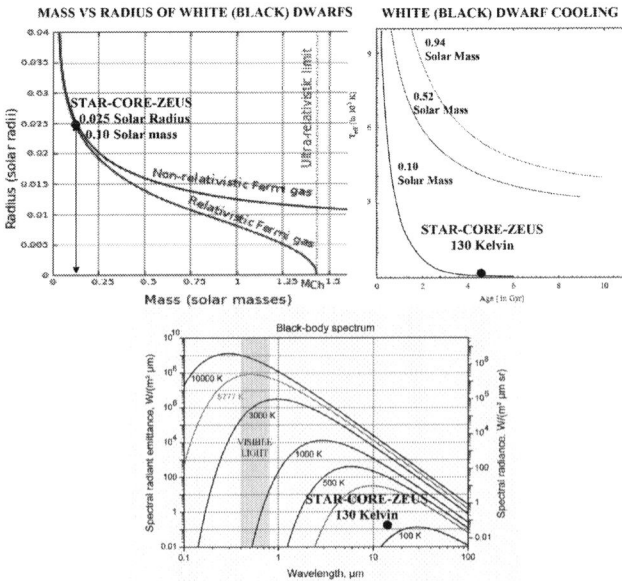

Rapid-Cooling of Small-Cores to Black-Dwarfs

Star-core-zeus, equivalent to Hoyle's black-dwarf, is probably only ten percent of a solar mass. Such an object must have cooled to invisibility much faster than the heavier hot white-dwarf population, which can still be observed.[1066, 1067]

However, this is still a controversial area of astrophysics. It is usually assumed that even the oldest white-dwarfs have not had enough time to cool below detectability. However, this is only true for white-dwarfs of more than twenty percent of a solar mass, which are detected simply because they are not invisible black-dwarfs.[1068]

There are theoretical difficulties in accurately modeling the cooling curves of very-low-mass, multi-billion year old white-dwarfs. An ultra-low-mass white-dwarf like star-core-zeus, with only ten percent of a solar mass, is predicted to cool much faster than the heavier general population. The amount of time necessary for Hoyle's white-dwarf to cool to an invisible black-dwarf is still unknown, but it is probably in the range of one to two billion years.

There is a mystery about a missing population of white-dwarfs that should exist with mass less than fifteen percent of a solar mass. Generally, as white-dwarfs cool, their optical luminosity decreases until their light is effectively extinguished. Sky surveys show the higher mass white-dwarfs are hotter and brighter than the lower mass white-dwarfs, which have been detected down to a luminosity of hundred-thousandth of the Sun's.

However, these surveys revealed something odd: there is a mysterious sudden cut-off in the population of dim white-dwarfs at fifteen percent solar. No white-dwarfs below this mass-limit have ever been observed, even though they are predicted to exist.[1069] This is an important clue to the upper-limit for the mass of star-core-zeus. The simple explanation is that they exist as invisible black-dwarfs, which by definition emit electromagnetic energy below present-day optical-detection-thresholds.

Theoretical mass-to-radius calculations show that less massive electron-degenerate objects occupy larger volumes because the radius of a white-dwarf is inversely-proportional to the cube-root of its mass. As white-dwarf mass is decreased, there is an exponential increase in its surface-to-volume ratio combined with an exponential fall in its density and its heat capacity.

For example, white-dwarf LHS1044 is sixty-six percent of a solar mass squeezed into a sphere of one-point-one percent of a solar radius. In contrast, white-dwarf LHS1734, which is only thirty percent of a solar mass, is forty-five percent bigger. The limit to the meaningful calculation of degenerate-mass-volume ratios was revealed with the discovery of a very low mass white-dwarf with only seventeen percent the mass of the Sun but with a radius nine-times the size of the Earth's.[1070]

Very-low-mass white-dwarfs have a larger radiative-surface to heat-capacity ratio, making their cooling much more efficient. Degenerate electron pressure is not temperature dependent, so these rapidly cooling white-dwarfs do not shrink. However, the strange properties of electron-degenerate matter, where coherent-thermal-vibration increases radiation efficiency and where heat capacity decreases with temperature, results in a positive-feedback-loop that accelerates heat-loss. Many small dark degenerate objects should exist in our galaxy, but because very-low-mass white-dwarfs cool so rapidly to black-body-temperatures insufficient to produce visible-light, they cannot be detected.

In addition, dark cloaks of supernova explosion debris, which are made of ionized carbon dust and other heavier elements, have been shown to block most of the electromagnetic radiation, even from bright star-cores. The conclusion is that a large number of undetected old cold low-mass black-dwarfs probably exist and the absence of optical evidence for Hoyle's star-core is not evidence of its absence.

Detection of Black Dwarfs

Generally, invisible massive objects in the galaxy are categorized by astronomers as machos, which are only detected by their gravitational effects. The gravitational micro-lensing effect of dark objects on visible star-light shows that machos probably make up half the invisible matter in the halo of our galaxy, and on an average, these dark objects weigh approximately half a solar-mass.[1071]

Sky surveys show that seventy percent of Sun-like stars in our local neighborhood wobble, revealing they are part of binary-star-systems. In ten percent of these binary-star-systems, the companion-star wobbling the primary star is invisible, indicating there is a dark massive object in orbit. Optical Doppler-shifts of the visible star have been used to measure the mass of potential black-dwarfs still in orbit around these primary stars. Four binary systems have been characterized in which one-solar-mass Sun-like stars are being wobble by dark-companions, which are about ten percent of a solar-mass.[1072] It is very likely that these dark invisible objects are old cold black-dwarfs.[1073]

In addition, a possible black-dwarf has been detected as an invisible solar-mass companion, perturbing a pulsar-neutron-star.[1074] The wobble of a low mass white-dwarf has revealed an invisible black-dwarf about twenty percent of a solar-mass in orbit. The detection of tiny wobbles in the position of other apparently single stars reveal they too are probably former binary-star-systems with a black-dwarf in orbit.

Magnetic White Dwarfs

In large stars, stellar magnetic fields are responsible for producing large-scale magnetic-structures comprising of a huge dense equatorial torus and bipolar-jets.[1075] Generally, when magnetic stars collapse, they become magnetic white-dwarfs. Sky surveys show that of the one hundred and twenty-two bright white-dwarfs discovered within twenty parsecs of the Sun, thirteen percent of them have detectable magnetic fields.[1076, 1077, 1078]

When a massive rapidly rotating magnetic star collapses in a supernova, either magnetic white-dwarfs or magnetic neutron-stars are produced.[1079, 1080] During the stellar-collapse, a surface magnetic field of one hundred gauss of a progenitor star will be amplified to a surface magnetic field of one million gauss, if the radius of the star shrinks by a factor of a hundred during the formation of a white-dwarf.

The first magnetic-white-dwarf detected was GJ742 due to its emission of circular-polarized-light, generated by its rapidly-rotating strong-surface-magnetic-field of approximately one-hundred-million gauss.

Generally, magnetic fields in white-dwarfs range from two thousand gauss, with about ten percent of white-dwarfs having magnetic-fields in excess of one million gauss. A hyper-magnetic white-dwarf has even been detected that has a magnetic field of an incredible one billion gauss.

All magnetic white-dwarfs have a similar characteristic structure.[1081] They resemble a child's spinning-top with a fat equatorial-toroid of charged-dust rotating rapidly around a small central ball of super-dense matter, with linear-axial-jets projecting from their poles.[1082] The structure is created by its rapidly rotating solenoid-like magnetic field in which closed magnetic loops connect toroidal magnetic-field-lines with the poles. The field lines are twisted into a tight magnetic helix at the rotation axis, due to the rapid rotation of the core.

This magnetic structure creates collimated axial-radio-jets of charged-particles, which stream away along magnetic-field-lines from the magnetic poles of the core and reach velocities near the speed-of-light. The changing magnetic-flux-density also generates strong radio-signals. Extremely powerful beams of radio waves are also emitted from the terminal-lobes formed at the end of the magnetic helix. An extremely magnetic white dwarf in a binary-star-system with a red dwarf star has recently been observed at AR Scorpii, beaming circular polarized UV light from its rotation poles.[1083]

A relationship between the population of lower-temperature white-dwarfs and their stronger magnetic-fields has also been discovered.[1084] Small magnetic white-dwarfs lose heat more rapidly by synchrotron radiation from the magnetic torus and tend to rapidly fade out of the visible spectrum to become invisible black-dwarfs. However, if star-core-zeus is a similar type of object, it should still be generating strong radio-signals, which are easy to detect.

The Birth of Our Solar-System and Star-Core-Zeus

Fred Hoyle proposed that at the birth of our solar-system, huge amounts of silicon, oxygen, iron, and other elements were ejected from the local supernova explosion of our companion-star. Some of this material was captured into orbit by the Sun's gravity, where it rapidly clumped-together to start the planet building process. This material also contaminated the Sun and increased its metallicity.

The Hubble Space Telescope has detected star-systems at a similar stage of planet formation. Generally, thirty percent of cool white dwarfs show evidence of planet formation in their vicinity, compared to less than one percent of main sequence stars.[1085] For example, four white-dwarfs were found with absorption spectra displaying high concentrations of iron, nickel, oxygen, silicon, and magnesium, evidence of a local cloud of planetary building materials.[1086]

Hoyle proposed that the asymmetric supernova explosion of the companion-star of the Sun caused the remains of its core to recoil at greater than solar-escape-velocity so that it was completely ejected from the solar-system and lost in space. It is certainly true that star-cores kicked out by asymmetric supernova explosions have been observed to move away from disrupted binary-star-systems at very high velocity.[1087]

However, the theoretical problem with this aspect of Hoyle's model was that if the momentum of star-core-zeus was large enough for it to be completely lost from the solar-system, then it would be highly unlikely that the momentum of the pre-planetary explosion-debris was small enough to be captured by the Sun and initiate planet-formation.

Conclusion

The companion-star of the Sun was probably an eight-to-ten solar-mass magnetic star with a rapid rotation rate. It was much larger and, therefore, much faster-evolving than our Sun. Four-point-six billion years ago, it blew up in a type-two supernova explosion. The supernova explosion of our binary-companion-star produced a huge explosion plume called the Fluff.

All that remained of the companion-star was star-core-zeus: a very-low-mass, rapidly-spinning hyper-magnetic white-dwarf. As the Fluff was blasted toward the bright star Cygnus, star-core-zeus recoiled away at relatively low velocity in the opposite direction, along the hot Tunnel toward Sirius. Hoyle suggested that his small white-dwarf became a cold invisible black-dwarf, which is now drifting in the galaxy far away from the Sun.

In contrast, this book presents the evidence that star-core-zeus cooled to a black-dwarf that remained in orbit with our Sun. Star-core-zeus was born as an ultra-low-mass white-dwarf, which did not have sufficient ballistic velocity to totally escape the gravitational well of the Sun. After star-core-zeus had traveled out no more than five-hundred AU in two thousand years, its outbound velocity had dropped to zero. Then like a ball thrown up into the air, it slowly swung around, gathered speed, and accelerated back under gravity toward the Sun.

Star-core-zeus settled into a highly eccentric elliptical orbit with our solar-system, around a new barycenter. At their closest approach, the Sun and star-core-zeus probably shot past each other at maximum velocity, near the present orbit of the Earth. The Sun and star-core-zeus then flew away from each other again, slowly decelerating.

The Sun and star-core-zeus have been orbiting each other on stretched-elliptical orbits every four thousand years since the formation of the solar-system. Efficient heat-loss meant that over a few billion years, star-core-zeus cooled from a hot visible white-dwarf to become a cold invisible black-dwarf.

Star-core-zeus is now probably a black body-radiator with a frosty temperature between one-hundred and one-hundred-and-fifty Kelvin. Even though it only produces a dim infrared signal, it still has a powerful magnetic field; so it should still produce a detectable radio-frequency signal.

Star-core-zeus is now invisible, but strange alignments and motions in our solar-system reveal its gravitational and magnetic influence on us, which shall be discussed in the next chapter.

CHAPTER 19

Odd Motions and a Hidden Magnetic Mass

● ● ●

THERE ARE ODD COINCIDENCES IN our solar-system. The general direction from the Sun towards the constellation of Gemini and the bright star Sirius, has collected a strange group of alignments. The elliptical orbit of the Earth is slightly stretched in that direction; the rotation axis of the Earth also leans over in that direction; the whole solar-system seems to be accelerating in that direction; and the solar-wind blows away from the Sun in that direction too.

The Elliptical Orbit of Earth around the Sun

Each year the Earth revolves around the Sun in a slightly eccentric elliptical orbit, traveling in an anti-clockwise direction from an imaginary view point above the north-pole of the Sun.[1088] The renaissance astronomer and astrologer Giovanni Cassini was first to measure the journey of the Earth around the Sun. Cassini organized the construction of a huge meridian-sun-dial within the dark nave of the great church of San Petronio in Bologna, Italy. This enormous pinhole-camera produced a small image of the Sun that traveled along a metal scale that spanned the floor of the church. The huge instrument allowed the position and size of the Sun to be accurately measured on each day of the year.[1089]

Cassini discovered that in January, the Sun moves three-point-four percent faster than its average motion, whereas in July it moves three-point-four percent slower. By measuring the relative diameter of the image of the Sun, he discovered the Earth is three percent closer to the Sun at the beginning of January.

Continuous measurement of the diameter of the Sun showed that the Earth arrives at aphelion, the furthest separation between the Earth and the Sun, on July 2, during the northern hemisphere summer when the solar disc diameter is thirty-one minutes and thirty-one seconds of arc. At aphelion, the Earth is one-hundred-and-fifty-two-million kilometers from the Sun and traveling at its slowest angular rate.

As the seasons turn to winter in the northern-hemisphere, the Earth arrives at perihelion, the nearest approach of the Earth to the Sun. On January 2, the solar disc diameter is maximum at thirty-two minutes and thirty-five seconds of arc, and Earth is at its perihelion position one-hundred-and-forty-seven-million kilometers from the Sun and traveling at its fastest angular rate.

It is a strange coincidence that at perihelion on January 2, the Earth passes the constellation of Gemini above an imaginary line connecting the Sun to the bright star Sirius, the approximate position predicted for the massive perturber of Uranus, Neptune, and the Kuiper Belt objects.

The Orientation of Earth's Rotation Axis

The rotation-axis of the Earth is tilted about twenty-three-point-five degrees from a right-angle to the plane of Earth's orbit around the Sun. It is another strange coincidence that the rotation-axis of Earth also leans toward a zone of the night-sky defined by the bright star Sirius and the constellations of Gemini and Orion. This is the location of the winter-solstice-point on the Earth's orbit around the Sun, a position known to astronomers as six-hours right-ascension.

The axis of the Earth maintains this orientation in space, throughout its year-long anti-clockwise journey around the Sun. This fixed orientation is responsible for the seasonal climates of Earth. The exception is a tiny clockwise shift in position of the angular direction of the celestial north and south poles, called axial-precession.

The orientation of Earth's rotation axis, combined with the position of the Earth on its orbit around the Sun, causes the passage from winter-spring-summer-autumn and back to winter. It is usually assumed that this process has been repeating like clockwork for millions of years, but this is not the case.

STRANGE ALIGNMENTS AND MOTIONS

There is a strange clustering of local alignments: the elongation of Earth's eliptical orbit, the tilt of the Earth's rotation axis, the magnetic-sheath & helio-tail surrounding solar system, and the hot supernova blast tunnel, all point to the general direction towards Sirius-Orion-Gemini. The blue-shifted light from Sirius shows we are flying towards Sirius and we are also accelerating.

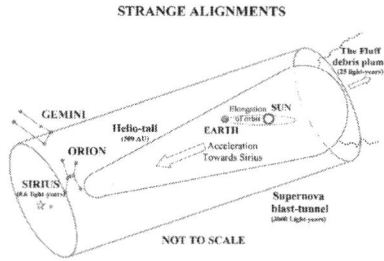

STRANGE ALIGNMENTS

NOT TO SCALE

The axial-precession of Earth is also accelerating, driven by the magnetic field of in-bound star-core-zeus.

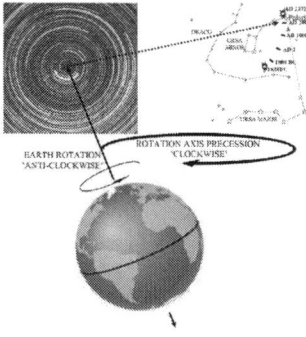

AXIAL PRECESSION

Image: an 8 hour exposure of the illusion that stars rotate around the North Celestial Pole, an effect due to the Earth turning on its axis

EARTH ROTATION 'ANTI-CLOCKWISE'

ROTATION AXIS PRECESSION 'CLOCKWISE'

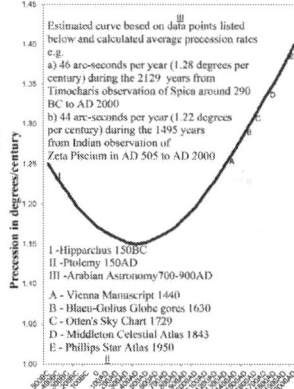

ACCELERATION OF PRECESSION
(Time in Centuries)

Estimated curve based on data points listed below and calculated average precession rates e.g.

a) 46 arc-seconds per year (1.28 degrees per century) during the 2129 years from Timocharis observation of Spica around 290 BC to AD 2000

b) 44 arc-seconds per year (1.22 degrees per century) during the 1495 years from Indian observation of Zeta Piscium in AD 505 to AD 2000

I - Hipparchus 150BC
II - Ptolemy 150AD
III - Arabian Astronomy 700-900AD

A - Vienna Manuscript 1440
B - Blaeu-Gelius Globe gores 1630
C - Otten's Sky Chart 1729
D - Middleton Celestial Atlas 1843
E - Phillips Star Atlas 1950

Precession in degrees/century

The axial-tilt of the Earth has been decreasing since the time of Cassini four hundred years ago. The eccentricity of Earth's orbit has also been decreasing from larger values: our orbit was much more eccentric only a few thousand years ago and has only recently declined to three percent eccentricity. Both the shape and the orientation of Earth's elliptical orbit are being changed not only by the gravitational perturbations of the other planets but also by an unknown force acting on the whole solar-system.[1090]

In 130 BC, Hipparchus measured the length of the seasons. His data shows that in his time, the eccentricity of Earth's orbit was four percent. Hipparchus measured the durations of the seasons by counting the days between the spring-vernal-equinox, summer-solstice, autumn-equinox, and the winter-solstice.

In year AD 2000, two-thousand-one-hundred-and-thirty years after the observations of Hipparchus, spring starting from the vernal-equinox was two days shorter; summer starting from the summer-solstice was over a day longer; autumn starting from the autumn-equinox was over two days longer; and winter starting from the winter-solstice was over a day shorter, than in the time of Hipparchus.

Three parameters influence season length: a shift in the axis of rotation of the Earth due to precession, a shift of the aphelion and perihelion points in Earth's orbit, and a variation in the shape of the Earth's orbit (its orbital eccentricity). Earth's orbit around the Sun has changed significantly between the time of Hipparchus in 130 BC and modern astronomy in the twenty-first century AD, but the precise combination of forces responsible is unknown.

Recent Changes in Earth's Axial Precession

The Earth rotates around its axis like a huge gyroscope, which maintains a constant orientation in space, unless external forces act to change its orientation. Isaac Newton proposed in his lunar-solar-precession-theory that the only forces that induce Earth to change its orientation were the combined torques from the gravitational pulls of the Sun and Moon on the Earth's equatorial bulge.

Conventional theory assumes that the tilted axis of the Earth has been slowly precessing in a clockwise direction at a constant rate due to these two torques. It is also assumed that the north-celestial-pole has made a complete three-hundred-and-sixty degree circuit of the heavens in approximately thirty-thousand years due to this effect.

The idea that the rate of precession is constant was originally introduced by Isaac Newton, but it turns out to be wrong. In his calculations,

Newton assumed the Earth is a sphere of uniform density, slightly flattened at the poles, with slightly more mass at the equator.

This is a mistake; almost all the mass of the Earth is concentrated symmetrically around the center of gravity at the Earth's core. Spacecraft have measured the surface-gravity of Earth and shown that the gravity at the equator is actually one percent less than at the poles.[1091] Therefore, it is impossible for the gravitational field of the Sun and Moon to act on the equatorial bulge, so this is not the origin of precession of the rotation axis of the Earth. Some other force must be responsible.

Recently Very-Long-Baseline-Interferometry (VLBI) of distant quasars have certainly shown the axis of the Earth precessing clockwise at a rate of approximately fifty arc-seconds per-year or about one-point-four degrees per-century. The problem is that axial-precession of Earth has been accelerating slightly.[1092]

Old star maps and other sources of ancient astronomy show that the acceleration of axial precession has been increasing since AD 400, which was described in my previous book *Cataclysms & Renewals*. Analysis of ancient measurements of the autumn-equinox-point by the ancient Greek, Indian, and Arab astronomers and the equinox-points on historical star maps over the last five hundred years clearly demonstrate the rate of precession is accelerating, and some mysterious force is acting on Earth to cause this acceleration.

Precession and Binary Motion

If the solar-system is part of a binary-star-system with a hidden companion star-core, then the Sun should also be displaying elliptical motion. The Sun and star-core should both be tracing out elliptical orbits around their common center of mass, known as the barycenter, which is always located between them. The effect of binary-system-motion is that the whole solar-system should be traveling on a curving flight path, and this could account for the apparent acceleration of axial-precession of the Earth.

Walter Cruttenden of the Binary Research Institute also believes Newton's lunar-solar-precession-theory is wrong, because it does not take into account the orbital motion of the Sun. For example, lunar-solar-precession-theory assumes that the Earth travels three-hundred-and-sixty degrees around the Sun from reference-star back to reference-star in a sidereal-year but less in a tropical-year from equinox-to-equinox (due to axial-precession).

However, Cruttenden demonstrated that lunar-solar-eclipse equations for predicting the position of the Moon and eclipses show that the Earth travels three-hundred-and-sixty degrees around the Sun in a tropical-year from equinox-to-equinox. This result challenges conventional ideas about the dynamics responsible for the precession of the equinoxes. In addition, when the duration in seconds of the sidereal-year with respect to reference-star Sirius was measured, it was also found to be the same as the tropical-year from equinox-to-equinox.[1093]

Cruttenden proposed that the Sun must be turning clockwise at the same rate that the rotation axis of the Earth is precessing clockwise.[1094] The Sun itself is moving on a clockwise curving trajectory, part of an elliptical orbit around a binary-star-system barycenter, located in the direction of Sirius.

Motion of the Solar-System Relative to Other Stars

The Sun is certainly not fixed in space, but its direction of motion can only be determined by measuring our motion relative to other stars. Herschel first analyzed this problem of the relative velocity of the solar-system in AD 1783 by measuring the changing positions of fourteen bright stars.

The absolute velocity of the solar-system in any direction is not easy to measure: there is no fixed reference point from which to measure our motion because all stars are in motion. In addition, the orbital velocity of the moving Earth around the Sun is about thirty kilometers-per-second, which also has to be subtracted from observed velocities of the stars surrounding us to arrive at the velocity of the solar-system relative to the stars.

The Sun and all the stars in our local spiral arm of the Milky Way swirl together in their related orbits round the center of the Galaxy. Our solar-system is located approximately twenty-seven-thousand light-years from galactic-center and forty light-years above the plane of the galactic disk.

The whole galactic-disk rotates producing an orbital velocity at the Sun's distance from galactic-center of about two-hundred-and-twenty kilometers-per-second. All the local stars surrounding the Sun are traveling with similar velocities around galactic-center.

The ESA Hipparcos Astrometry Satellite launched in the 1990s measured the positions, distances, motions, brightness, and colors of about one-hundred-and-twenty-thousand stars, two-hundred times more accurately than ever before. The Hipparcos and Tycho Catalogs of star positions and velocities were published by ESA in AD 1997.

This data has been used to construct the trajectories of all the local stars in the neighborhood of the Sun, which seem to be relatively stationary with respect to the Sun. This was called the local-standard-of-rest, which is calculated from the theoretical rotation velocity of an average circular orbit in the galactic-plane around galactic-center, at the radial distance of the Sun.

However, most of the local stars still move twice as fast as the Sun, with typical velocities of eight AU per year, relative to the local-standard-of-rest. The Sun's velocity relative to the local-standard-of-rest is four AU per year, which is low compared with other local stars.

Analysis of the apparent velocity-vectors of the stars surrounding us revealed that stars of the Sirius super-cluster are catching up with us by about four AU per year, as they travel toward Cygnus. This is equivalent to the solar-system moving in the opposite direction toward the Sirius super-cluster, at a relative velocity of four astronomical units per year.

Unfortunately, the accuracy of velocity estimates in the Hipparcos data is limited to about 10 kilometers-per-second, equivalent to about two AU-per-year.[1095] So far the results on the proper motion of the solar-system relative to local stars have not been accurate enough to prove or disprove any elliptical motion of the solar-system. It can be calculated that the gravitational attraction between the Sun and star-core-zeus, should produce an average velocity between one to two astronomical units per year.

However, the new data from the ESA spacecraft called Gaia launched in 2013 will have sufficient accuracy to determine the solar -system elliptical motion due to star-core-zeus, but it will not be available until 2018.

Acceleration toward Sirius

If there is a massive star-core close to us in the angular direction of Sirius, the whole solar-system should be falling in that direction and accelerating. The gravitational field of star-core-zeus should not just cause a velocity-vector, but it should also cause a detectable acceleration-vector. Analysis of the proper motion of the Sun relative to local stars indicates that there is a significant velocity-vector of the solar-system toward the approximate direction of the bright star Sirius.

The balmer-hydrogen-absorption-lines in the starlight coming from Sirius is blue-shifted, indicating the Sun and Sirius are flying toward each other. Data from around 1970 showed the Balmer alpha six-five-six nanometer absorption-line was blue-shifted point-zero-one-seven nanometers, indicating that the Sun and Sirius were traveling toward each other at a velocity of seven-point-seven kilometers-per-second, at that time.

However, if star-core-zeus is hidden in the general direction of Sirius, the Sun should not only be traveling in the direction of Sirius, but it should also be falling under gravity and accelerating in that direction too.

During my review of the historical published measurements of the radial velocity of Sirius, I made a startling discovery. The published radial velocity measurements over the previous hundred years show that we are definitely accelerating toward Sirius. There is an anomalous acceleration in the radial velocity of Sirius, which has increased by at least twenty-five percent, over the previous one hundred years.

In AD 1905 the radial velocity of the solar-system toward Sirius was minus-seven-point-three-six kilometers per second (minus indicates a closing-velocity in which the Sun and a star are heading toward each other).[1096] About sixty years later in AD 1967 the radial velocity of the solar-system toward Sirius had increased to minus-seven-point-six kilometers-per-second.[1097] After another ten years, in AD 1994 the radial velocity had increased further to minus-eight kilometers-per-second.[1098] In AD 2005 the closing velocity had increased again to minus-eight-point-six kilometers-per-second and it has continued to increase since that time.[1099] The radial velocity of Sirius is currently being measured again by the ESA space-craft Gaia, and new data points should be published in AD 2017.

Generally, the data supports the hypothesis that star-core-zeus and the Sun are falling toward each other. Star-core-zeus is probably currently hidden about two hundred and fifty AU from the Sun. The whole solar-system is accelerating toward the center of gravity between the Sun and star-core-zeus, located about fifty AU from the Sun, in approximately the same direction as Sirius.

OUR ACCELERATION TOWARDS SIRIUS

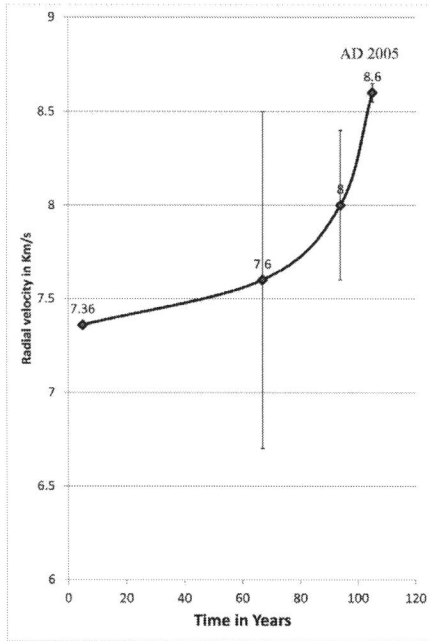

Data Sources
In 1905: Radial Velocity Sirius was -7.36 Km/s
Campbell W., "The variable radial velocity of Sirius," Astrophys. J, 21, (1905): 176-184. Campbell W., "The variable radial velocity of Sirius, and the inclination of its orbit-plane," Publ. Astron Soc. Pac. 17 (1905): 66-69.
In 1967 (or a few years before): Radial Velocity Sirius was -7.6 Km/s
SIMBAD, quoting Evans D. S., The revision of the general catalogue of radial velocities by 1 A.U Symp., held in Toronto, Canada. 30, (1967) 57-62 held on microfiche by " Centre de donnees Stellairies" Strasbourg.
In 1994 (or a few years before): Radial Velocity Sirius was -8.0 Km/s
Hoffleit, D. and Warren, W.H. Jr., The Bright Star Catalogue, 5th Revised Edition, Version 2 (1994)
In 2005 (or a few years before): Radial Velocity Sirius was -8.6 Km/s
Barstow M., et al, "Hubble Space Telescope Spectroscopy of the Balmer lines in Sirius B" Mon. Not. R. Astron. Soc. 362 (2005): 1134-1142 DOI: 10.1111/j.1365-2966.2005.09359.x   arXiv:astro-ph/0506600

The Magnetic Helio-Sheath and the Solar Wind

Another remarkable coincidence is that the orientation of the magnetic-helio-sheath surrounding the solar-system also approximately coincides with the same Sun-Sirius alignment.

At the end of the twentieth century, the old model of solar-system-magnetism placed the Sun and planets in the middle of a spherical magnetic field generated by the Sun. The idea was that open magnetic field lines extended equally in all directions from the Sun, creating a huge electrically-charged magnetic-bubble about one hundred AU in diameter, which was named the helio-sphere.

Magnetic field lines are generated by varying electric-fields and moving electric-charges. The Sun pumps out the charged particles of the solar-wind in all directions, which stream away along the open magnetic field lines of the local interplanetary-magnetic-field.[1100] In the region of the orbit of Earth, the anti-clockwise rotation of the Sun induces spiral pleats in our local interplanetary-magnetic-field.[1101]

The old model predicted that the super-sonic solar-wind streaming away from the Sun at approximately five-hundred kilometers-per-second must slow down when it collides with the gases in the interstellar medium of our galaxy. At this boundary, a standing shock-wave named the termination-shock was predicted to form where the velocity of the solar-wind abruptly slowed-down below the speed-of-sound in the local medium.

In addition, it was supposed that the rotation of our Milky Way galaxy is dragging our solar-system through the local interstellar medium, which carries an inter-stellar-magnetic-field. The interaction of the inter-planetary-magnetic-field generated by the Sun, with the inter-stellar-magnetic-field from the surrounding stars, was believed to create a stretched tear-drop-shaped magnetic-structure called the helio-sheath.

The magnetic-helio-sheath was predicted to resemble the coma of a huge comet about five hundred AU long and a hundred AU wide. The tail of the helio-sheath, called the helio-tail, was expected to trail behind the solar-system in the opposite direction to the path of the Sun through the Milky Way.[1102]

At the end of the twentieth-century, the velocity and direction of travel of the solar-system had already been calculated from the proper motions and radial velocities of more than forty-thousand nearby stars. The angular direction of motion of the solar-system was calculated to be toward the solar-apex in the constellation of Hercules, southwest of the star Vega.

This direction in space can be visualized as the direction of Earth from the Sun at the end of June, two-hundred-and-seventy-degrees anti-clockwise from the spring-vernal-equinox in the direction of Earth-orbit but thirty degrees above the orbital plane of Earth.[1103] The significance of this position shall become clear later.

The speed of the Sun toward the solar-apex was estimated to be about twenty kilometers-per-second relative to the local-standard-of-rest, the average motion of the local stars. This velocity is only ten per-cent of the orbital speed of the Sun, around the galactic-center of the Milky Way.

The old model predicted that the helio-sheath should resemble a comet traveling toward the solar-apex, with a bow-shock at the front, where the helio-sphere ploughed through the interstellar medium. Its long comet-like helio-tail was expected to stream behind, stretching away in exactly the opposite direction to the solar-apex, toward six hours (ninety-degrees) right-ascension and minus-thirty degrees declination, which is roughly the direction toward the constellation of Canis Major, which contains the bright star Sirius.

This old model of the magnetic solar-system survived for a genera-tion of astronomers, until the twenty-first century spacecraft started to produce strange new data.

Mysteries of the Magnetic-Helio-Tail

The first hint of a problem came from Pioneer-10, which was heading into the tip of the helio-tail. After the spacecraft passed the orbit of

Neptune in AD 1983, it started to send back signals of an anomalous acceleration before it was lost.[1104]

In AD 2004, data from the Extreme Ultraviolet Explorer (EUVE) spacecraft showed the bow-shock was not in front of the solar-system, where it had been expected to be found. It was deflected twenty-three degrees to an enigmatic location, around eighteen-hours right-ascension and only plus-seven-degrees of declination.[1105, 1106] The whole helio-sheath seemed to be strangely twisted, twenty-three degrees away from the direction of travel of our solar-system relative to galactic-center.

The two Voyager spacecraft, traveling in the opposite direction to Pioneer-10, confirmed this anomalous orientation. The termination-shock was traversed by Voyager-1 in AD 2004 at ninety-four AU but by Voyager-2 in AD 2007 at eighty-four AU out from the Sun. The different termination-shock distances found by Voyager-1 and Voyager-2 were quite unexpected and indicated an unpredicted asymmetry.

Then when the local inter-stellar-magnetic-field was measured, it was found to be almost three-times-stronger than the galactic average. Even more startling was the direction of the field lines, which ran approximately parallel to an imaginary line connecting the Sun and Sirius. The source of this strong magnetic field was another mystery.[1107]

In March 2005, Solar Wind Anisotropies (SWAN) spacecraft and Solar and Heliospheric Observatory (SOHO) spacecraft also showed that the helio-sheath was either distorted or simply not aligned to the direction of travel of the solar-system. It was also a surprise to discover that the hydrogen-flow inside the helio-sphere deviated by about four degrees from the direction of local-inter-stellar-medium-flow beyond the helio-sphere.[1108]

In 2008, NASA's Interstellar-Boundary-Explorer spacecraft called IBEX was launched to sort out the problem. Early data from IBEX confirmed that the relative motion of the Sun with respect to the local-interstellar-medium is twenty-three kilometers-per-second.[1109] This was very similar to the velocity toward the solar-apex of twenty kilometers-per-second, calculated from proper motions and radial velocities of local stars.

However, this velocity was much slower than the fast magneto-sonic speed, calculated from the velocity of the solar-wind streaming away from the Sun in all directions, which in the Earth's vicinity flies past at speeds around five-hundred kilometers-per-second. It was also a surprise that no termination-shock was detected by IBEX, where the supersonic wind was expected to slow-down suddenly. Another surprise was that no bow-shock was forming ahead of the heliosphere either.

The data suggested that a mysteriously strong local magnetic field was preventing the supersonic solar-wind that was streaming out from the Sun, from colliding with the interstellar-medium. Based on IBEX data, maps of Energetic Neutral Atoms (ENAs) flowing from the outer helio-sphere revealed a strange bright ring or ribbon around the sky.[1110] This is strong evidence that a local alien magnetic field is shaping the helio-sheath and deflecting the direction of the helio-tail.[1111]

The IBEX spacecraft also confirmed the enigmatic orientation of the helio-sheath.[1112] By combining observations from the first three years of IBEX data, the structure and boundaries of the helio-tail were mapped: the tip of the helio-tail was enigmatically centered around six-hours right-ascension, minus-six degrees declination, a deflection from the direction predicted by the old model.[1113]

There were further strange results. A slow stream of particles was expected to be detected traveling down the middle of a straight tail. It was a surprise when IBEX data showed there were two lobes of slower particles on the sides, and two lobes of faster particles above and below, giving a four-leaf-clover shape to the helio-tail.

In addition, the four-leaf clover structure was not oriented to the poles and equator of the Sun. The entire structure was twisted, as if it was under the control of an alien magnetic field from outside the solar-system. The helio-tail was being aligned with an alien object, hidden outside the solar-system, which was generating the powerful magnetic field.

These anomalies also corresponded with a weird clustering of cosmic rays, which were expected to arrive at ground-based observatories from all sky-directions.[1114] An enigmatic concentration of cosmic rays were coming from the same direction as the tip of the helio-tail detected by IBEX, the position of the alien object, which was perturbing the local interstellar magnetic field.[1115]

In 2014, new data from the Hubble Space Telescope also confirmed the unexpected location of the tip of the helio-tail. A spectral absorption-line of ionized-hydrogen, known to astronomers as the Lyman-alpha-line, allowed the detection of the hydrogen and hydrogen ions streaming away from the Sun in the direction of the helio-tail. By looking for this absorption line in star-light, from stars near the expected position of the tip of the helio-tail, the general direction of the helio-tail could be assessed.

The column-density of neutral-hydrogen-atoms flowing in the helio-tail was sufficient to give a clear signal in the light coming from stars in a triangular region of sky marked out by the bright star Sirius and the ecliptic stars of the constellation of Orion and across to the left horn of Taurus.[1116]

There is a clustering of helio-tail detections in the Lyman triangle around six-hour right ascension, the position of the winter-solstice. The tip of the helio-tail seems to point approximately toward the direction of the Winter Solstice and about six-degrees below the celestial equator (about thirty degrees below the ecliptic) in the direction of Sirius-Orion.[1117, 1118, 1119, 1120]

It seems that magnetic star-core-zeus is located at the tip of the helio-tale, forming a magnetic structure with the Sun, which resembles the fuselage of an aeroplane. Closed field-lines between star-core-zeus and the Sun allow the supersonic-solar-wind to curve around the outside of the helio-sheath in a great closed-loop, rather than collide with the interstellar medium.

The magnetic-sheath surrounding our solar-system is like a huge magnetic finger pointing at the space between Gemini, Sirius, and Orion, where star-core-zeus is stalking us from the darkness beyond Neptune.

THE CLUSTER OF 3C-161, THE HELIO-TAIL, THE HOT TUNNEL ENTRANCE AND THE WINTER SOLSTACE REVEALS THE LOCATION OF STAR-CORE-ZEUS

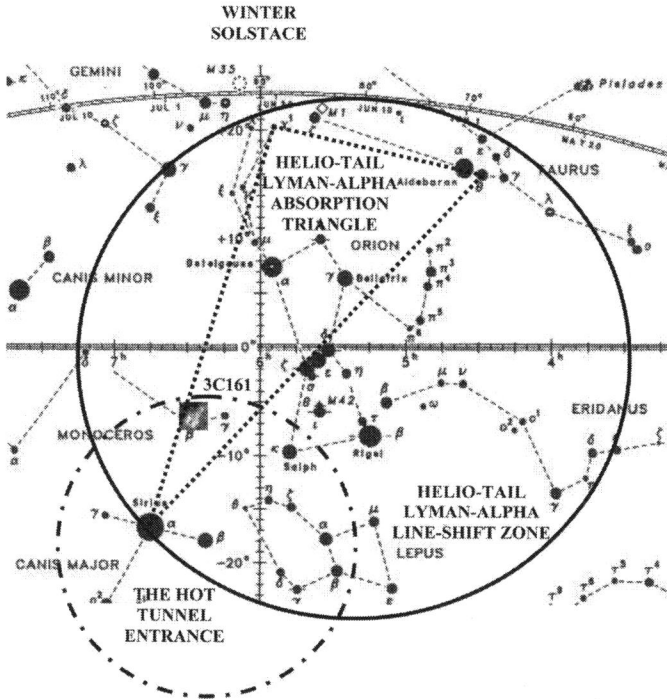

Data Source:
3C-161: Pearson, T., 'Compact Radio Sources In The 3C Catalog,' *The Astronomical Journal* 90 (1985) :738-755
THE HOT TUNNEL ENTRANCE: Lallement, R., '3D maps of the local interstellar medium; searching for the imprints of past events, 13th Annual International Astrophysics Conference: Voyager, IBEX, and the Interstellar Medium', IOP Publishing, *Journal of Physics: Conference Series* 577 (2015) 012016
HELIO-TAIL LYMAN-ALPHA ABSORPTION TRIANGLE: Wood, B., 'A New Detection of Lyα Absorption from the Heliotail', *The Astrophysical Journal*, 780 (2014) (12pp)
HELIO-TAIL LYMAN-ALPHA LINE-SHIFT ZONE Katushkina, O., et al 'Direction of interstellae hydrogen flow in the heliosphere: theoretical modelling and comparison with SOHO/SWAN data', MNRAS 446 (2015): 2929-2943

More than a Strange Coincidence of Alignments

It is more than a strange coincidence of alignments that the magnetic-sheath surrounding our solar-system also has the same orientation as the supernova-blast Tunnel and Fluff. The hot tunnel entrance is centered on a star called Mirzam adjacent to Sirius, which is also known as beta Canis Major.

The fundamental pattern surrounding our solar-system is probably the result of the four-point-six-billion year old shock wave from the asymmetric supernova explosion, which destroyed the companion-star of the Sun and created star-core-zeus.

When the companion-star blew up in an asymmetric type-two supernova, most of the debris was blasted toward the Sun and beyond. The Fluff is the remains of the hot convective region of the companion-star that was blasted away toward Cygnus.

This mass of hot material acted like massive rocket-exhaust, causing the hot super-dense star-core of the companion to recoil in the opposite direction. As the star-core went ballistic, it formed the ultra-hot linear tunnel through the Local Bubble, which runs in the angular direction of the bright star Sirius and its neighboring star called Mirzam (beta Canis Major). The aphelion position of star-core-zeus is now in this approximate direction.

Magnetic star-core-zeus is approaching from the space between the constellations of Gemini and Canis Major and moving toward the constellation of Orion, on its way to the Sun. The arrangement of the large scale structures surrounding the solar-system seem to coincide with the predicted position of the highly elliptical and inclined orbit of star-core-zeus.

The orientation of the axis of rotation of the Sun also seems to be associated with this grand alignment. The Sun tilts seven-and-a-quarter degrees from the perpendicular of the average orbital plane of the planets. The Sun's north-rotational-pole leans almost exactly in the opposite direction to Sirius. The axis of rotation of the Sun probably lies in the plane of the paired binary-system orbits of the Sun and star-core-zeus, whose perihelion position is above the north-rotation-pole of the Sun. In addition, the major-axis of the elliptical orbit of the Earth also approximately coincides with the orientation of the tail of the magnetic helio-sheath, the Tunnel, and the Fluff.

A grand-alignment occurs on January 2 and July 1 every year, when the Earth is respectively at perihelion and aphelion, and the Sun, Sirius, the Tunnel, the Fluff, the magnetic helio-sheath, and the axis of rotation of both the Earth and Sun, all fall into one plane. This is the plane of the orbit of star-core-zeus.

Conclusion

The mysterious motions and strange coincidences in orientation of the solar-system reveal the presence of star-core-zeus. In the next chapter, we shall consider strange space phenomena and climate changes, which are warnings of the coming fly-by of star-core-zeus and the end of our age of the world.

CHAPTER 20

The Return of Star-Core-Zeus

● ● ●

Magnetic-field changes, increases in solar-radiation intensity, and the current global-warming, all suggest that the solar-system is already under the influence of star-core-zeus. Industrial-carbon-dioxide only adds a minor extra factor to this natural cycle of cataclysm. A few centuries of climate-change heralded each one of the previous three cataclysms. Climate-change seems to be caused by the approaching magnetic star-core, which induces changes in the interplanetary-magnetic-field. In addition, recent astronomical surveys have already detected a mysterious object, which is probably star-core-zeus.

Magnetic Star-Core-Zeus

Star-core-zeus is a sphere of super-dense degenerate-electron matter, about two-to-three Earth diameters in size and ten percent of the mass of the Sun. However, star-core-zeus looks like an enormous spinning-top, due to its bagel-shaped magnetic torus of dust and debris that surrounds its equator and its thin magnetic polar-jets that resemble incandescent spindles.

The whole complex structure of star-core-zeus is held together by its intense rapidly rotating magnetic field. This type of magnetic structure has been observed at all scales in the cosmos from magnetic super-massive black-holes at the centers of galaxies to magnetic neutron stars and white dwarfs.[1121, 1122]

The Enigmas of Earth Magnetism

Magnetometers on satellites have recently confirmed the magnetic-field-strength of Earth is declining steadily: no-one knows why. European-Space-Agency swarm-satellites confirmed the terrestrial magnetic field is weakening at five percent-per-century.[1123] This new data contradicts the old model that the Earth's magnetic field is being generated by a self-sustaining dynamo deep in the mantle. It is currently decaying with a half-life of only fourteen-hundred years, and the last time it was at full-charge was less than four thousand years ago.

The magnetic poles of the Earth are also drifting toward the geographic poles as the field-strength falls.[1124] The north-magnetic-pole has been tracked, moving across northern Canada toward the north-geographic-pole in the Arctic Ocean.[1125]

Something is going on: the fluctuating magnetic field of the Earth is directly connected with climate-change.[1126, 1127, 1128, 1129, 1130, 1131, 1132] The climate-history data shows a repeating pattern of magnetic-anomalies, global-warming, and drought, prior to a cataclysm.

Star-core-zeus is surrounded by a powerful dipolar magnetic field and carries a substantial static electric charge. Changes in axial orientation and pole positions of the Earth are caused by interaction with the powerful magnetic and electro-static fields of star-core-zeus. Star-core-zeus is already causing the acceleration in the precession of the equinoxes.

During a fly-by of Earth, like-magnetic-pole-repulsion and electro-static-repulsion are powerful enough to flip our planet. Our planet can tumble over in space, like a floating ball compass perturbed by a strong magnetic field. Earth was turned up-side-down in the previous two fly-bys: these planetary inversions that happened in 5600 BC and in 1628 BC were described in my previous book *Cataclysms & Renewals*. On each fly-by, the magnetic field of the Earth was also recharged by magnetic induction, when exposed to the powerful magnetic field of star-core-zeus.

Star-Core-Zeus and the Interplanetary-Magnetic-Field

In contrast to the weakening magnetic-field of Earth, the strength of the interplanetary-magnetic-field is increasing rapidly: something very odd is going on.

Lockwood's group at the Rutherford Appleton Laboratory, Oxford, United Kingdom, discovered that the interplanetary-magnetic-field has more than doubled in strength in the last hundred years.[1133] Surrogate measurements of the interplanetary-magnetic-field indicate that the field strength has been increasing since the mid-nineteenth century: the same period of time we have assumed for man-made global-warming.[1134]

Data from various space missions from AD 1964 combined with the data from the spacecraft Ulysses launched in AD 1990 led to the discovery of an alarming increase in the strength of the interplanetary-magnetic-field. Measurements of the near-Earth radial-component of the interplanetary-magnetic-field have revealed that the magnetic flux in the solar-corona and the total solar-magnetic-flux leaving the Sun has risen by forty percent in only thirty-three years.

The total solar-magnetic-flux derived from historic geomagnetic data from AD 1868 to AD 1996, combined with interplanetary observations from AD 1964 to AD 1996, show that the interplanetary-magnetic-field has increased by an incredible two-point-three-times since AD 1901. Both the interplanetary-magnetic-field and solar-magnetism have more than doubled over the twentieth-century, but nobody knows why.

What we do know is that the increasing interplanetary-magnetic-field strength is correlating with global-warming: the increase in temperature of Earth's atmosphere and oceans.[1135] Global warming strongly correlates to weird new phenomena in the solar-system but not man-made carbon-dioxide in our atmosphere.[1136, 1137, 1138, 1139]

For example, the Arctic-surface air-temperature has been shown to be driven by total solar irradiance, which directly correlates with the magnetic-flux in the solar-corona, the ultra-hot outer transparent atmosphere of the Sun. It is the increasing strength of the magnetic-field in the solar-corona and the solar-system that is driving global-warming and climate-change.[1140]

In addition, we are still ignorant about how the solar corona is being heated. The temperature of the photosphere at the surface of the Sun is six-thousand Kelvin, heated mainly by convection of heat from the fusion-reactions in the solar-core. However, just above the photosphere surface, there is a five hundred kilometer thick cooler layer called the temperature minimum, which only has a temperature of four-thousand Kelvin, two-thirds of the temperature of the photosphere.

Above this layer, the outer solar corona is one-million Kelvin, more than two-hundred-and fifty times hotter. No scientist has a good explanation for this heating or why the temperature of the solar-corona rises steeply with increasing altitude to the ultra-hot temperature of five-million Kelvin, even further out from the Sun.[1141] It is this ultra-hot plasma of the corona, which expands out to become the super-heated solar-wind.

The solar coronal heating seems to be connected to the combined electrical and magnetic properties of the Sun and solar-system. However, it is still not known what process is making the outer-layers of the solar-atmosphere so much hotter than the inner-layers. It seems the Sun's corona is heated by the external interplanetary-magnetic-field.

The total energy output of the Sun is determined by the magnetic field inside and outside the Sun.[1142] The generation of the internal magnetic field of the Sun is connected to differential rotation rates at different solar-latitudes and convection-cycles of electrically-charged-plasma, which gives rise to the solar electro-magnetic dynamo.[1143]

Two processes seem to be responsible for maintaining the solar magnetic field. One originates in the interior, around a narrow shell between the inner radiative zone and outer convective zone of the Sun, which generates a toroidal magnetic field around the solar equator. The other process is at the surface of the Sun, concentrated near the sunspots, and is directly connected to the external interplanetary-magnetic-field, which stretches away from the Sun.[1144]

It is thought that the thermostat of the Sun is controlled by the magnetic field external to the Sun, which is connected to the interplanetary-magnetic-field. The external-magnetic-field perturbs the internal toroidal field of the Sun to generate a poloidal magnetic field that follows the lines of longitude from solar-pole to solar-pole. This perturbation induces an auto-activating Tayler-magnetic instability that induces strong electric current flows through the conductive solar-plasma, which in turn stimulates a stronger magnetic field and which in turn generates a further electric current flow.

There is also a regular sun-spot-cycle of solar-intensity peaks of eleven years in duration in which the polarity of the Sun's magnetic field is reversed.[1145] Every eleven years, the peak numbers of sun spots correspond to a peak in the interplanetary-magnetic-field strength and a peak in solar irradiance at Earth-surface.

The sun-spot-cycle repeats the same magnetic polarity for the Sun every twenty-two years. This magnetic-resonance is in harmony with an orbit resonance, which produces a planetary alignment of Venus, Earth, and Jupiter every forty-four years.[1146, 1147, 1148]

The hot ionized solar-wind, which is blasting away from the Sun's corona at up to eight-hundred-thousand kilometers-per-second, carries the one-hundred-thousand nano-Tesla magnetic dipole field of the Sun. This coronal-magnetic-field is transmitted out into the solar-system to become the interplanetary-magnetic-field.

If space surrounding the Sun was an absolute vacuum, then the magnetic-dipole-field of the Sun should decline rapidly reducing in strength by the cube of the distance so that by the time it reaches the Earth, it should be no greater than one nano-Tesla.

However, satellite observations above Earth show something completely different. The local interplanetary-magnetic-field surrounding Earth is over one-hundred-times bigger than expected, and it is getting bigger. Scientists do not understand what is amplifying the extended dipole-field of the Sun or the interplanetary-magnetic-field. It is very likely that star-core-zeus is responsible.

There is no doubt that the magnetic field of the Sun plus the inter-planetary-magnetic-field directly affect the climate of Earth in two ways.[1149, 1150, 1151, 1152] The increasing field-strength of the interplanetary-magnetic-field is correlating with greater solar-radiation-intensity, leading to more heat being received by Earth from the Sun and significant effects on our weather.

The increasing strength of the interplanetary-magnetic-field also reduces the number of cosmic-rays, which are high-energy-protons from the cosmos and which strike our atmosphere. Peaks in the interplanetary-magnetic-field strength correspond to troughs in the cosmic-ray hourly-count, related to the number of high-energy-protons entering our atmosphere.[1153]

Cosmic-rays trigger cloud-formation, so reducing cosmic-rays reduces the total cloud cover over Earth.[1154, 1155] The interplanetary-magnetic-field behaves like a giant magnetic-deflector-shield, which prevents high-energy charged-particles ionizing the upper-atmosphere and seeding new clouds. Less low-altitude cloud-cover on Earth leads to a lower total planetary reflectivity (known as albedo) and more effective solar heating.[1156, 1157, 1158, 1159]

In summary, global-warming is being driven by a hotter Sun and lower Earth albedo, both caused by the magnetic field of star-core-zeus as it approaches the Sun. The magnetic field lines connecting the two magnetic objects are getting progressively denser, and the interplanetary-magnetic-field in the whole solar-system is increasing in strength. The most significant observation is that it is not just the Earth that is experiencing global-warming; the whole solar-system is heating up.

The Sun Is Getting Hotter and Global-Warming on Mars

The average solar-UV-output is increasing, indicating that the Sun is getting hotter. Spectro-radiometer measurements of solar-UV at the high-mountain observatory at Hoher Sonnblick in Austria showed that between AD 1997 and AD 2011, the three-hundred-and-fifteen nanometer UV-light intensity increased by one-point-five percent per-year, even when atmospheric UV-blocking ozone concentrations were increasing.[1160]

In Greece, the average UV irradiance between AD 1994 and AD 2014 was increasing by one percent per-year.[1161] The average total-solar-irradiance in watts-per-square-meter at Earth's surface has been increasing since AD 1700. Each peak and each trough of the sun-spot-cycle is getting hotter too, producing a larger mean-radiation-intensity for each sun-spot-cycle.[1162, 1163]

Global warming is not just occurring on Earth either, it is happening throughout the solar-system.[1164] NASA's Mars-Odyssey orbiter revealed that the Martian ice-caps are melting, and Mars is suffering global warming too.[1165, 1166, 1167] The albedo of the poles and highlands of Mars has declined over twenty years, due to disappearing ice.[1168, 1169] This observation was discovered by comparing pictures of the Martian surface taken by the Viking spacecraft in AD 1977, with pictures taken by the Mars Global Surveyors in AD 1999.[1170, 1171, 1172, 1173]

The darkening of the Southern Highlands of Mars is especially obvious. Between AD 1999 and AD 2005, there was a rapid and sustained retreat in the south-polar residual-ice over four Mars years, and the sublimation is ongoing. Seasonal Martian ice-caps are certainly getting smaller every year, and the permanent deposits of frozen carbon-dioxide near the south pole of Mars have shrunk.

This Mars-global-warming is equivalent to about one-degree-Celsius over forty years, and it is inducing more dust storms. New gullies have appeared on Martian sand-dunes, as sub-surface solid carbon-dioxide is disappearing due to progressive atmospheric heating.

A Massachusetts Institute of Technology researcher reported further evidence of solar-system-warming. NASA's Hubble Space Telescope and other ground-based instruments revealed that Neptune's largest-moon Triton has also heated up significantly since the Voyager space probe visited in AD 1989.[1174, 1175, 1176] The warming trend is causing part of Triton's surface of frozen nitrogen to turn into gas, making its thin atmosphere much denser.[1177, 1178, 1179]

There is evidence of global warming on Jupiter.[1180, 1181] Uranus is getting hotter.[1182, 1183, 1184] Climate change is occurring on Neptune.[1185, 1186] Global warming is occurring on Pluto too.[1187, 1188, 1189, 1190, 1191, 1192]

The increasing temperature throughout our solar-system is connected. It is caused by the approach of magnetic star-core-zeus, which is inducing the increase in strength of the interplanetary-magnetic-field and increasing the heat output of the Sun.

Zeus Is a Radio-Star

Star-core-zeus should produce powerful radio-signals due to its intense magnetic-field just like planet-Jupiter, which pumps out strong radio-signals due to its strong magnetic-field.

All-sky-surveys by radio-telescopes since AD 1950 have detected a number of powerful sources of radio-frequency-radiation in the sky. Optical observations have confirmed that many of these radio-signals come from incredibly remote radio-galaxies far outside our Milky Way. It is currently assumed that magnetic super-massive black-holes at the center of these distant galaxies are responsible for the powerful radio broadcasts.

Other radio-sources have been visually-identified to be coming from large spinning magnetic-stars, neutron-stars, or black-holes in our own galaxy.[1193] These magnetic-objects are surrounded by rapidly-rotating, bagel-shaped equatorial clouds, which are filled with hot electrically-charged ionized-gas that pumps out radio-frequency synchrotron radiation.[1194]

However, other enigmatic powerful radio-sources cannot be identified optically with telescopes. They are just assumed to be coming from distant galaxies rather than magnetic-black-dwarfs in our galaxy or even dark-magnetic-objects local to our solar-system.

The former companion-star of our Sun was a large rapidly-rotating magnetic-star, which died in a supernova explosion at the birth of the solar-system. When it collapsed into a magnetic-white-dwarf, star-core-zeus was born with an intense stellar-magnetic-field. Star-core-zeus is now a very cool invisible radio-star, but its powerful equatorial magnetic-field should give rise to non-thermal polarized radio-frequency synchrotron-radiation, generating powerful radio-signals in the thirty-five to five-thousand megahertz range.[1195]

The field-lines at the poles of magnetic-white-dwarfs with high rates of spin also become twisted to form linear axial-radio-jets, composed of a helical magneto-plasma. An electric-wind blasts through the structure at relativistic velocities of one-thousand kilometers-per-second, forming an intense plasma-beam. The structure also behaves like a huge aerial, emitting very powerful plane-polarized radio-signals perpendicular to the jet-axis.[1196, 1197]

The radio-jets of magnetic white-dwarfs terminate at a shock-front with the interstellar medium, forming a radio-lobe. These resemble independent bright-beacons of circular-polarized radio-energy, which hover above the rotation-poles.[1198]

Star-core-zeus is likely to have all these magnetic features, including two axial radio-lobes, which should emit intense cones of circular-polarized radio-frequency energy. If one radio-lobe of star-core-zeus is pointing toward the Earth, it should look like a bright radio-source, offset from the synchrotron-radiation coming from its equatorial torus.

The radio frequency output of star-core-zeus has definitely been detected and recorded in different astronomy-databases, since the dawn of radio-astronomy over sixty-years ago. However, the problem is that the sky is full of radio-sources and radio-noise.

An Orbital Model of Star-Core-Zeus

To positively identify the radio-signal coming from our magnetic black-dwarf, the first step was to develop an accurate orbital-model. If the current approximate location of star-core-zeus could be predicted, then its radio signal could be identified in that region of the night-sky.

In the remainder of this description of the search for signals from star-core-zeus, I shall use celestial-coordinates. Positions in the sky are identified by two coordinates: right ascension (RA) and declination (DEC), which are explained in the end-note.[1199]

In my previous book *Cataclysms & Renewals*, I described ancient astro-mythologies that contained detailed information about ancient observations of star-core-zeus, when it crossed the sky about three-thousand-six-hundred-years ago. Using the clues provided by the ancient astronomers, combined with data from modern astronomy, I generated a three-dimensional computer-model of the orbit of star-core-zeus, using commercially available astronomy software (Starry-Night Backyard).[1200]

In order to build the model, I had to make a number of assumptions about star-core-zeus. My first assumption was the orbital-period of star-core-zeus is around four-thousand years, based on the fundamental harmonic in the climate-history data, described in Chapter One. My second assumption was that aphelion of star-core-zeus is in the angular direction of Sirius, based on the ancient red-Sirius observations. The third assumption was that the perihelion distance of star-core-zeus from the Sun is approximately one AU, to allow close-Earth fly-bys. These three assumptions automatically located star-core-zeus' perihelion above the Sun's north pole and above the end-June position of the orbit of the Earth around the Sun.

The fine-tuning of the orbital-elements of the computer model, which control the path of star-core-zeus around the Sun, was done by trial and error, until the model matched the sequence of ancient observations of star-core-zeus as it traversed the constellations just before the Cataclysm of Fire in 1628 BC.

Around three-thousand-six-hundred years ago, ancient astronomers in the northern hemisphere of Earth actually observed star-core-zeus crossing the sky from Sirius via Orion, Taurus, the Pleiades, and Draco. This is a retrograde direction, the opposite direction to the average motion of the planets. These parameters were then fixed for the computer-simulation to construct a dynamic electronic model of orbiting star-core-zeus.[1201]

The computer-simulation predicted that the orbit of star-core-zeus is a highly eccentric ellipse, with a major axis of about five-hundred AU long, inclined one-hundred-and-thirteen degrees to the plane of Earth's orbit. As described earlier, scattered-objects have recently been discovered to orbit the Sun, in a very similar orbital plane.

The prediction that the orbital plane of star-core-zeus was quite separate from the orbital plane of the planets was consistent with the stability of the planetary orbits of the solar-system. The binary-orbital-plane of the Sun and star-core-zeus is probably angled approximately sixty-seven degrees to the average plane of the planetary orbits.

The distance between the orbit of Earth and the orbit of star-core-zeus at the orbital intersection was assumed to be approximately four million kilometers, taking into account Earth-orbit-eccentricity.

This model predicts that after each perihelion fly-by of the Sun, star-core-zeus passes through the inner solar-system disc near the orbit of Earth, at a very high velocity of about fifty-kilometers-per second (one-hundred-and-eighty-thousand kilometers-per-hour).

Star-core-zeus covers the one-million kilometers of its closest approach to Earth in about five hours, briefly applying equal and opposite gravitational force on approach and departure, so it does not pull Earth out of the average orbital plane of the planets.

The computer-model gave the current position of star-core-zeus between Sirius and Orion, at around six-hours twenty-seven-minutes right ascension (RA) and minus-five-degrees fifty-three-minutes declination (DEC), in epoch J2000.0. The result of the computer-model positioning, allowed the search for the radio-signal of star-core-zeus to commence.

The Mystery Radio Source 3C-161

The Internet has made basic astronomy research available to everyone. Skyview is a virtual telescope service developed by NASA, which allows remote access of many modern astronomy databases.[1202] Using this excellent interface, I discovered a radio-star that is very likely to be star-core-zeus.

The 3C-catalog of bright radio sources was compiled at the dawn of radio-astronomy in the early 1950s. A bright radio-source named 3C-161 was soon detected because it was one of the most intense radio sources in the sky.[1203, 1204]

Radio-source 3C-161 is located just below the dense band of stars of the Milky Way, in an area of sky near the constellations of Gemini, Canis Major, and Monoceros, between the bright star Sirius and the constellation of Orion. 3C-161 also sits at the tip of the helio-tail of the magnetic helio-sheath surrounding the solar-system, which was discussed in the previous chapter. However, the real breakthrough is that 3C-161 is located exactly at the point predicted by the computer-simulation, for the current location of star-core-zeus!

However, when this powerful radio-source was first discovered, 3C-161 was simply labeled as a radio-star, and later it was dismissed as a distant radio-galaxy.[1205] However, no distant galaxy or local object has ever been positively identified as associated with the mysteriously powerful signal.

A telescope search for an object at the center of intensity of radio-source 3C-161 failed to identify anything that could be responsible for such a strong radio-signal. After the total lack of success in pin-pointing any optical object at the center of radio source 3C-161, it was simply cataloged as a mystery radio source, whose origin was unknown. No one knew whether 3C-161 was near the solar-system or incredibly far away in another galaxy.

More than sixty years have elapsed since the powerful radio signal of 3C-161 was first identified, but no optical counterpart of 3C-161 has ever been confirmed. However, in AD 2015 an amateur astronomer observed a tenth-magnitude light, which had not been seen before, at the co-ordinates of 3C-161.[1206]

In AD 1987, a low-resolution radio-sky map compiled from signals broadcast at 34.5 megahertz and detected using the GEETEE radio-telescope in India showed 3C-161 as a bright oval patch of radio output, covering a large area of sky, at least twice the visual area of the Moon.[1207]

Star-core-zeus should produce synchrotron-radiation from electrons that are accelerated in its powerful magnetic field. This radio-frequency radiation should be detected as a continuum-spectrum over a frequency range from one megahertz to ten gigahertz.

POWERFUL 3C-161 SIGNALS FROM STAR-CORE-ZEUS

DUST CLOUDS HIDE STAR CORE ZEUS

A 'Gaint Molecular Cloud' rich in Hydrogen, Carbon and Oxygen surrounds 3C-161 hiding Star-Core-Zeus from view.

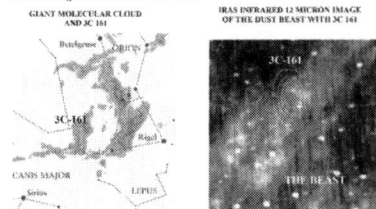

GIANT MOLECULAR CLOUD AND 3C 161

IRAS INFRARED 12 MICRON IMAGE OF THE DUST BEAST WITH 3C 161

The Giant Molecular Cloud (white patch on negative) centred on 3C161 obscures back-ground star-light. A negative image of clear summer sky around Orion and Sirius taken by the Author in Egypt.

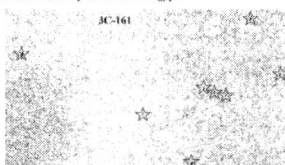

SHAPE-SHIFTING 3C-161

The powerful radio-source 3C-161 shape-shifts so rapidly, that the changes in its angular dimensions, prove that it cannot be a huge remote galaxy-size object. Data. (1) Pearson, T., et al., "Compact Radio Sources in the 3C Catalog" *The Astronomical Journal* 90 (1985):745 (2) Greisen & Liszt "Small-scale structure of interstellar H1 Clouds" *Astrophysical Journal*, 303 (1986): 702-717. (3) Goss et al *Mon Not Roy Astro Soc* 388 2008): 165-175

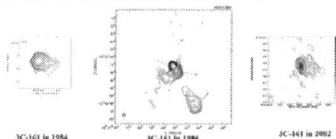

3C-161 in 1984   3C-161 in 1986   3C-161 in 2002

There is direct evidence the object generating the powerful radio signal of 3C 161 is very close to us. If 3C-161 was really shining through the whole Milky Way, the hydrogen cloud velocity, derived from 21cm neutral hydrogen doppler-shift, would be about +40Km/s. However, the hydrogen cloud between 3C-161 and the Sun is travelling towards us at about -2 Km/s, the same velocity predicted for Star-Core-Zeus. Data: Barkume, K., "Small Scale Structures in the Interstellar medium" Thesis, Mathematics and Natural Sciences, Reed College, Portland Oregon USA, 2003.

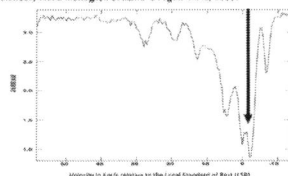

3C-161 PARALLAX DISTANCE MEASUREMENT

The Right Ascension (RA) shift in 3C-161 reveals that it is only 229 AU away from the Sun

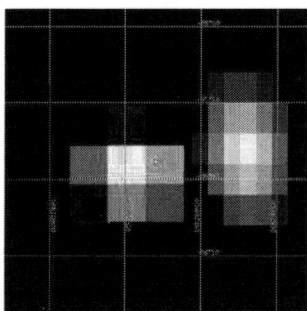

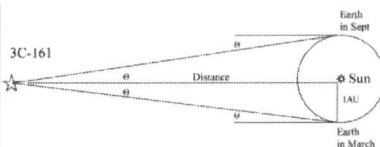

Observed shift in 3c 161 (2Θ) is approximately 2 RA minutes
≈ approximately 0.5 degree
Parallax angle Θ = 0.25 degree
Calculated Distance to 3c 161 = 1/tan Θ = 229 AU

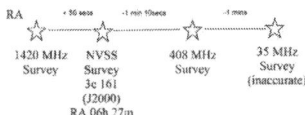

1420 MHz Survey   NVSS Survey 3c 161 (J2000) RA 06h 27m   408 MHz Survey   35 MHz Survey (inaccurate)

The 3C-161 radio signal detected by the GEETEE radio-telescope matched this prediction, with a continuum spectrum of synchrotron radiation covering this radio frequency range. 3C-161 also produced a bright polarized emission, consistent with the circumferential magnetic field of a radio-lobe, the terminal-shock structure of a radio jet.

Since then, 3C-161 has been resolved with increasing accuracy at higher frequencies. It was clearly visible at thirty-five megahertz, four-hundred-and-eight megahertz, one-thousand-four-hundred-and-twenty megahertz, and four-thousand-eight-hundred-and fifty megahertz; and it was resolved to almost a point source at one-point-four gigahertz using VLA radio-telescopes. 3C-161 has been detected in many later sky surveys as a bright radio source, but it is still cataloged by its celestial co-ordinates only and labeled as an unidentified-object.

However, 3C-161 has some very strange properties. Over the last fifty years, different observations of 3C-161 have shown unexpected variations in its signal-strength. Sometimes the radio-source generated a strong signal, for example, nineteen Janskies at a wavelength of twenty-one centimeters from electron-spin-inversion in hydrogen atoms. At other times, only a faint transmission could be detected. There were also occasions when 3C-161 could not be detected at all. For example, in AD 2000, a VBLI scan failed to find 3C-161 at its expected co-ordinates.[1208]

Another mystery about 3C-161 is that different detailed observations, made in surveys years-apart, showed that its interferometry-resolved radio-image had undergone major changes of morphology.

The problem with these shape-changes is that if 3C-161 really is a galaxy located millions of light-years away from us: it was changing shape at greater than the speed-of-light. This data refuted the idea that 3C-161 is a massive but distant radio galaxy: it must be a local invisible object.

The Motion of 3C-161 and Parallax

As the Earth travels around the Sun, there is an angular shift in the position of local objects relative to the distant stars in directions parallel to the orbital plane of Earth, giving rise to variations in its right-ascension co-ordinate.

This shift is known as parallax and is caused by our constantly changing angle of observation, as the Earth orbits the Sun in a year. The effect of parallax allows astronomers to calculate the distances to near-by stars. The maximum parallax shift occurs when the Earth is on opposite sides of the Sun, relative to the angular location in the sky of the object under study.

The computer-simulation predicted star-core-zeus is about two-hundred-and-fifty AU away from Earth, so the effect of parallax should produce displacement of the 3C-161 signal, as Earth changes location by a maximum of two AU during the year, as it revolves from one side of the Sun to the other.

Based on this geometry, the detectable shift in position of star-core-zeus in the plane of the ecliptic relative to the distant stars should be in the region of two minutes of right-ascension. This is equivalent to a shift of half a degree-of-arc, relative to the distant stars, equivalent to a parallax angle of a quarter of a degree.

My break-through in identifying 3C-161 as a signal coming from star-core-zeus came from comparing different radio-sky surveys that had observed 3C-161 in different months of the year: 3C-161 certainly displays a right-ascension shift, meaning the radio-source is displaying a local parallax-shift in the plane of the ecliptic.

For example, the location of 3C-161 shifted between the 408 MHz radio-survey and 1420 MHz Bonn radio-survey by about two minutes of right ascension. Other sky surveys support the conclusion that 3C-161 displays this significant parallax.[1209] The result shows that radio-source 3C-161 is at the same distance predicted for star-core-zeus by the computer-simulation, which is about two-hundred-and-fifty AU away from Earth.

In addition, the radio source 3C-161 seems to be displaying some proper-motion, traveling north at around three arc-seconds per year, toward the ecliptic plane of our solar-system. 3C-161 was first located in 1955 at a J2000-adjusted declination of minus-five degrees fifty-six minutes of arc. Fifty years later in 2006, the 74-megahertz VLA survey gave the position of 3C-161 as a declination of minus-five degrees fifty-*three* minutes of arc, proper-motion of three arc-minutes (one-hundred-and-eighty arc-seconds) of declination over approximately fifty-years. The best explanation is that 3C-161 is the radio output of star-core-zeus, and the very slow proper-motion is due to the orbital motion of star-core-zeus with the Sun.

This is the expected ultra-slow proper motion for an object approaching the Sun in a highly eccentric elliptical orbit. A typical object in the

Kuiper Belt, traveling in an approximately circular orbit between thirty AU and fifty AU from the Sun, moves at three arc-seconds-per-hour. However, Eris, the most distant object so far observed in the solar-system, which is currently ninety-six AU from the Sun, moves at only one-point-five arc-seconds per hour. Beyond two hundred AU from the Sun, even an object traveling in a circular orbit would appear almost stationary.

More Evidence That 3C-161 Is Local to the Sun

Many astronomers still assume that 3C-161 is extra-galactic. No optical nor IR counterpart of 3C-161 had ever been confirmed, so there is no red-shift data to indicate if 3C-161 is either near the solar-system or faraway in another galaxy.[1210] However, some unexpected properties of the continuum-radio-frequency-radiation arriving from 3C-161 were discovered, when an attempt was made to study the interior of the Milky Way, using the radiation from 3C-161, as if it was an extra-galactic torch-beam.[1211]

In this study, the bright radio source 3C-161 was assumed to be shining through the outer reaches of our rotating Milky Way, from outside our galaxy. It was assumed the bright radio beam of 3C-161 had passed all the way through our galaxy, so that all dust and gas of the Milky Way that should be moving in front of the radio beam from 3C-161 could be studied. This experiment is a bit like using a torch-light beam at night-time to study a swirling cloud of mist.

Genuinely distant radio-sources reveal line-of-sight H-one-neutral-hydrogen absorption moving in front of them, as a result of clouds of hydrogen gas swirling around our Milky Way galaxy. Red-shifted or blue-shifted twenty-one-centimeter-absorption-lines are produced by the motion of hydrogen-gas in high velocity clouds or intermediate velocity clouds in our galaxy.[1212]

The average gas-velocity in our galaxy is approximately thirty-five kilometers-per-second. Hydrogen-absorption-lines are either red-shifted by clouds flying away from us, at a velocity range from minus-ten to minus-forty kilometers-per-second, or are blue-shifted by clouds flying toward us, at velocity range from plus-ten to plus-forty kilometers-per-second.

If the object that was producing the 3C-161 signal was really light-years far-away and 3C-161 was shining like a bright radio-torch-beam through our Milky Way, it should be illuminating rapidly moving gas-clouds, and we would expect to see these red-shifted or blue-shifted hydrogen-absorption-lines in the continuum-radiation from 3C-161.

The main Doppler-shift-signal expected from 3C-161 was predicted to be a red-shifted H-one-absorption, from the swirling neutral atomic-hydrogen-clouds traveling away from us in the galactic-plane, at velocities from twenty to forty kilometers-per-second.

However, when the hydrogen-absorption-lines in the continuum-radio-frequency-spectrum of 3C-161 were analyzed, there was a great surprise. The continuum radiation arriving from radio source 3C-161 had no red-shifted absorption lines at all! In addition, there was also a strange anomaly: there was a dominant slightly-blue-shifted H-one-absorption-signal, which was at least ten-times greater than all the other signals combined.

The anomaly seemed to be coming from a dense local cloud of hydrogen gas, which was hardly moving relative to the solar-system or 3C-161. This hydrogen cloud had to be located between us and 3C-161 and had to be so close to our solar-system that both 3C-161 and the cloud were matching-velocity with us, at approximately the twenty kilometers-per-second velocity of our local standard of rest.

The blue-shift of this odd dominant H-one-absorption-signal meant that 3C-161 is approaching us between one and two kilometers-per-second, between a quarter and a half-an-astronomical-unit per-year. This is an astonishing coincidence: the computer-simulation gave the current radial-velocity of star-core-zeus toward the Sun, as inbound at one to two kilometers-per-second.

In other words, the strange cloud of hydrogen illuminated by 3C-161 is moving toward us at the expected orbital velocity of star-core-zeus. The only reasonable explanation is that 3C-161 is a signal coming from star-core-zeus, and it is very close to our solar-system.

Although star-core-zeus is an invisible cold black-dwarf, the electrons accelerated by its intense magnetic field were producing the powerful radio-frequency signals of 3C-161. Radio-star 3C-161 is star-core-zeus!

Feeling the Heat of Star-Core-Zeus

For many years, not only radio telescopes but also infrared telescopes have been detecting star-core-zeus, but these signals have been misunderstood and misinterpreted. Unfortunately, star-core-zeus is inbound toward the Sun from a very congested region of sky near the Milky Way, which is so full of other stars and dust clouds that identification is very difficult.

Star-core-zeus is a condensed stellar-object with ten-percent of a solar mass, so it is only two-to-three Earth-diameters in size. If it is located between one-hundred astronomical units and one-thousand astronomical units from Earth, then its apparent size from Earth is only ten to a hundred mili-arc-seconds across.

Unfortunately, this is at the limit of resolution for most space-based and ground-based optical telescopes, even with computer-driven adaptive-optics. Star-core-zeus is still too far away, too dim, and too small to be resolved into an image by most optical telescopes.

The solution was to hunt for its heat-signature. When the supernova explosion destroyed the companion-star, star-core-zeus was ejected as a very hot sphere of electron-degenerate matter. However, over the following four point six billion years, star-core-zeus cooled to very low temperatures and its light faded. However, star-core-zeus should be still warm enough to radiate detectable infrared radiation.

Although cooling curves of ultra-low-mass white-dwarfs are notoriously unreliable, star-core-zeus is probably still warm, with a temperature between one-hundred and three-hundred kelvin (equivalent to twenty-seven degrees Celsius). Star-core-zeus should be a blackbody-radiation-source with a mid-infra-red output-peak in the wavelength range from ten-to-thirty microns.

The computer-simulation and the 3C-161 parallax data places star-core-zeus approximately two-hundred-and-fifty-AU from the Sun. If star-core-zeus is two-Earth diameters in size and located about two-hundred-and-fifty AU from the Sun, the infra-red signal should resolve to a disc less than one hundred mili-arc-seconds in diameter. The challenge is to find such a heat-signal against the background infrared-glare of the Milky Way.

In addition, the weak photon-emission from the star-core is probably obscured by thick clouds of supernova debris in the equatorial torus surrounding star-core-zeus. However, the dusty torus itself should be warm and also radiate infrared, which should give away its position. In fact, its torus should be ten to a hundred times larger than the black-dwarf, and its infra-red signal should resolve to a diffuse-disc up to ten arc-seconds in diameter.

In 1983, the old IRAS infra-red space-telescope surveyed the whole sky between the electromagnetic frequencies of three-to-thirty Tera-Hertz, the frequency range of radiant heat. The data was collected in four wavelength bands: one-hundred, sixty, twenty-five, and twelve microns, corresponding to increasing temperature of a radiating object. However, the resolution of this detection system was only sixty arc-seconds.

IRAS did detect a mystery source of heat between Sirius and Orion, near 3C-161. The source was labeled IRAS 06240-0559, but its nature has never been identified. It was radiating mid-infra-red between twenty-five and sixty microns. At twenty-five microns, a warm-zone was detected at right-ascension six hours twenty-nine minutes twenty-five seconds, DEC minus-five degrees forty-five minutes and zero seconds, in epoch J2000. The warm object was less than six minutes-of-arc across.

In contrast, at the shortest and warmest wavelength of twelve microns, equivalent to about four hundred Kelvin, the object was invisible against the background of warmer dust clouds. Based on the properties of simple blackbody radiators, this IR-radiating-object probably had a surface temperature around three-hundred Kelvin, in the correct temperature range for star-core-zeus.

Over ten years later, the mystery source IRAS 06240-0559 was re-measured by the Japanese using their Infrared-Telescope-in-Space (called IRTS). In 1995, the object was found to have shifted by twenty seconds-of-arc from its earlier position detected by IRAS.[1213] This possible parallax motion was a further clue that this mid-infra-red source could be star-core-zeus. However, at the end of the twentieth century, infra-red telescopes were simply not sensitive enough nor had a high enough resolving power to image star-core-zeus.

The Beast Located at DEC – 6 6 6

During a search for star-core-zeus in a twelve micron-infrared-survey data from the old IRAS satellite, I made a strange discovery: the huge head of a horned beast was revealed below the mystery source IRAS 06240-0559.

The hideous face was four-times the angular diameter of the Moon, and the wavelength of the infrared signal revealed the cloud was the same temperature as warm blood.[1214] This Beast is biting our helio-tail, and its co-ordinates come straight from Biblical horror: the face of the Beast is located at a declination of minus six degrees, six minutes, and six seconds. I put an image of the Beast on the front cover of my first book *Cataclysms & Renewals*.

The revelation of St John at the end of the Bible described the end of the world and the sign of the Beast. Its number 6 6 6 may have originated from Babylonian astronomers, who were well aware of its sky coordinates and that it heralded the arrival of star-core-zeus and the chaos that ended each Age of the World.

It is difficult to determine the exact nature of the Beast, but it appears to be a warm local dust cloud held in place by the magnetic field connecting the Sun and star-core-zeus. It is possible that when star-core-zeus gets closer to the Sun, the cloud is heated by the solar-wind making it glow brighter. People in the second millennium BC must have gaped in terror at this enormous dark-red evil-looking face of the Beast, staring at them from the night sky.

The CMB Axis of Evil

The location of the Beast also provided a solution to an enigma known as the cosmic-microwave-background Axis-of-Evil. Since the end of the twentieth century, cosmologists have been studying small fluctuations in cosmic-microwave-background-radiation, seeking information on the big bang birth of the universe. This radiation was detected by three different satellite-based microwave-telescopes, known as COBE, WMAP, and Planck.

Generally, the cosmic microwave background radiation arrives with almost equal intensity from all directions, but there are ultra-small scale fluctuations in the temperature data, which reveal structure in the after-glow of big bang of the whole universe. These fine details in the signals allowed the refinement of models of the expansion-period of the universe after big bang.

However, the analysis of the cosmic-microwave-background-radiation revealed an enigmatic symmetry, which was so startling to the cosmologists that they named it the Axis of Evil. A strange pattern of data-clustering resolved into dipoles and higher order symmetries.

Astronomers were shocked to discover that the fluctuations were orientated with respect to the equinoxes of the Earth. This was totally unexpected and inexplicable: the signal was from the birth of the universe, but it was aligned relative to the orientation of the rotation-axis of our own planet.

In addition, this alignment was being actively maintained. After more than a decade of measurement, even though the equinox-points were shifting slowly due to the precession of the rotation-axis of the Earth, the pattern in the cosmic-microwave-background-radiation from big bang remained aligned to the equinoxes.

The Axis-of-Evil and related anomalies can be explained by the shape of the local dust cloud near our solar-system and the orientation of the magnetic field connecting star-core-zeus and Sun. In the chapter on precession in my first book *Cataclysms and Renewals*, I explained the ball-compass-model and how the rotation axis of Earth shifts to lean toward the magnetic star-core so that star-core-zeus is always located at approximately six hours of right-ascension.

The so-called Axis of Evil is simply an artifact of the equatorial coordinate system of our star-maps, which are drawn relative to the vernal-equinox-point. As magnetic star-core-zeus changes position, it shifts the orientation of the tilted rotation axis of the Earth and causes the precession of the equinox (by definition, the equinox-points are always located at ninety degrees from the direction of tilt). The hot dipole-lobe in the CMB data points toward the Beast, which is located at the tip of the helio-tail and centered around six hours right-ascension and declination -6 6 6.

Interference from local electromagnetic signals generated by warm dust held in the magnetic field of star-core-zeus is contaminating the cosmic microwave background data and producing the Axis of Evil.

WISE Images of Star-Core-Zeus

Although the old space-based infrared telescopes IRAS, IRTS, and the Spitzer were sensitive enough to detect the heat of star-core-zeus, they did not have the resolving power to form an image. They needed a very large aperture to resolve and focus an object with an angular size of less than zero-point-one of an arc-second.

The breakthrough in getting an infra-red image of star-core-zeus came in AD 2013 with the release of the data from NASA's Wide-field Infrared Survey Explorer (WISE) onto Skyview. In AD 2010, the infra-red satellite had mapped the sky at three-point-four, four-point-six, twelve, and twenty-two microns with an average resolution of six arc-seconds. In addition, WISE was much more sensitive than earlier infra-red satellite telescopes and could resolve energy from point-sources in uncluttered regions of the sky, down to the micro-Jansky range.[1215]

WISE detected star-core-zeus as a point source coinciding with 3C-161, at right-ascension six hours, twenty-seven minutes, nine seconds, with a declination of minus five degrees, fifty-three minutes, and fourteen seconds (J2000.0: 06 27 09.36 -05 53 14.2). The object was imaged as a bright spherical cloud with a hot center with a diameter of twelve arc seconds and a cooler cloudy region that was slightly flattened with an approximate diameter fifty arc-seconds. The front cover of this book *Star-Core-Zeus* is a low-resolution infrared-image of this object from WISE.

IMAGES OF STAR-CORE-ZEUS

Star-Core-Zeus is a massive cold dark sphere, only two to three Earth diametres in size, cloaked in dust clouds and currently located 250AU from the Sun. However the WISE infra-red satellite detected its weak 22 micron heat output, shining through the clouds at the same position as 3C-161.

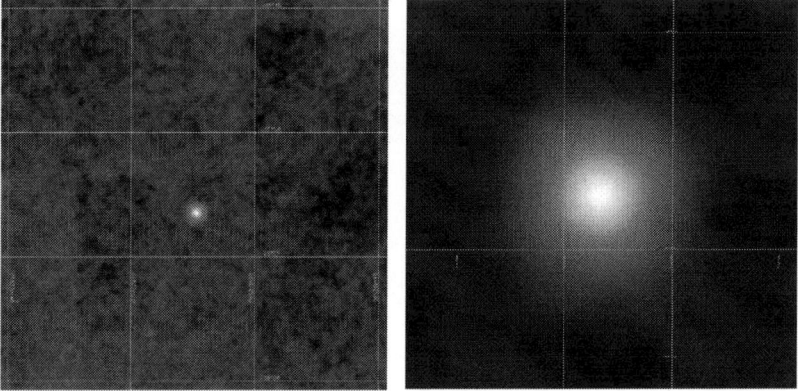

When Star-Core Zeus gets close to the Sun it will look like this:

The First Pictures of Star-Core-Zeus

Generally, Earth-based ten-meter infrared-telescopes are limited to a resolution of zero-point-one arc-seconds, a resolution too low to focus an image of star-core-zeus. However, in AD 2016 the ESA spacecraft Gaia was performing micro-arc-second global astrometry on stars, some as dim as twenty-magnitude. The Gaia CCD detectors have a pixel size of sixty milli-arc-seconds, so they have the capability to detect star-core-zeus.[1216]

The new James Webb Space Telescope (JWST) will be launched in AD 2018. It has a six-point-five meter primary-mirror, and its mission is to orbit the Sun a million miles from Earth. It will have better infrared sensitivity than WISE, and its instruments will offer better resolution and wavelength coverage than earlier space telescopes, so it may be the source of the first high-resolution pictures of star-core-zeus.[1217, 1218]

CHAPTER 21

The Star-Core-Zeus Fly-By

● ● ●

STAR-CORE-ZEUS IS RETURNING TO THE Sun from the region of the night-sky defined by Gemini, Sirius, and Orion. A quadrant in the same region of the night-sky has been identified by other astronomers, mapping between six and seven hours of right-ascension and zero and minus-ten degrees of declination as the likely location of a massive extra-solar-system object. Star-core-zeus is probably less than two-hundred-and-fifty AU away from us and is inbound along the hot tunnel, which was originally blasted out by the ancient supernova of the companion-star four-point-six billion years ago.

Ancient Observations of Star-Core-Zeus

The periodicity of star-core-zeus is recorded in our climate history data: severe disruptions of the global climate occurred in 13,600 BC, 9600 BC, 5600 BC, and 1628 BC. The four-thousand-year terrestrial climate-cycle shows that star-core-zeus and the Sun return to their point of closest approach every four thousand years.

According to astro-mythology, star-core-zeus started its approach toward the Sun from the direction of the bright-star Sirius. The archaic legends about Tishtrya, which were recorded just after the Great Flood, even described the trajectory of star-core-zeus across the night-sky in 5600 BC.

Star-core-zeus was hidden for thousands of years near Sirius, before it slowly drifted into Orion. It then moved on more rapidly toward the constellation of Taurus and the Pleiades, where it became clearly visible. Tishtrya then traversed the sky rapidly up to the northern constellations and its perihelion, before it flew through the constellation of Draco-the-Dragon and plunged down at maximum velocity toward the Earth.

Just before the fly-by that caused the Deluge in 5600 BC, Tishtrya was observed in the zodiac constellation of Aquarius. It can be deduced from diagrams of sighting angles that when Tishtrya was seen plunging down to the ecliptic in front of Aquarius, Earth must have been located between the April and May positions of its orbit, so that the Great Flood appeared to fall from the heavens, from this region of the night-sky. Tishtrya probably passed Earth at a separation of only three million kilometers.[1219]

To the ancient Egyptians of the sixth millennium BC who witnessed the fly-by that caused the Great Flood, star-core-zeus looked like a dark-blue eye hanging in the sky, surrounded by black eyeliner: it was worshipped as the Eye of Horus. The ancient Aryans saw star-core-zeus as a huge flying-horse, while other ancient peoples saw an enormous black dragon or thunderbird, which destroyed the third age of the world.

Around 1650 BC, toward the end of the fourth age of the world, priest-astronomers of Babylon also recorded early sightings of the return of star-core-zeus. They gave it the name "Nibiru" and wrote that it was observed as a hazy object seen high in the midnight-sky at midwinter, as a stationary star located between Sirius and Orion. The mystery is that Nibiru should have been too far away at this time to have been visible to the naked-eye: these ancient astronomers must have been using some form of simple telescope.

Nibiru was traveling in a curving trajectory from the direction of Sirius toward the Sun. As star-core-zeus crept up on the solar-system, it drifted across the Milky Way from Orion toward Taurus and became brighter as it arrived in the Pleiades, the constellation the Old Babylonians called MUL.MUL. It appears to be another mystery that MUL.MUL was observed in the southern sky of this era, but I described that our Earth was inverted in the previous age of the world in my first book *Cataclysms & Renewals*.

As Nibiru crossed the ecliptic plane at a position marked by the Pleiades, it was passing below the orbit of Neptune on its way to the

Sun. By this time, Nibiru was clearly visible to the naked eye as a wandering star or planet. Later star-core-zeus appeared to change direction and moved north through the polar constellations. To have been seen in such locations, star-core-zeus must have been traveling in a highly eccentric orbit, which was inclined close to right-angles to the ecliptic.

Nibiru drifted on to the northwest until it passed through the constellation of Draco (the Dragon). When Nibiru (star-core-zeus) made its final approach to Earth from near the celestial-north-pole in the early spring of 1628 BC: it was said to be a terrifying sight.

Star-core-zeus (Nibiru) passed very close to the Earth during the Cataclysm of Fire of 1628 BC. Contemporary images of star-core-zeus represented it as an object in the sky with a similar angular size as the Moon. If star-core-zeus was two Earth diameters in size, then it must have passed the Earth at a separation of only ten times the distance of the Earth to the Moon, which is approximately four million kilometers.

The mythology of the most recent fly-by in 1628 BC suggests that when star-core-zeus made its final approach, it was seen during the daytime as bright as a second sun. At this point, it was descending from above the orbital plane of the Earth and reflecting sunlight down to us. Star-core-zeus must have intersected the ecliptic-plane inside the orbit of the Earth, because it was observed near the Sun in daytime.

The terrible consequences of the fly-bys of Earth are described in my first book *Cataclysms & Renewals*. In 1628BC, when star-core-zeus destroyed civilizations of the Middle Bronze Age, it shot across the sky with its equatorial torus almost exactly side-on to the Earth. The light from star-core-zeus was scattered by the dusty torus, so it appeared to be a dark-red ball similar to the color of sunset, flying on vast black wings that stretched from horizon to horizon.

The huge scale of star-core-zeus dwarfed the imagination of awe-struck observers. However, they made images of star-core-zeus based on objects familiar to their experience. The Middle Kingdom Egyptians and Babylonians thought star-core-zeus resembled a giant red ball that discharged snake-like thunder-flashes, which was gripped by a giant eagle or griffin hovering on vast outstretched wings.

THE ORBIT OF STAR-CORE ZEUS

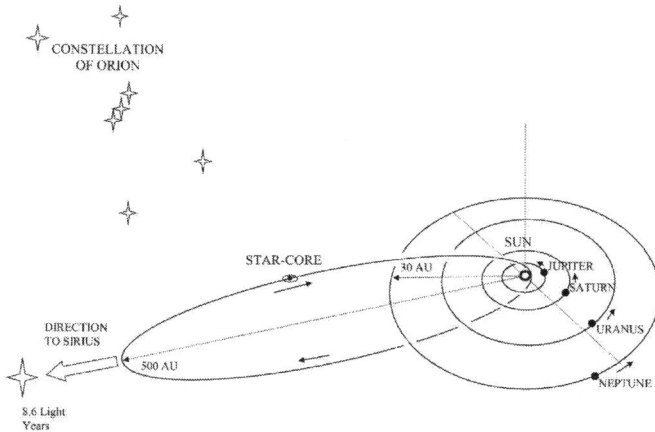

By assuming a periodicity around 4000 years and a 30th April 1628BC fly-by, the modelling the recorded observations of ancient civilisations provided the orbital elements of Star-Core-Zeus. **Periodicity: 4001 years, Mean Distance on 09/11/2012 (a): 251.98 AU, Eccentricity (e): 0.9969519, Inclination (i): 113.5 degrees, Ascending node: 82.00 degrees, Arg of pericentre: 138.00 degrees, Mean anomaly (L): 326.5755838 degrees , Epoch: 2452230 Julian Days.**

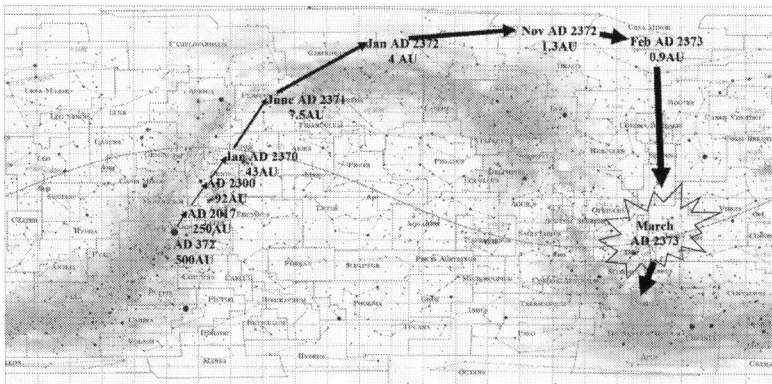

From the mid-second millennium BC onward, the famous winged-disc symbol was painted and carved all around the world. Not only had the Egyptians and Mesopotamians witnessed the huge object in the sky, the art of the Central Americans, Hittites, Persians, and Chinese confirmed that the fly-by of star-core-zeus had been seen by all the peoples of the world.

After the Cataclysm of Fire in 1628 BC, star-core-zeus receded away from the solar-system into the southern heavens in the direction of Sirius. Ancient historical documents recorded that from about 1000 BC to about AD 400, the light of Sirius was dimmed to a deep red. During most of star-core-zeus's out-bound journey away from the Sun, it seems that the dust cloud surrounding it eclipsed and scattered the blue-white starlight of Sirius so that only the red light of the star was seen from Earth.

During the next two thousand years, the dust clouds surrounding star-core-zeus scattered and absorbed the light coming from *Sirius*, causing it to shine with a dimmer red-brown light. Recent research has shown that the diffuse absorption that reddens starlight is caused by fullerenes, which are generated in the cooling carbon-gas after supernova explosions.[1220]

In AD 372 star-core-zeus reached its aphelion, its maximum separation from the Sun, which is located in the approximate direction of Sirius. The change in the color of Sirius from red back to white occurred as star-core-zeus swung around and commenced its return journey to the Sun. Sirius was fully unveiled around 450 BC as a bright blue-white star. I provided a full description of the history of Red Sirius in my first book *Cataclysms & Renewals*.

From Ancient Lore to Modern Astronomy

Star-core-zeus revolves in a highly eccentric orbit around the binary center of mass of our solar-system, located fifty AU away from the Sun, in the angular direction of Sirius.

Simple binary orbital equations show that if star-core-zeus is ten percent of the mass of the Sun, then it was massive enough to make the whole solar-system move in a curved flight path too. If star-core-zeus is approaching us from the direction of Sirius-Orion, then the whole solar-system must be traveling on a curving flight path and accelerating around a binary-center-of-gravity (known as a barycenter), located in the same direction.

However, due to the relative masses of star-core-zeus and the Sun, the distance the Sun travels to the barycenter during one cycle of their mutual orbit is only ten percent of the distance that star-core-zeus travels. The maximum distance of the Sun from the barycenter of the binary-system is fifty AU when the Sun and star-core-zeus are at aphelion, and they are maximally separated by five-hundred AU.

The model predicts that the Sun and planets are accelerating on a gentle clockwise curve, on an orbital path that slopes down about six degrees below the ecliptic plane, in the angular direction of Sirius-Orion. This motion is the origin of the acceleration that is detected in the rate of precession of the axis of rotation of the Earth. For a more detailed description, see the precession chapter in my first book *Cataclysms & Renewals*.

As star-core-zeus approaches the Sun, it totally disrupts the scatter-disc-objects. It is very significant that the Kuiper Belt objects that should have been orbiting beyond the edge of our solar-system more than fifty AU from the Sun are all missing. Any solar-system object that did wander beyond the fifty AU limit has been scattered, ejected, or captured.

Archaic oral traditions maintained that the direction of motion of star-core-zeus across the constellations was retrograde, meaning in the opposite direction to other planets crossing the night sky. The orbital model predicts that the component of star-core-zeus's orbit in the plane of the solar-system is in the opposite direction to the motion of Earth around the Sun.

As star-core-zeus approaches the inner solar-system, it travels above the solar-system disc until it reaches perihelion, its closest approach to the Sun, which is its closest approach to the barycenter of our binary system. The perihelion point is about point-nine-seven-five AU above the solar-northern-hemisphere.

After star-core-zeus and the Sun pass each other, star-core-zeus then dives down toward the ecliptic plane and about a month later zooms by Earth. The orbital intersection lies point-zero-two-five AU inside the path of the Earth's orbit around the Sun, between the orbits of Earth and Venus, about three million kilometers away from us in June. This place-of-crossing of star-core-zeus and Earth is very near the position of the second-of-July-aphelion-point on Earth's orbit, which is on the opposite of the Sun to Sirius. The Old Babylonians also wrote about Nibiru and this place-of-crossing.

There is also another coincidence. The length of the major axis of the orbit of the Earth from aphelion to perihelion, which is aligned toward the angular direction of Sirius-Orion, is approximately point-zero-three AU longer than the minor axis of the Earth's orbit. The average orbital velocity of the solar-system in the binary system is also point-zero-three AU per year toward the angular direction of Sirius-Orion, because periodicity of our binary system is four thousand years.

The relationship between these variables suggest that as the Sun and star-core-zeus approach each other, the Earth travels in a spiral motion, advancing point-zero-three AU per year in the direction of star-core-zeus, as the star-core approaches us from the angular direction of Sirius-Orion.

Observing the Inbound Star-Core

Star-core-zeus is currently located in the triangle of night-sky marked by Sirius and the constellations of Gemini and Orion. This is very near the edge of the Milky Way, so it is hard to distinguish star-core-zeus in the dense background clutter of stars and dust of our galaxy.

Star-core-zeus is about two-hundred-and-fifty AU away, equivalent to about eight times the distance of Neptune. Star-core-zeus is advancing toward us, and during the next two centuries, it will travel about one hundred AU. Star-core-zeus will be one-hundred-and-sixty AU away from the Sun in AD 2200. By that time, star-core-zeus will be visible to all ground-based telescopes as it drifts across the sky toward Orion.

Another hundred years later in AD 2300, star-core-zeus will reach the angular position of the belt stars of Orion and will be only ninety-two AU from us, equal to three times the distance to Neptune. After another fifty years, star-core-zeus will be moving out of the constellation of Orion into Taurus and converging rapidly on the Sun.

By January 2370, star-core-zeus will be detectable to anyone with binoculars as it passes the horns of Taurus. By this time, it will be just outside the limits of our solar-system, about forty-three AU from the Sun. By December 2370, star-core-zeus will be clearly visible to the naked eye as a bright new star in the Pleiades, and its motion relative to fixed stars will then be obvious. As star-core-zeus moves out of the Pleiades, it will actually be climbing above the ecliptic plane between the orbits of Saturn and Jupiter, only seven-point-five AU from the Sun.

As star-core-zeus passes above the orbit of Jupiter, its shape will be clearly visible to the naked eye. By January 2372, star-core-zeus will be only four AU away and approaching the Sun, from high above the ecliptic plane. By November 2372, star-core-zeus will be terrifyingly near, only one-point-three AU from us, and flying like a fiery portent in the midnight sky, through the constellation of Draco-the-dragon.

In February 2373, star-core-zeus will commence its rapid descent toward the orbital track of the Earth. On its final approach, star-core-zeus will be traveling at its maximum velocity of over sixty kilometers-per-second, that is, around two-hundred-and-twenty-thousand kilometers per hour. It will still take three to four weeks for star-core-zeus to plunge down from its perihelion position to cross the ecliptic plane adjacent to Earth. Then star-core-zeus will be as bright as a second sun shining in the daylight sky.

The Danger Month for a Fly-By

On each binary orbit, star-core-zeus curves over the north of the Sun, before it dives down through the ecliptic plane near the orbit of Earth. The destructiveness of the event depends upon the position of Earth on its orbit around the Sun. If the Earth is crossing the orbital intersection at the same time as star-core-zeus, there will be a devastating near-collision. Star-core-zeus will roar past our planet with a separation of less than point-zero-three AU, just inside the orbital track of the Earth.

The cataclysm that shall end the fifth age of the world shall occur in AD 2373. The intersection between the orbits of star-core-zeus and Earth is near the June-July boundary on Earth's orbit. This place-of-crossing is located on the exact opposite side of the Sun to the bright star Sirius. In the year of a fly-by, our planet is safest at the end of December but in extreme danger at the end of June.

According to the tree ring data, the last catastrophic fly-by of star-core-zeus occurred in the northern hemisphere, during the late spring of 1628 BC.[1221] According to various myths and traditions (for example, the Jewish Passover), the fly-by of star-core-zeus happened in April, so Earth was quite far from the intersection at the time. In contrast, Venus seems to have performed a gravity-assist turn around the Earth during the Cataclysm of Fire, so it was probably responsible for most of the destruction that occurred at the time, which was described *in my first book Cataclysms & Renewals.*

Four thousand years earlier in 5600 BC, the month of the fly-by can be determined by the remains of ancient forests that were ripped up and buried on the east coast of the United Kingdom, during the drowning of Doggerland. Eight-thousand-year-old roots and trunks of fir, oak, alder, and hazel trees were discovered on the seashore between Sutton and Cleethorpes.

These remains had been rapidly entombed, preserving leaves plus immature berries and nuts. The condition of the ancient early summer vegetation suggested it was probably in early June, when star-core-zeus fly-by buried these trees. Star-core-zeus caused a serious catastrophe, which was described all over the world in legends of the Deluge and Great Flood. June was even given as the month of the Great Flood in some ancient texts.[1222]

Four thousand years before the Great Flood, the second age of the world at the end of the ice-age ended suddenly in the cataclysm of 9600 BC. This cataclysm was caused by a violent near-collision with star-core-zeus. Trashed summer vegetation and forests were dumped and buried in huge mounds of muck. The stomachs of mammoths discovered in northern Siberia that had been preserved in permafrost also contained flowers common in late June or early July.

All the evidence supports the concept that the orbital intersection between the Earth and star-core-zeus was located near the July-second position on Earth's orbit around the Sun. However, the orbital model is not accurate enough to confirm whether we will be safe or in extreme danger.

The Quest at the End of the Fifth World Age

Thank you for your time and dedication in studying *this book Star-Core-Zeus*. However, the book you have just finished reading is not a conclusion but only the start of the quest.

Star-Core-Zeus and my first book in the trilogy *Cataclysms & Renewals* are a call to you and other thinkers to question research and propagate the message. Join in the search for star-core-zeus, and do your bit to save civilization. As quests go, this is the biggest one of our age.

The advent of virtual Internet astronomy allows you to access and analyze the huge amounts of data that are being collected by terrestrial and orbiting telescopes.[1223] It falls upon you and the coming generations to search for star-core-zeus, fully understand the dangers, and take whatever counter-measures are possible. We can only properly assess the risk star-core-zeus poses to our nations and civilizations, if we face the reality that we live in a binary-star-system.

We have two chances that our civilization could survive the next fly-by. We may be lucky that star-core-zeus plunges through the ecliptic plane in January, when its effect will be less severe. Another chance is the changes to Earth's orbit, caused by the Venus fly-by during the Late Bronze Age Catastrophe, which was detailed in my first book *Cataclysms & Renewals*.

If our planet was moved further from the orbital intersection with star-core-zeus, we may be safer. Changes in the duration of the year during that cataclysm suggest the orbital radius of our planet increased at that time by about twenty million kilometers, so if we are lucky, the intersection now lies about twenty-five million kilometers from our orbit. However, we may have been moved closer.

What is known is that the Sun and star-core-zeus shall meet again at the end of the fifth age of our world. If a close fly-by of star-core-zeus occurs, its effects will be devastating. The next cataclysm may cause an abrupt alteration of the orbital path of Earth around the Sun. It may cause a sudden shift of the geographic poles and the equator across the surface of the Earth. It may also induce a sudden change in the orientation of the axis of rotation of the Earth in space.

As it approaches our planet, all electronic systems will fail, burnt-out in an intense electro-magnetic over-load caused by star-core-zeus's powerful electric and magnetic flux. Weather will become unbelievably destructive: there will be raging fires and floods. The intense gravity of star-core-zeus will cause terrible earthquakes, which will destroy all the cities. As it passes overhead, it will make the oceans rise and the continents buckle. Some lands may be drowned forever while some sea-beds may become new lands.

The coming cataclysm will be witnessed by the great grandchildren of our great grandchildren's great grandchildren. Only the informed, prepared, and lucky few will survive to witness the dawn of the sixth age and the renewal of our world.

= THE END =

The Appendices

This is the end of the book but only the beginning of the research into star-core-zeus. One exciting topic is the role star-core-zeus has played in the origin of life, which is described in the following Appendix A and Appendix B.

In addition, the astronomy community around the world is now convinced that there is a massive object lurking beyond the solar-system, which has been variously referred to as Planet-X, Planet-9, or Nibiru. Some of the ongoing astronomy studies are described in Appendix C.

APPENDIX A

Supernova-Biochemistry in Space

● ● ●

How DID LIFE DEVELOP FROM non-living matter? The astounding answer to this question is star-core-zeus.

Cosmo-Chemical-Creation

There is a growing body of scientific evidence for a special type of cosmo-chemistry prior to the emergence of life on Earth. Binary-star-systems, supernova debris, and young UV-emitting star-cores add up to supernova-biochemistry in Space.

Carbon, oxygen, nitrogen, phosphorus, sulfur, and hydrogen are some of the most abundant elements in large stars, which are blasted into space during supernova explosions. Carbon, oxygen, nitrogen, phosphorus, sulfur, and hydrogen are also the basic elements of life. Just prior to the birth of our solar-system four-point-six-billion years ago, the supernova explosion, which destroyed the companion-star of our Sun, scattered these elements as a hot elemental plasma.

As the huge mass of material cooled, the clouds surrounding star-core-zeus became a vast chemical reactor, where elements combined to form silicon-compounds, organic-carbon-molecules, and water. The products of this gigantic synthesis aggregated as minerals, glasses, dusts, oils, and water droplets, which were captured by the Sun.

Chemical Synthesis in Supernova Debris

The shock-fronts of these supernova explosions concentrate hot elemental matter to form enormous chemical-reactors, powered by the radiation emitted from hot and magnetic star-core-remnants. Far-infrared and sub-millimeter observations show that after supernova explosions, hot star-core-remnants are surrounded by dark dust clouds, which contain huge masses of complex silicon-based and carbon-based molecules.

For example, Supernova 1987A produced dark carbon-rich dust clouds, which weighed about half the mass of the Sun. Rapid cooling of this supernova debris occurred in less than twenty-five years, and during this time, chemical-synthesis of huge quantities of carbon-macromolecules had occurred.[1224]

Elemental phosphorus is routinely produced in stars over eight-times the mass of our Sun, synthesized by neutron-capture on silicon. Large amounts of phosphorus, the energy element of life, were produced in the type-2-supernova explosion debris of Cassiopeia A.[1225] The same supernova also produced large amounts of carbon, sulfur, nitrogen, oxygen, and other essential elements for life.

Various materials were made from the supernova-debris, under different reaction conditions and during the different stages of cooling. The chemical processes ranged from UV-driven vapor-phase free-radical-reactions, to thermal reactions in the aqueous solution of liquid water droplets, to exothermic reactions in the cold vacuum of space.[1226]

Organic compounds have also been detected spectroscopically in dust surrounding other stars. Emission lines corresponding to nitrile compounds containing carbon and nitrogen have been detected by the Atacama Large Millimeter Array telescope (ALMA) around a star called HL Tau.[1227]

Not only were small organic molecules produced, the chemical-reactors manufactured fullerenes and high-molecular-weight polymers. Complex solid-gas-phase synthetic-chemistry led to substituted-aromatic-compounds, long-chain-hydrocarbons, and large biological macromolecules, including proteins.

Convection-churning of the dense dark clouds of material allowed macromolecules to accumulate in the shade, preventing their photolytic-break-down. The reaction products eventually condensed as hydrocarbon solids and aqueous droplets containing high concentrations of complex molecules. This matter became so dense and dark that it blocked out further UV-irradiation, preventing degradation.

Supernova-Derived Chondrite-Meteorites

The wide range of products produced in the supernova-debris-reactor of our former companion-star aggregated as the archaic chondrite-meteorites, which have been circling the Sun since the birth of the solar-system.[1228]

In addition to rocky silicate-minerals, these complex stony objects also contain all the elements of life: carbon, hydrogen, oxygen, nitrogen, sulfur, and phosphorous. Five percent of all meteorites that fall to Earth also contain complex mixtures of organic carbon compounds, so they are called carbonaceous-chondrite-meteorites.

By weight these meteorites contain up to three percent carbon and are also made of hydrated rock that is up to twenty percent water. The hydrated rock particles are mixed with the organic compounds, which are mainly in the form of high molecular weight carbon polymer tar that has never been exposed to very high temperatures.[1229] The range of complex organic materials in the matrix records the wide range of cosmo-chemistry that occurred.[1230]

Crude-Oil Precursors in Meteorites

In 1955, Sir Fred Hoyle proposed crude-oil was produced in space from stellar carbon and hydrogen, which had then rained down on Earth during the formation of our planet, as a huge deluge of carbonaceous-chondrite meteors.[1231]

According to Hoyle, there are enormous reserves of crude-oil at great depths in the Earth's crust, far exceeding the comparatively tiny quantities that have been recovered in our industrial age. This is vastly more oil than could ever have been produced by decaying marine organisms, a dogma that is used to explain the origin of crude-oil on Earth and led to speculation about a crisis of peak-oil.

Crude-oil is often found associated with supernova-derived metals such as uranium, mercury, vanadium, nickel, and iron. For example, uranium, iron, nickel, and rare-earth-metals, together with heavy bitumens, lighter hydrocarbons, and methane, are found together in granite and gneiss rocks of the nepheline-syenite complex in the Kola Peninsula, in the far northwest of Russia.[1232] Oil has been found down to more than eleven kilometers underground in this region.

Crude-oil contains nickel-porphyrins and vanadium-porphyrins, which are made of supernova-derived nickel and vanadium atoms surrounded by an aromatic porphyrin ring of unsaturated carbon atoms, also known as a cyclic tetrapyrrole.[1233] The same nickel-porphyrins and vanadium-porphyrins have been isolated from carbonaceous-chondrite-meteorites.[1234]

There is a close structural similarity between these molecules and chlorophyll-A from green-plants, which also has a porphyrin structure, but with magnesium replacing vanadium. Prof. Alfred Treibs originally extracted the first vanadium-porphyrin compound from crude-oil in AD 1936 and noted the close structural similarity between this molecule and chlorophyll-A from plants. Professor Treibs mistakenly concluded that crude oil came from plants.

Since that time others have speculated that the various vanadium-porphyrins and nickel-porphyrins found in crude-oil are common in marine micro-organisms, even in the absence of examples. This led to a mistaken belief that crude-oil was a breakdown product of either plants or marine organisms.[1235, 1236]

No marine organism has ever been found that could have produced these porphyrin compounds in the eighty years that have elapsed since the original molecular characterization. These ideas are wrong but remain as unchallenged dogma that they are conclusive proof for the biological origin of crude-oil.

Sir Robert Robinson, one of Britain's leading synthetic organic chemists of his time, noted that the composition of petroleum does not match what could be expected from degradation of biological materials. His view was that ancient crude oils originated with the formation of Earth but later may have been contaminated with small amounts of biological material.[1237, 1238]

Hydrocarbons in carbonaceous-chondrites are the precursors to crude-oil found on Earth. Porphyrins, isoprenoids, pristane, phytane, cholestane, terpanes, and chlorins found both in terrestrial crude oil and carbonaceous-chondrite-meteorites are identical. In addition, optically-active crude-oil compounds are very similar to optically-active meteoric compounds.[1239]

The Russians have published thousands of papers on the non-biological origin of crude-oil.[1240, 1241, 1242, 1243] In their view, archaic crude-oil is vertically migrating from deep levels in the crust, up into more recent geological strata. When oil is discovered in strata identified as Cambrian, Devonian, Permian, or Cretaceous, the age of the strata in which the oil is discovered does not date the actual age of the crude-oil.

The Russians discovered that if oil or gas is present in any sub-surface horizon, then more hydrocarbons will also be found in much deeper underlying horizons. For example, the oil deposits in the Volga-Ural region were discovered in the biologically-contaminated domanik-beds of the upper-devonian series. However, the main oil deposits were pooled at much deeper levels, directly on top of the Precambrian crystalline basement surface.

In the Caspian-district, oil and gas fields are even deeper and lie within the crystalline basement rock. Another example of deep oil is the western-Siberian cratonic-rift sedimentary-basin. On the northern flank of the Dnieper-Donets basin, the main oil deposit is far below the carboniferous sediments, actually located within the crystalline lower basement-rocks.[1244]

There are many examples of the direct connection between accessible oil deposits and deep-fault-zones. Super-giant oil fields such as the Ghawar oil field in Saudi Arabia actually bled out of deep Permian faults. The western continental shelf of the Indian sub-continent is part of a Permian fault system and is also rich in crude oil. Another example is the petroleum-bitumen accumulations located in basal Paleozoic strata in the southern Fergana area of Uzbekistan, which is associated with the deep Permian Tien-Shan fault. Deep hydrocarbons and vertical migration was also discovered in the western Gulf of Mexico.

The terrestrial hydrocarbon content of the crust of Earth can be explained by heavy bombardments of CI and CM carbonaceous chondrite meteorites. More than seventy percent of the tar from carbonaceous-chondrite-meteorites is kerogen and bitumen, with molecular weights greater than a thousand Daltons. Much of this high molecular weight material is almost identical to kerogen and bitumen found in coal, crude-oil, and shale on Earth.

The presence of similar chemical mixtures in both layered coal seams and crude oil deposits suggests that there were even cycles of deposition of crude oil from space, after the formation of the primordial crust. This process would also account for the unusually high abundance of uranium, gold, platinum, and other supernova materials found near the surface of Earth in association with hydrocarbons. In Devon and Lancashire in the United Kingdom, uranium-rich nodules were associated with extra-terrestrial bitumen-like hydrocarbons with a carbon-13 isotope abundance similar to crude-oil.

The Carbon-13/Carbon-12 Ratio in Crude Oil and Meteorites

The analysis of the carbon-13-to-carbon-12-ratio of various terrestrial and extra-terrestrial carbon compounds allows origins and relationships to be established. Crude-oil and the macromolecular carbon in chondrite-meteorites have an identical carbon-13-to-carbon-12-ratio of 1/92, which is less carbon-13 than in plants or atmospheric carbon-dioxide.[1245, 1246] The conclusion is that crude oil comes from Space, not from plants.

Atmospheric carbon-dioxide has a C13/C12 ratio of 1/90. Land-plants have slightly less carbon-13 than the atmosphere, with a C13/C12 ratio of 1/91. The origin of the difference in C13/C12 ratio between the atmosphere and plants is due to photosynthesis that selects for the lighter C12 carbon-dioxide and rejects the heavier C13 version.[1247]

Methane clathrate, the methane-ice found under the sea floor, is a microbiological breakdown product of crude-oil and has even less carbon-13, with a C13/C12 ratio of 1/95. Microbes feeding on crude oil also generally select for carbon-12, so carbon-13-depleted methane is produced as their waste product.

Complicating matters is the fact that carbonate-rock particles in CI-meteorites have much more carbon-13 than the carbon in macromolecular compounds found in chondrite-meteors. CI-meteoric-carbonate has an unusually high abundance of carbon-13, with a C13/C12 ratio of 1/84.[1248] Some comet-dust has an even larger proportion of carbon-13, with a C13/C12 ratio of 1/50.

The significantly larger than atmospheric amounts of carbon-13 in extra-terrestrial carbonate and in limestone and chalk rocks found on Earth reveals their likely origin in space. Limestone standard rocks, dolomite, cretaceous-chalk, and Permian-carbonate-rocks, have a C13/C12 ratio of 1/89, while the start-Triassic carbonate-anomaly-rocks have even more carbon-13, with a C13/C12 ratio of 1/88.

Carbon Macromolecules in Meteorites

Carbonaceous-chondrite-meteorites carry isotopic evidence and molecular evidence of a supernova origin. Silicon-carbide, nano-diamond, graphite, and fullerenes are physically associated with extra-terrestrial isotopes of helium, xenon, and neon. They also contain metallic nickel-iron-droplets and glassy-beads.

The large carbonaceous Allende-meteorite not only contained macro-molecular carbon-compounds but also magnesium-26, the decay product of supernova-produced aluminum-26. It also carried an isotope mixture of nitrogen, calcium, barium, xenon, krypton, and neodymium, plus trace amounts of isotopes of chromium, iron, nickel, vanadium, manganese, and cobalt, which all confirmed that this meteorite had condensed directly from the ultra-hot material ejected from a type-two supernova.[1249]

A complex mixture of carbon compounds originally condensed from the dense molecular cloud of debris, generated by the destruction of the companion-star of the Sun.[1250] Different reaction conditions in different parts of the supernova debris produced different classes of carbon-macromolecules.[1251]

The production of carbon-macromolecules probably occurred as the explosion-debris-plume cooled. A collection of free-radical chemical reactions occurred in a gas/vacuum phase at around five-hundred Kelvin. The reactions were catalyzed by UV light from the remnant star-core, which converted a mixture of carbon monoxide, nitrogen, and hydrogen into substituted-hydrocarbons.[1252]

Over a hundred kilograms of a carbonaceous-chondrite-meteorite crashed into the ground at Murchison, Australia, in AD 1969 and provided a huge amount of material for detailed scientific study. Analysis of large carbonaceous-chondrite-meteorites, such as the Murchison-meteorite, Murray-meteorite, and Tagish-lake-meteorite, shows that around ninety-five percent of the mass of carbonaceous-chondrite-meteorites is hydrated rock, with small amounts of various supernova manufactured metals. Two-to-five percent of the mass of the meteorites is a black-tar made of carbon-based-macromolecules and smaller organic compounds.

The complex mixture of carbon compounds contains volatile molecules that give off a distinctive organic aroma. Organic solvents have been used to extract the soluble fraction, which contains an extensive range of organic molecules, many of which are temperature-sensitive. The range of temperature sensitive soluble molecules extracted from the matrix material shows that it formed at around five hundred Kelvin and then cooled and was not reheated significantly.[1253]

So far more than five-hundred different types of carbon-compounds and substituted-carbon-structures have been identified, and many resemble known bio-molecules. The compound-classes include aliphatic-hydrocarbons, aromatic-hydrocarbons, carboxylic-acids, sulfonic-acids, phosphonic-acids, alcohols, aldehydes, ketones, sugars, amines, amides, nitrogen-heterocycles, and sulfur-heterocycles. The extracts even contain more complex compounds such as amino-acids, which are the building blocks of proteins.[1254, 1255]

About ninety percent of the black-tar found in these meteorites is made of carbon-based long-chain-polymers and high-molecular-weight macromolecules, sometimes with carbon-atoms substituted with nitrogen, oxygen, or sulfur.[1256, 1257, 1258] These large organic chemical compounds and polymers are insoluble in organic solvents. However, some of the material has been extracted with strong acids and then studied, but the extreme conditions also degrade macromolecules. Mass-spectrometric techniques have been used to determine the chemical-structures and isotope-ratios in the acid-extracts.

Elemental ratio analysis has demonstrated that much of the carbon in the macromolecules is held together by reactive carbon=carbon double-bonds, in cyclic structures like graphite and fullerene. Elemental analysis shows that for every one hundred carbon atoms of the carbon-tar in carbonaceous meteorites, there are approximately sixty-to-seventy-five hydrogen atoms, thirteen-to-fifteen oxygen atoms, four-to-five nitrogen atoms, and three-to-four sulfur atoms. In addition, some of the carbon-tar resembles degraded protein-like molecules.

The carbon-macromolecules from carbonaceous-chondrite- meteorites have isotopic differences from similar molecules found on Earth. Meteoric compounds contain more deuterium relative to hydrogen and more nitrogen-15 relative to nitrogen-14 than on Earth.[1259] The isotopic-differences between different carbon-components in different meteorites suggest that they formed in different reaction conditions in different parts of the supernova explosion plume.

A black tar-like organic material was broadly distributed throughout the Murchison-meteorite, which made up about five percent of its mass. The tar was intermixed with fine grains of rocky-hydrous-silicates, which formed a matrix into which the glassy chondrules were also embedded.

Thirty percent of the tar was soluble in organic solvents and revealed a complex mixture of organic compounds, many of which occur in living systems. The organic compounds from the Murchison-meteorite were all found to have more carbon-13 and deuterium (the heavy isotope of hydrogen) than biological molecules from Earth.

Seventy percent of the tar was a complex mixture of macromolecules. Scanning electron microscope images of the acid-residue also showed an abundance of submicron-sized spherical carbonaceous particles, resembling interplanetary dust.

The macromolecular-material from the Murchison-meteorite, comprises of aromatic units connected by aliphatic and heteroatom-containing linkages. The acid-extractable fraction of this material contained small aromatic units enriched in carbon-13, while the residual fraction was made up of large aromatic macromolecules depleted in carbon-13. The compound-specific carbon isotope trends with molecular size seem to reflect mixing of products from two different reaction conditions in space. Organic macromolecules have also been isolated from the Tagish Lake meteorite and have been shown to have similar characteristics.[1260]

Small Organic Molecules in Meteorites

Generally, about ten-to-twenty percent of the carbon material in carbonaceous-chondrite-meteorites is in the form of small solvent-soluble or water-soluble organic carbon molecules. Analytical chemistry revealed the molecules are aromatic, hydro-aromatic, and hetero-aromatic compounds that contain alkyl branches, ether links and hydroxy, and amine and carboxy functional groups.

The complex mixture of small soluble compounds includes a diverse selection of amino-acids, lipids, long-carbon-chain carboxylic acids, sugar-precursors, alcohols, and aromatic nitrogen-substituted bases; all basic molecular ingredients of life.

Aliphatic hydrocarbons are also found in meteorites, which range in molecular size from methane gas, through petrol-like octane and decane, to hydrocarbons with polymer back-bones up to thirty carbon atoms. Hydrocarbons with twelve to twenty-six carbon-atom chains were extracted from six chondrite-meteors: Murchison, Orgueil, Cold Bokkeveld, Vigarano, Ornans, and Bishunpur. On average, they had the same carbon-13-to-carbon-12 isotope ratio, as crude-oil from Earth.[1261] Meteorites were also recovered from the ice fields of Antarctica, known as the CR2-carbonaceous-chondrite-meteorites, which had a black organic material that was mainly water-soluble hydrophilic carbon-compounds, very similar to the organic molecules of life.

Interplanetary-dust-particles that have been captured by high flying aircraft resemble the components of carbonaceous-chondrite-meteorites. They too contain complex organic polymers and macro-molecules. These dust particles are only five to fifty micrometers in diameter, so they are sufficiently small to descend slowly through the atmosphere of Earth. They preserve their complex molecular cargoes without thermal degradation, because they efficiently radiate heat on entry to the atmosphere.

At the beginning of 2004, the Stardust spacecraft flew through the dusty tail of the Comet 81P/Wild 2 and returned to Earth in 2006 with samples of comet-dust.[1262] It was found that the comet-dust was quite similar to the interplanetary-dust-particles and contained complex compounds including the amino-acid glycine.[1263, 1264, 1265, 1266, 1267]

Amino-Acids in Meteorites

The first real clue that organic material from space was responsible for life on Earth was the discovery of amino-acids, the chemical building blocks of proteins, in the soluble organic material from carbonaceous-chondrite-meteorites and interplanetary-dust-particles.[1268, 1269]

Over one hundred different amino-acids have now been characterized in meteorites, and twenty-one of these amino-acids are identical to the amino-acids used in the proteins of living systems. Relative amino-acid concentrations of carbonaceous chondrites suggest variants of a single synthetic process.[1270, 1271, 1272, 1273]

In CR2-carbonaceous-chondrite-meteorites, large quantities of nitrogen-rich amino-acids such as glycine, alanine, tyrosine, and serine have been characterized. The top ten amino-acids, which are abundant in meteorites, are also found in proteins: glycine, alanine, serine, proline, valine, leucine, isoleucine, aspartic acid, glutamic acid, and tyrosine.

Six types of amino-acid, which were the most abundant in the Murchison-meteorite, were the same as the most abundant six amino-acids in the proteins of the most archaic microbes. Proteins are polymers of amino-acids, so it was an exciting discovery to find a dipeptide of glycine in the Murchison-meteorite.[1274] In addition, the amino acid isovaline found in meteorites was shown to be a catalyst for the condensation of formaldehyde and glycolaldehyde into sugar.

Cell Membrane Material in Meteorites

Lipids, which are long-carbon-chain carboxylic-acids with detergent-like polar and non-polar regions on the same molecule, are the building material of the membranes of living cells. Lipids have also been isolated from the soluble carbon material from carbonaceous-chondrite-meteorites.

Extraction of these organic compounds from the Murchison Meteorite with organic solvents yielded detergent like molecules that self-assembled to form micro-vesicles, which actually resembled living cells.[1275] Extra-terrestrial polycyclic aromatic hydrocarbons mixed with the lipids stabilized the membranes and also made these vesicles fluorescent.

Similar long chain organic compounds have been recently discovered on the surface of Mars. They also resemble the fatty acids found in primitive cell membranes.[1276] This lipid mixture from Space was probably the original building material for the biological membranes of the first living cells on Earth.

DNA building blocks in Meteorites

Researchers were also astonished to discover some simple nitrogen substituted aromatic compounds, including adenine and guanine in the ancient carbonaceous-chondrite-meteorites. Adenine had been probably synthesized from cyanide (HCN) in the presence of UV light.[1277] These organic bases are components of DNA, the information storage molecule of living systems.[1278] However, so far, neither DNA nor RNA polymers have been found in meteorites.

The Puzzle of the Chiral Compounds of Life

Before we return to the main theme of the cosmic origin of molecular biology, the puzzle of chiral compounds of life on Earth needs to be explained.

In the mid-nineteenth century, Louis Pasteur studied the optical activity of solutions of organic compounds, derived from living things. When a beam of plane-polarized light was passed through a solution of either sugar or amino-acids made by living systems, the angle of plane-polarized light was rotated.

It was then discovered that the plane of polarization of the electro-magnetic radiation was rotated in different directions and to different extents by different solutions of molecules from living systems. Solutions of amino-acids from living systems rotated plane-polarized light counter-clockwise (the levo-rotatory or L effect), while sugars from living systems rotated the plane-polarized light clockwise (the dextro-rotatory or D effect).

The origin of this optical activity was the three-dimensional structure of the substituted carbon atoms of the organic molecules. When four different chemical side groups are arranged tetrahedrally around a carbon atom, the structure gives rise to two possible three-dimensional mirror-image forms.

Such substituted carbon atoms can have a left or right mirror-image-form, like your left and right hands or left and right feet. The three-dimensional-structures were called chiral when they could not be made identical with their mirror image, by either rotation or translation. Each mirror image is called a chiral-form.

Although chiral molecules can be formed in a number of different three-dimensional arrangements from the same atomic components and bonds living systems only contain one chiral form of all the possible three-dimensional structures.

Amino-acids and sugars of living systems (with the exception of glycine) are all chiral molecules. Living organisms only produce left-handed L-amino-acids and right-handed D-sugars.[1279] Biopolymers made from these molecules always contain only one type of chiral form, out of all the possible three-dimensional structures. In contrast, normal chemical reactions produce mixtures of chiral molecules with all the possible three-dimensional arrangements of the same atomic components and bonds.

The origin of the biopolymers, which are polymers of only one chiral form, is a central mystery of molecular biology. A chiral polymer can be produced in many different three-dimensional forms from different combinations of chiral amino-acids. Ignoring the rare exceptions, it is known that biopolymers from living systems essentially have only one chiral form derived from one type of chiral monomer.

These specific chiral forms of biological polymers are essential for living systems. It has been established that mirror-image amino-acids are not tolerated during the formation of the secondary and tertiary structures of proteins. Experiments have also shown that polymerization of RNA is actively inhibited by mixtures of D-sugars contaminated with L-sugars.[1280] This cross-inhibitory effect has also been demonstrated in protein-synthesis with contaminating D-amino-acids.

Early concepts about the origin of life were focused on the synthesis of small organic molecules, including the monomers of proteins, RNA and DNA, in the atmosphere of the early Earth. It used to be assumed that amino-acids, sugars, aromatic bases, and fatty-acids formed spontaneously in warm clouds of water-vapor, hydrogen, ammonia, and carbon-monoxide, which had been exposed to repeated electrical discharges. However, further research demonstrated that these reaction conditions never selected for only one chiral form of a molecule.

The origin of the specific chirality of life remained a mystery. If both mirror-image-forms of the building materials of life had been available on the early Earth, mirror-life could also have easily evolved independently. It remained an enigma why and how life developed such specific chirality.

Chiral Amino-Acids in Meteorites

The puzzle of the chirality of life was only solved when molecules with the same chirality bias as the living systems on Earth were found in carbon-based compounds isolated from meteorites and interplanetary dust.[1281]

There was a strange excess of L-amino-acids in all carbonaceous-chondrite-meteorites, which is the same chirality as living systems. The absence of mirror-life on Earth also supported the hypothesis that only one chiral form of the chiral biopolymers was available when life emerged on Earth.

Alanine was the first amino-acid isolated from the Murchison-meteorite. It was found mainly in the left-hand chiral-form, the same form that is found in proteins of living organisms. Later a wide range of amino acids were isolated from the Murchison-meteorite with a similar excess of the left-handed chiral form.

When these amino-acids were originally synthesized in space, only the left-handed chiral form had been made. However, chiral-amino-acids are known to slowly degrade by racemization so that over very long periods of time, they eventually turn into near equal mixtures of both chiral forms.[1282]

The relative excess of one chiral form of amino-acids in the four-point-six billion year old Murchison-meteorite suggested that the original chiral synthesis had occurred billions of years ago. Isotopic analyses of samples from the Murchison-meteorite also showed that the L-forms of alanine, aspartic acid, and glutamic acid had significantly higher carbon-13 content than their terrestrial counterparts, so they were definitely not laboratory contaminants, which had been made recently by micro-organisms from Earth.[1283, 1284, 1285, 1286, 1287]

A chiral selection process had clearly existed in space at the dawn of our solar-system, before the formation of the Earth and certainly long before the production of proteins, RNA, and DNA by living systems.[1288]

CIRCULARLY-POLARIZED UV-LIGHT
& PHOTO-CHEMICAL SYNTHESIS
OF CHIRAL MOLECULES IN SPACE

After the supernova, the hyper-magnetic core of the Companion Star, generated polar jets of circular-polarized UV-light, of opposite polarity at each rotation pole. This radiation favoured the net synthesis of the L-chiral form of aminoacids, found in Life on Earth.

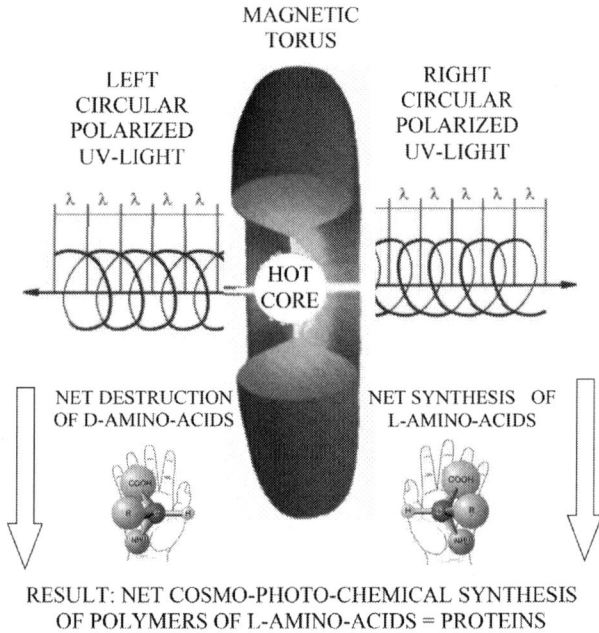

MAGNETIC
TORUS

LEFT
CIRCULAR
POLARIZED
UV-LIGHT

RIGHT
CIRCULAR
POLARIZED
UV-LIGHT

HOT
CORE

NET DESTRUCTION
OF D-AMINO-ACIDS

NET SYNTHESIS OF
L-AMINO-ACIDS

RESULT: NET COSMO-PHOTO-CHEMICAL SYNTHESIS
OF POLYMERS OF L-AMINO-ACIDS = PROTEINS

The revolutionary conclusion was that the original biological molecules of life, including macromolecules like proteins and porphyrins, had been made in space. Extra-terrestrial chiral-asymmetry had preceded biochemistry on Earth. However, the question still remained how the L-chiral-form of amino-acids had actually been made.

Circular-Polarized UV and Chiral-Amino-Acid Synthesis
Anyone who has enjoyed a 3D IMAX movie has experienced the selection effect of circular-polarized-light. The IMAX screen produces two

images, which are circular-polarized in opposite directions. The circular-polarizing filters in the viewing spectacles filter clockwise for one eye and filter anti-clockwise for the other eye so that only one image reaches the retina of each eye. It is the combination of the two images in the brain that creates the illusion of a three-dimensional virtual-image.

When four-point-six billion-year-old carbonaceous-chondrite-meteorites are cut, the fresh surfaces also have optical-activity and behave like an IMAX screen. There is a related L-chirality circular-polarization-bias in both the silicate material and carbon matrix material, at the cut-surface of these meteorites.[1289]

This data revealed that there must have been a bright source of circular-polarized UV-light irradiating the material that later clumped to form the meteorites and eventually the planets, at the birth of the solar-system. The L-chirality bias on the cut-surfaces of meteorites is the same as the L-chirality bias in meteoric amino-acids and the L-chirality in life on Earth.

The explanation for these phenomena is that solid-gas-phase reactions in the presence of circular-polarized UV-light produce chiral products. Circular-polarized far-UV synchrotron-radiation, which is similar to the radiation produced by magnetic stellar-remnants in our galaxy, has been demonstrated in the laboratory to selectively catalyze the synthesis of one chiral-form of an amino-acid. The frequency and rotation-direction of the circular-polarized UV-light was found to precisely control the outcome of these asymmetric photochemical reactions.[1290]

Laboratory experiments showed that circular-polarized UV-light could selectively support the production of one chiral form of an amino-acid by either asymmetric-photochemical-synthesis, asymmetric-photochemical-degradation, or asymmetric-photo-isomerization.[1291, 1292, 1293]

For example, the amino-acid L-leucine has been synthesized in solid-gas phase, using right-circular-polarized-UV-light with a wavelength around one-hundred-and-ninety nanometers. In other experiments, L-alanine and seven other amino-acids were synthesized from a special ice formed at seventy-seven degrees Kelvin from a mixture of carbon-monoxide, carbon-dioxide, water, ammonia, and methanol, which was then exposed to right-circular-polarized-UV-light.[1294, 1295]

Generally, when using circular-polarized-UV-light with wavelengths around one-hundred-and-ninety nanometers, right-circular-polarization results in the selective synthesis of a small excess of L-amino acids, whereas left-circular-polarization results in the selective degradation of D-amino-acids. Multiple exposures of both right- and left-polarized-UV have a cumulative effect of producing more and more L-amino acid. The experimental results support the concept that this type of cosmic-photochemistry was responsible for the excess of L-amino-acids found in space and in living systems on Earth.[1296]

Protein Synthesis in Space

There is some evidence that even the synthesis of proteins occurred in the supernova debris cloud. Free-radical polymerization is commonly used in the plastics industry and is based on the reactivity of lone-pair-electrons decomposed by photon-radiation to initiate the addition of one monomer unit to another. Recently, photon-activated-polymerization has been show to work with N-substituted aromatic-carbon-molecules, which are known to exist in supernova debris.[1297, 1298]

Solid-state vacuum-dispersed reactions driven by circular-polarized-UV-light can produce chiral polymers of L-amino-acids, which are very similar to natural proteins. One example of this type of photochemical synthesis of protein was catalyzed by a transient pulse of right-circular-polarized UV with a wavelength around one-hundred-and-eighty nanometers. In another example, one-hundred-and-fifty-seven nano-meter UV drove gas-phase peptide synthesis.[1299, 1300, 1301]

In addition, it has been shown that the secondary structures of peptides and proteins selectively absorb circular-polarized-UV-light between approximately one-hundred-and-eighty nanometers and two-hundred-and-sixty nanometers. The different secondary structural types found in proteins—helix, parallel and antiparallel beta sheet—absorb circular-polarized-UV-light at specific wavelengths.[1302]

It has also been experimentally demonstrated that the polymerization of proteins by the formation of peptide-bonds between one chiral form of amino-acids could occur in molecular clouds in space. Dry solid-gas phase reactions at temperatures around five hundred degrees Kelvin converted amino-acids of the L-chiral form to protein macro-molecules in the absence of any enzymes.[1303, 1304]

In addition, it has been demonstrated that a solution of L-amino-acids in the presence of a three-atom carbon-oxygen-sulfur compound called carbonyl-sulfide, in the presence of catalytic iron-ions or nickel-ions, can lead to rapid synthesis of peptides and proteins.[1305] Such conditions could have existed in the supernova debris of the companion star of the Sun, which was illuminated by the circular-polarized UV-light of star-core-zeus, when it was young and hot.

There is a large amount of evidence that the original chiral-selection of molecular-biology occurred at the birth of the solar-system as a result of chiral-selection in space, during the photo-chemical synthesis of amino acids and proteins in the presence of circular-polarized UV-light.[1306]

Long ago, complex protein-like polymers collected in the high-molecular-weight substituted-hydrocarbon-matter of carbonaceous chondrite meteors. The chirality of living systems was derived from the chirality of these original cosmic-proteins, which had been synthesized in the vacuum of space just before our planet formed.

Synthesis of Chiral Sugars in Space

A mixture of simple ices of water, methanol, and ammonia, irradiated with circular-polarized UV-light yields a wide variety of sugars, including D-ribose.[1307] In addition, D-sugars found in living systems can be produced in reactions catalyzed by meteoritic L-amino-acids. For example, using extra-terrestrial L-amino-acid as a catalyst, formaldehyde reacted with glycol-aldehyde to produce D-glyceraldehyde, the building block of D-sugar.

Extra-terrestrial chiral amino-acids may have catalyzed the synthesis of the chiral polysaccharides of living systems. Extra-terrestrial

L-L dipeptides act as catalysts that strongly favor the production of D-erythrose and D-ribose.[1308, 1309, 1310, 1311] Sugars could have been synthesized in space in water droplets condensing out of the supernova explosion debris.

Circular-Polarized UV-Light and White-Dwarfs

Four-point-six billion years ago, star-core-zeus probably radiated circular-polarized UV-light at the debris in the supernova explosion plume of our former companion-star. It is well known that circular-polarized electro-magnetic radiation is produced by electrons accelerated in the powerful magnetic fields of rapidly-rotating collapsed-stellar-objects, such as magnetic-white-dwarfs.[1312]

Magnetic-white-dwarfs in the temperature range between seven-thousand and ten-thousand kelvin emit circular-polarized radiation in the ultra-violet part of the spectrum.[1313, 1314, 1315] Magnetic-white-dwarfs in this temperature range produce polar-jets of intense circular-polarized UV radiation, with wavelengths in the one-hundred-and-fifty to three-hundred nano-meter range.[1316]

Large numbers of white-dwarfs have been studied, and it is known that up to fifty percent of the UV-radiation produced by them is uniformly circular-polarized and comes from their polar-jets.[1317, 1318] The direction of the circular-polarization is opposite at each pole of the white-dwarf: one pole radiates uniform *right*-circular-polarized-UV, while simultaneously the other pole radiates uniform *left*-circular-polarized-UV.[1319] An example of this phenomenon was detected with the magnetic-white-dwarf GD229, which has an intense magnetic field of five-hundred mega-gauss and pumps out intense circular-polarized-UV as continuum-radiation.[1320]

Soon after its violent birth, star-core-zeus was a highly-magnetic, rapidly-rotating star-core remnant, with a temperature around seven-thousand Kelvin and radiating circular-polarized-UV-light with a peak intensity at two-hundred nano-meters. Its circular-polarized-UV-light catalyzed a wide range of free-radical reactions in the clouds of explosion debris from the companion-star and stimulated the production of complex chiral biopolymers, hydrocarbon, lipids, polyphosphates, and small-organic molecules.

Conclusion

This Appendix A on cosmo-chemistry shows that the creation of the building blocks of life was not an improbable accident: it was the direct consequence of the life and death of a binary star-system. The matter of companion-stars is the raw material from which biological polymers are pre-fabricated in Space.

Four-point-six-billion years ago, complex free-radical chemistry occurred in the vacuum of space, driven by the circular-polarized-UV-light of hot star-core-zeus. It produced all the bio-molecules necessary for the spontaneous emergence of self-organizing and reproducing living systems on Earth. Huge mounds of proteins, lipids, and other complex molecules from the cosmo-chemical-creation were then dumped on our planet.

Somewhere on Earth, probably in the wet sludge of a small warm geothermal pond, this complex mixture of macromolecules spontaneously created the first living cell. Life on Earth must have developed very rapidly, before all this polymeric material had a chance to degrade.

The extraordinary assembly of the first living cell on Earth from the components pre-fabricated by star-core-zeus in space shall be considered in Appendix B.

APPENDIX B

Supernova-Life on Archaic-Earth

● ● ●

THE ORIGIN OF LIFE IS a huge mystery that baffles scientists. Where and how did the transition from chemistry to biology occur?[1321, 1322] How did a dilute mixture of weakly interacting molecules, concentrate into a complex organization inside a cell membrane? Where did proteins come from? How did the auto-catalytic networks of life's biochemistry start to function? What was the power-source of the first living cell? How did the first cell reproduce?

This Appendix B provides extraordinary answers to these fundamental questions. The first biopolymers and proteins were produced in vast quantities in the cooling debris surrounding star-core-zeus. This allowed the rapid assembly of pre-fabricated complex molecular-components on the surface of Earth, which quickly initiated supernova-life on our planet.

Old models for the origin of life on Earth were focused on the synthesis of small organic molecules in the primordial atmosphere of archaic Earth. The idea was that the first biological molecules were made in clouds of water-vapor, hydrogen, ammonia, and carbon-monoxide, which had been exposed to repeated lightning discharges. On rare occasions amino-acids, sugars, aromatic bases, and fatty acids were made and infrequently combined into larger molecules.

This scenario is highly unlikely, and the fatal problem is that these conditions could never generate the chiral-biopolymers needed for life. In addition, the constant exposure to sunlight and a hot wet atmosphere would soon destroy any complex organic molecules which may have been produced.

Archaic Earth

We can speculate that soon after the Earth cooled, the sky was orange, the shallow ocean was green, and the land was a multitude of rocky platforms and bubbling geothermal pools, covered in dark extra-terrestrial sludge. During the formation of Earth, enormous amounts of water, carbon-dioxide, iron-sulfide (Fe=S), iron-pyrite (S-Fe-S), and macromolecular hydrocarbon were dumped on the recently cooled granite surface of the young Earth.[1323]

Between four-point-six and four-point-five billion years ago, carbon macromolecules, chiral bio-polymers, and other complex organic chemicals, plus reduced iron compounds, rained down from space. Huge dumps of this material formed a black oily-sludge containing membrane-components, energy-molecules, hydrocarbon feed-stock, and even primitive enzymes. There is good evidence from ancient zircon crystals that Earth already had a crust of rock and shallow seas of liquid water, more than four-point-four billion years ago.[1324, 1325, 1326, 1327, 1328]

We know this is a possible scenario because of the enormous amounts of carbon-macromolecules in the earliest sediments, the huge amounts of related material in crude-oil and shale deposits, and the carbon macro-molecules, which still fall to Earth in the carbonaceous chondrite meteorites.

Zircon crystals also record that the archaic atmosphere of Earth had hydrogen-sulfide, hydrogen, water-vapor, carbon-dioxide, and nitrogen, plus some helium and other noble gases. It is very significant that the basic metabolic processes of life, such as glycolysis and the Krebs cycle, produce the biological equivalents of hydrogen-sulfide, hydrogen, water-vapor, and carbon-dioxide. In the archaic atmosphere of Earth, these metabolic reactions probably functioned backward, meaning that the first cells probably consumed these gases to make sugar.

The young Sun produced less thermal radiation than today, but there may have been more UV-light from the Sun, due to the absence of ozone.[1329, 1330, 1331, 1332, 1333] The presence of enormous quantities of the reduced ferric-ion (Fe^{2+}) in sedimentary rocks of this archaic period demonstrates that there was no oxygen and no ozone in the atmosphere. However, we have no information on the density of the cloud-cover.

As early as four-point-six billion years ago, huge volumes of salt water were delivered by meteorites to fill the first seas. Radio-isotope dating of meteoric material has shown that droplets of water containing sodium-chloride had formed at the birth of our solar-system.[1334]

Modern oceans are slightly basic but four-point-five billion years ago, the first shallow seas on Earth were dilute carbonic-acid at pH-six. The sea was a cloudy-green because it was a solution of ferrous (Fe^{2+}) salts with sulfur and phosphorus in an emulsion with alcohols, detergent like lipids, hydrocarbon oils, and other complex compounds.

The sea-floor-sediments from this early period were dark-carbonaceous-shales, containing enormous quantities of macromolecular-hydrocarbon and iron-sulfur compounds with a characteristic sulfur-33 isotope-signature. Iron-sulfur precipitates from this seawater produced the banded-iron-formations. These intensely-magnetic red-and-black-striped archaean-sedimentary-rocks were closely associated with carbon-rich-shales and the first granite rocks of the Earth's crust.

On the north-eastern shore of Hudson bay Canada, banded-iron-formations occur with a type of archaic rock called amphibolite, which is four-point-three-billion years-old.[1335] It had originally formed in solid crust at a depth of twenty kilometers, evidence that the original continental crust of Earth already existed in this archaic time.

Billions of tons of these materials had been produced in the supernova plume of the companion star. Huge quantities of iron-sulfide and iron-pyrite are found in all rock-strata, down to the deepest levels of the crust. In addition, huge amounts of iron-sulfide, iron-pyrite, and carbon macro-molecules continued to be delivered to Earth by star-core-zeus over the following billions of years.

The evidence of later deliveries of material from space can be found in not only four-billion-year-old archaean hydrocarbon-rich dark sediments but also in later rocks of the Proterozoic period, up to two-point-five billion years ago. There is evidence that iron-sulfide, iron-pyrite, and carbon macro-molecules continued to be deposited through the Cambrian and Devonian periods.[1336] Iron-pyrite and iron-sulfide are also strangely abundant in marine-chert sedimentary-rocks that mark the Permian-Triassic extinction-boundary.

In the dark fossil-rich Jurassic-sediments at Black Ven in Dorset, huge amounts of extra-terrestrial iron-pyrite were discovered in the sedimentary rocks in the form of two-to-three centimeter discs and button-mushroom shaped pebbles formed by hot-high-speed-atmospheric-entry. These sediments were also associated with organic compounds of extra-terrestrial origin, which are the source of the crude-oil in the Wytch Farm oilfield.

In the later Cretaceous period, iron-pyrite and calcium-carbonate were regularly dumped on our planet from space. Iron-pyrite appears in pebble-like balls called marcasite in cretaceous-chalk that is deposited in distinct strata, as if it had periodically dropped from the sky.

Even the comet tail of Venus still has large quantities of iron-sulfide and iron-pyrite.

Supernova-Life

Supernova-life commenced when the first cell self-assembled from these specialized materials, which had been pre-fabricated in space. The limited stability of chiral biopolymers suggests that the first living cell may have come into being more than four-point-five billion years ago, soon after the supernova explosion debris rained down on the young Earth.

The first living cell probably emerged in dark warm organic sludge in a rock pool. During these self-assembly events, cell-membranes probably formed first and concentrated pre-existing complex molecules. A spontaneous and lucky combination of supernova-produced molecules resulted in the first simple viable self-organizing, self-replicating, complex molecular system, which we would define as life.[1337] The biochemistry and molecular biology of all living things on Earth is so closely related that all life must have arisen from this single event.[1338]

Evidence of Life in Archaic Surface Rocks

The earliest indirect evidence of life on Earth comes from a four-point-one billion-year-old zircon crystal recovered from rocks in Western Australia. It has a carbon-contaminant with an unusually low proportion of carbon-13 relative to carbon-12, which was probably due to the carbon-12 isotope being selectively accumulated by living organisms.[1339] Tube-like micro-structures, which seem to be the remains of early micro-organisms, have been discovered in four billion-years-old quartz layers at Nuvvuagittuq, Quebec, Canada.[1340]

Carbon, iron, sulfur, and nitrogen isotopes are all fractionated by living cells, and the earliest example of this fractionation is recorded in the three-point-nine billion-year-old carbonate-rich archaean rocks of Isua, West Greenland.[1341] These sedimentary rocks contain graphite inclusions with an abundance-ratio of carbon-13-to-carbon-12, which suggests they were formed by early life.[1342, 1343, 1344]

Stromatolites, archaic cities the size of pebbles build by microbes, are the earliest direct evidence of life. These mineral constructions contain intricately-layered microscopic-structures, which were produced by complex communities of archaic microbes. The most archaic stromatolites are only a few centimeters in diameter and date to three-point-seven billion-years-ago.[1345, 1346]

Three-point-five billion-year-old microbe-fossils have been found preserved in sandstone in Western Australia.[1347] By this time, prokaryotic life was already very complex and active on the surface of the Earth. Large mushroom-shaped stromatolites were growing in shallow water, with specialized micro-organisms in the interior metabolizing hydrocarbons, while photosynthetic cyanobacteria living on the domed surfaces had started to convert carbon-dioxide in the atmosphere to oxygen.[1348, 1349]

Deep Underground: Archaic Life Feeding On Crude-Oil

There is evidence of the earliest forms of life deep underground too.[1350] Deep reservoirs of crude-oil are being degraded by specialized micro-organisms to produce methane, saturated crude-oil alkanes up to thirty carbon atoms in length, and other unsaturated by-products. The same microbiology is also responsible for the occurrence of hydrocarbon gases such as methane, ethane, propane, and butane.

Kerogens are high molecular-weight unsaturated-carbon-macromolecules that contain many carbon=carbon double-bonds. Related types of kerogens are found in crude oil, coal, and carbonaceous meteorites. The carbon-to-hydrogen ratio in meteoric kerogens reveals that much of the carbon is held together by reactive carbon=carbon double-bonds. Generally, for every one-hundred carbon atoms in meteoric carbon-macromolecules, there are approximately sixty hydrogen atoms, thirteen oxygen atoms, five nitrogen atoms, and three sulfur atoms.

Meteoric kerogens were the original feed-stock for life on Earth. The first living cells chemically-reduced and hydrogenated this type of extra-terrestrial material to generate energy. In crude-oil, which is the breakdown product of these large meteoric carbon-macromolecules, for every one hundred carbon atoms, there are now approximately *one hundred and seventy* hydrogen atoms, one oxygen atom, two nitrogen atoms, and three sulfur atoms. The microbes have been adding a lot of hydrogen to the meteroic kerogen but have been taking away the nitrogen and oxygen. The waste products of these ancient microbes were methane gas and saturated shorter-chain hydrocarbon molecules.

Primordial kerogens and other hydrocarbons were built into Earth when our planet was formed. They have been recovered from deep-impact structures, such as the three-hundred-kilometer-diameter dinosaur-kill crater at Chicxulub in Mexico. Twenty-five billion barrels-of-oil were found there, which had gushed up through fractures from the much deeper strata. Another example of deep-oil rising up through impact-fractures is the thirteen-kilometer-wide Ames structure in Oklahoma, United States.[1351]

A twelve-kilometer-deep borehole into proterozoic and archaean rock complexes under the Kola Peninsula in northwest Russia also revealed methane, ethane, propane, and butane that were being produced by micro-organisms feeding on crude-oil very deep underground, in ancient micro-environments rich in nitrogen, hydrogen, and helium.

In the Gulf of Mexico in AD 2009, the oil-rig called Deep water Horizon drilled the deepest oil well in history. Floating more than a kilometer above the sea-floor, it drilled an eleven kilometers deep hole into the crust. In AD 2010, while drilling a similar hole, an ultra-high pressure oil and methane blowout caused an explosion and fire that destroyed the rig.[1352]

There is a three-hundred-and-sixty-million-year-old deep-impact-structure in central Sweden, called the Siljan Ring. A seven-kilometer-deep hole was drilled and crude-oil was also discovered. However, the significant discovery was that the black-gunk was full of primitive bacteria. Several strains of thermophilic bacteria and archaea were cultured from this material, which thrived at temperatures up to one hundred-and-fifty degrees Celsius.[1353, 1354]

Based on this type of data, it has been calculated that ninety-percent of the global biomass is located in the sub-surface rocks of our planet. There is a huge quantity of micro-organisms deep in the Earth: the total biomass of bacteria and archaea up to ten kilometers below the surface, which probably weighs more than five-hundred-billion kilograms.[1355]

Living micro-organisms have been found in samples of rock that are more than three billion years old. Generally, the most abundant sources of these micro-organisms are found in ancient sedimentary rocks that are rich in hydrocarbons.[1356, 1357] Where hydrocarbons are abundant, each cubic-centimeter of rock contains up to a million ancient bacteria and archaea.

These micro-organisms lack a nucleus and grow well at high temperatures. They produce methane from hydrocarbon, so they are classed as methanogenic-extremophiles. They grow well in atmospheres containing hydrogen-sulfide, hydrogen, and their methane waste but are poisoned by oxygen.[1358]

As a result of microbiological activity, hydrocarbons in crude-oil are generally more chemically-reduced and more saturated than meteoric carbon macromolecules. Crude-oil contains shorter carbon chains, about three-times more hydrogen-substitution, but less oxygen and nitrogen than meteoric material.

The hydrocarbons in crude oil are mostly alkanes, cyclo-alkanes, and various aromatic hydrocarbons. There are smaller amounts of other organic compounds, which contain nitrogen, oxygen, and sulfur, plus trace amounts of metals such as iron, nickel, copper, and vanadium.

Methanogenic-archaean-microbes living in the crust of the Earth digest carbon macro-molecules from geological hydrocarbon deposits by chemical-reduction and hydrogen-substitution of carbon=carbon double-bonds. They preferentially metabolize carbon-12 macromolecules, so the carbon-13 abundance of their waste methane is very low, with a C13/C12 ratio of 1/95, compared to the C13/C12 ratios of crude oil and meteoric hydrocarbon of 1/92. Generally, hydrocarbons containing a lower proportion of the carbon-13 isotope are evidence of microbiological processing.

Methane-hydrates (for example, methane-clathrate) are the main waste product of a huge population of ancient microbes that live under the sea-floor, particularly on the drowned continental shelves. Primitive bacteria and archaea have been found living two-to-three kilometers below this type of sea-floor, feeding on coal and producing methane.[1359]

Some methane hydrates also contain long-chain saturated-hydro-carbon-oil too, another waste product of these organisms. The methane eventually migrates up through the crust and into the sea-bottom sediments, forming methane-clathrate-ice on contact with high-pressure low-temperature water.

These micro-organisms living deep in the continental crust and under the sea-floor originally lived on the surface and are descendants of the first supernova-life on Earth. These early communities of living cells were buried under further fallout dust from space and buried even deeper by the subsequent geological processes. However, they continued to thrive and evolve in the sub-surface ecosystems. The chemotrophic metabolism of these underground communities of micro-organisms is an echo of the earliest chemistry of life.

Where Did Life First Emerge?

The creation of life on Earth was a unique event, which probably occurred very soon after the solid surface of our planet was established.

The current scientific-fashion is to assume deep-ocean-thermal-vents were the incubator of the first living systems.[1360]

However, although this is an interesting hypothesis, it ignores the fact that deep-ocean-thermal-vents are only a recent ecosystem, not more than two-hundred and fifty million years old. It is also unlikely that life was first established in such a corrosive and destructive environment.

The first functional replicating cell probably formed on the young rocky surface of our planet in water with a salt balance similar to the salt balance found in all living cells. The average intra-cellular-medium is a solution of mainly potassium salts, together with some calcium and sodium salts, and is also rich in phosphates. The enigma is that this mixture of salts is obviously absent in rain-water. It is also very different from the mixture of salts in ocean-water and meteoric-salt-water, where sodium is the dominant ion.[1361]

The Russian solution to this problem is that life emerged in the warm geothermal pools, which were rich in potassium salts. The first cell of supernova-life probably appeared in the dark sludge in these geothermal pools, where materials could be incubated and concentrated.[1362, 1363]

The archaic atmosphere lacked oxygen but was rich in hydrogen-sulfide, hydrogen, nitrogen, carbon-dioxide, and water vapor plus helium and other noble gases. The high concentration of carbon-dioxide and water vapor made acidic rain, which percolated down into the original crust, dissolving minerals out of the rocks.

Deep underground the dilute acid was heated near magma chambers and then steamed back up to the surface. On the way, the super-heated water dissolved potassium salts out of the early granite like-rocks, making potassium-rich geothermal-water. The cool atmospheric temperature caused rapid condensation, and repeated evaporation and condensation concentrated a wide range of materials in the warm water.

Present-day geothermal-pools on the Kamchatka Peninsula in the far-east of Russia produce warm water with a high potassium concentration, which is also rich in hydrogen-sulfide and phosphates. Most ancient enzymes require high potassium-ion-concentrations to function, but cells with even leaky membranes can survive in warm potassium-rich water. The phosphate content of this warm geothermal water is also similar to that in living cells.

Today, oxygen in the atmosphere oxidizes the hydrogen-sulfide from the geothermal pools into sulfuric acid, making the environment acidic and toxic for most micro-organisms. However, in the archaic reducing atmosphere of Earth, these pools had a neutral-pH and were rich in hydrogen-sulfide.

During the scientific study of this environment, a new group of very rare and archaic micro-organisms called korarchaeota were discovered, which are very different from the archaea and bacteria.[1364] Although the korarchaeota were first found in Kamchatka-Russia in the potassium-rich hot-pools near the geothermal vents, they were later isolated from similar geothermal hot-pools in Iceland. Korarchaeota have also been found in anoxic estuary sediments in the sulfate-methane transition zone.[1365, 1366, 1367]

Pre-Life Chemistry

At the birth of our planet, there was no oxygen in the atmosphere to support internal-combustion to generate energy in living cells: only hydrogen sulfide and hydrogen were available. In these archaic times, huge quantities of iron-pyrite, iron-sulfide, and hydrocarbon lay dumped on the surface of Earth. Iron-sulfide is a water-soluble compound made of one atom of iron double-bonded to one atom of sulfur ($Fe=S$), whereas iron-pyrite is water insoluble and made of one atom of iron bonded to two atoms of sulfur ($S-Fe-S$) in the form of a lattice.

When primordial life first emerged, their metabolism was based on energy-generating chemical-reduction, which used extra-terrestrial hydrocarbon, iron-pyrite, and iron-sulfide and consumed hydrogen and hydrogen sulfide from the atmosphere. Most deep-oil deposits in the crust still contain iron sulfur compounds, hydrogen sulfide, and hydrogen, creating an environment that continues to support the earliest forms of life.

Chemical reduction-oxidation reactions, generally known as redox-reactions, are central to the electro-chemical processes in all living cells. In redox reactions, electrons are transferred from one atom to another. The atom that loses an electron is said to be oxidized (or had its oxidation-state increased), while the atom that gains an electron is said to be reduced (or had its oxidation-state reduced). Redox chemical reactions run faster at higher temperature and pressure in the presence of water but are rapidly poisoned by the presence of oxygen. Highly complex electron-transfer reactions are a key characteristic of all life.

The main pre-life redox reactions on archaic Earth were much simpler. Electrons were removed from iron-atoms in iron pyrite and iron-sulfide and added to double-bonded carbon atoms of extra-terrestrial hydrocarbons. In iron pyrite, the oxidation state of iron is plus-two, and the oxidation state of sulfur is minus-one. In iron sulfide, the oxidation state of iron is also plus-two, but the oxidation state of sulfur is minus-two.

Pre-life chemistry was determined by the abundance of cosmic unsaturated hydrocarbons, iron pyrite, and iron sulfide on the surface of ancient Earth and the large amount of hydrogen sulfide and molecular hydrogen in the ancient atmosphere. In three steps catalyzed by iron-pyrite (FeS_2), unsaturated bonds in extra-terrestrial hydrocarbons were reduced with hydrogen sulfide (H_2S) to yield a steady supply of energy. For each hydrocarbon double-bond reduction, one molecule of hydrogen sulfide (H_2S) was consumed and one molecule of iron-sulfide (FeS) was converted into iron-pyrite (FeS_2).[1368]

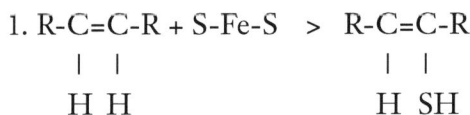

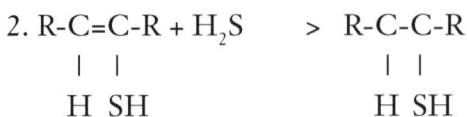

```
1. R-C=C-R + S-Fe-S  >  R-C=C-R
     |  |                   |  |
     H  H                   H  SH


                          + Fe=S


                          H  SH
                          |  |
2. R-C=C-R + H₂S     >    R-C-C-R
     |  |                   |  |
     H  SH                  H  SH


                          + energy
```

$$
\begin{array}{ccc}
\text{H} & \text{SH} & \text{H} & \text{H} \\
| & | & | & | \\
\text{3. R-C-C-R} + 2\text{Fe=S} & > & \text{R-C-C-R} \\
| & | & | & | \\
\text{H} & \text{SH} & \text{H} & \text{H}
\end{array}
$$

$$+ 2(\text{S-Fe-S}) + \text{energy}$$

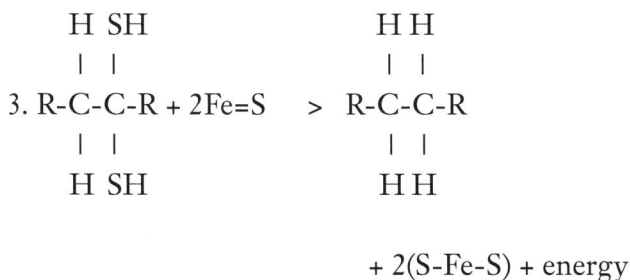

R-CH=CH-R included extraterrestrial unsaturated hydrocarbons, unsaturated heterocyclics, and protein-like polymers. Similar redox reactions can be driven by iron-sulfide, hydrogen-sulfide, or molecular-hydrogen. They all yield energy and result in the hydrogenation and sometimes cleavage of carbon=carbon double bonds of carbon-macromolecules.

They also result in the hydrogenation and sometimes cleavage of carbon=nitrogen double bonds. This type of chemistry not only explains the constituents of crude oil but also the origin of basic biochemistry and the global nitrogen cycle.

As life evolved, hydrogen-sulfide (H_2S) was replaced by hydrogen-sulfur-co-enzyme-A (HS-CoA). The iron-pyrite (FeS_2) catalyst was replaced by iron, nickel, or vanadium containing enzymes.[1369]

Extra-Terrestrial Lipid and the Formation of Cells

Lipids are long-chain hydrocarbon molecules with terminal polar carboxylic acid groups, which function as detergent-like molecules. Lipids are partially soluble in water and partly soluble in non-polar organic solvents.

It was a surprise when it was discovered that a mixture of lipid molecules could be extracted from carbonaceous-chondrite-meteorites. It was an even greater surprise to discover this material could spontaneously self-assemble in water and form semi-permeable monolayers and bi-layer membranes. With agitation and concentration, these membranes went on to roll-up into three dimensional structures such as tubes and cell-like vesicles. Laboratory experiments have even shown that such vesicles readily encapsulate macromolecules such as proteins.[1370]

These types of results support an astonishing model in which a heavy fall-out of extra-terrestrial material created an emulsion of dark molecular scum on the bubbling geothermal pools. The concentrated emulsion contained detergent-like lipids, polymers of amino acids, and other complex molecules, which floated on water or collected at the bottom. Lipid vesicles self-assembled, enclosing a variety of substituted hydrocarbon polymers, iron-sulfide, and proteins in high concentrations, all suspended or dissolved in a warm solution of potassium and phosphate.

The formation of a lipid cell-membrane is essential for all living cells. The original cell membranes probably had a lipid bi-layer that trapped macro-molecules but was still leaky to small molecules.

Chemistry Becomes Biochemistry

In one very rare event, which we still do not understand, the first auto-catalytic self-sustaining living-cell spontaneously started to function.[1371] This first cell eventually grew fat on extra-terrestrial polymer food, until it got so big that it mechanically split into two vesicles and continued to grow.

This basic process allowed cells to grow, divide, multiply, and evolve. The biochemistry and molecular biology of all living things is so closely related that life must have arisen from one single ancestor cell, which was the first to develop such a simple but effective replication process.[1372]

Iron and hydrocarbon rich archaean-rocks contain an ancient record of the origin of biochemistry. The first cells left behind the micro-structures discovered in four billion-years-old quartz layers, at Nuvvuagittuq, Quebec, Canada. These tube-like structures have been examined and they still contain the remains of iron sulfur compounds.[1373]

The electro-chemical reactions of the archaic biochemistry of the first cells was based on extra-terrestrial iron-sulfide, iron-pyrite, and unsaturated-hydrocarbons, in an atmosphere rich in water-vapor, carbon-dioxide, hydrogen-sulfide, and molecular-hydrogen.[1374]

Iron-sulfide allowed the first cells to have the electron-donating reducing-power to convert nitrogen to ammonia and to convert positively-charge-protons to molecular hydrogen.[1375, 13761377] The first living cells managed reduction reactions with iron-sulfide and hydrogen-sulfide, using simple catalysts of supernova-derived metals, such as iron, nickel, vanadium, molybdenum, manganese, and tungsten. Silicate-rocks containing zinc and sulfur also had catalytic properties, which accelerated these reactions.

Cells then improved on this pre-life chemistry, by chelating iron, iron-sulfur, and other supernova derived metals with extra-terrestrial protein-like polymers to make primitive enzymes. For example, archaic nitrite-reductases have iron-sulfur clusters wrapped in a protein chain, which was an improvement on the pre-life iron-pyrite catalyst. Proteins with more electrically charged amino acids have a natural affinity to bind to iron-pyrite.

Reduced-ferric-iron was also used as the electron-donor in the reaction-center of early proteins used for molecular synthesis. Archaean cells still use ferric-iron catalysis plus phosphorous reagents to catalyze glycolysis. Oxidized-iron complexed with protein or porphyrin like molecules became the terminal electron acceptor for energy-generating respiration.[1378]

The free-radical chemistry catalyzed by supernova-derived nickel, which was used to produce methane, was later improved by micro-organisms with a creation of nickel-protein enzymes.[1379] Some ancient-enzymes such as nitrogenases used vanadium-iron active-centers, which was another adaptation of a supernova-derived catalyst.[1380]

As archaic life evolved, HS-CoA replaced the H_2S, NAD-H, and $FADH_2$ replaced H_2, Fe-Ni containing enzymes replaced the FeS_2 catalyst, and cosmic phosphates were replaced by ATP. However, iron-sulfide, hydrogen-sulfide, and molecular-hydrogen are still used by microbes deep underground to breakdown hydrocarbons.[1381] Even today archaic hyper-thermophilic bacteria and archaea living in deep deposits of heavy crude-oil, rich in hydrogen-sulfide, are breaking-down oil and nitrates to produce lighter oils, ammonia, methane, and hydrogen gas.

The simple chemistry evolved to produce acetaldehyde, a common intermediate of metabolism in most living cells and a central reaction in basic biochemistry. Similar reactions produced 2-mercapto-ethylamine, a building block of HS-coenzyme-A (HS-CoA), life's upgrade on hydrogen-sulfide chemistry, which is an essential component of metabolism of almost all living things.

Iron-sulfide and hydrogen-sulfide was also used to reduce unsaturated hydrocarbons to 2-ketoacids, converting oxaloacetate to fumarate and succinate. This was the probable origin of the archaic citric-acid redox-cycle of biochemistry, known as the Krebs Cycle or TCA Cycle, which is learnt by every biochemistry student.

In the primitive metabolic-reactions of the first micro-organisms, iron-sulfide plus hydrocarbon generated energy and methane. An end product of this metabolic reaction was insoluble iron-pyrite, an atom of iron combined with two atoms of sulfur.[1382]

However, the name iron-pyrite actually means iron-firestone because it can be used to start fires. Iron-pyrite was also used to drive biochemistry in the opposite direction by capturing electrons to produce iron-sulfide.[1383] Iron-pyrite was probably the energy source for the first synthetic reactions of living cells.

These basic biochemical systems continued to evolve underground, shaped by anoxic subterranean environments and various macro-molecular carbon feed-stocks. Over billions of years complex alien carbon-macromolecules were buried and transformed by micro-organisms to become crude oil and tars on which the global economy depends. We still drive cars and power our industry with the same carbon rich sludge that created life on Earth.

The Phosphate Energy Transfer Molecules

Phosphates are the universal energy transfer molecules in almost all biological systems. It is very significant that phosphorus is another abundant supernova-produced element in the solar-system.

Large amounts of phosphorus landed on Earth at the formation of our planet.[1384] Schreibersite, $(Fe, Ni)_3P$, is a iron-nickel-phosphide mineral, which originated from the rupture of the outer-thermonuclear-reaction-shells of the former companion-star of the Sun. Huge amounts of Schreibersite crashed onto the young Earth in nickel-iron meteorites, during the formation of our planet. Later when Schreibersite-rich meteors landed in rain water pools of dilute carbonic acid, a natural electro-chemical fuel cell was created, which produced a solution of chemically reactive phosphates.[1385]

Carbonaceous chondrite meteorites like Murchison also contain polyphosphates, pyrophosphate, and significant amounts of methyl-, ethyl-, propyl-, and butyl phosphorous acids, which were originally synthesized in the supernova explosion plume. When these phosphorous compounds dissolved in the archaic acidic-rainwater, the pyrophosphates produced reactive intermediates called phosphites.

These materials represent the first chemical steps toward the ubiquitous energy system of living cells based on adenosine tri-phosphate (ATP), which contains reactive phosphate-groups.[1386]

Proteins from Space and Archaic Protein-Metabolism

Proteins are made of the same amino acids found in meteorites. Archaic proteins in ancient micro-organisms have similar amino-acid abundance-ratios to those found in meteorites. The six most abundant amino-acids that have been isolated from meteorites are glycine, leucine, alanine, aspartic-acid, valine, and serine. These same six amino acids are the most frequently used amino acids in the oldest proteins of the earliest bacteria and archaea.[1387]

Thorarchaeota and Korarchaeota (described earlier) are separate from other archaeal groups and appear to have preserved relic-metabolic pathways from very early life on Earth. It is very significant that the ancient microbes from the geothermal pools have genes for a strange archaic metabolic pathway for digesting protein and amino-acids, to produce acetate and energy. These micro-organisms may be descendants of the first micro-organisms that originally fed on supernova-produced extra-terrestrial protein.[1388, 1389, 1390]

Life Started Backward

All living things alive today are highly-complex far-from-equilibrium energy-consuming molecular-machines, which are controlled by highly integrated and inter-dependent molecular systems. Scientists have great difficulty explaining how life commenced, because it is hard to model a simpler functional living system.

A major barrier to understanding the origin of life has been mistaken assumptions about the initial conditions. Today, living cells are so complex and well adapted; they can take in simple gases, salts, and water and extract energy from simple chemical-fuels or photons to synthesize highly complex molecules. Generally, we assume that the first cells functioned in a similar way, consuming energy and fighting entropy, to convert components of its chaotic environment into complex structures and systems.

This assumption is wrong: Life started backward. In the first cells, most metabolic pathways ran backward. Even the information flow ran backward: it was the original cosmic protein-like polymers that formed the templates for the creation of RNA.

Life started as a simple adaptation of pre-existing chemical-degradation-processes: the conversion of extra-terrestrial macro-molecular unsaturated carbon compounds into methane and crude oil, in the presence of iron-sulfur compounds, phosphate compounds, hydrogen sulfide, and hydrogen. Life arose out of catalytic chemistry, originally based on iron-pyrite, which guided the controlled demolition of complex macro-molecules, which had been synthesized in space, to yield energy and useful smaller molecules. The key to understanding the origin of life was the reversibility of these catalytic pathways.

Glycolysis Ran Backward to Make Sugar

In almost all living systems, glycolysis is a basic metabolic pathway that breaks down sugar into sugar-phosphates, pyruvate, and energy. However, glycolysis in archaea and bacteria is based on different enzymes of different origin, revealing that the current process of glycolysis became operational long after the first organisms evolved.

Glycolysis used to run backward to make sugar. The discovery of the starting materials for the synthesis of sugar; di-hydroxy-acetone, ethylene-glycol, glyceric-acid, di-hydroxy-butyric-acids, and glycerol, in both the Murchison-meteorite and the Murray-meteorite, suggests these were the starting materials for a process that ran in the opposite direction. Backward-glycolysis was driven by the abundance of these extra-terrestrial starting-materials, together with phosphates and iron-sulfur compounds, plus hydrogen-sulfide and hydrogen in the archaic atmosphere, to produce sugar. The conversion of pyruvate and related starting-materials into sugar was catalyzed by supernova-derived metals.

The Krebs TCA-Cycle Ran Backward

In almost all living systems, the TCA-cycle is a cycle of chemical reactions regulated by protein-enzymes, which is used by almost all oxygen-breathing organisms, to generate energy from the oxidation of carbohydrates and fats.

The TCA-cycle functions by oxidizing various carbon-based feedstocks to produce polyphosphate energy molecules and carbon-dioxide waste. Energy capture from the TCA-cycle oxidation process is achieved using a transfer molecule called acetyl-CoA, which captures energy as a high-energy phosphate and which can then be used in the synthesis of ATP (adenosine-tri-phosphate).

However, in the absence of oxygen, the TCA-cycle originally ran backward. The original biochemical process controlled the consumption of extra-terrestrial polyphosphates and powered the conversion of extra-terrestrial proteins into sugars, carbohydrates, and fats, in the presence of hydrogen-sulfide and hydrogen.

Again supernova derived metals played a central role. They catalyzed the break-down of extra-terrestrial proteins into de-aminized amino acids, which entered the TCA-cycle coupled to a recycled intermediate called HS-CoA, life's equivalent of hydrogen-sulfide, in the form of acetyl-CoA. The acetyl groups were then reduced and assembled to produce glucose.[1391]

Acetyl-CoA is found in all living systems, including the methanogenic archaea and acetogenic bacteria, the most ancient prokaryotes characterized. The acetyl-CoA biochemical pathway is a short linear reaction path at the cross roads to both carbon-metabolism and energy-metabolism.

Acetyl-CoA is a critical intermediate for the synthesis of most organic molecules.

All the enzymes in the ancient acetyl-CoA pathway, used by both bacteria and archaea, contain ancient supernova derived elements such as iron, nickel, and sulfur. These enzymes are much older than the enzymes of the membrane-associated proton-pumps of bacteria and archaea, suggesting that the acetyl-CoA system predates the membrane coupled energy systems on which life now depends.[1392, 1393, 1394]

Four-point-five billion year old biochemistry was based on polyphosphate and HS-CoA to convert extra-terrestrial proteins to sugars. HS-CoA is also an energy-transfer-molecule used by all living systems. HS-CoA is a compound made from ADP (adenosine-di-phosphate), isobutanol, and leucine, an amino acid. ADP (adenosine-di-phosphate) comprises of adenine, a nitrogen-substituted aromatic hetero-cycle, ribose-sugar, and two phosphates, the breakdown product of the energy molecule ATP.[1395]

The DNA-RNA-Protein Cycle Ran Backward

Basic biology classes teach that DNA is the essential information molecule of life. Genetic codes written in DNA are transcribed into RNA messages, which direct the synthesis of proteins, which catalyze the reactions of life, some of which are responsible for the synthesis of DNA and RNA.

The problem with understanding the origin of this cycle is in determining which type of biopolymer was developed first by early life, to direct the synthesis of all other biopolymers in the cycle? It is impossible to imagine how this complex cycle could have appeared spontaneously, when the first cell started to function.

Despite these difficulties, the old "RNA World" hypothesis was that RNA was the first biological polymer.[1396] However, although the basic nitrogen-containing heterocycles needed to make RNA have been found in carbonaceous chondrite meteorites, neither ribose nor nucleic-acid chains of RNA have ever been found in meteoric material. Ribose is a pentose sugar that is very difficult to synthesize and is very unstable in aqueous solution and to heat.[1397]

The solution to this paradox is that in ancient times, the biological pathways in the first cells were based on extra-terrestrial proteins, which were abundant in the archaic environment. RNA was a much later adaptation based on the polymerization of energy-transfer-molecules like HS-CoA, which used extra-terrestrial protein as a template. HS-CoA was probably originally derived from extra-terrestrial protein.

Transfer-RNA could have developed from molecules related to acetyl-CoA, which resembles structures in both protein and RNA. There is also an ancient class of polymer resembling acetyl-CoA, protein, and transfer-RNA called peptide-nucleic-acid (PNA), which could have been the precursor of both RNA and DNA.[1398]

The DNA and RNA system developed much later from backward protein synthesis. Ribosomes originally used to make RNA polymers from nucleobase-ribose-phosphate-amino-acid monomers polymerized on an extra-terrestrial protein template. When DNA-transcription systems first evolved, they probably also started by running backward, copying DNA from RNA. DNA-replication enzymes are very diverse, so they must also have evolved much later.

The Story of LUCA: the Last Universal Common Ancestor

So far a bottom-up approach to the origin of life from chemistry and biochemistry has been described. The uniformity of biochemistry and molecular biology across the three great domains of life, known as *archaea*, *bacteria*, and *eukarya*, shows that life could only have arisen from one starting point, from which all living systems evolved.[1399] The other way to approach the problem of the origin of life is a top-down approach from organisms alive today to LUCA, the Last Universal Common Ancestor of all life.

LUCA is a hypothetical micro-organism that existed on Earth more than three point five billion years ago.[1400] A tree-of-life has been constructed from the analysis of related genetic sequences of small subunit ribosomal RNA, from large numbers of different species, to represent the degree of genetic relatedness between different micro-organisms. Extrapolating back from the common metabolic pathways and molecular biology of bacteria and archaea alive today, it is possible to model LUCA as a small cell enclosed in a lipid bi-layer membrane, which contained all the macromolecules and metabolites necessary for life.[1401]

LUCA had energy systems based on phosphate polymers (ATP and Acetyl CoA) and the TCA-cycle for the degradation of hydrocarbons. However, the electro-chemi-osmotic energy systems across membranes, used by living cells today, must have been a later development, because archaea have different types of membranes and different proton pumps from bacteria. The membrane proton-gradient energy-systems were later adaptations of the original iron-sulfide and hydrocarbon energy system of the first cell.

Recently, a deeper analysis of the components of LUCA has been achieved by the analysis of over six million different genes.[1402] There were only sixty protein coding genes before the original separation of archaea and prokaryotes, which occurred over three billion years ago. Two-thirds of these genes coded for protein-translation, membrane-enzymes, redox-enzymes, and enzymes for processing nucleotides.

The data shows that LUCA was an anaerobic micro-organism producing methane, probably living in a subterranean environment. It had redox-chemistry, iron-sulfide biochemistry, and free-radical reaction pathways, acetyl-CoA synthase, and ancient enzymes with molybdenum-reaction centers. LUCA had a functional DNA-to-RNA transcription system and an RNA-to-protein translation system but no DNA replication system.

The first cells, living more than four billion years ago, seem to have got their proteins and lipids from the environment. The very first archaic microbes that pre-dated LUCA were made of extra-terrestrial proteins enclosed in a cell-membrane of extra-terrestrial lipid and had neither DNA nor RNA.

Evolution of Life in Quantum Jumps

Taking into account all the information in the previous sections, a model can be built for the evolution of life as a series of quantum jumps in complexity.

Life Version 1.0 emerged around four-point-five billion years ago built from prefabricated macromolecules. It had a simple metabolism for generating energy based on chemical reduction of extra-terrestrial carbon-macromolecules using iron-sulfide and hydrogen-sulfide in the presence of metal catalysts.

After a slow period of subterranean evolution, about four billion years ago Life Version 2.0 appeared. It resembled LUCA, the precursor of archaea, bacteria, and other primitive micro-organisms. It lived in sub-surface oil deposits but then underwent rapid development, when it was returned to the surface of Earth. The big breakthroughs for life were the developments of the DNA-RNA-protein system, photosynthesis, and oxygen respiration.

The next quantum jump occurred around two-point-five billion years ago with the creation of Life Version 3.0: the eukaryote revolution. Larger and more complex cells were created by fusion of multiple microbes. Parasitic microbes living inside the intercellular environment of other microbes evolved into the cell nucleus and organelles.[1403] Some soil bacteria still retain evidence of this transition from archaea to the eukaryotes about two-billion years ago.

Life Version 4.0 was the innovation of multi-cellular organisms, which developed about two-point-one billion years ago.

Alien Life in Other Star Systems?

We have traced the origin of life on Earth, back through biochemistry and chemistry, to the nucleosynthesis of elements in a supernova explosion in a binary-star-system. The radical new idea in this book is that the death of a companion-star led directly to the birth of planets and the origin of life. The study of exo-planets suggests this process is happening all over the universe.

The most likely places to find life will be on earth-like rocky planets, which orbit a host-star with high metallicity, indicating a supernova explosion of a local companion-star. Any exo-planets orbiting in the habitable-zone could have the environmental conditions favorable for assembling prefabricated chiral macro-molecules from the supernova-debris into living systems. The presence of methane or oxygen in the planetary atmosphere is a marker of life.

The simple conclusion is that life is probably common on exo-planets orbiting stars that are the remains of old binary-star-systems. Star-core-zeus is the story of life in the whole universe.

APPENDIX C

Chaos in the Kuiper Belt

● ● ●

THE HUNT FOR THE SUPER-MASSIVE object that is causing chaos at the outer edge of the Kuiper Belt suddenly became a fashionable area of astronomy-research in 2016.

The Kuiper Belt and the Scattered-Objects

Some of the first icy-objects to be discovered that had been scattered out of the Kuiper Belt were 1995TL8 and 2000YW134. Both had unusual orbits with inclinations of approximately twenty degrees to the ecliptic plane and eccentricities around thirty percent.

Sedna and 2000CR105 were even more perturbed, with very high eccentricities around seventy percent. The closest that Sedna gets to the Sun is seventy-six AU and a similar scattered-object 2012VP113 has a perihelion out at eighty AU. The aphelia of both objects is hundreds AU away from the Sun.

Eris, the body that got Pluto relegated to dwarf planet status, has also been perturbed by some massive object, which threw it into a highly eccentric orbit, inclined forty-four degrees to the solar-system disc. Buffy, the nick-name for 2004X190, an icy-object that orbits the Sun every four-hundred-and-forty years, has also been kicked out of the ecliptic plane. An undetected but massive object lurking further out must have thrown Buffy into this orbit, which is inclined at forty-seven degrees to the ecliptic plane.

Further discoveries have shown that generally there is a strange pattern in the orbital parameters of the scattered-objects that have perihelia greater than thirty AU and semi-major axes greater than one-hundred-and-fifty AU. Many of these objects have been thrown out of the ecliptic plane into highly inclined and eccentric orbits with related orientations.

There is also a pattern emerging in the orbital periods of the scattered-objects, which is becoming clearer with each new discovery. The scattered-objects—2012VP113, 2004VN112, 2010 GB174, and 2013RF98—have similar orbital periods in the region of four thousand to six thousand years, whereas Sedna and 2007TG422 have almost the same orbital period in the region of twelve-thousand years: some sort of orbital resonance is at work.

Six of the scattered-objects—Sedna, 2012VP113, 2007TG422, 2004VN112, 2013RF98, and 2010GB174—were studied in detail. They all have perihelia located to the south of the ecliptic plane of the solar-system and have clustered ascending-nodes (Ω). The ascending-node is one of the two intersection points on the plane of an object's orbit, where the object passes from below the solar-system plane to above it (i.e., as it moves in a solar northward direction), as it travels around its orbit. The longitude-of-the-ascending-node is an angle measured in the direction of the orbital motion of Earth from the spring-vernal-equinox point to the ascending-node.

The perihelia of all six scattered-objects are clustered together, and their arguments-of-perihelion (ω) are tightly confined around three-hundred-and-ten degrees. The argument-of-perihelion is the angle in the object's orbital plane, between its ascending-node and its perihelion, measured in the direction of travel of the object in its orbit around the Sun. This is another way of saying that the orbits of the objects are tilted in a similar way with respect to the solar-system plane so that all their orbital ellipses approximately intersect with the solar-system plane at only two points.

All six scattered-objects also have longitudes-of-perihelion clustered around 71±16 degrees. The longitude-of-perihelion (ϖ) is defined as equal to the sum of the argument-of-perihelion ω angle, plus the ascending-node Ω angle ($\varpi = \omega + \Omega$). In simple terms, all six scattered-objects move away from their perihelion points that are clustered near the Sun and to south of the ecliptic and travel up and fan out into the northern sky on related orbits, whose orbital planes are all orientated in approximately the same plane.

Planet-9 or Star-Core-Zeus

In January 2016, Caltech astronomers Batygin and Brown published their computer model to explain the strangely related alignments of the orbits of the six scattered-objects. They suggested scattering was being caused by an undiscovered massive object which was orbiting beyond the Kuiper Belt.[1404, 1405]

Batygin and Brown tried various parameters for their computer model of the solar-system, in which they attempted to reproduce the pattern of orbits of the six-scattered-objects, which they represented in their model with nominal test-masses, by including an additional massive perturbing object, which they called Planet-9.

Batygin and Brown assumed the following basic parameters for their Planet-9: a mass greater than ten Earths: a semi-major axis (a) of 700 AU, an eccentricity (e) of 0.6, an aphelion at 1200 AU, a perihelion at 200 AU, an aphelion-to-perihelion distance of 1400 AU, an orbital period (P) of ten thousand to twenty thousand Earth years, an orbital inclination to the solar-system plane (i) of 30 degrees, and an initial argument-of-perihelion (ω) of 150 degrees.

With further modifications, Batygin and Brown arrived at a rough approximation for an orbit of the massive perturber, which could be causing the observed pattern of scattering. However, they showed there were a wide range of options for the mass and the orbital elements of this hidden perturbing mass.

Their computer simulation suggested that the orbit of their Planet-9 lay in approximately the same plane as the average plane of the orbits of the six scattered-objects. The plane of the orbit of the six scattered-objects was close to the plane of the Milky Way, not in the ecliptic plane of our solar-system. Their prediction for the location of the aphelion of Planet-9 lay on the opposite side of the Sun to the average location of the aphelia of the six scattered-objects.

After adjusting the parameters of their model, one possible orbit of their Planet-9 was generated: an eccentric-ellipse stretching away to the south of the solar-system to a distant aphelion, with its plane significantly inclined to the plane of the solar-system. Batygin and Brown had independently arrived at aspects of an orbit, which were very similar to those already established for star-core-zeus.

Their computer-simulation also generated best-fit parameters for Planet-9 to produce the observed orbits of the six scattered-objects. Planet-9 probably had a semi-major axis of two-hundred-and-fifty AU and perihelion-aphelion separation of around five-hundred AU, just like star-core-zeus. They also estimated the perihelion position of Planet-9 was probably located between sixteen and eighteen hours right-ascension, in the direction of the May-June position of Earth's orbit around the Sun, again like the orbit of star-core-zeus.

The computer models of Batygin and Brown also predicted that Planet-9 was currently located in one of two zones where it crossed the Milky Way. They estimated that the ascending-node of their Planet-9 was probably located between sixty and ninety degrees from the vernal-spring-equinox. In other words, Planet-9 must approach the Sun from its aphelion in the angular direction of Sirius and then cross the region of sky defined by Sirius-Orion-Taurus, just like star-core-zeus.

Batygin and Brown estimated that Planet-9 is currently located in a quadrant of the night-sky defined by six-to-four hours of right-ascension and declination from minus-ten to minus-twenty degrees, below the ecliptic plane of the solar-system.[1406] This is the same area as the triangular zone of the night-sky that is marked by the bright star Sirius and the constellations of Gemini and Orion, which was described as the location of star-core-zeus in earlier chapters.

However, the big theoretical problem with Planet-9, in contrast to star-core-zeus was that Batygin and Brown believed that their Planet-9 had always remained far outside the Kuiper Belt and never entered the inner solar-system. The problem was that if Planet-9 really had this type of distant-orbit, it must have an enormous angular momentum, more than one hundred times greater than the Sun.[1407]

One team of astronomers proposed that if Planet-9 had such enormous angular momentum, it must be an exo-planet captured from another star.[1408] Batygin and Brown failed to respond with a viable explanation for the origin of their Planet-9 orbit, because the solar-nebular-hypothesis for the formation of the solar-system, predicted Planet-9 should not exist at all.

It was impossible for Planet-9 to have picked up enough energy to get so far away from the Sun, but neither return to the inner solar-system where it formed nor depart from the solar-system altogether. If Planet-9 really was a planet, which had accreted in a dense part of the primordial solar-nebular, what was it doing so far out from the Sun?

The Sky Survey Search for Planet-9

Batygin and Brown went in search of Planet-9 in the astronomy sky-survey-data from WISE, Catalina, and Pan STARRS. They eliminated most zones of the sky as a possible hiding place for the massive local perturber.

NASA's Widefield Infrared Survey Explorer (WISE) had completed an all-sky survey looking for the heat of brown dwarfs or giant planets bigger than Saturn. Using computers to analyze the WISE data, Batygin and Brown thought they had eliminated the possibility of any larger-than-Saturn object as far out from the Sun as ten-thousand AU, any Neptune-size object as far out as seven hundred AU, or any earth-size object only two hundred AU from the Sun, in most regions of the sky. However, they were mistaken: star-core-zeus had already been detected by WISE.

The Catalina Sky Surveys, which looked for near-Earth asteroids and were sensitive to slow-moving objects, covered a large part of the sky out to distances of ten-thousand AU. However, Batygin and Brown failed to detect the perturber in the regions of the sky covered by the Catalina Sky Surveys.

They explained away their failure with control-studies. This revealed that even though the computer managing the Catalina Sky Survey data could detect known bright Kuiper Belt objects crossing an empty field of view, it failed to detect known objects crossing the bright star field of the Milky Way.

It turned out that the computers analyzing both the WISE data and Catalina data were effectively blind between seven-hour and four-hour right ascension, in the region of the galactic-disc of the Milky Way. The Panoramic Survey Telescope and Rapid Response System based on Haleakala, Maui (Pan-STARRS), was also effectively blind in the galactic plane of the Milky Way, due to the light and heat from this dense region of stars, dust-clouds, and gas.

The only area that was not properly searched by Batygin and Brown was the quadrant of sky, south of the ecliptic plane of the solar-system, defined by right-ascension of 7-hour-to-5-hour and declination of zero-to-minus-15-degrees. Batygin and Brown missed star-core-zeus that is broadcasting its powerful 3C161 radio-signal from the middle of this region of the night-sky and its associated WISE IR-signal.

The new mystery of Niku and Other High-Inclination-Objects
The Planet-9 computer-model of the Caltech astronomers Brown and Batygin was invalidated later in 2016 by new discoveries. A group of objects, with highly-inclined retrograde-orbits, were found traveling deep inside the solar-system by the Outer solar-system Survey of Pan-STARRS. The massive perturber must penetrate the inner solar-system after all.

A retrograde trans-Neptune-object called Niku, the nick-name of 2011KT19, was detected high above the ecliptic plane, traveling inside the orbit of Neptune, twenty-six AU from the Sun. Niku was first discovered in the Catalina Sky Survey as a trans-Neptunian object and then confirmed in 2015 in images taken with the Pan-STARRS telescope in Hawaii.[1409]

Niku passed perihelion about twenty-four AU from the Sun in 1999 and is now traveling away from the Sun from inside the orbit of Neptune to its aphelion located out at forty-seven AU from the Sun, close to the aphelion of Pluto. Niku's orbital period has been calculated as two-hundred-and-twelve years. The orbital dynamics of Niku were also very similar to that of Drac (2008 KV42).

The trans-Neptune-objects and centaurs all exhibit a surprising clustering of ascending-nodes and occupy a common orbital plane. However, simulations show that these alignments were very unstable and orbital precession should separate such clusters of objects within a few million years, unless something very massive is constantly forcing these high-inclination-orbits into the same common plane.

Niku orbits in a plane inclined one-hundred and ten degrees from the plane of the solar-system, which is almost the same as the inclination predicted for star-core-zeus of one-hundred and thirteen degrees.[1410] Niku also orbits in the same retrograde direction as predicted for star-core-zeus.[1411]

Star-core-zeus is responsible for all the unusual orbits of these newly discovered objects: they can be explained by binary-star-system dynamics between star-core-zeus and the Sun. The scattered-objects were thrown into their orbits when they encountered the barycenter of our binary system, located at binary aphelion fifty AU from the Sun in the direction of Sirius.

More Scattered Objects

By the end of 2016, the hunt for Planet-9 was heating up. A new class of high-inclination-Centaurs lurking in the distant solar-system whose orbits cross those of the outer planets beyond Jupiter had been discovered. Two more trans-Neptune-objects were being tracked, and they added to the evidence for a huge perturbing mass lurking beyond the Kuiper Belt.[1412]

Another new object called 2013FT28 was discovered with a highly eccentric elliptical orbit whose orientation was the same as star-core-zeus, with an aphelion about five-hundred AU from the Sun in the approximate angular direction of Sirius.[1413] 2013FT28 is anti-aligned to the average orbits of the six scattered-objects.

Astronomers around the world are currently searching for the massive perturber in the region of the night-sky around the bright star Sirius and the constellation of Orion.[1414] However, I have already identified star-core-zeus as the infrared-emitting object at (J2000.0: 06 27

09.36, -05 53 14.2) in the WISE database, corresponding to the power-ful 3C-161 radio signal broadcasting between Sirius and Orion.

=END OF THE APPENDICES=

NOTES

[1] The 'isotopes' of a chemical element, all have the same number of protons, which give rise to its chemical properties, but have different numbers of neutrons. Isotopes are identified by the name of the element and its mass number; equivalent to its total number of protons plus neutrons. An element with too many neutrons is unstable and can decay radioactively by ejecting particles from its atomic nucleus.

[2] Holms, Rupert, *Cataclysms & Renewals* (London: Rupert Holms & Co., 2015), printed and distributed by www.createspace.com, title/5104182;https://www.amazon.co.uk/gp/offer-listing/1517587220/ref=sr_1_1_olp?ie=UTF8&qid=1482494698&sr=8-1&keywords=cataclysms+%26+renewals.

[3] 'Perihelion' is the point on the orbit of an object where it is nearest to the Sun. The word 'Perihelion' was derived from the Greek word, '*peri*' meaning 'around' and '*helios*,' which was the name of the Greek god of the Sun.

[4] Jouzel, Jean, "A Brief History of Ice-Core Science over the Last 50 Yr," *Climate of the Past* 9 (2013): 2525–47, doi:10.5194/cp-9-2525-2013.

[5] Petit, J. R. et al., "Climate and Atmospheric History of the Past 420,000 Years from the Vostok Ice Core, Antarctica," *Nature* 399 (1999): 429–36.

[6] Fischer, Hubertus et al., "Ice-core Records of Atmospheric CO_2 around the Last Three Glacial Terminations," *Science* 283 (1999): 1712–14.

[7] Bond, Gerard et al., "Correlations between Climate Records from North Atlantic Sediments and Greenland Ice," *Nature* 365 (1993): 143–47, doi:10.1038/365143a0.

[8] *Summary for Policymakers*: The globally averaged combined land and ocean surface temperature data as calculated by a linear trend, show a warming of 0.85 [0.65 to 1.06] °Celsius, over the period 1880 to 2012, when multiple independently produced datasets exist. The total increase between the average of the 1850–1900 period and the 2003–2012 period is 0.78 [0.72 to 0.85] °C, based on the single longest dataset available. http://www.ipcc.ch/pdf/assessment-report/ar5/wg1/ WG1AR5_SPM_FINAL.pdf.

[9] Alley, R. B. et al., "Abrupt Climate Change," *Science* 299 (2003): 2005–10.

[10] Steffensen, J. P. et al., "High-resolution Greenland Ice-core Data Show Abrupt Climate Change Happens in few Years," *Science* 321 (2008): 680–84, doi:10.1126/science.1157707.

[11] Chen, T., "Synchronous Centennial Abrupt Events in the Ocean and Atmosphere during the Last Deglaciation," *Science* 349 (2015): 1537–41.

[12] Barker, S. et al., "800,000 Years of Abrupt Climate Variability," *Science* 334 (2011): 347–51.

[13] Mecler, N., "An Extended Yardstick for Climate Variability," *Nature* 534 (2016): 626–28.

[14] Cheng, H. et al., "The Asian Monsoon over the Past 640,000 Years and Ice Age Terminations," *Nature* 534 (2016): 640–46.

[15] Schmittner, A., "The Smoking Gun for Atlantic Circulation Changes," *Science* 353 (2016): 445–46.

[16] Henry, L. G., et al., "North Atlantic Ocean Circulation and Abrupt Climate Change during the Last Glaciation," *Science* 353 (2016): 470–74.

[17] Committee on Abrupt Climate Change, National Research Council, *Abrupt Climate Change: Inevitable Surprises* (Washington, DC: National Academy Press, 2002), ISBN-10: 0-309-07434-7; ISBN-13: 978-0-309-07434-6G.

[18] Crowley, T., "Cycles, Cycles Everywhere," *Science* 295 (2002): 1473–74.

[19] Raymo, M. E. and Huber, P., "Unlocking the Mysteries of the Ice Ages," *Nature* 451 (2008): 284–85.

[20] Petit, J. R. et al., "Climate and Atmospheric History of the Past 420,000 Years from the Vostok Ice Core, Antarctica," *Nature* 399 (1999): 429–36.

[21] Lorius, C. et al., "A 30,000-yr Isotope Climatic Record from Antarctic Ice," *Nature* 280 (1979): 644–48.

[22] Greenland Ice-core Project (GRIP) Members, "Climate Instability during the Last Interglacial Period Recorded in the GRIP Ice-core," *Nature* 364 (1993): 203–7.

[23] Bianchi, G. G., "Holocene Periodicity in North Atlantic Climate and Deep-ocean Flow South of Iceland," *Nature* 397 (1999): 515–17.

[24] Oppo, D., "Millennial Climate Oscillation," *Science* 278 (1997): 1244–46.

[25] Wolff, E. W. et al., "Millennial-scale Variability during the Last Glacial: The Ice-core Record," *Quaternary Science Reviews* 29 (2010): 2828–38.

[26] Bond, G. et al., "A Pervasive Millennial-Scale Cycle in North Atlantic Holocene and Glacial Climates," *Science* 278 (1997): 1257–66.

[27] Kerr, R., "Does a Climate Clock Get a Noisy Boost," *Science* 290 (2000): 697–98.

[28] Jouzel, J. et al., "Orbital and Millennial Antarctic Climate Variability over the Past 800,000 Years," *Science* 317 (2007): 793–96.

[29] Petit, J. R. et al., "Climate and Atmospheric History of the Past 420,000 Years from the Vostok Ice Core, Antarctica," 429–36.

[30] Monnin, E. et al., "Atmospheric CO_2 Concentrations over the Last Glacial Termination," *Science* 291 (2001): 112–14.

[31] Fischer, H. et al., "Ice-Core Records of Atmospheric CO_2 around the Last Three Glacial Terminations," 1712–14.

[32] Siegenthaler, U. et al., "Stable Carbon Cycle–Climate Relationship during the Late Pleistocene," *Science* 310 (2005): 1313–17.

[33] Allen, K. A., "When Carbon Escaped from the Sea," *Nature* 518 (2015): 176–77.

[34] Martinez-Boti, M. A. et al., "Boron Isotope Evidence for Oceanic Carbon Dioxide Leakage during the Last Deglaciation," *Nature* 518 (2015): 219–22.

[35] Tolstoy, M., "Mid-ocean Ridge Eruptions as a Climate Valve," *Geophysical Research Letters* 42 (2015): 1346–51, doi:10.1002/2014GL063015.

[36] Committee on the Effects of Solar Variability on Earth's Climate; Space Studies Board; Division on Engineering and Physical Science; National Research Council, *The Effects of Solar Variability on Earth's Climate: A Workshop Report* (Washington, DC: The National Academies Press, 2013), http://www.nap.edu/catalog.php?record_id=13519.

[37] Leconte, J., "Increased Insolation Threshhold for Runaway Greenhouse Processes on Earth-like Planets," *Nature* 504 (2013): 268.

[38] Haigh, J. D., "The Effects of Solar Variability on the Earth's Climate," *Philosophical Transactions of the Royal Society A* 361 (2003): 95–111, doi:10.1098/rsta.2002.1111.

[39] Krivova, N. and Solanki, S., "Models of Solar Irradiance Variations: Current Status," *Journal of Astrophysics and Astronomy* 29 (2008): 151–58.

[40] [Precession of the rotation axis of our planet influences the timing of the seasons with respect to the timing of maximum insolation. The harmonics in the climate history data have been erroneously dismissed as nothing more than the result of the slow variations in orbital eccentricity, axial precession and axial tilt of the Earth, which combine to effect the timing and amount of seasonal insolation.

Increases in the tilt-angle of the planet's rotation axis away from perpendicular to Earth's orbital plane, increases the intensity of seasonality. The 'tilt' angle away from perpendicular of the orbit of Earth around the Sun, is always equal to the angle of 'obliquity': the angle between the equatorial plane of Earth and the ecliptic plane of the orbit of Earth around the Sun. For example, an increase in 'tilt' or 'obliquity' from 22.1 to 24.5 degrees, increases summer insolation by 24 watts per square metre and also the duration of summer by about 3 percent.]

[41] Marshall, S. J., "Solution Proposed for Ice-age Mystery," *Nature* 500 (2013): 159–60.

[42] Huybers, P., "Combined Obliquity and Precession Pacing of late Pleistocene Deglaciations," *Nature* 480 (2011): 229–32.

[43] Huybers, P., "Early Pleistocene Glacial Cycles and the Integrated Summer Insolation Forcing," *Science* 313 (2006): 508–11.

[44] Abe-Ouchi, A. et al., "Insolation-driven 100,000-Year Glacial Cycles and Hysteresis of Ice-sheet," *Nature* 500 (2013): 190–93.

[45] Petit, J. R. et al., "Climate and Atmospheric History of the Past 420,000 Years from the Vostok Ice Core, Antarctica," *Nature* 399 (1999): 429–36.

[46] Haxton, W., "What Makes the Sun Shine," *Nature* 512 (2014): 378–80.

[47] National Institutes of Natural Sciences, News, "Mystery of Coronal Heating Problem: Magnetically Driven Resonance Helps Heat Sun's Atmosphere," *ScienceDaily*, August 24, 2015, https://www.sciencedaily.com/releases/2015/08/150824064742.htm.

[48] Matthews, S. et al., "Magnetic Coupling in the Solar-system," *A&G News and Reviews in Astronomy & Geophysics* 50 (2009): 2.31–2.35, doi:10.1111/j.1468-4004.2009.50231.x, http://astrogeo.oxfordjournals.org/content/50/2/2.31.full.

[49] Steig, E. J., "Sources of Uncertainty in Ice-core Data," A Contribution to the "Workshop on Reducing and Representing Uncertainties in High-Resolution Proxy Data" at International Center for Theoretical Physics, Trieste, Italy, June 9–11, 2008, sponsored by University of Washington, Seattle.

[50] Billups, K., "Timing Is Everything during Deglaciations," *Nature* 522 (2015): 163–64.

[51] Meese, D. A., et al., "The Greenland Ice Sheet Project 2 Depth-age Scale: Methods and Results," *Journal of Geophysical Research* 102 (1997) C12: 26,411–423.

[52] Baillie, M. G. L., "Volcanoes, Ice-cores and Tree-rings: One Story or Two?," *Antiquity* 84 (2010): 202–15.

[53] Blaauw, M., "Out of Tune: The Dangers of Aligning Proxy Archives," *Quaternary Science Reviews* 36 (2012): 38–49.

[54] Ackert Jr., R. P., et al., "Patagonian Glacier Response during the Late Glacial-Holocene Transition," *Science* 321 (2008): 393.

[55] Fairbanks, R., et al., "Radiocarbon Calibration Curve Spanning 0 to 50,000 Years BP Based on Paired $^{230}Th/^{234}U/^{238}U$ and ^{14}C Dates on Pristine Corals," *Quaternary Science Reviews* 24 (2005): 1781–96.

[56] Reimer, P. J., et al., "INTCAL04 Terrestrial Radiocarbon Age Calibration, 26-0 ka BP," *Radiocarbon* 46 (2004):1029–58.

[57] Edwards, R. L., et al., "A Large Drop in Atmospheric $^{14}c/^{12}C$ and Reduced Melting in the Younger Dryas, Documented with ^{230}Th Ages of Corals," *Science* 260 (1993): 962–68.

[58] Goslar, T., et al., "High Concentration of Atmospheric ^{14}C during the Younger Dryas Cold Episode," *Nature* 377 (2002): 414–17, doi:10.1038/377414a0.

[59] Bard, E., et al., "Calibration of the ^{14}C Timescale Over the Past 30,000 Years Using Mass Spectrometric U–Th Ages from Barbados Corals," *Nature* 345 (1990): 405–10.

[60] Marchitto, T. M., et al., *Baja California 38KYr Radiocarbon Activity Reconstruction*, IGBP PAGES/World Data Center for Paleoclimatology, Data Contribution Series # 2009-139 (Boulder, CO and Asheville, NC: World Data Center for Paleoclimatology and NOAA Paleoclimatology Program), http://www1.ncdc.noaa.gov/pub/data/paleo/contributions_by_author/marchitto2007b/marchitto2007b.txt.

[61] Hughen, K., et al., "14C Activity and Global Carbon Cycle Changes Over the Past 50,000 Years," *Science* 303 (2004): 202–7.

[62] Hughen, K., et al., "Marine-derived [14]C Calibration and Activity Record for the Past 50,000 Years Updated from the Cariaco Basin," *Quaternary Science Reviews* 25 (2006): 3216–27.

[63] Grootes, P., et al., "Comparison of Oxygen Isotope Records from the GISP2 and GRIP Greenland Ice-cores," *Nature* 366 (1993): 552–54.

[64] Boulton, G., "Two Cores Are Better than One," *Nature* 366 (1993): 507–8.

[65] Raisbeck, G. M., et al., "Direct North-South Synchronization of Abrupt Climate Change Record in Ice-cores using Beryllium 10," *Climate of the Past* 3 (2007): 541–47.

[66] Kapsner, W., et al., "Dominant Influence of Atmospheric Circulation on Snow Accumulation in Greenland over the Past 18,000 Years," *Nature* 373 (1995): 52–54.

[67] Cuffrey, K. M., et al., "Large Arctic Temperature Change at the Wisconsin-Holocene Glacial Transition," *Science* 270 (1995): 455–57.

[68] Ahn, J., et al., "A Record of Atmospheric CO_2 Concentrations during the Last 40,000 Years from the Siple Dome, Antarctica Ice Core," *Journal of Geophysical Research* 109 (2004): D13305.

[69] Chen, T., "Synchronous Centennial Abrupt Events in the Ocean and Atmosphere during the Last Deglaciation," *Science* 349 (2015): 1537–41.

[70] Marcott, S. A., "Centennial-scale Changes in the Global Carbon Cycle during the Last Deglaciation," *Nature* 514 (2014): 616–19.

[71] Rahmstor, S., "Ocean Circulation and Climate during the Past 120,000 Years," *Nature* 419 (2002): 207–14, doi:10.1038/nature01090.

[72] North Greenland Ice-core Project Members, "High-resolution Record of Northern Hemisphere Climate Extending into the Last Interglacial Period," *Nature* 431 (2004): 147–51.

[73] Severinghaus, J. P., et al., "Timing of Abrupt Climate Change at the End of the Younger Dryas Interval from Thermally Fractionated Gases in Polar Ice," *Nature* 391 (1998): 141–46. (See Figure 2 on page 142).

[74] Kobashi, T., et al., "Argon and Nitrogen Isotopes of Trapped air in the GISP2 Ice-core during the Holocene Epoch (0–11,500 B.P.): Methodology and Implications for Gas Loss Processes," *Geochimica et Cosmochimica Acta* 72 (2008): 4675–86.

[75] Meyer, B. S., Bojazi, M. J., The, L.-S., and El Eid, M. F., et al., "Presolar Silicon Carbide X grains, Explosive Hydrogen Burning and the Evolution of Massive Stars," *74th Annual Meteoritical Society Meeting, Abstract* 5457 (2011), http://www.lpi.usra.edu/meetings/metsoc2011/pdf/5457.pdf.

[76] Johnson, T. C., et al., "A High Resolution Paleoclimate Record Spanning the Past 25000 Years in Southern East Africa," *Science* 296 (2002): 113–32.

[77] Thompson, L. G. et al., "Kilimanjaro Ice-core Records: Evidence of Holocene Climate Change in Tropical Africa," *Science* 298 (2002): 589–93.

[78] Peterson, L. C., et al., "Rapid Changes in the Hydrologic Cycle of the Tropical Atlantic during the Last Glacial," *Science* 290 (2000): 1947–51.

[79] Mayewski, P. A., et al., "Greenland Ice-core 'signal' Characteristics: An Expanded View of Climate Change," *Journal of Geophysical Research* 98 D7 (1993): 12839–847.

[80] Mayewski, P. A., et al., "Major Features and Forcing of High Latitude Northern Hemisphere Atmospheric Circulation over the Last 110,000 Years," *Journal of Geophysical Research* 102, no. C12 (1997): 26345–366.

[81] Winckler, G., and Fischer, H., "30,000 Years of Cosmic Dust in Antarctic Ice," *Science* 313 (2006): 491.

[82] Firestone, Richard, West, Allen, and Warwick-Smith, Simon, *The Cycle of Cosmic Catastrophes* (Rochester, VT: Bear & Company, 2006), ISBN-13: 978-1-59143, www.cosmiccatastrophes.com.

[83] Bond, G., et al., "Correlations between Climate Records from North Atlantic Sediments and Greenland Ice," *Nature* 365 (1993):143–47.

[84] Barker, S., et al., "Icebergs not the Trigger for North Atlantic Cold Events," *Nature* 520 (2015): 333–36.

[85] Dansgaard, W., et al., "Evidence for General Instability of Past Climate from a 250-kyr Ice-core Record," *Nature* 364 (1993): 218–20, doi:10.1038/364218a0.

[86] Barker, S., et al., "800,000 Years of Abrupt Climate Variability," *Science* 334 (2011): 347–51.

[87] Billups, K., "Timing Is Everything during Deglaciations," *Nature* 522 (2015): 163–64.

[88] Cooper, A., et al., "Abrupt Warming Events Drove Late Pleistocene Holarctic Megafaunal Turnover," *Science* 349 (2015): 602–6.

[89] Barker, P. A. et al., "A 14000 Year Oxygen Isotope Record from Diatom Silica in Two Alpine Lakes on Mt Kenya," *Science* 292 (2001): 2307–10.

[90] Gasse, F., "Hydrological Changes in Africa," *Science* 292 (2001): 2259–60.

[91] Thompson L. G., et al., "Kilimanjaro Ice-core Records: Evidence of Holocene Climate Change in Tropical Africa," 589–93.

[92] Legrand, M. R., and De Angelis, M., "Origins and Variation of Light Carboxylic Acids in Polar Precipitation," *Journal of Geophysical Research (Atmospheres)* 100 D1 (1995): 1445–62.

[93] Legrand, M. R., et al., "Large Perturbations of Ammonium and Organic Acids Content in the Summit Greenland Ice-core: Fingerprint from Forest Fires?," *Geophysical Research Letters* 19 (1992): 473–475.

[94] Bond, G., "Correlations between Climate Records from the North Atlantic Sediments and Greenland Ice," *Nature* 365 (1993):143–47.

[95] Sowers, T., et al., "Ice-core Records of Atmospheric N_2O Covering the last 106,000 Years," *Science* 301 (2003): 945–48.

[96] Firestone, Richard., West, Allen., and Warwick-Smith, Simon, *The Cycle of Cosmic Catastrophes*2006) ISBN-13:978-1-59143 www.cosmic-catastrophes.com

[97] Lowell, T. V., et al., "Interhemispheric Correlation of Late Pleistocene Glacial Events," *Science* 269 (1995): 1541–49.

[98] Kellogg, T. B., "Late Pleistocene interactions of East and West Antarctic Ice-flow Regimes: Evidence from the McMurdo Ice Shelf," *Journal of Glaciology* 42 (1996): 486–500.

[99] Rohling, E. J., et al., "Sea-level and Deep-Sea-Temperature Variability Over the Past 5.3 Million Years," *Nature* 508 (2014): 477–82.

[100] Mohtadi, M., "North Atlantic Forcing of Tropical Indian Ocean Climate," *Nature* 509 (2014): 76–80.

[101] Pahnke, K., et al., "340,000 Year Centennial-Scale Marine Record of Southern Hemisphere Climatic Oscillation," *Science* 301 (2003): 948–52.

[102] Clarke, G., et al., "Superlakes, Megafloods, and Abrupt Climate Change," *Science* 301 (2003): 922–23.

[103] Ellison, C. R., et al., "Surface and Deep Ocean Interactions during the Cold Climate Event 8200 Years Ago," *Science* 312 (2006): 1929–32.

[104] Ryan, W. B. F. et al. "An Abrupt Drowning of the Black Sea Shelf," *Marine Geology* 138 (1997): 119–26, doi:10.1016/S0025-3227(97)00007-8.

[105] Törnqvist, T. E., and Hijma, M. P., "Links between Early Holocene Ice-sheet Decay, Sea-Level Rise and Abrupt Climate Change," *Nature Geoscience* 5 (2012): 601–6, doi:10.1038/ngeo1536.

[106] Gavin, D. G., et al., "Abrupt Holocene Climate Change and Potential Response to Solar Forcing in Western Canada," *Quaternary Science Reviews* 30 (2011): 1243–55 (see fig 2, page 1246).

[107] Kerr, R. A., "Atlantic Mud Shows How Melting Ice Triggered an Ancient Chill," *Science* 312 (2006):1860.

[108] Pahnke, K., and Zahn, R., "Southern Hemisphere Water Mass Conversion Linked with North Atlantic Climate Variability," *Science* 307 (2005): 1741–46.

[109] Bintanja, R., et al., "Modelled Atmospheric Temperatures and Global Sea Levels Over the Past Million Years," *Nature* 437 (2005): 125–28, doi:10.1038/nature03975.

[110] Nakada, M., and Lambeck, K., "The Melting History of the Late Pleistocene Antarctic Ice Sheet," *Nature* 333 (1988): 36–40.

[111] Lambeck, K. and Chappell, J., "Sea Level Change Through the Last Glacial Cycle," *Science* 292 (2001): 679–86 (see p. 683).

[112] Duplessy, J. C., et al., "Changes in Surface Salinity of the North Atlantic Ocean during the Last Deglaciation," *Nature* 358 (1992): 485–88, doi:10.1038/358485a0.

[113] Nakada, M., and Lambeck, K., "The Melting History of the Late Pleistocene Antarctic Ice Sheet," *Nature* 333 (1988): 36–40.

[114] Grant, K. M., et al., "Rapid Coupling between Ice Volume and Polar Temperature over the Past 150,000 Years," *Nature* 491 (2012): 744–47.

[115] Fairbanks, R. G., "A 17,000-year Glacio-eustatic Sea Level Record: Influence of Glacial Melting Rates on the Younger Dryas Event and Deep-ocean Circulation," *Nature* 342 (1989): 637–42.

[116] Chappell, J., et al., "Reconciliation of late Quaternary Sea Levels Derived from Coral Terraces at Huon Peninsula with Deep Sea Oxygen Isotope Records," *Earth and Planetary Science Letters* 141 (1996): 227.

[117] Grant, K. M., et al., "Sea-Level Variability over Five Glacial Cycles," *Nature Communications* 5 (2014): 5076 (online article number).

[118] Weyer, E. M., "Pole Movement and Sea Levels," *Nature* 273 (1978): 18–21.

[119] Lambeck, K.,.et al., "Sea Level and Global Ice Volumes from the Last Glacial Maximum to the Holocene," *PNAS* 111 (2014): 15296–303.

[120] Milliman, J. D., and Emery, K. O., "Sea Levels during the Past 35,000 Years," *Science* 162 (1968): 1121–23.

[121] Yokoyama, Y., et al., "Timing of Last Glacial Maximum from Observed Sea Level Minima," *Nature* 406 (2000): 713–16, doi:10.1038/35021035.

[122] Clark, P. U., et al., "Rapid Rise of Sea Level 19,000 Years Ago and Its Global Implications," *Science* 304 (2004):1141–44.

[123] Lambeck, K., et al., "Into and Out of the Last Glacial Maximum: Sea-level Change during Oxygen Isotope Stages 3 and 2," *Quaternary Science Reviews* 21 (2002): 343–60.

[124] Bard, E., et al., 'Deglacial Sea-Level Record from Tahiti Corals and the Timing of Global Meltwater Discharge," *Nature* 382 (1996): 241–44.

[125] Stanford, J. D., et al., "Timing of Melt Water Pulse 1A and Climate Responses to Melt Water Injections," *Paleoceanography* 12 (2006): PA4103 1-9, doi:1029/2006PA001340.

[126] Blanchon, P., and Shaw, J., "Reef Drowning during the Last Deglaciation: Evidence for Catastrophic Sea-Level Rise and Ice-Sheet Collapse," *Geology* 23 (1995): 4–8, doi:10.1130/0091-7613(1995)023<0004:RDD TLD>2.3.CO;2.

[127] Hanebuth, T., et al., "Rapid Flooding of the Sunda Shelf: A Late-Glacial Sea-Level Record," *Science* 288 (2000): 1033–35.

[128] Smitha, D. E., et al., "The Early Holocene Sea Level Rise," *Quaternary Science Reviews* 30 (2011):1846–60.

[129] Lohne, O. S., et al., "Calendar Year Age Estimates of Allerod-Younger Dryas Sea-level Oscillations at Os, Western Norway," *Journal of Quaternary Science* 19 (2004): 443–64.

[130] Carlson, A. E., and Clark, P. U., "Ice Sheet Sources of Sea Level Rise and Freshwater Discharge during The Last Deglaciation," *Reviews of Geophysics* 50 (2012): RG4007 1-72 [8755-1209/12/2011RG000371].

[131] Cronin, T. M., et al., "Rapid Sea Level Rise and Ice Sheet Response to 8,200-Year Climate Event," *Geophysical Research Letters* 34 (2007): L20603 1–6, doi:10.1029/2007GL031318.

[132] Kendall, R. A., et al., "The Sea-Level Fingerprint of the 8.2 ka Climate Event," *Geology* 36 (2008): 423–26, doi:10.1130/G24550A.1.

[133] Zhimin, Z., et al., "Stepwise Paleoceanographic Changes during the Last Deglaciation in the Southern South China Sea: Records of Stable Isotope and Microfossils," *Science in China [Series D]* 41 (1998): 187–94.

[134] Stanley, D. J. and Warne, A. G., "Worldwide Initiation of Holocene Marine Deltas by Deceleration of Sea-level Rise," *Science* 265 (1994): 228–31.

[135] Fisk, H. N., and McFarlan, E. Jr., "Late Quaternary Deltaic Deposits of the Mississippi River," *'Crust of the Earth' Geological Society of America Special Papers* 62 (1955): 279–302.

[136] Holmes, D., "Rise of the Nile Delta," *Nature* 363 (1993): 402–3.

[137] Stanley, D. J. and Warne, A. G., "Sea Level and Initiation of Predynastic Culture in the Nile Delta," *Nature* 363 (1993): 435–38.

[138] Tornqvist, T. E., *Fluvial Sedimentary Geology and Chronology of the Holocene Rhine-Meuse Delta, The Netherlands*, Nederlandse geografische studies 166, Thesis (Ph. D.)--Universiteit Utrecht, 1993 (Utrecht, Netherlands: Koninklijk Nederlands Aardrijkskundig Genootschap, 1993), ISBN: 9068091794 (NGS), ISBN: 9062661068 (thesis), ISBN: 9789068091793 (NGS), ISBN: 9789062661060 (thesis).

[139] Stanley, D. J., and Chen, Z., "Yangtze Delta, Eastern China: 1. Geometry and Subsidence of Holocene Depocenter," *Marine Geology* 112 (1993): 1–11.

[140] Bickel, P. M., "Changing Sea Levels Along the California Coast: Anthropological Implications," *Journal of California Anthropology* 5 (1978): 7–20.

[141] Achyuthan, H., and Baker, V. R., "Coastal Response to Changes in Sea Level Since the Last 4500 BP on the East Coast of Tamil Nadu, India," *Radiocarbon* 44 (2002): 137–44.

[142] Bond, G., et al., "Evidence for Massive Discharges of Icebergs into the North Atlantic Ocean during the Last Glacial Period," *Nature* 360 (1992): 245–48.

[143] Adkins, J., et al., "Variability of the North Atlantic Thermohaline Circulation during the Last Interglacial Period," *Nature* 390 (1997): 154–56.

[144] Stott, L., et al., "Super ENSO and Global Climate Oscillations at Millennial Time Scales," *Science* 297 (2002): 222–26.

[145] Peterson, L. C., et al., "Rapid Changes in the Hydrologic Cycle of the Tropical Atlantic during the Last Glacial," *Science* 290 (2000): 1947–51.

[146] Cornwall, W., "Ghosts of Oceans Past," *Science* 350 (2015): 752–55.

[147] Hanebuth, T., et al., "Rapid Flooding of the Sunda Shelf: A late-Glacial Sea-Level Record," *Science* 288 (2000): 1033–35.

[148] Lee, J. S., *The Geology of China* (London: Thomas Murby & Co., 1939).

[149] Forrest, H. E., *The Atlantean Continent: Its Bearing on the Great Ice Age and the Distribution of Species*, 2nd ed. (London: Witherby, 1935), 190–92.

[150] Brewster, E. T., *This Puzzling Planet: The Earth's Unfinished Story* (Indianapolis, IN: The Bobbs-Merrill Company, 1928), 134–35.

[151] Umbgrove, J. H. F., *The Pulse of the Earth*, 2nd ed. (The Hague: Martinus NiJhoff, 1947), xxii, 35–38.

[152] Brooks, C. E. P., *Climate Through the Ages* (New York: Ernest Benn, 1949), 247–52.

[153] Termier, P., "Atlantis," *Bulletin de l'Institut océanographique (Monaco)* 256 (1913): 219.

[154] Termier, P., *Atlantis* (Washington, DC: Rep. Smithsonian Inst. 1916), 219–34.

[155] Forrest, H. E., *The Atlantean Continent: Its Bearing on the Great Ice Age and the Distribution of Species*, 2nd edn. (London, 1935) see p234.

[156] Scharff, R. F., *European Animals* (London: Archibald Constable & Co., Ltd., 1907), 126.

[157] Hopkins, D. M., et al., eds., *Paleoecology of Beringia* (New York: Academic Press, 1982).

[158] Luternauer, J. L., et al., "Late Pleistocene Terrestrial Deposits on the Continental Shelf of Western Canada: Evidence for Rapid sea-level Change at the End of the Last Glaciation," *Geology* 17 (1989): 357–60, doi:10.1130/0091-7613(1989)017<0357:LPTDOT>2.3.CO;2.

[159] Wallace, A. R., *The Geographical Distribution of Animals; with a Study of the Relationships of Living and Extinct Faunas as Elucidating the Past Changes of the Earth's Surface*, 2 vols. (London, 1876.); see vol. 1, pp. 328–29.

[160] Carson, U. R. L., *The Sea Around Us* (London: Staples Press Limited, 1951), 64.

[161] Blanford, H. F., "On the Age and Correlations of the Plant-bearing Series of India and the Former Existence of an Indo-Oceanic Continent," *Geological Society London* 31 (1875): 534–40.

[162] Sewell, R. B., "Geographic and Oceanographic Research in Indian Waters," *Memoirs of Royal Asiatic Society* 9 (1935): 1–7.

[163] Wadia, D. N., *Geology of India* (London: Macmillan, 1953), xx, 37.

[164] Fairbridge, R. W., "Global Climate Change during the 13,500 b.p. Gothenburg Geomagnetic Excursion," *Nature* 265 (1977): 430–31.

[165] Morner, N. A., "The Gothenburg Magnetic Excursion," *Quaternary Research* 7 (1977): 413–27.

[166] Snowball, P. and Sandgren, P., "Geomagnetic Field Intensity Changes in Sweden between 9000 and 450 Cal BP: Extending the Record of 'Archeomagnetic Jerks' by Means of Lake Sediments and the Pseudo-Thellier Technique," *Earth and Planetary Science Letters* 227 (2004): 361–75.

[167] Morner, N. A., "Annual and Inter Annual Magnetic Variations in Varved Clay," *Journal of Interdisciplinary Research* 9 (1978): 229–41.

[168] Merrill, Ronald, *Our Magnetic Earth: The Science of Geomagnetism* (Chicago, IL: The University of Chicago Press, 2010).

[169] Sagnotti, L., et al., "Extremely Rapid Directional Change during Matuyama-Brunhes Geomagnetic Polarity Reversal," *Geophysical Journal International* 199 (2014): 1110–24, doi:10.1093/gji/ggu287.

[170] Thiagarajan, N., et al., "Abrupt Pre-Bolling Allerod Warming and Circulation Changes in the Deep Ocean," *Nature* 511 (2014): 75–78.

[171] Marcott, S. A., "Centennial-scale Changes in the Global Carbon Cycle during the Last Deglaciation," *Nature* 514 (2014): 616–19.

[172] Maslin, M., et al., "Linking Continental Slope Failures and Climate Change," *Geology* 32 (2004): 53–56.

[173] Palacios, D., et al., "Evidence of Glacial Activity during the Oldest Dryas in the Mountains of Spain," *The Lyell Collection, The Geological Society of London* 433 (2016), Print ISSN 0305-8719, Online ISSN 2041-4927, doi:10.1144/SP433.10; http://sp.lyellcollection.org/content/early/2016/01/13/SP433.10.abstract.

[174] Shakun, J. D., and Carlson, A. E., "A Global Perspective on Last Glacial Maximum to Holocene Climate Change," *Quaternary Science Reviews* 29 (2010): 1801–16.

[175] Alley, R. B., "The Younger Dryas Cold Interval as Viewed from Central Greenland," *Quarternary Science Reviews* 19 (2000): 213–26.

[176] Allan, D. S., and Delair, J. B., *When the Earth Nearly Died; Compelling Evidence of a Catastrophic World Change 9500 BC* (Bath: Gateway Books, 1995).

[177] Smith, L., et al., "Siberian Peatlands: A Net Carbon Sink and Global Methane Source Since the Early Holocene," *Science* 303 (2004): 353–56.

[178] Severinghaus, J. P., and Brook E. J., "Abrupt Climate Change at the End of the Last Glacial Period Inferred from Trapped Air in Polar Ice," *Science* 286 (1999): 930–34.

[179] Taylor, K. C., "The Holocene-Younger Dryas Transition Recorded at Summit, Greenland," *Science* 278 (1997): 825–26.

[180] Gronvold, K. et al., "Ash Layers from Iceland in the Greenland GRIP Ice-Core Correlated with Oceanic and Land Sediments," *Earth and Planetary Science Letters* 135 (1995): 149–55.

[181] Haynes, G., ed., *American Megafaunal Extinctions at the End of the Pleistocene, Vertebrate Paleobiology and Paleoanthropology series* (New York: Springer Science, 2009), ISBN: 978-1-4020-8792-9.

[182] Cooper A., et al., "Abrupt Warming Events Drove Late Pleistocene Holarctic Megafaunal Turnover," *Science* 349 (2015): 602–6.

[183] Firestone, Richard., West, Allen., and Warwick-Smith, Simon, *The Cycle of Cosmic Catastrophes* (Rochester, Vermont, USA: Bear & Company 2006) ISBN-13:978-1-59143 www.cosmiccatastrophes.com.

[184] Firestone, R. B., et al., "Evidence for an extraterrestrial impact 12,900 years ago that contributed to the megafaunal extinctions and the Younger Dryas cooling," *Proceedings of the National Academy of Sciences of the United States of America* 104 (2007):16016–21.

[185] Kerr, R. A., "Experts Find No Evidence for a Mammoth-Killer Impact," *Science* 319 (2008): 1331–32.

[186] Kloosterman, J. B. H., "An Allerod Conflagration?" *Catastrophist Geology* 2 (1977): 13–15.

[187] Kloosterman, J. B. H., "The Usselo Horizon, a Worldwide Thin Layer Rich in Charcoal of Alleroed Age," *New solar-system Models, Symposium Bergamo* (1999): 52–53.

[188] Rasmussen, S. O., et al., "Synchronization of the NGRIP, GRIP, and GISP2 ice-cores across MIS 2 and palaeoclimatic implications," *Quaternary Science Reviews* 27 (2008): 18–28.

[189] Delmas, R. J., "A natural Artifact in Greenland Ice-core CO_2 Measurements," *Tellus* 45B (1993): 391–96.

[190] Johnson, T., et al., "A High-Resolution Paleoclimate Record Spanning the Past 25,000 Years in Southern East Africa," *Science* 296 (2002): 113–32.

[191] Thompson L., et al., "Kilimanjaro Ice-Core Records: Evidence of Holocene Climate Change in Tropical Africa," 589–93.

[192] Gabrielli, P., et al., "Meteoric Smoke Fallout over the Holocene Epoch Revealed by Iridium and Platinum in Greenland Ice," *Nature* 432 (2004): 1011–14.

[193] Golledge, N. R., et al., "First Cosmogenic [10]Be Age Constraint on the Timing of Younger Dryas Glaciation and Ice Cap Thickness, Western Scottish Highlands," *J Quaternary Science* 22 (2007): 785–91.

[194] Marcantonio, F., et al., "Abrupt Intensification of the SW Indian Ocean Monsoon during the Last Deglaciation: Constraints from Th, Pa, and He Isotopes," *Earth and Planetary Science Letters* 184 (2001): 505–14.

[195] Cuffey, K. M., et al., "Large Arctic Temperature Change at the Wisconsin-Holocene Glacial Transition," *Science* 270 (1995): 455–58, doi:10.1038/467160a.

[196] Buizert, C., et al., "Greenland Temperature Response to Climate Forcing during the Last Deglaciation," *Science* 345 (2014): 1177.

[197] White, W. C., and Mayewski, P., "Abrupt Accumulation Increase at the Younger Dryas Termination in the GISP2 Ice-Core," *Nature* 362 (1993): 527–29.

[198] Bondevik, S., et al., "Changes in North Atlantic Radiocarbon Reservoir Ages during the Allerød and Younger Dryas," *Science* 312 (2006): 1514–17.

[199] Peteet, D. M., "Global Younger Dryas?," *Quaternary International* 28 (1995): 93–104, doi:10.1016/1040-6182(95)00049-O.

[200] Mehl A. E., and Zárate M. A., "Late Glacial–Holocene Climatic Transition record at the Argentinian Andean Piedmont between 33 and 34°S," *Climate of the Past* 10 (2014): 863–76, doi:10.5194/cp-10-863-2014.

[201] Kirkbride, M. P., "Climate Change: A Glacial Test of Timing," *Nature* 467 (2010): 160–61.

[202] Rasmussen, S. O., et al., "A New Greenland Ice-core Chronology for the Last Glacial Termination," *Journal of Geophysical Research* 111 (2006): D06102, 1 of 16, doi:10.1029/2005JD006079.

[203] Fairbanks, R. G., "The Age and Origin of the Younger Dryas Climate 'event' in Greenland Ice-cores," *Paleoceanography* 6 (1990): 937–48.

[204] Ivy-Ochs, S., et al., 'Moraine Exposure Dates Imply Synchronous Younger Dryas Glacier Advances in the European Alps and in the Southern Alps of New Zealand," *Geografiska Annaler* 81 (1999): 313.

[205] Denton, G. H., and Hendy, C. H., "Younger Dryas Age Advance of Franz Josef Glacier in the Southern Alps of New Zealand," *Science* 264 (1994): 1434.

[206] Strelin, J. A., and Malagnino, E. C., "Late Glacial History of Lago Argentino, Argentina, and Age of the Puerto Bandera Moraines," *Quaternary Research* 54 (2000): 339–47.

[207] Ackert, et al., "Patagonian Glacier Response," *Science* 321 (2008): 392–95. DOI: 10.1126/science.1157215

[208] Alley, R. B. et al., "Abrupt Increase in Greenland Snow Accumulation at the End of the Younger Dryas Event," *Nature* 362 (1993): 527–29, doi:10.1038/362527a0.

[209] http://www.ncdc.noaa.gov/paleo/icecore/greenland/summit/document/.

[210] Severinghaus, J. P. et al., "Timing of Abrupt Climate Change at the End of the Younger Dryas Interval from Thermally Fractionated Gases in Polar Ice," *Nature* 391 (1998): 141–46.

[211] Alley, R. B. et al., "Holocene Climatic Instability: A Prominent, Widespread Event 8200 Yr. Ago," *Geology* 25 (1997): 483–86.

[212] Stager, J. C., and Mayewski, P. A., "Abrupt Early to Mid-Holocene Climatic Transition Registered at the Equator and the Poles," *Science* 276 (1997): 1834–36.

[213] Ryan, W. B. F., Pitman III, W. C., et al., "An Abrupt Drowning of the Black Sea Shelf," *Marine Geology* 138 (1997): 119–26.

[214] Johnson, A., "A Wave in the Earth," *Science* 274 (1996): 735.

[215] Arvidsson, R., "Fennoscandian Earthquakes: Whole Crustal Rupturing Related to Postglacial Rebound," *Science* 274 (1996): 744–46.

[216] Nisbet, E. G., and Piper, D. J. W., "Giant Submarine Landslides," *Nature* 392 (1998): 329.

[217] Dawson, S., et al., "Environmental Catastrophes and Recoveries in the Holocene," *Conference Report*, Dept. Geography & Earth Sciences, Brunel University, UK, 2002.

[218] Fujii, Y., and Watanabe, O., "Microparticle Concentration and Electrical Conductivity of a 700m Ice-Core from Mizuho Station Antarctic," *Annals of Glaciology* 10 (1988): 38–42.

[219] Reimer, P. J., Baillie, M. G. L., et al., "IntCal04 Terrestrial Radiocarbon Age Calibration, 0-26 Cal Kyr BP," *Radiocarbon* 46 (2004): 1029–58.

[220] Kleiven, F., et al., "Multi-Proxy Evidence for Reduced North Atlantic Deep Water Flux Across the 8.2 kyr B.P. Event from Core MD03-2665 at the Eirik Drift," *American Geophysical Union Fall Meeting Abstracts* 12/2005.

[221] Daley, T., et al., "Terrestrial Climate Signal of the '8200 yr B.P. Cold Event' in the Labrador Sea Region," *Geology* 37 (2009): 831–34, doi:10.1130/G30043A.1.

[222] Barber, D., et al., "Forcing of the Cold Event of 8200 Years Ago by Catastrophic Drainage of Laurentide Lakes," *Nature* 400 (1999): 344–48.

[223] Meese, D., et al., "The Accumulation Record from the GISP2 Core as an Indicator of Climate Change throughout the Holocene," *Science* 266 (1994):1680–82.

224 Kleiven, F., et al., "Reduced North Atlantic Deep Water Coeval with the Glacial Lake Agassiz Freshwater Outburst," *Science* 319 (2008): 60–64.

225 Alley, R. B., and Agustsdottir A. M., "The 8k Event: Cause and Consequences of a Major Holocene Abrupt Climate Change," *Quarterly Science Reviews* 24 (2005): 1123–49.

226 Sepp, H., et al., "Spatial Structure of the 8200 Cal Yr BP Event in Northern Europe," *Climate of the Past Discussions* 3 (2007): 165–95.

227 Long, D., et al., "A Holocene Tsunami Deposit in Eastern Scotland," *Journal of Quaternary Science* 4 (1989): 61–66.

228 Briggs, H., "Giant Wave Hit Ancient Scotland," *BBC News*, September 7, 2001, news.bbc.co.uk/2/hi/in_depth/sci_tech/2001/glasgow_2001/1531049.stm.

229 Leroy, S., and Stewart, I. S., eds., "The Storegga Slide and Tsunami in the North Atlantic Region," *Abstracts Volume, 2002. Conference: Environmental Catastrophes and Recoveries in the Holocene;* August 29–September 2, 2002, Department of Geography & Earth Sciences, Brunel University, Uxbridge, UK.

230 Derbyshire, D., and Highfield, R., "Tsunami Turned Britain into an Island Overnight," Telegraph.co.uk, September 13, 2001, http://www.telegraph.co.uk/news/worldnews/europe/norway/1339878/Tsunami-turned-Britain-into-an-island-overnight.html.

231 Dury, G. H., *The British Isles—A Systematic and Regional Geography*, 2nd ed. (London: Heinemann, 1963).

232 Kerr, R., "Did a Mega Flood Slice Off Britain," *Science* 317 (2007): 307.

[233] Devoy, R., "Flandrian Sea Level Changes in the Thames Estuary and the Implications for Land Subsidence in England and Wales," *Nature* 270 (1977): 712–15.

[234] Hvan-Andel, T., "Late Quaternary Sea-Level Changes and Archaeology," *Antiquity* 63 (1989): 733–45.

[235] Ryan, W., and Pitman, W., *Noah's Flood: The New Scientific Discoveries about the Event that Changed History* (New York: Simon & Schuster, 1998).

[236] Nissen, H. J., *The Early History of the Ancient Near East: 9000–2000 B.C.*, translated from German by Elizabeth Lutzeier (Chicago IL: University of Chicago Press, 1988).

[237] Lambek, K., and Chappell, J., "Sea Level Change Through the Last Glacial Cycle," *Science* 292 (2001): 679–86.

[238] Broecker, W., "Massive Iceberg Discharges as Triggers for Global Climate Change," *Nature* 372 (1994): 421–24.

[239] Sletto, B., "Nebraska Sand Hills," *Earth* (1997): 43–49.

[240] Zdanowicz, C. M., et al., "Mount Mazama Eruption; Calendrical Age Verified and Atmospheric Impact Assessed," *Geology* 27 (1999): 621–24.

[241] Geyh, M. A., et al., "Sea Level Changes during Holocene in the Strait of Malacca," *Nature* 278 (1979): 441.

[242] Bard, E., "Deglacial Sea Level Record from Tahiti Corals and the Timing of Global Melt Water Discharge," *Nature* 382 (1996): 241–44.

[243] Blanchon, P., "Reef Drowning during the Last Deglaciation: Evidence for Catastrophic Sea Level Rise and Ice Sheet Collapse," *Geology* 23 (1995): 4–8.

[244] Wagner, F., et al., "Rapid Atmospheric CO_2 Changes Associated with the 8,200-years-B.P. Cooling Event," *PNAS* 99 (2002): 12011–14.

[245] Clarke, G., et al., "Superlakes Megafloods and Abrupt Climate Change," *Science* 301 (2003): 922.

[246] Barber, D. C., et al., "Forcing of the Cold Event of 8,200 Years Ago by Catastrophic Drainage of Laurentide Lakes," *Nature* 400 (1999): 344–48, doi:10.1038/22504.

[247] Meese, D. A., et al., "The Accumulation Record from the GISP2 Core as an Indicator of Climate Change Throughout the Holocene." *Science* 266 (1994): 1680–82, doi:10.1126/science.266.5191.1680.

[248] Siani, G., et al., "Mediterranean Sea Surface Radiocarbon Reservoir Age Changes since the Last Glacial Maximum," *Science* 294 (2001): 1917–20.

[249] Stager, J. C. and Mayewski, P. A., "Abrupt Early to Mid-Holocene Climatic Transition Registered at the Equator and the Poles," *Science* 276 (1997): 1834–36, doi:10.1126/science.276.5320.1834.

[250] Alley, R. B., et al., "Holocene Climatic Instability: A Prominent, Widespread Event 8200 Yr Ago." *Geology* 25 (1997): 483–86.

[251] Steig, E., "Mid-Holocene Climate Change," *Science* 286 (1999): 1485–87.

[252] Baker, L., "Abrupt Onset and Termination of the African Humid Period: Rapid Climate Responses to Gradual Insolation Forcing," *Quarterly Science Reviews* 19 (2000): 347–61.

[253] Lachniet, M. S., "Tropical Response to the 8200 yr B.P. Cold Event? Speleothem Isotopes Indicate a Weakened Early Holocene Monsoon in Costa Rica," *Geology* 32 (2004): 957–60.

254 deMenocal, P. B., "Cultural Responses to Climate Change during the Late Holocene," *Science* 292 (2001): 667–73.

255 LaMoreaux, P. E., "Worldwide Environmental Impacts from the Eruption of Thera," *Environmental Geology* 26 (1995): 172–81.

256 Friedrich W. L., et al., "Santorini Eruption Radiocarbon Dated to 1627–1600 B.C.," *Science* 312, (2006): 548.

257 Manning, E. T., "Chronology for the Aegean Late Bronze Age 1700–1400 B.C.," *Science* 312 (2006): 565–69.

258 Grudd, H., et al., "Swedish Tree Rings Provide New Evidence in Support of a Major Widespread Environmental Disruption in 1,628 BC," *Geophysical Research Letters* 27 (2000): 2957–60.

259 Pearce, N. J. G. et al., "Identification of Aniakchak (Alaska) Tephra in Greenland Ice-Core Challenges the 1645 BC Date for Minoan Eruption of Santorini," *Geochemistry Geophysics Geosystems* 5 (2004): Q03005.

260 Hammer, C. U., et al., "The Minoan Eruption of Santorini in Greece Dated to 1645 BC?," *Nature* 328 (1987): 517.

261 Fujii, Y., and Watanabe, O., "Microparticle Concentration and Electrical Conductivity of a 700 m Ice-core from Mizuho Station, Antarctica," *Annals of Glaciology* 10 (1988): 38–42.

262 Bruins, H. J., and Van der Plicht, J., "The Minoan Santorini Eruption and Tsunami Deposits in Crete (Palaikastro): Geological, Archaeological, 14C Dating and Egyptian Chronology," *Radiocarbon* 51 (2009): 397–411.

263 Baillie, M., and Munro, M., "Irish tree rings, Santorini and Volcanic Dust Veils," *Nature* 332 (1988): 344–46, doi:10.1038/332344a0.

[264] Baillie, M. G. L., "Irish Tree Rings and an Event in 1,628 BC," *Thera and the Aegean World III*, vol. 3, edited by Hardy, D. A. (London: The Thera Foundation, 1990), 160–66, http://www.therafoundation.org/articles/chronololy/irishtreeringandaneventin1.628bc.

[265] Lamarche, V. C., and Hirschboeck, K. K., "Frost Rings in Trees as Records of Major Volcanic Eruptions," *Nature* 307 (1984): 121–26, doi:10.1038/307121a0.

[266] Hughes, M. K., "Ice Layer Dating of the Eruption of Santorini," *Nature* 335 (1988): 211–12.

[267] Baillie, M. G. L., "Volcanoes, Ice-cores and Tree-rings: One Story or Two?," *Antiquity* 84 (2010): 202–15.

[268] Grudd, H., et al., "Swedish Tree Rings Provide New Evidence in Support of a Major Widespread Environmental Disruption in 1,628 BC," *Geophysical Research Letters* 27 (2000): 2957–60.

[269] Manning, S. W., et al., "Anatolian Tree Rings and a New Chronology for the East Mediterranean Bronze-Iron Ages," *Science* 294 (2001): 2532–35.

[270] Pang, K. D., "Extraordinary Floods in Early Chinese History and Their Absolute Dates," *Journal of Hydrology* 96 (1987): 139–55.

[271] Thompson, L. G., et al., "A 25000 Year Tropical Climate History from Bolivian Ice-Cores," *Science* 282 (1998): 1858–64.

[272] Thompson, L. G., et al., "Kilimanjaro Ice-core Records: Evidence of Holocene Climate Change in Tropical Africa," 589–93.

[273] Stager, J. C., and Mayewski, P. A., "Abrupt Early to Mid-Holocene Climatic Transition Registered at the Equator and the Poles," *Science* 276 (1997): 1834–36.

[274] Cullen, H. M., et al., "Climate Change and the Collapse of the Akkadian Empire: Evidence from the Deep Sea," *Geology* 28 (2000): 379–82.

[275] deMenocal, P. B., "Cultural Responses to Climate Change during the Late Holocene," *Science* 292 (2001): 667–73.

[276] Delibrias, G., and Guillier, M., "The Sea Level on the Atlantic Coast and the Channel for the Last 10,000 Years by 14C Method," *Quaternaria* 14 (1971): 131–35.

[277] Devoy, R. J. N., "Flandrian Sea Level Changes and Vegetational History of the Lower Thames Estuary," *Philosophical Transactions of the Royal Society B* 285 (1979): 712.

[278] Sidell, J., et al. *The Holocene Evolution of the London Thames*, Museum of London Archaeology Service MoLAS Monograph 5 (London: MOLA (Museum of London Archaeology), 2000).

[279] Lamb, H. H., *Climate History and the Modern World* (London: Routledge, 1982).

[280] Enkin, R., et al., "A New High-Resolution Radiocarbon Bayesian Age Model of the Holocene and Late Pleistocene from Core MD02-2494 and Others, Effingham Inlet, British Columbia, Canada; with an Application to the Paleoseismic Event Chronology of the Cascadia Subduction Zone," *Canadian Journal of Earth Sciences* 50 (2013): 746–60, dx.doi.org/10.1139/cjes-2012-0150.

[281] Geyh, M. A., et al., "Sea-level Changes during the Late Pleistocene and Holocene in the Strait of Malacca," *Nature* 278 (1979): 441.

[282] Shennan, I., et al., eds., *Handbook of Sea-Level Research*, American Geophysical Union (New York: Wiley, 2015), ISBN: 978-1-118-45258-5.

283 Bryant, E. A., et al., "Cosmogenic Megatsunami in the Australia Region: Are They Supported by Aboriginal and Mairo Legends?," in *Myth and Geology*, eds. Piccardi, L., and Masse, W. B. (London: Geological Society, Special Publications, 273 (2007)), 203–14.

284 Staubwasser, M., and Weiss, H., "Holocene Climate and Cultural Evolution in Late Prehistoric–Early Historic West Asia," *Quaternary Research* 66 (2006): 372–87.

285 Manning, S. W., et al., "Anatolian Tree Rings and a New Chronology for the East Mediterranean Bronze-Iron Ages," *Science* 294 (2001): 2532–35, doi:10.1126/science.1066112.

286 An, C. B., et al., "Climate Change and Cultural Response Around 4000 cal yr B.P. in the Western Part of Chinese Loess Plateau," *Quaternary Research* 63 (1995): 347–52.

287 Holms, Rupert, *Cataclysms & Renewals* (London: Rupert Holms & Co, 2015), printed and distributed by www.createspace.com, title/5104182.

288 Ruddiman, W. F., et al., "Late Holocene climate: Natural or anthropogenic?," *Reviews in Geophysics* 54 (2016): 93–118, doi:10.1002/2015RG000503.

289 Marcott, S. A., et al., "A Reconstruction of Regional and Global Temperature for the Past 11300 Years," *Science* 339 (2013): 1198–201; Renssen, H., et al., "The Spatial and Temporal Complexity of the Holocene Thermal Maximum," *Nature Geoscience* 2 (2009): 411–14.

290 Odada, E., and Olago, D., "Holocene Climatic, Hydrological and Environmental Oscillations in the Tropics with Special Reference to Africa, Odada and Olago," in *Climate Change and Africa* (Cambridge: Cambridge University Press, 2005), 3–22; Gasse, F., "Hydrological

Changes in the African Tropics since the Last Glacial Maximum," *Quaternary Science Reviews* 19 (2000): 189–211.

[291] Servant, M., et al., 'Tropical Forest Changes during the Late Quaternary in African and South American Lowlands," *Global and Planetary Change* 7 (1993): 25–40.

[292] Haberle, S., "Upper Quaternary Vegetation and Climate History of the Amazon Basin: Correlating Marine and Terrestrial Pollen Records,'" *Proceedings of the Ocean Drilling Program, Scientific Results* 155 (1997): 381–96.

[293] Marret, F., "Abrupt Changes and Permanence of Rain-forests from Atlantic Central Africa during the Holocene," *Conference Proceedings: Environmental Catastrophes and Recoveries in the Holocene* (Uxbridge: Brunel University, September 2002).

[294] Kuper, R., and Kropelin, S., "Climate Controlled Holocene Occupation in the Sahara: Motor of Africa's Evolution," *Science* 313 (2006): 803–7.

[295] Holmes, D. L., "Rise of the Nile Delta," *Nature* 363 (1993): 402–3.

[296] Stanley, D. J., and Warne, A. G., "Sea Level and Initiation of Predynastic Culture in the Nile Delta," *Nature* 363 (1993): 435–38.

[297] The refuted model of ice-covered Europe is described in: H. E. Wright, "Late Pleistocene Climate of Europe: A Review," *Geological Society of America Bulletin* 72 (1961): 933, doi:10.1130/0016-7606(1961)72[933:LPC OEA]2.0.CO;2.

[298] Allen, J., et al., "Rapid Environmental Changes in Southern Europe during the Last Glacial Period," *Nature* 400 (1999): 740–43.

[299] Tzedakis, P. C., et al., "Buffered Tree Population Changes in a Quaternary Refugium: Evolutionary Implications," *Science* 297 (2002): 2044–47.

[300] Varela, S., et al., "Were the Late Pleistocene Climatic Changes Responsible for the Disappearance of the European Spotted Hyena Populations? Hindcasting a Species Geographic Distribution Across Time," *Quaternary Science Reviews* 29 (2010): 2027–35.

[301] Renssen, H., et al., "Thermal Gradients in Europe during the Last Glacial-interglacial Transition," *Netherlands Journal of Geosciences* 81 (2002): 113–22.

[302] Reille, M., and Andrieu, V., "The Late Pleistocene and Holocene in the Lourdes Basin, Western Pyrénées, France: New Pollen Analytical and Chronological Data," *Vegetation History and Archaeobotany* 4 (1995): 1–21.

[303] Whittington, G., et al., "Lateglacial and Early Holocene Climates of the Atlantic Margins of Europe: Stable Isotope, Mollusc and Pollen Records from Orkney, Scotland," *Quaternary Science Reviews* 122 (2015): 112–30.

[304] Schreudera, L. T., et al., "Late Pleistocene Climate Evolution in Southeastern Europe Recorded by Soil Bacterial Membrane Lipids in Serbian Loess," *Palaeogeography, Palaeoclimatology, Palaeoecology* 449 (2016):141–48.

[305] Jahns, S., "On the Late Pleistocene and Holocene History of Vegetation and Human Impact in the Ucker Valley, North-Eastern Germany," *Veget Hist Archaeobot* 10 (2001): 97–104.

[306] Kaiser, K., et al., "Late Quaternary Evolution of Rivers, Lakes and Peatlands in Northeast Germany Reflecting Past Climatic and

Human Impact-an Overview," *E&G Quaternary Science Journal* 61 (2012): 103–32, doi:10.3285/eg.61.2.01.

[307] Jorgensen, P., et al., "Glacial Survival of Boreal Trees in Northern Scandinavia," *Science* 335 (2012): 1083–86.

[308] Nesje, A., et al., "Were Abrupt Lateglacial and Early-Holocene Climatic Changes in Northwest Europe Linked to Freshwater Outbursts to the North Atlantic and Arctic Oceans?," *The Holocene* 14 (2004): 299–310.

[309] Davisa, B., et al., "The Temperature of Europe during the Holocene Reconstructed from Pollen Data," *Quaternary Science Reviews* 22 (2003): 1701–16.

[310] Väliranta, M., et al., "Plant Macrofossil Evidence for an Early Onset of the Holocene Summer Thermal Maximum in Northernmost Europe," *Nature Communications* 6 (2015): Article number: 6809, doi:10.1038/ncomms7809.

[311] Brewer, S., et al., "Mid-Holocene Climate Change in Europe: A Data-model Comparison," *Climate of the Past* 3 (2007): 499–512, www.clim-past.net/3/499/2007/; Wanner, H., et al., "Mid- to Late Holocene Climate Change: An Overview," *Quaternary Science Reviews* 27 (2008): 1791–828.

[312] Tzedakis P. C., et al., "Buffered Tree Population Changes in a Quaternary Refugium: Evolutionary Implications," *Science* 297 (2002): 2044–47.

[313] Geirsdóttira, Á. et al., "Holocene and Latest Pleistocene Climate and Glacier Fluctuations in Iceland," *Quaternary Science Reviews* 28 (2009): 2107–18.

[314] Black, J. L., "Holocene Climate Change in South-Central Iceland: A Multi-proxy Lacustrine Record from Glacial Lake Hvitarvatn" (Ph.D. diss. 3315776, Dept Geology, University of Colorado at Boulder, 2008), gradworks.umi.com/33/15/3315776.html.

[315] Hantemirov, R. M., and Shiyatov, S. G., "A Continuous Multi-Millennial Ring-Width Chronology in Yamal, North-Western Siberia," *The Holocene* 12 (2002): 717–26.

[316] MacDonald, G. M., et al., "Climate Change and the Northern Russian Treeline Zone," *Philosophical Transactions of the Royal Society B* 363 (2008): 2285–99, doi:10.1098/rstb.2007.2200.

[317] Guthrie, R. D., *Frozen Fauna of the Mammoth Steppe* (Chicago, IL: University of Chicago Press, 1990).

[318] Kienast, F., et al., "Palaeobotanical Evidence for Warm Summers in the East Siberian Arctic during the Last Cold Stage," *Quaternary Research* 63 (2005): 283–300.

[319] Groisman, P., and Gutman, G., eds., *Regional Environmental Changes in Siberia and Their Global Consequences* (New York: Springer, 2013).

[320] Kienast, F., et al., "Palaeobotanical Evidence for Warm Summers in the East Siberian Arctic during the Last Cold Stage," *Quaternary Research,* 63 (2005): 283–300.

[321] Badyukova, E. N., "Age of Khvalynian Transgressions in the Caspian Sea Region," *Marine Geology; Oceanology* 47 (2007): 400–405.

[322] Badyukova, E. N., "Evolution of the Northern Caspian Sea Region and the Volga Delta in the Late Pleistocene-Holocene," *Marine Geology; Oceanology* 50 (2010): 953–60.

[323] Macklina, M., et al., "The influence of Late Pleistocene Geomorphological Inheritance and Holocene Hydromorphic Regimes on Floodwater Farming in the Talgar Catchment, Southeast Kazakhstan, Central Asia," *Quaternary Science Reviews* 129 (2015): 85–95.

[324] Arslanova, Kh. A., "On the Age of the Khvalynian Deposits of the Caspian Sea Coasts According To ^{14}C and ^{230}Th/^{234}U Methods," *Quaternary International* 409 (2016): 81–87.

[325] Deplazes, G., et al., "Links between Tropical Rainfall and North Atlantic Climate during the Last Glacial Period," *Nature Geoscience* 6 (2013): 213–17.

[326] Wang, Y., et al., "Millenial and Orbital Scale Changes in the East Asian Monsoon Over the Past 224000 Years," *Nature* 451 (2008): 1090–93.

[327] Konecky, B., "Monsoon Matters," *Nature* 517 (2015): 445–46.

[328] Lu, H. Y., et al., "Chinese Deserts and Sand Fields in Last Glacial Maximum and Holocene Optimum," *Chinese Science Bullitin; Geology* 58 (2013): 2775–83, doi:10.1007/s11434-013-5919-7.

[329] Zhuo, Z., et al., "Paleoenvironments in China during the Last Glacial Maximum and the Holocene Optimum," *Episodes* 21 (1998): 152–58.

[330] Wang, Y., et al., "A High Resolution Absolute Dated Late Pleistocene Monsoon Record from Hulu Cave China," *Science* 294 (2001): 2345–48.

[331] Whitmore, T. C., "Fleeting Impressions of Some Chinese Rain Forests," *Commonwealth Forestry Review* 61 (1982): 51–58.

[332] Hua, Z., "The Floras of Southern and Tropical Southeastern Yunnan Have Been Shaped by Divergent Geological Histories," *Plos One* 8 (2013): e64213 1–8, http://dx.doi.org/10.1371/journal.pone.0064213.

[333] Hua, Z., "Advances in Biogeography of the Tropical Rainforest in Southern Yunnan, Southwestern China," *Tropical Conservation Science* 1 (2008) : 34–42, https://news.mongabay.com/2008/03/chinas-tropical-rainforests-decline-67-in-30-years/.

[334] Zhu, H., and Roos, M. C., "The Tropical Flora of S China and Its Affinity to IndoMalesian Flora," *Telopea* 10 (2004): 639–48.

[335] Partin, J. W. et al., "Millennial-scale Trends in West Pacific Warm Pool Hydrology since the Last Glacial Maximum," *Nature* 449 (2007): 452–55.

[336] Wang, Y., et al., "The Holocene Asian Monsoon: Links to Solar Changes and North Atlantic Climate," *Science* 308 (2005): 854–57.

[337] Zhongyuan, C.,"Holocene Climate Fluctuations in the Yangtze Delta of Eastern China and the Neolithic Response," *The Holocene* 15 (2005): 915–24.

[338] Carolin, S. A., et al., "Varied Response to Western Pacific Hydrology to Climate Forcings over the Last Glacial Period," *Science* 340 (2013): 1564–66.

[339] Yafeng, S., et al., "Mid-holocene Climates and Environments in China," *Global and Planetary Change* 7 (1993): 219–33, doi:10.1191/0959683605hl862rr.

[340] Brian Fagan, *The Great Warming: Climate Change and the Rise and Fall of Civilizations* (New York: Bloomsbury, 2008).

[341] Shi-Yong, Y., et al., "Quantitative Reconstruction of Mid- to Late-Holocene Climate in NE China from Peat Cellulose Stable Oxygen and Carbon Isotope Records and Mechanistic Models," *The Holocene* 23 (2013): 1507–16.

[342] Zhao, M., et al., "Major Mid-late Holocene Cooling in the East China Sea Revealed by an Alkenone Sea Surface Temperature Record," *Journal of Ocean University of China* 13 (2014): 935–40.

[343] Madsen, D., Chen, F., and Gao, X., eds., "Late Quaternary Climate Change and Human Adaptation in Arid China," *Developments in Quaternary Science* 9 (2007): 1–237, ISBN: 978-0-444-52962-6.

[344] Zhang, H., et al., "Late Holocene Climate Change and Anthropogenic Activities in North Xinjiang: Evidence from a Peatland Archive, the Caotanhu Wetland," *The Holocene* 25 (2015): 323–32.

[345] Kotlia, B., et al., "Stalagmite Inferred High Resolution Climatic Changes through Pleistocene-Holocene Transition in Northwest Indian Himalaya," *Journal of Earth Science and Climatic Change* 7 (2016): 338, doi:10.4172/2157-7617.1000338.

[346] Premathilake, R.,"Late Quaternary Climate History of the Horton Plains, Central Sri Lanka, Premathilake and Risberg," 22 (2003): 1525–41.

[347] Chauhan, O., "Past 20,000-year History of Himalayan Aridity: Evidence from Oxygen Isotope Records in the Bay of Bengal," *Current Science* 84 (2003): 90–93.

[348] Juyal, N., and Sundriyal, S., "Late Quaternary Climate Studies in Himalaya," *Glimpses of Geosciences Research in India: The Indian Report to IUGS* 2004–2008, *Indian National Academy of Sciences* (2008): 51–55.

[349] Merlis, T., et al., "The Tropical Precipitation Response to Orbital Precession," *Journal of Climate* 26 (2013): 2010–21.

[350] Schneider, T., et al., "Migrations and Dynamics of the Intertropical Convergence Zone," *Nature* 513 (2014): 45–53.

[351] http://whc.unesco.org/en/list/1342.

[352] Lawler, A., "In Search of Green Arabia," *Science* 345 (2014): 994–97.

[353] Deplazes, G., et al., "Links between Tropical Rainfall and North Atlantic Climate during the Last Glacial Period," *Nature Geoscience* 6 (2013): 213–17, doi:10.1038/ngeo1712.

[354] Parker, A., et al., "Holocene Vegetation Dynamics in the Northeastern Rub' al-Khali Desert, Arabian Peninsula: A Phytolith, Pollen and Carbon Isotope Study, *Journal of Quaternary Science* 19 (2004): 665–76; Fleitmann, D. et al., "Holocene forcing of in the Indian Monsoon Recorded in a Stalagmite from Southern Oman," *Science* 300 (2003): 1737–39.

[355] Preusser, F., "Chronology of the Impact of Quaternary Climate Change on Continental Environments in the Arabian Peninsula," *Geoscience* 341 (2009): 621–32.

[356] Fleitmann, D., et al., "Holocene ITCZ and Indian Monsoon Dynamics Recorded in Stalagmites from Oman and Yemen (Socotra)," *Quaternary Science Reviews* 26 (2007): 170–88.

[357] deMenocal, P., et al., "Influences of High-and Low- latitude Processes on African Terrestrial Climate: Pleistocene Eolian Records from Equatorial Atlantic Ocean Drilling Program Site 663," *Paleoceanography* 8 (1993): 209–42.

[358] Tierney, J., and deMenocal, P. B., "Abrupt Shifts in Horn of Africa Hydroclimate Since the Last Glacial Maximum," *Science* 342 (2013) 843–46.

[359] Battarbee, R., Gasse, F., and Stickley, C., eds., *Past Climate Variability through Europe and Africa* in Developments in Paleoenvironmental Research' series (New York: Springer, 2004), ISBN: 978-1-4020-2121-3.

[360] Foley, J., et al., "Regime Shifts in the Sahara and Sahel: Interactions between Ecological and Climatic Systems in North Africa," *Ecosystems* 6 (2003): 524–39.

[361] Umer, M., et al., "Late Pleistocene and Holocene Vegetation History of the Bale Mountains, Ethiopia," *Quaternary Science Reviews* 26 (2007): 2229–46.

[362] Street, F., and Grove, A., "Environmental and Climatic Implications of late Quaternary Lake-level Fluctuations in Africa," *Nature* 261 (1976): 385–90.

[363] Kutzbach, J. E. et al., "Vegetation and Soil Feedbacks on the Response of the African Monsoon to Orbital Forcing in the Early to Mid-Holocene," *Nature* 384 (1996): 623–26.

[364] Claussen, M., and Gayler, V., "The Greening of the Sahara during the Mid-Holocene: Results of an Interactive Atmosphere-Biome Model," *Global Ecology and Biogeography Letters* 6 (1997): 369–77, doi:10.2307/2997337.

[365] deMenocal, P., et al., "Abrupt Onset and Termination of the African Humid Period: Rapid Climate Responses to Gradual Insolation Forcing," *Quaternary Science Reviews* 19 (2000): 347–61.

[366] Hoelzmann, P., et al., "Mid-Holocene Land-surface Conditions in Northern Africa and the Arabian Peninsula: A Data set for the Analysis of Biogeophysical Feedbacks in the Climate System," *Global Biogeochem Cycles* 12 (1998): 35–51.

[367] Kropelin, S., et al., "Climate-Driven Ecosystem Succession in the Sahara: The Past 6000 Years," *Science* 320 (2008): 765–68.

[368] Gasse, F., "Hydrological Changes in the African Tropics Since the Last Glacial Maximum," *Quaternary Science Reviews* 19 (2000): 189–211.

[369] Schuster, M., et al., "Holocene Lake Mega-Chad Palaeoshorelines from Space," *Quaternary Science Reviews* 24 (2005): 1821–27.

[370] Weldeab, S., et al., "155,000 Years if West African Monsoon and Ocean Thermal Evolution," *Science* 316 (2007): 1303–7.

[371] Alley, R., et al., "Abrupt Climate Change," *Science* 299 (2003): 2005–10, doi:10.1126/science.1081056.

[372] Rial, J., et al., "Nonlinearities, Feedbacks and Critical Thresholds within the Earth's Climatic System," *Climatic Change* 65 (2004): 11–38.

[373] deMenocal, P., et al., "Abrupt onset and termination of the African Humid Period: Rapid climate response to gradual insolation forcing," *Quat. Sci. Rev* 19 (2000) 347-361.

[374] McGee, D., et al., "The Magnitude, Timing and Abruptness of Changes in North African Dust Deposition over the Last 20,000 Yr," *Earth and Planetary Science Letters* 371/372 (2013): 163–76.

[375] Garcin, Y., et al., "East African Mid-Holocene Wet-dry Transition Recorded in Palaeo-Shorelines of Lake Turkana Northern Kenya Rift," *Earth and Planetary Science Letters* 331 (2012): 322–34.

[376] Kropelin, S., et al., "Climate-Driven Ecosystem Succession in the Sahara: The Past 6000 years," *Science* 320 (2008): 765–68.

[377] Kuper, R., et al., "Sahara: Motor of Africa's Evolution," *Science* 313 (2006): 803–7, doi:10.1126/science.1130989.

[378] Hoelzmann, P., et al., "Palaeoenvironmental Changes in the Arid and Sub Arid Belt (Sahara-Sahel-Arabian Peninsula) from 150 kyr to Present," in *Past Climate Variability through Europe and Africa in 'Developments in Paleoenvironmental Research,'* eds. Battarbee, R., Gasse, F., and Stickley, C. (New York: Springer, 2004), 219–56, ISBN: 978-1-4020-2121-3.

[379] Street-Perrott, F., et al., "Drought and Dust Deposition in the West African Sahel: A 5500-Year Record from Kajemarum Oasis, Northeastern Nigeria," *Holocene* 10 (2000): 293–302.

[380] Holmes, J., "How the Sahara Became Dry," *Science* 320 (2008): 752–53

[381] Anderson, P. M., et al, "Results and Paleoclimate Implications of 35 Years of Paleoecological Research in Alaska," in *The Quaternary Period in the United States. Developments in Quaternary Science*, eds. Gillespie A. E., Porter, S. C., and Atwater, B. F. (Amsterdam: Elsevier, 2004), 427–40.

[382] Guthrie, R., *Frozen Fauna of the Mammoth Steppe* (Chicago IL, USA: Univ Chicago Press 1990).

[383] Ager, T., "Late Quaternary Vegetation and Climate History of the Central Bering Land Bridge from St. Michael Island, Western Alaska," *Quaternary Research* 60 (2003): 19–32.

[384] Kapp, R., "Late Pleistocene and Postglacial Plant Communities of the Great Lakes Region," in *Geobotany I*, ed. Romans, R. (New York: Springer, 1977), 1–27, ISBN: 978-1-4757-1674-0.

[385] Fischer, H., et al., "Millennial Changes in North American Wildfire and Soil Activity Over the Last Glacial Cycle," *Nature Geoscience* 8 (2015): 723–27, doi:10.1038/ngeo2495.

[386] Springer, K., et al., "Dynamic Response of Desert Wetlands to Abrupt Climate Change," *PNAS* 112 (2015): 14522–526, doi:10.1073/pnas.1513352112.

[387] Broecker, W., and Putnam, A., "How Did the Hydrologic Cycle Respond to the Two-Phase Mystery Interval?," *Quaternary Science Reviews* 57 (2012): 17–25.

[388] Caissie, B., et al., "Last Glacial Maximum to Holocene Sea Surface Conditions at Umnak Plateau, Bering Sea, as Inferred from Diatom, Alkenone, and Stable Isotope Records," *Paleoceanography* 25 (2010): PA1206, 1–16, doi:10.1029/2008PA001671.

[389] Gavin, D., et al., "Abrupt Holocene climate change and potential response to solar forcing in western Canada," *Quaternary Science Reviews* 30 (2011): 1243-1255(see1246 (figure 2).

[390] Lowell, T., et al., "Interhemispheric Correlation of Late Pleistocene Glacial Events," *Science* 269 (1995): 1541–49.

[391] Ford, H. et al., "Reduced El Nino-Southern Oscillation during the Last Glacial Maximum," *Science* 347 (2015): 255–58.

[392] Tudhope, A., et al., "Variability in the El Nino Southern Oscillation through a Glacial-interglacial Cycle," *Science* 291 (2001): 1511–17.

[393] Felis, T., et al., "Pronounced Interannual Variability in Tropical South Pacific Temperatures during Heinrich Stadial 1," *Nature Communications* 3 (2012): 965, http://dx.doi.org/10.1038/ncomms1973.

[394] Rein, B., et al., "El Nino Variability Off Peru during the Last 20,000 Years," *Paleoceanography* 20 (2005): PA4003, http://dx.doi.org/10.1029/2004PA001099.

[395] Sandweiss, D., et al., "Quebrada Jaguay: Early South American Maritime Adaptations," *Science* 281 (1998): 1830–32, doi:10.1126/science.281.5384.1830.

[396] Carre, M., et al., "Holocene History of ENSO Variance and Asymmetry in the Eastern Tropical Pacific," *Science* 345 (2014): 1045–47; [Climatologists also refer to El Nino, as ENSO: the El Nino Southern Oscillation.]

[397] Wuethrich, B., "El Nino Grew Strong as Cultures Were Born," *Science* 283 (1999): 467–68.
[A climate record cored high in the Ecuadorian Andes from the bottom of a lake, suggests a much-weaker El Nino between five thousand and twelve thousand years ago, maybe none at all. Older climate records show that before twelve thousand years ago, El Nino was similar to present. The onset of the modern El Nino less that five thousand years ago may have stimulated the emergence of civilizations around the Pacific.]

[398] Hughen, K., et al., "Marine-Derived 14C Calibration and Activity Record for the Past 50,000 years Updated from the Cariaco Basin," *Quat. Sci. Rev.* 25, (2006) 3216–27.

[399] Moy, C., et al., "Variability of El Nino/Southern Oscillation Activity at Millennial Timescales during the Holocene Epoch," *Nature* 420 (2002): 162–65.

[400] McGregor, H., and Gagan M., "Western Pacific Coral d[18]O Records of Anomalous Holocene Variability in the El Nino Southern Oscillation," *Geophysical Research Letters* 31 (2004): L11204, 1 of 4, doi:10.1029/2004GL019972.
[Skeletal oxygen isotope ratios in Holocene Porites corals from northern Papua New Guinea recorded decreases in sea surface temperature (SST) and rainfall during El Nino events.
Seven fossil coral d[18]O records spanning the period 7.6–5.4 ka (5,600BC to 3400BC in the fourth-age) showed only 8–12 El Nino events/century, and a 15% reduction in El Nino Amplitude.]

[401] Rodbell, D., et al., "A 15,000-year Record of El Nino-driven Alluviation in Southwestern Ecuador," *Science* 283 (1999): 516–20.

[402] Sandweiss, D., et al., "Transitions in the Mid-Holocene," *Science* 283 (1999): 499–500.

[403] The Altiplano salt flat is known locally as: Salar de Uyuni.

[404] Baker, P., et al., "The History of South American Tropical Precipitation for the Past 25,000 years," *Science* 291 (2001): 640–43.

[405] Baker, P., et al., "Tropical Climate Changes at Millennial and Orbital Timescales on the Bolivian Altiplano," *Nature* 409 (2001): 698–701.

[406] Jomelli, V., et al., "A Major Advance of Tropical Andean Glaciers during the Antarctic Cold Reversal," *Nature* 513 (2014): 224–28, doi:10.1038/nature13546.

[407] Nunez, L., et al., "Human Occupations and Climate Chang in the Puna de Atacama, Chile," *Science* 298 (2002): 821–24.

[408] Hermanowskia, B., "Palaeoenvironmental Dynamics and Underlying Climatic Changes in Southeast Amazonia (Serra Sul dos Carajás,

Brazil) during the Late Pleistocene and Holocene," *Palaeogeography, Palaeoclimatology, Palaeoecology* 365/366 (2012): 227–46.

[409] Stevaux, J., "Climatic Events during the Late Pleistocene and Holocene in the Upper Parana River: Correlation with NE Argentina and South-Central Brazil," *Quaternary International* 72 (2000): 73–85.

[410] Buso Jr. A., et al., "Late Pleistocene And Holocene Vegetation, Climate Dynamics, and Amazonian Taxa In The Atlantic Forest, Linhares, SE Brazil," *Proceedings of the 21st International Radiocarbon Conference, (University of Arizona)* edited by Jull, A., and Hatté, C., *Radiocarbon* 55 (2013): 1747–62.

[411] Glasser, N., et al., "Late Pleistocene and Holocene Palaeoclimate and Glacier Fluctuations in Patagonia," *Global and Planetary Change* 43 (2004): 79–101.

[412] Putnum, A., et al. "Glacier Advance in the Southern Middle-Latitudes during the Antarctic Cold Reversal," *Nature Geoscience* 3 (2010): 700–704.

[413] Heusser, C., "Late Quaternary Vegetation and Climate of Southern Tierra del Fuego," *Quaternary Research* 31 (1989): 396–406.

[414] Ackert, Jr. R., et al., "Patagonian Glacier Response during the Late Glacial-Holocene Transition," *Science* 321 (2008): 392–95.

[415] Markgraf, V., et al., "Holocene Palaeoclimates of southern Patagonia: Limnological and Environmental History of Lago Cardiel, Argetnina," *Holocene* 13 (2003): 581–91.

[416] [On December 1, 2011, the West Antarctic Ice Sheet (WAIS) Divide ice core project, funded by the National Science Foundation (NSF), reached its final depth of 3.4 kilometers down into West Antarctic Ice

Sheet (WAIS) Divide, recovering one of the longest ice-core to date from the polar regions. The 12.2-centimeter (4.8-inch) diameter cylinders of ice that make up the ice core. Annual layers of snow were detected using electrical conductivity methods the estimate the thickness of annual layers, depth and age of sample the adjusted to 'Greenland Ice Core Chronology 2005' by matching methane peaks. The result was uniquely detailed information on past environmental conditions in the region during the last sixty-eight thousand years, including the atmospheric concentration of greenhouse gases, surface air temperature, wind patterns, the extent of sea ice around Antarctica, and the average temperature of the ocean. http://www.waisdivide.unh.edu.]

[417] WAIS Divide Project Members, "Onset of Deglacial Warming in West Antarctica Driven by Local Orbital Forcing," *Nature* 500 (2013): 440–44.

[418] Weber, M., et al., "Millennial-scale Variability in Antarctic Ice-sheet Discharge during the Last Deglaciation," *Nature* 510 (2014): 134–38.

[419] Huybers, P., and Denton, G., "Antarctic Temperature at Orbital Timescales Controlled by Local Summer Duration," *Nature Geoscience* 1 (2008): 787–92.

[420] Kawamura, K., et al., "Northern Hemisphere Forcing of Climate Cycles in Antarctica over the Past 360,000 Years," *Nature* 448 (2007): 912–16.

[421] Wagner, B., and Melles, M., "The Heterogenity of Holocene Climatic and Environmental History along the East Antarctic Coastal Regions," *U.S. Geological Survey and the National Academies; Extended Abstract* 161 (2007), USGS OF-2007-1047, 10th International Symposium on Antarctic Earth Sciences. See Figure 2. 'Comparison of paleoclimate information from several coastal regions in East Antarctica and from East Antarctic ice cores.'

[422] Masson, V., et al., "Holocene Climate Variability in Antarctica Based on 11 Ice-Core Isotopic Records," *Quaternary Research* 54 (2000): 348–58.

[423] Kulbe, T., et al., "East Antarctic Climate and Environmental Variability over the Last 9400 Years Inferred from Marine Sediments of the Bunger Oasis," *Arctic, Antarctic, and Alpine Research* 33 (2001): 223–30.

[424] Thiagarajan, N., "Abrupt Pre-Bolling-Allerod Warming and Circulation Changes in the Deep Ocean," *Nature* 511 (2014): 75.

[425] Deschamps, P., et al., "Ice-sheet Collapse and Sea-level Rise at the Bolling Warming 14600 Years Ago," *Nature* 483 (2012): 559–64.

[426] Clark, P., "Sea-level Fingerprinting as a Direct Test for the Source of Global Meltwater Pulse 1A," *Science* 295 (2002): 2438–41.

[427] Wagner, B., "Late Pleistocene and Holocene History of Lake Terrasovoje, Amery Oasis, East Antarctica, and Its Climatic and Environmental Implications," *Journal of Paleolimnology* 32 (2004): 321–39.

[428] Johnson, J., et al., "Rapid Thinning of Pine Island Glacier in the Early Holocene," *Science* 343 (2014): 999–1001.

[429] Clapperton, C., "Quaternary Glaciations in the Southern Ocean and Antarctic Peninsula Area," *Quaternary Science Reviews* 9 (1990): 229–52.

[430] Adams, J., "Europe during The Last 150,000 Years," Environmental Sciences Division, Oak Ridge National Laboratory, Oak Ridge, TN, USA, http://www.esd.ornl.gov/projects/qen/nercEUROPE.html.

431 Hooghiemstra, H., et al., "Vegetational and Climatic Changes at the Northern Fringe of the Sahara 250,000-5000 BP," *Review of Palaeobotany and Palynology* 74 (1992): 1–53.

432 Dobson, Mike and Kawamura, Yoshinari, "Origin of the Japanese Land Mammal Fauna: Allocation of Extant Species to Historically-Based Categories," *Daiyonki Kenkyu (The Quaternary Research)* 37 (1998): 385–95 [in English with Japanese abstract].

433 Ager, T., "Late Quaternary Vegetation and Climate History of the Central Bering Land Bridge from St. Michael Island, Western Alaska," *Quaternary Research* 60 (2003) 19–32.

434 Jo, K., "Mid-latitude Interhemispheric Hydrologic Seesaw over the Past 550,000 Years," *Nature* 508 (2014): 378–82.

435 Heusser, C., "Late Quaternary Vegetation and Climate of Southern Tierra del Fuego," *Quaternary Research*, 31 (1989) 396–406.

436 Lowe, J., and Walker, M., *Reconstructing Quaternary Environments*, 3rd ed. (London: Routledge, 2015).

437 Street-Perrott, F. A., "Palaeoperspectives: Changes in Terrestrial Ecosystems," *Ambio-Stockholm* 23 (1994): 37–43 (Conference Paper for Third Scientific Advisory Council Meeting, Integrating Earth System Science; (1993) Ensenada; Mexico (7 pages) ISSN: 0044-7447 International Geosphere-Biosphere Programme.

438 Mayewski, P., et al., "Holocene Climate Variability," *Quaternary Research* 62 (2004): 243–55.

439 http://www.esd.ornl.gov/projects/qen/nercAFRICA.html.

[440] Arz, H., et al., "Mediterranean Moisture Source from an Early-Holocene Humid Period in the Northern Red Sea," *Science* 300 (2003): 118–21.

[441] Bowler, J., "Late Quaternary Climates of Australia and New Guinea," *Quaternary Research* 6 (1976): 359–94.

[442] Stuijts, I., "Evidence for Late Quaternary Vegetational Change in Sumatran and Javan Highlands," *Review of Palaeobotany and Palynology* 55 (1988): 207–16.

[443] Masson, V. et al., "Holocene Climate Variability in Antarctica Based on 11 Ice-Core Isotope Records," *Quaternary Research* 54, no. 3 (2000): 348–58.

[444] Wagner, B., "Late Pleistocene and Holocene History of Lake Terrasovoje, Amery Oasis, East Antarctica, and Its Climatic and Environmental Implications," *Journal of Paleolimnology* 32 (2004): 321–39.

[445] *Our Planet*, "The Collection," *New Scientist*, 2, no. 4 (2015): 30, ISSN 2054-6386.

[446] Hantemirov, R., and Shiyatov, S., "A Continuous Multi Millennial Ring-width Chronology in Yamal, North-western Siberia," *The Holocene* 12 (2002): 717–26.

[447] Seppa, H., and Birks, H., "Holocene Climate Reconstructions from the Fennoscandian Tree-Line Area Based on Pollen Data from Toskaljavri," *Quaternary Research* 57 (2002): 191–99.

[448] Birks, H., "Holocene Vegetational History and Climatic Change in West Spitsbergen – Plant Macrofossils from Skardtjorna, an Arctic Lake," *The Holocene* 1 (1991): 209–18.

[449] Hjort, C., et al., "Radiocarbon Dated Common Mussels Mytilus Edulis from Eastern Svalbard and the Holocene Marine Climate Optimum," *Polar Research* 14 (1995): 239–43.

[450] Sletto, B.,"Desert in Disguise," *Earth* 6, no. 1 (1997): 42–49.

[451] Loope, D., and Swinehart, J., "Thinking Like A Dune Field: Geologic History in the Nebraska Sand Hills," *Great Plains Research* 10 (2000): 5–35.

[452] Svendsen, J., and Mangerud, J., "Holocene Glacial and Climatic Variations on Spitsbergen, Svalbard," *The Holocene* 7 (1997): 45–57.

[453] Allen, J., et al., "Rapid Environmental Changes in Southern Europe during the Last Glacial Period," *Nature* 400 (1999): 740–41.

[454] Sandford, R., et al., "Amazon Rain-Forest Fires," *Science* 277 (1985): 53–55.

[455] Warlow, P., "Geomagnetic Reversals?," *Journal of Physics A Mathematical and General* 11 (1978): 2107–31.

[456] Hapgood, C., *The Path of the Pole* (Kempton, IL: Adventures Unlimited Press, 1999 (1968)), ISBN: 0-932813-71-2.

[457] White. J., *Pole Shift* (Virginia Beach, VA: A.R.E. Press, 1994 (1980)).

[458] Ager, T., "Late Quaternary Vegetation and Climate History of the Central Bering Land Bridge from St. Michael Island, Western Alaska," *Quaternary Research* 60 (2003) 19–32.

[459] Donn, W., "The Enigma of High-latitude Paleoclimate," *Palaeogeography, Palaeoclimatology, Palaeoecology* 40 (1982): 199–212.

[460] André, M. -F., "Holocene Climate Fluctuations and Geomorphic Impact of Extreme Events in Svalbard," *Geografiska Annaler. Series A, Physical Geography: Papers from Symposium: Arctic and Alpine Geomorphology and Environmental Change* 77 (1995): 241–50.

[461] Lowell, T. V., et al., "Interhemispheric Correlation of Late Pleistocene Glacial Events," *Science* 269 (1995): 1541–49.

[462] Guilderson, T., et al., "Tropical Temperature Variations Since 20,000 Years Ago; Modulating Inter-hemispheric Climate Change," *Science* 263 (1994): 663–65.

[463] Lorius, C., et al., "A 30,000-yr Isotope Climatic Record from Antarctic Ice," *Nature* 280 (1979): 644–48.

[464] Dansgaard, W., et al., "The Abrupt Termination of the Younger Dryas Climate Event," *Nature* 339 (1989): 532–34.

[465] http://www.ncdc.noaa.gov/paleo/icecore/antarctica/vostok/vostok_data.html.

[466] Svendsen, J., and Mangerud, J., "Holocene Glacial and Climatic Variations on Spitsbergen, Svalbard," *The Holocene* 7 (1997): 45–57.

[467] Ager, T., "Late Quaternary Vegetation and Climate History of the Central Bering Land Bridge from St. Michael Island, Western Alaska," *Quaternary Research* 60 (2003) 19–32.

[468] Jones, M., and Yu, Z., "Rapid Deglacial and Early Holocene Expansion of Peatlands in Alaska," *Proceedings of the National Academy of Sciences of the United States of America* 107 (2010): 7347–52.

[469] Strain, M., *The Earth's Shifting Axis* (Shrewsbury, MA: ATL Press Inc Science Publishers, 1997).

[470] Latitude Shift: see Velikovsky, I., *Worlds in Collision* (London: Victor Gollancz Ltd., 1950), 303, quoting Kugler, F. X., *Die babylonische Mondrechnung: Zwei Systeme der Chaldaer uber den Lauf des Mondes und der Sonne* (London: Forgotten Books, 1900), 80 and Kugler, F. X., *Sternkunde und Sterndienst in Babel*, vol. I (Münster, Germany: Aschendorff, 1907), 226–27.

[471] [Tropics of Cancer and Capricorn: On the Tropic of Cancer, 23.5° North of the Equator, the sun was directly overhead at noon on the northern summer solstice on June 21. On the Tropic of Capricorn, 23.5° South of the Equator, the sun was directly overhead at noon on the southern summer solstice on December 21.]

[472] Dentona, G., "The Role of Seasonality in Abrupt Climate Change," *Quaternary Science Reviews* 24 (2005): 1159–82.

[473] Rocek, T., and Bar-Yosef, O., eds., *Seasonality and Sedentism: Archaeological Perspectives from Old and New World Sites*, Peabody Museum Bulletins (Cambridge, MA: Harvard University Press, 2004), ISBN: 9780873659567.

[474] Stevens, L., et al., "Proposed Changes in Seasonality of Climate during the Lateglacial and Holocene at Lake Zeribar, Iran," *The Holocene* 11 (2001): 747–55, doi:10.1191/09596830195762.

[475] Atkinson, T., et al., "Seasonal Temperatures in Britain during the Past 22,000, Reconstructed Using Beetle Remains," *Nature* 325 (1987): 587–92.

[476] Renssen, H., et al., "Thermal Gradients in Europe during the Last Glacial-Interglacial Transition," *Netherlands Journal of Geosciences* 81 (2002): 113–22.

[477] Friedrich, M., et al., "The 12460 Year Hohenheim Oak and Pine Tree-Ring Chronology from Central Europe. A Unique Annual Record for

Radiocarbon Calibration and Paleoenvironment Reconstructions," *Radiocarbon* 46 (2004): 1111–22; http://www.wsl.ch/dendro/dendrodb. html; http://web.utk.edu/~grissino/; http://www.ncdc.noaa.gov/paleo/ treering.html.

[478] Kutzbach, J., and Street-Perrott, F., "Milankovitch Forcing of Fluctuations in the Level of Tropical Lakes from 18 to 0 kyr BP," *Nature* 317 (1985): 130–34, doi:10.1038/317130a0.

[479] Meese, D., et al., "The Accumulation Record from the GISP2 Core as an Indicator of Climate Change Throughout the Holocene," *Science* 266 (1994): 1680–82.

[480] Ma, Chao, "Theory o Chaotic Orbital Variations Confirmed by Cretaceous Geological Evidence," *Nature* 542 (2017): 468–70.

[481] Paillard, D.,"Predictable Ice Ages on a Chaotic Planet," *Nature* 542 (2017): 419–20.

[482] Imbrie, J., and Imbrie, K., *Ice Ages, Solving the Mystery* (Cambridge, MA: Harvard University Press, 1979).

[483] Adhemar, J., *Revolutions of the Sea* (Paris, 1842).

[484] Kutzbach, J., and Otto-Bliesner, B., "The Sensitivity of the African-Asian Monsoonal Climate to Orbital Parameter Changes for 9000 yr B.P. in a Low-resolution General Circulation Model," *Journal of the Atmospheric Sciences* 39 (1982): 1177–88.

[485] Broeker, W., and Denton, G., "What Drives Glacial Cycles?," *Scientific American* 262 (1990): 49–56.

[486] National Research Council, *Abrupt Climate Change: Inevitable Surprises* (Washington, DC: National Academy Press, 2002).

[487] Tzedakis, P., "A Simple Rule to Determine Which Insolation Cycles Lead to Interglacials," *Nature* 542 (2017): 427–32.

[488] Muck, O., *The Secret of Atlantis* (London: Collins, 1978).

[489] Emery, K., and Uchupi, E., *The Geology of the Atlantic Ocean* (New York: Springer, 1984), edition ISBN-10: 0387960325; ISBN-13: 978-0387960326.

[490] Allan, D., and Delair, J., *When the Earth Nearly Died (Compelling Evidence of a Catastrophic World Change 9500 BC)* (Bath: Gateway Books, 1995).

[491] Firestone, Richard., West, Allen., and Warwick-Smith, Simon, *The Cycle of Cosmic Catastrophes*2006) ISBN-13:978-1-59143 www.cosmic-catastrophes.com.

[492] Firestone, R., et al., "Evidence for an Extraterrestrial Impact 12900 Years Ago that Contributed to the Mega Faunal Extinctions and the Younger Dryas Cooling," *PNAS* 104 (2007): 16016–21.

[493] Kerr, R., et al., "Experts Find No Evidence for a Mammoth-Killer Impact," *Science* 319 (2008): 1331–32.

[494] Barger, V., and Olsson, M., *Classical Mechanics, A Modern Perspective* (New York: McGraw-Hill, 1973), 265–74.

[495] Ollier, C., and Pain, C., *The Origin of Mountains* (London: Routledge, 2000), ISBN: 0-203-00590-2, ISBN: 0-415-19889-5, ISBN: 0-415-19890-9.

[496] Collins, W., "Hot Orogens, Tectonic Switching, and Creation of Continental Crust," *Geology* 30 (2002): 535–38.

[497] Cawood, P., et al., "Accretionary Orogens Through Earth History," *Geological Society London Special Publications* 318 (2009): 1–36.

[498] Wegener, Alfred, *The Origin of Continents and Oceans* (New York: Dover), ISBN: 0-486-61708-4. Translated from the fourth revised German edition by John Biram. Alfred Wegener, "Die Entstehung der Kontinente," *Geologische Rundschau* (in German) 3 (1912): 276–92, doi:10.1007/BF02202896.

[499] Wegener, Alfred, *Die Entstehung der Kontinente und Ozeane* [*The Origin of Continents and Oceans*], 1922 (in German), ISBN: 3-443-01056-3. LCCN unk83068007.

[500] Lowman, Paul, *Exploring Space Exploring Earth: New Understanding of the Earth from Space Research* (Cambridge: Cambridge University Press, 2002), 38.

[501] Allan, D. S. and Delair, J. B., *When the Earth Nearly Died: Compelling Evidence of a Catastrophic World Change 9500 BC* (Bath: Gateway Books, 1995), 69–71, Table 1C.

[502] Willis, B., *Research in China*, 2 vols (Washington, DC: Carnegie Institute, 1907).

[503] Lee, J. S., *The Geology of China* (London,1939), 207.

[504] Wadia, D. N., *Geology of India* (London,1953) see pp, 22–23.

[505] Berkey, C., and Morris, F., *Geology of Mongolia: A Reconnaissance Report based on the Investigations of the Years 1922–1923; Central-Asiatic Expeditions* (New York: Amer Mus Nat Hist, 1927), 35.

[506] Lee, J. S., *The Geology of China* (London,1939) see p, 201.

[507] Ibid., 396–97.

[508] Embleton, C., and King, C., *Glacial and Periglacial Geomorphology (2nd ed.), Volume 1: Glacial Geomorphology, Volume 2: Periglacial Geomorphology* (London: Edward Arnold, 1975), 30, ISBN: O713157917;O71315793 3.

[509] Lee, J. S., *The Geology of China* (London, 1939) see pp, 206–7.

[510] Krishnan, M. S., *Geology of India and Burma* (Madras: Madras Law Journal Office, 1949), 511.

[511] Petterson, M., "A Review of the Geology and Tectonics of the Kohistan Island Arc, North Pakistan," *Geological Society, London, Special Publications* 338 (2010): 287–327, doi:10.1144/SP338.14.

[512] Wadia, D., *The Structure of the Himalayas and of the North India Foreland*, Presidential Address, 25th Indian Sci Congr (Calcutta, 1938.), 26. Geology section quoting the Geological Survey of India.

[513] Heim, A., and Gansser, A., *The Throne of the Gods: an Account of the First Expedition to the Himalayas* (New York: The Macmillan Company, 1939), 218.

[514] Finsterwalder, R., *Die Formen der Inanga Parbat-Gruppe* (Berlin: Zeit Ges Erdk, 1936).

[515] Wadia, D., *Geology of India* (London, 1953), 405.

[516] Oldham, R., "The Structure of the Gangetic Plain," *Memoirs of the Geological Survey of India* 42 (1917): pt. 2.

[517] Glennie, E., *Gravity Anomalies and Structure of the Earth's Crust*, Prof Papers Geol Surv India, no. 27, 1932.

[518] Krishnan, M., *Geology of India and Burma* (Madras, 1949).

[519] Gentil, L., "La Geologic du Maroc," *Congr Geol Internal*, 1914, see p. 703.

[520] McMaster, R., and La-Chance, T., "Seismic Reflectivity Studies on Northwestern African Continental Shelf: Strait of Gibraltar to Mauritania," *American Association of Petroleum Geologists* 52 (1968): 2387–95.

[521] Furon, R., *Geology of Africa* (Edinburgh: Oliver and Boyd, 1963), 72.

[522] Baker, B., et al., "Geology of the Eastern Rift System of Africa," *Geological Society of America Special Papers* (1972): Paper 136.

[523] Dixey, F., *The East African Rift System*. Overseas Geol Surv Min Resour Divn, suppi 1 (London: H.M. Stationery Off, 1956).

[524] McConnell, R., "Geological Development of the Rift System of Eastern Africa," *Bulletin of the Geological Society of America* 83 (1972): 2549–72.

[525] Ewing, M., et al. *Columbia Research News*, March 1957.

[526] Flint, R., *Glacial Geology and the Pleistocene* (New York: Epoch, 1947), 523.

[527] Tennison-Woods, J., *Geological Observations in South Australia, Principally in the Southeast of Adelaide* (London: Longman, Green, Longman, Roberts, & Green, 1862), 208.

[528] Brown, D., et al., *The Geological Evolution of Australia and New Zealand* (Oxford: Pergamon Press, 1968), 348.

[529] Forest, H., *The Atlantean Continent: Its Bearing on the Great Ice Age and the Distribution of Species*, 2nd edn. (London,1935).

[530] Daly, R., *Our Mobile Earth* (London & New York: D. Appleton and Company, 1926), 228–31.

[531] Price, G., *Commonsense Geology* (Mountain View, CA: Pacific Press Publishing Association, 1946.), 20.

[532] Weaver, C., "Geology of the Coast Ranges North of San Francisco Bay," *Mem Geol Surv Amer* 35 (1949): 1–242, see p. 166.

[533] Fenneman, N., *The Physiography of the Western United States* (New York, 1931).

[534] Putnam, W., *Geology* (New York, 1964), 117.

[535] Zeil, W., *The Andes: A Geological Review* (Berlin, 1979), 173.

[536] Garzione, C. N. et al., "Rise of the Andes," *Science* 320 (2008): 1304–7.

[537] Fritz, S., et al., "Quaternary Glaciation and Hydrologic Variation in the South American Tropics as Reconstructed from the Lake Titicaca Drilling Project," *Quaternary Research* 68 (2007): 410–20.

[538] Kroll, O., et al., "The Endemic Gastropod Fauna of Lake Titicaca: Correlation between Molecular Evolution and Hydrographic History," *Ecology and Evolution* 2 (2012): 1517–30, doi: 10.1002/ece3.280 PMCID: PMC3434920.

[539] Fairbridge, R., ed., "The Encyclopaedia of World Regional Geology, Part I: Western Hemisphere, including Antarctica and Australia," in *Encyclopaedia of Earth Sciences*, vol. 7 (Stroudsburg, 1975), 266, 464.

[540] Trumpy, R., *Geology of Switzerland: A Guide Book, Part 4: An Outline of the Geology of Switzerland* (Basel, 1980), 93.

[541] Daly, *Our Mobile Earth* (London & New York, 1926) see pp, 232–42.

[542] Rutten, M., *The Geology of Western Europe* (Amsterdam, 1969), 211.

[543] Ibid., 382–88.

[544] Ibid., 177.

[545] Lubbock, J., *The Scenery of Switzerland and the Causes to Which it Was Due* (London, 1896), 291–92, 369.

[546] Heer, O., *The Primaeval World of Switzerland* (2 vols), trans. W. Dallas and ed. J. Heywood (London, 1875), vol 2, p. 224.

[547] Forest, H., *The Atlantean Continent: Its Bearing on the Great Ice Age and the Distribution of Species*, 2nd ed.n. (London,1935) 234.

[548] Gregory, J., *The Nature and Origin of Fiords* (London, 1913).

[549] Peteressen, K., "How the Norway Fiords Were Made," *Nature* 32 (1885): 177–80.

[550] Tayler, J., "On the Making of Fiords," *Royal Geographical Society of London* 11 (1870).

[551] Sokolov, V., *Stratigraphy of Spitzbergen* (Boston Spa, 1977), 273.

[552] Hitchcock, C., "New Zealand in the Ice Age," *American Geologist* 27 (1901): 271–81.

[553] Suggate, R., "The Alpine Fault," *Transactions of the Royal Society of New Zealand* (geology section) 2 (1963): 105–29.

[554] Tayler, J., "On the Making of Fiords," *Royal Geographical Society of London* 11 (1870): 228–30.

[555] Gregory, J., "The Fiords of the Hebrides," *Geography Journal* 69 (1927): 93–216.

[556] Peteressen, K. "How the Norway Fiords Were Made,", *Nature* 23 (1885): 177–80.

[557] Gregory, J., *The Nature and Origin of Fiords* (London, 1913).

[558] [There are published examples highlands elevated at the end of the Pleistocene from Jan Mayen Island, Bear Island, Spitsbergen, Kong Karl Land, Franz Josef Land, Kola Peninsula, Kanin Peninsula, Novaya Zemlya, the Laptev Sea, the New Siberian Islands, the Chukchee coast, Anadyr Bay, the northern Ural mountains, St Lawrence Islands, the Seaward Peninsula, the Alaskan Range, Aleutian Islands and the Canadian Archipelago.

[559] Significant elevations in Asia including; the Altai Mountains, Tibetan Plateau, Tien Shan, Gobi Basin, Pamirs, Hindu Kush, Karakoram, Kailas Mountains, Alai Mountains, Himalayas and Pir Panjal, the Kamchatka Peninsula, Bayan Kara Shan, Minya Konka, Yunnan Province, Great Khingan Shan and the Sikhote-Alin Mountains; are described in the literature.]

[560] Scrivenor, J., *The Geology of Malaya* (London, 1931), 119–20.

[561] Umbgrove, J., *The Pulse of the Earth*, 2nd edn. (The Hague,1947) 235.

562 Smith, W., *Geology and Mineral Resources of the Philippine Islands* (Manila, 1924), 89–90, 92, 467.

563 Brouwer, H., *The Geology of the Netherlands East Indies* (New York, 1925), 40.

564 Brouwer, H., *Geological Explorations in the Islands of Celebes: Summary of the Results* (Amsterdam, 1947), 17, 49.

565 Hobbs, W., "The Correlation of Fracture Systems and the Evidence for Planetary Dislocations within the Earth's Crust," *Transactions of the Wisconsin Academy of Sciences, Arts, and Letters* 15 (1905): 15–29 see p. 15.

566 Vening-Meinesz, F., "Shear Patterns of the Earth's Crust," *Transactions, American Geophysical Union* 28 (1947): 161.

567 Hobbs, W., "Repeating Patterns in the Relief and Structure of the Land," *Bulletin of the Geological Society of America* 22 (1911): 123–76; see p. 163.

568 Umbgrove, J., *The Pulse of the Earth*, 2nd ed. (The Hague, 1947), 307.

569 Vening-Meinesz, F., "Spanningen in de aardrost tengevolge van poolverschuivingen" *Nederlandsche Akademie van Wetenschappen Verslagen* LII (1943).

570 Anonymous, "Submarine Canyons" *Geographical review* 27 (1937): 681–683.

571 Hess, H., and P MacClintock, P., "Submerged Valleys on Continental Slopes and Changes of Sea Level," *Science* 83 (1936): 332–34.

[572] Bucher, W., *The Deformation of the Earth's Crust* (Princeton, 1933), 144.

[573] Geikie, J., *The Great Ice Age*, 2nd ed. (London, 1877), 73.

[574] Poldervaart, A., "Symposium on the Crust of the Earth," *Geological Society of America Special Papers* 62 (1955): 319.

[575] Umbgrove, J., *The Pulse of the Earth*, 2nd ed. (The Hague, 1947).

[576] Turtle, E., et al., "Appendix 2: Ionian Mountains Identified to Date," in *Io after Galileo*, eds. R. Lopes and J. Spencer (New York: Springer-Praxis, 2007), 325–30, ISBN: 3-540-34681-3.

[577] Lowman, P., *Exploring Space Exploring Earth: New Understanding of the Earth from Space Research.* (Cambridge, UK: Cambridge University Press, 2002) pp, 283–84.

[578] Wegener, A., *The Origin of Continents and Oceans*, trans. J. Biram (New York: Dover, 1966).

[579] Romano, M., and Cifelli, R., "100 Years of Continental Drift, One Hundred Years Ago, Alfred Wegener Laid the Foundations for the Theory of Plate Tectonics," *Science* 350 (2015): 915–16.

[580] Hambrey, M., and Harland, W., *Earth's Pre-Pleistocene Glacial Record*, Project 38: Pre-Pleistocene Tillites (Cambridge: Cambridge University Press, 1981), 76.

[581] Rubidge, B., "Re-uniting Lost Continents – Fossil Reptiles from the Ancient Karoo and Their Wanderlust," *South African Journal of Geology* 108 (2005): 135–72, doi:10.2113/108.1.135.

[582] McKenzie, G., *Gondwana Six: Stratigraphy, Sedimentology, and Paleontology, Volume 2* (Washington, DC: American Geophysical Union, 1987).

[583] Hess, H., "History of Ocean Basins," in *Petrologic Studies: A Volume to Honor A. F. Buddington*, ed. Engel, A., et al. (Boulder, CO: Geological Society of America, 1962), 599–620.

[584] Vine, F. J., "Spreading of the Ocean Floor: New Evidence," *Science* 154 (1966): 1405–15, doi:10.1126/science.154.3755.1405F.

[585] Jeffreys, H., *The Earth, Its Origin, History and Physical Constitution* (Cambridge: Cambridge University Press, 1924; 5th ed. 1970; 6th ed. 1976).

[586] Oreskes, N., "How Plate Tectonics Clicked," *Nature* 501 (2013): 27–29.

[587] Gerya, T., et al., "Plate Tectonics on the Earth Triggered by Plume-induced Subduction Inititation," *Science* 527 (2015): 211–25.

[588] Mallard, C., "Subduction Controls the Distribution and Fragmentation of Earth's Tectonic Plates," *Nature* 535 (2016): 140–43.

[589] Dick, H., et al., "An Ultraslow-spreading Class of Ocean Ridge," *Nature* 426 (2003): 405–12.

[590] Burke, K., and Wilson, J., "Is the African Plate Stationary?," *Nature* 239 (1974): 313–16.

[591] Vine, F., "Spreading of the Ocean Floor: New Evidence," *Science* 154 (1966): 1405–15. doi:10.1126/science.154.3755.1405.

[592] Choi, D., "Late Premian-Early Triassic Paleogeography of Northern Japan: Did Pacific Microplates Accrete to Japan?," *Geology* 12 (1984): 728–831.

[593] Harrison, T., et al., "Heterogeneous Hadean Hafnium: Evidence of Continental Crust at 4.4 to 4.5 Ga," *Science* 310 (2005): 1947–50.

[594] Patterson, C., "Age of Meteorites and the Earth," *Geochimica et Cosmochimica Acta* 10 (1956): 230–37, doi:10.1016/0016-7037(56)90036-9.

[595] Tivey, M., et al., "Downhole Magnetic Measurements of ODP Hole 801C: Implications for Pacific Oceanic Crust and Magnetic Field Behavior in the Middle Jurassic," *Geochemistry Geophysics Geosystems* 6 (2005): Q04008, doi:10.1029/2004GC000754 ISSN: 1525-2027.

[596] Floyd, P., et al., "Tholeitic and Alkalic Basalts of the Oldest Pacific-Ocean Crust," *Terra Nova* 3 (1991): 257–64.

[597] Renz, O., "Early Cretaceous Cephalopoda from the Blake-Bahama Basin (Deep Sea Drilling Project Leg 76, Hole 534a) and Their Correlation in the Atlantic and Southwestern Tethys," www.deep-seadrilling.org/76/volume/dsdp76_27.pdf.

[598] Bercovici, D., and Ricard, Y., "Plate Tectonics, Damage and Inheritance," *Nature* 508 (2014): 513–16.

[599] Witze, A., "The Fiery Birth of Earth's Largest Ocean Exposed. A Volatile Arrangement of Tectonic Plates Millions of Years Ago Gave Us the Pacific," *Nature* (2016), doi:10.1038/nature.2016.20334.

[600] http://www.mantleplumes.org.

[601] Ryberg, T. et al., "Crustal structure of Northwest Namibia: Evidence for Plume-rift-continent Interaction," *Geology* 43 (2015): 739–42, doi:10.1130/G36768.1.

[602] Hand, E., "Mantle Plumes Seen Rising from Earth's Core," *Science* 349 (2015): 1032–33.

[603] Gillis, K., et al., "Primitive Layered Gabbros from Fast-spreading Lower Oceanic Crust," *Nature* 505 (2014): 204–7.

[604] Smith, D., et al., "Hydroacoustic Monitoring of Seismicity at the Slow-spreading Mid-Atlantic Ridge," *Geophysical Research Letters* 29 (2002): 1518, doi:10.1029/2001GL013912.

[605] Fox, C., et al., "Potential for Monitoring Low-Level Seismicity on the Juan de Fuca Ridge Using Military Hydrophone Arrays," *Marine Technology Society* 27 (1993): 22–29.

[606] Fox, C., et al., "Acoustic Detection of a Sea-floor Spreading Episode on the Juan-de-Fuca Ridge using Military Hydrophone Arrays," *Geophysical Research Letters* 22 (1995): 131–34, doi:10.1029/94GL02059.

[607] Olive, J., et al., "Sensitivity of Seafloor Bathymetry to Climate-Driven Fluctuations in Mid-Ocean Ridge Magma Supply," *Science* 350 (2015): 310–13.

[608] Ollier, C., and Pain, C.,*The Origin of Mountains*, (London, UK:Routledge 2000)
ISBN 0-203-00590-2, ISBN 0-415-19889-5, ISBN 0-415-19890-9
p323–26.

[609] Sullivan, W., "Science Using New Tools to Verify Continental Drift," *The New York Times*, July 5, 1983.

[610] Lowman, P. *Exploring Space Exploring Earth: New Understanding of the Earth from Space Research* (Cambridge: Cambridge University Press, 2002).

[611] Henbest, N., "Continental Drift: The Final Proof," *New Scientist*, May 31, 1984, 6. [The same article was republished in Issue Number 2578 on November 15, 2006, as part of the fiftieth anniversary celebrations of *New Scientist*].

[612] Lowman, P., *Exploring Space Exploring Earth: New Understanding of the Earth from Space Research* (Cambridge: Cambridge University Press, 2002).

[613] Lowman, P., "Plate Tectonics and Continental Drift: A Skeptic's View," in *The Blue Planet: An Introduction to Earth System Science*, eds. B. Skinner and S. Porter (New York: John Wiley & Sons, 1995), 187–89.

[614] DeMets, C., et al., "Geologically Current Plate Motions," *Geophysical Journal International* 181 (2010): 1–80.

[615] Pratt, D., "Problems with Plate Tectonics," *New Concepts in Global Tectonics Newsletter* 21 (2001): 10–24.

[616] Conrad, C., "How Climate Influences Sea-Floor Topography," *Science* 347 (2015): 1204–5.

[617] Tolstoy, M., "Mid-ocean Ridge Eruptions as a Climate Valve," *Geophysical Research Letters* (2015), doi:10.1002/2014GL063015.

[618] Crowley, J., "Glacial Cycles Drive Variations in the Production of Oceanic Crust," *Science* 347 (2015): 1237–40. See data in fig 3, p. 1239.

[619] Lund, D., "Enhanced East Pacific Rise Hydrothermal Activity during the Last Two Glacial Terminations," *Science* 351 (2016): 478–82.

[620] Phillips J. D., et al., "Mid-Atlantic Ridge near 43°N Latitude," *Journal of Geophysical Research* 74 (1969): 3069–82.

[621] Meyerhoff, A., et al., *Surge Tectonics: A New Hypothesis of Global Geodynamics*, Series: Solid Earth Sciences Library Volume 9 (New York: Springer, 1996), ISBN: 978-94-009-1738-5.

[622] Aumento, F., and Loncarevic, B., "The Mid-Atlantic Ridge Near 45°N. Fission Track and Ferromanaganese Chronology," *Canadian Journal of Earth Sciences* 6 (1969): 1431–40.

[623] MacDougal, D., "Deep Sea Drilling: Age and Composition of an Atlantic Basaltic Intrusion," *Science* 171 (1971): 1244–45.

[624] Quartau, R., et al., "The Insular Shelves of the Faial-Pico Ridge (Azores archipelago): A Morphological Record of Its Evolution," *Geochemistry Geophysics Geosystems* 16 (2015): 1401–20, doi:10.1002/2015GC005733.

[625] Norton, I., et al., "Plate Motion of Iberia Relative to Europe in the Cretaceous: Problems with the Fit at MO Time," in *Rift Renaissance Abstract Book*, August 19–21, 2008 (London: Geological Society UK, 2008), 21, www.geolsoc.org.uk/~/media/Files/.../Conference%20 Programme.ashx.

[626] Peron-Pinvidic, G., and Manatschal, G., "Constraints on Magma-Poor Rifting Evolution and Continental Breakup from the Iberia-Newfoundland Conjugate Margins," in *Rift Renaissance Abstract Book*, August 19–21, 2008 (London: Geological Society UK, 2008), 23, www.geolsoc.org.uk/~/media/Files/.../Conference%20Programme. ashx.

[627] Crosby, A., et al., "Evolution of the Newfoundland–Iberia Conjugate Rifted Margins," *Earth and Planetary Science Letters* 273 (2008): 214–26.

[628] Moorbath, S., and Welke, H., "Isotopic Evidence for the Continental Affinity of the Rockall Bank, North Atlantic," *Earth and Planetary Science Letters* 5 (1969): 211–16.

[629] Pratt, D., "Plate Tectonics: A Paradigm Under Threat," *Journal of Scientific Exploration* 14 (2000): 307–52.

[630] Pratt, D., "Organized Opposition to Plate Tectonics: The New Concepts in Global Tectonics Group," http://davidpratt.info/ncgt-jse.htm; http://www.naturalphilosophy.org/php/index.php?tab0=Sci entists&tab1=Scientists&tab2=Display&id=902.

[631] Hoernle, K., "70 m.y. History (139–69 Ma) for the Caribbean Large Igneous Province," *Geology* 32 (2004): 697–700, doi:10.1130/G20574.1.

[632] Wade, S., et al., "The Velingara Circular Structure – A Meteorite Impact Crater?" *Focus Earth ESA Bulletin* 106 (2001): 135–39.

[633] Planetary Visions Ltd., University College, London.

[634] Burke, K., and Wilson, J., "Is the African Plate Stationary?," *Nature* 239 (1974): 313–16.

[635] Duarte, J., et al., "Thrust-wrench Interference Tectonics in the Gulf of Cadiz (Africa-Iberia Plate Boundary in the North-East Atlantic): Insights from Analog Models," *Marine Geology* 289 (2009): 135–49.

[636] Kenyon, N., et al., eds., "Geological Processes in the Mediterranean and Black Seas and North East Atlantic: Preliminary Results of

Investigations during the TTR-11 Cruise of RV Professor Logachev July–September 2001," *Intergovernmental Oceanographic Commission Technical Series* 62, SC-2002/WS/62 UNESCO 2002.

[637] Dunn, R. at al., "Three-dimensional Seismic Structure and Physical Properties of the Crust and Shallow Mantle Beneath the East Pacific Rise at 9° 30'N," *Journal of Geophysical Research* 105 (2000): 23537–55.

[638] Laursen, L., "Russian Claim Heats Up Battle to CONTROL ARCTIC SEA FLOOR (New Data on Undersea Mountains Support Conflicting Claims to the North Pole)," *Science* 349 (2015): 678.

[639] Fargion, D., and Arnon, D., "Tidal Effects of Passing Planets and Mass Extinctions," (1998) arXiv:astro-ph/9802265.

[640] LITHOPROBE: Canada's national, collaborative, multidisciplinary Earth science research project established to develop a comprehensive understanding of the evolution of the northern half of the North American continent. http://lithoprobe.eos.ubc.ca/about/forms-docs/phaseproposal5.html.

[641] Santosh, M., et al., "Hadean Earth and Primordial Continents: The Cradle of Prebiotic Life," *Geoscience Frontiers* 8 (2017): 309e327.

[642] Raup, D., and Sepkoski, J., "Periodicity of Extinctions in the Geologic Past," *Proceedings of the National Academy of Sciences of the United States of America* 81 (1984): 801–5.

[643] Erwin, D., *Extinction: How Life on Earth Nearly Ended 250 Million Years Ago*, (Princeton, NJ and Oxford: Princeton University Press, 2006).

[644] Benton, M., *When Life Nearly Died (The Greatest Mass Extinction of all Time)* (London: Thames and Hudson, 2003).

[645] Miller, K., et al., "The Phanerozoic Record of Global Sea-Level Change," *Science* 310 (2005): 1293–98.

[646] Sloss, L., "Sequences in the Cratonic Interior of North America," *Geological Society of America Bulletin* 74 (1963): 93–114, doi:10.1130/0016-7606(1963)74[93:SITCIO]2.0.CO;2.

[647] Clarkson, M., et al., "Dynamic Anoxic Ferruginous Conditions during the End-Permian Mass Extinction and Recovery," *Nature Communications* 7 (2016): 12236, doi:10.1038/ncomms12236. www.nature.com/naturecommunications.

[648] Steiner, M., et al., "Fungal Abundance Spike and the Permian-Triassic Boundary in the Karoo Supergroup (South Africa)," *Palaeogeography, Palaeoclimatology, Palaeoecology* 194 (2003): 405–14.

[649] Grasby, S., et al., "Catastrophic Dispersion of Coal Fly Ash into Oceans during the Latest Permian Extinction," *Nature Geoscience* 4 (2011): 104–7, doi:10.1038/ngeo1069.

[650] Scott, A. C. and Fleet, A. J., eds., "Coal and Coal-bearing Strata as Oil-prone Source Rocks?," *Geological Society Special Publication* 77 (1994): 1–8.

[651] Kerr, R., "Mega-Eruptions Drove the Mother of Mass Extinctions," *Science* 342 (2013): 1424.

[652] Courtillot, V., et al., "On Causal Links between Flood Basalts and Continental Breakup," *Earth and Planetary Science Letters* 166 (1999): 177–95.

[653] Zhou, M., et al., "A Temporal Link between the Emeishan Large Igneous Province (SW China) and the end-Guadalupian Mass Extinction," *Earth and Planetary Science Letters* 196 (2002): 113–22.

[654] Chung, S., et al., "The Emeishan Flood Basalt in SW China: A Mantle Plume Initiation Model and Its Connection with Continental Break-Up and Mass Extinction at the Permian-Triassic Boundary," *Mantle Dynamics and Plate Interaction in East Asia. AGU Geodynamics Series* 27 (1998): 47–58.

[655] Duncan, R., "Deadly Combination," *Nature* 527 (2015): 172.

[656] Palmer, M., and Edmond, J., "The Strontium Isotopic Budget of the Modern Ocean," *Earth and Planetary Science Letters* 92 (1989): 11–26.

[657] Tomomi-Kani, T., et al., "The Paleozoic Minimum of 87Sr/86Sr Ratio in the Capitanian (Permian) Mid-oceanic Carbonates: A Critical Turning Point in the Late Paleozoic," *Journal of Asian Earth Sciences* 32 (2008): 22–33.
NOTE the 87Sr/86Sr minimum, means a sudden concentration <u>maximum of 86Sr.</u>

[658] Cao, C., et al., "Biogeochemical Evidence for Euxinic Oceans and Ecological Disturbance Presaging the End-Permian Mass Extinction Event," *Earth and Planetary Science Letters* 281 (2009): 188–201.

[659] Becker, et al., "Impact Event at the Permian-Triassic Boundary: Evidence from Estraterrestrial Noble Gases in Fullerenes," *Science* 291 (2001): 1530–33.
doi: 10.1126/science.1057243

[660] Erwin, D., *Extinction: How Life on Earth Nearly Ended 250 Million Years Ago*, (Princeton, NJ, USA and Oxford, UK: Princeton University Press, 2006).

[661] Poreda, R., and Becker, L., "Fullerenes and Interplanetary Dust at the Permian-Triassic Boundary," *Astrobiology* 3 (2003): 75–90.

662 Kerr, R., "Whiff of Gas Points to Impact Mass Extinction," *Science* 291 (2001): 1468.

663 Ehrenfreund, P., and Foing, B., "Fullerene Solves an Interstellar Puzzle," *Nature* 523 (2015): 296–323.

664 Kemp, A., et al., "The Uranium-Thorium and Rare Earth Element Geochemistry of Reduction Nodules from Budleigh Salterton, Devon," Annual Conference of the Ussher Society January 1994. *Proceedings of the Ussher Society* 8, no. 3 (1994): 214–18.

665 Parnell, J., and Eakin, P., "The Replacement of Sandstones by Unraniferous Hydrocarbons: Significance for Petroleum Migration," *Mineralogical Magazine* 51 (1987): 505–15.

666 Cao, C., et al., "Biogeochemical Evidence for Euxinic Oceans and Ecological Disturbance Presaging the End-Permian Mass Extinction Event," *Earth and Planetary Science Letters* 281 (2009):188–201.

667 Payne, J., "Large Perturbations of the Carbon Cycle during Recovery from the End-Permian Extinction," *Science* 305 (2004): 506–9.

668 [The Strange Origin of Carbonate Rocks. One proposal is that methane released from undersea methane hydrates (methane clathrate), caused the whole Permian atmosphere to burn like a methane gas furnace. This global inferno produced huge amounts of carbon dioxide and water vapor, which caused a hot rain of carbonic acid into the Permian seas. As the temperature of sea-water increased, the solubility of carbon-dioxide decreased, so that it became super-saturated with carbon dioxide and almost pure calcium-carbonate suddenly precipitated.

The weakness of this argument, is that methane clathrate on the seafloor has a low-C13-high-C12 abundance but the calcium-carbonate at the Permian-Triassic boundary has a high-C13-low-C12 abundance. It addition, concentration of calcium ions in sea-water is too low to account for the amount of calcium carbonate that was precipitated. A complicating factor is that calcium-carbonate is only insoluble in warm water in the absence of carbon-dioxide. Calcium-carbonate can react with carbon-dioxide dissolved in warm water to form soluble calcium-bicarbonate. The water must have been hot enough to outgas enough carbon-dioxide for the insoluble calcium carbonate to remain stable.]

[669] [Carbon-13 ratios are conventionally expressed in parts-per-thousand, relative to Carbon-12 of a standard limestone: a fossil skeleton of a Creaceous Belemnite called *Belemnitella americana* from the Peedee formation in South Carolina USA (the PDB scale). This material has high abundance of carbon-13: 13C/12C = 0.0112372, meaning one C13 atom for every 88.99 C12 atoms. Standard Belemnite was established as the standard δ13C value of zero.

Variations relative to the standard are reported as positive or negative variations in ‰, parts-per-thousand, (percent × 10). Relative to this standard, most terrestrial material has a negative δ13C. A negative delta value means that the C13 abundance in the sample is less than that of the standard.

However PDB δ13C notation is very confusing. For descriptive purposes it is simpler to express C13 abundance as a fraction of C12 abundance e.g. 1/89. For example land plants have a Delta of -11, which means the sample has less C13 than the standard, by 11 per thousand or 1.1 %; equivalent to C13/C12 = 1/90. Terrestial crude oil has even less C13 than the standard: a negative delta of -32; equivalent to C13/C12 = 1/92, which is the same as the C13/C12 ratio in carbonaceous chondrite meteors. In contrast, Comet West had ratio of C13/C12 = 1/50.]

[670] [The C13/C12 Ratio Series (from low-C13 to high-C13): Methane clathrate 1/95, Crude oil & meteoric carbon 1/92, Land plants 1/91, atmospheric CO_2 1/90, Limestone standard & Permian carbonate rock

1/89, start-Trassic carbonate anomaly 1/88, CI-meteoric-carbonate 1/84.]

[671] Hayes, J., and Waldbauer, J., "The Carbon Cycle and Associated Redox Processes through Time," *Philosophical Transactions of the Royal Society B: Biological Sciences* 361 (2006): 931–50.

[672] Payne J., "Large Perturbations of the Carbon Cycle during Recovery from the End-Permian Extinction," *Science* 305 (2004): 506–9.

[673] Kerridge, F., "Carbon, Hydrogen and Nitrogen in Carbonaceous Chondrites: Abundances, and Isotopic Compositions in Bulk Samples," *Geochimica et Cosmochimica Acta* 49 (1985): 1707–14.

[674] Alexander, C., et al., "The Prevenances of Asteroid, and Their Contributions to the Volatile Inventories of the Terrestrial Planets," *Science* 337 (2012): 721–23.

[675] Grady, M., et al., "The Carbon and Oxygen Isotopic Composition of Meteoritic Carbonates," *Geochimica et Cosmochimica Acta* 52 (1988): 2855–66.

[676] Lodders, K., "Solar System Abundances and Condensation Temperatures of the Elements," *The Astrophysical Journal* 591 (2003): 1220–47.

[677] Asplund, M., et al., "The Chemical Compostion of the Sun," *Annual Review of Astronomy and Astrophysics* 47 (2009): 481–522.

[678] Hand, E., "Acid Oceans Cited in the Earth's Worst Die-off," *Science* 348 (2015): 165–66.

[679] Benton, M., *When Life Nearly Died (The Greatest Mass Extinction of all Time)* (London: Thames and Hudson, 2003).

[680] Sanford, W., et al., "Evidence for High Salinity of Early Cretaceous sea Water from the Chesapeake Bay Crater," *Nature* 503 (2013): 252–56.

[681] George Howard Darwin, *The Scientific Papers of Sir George Darwin* (Cambridge: Cambridge University Press, 1907, reprinted. by Cambridge University Press, 2009), ISBN: 978-1-108-00449-7.

[682] Daly, R., *Our Mobile Earth* (New York: Scribner's, 1926).

[683] Baldwin, R., *The Face of the Moon* (Chicago, IL: University of Chicago Press, 1949).

[684] Hartmann, W., and Davis, D., "Satellite-sized Planetesimals and Lunar Origin," *Icarus* 24 (1975): 504–14, doi:10.1016/0019-1035(75)90070-6.

[685] Hartmann, W., et al., eds., *Origin of the Moon* (Houston: Lunar and Planetary Institute, Tucson Arizona, 1986).

[686] Canup, R., "Lunar-forming Impacts: Processes and Alternatives," *Philosophical Transactions of the Royal Society A* 372, no. 2024 (2014): 20130175, doi:10.1098/rsta.2013.0175.

[687] Avice, G., and Marty, B., "The Iodine–Plutonium–Xenon Age of the Moon–Earth System Revisited," *Philosophical Transactions of the Royal Society A* 372, no. 2024 (2014): 20130260, doi:10.1098/rsta.2013.0260.

[688] Ward, W., "On the Evolution of the Protolunar Disc," *Philosophical Transactions of the Royal Society A* 372, no. 2024 (2014): 20130250, doi:10.1098/rsta.2013.0250.

[689] Salmon, J., and Canup, R., "Accretion of the Moon from Non-canonical Discs," *Philosophical Transactions of the Royal Society A* 372, no. 2024 (2014): 20130256, doi:10.1098/rsta.2013.0256.

[690] Sleep, N., et al., "Terrestrial Aftermath of the Moon-forming Impact," *Philosophical Transactions of the Royal Society A* 372, no. 2024 (2014): 20130172, doi:10.1098/rsta.2013.0172.

[691] Hartmann, W., "The Giant Impact Hypothesis: Past, Present (and Future?)," *Philosophical Transactions of the Royal Society A* 372, no. 2024 (2014): 20130249, doi:10.1098/rsta.2013.0249.

[692] Stevenson, D., and Halliday, A., eds., "Discussion Meeting Issue: 'Origin of the Moon: Challenges and Prospects,'" *Philosophical Transactions of the Royal Society A* 372, no. 2024 (2014), doi:10.1098/rsta.2014.0289.

[693] Wieczorek, M., and Philips, R., "The Procellarum KREEP Terrane: Implications of Mare Volcanism and Lunar Evolution," *Journal of Geophysical Research* 105 (2000): 20417–30.

[694] Tatsumoto, M., and Rosholt, J., "Age of the Moon: An Isotopic Study of Uranium-Thorium-Lead Systematics of Lunar Samples," *Science* 167 (1970): 461–63, doi:10.1126/science.167.3918.461.

[695] Carlson, R., et al., "Rb-Sr, Sm-Nd and Lu-Hf Isotope Systematics of the Lunar Mg-Suite: The Age of the Lunar Crust and Its Relation to the Time of Moon Formation," *Philosophical Transactions of the Royal Society A* 372, no. 2024 (2014): 20130246, doi:10.1098/rsta.2013.0246.

[696] Papike, J. et al., "Lunar Samples," *Reviews in Mineralogy and Geochemistry* 36 (1998): 5.1–5.234.

[697] Cuk, M., and Steward, S., "Making the Moon from a Fast-Spinning Earth: A Giant Impact Followed by Resonant Despinning," *Science* 338 (2012): 1047–52.

[698] Canup, R., "Solar-System: An Incredible Likeness of Being" *Nature* 520 (2015): 169–70, doi:10.1038/520169a.

[699] Ringwood, A., "Terrestrial Origin of the Moon," *Nature* 322 (1986): 323–28.

[700] Zhang, J., et al., "The Proto-Earth as a Significant Source of Lunar Material," *Nature Geoscience* 5 (2012): 251–55.

[701] Young, E., et al., "Oxygen Isotopic Evidence for Vigorous Mixing during the Moon-froming Giant Impact" *Science* 351 (2016): 493–96.

[702] Drozd, R., "Krypton and Xenon in Lunar and Terrestrial Samples" (Ph.D. Thesis Washington Univ., Seattle, 1974). Category: Lunar and Planetary Exploration.

[703] Melosh, H., "New Approaches to the Moon's Isotopic Crisis," *Philosophical Transactions of the Royal Society A* 372 (2014): 20130175.

[704] Konig, S., et al., "The Earth's Tungsten Budget during Mantle Melting and Crust Formation," *Geochimica et Cosmochimica Acta* 75 (2011): 2119–36.

[705] Touboul, M., et al., "Late Formation and Prolonged Differentiation of the Moon Inferred from W isotopes in Lunar Metals," *Nature* 450 (2007): 1206–9.

[706] Touboul, M., et al., "Tungsten Isotopic Evidence for Disproportional Late Accretion to the Earth and Moon," *Nature* 520 (2015): 530–33, doi:10.1038/nature14355.

[707] Dahl, T., "Identifying Remnants of Early Earth," *Science* 352 (2016): 768.

[708] Rizo, H., et al., "Preservation of Earth-forming Events in the Tungsten Isotope Composition of Modern Flood Basalts," *Science* 352 (2016): 809.

[709] Boyet, M., and Carlson, R., "^{142}Nd Evidence for Early (>4.53 Ga) Global Differentiation of the Silicate Earth," *Science* 309 (2005): 576–81.

[710]

Element	Moon-Earth abundance ratio	Refractory(Re) or Volatile (Vo)
	(1.0 means the same)	
barium (Ba)	**6.0**	Re >1300 K
uranium (U)	**5.0**	Re >1300 K
thorium (Th)	**4.2**	Re >1300 K
titanium (Ti)	**2.0**	Re >1300 K
iridium (Ir)	1.1×10^{-1}	Re >1300 K
sulfur (S)	**4.4**	Vo 1300-600 K
gallium (Ga)	3.0×10^{-1}	Vo 1300-600 K
copper (Cu)	1.1×10^{-1}	Vo 1300-600 K
sodium (Na)	8.0×10^{-2}	Vo 1300-600 K
germanium (Ge)	6.9×10^{-2}	Vo 1300-600 K
potassium (K)	6.5×10^{-2}	Vo 1300-600 K
rubidium (Rb)	3.5×10^{-2}	Vo 1300-600 K
zinc (Zn)	8.5×10^{-3}	Vo 1300-600 K
bismuth (Bi)	11.5×10^{-3}	Vo <600 K
lead (Pb)	9.0×10^{-2}	Vo <600 K
indium (In)	3.8×10^{-2}	Vo <600 K

[711] Melosh, H., " New Approaches to the Moon's isotopic crisis," *Philosophical Transactions of the Royal Society A* 372 (2014) issue 2024: 20130175.

[712] Weiss, B., and Tikoo, S., "The Lunar Dynamo," *Science* 346 (2014): 1198.

[713] Wieczorek, M., et al., "The Crust of the Moon as Seen by GRAIL," *Science* 339 (2013): 671–75. Jolliff, B., et al., "Major Lunar Crustal Terranes: Surface Expressions and Crust-mantle Origins," *Journal of Geophysical Research* 105 (2000): 4197–216.

[714] Sedgwick, W. F., "On the Figure of the Moon," *Messenger of Mathematics* 27 (1898): 171–73.

[715] Jeffreys, H., "On the Figures of the Earth and Moon," *Geophysical Journal International* 4 (1937): 1–13.

[716] Urey, H., et al., "Note on the Internal Structure of the Moon," *Astrophysics Journal* 129 (1959): 842–48.

[717] Stevenson, D., "Origin and Implications of the Degree Two Lunar Gravity Field," *Proceedings of the Lunar and Planetary Science Conference* 32 (2001): 1175.

[718] Garrick-Bethell, I., "The Tidal-Rotational Shape of the Moon and Evidence for Polar Wander" *Nature* 512 (2014): 181–84.

[719] Konopliv, A., et al., "Improved Gravity Field of the Moon from Lunar Prospector," *Science* 281 (1998): 1476–80.

[720] Konopliv, A., et al., "Improved Gravity Field of the Moon from Lunar Prospector," *Science* 281 (1998): 1476–80.

[721] Solomon, S., "Mare Volcanism and Lunar Crustal Structure," *Proceedings of the Lunar and Planetary Science Conference* 6 (1975): 1021–42.

[722] Solomon, S., and Head, J., "Lunar Mascon Basins: Lava Filling, Tectonics, and Evolution of the Lithosphere," *Reviews of Geophysics and Space Physics* 18 (1980): 107–41.

[723] Miljkovic, K., "Asymmetric Distribution of Lunar Impact Basins Caused by Variations in Target Properties," *Science* 342 (2013): 724–26.

[724] Neumann, G., et al., "The Lunar Crust: Global Signature and Structure of Major Basins," *Journal of Geophysical Research* 101 (1996): 16,841–863.

[725] Andrews-Hanna, J., "The Origin of the Non-Mare Mascon Gravity Anomalies in Lunar Basins," *Icarus* 222 (2013): 159–68.

[726] Wiechert, U., et al., "Oxygen Isotopes and the Moon-Forming Giant Impact," *Science* 294 (2001): 345–48.

[727] Hiesinger, H., et al., "Ages of Mare Basalts on the Lunar Nearside," *Journal of Geophysical Research* 105 (2000): 29,239–275.

[728] Apollo 15 Preliminary Science Report, "Preliminary Geologic Investigation of the Apollo 15 Landing Site," *NASA* (1972): SP-289.

[729] Peeples, W., "Orbital Radar Evidence for Lunar Subsurface Layering in Maria Serenitatis and Crisium," *Journal of Geophysical Research* 83 (1978): 3459.

[730] http://www.space.com/14740-footprints-moon.html.

[731] Hapke, B., "Photometric and Other Laboratory Studies Relating to the Lunar Surface," in *The Lunar Surface Layer -Materials and Characteristics* eds. J. Salisbury and P. Glaser (New York: Academic Press, 1964), 332.

[732] Hapke, B. W., "Optical Properties of the Moon's Surface," in *The Nature of the Lunar Surface*, ed. W. Hess (Baltimore, MD: Proceedings of The 1965 International Astronomical Union – National Aeronautics and Space Administration Symposium, Johns Hopkins Press, 1965), 141.

[733] Hawkins, G. S., ed., "Meteor Orbits and Dust" (The Proceedings of a Symposium, National Aeronautics and Space Administration, Washington, D.C., Publication SP-135 and Smithsonian Institution, Cambridge, Massachusetts, Smithsonian Contribution) 10 *Astrophysics*11 (1967)

[734] News. Ainsworth, D., *Martian Moon Phobos Hip-Deep In Powder* (Pasadena, CA: Jet Propulsion Laboratory, California Institute Of Technology, NASA, 1998), http://www.jpl.nasa.gov/releases/98/mgsphobos.html.

[735] Shepard, M., *Asteroids, Relics of Ancient Time* (Cambridge: Cambridge University Press, 2015), 260.

[736] Touboul, M., et al., "Tungsten Isotopes in Ferroan Anorthosites: Implications for the Age of the Moon and Lifetime of Its Magma Ocean," *Icarus* 199 (2009): 245–49.

[737] Wood, J., et al., "Lunar Anorthosites," *Science* 167 (1970): 602–4, doi:10.1126/science.167.3918.602.

[738] Ohtake, M., "The Global Distribution of Pure Anorthosite on the Moon," *Nature* 461 (2009): 236–41, doi:10.1038/nature08317.

[739] Carlson, R., "Earth's Building Blocks," *Nature* 541 (2017): 468–70.

[740] Dauphas, N., "The Isotopic Nature of the Earth's Accreting Material through Time," *Nature* 541 (2017): 521.

[741] [The Allende Metereorite: The fall of Pueblito de Allende Stony Meteorite Shower, Chihuahua, Mexico (φ = 26°58'N, λ = 105°19'W) occurred February 8, 1969, 7h 05m GMT. A huge fireball lit up thousands of square miles of Northern Mexico and Southwestern United States. The fireball travelled from south to north and a meteorite shower spread over 50 square kilometers area. There were several impact sites; the biggest one is 60 cm across and 15 cm deep. Search and preliminary investigation of the meteorites were carried out by Dr. E. King (NASA), Drs. B. Mason and R. Clarke (Smithsonian Institution, Washington, USA). Over 100 kg of carbonaceous chondrite, type III fragments were recovered.]

[742] Markl, G., and Höhndorf, A., "Isotopic Constraints on the Origin of AMCG-suite Rocks on the Lofoten Islands, N Norway," *Minerology and Petrology* 78 (2003): 149–71.

[743] Wanvik, J. -E., "Norwegian Anorthosites and Their Industrial Uses, with Emphasis on the Massifs of the Inner Sogn-Voss Area in Western Norway," *NGU-Bulletin* 436 (2000): 103–12.

[744] Hui, H. et al., "Water in Lunar Anorthosites and Evidence for a Wet Early Moon," *Nature Geoscience* 6 (2013): 177–80, doi:10.1038/ngeo1735.

[745] Saal, A., et al., "Hydrogen Isotopes in Lunar Volcanic Glasses and Melt Inclusions Reveal a Carbonaceous Chondrite Heritage," *Science* 340 (2013): 1317–20.

[746] McCubbin, F. M., et al., "Nominally Hydrous Magmatism on the Moon," *Proceedings of the National Academy of Sciences of the United States of America* 107 (2010): 11223.

[747] Saal, A., et al., "Volatile Content of Lunar Volcanic Glasses and the Presence of Water in the Moon's Interior," *Nature* 454v (2008): 192.

[748] Hauri, E., et al., "High Pre-Eruptive Water Contents Preserved in Lunar Melt Inclusions," *Science* 333 (2011): 213–15.

[749] NASA news, "LCROSS Impact Data Indicates Water on Moon," http://www.nasa.gov/mission_pages/LCROSS/main/prelim_water_results.html.

[750] News, "Lopsided Ice Points to Moon's Polar Shift," *Science* 347 (2015): 1398.

[751] Wieczorek M., et al., "The Crust of the Moon as Seen by GRAIL," *Science*, 339, (2013): 671–75. doi:10.1126/science.1231530

[752] http://www.nasa.gov/mission_pages/grail/main/#.V7wWPpgrK5g.

[753] Besserer, J., et al., "Grail Constraints on the Vertical Density Structure of the Lunar Crust," *45th Lunar and Planetary Science Conference* (2014), https://www.hou.usra.edu/meetings/lpsc2014/pdf/2407.pdf.

[754] Andrews-Hanna, J., et al., "Structure and Evolution of the Lunar Procellarum Region as Revealed by GRAIL Gravity Data," *Nature* 514 (2014): 68–71.

[755] Gibney, E., "Moon's Largest Plain Is Not an Impact Crater," *Nature* (2014), doi:10.1038/nature.2014.16041.

[756] News; Clery, Daniel, "Impact Theory Gets Whacked," *Science* 342 (2013): 183–85.

[757] Taylor, J., andWieczorek, M., "Lunar Bulk Chemical Composition: A Post-Gravity Recovery and Interior Laboratory Reassessment," *Philosophical Transactions of the Royal Society A* 372 (2014): 20130242, doi:10.1098/rsta.2013.0242.

[758] Pahlevan, K., "Isotopes as Tracers of the Sources of the Lunar Material and Processes of Lunar Origin," *Philosophical Transactions of the Royal Society A* 372 (2014): 20130257, doi:10.1098/rsta.2013.0257.

[759] Melosh, H., "New Approaches to the Moon's Isotopic Crisis," *Philosophical Transactions of the Royal Society A* 372 (2014): 20130168, doi:10.1098/rsta.2013.0168.

[760] Walker, R., "Siderophile Element Constraints on the Origin of the Moon," *Philosophical Transactions of the Royal Society A* 372 (2014): 20130258, doi:10.1098/rsta.2013.0258.

[761] Armytage, R., et al., "Silicon Isotopes in Lunar Rocks: Implications for the Moon's Formation and the Early History of the Earth," *Geochimica et Cosmochimica Acta* 77 (2012): 504–14.

[762] Wiechert, U., et al., "Oxygen Isotopes and the Moon-Forming Giant Impact," *Science* 294 (2001): 345–48.

[763] Day, J., and Moynier, F., "Evaporative Fractionation of Volatile Stable Isotopes and Their Bearing on the Origin of the Moon," *Philosophical Transactions of the Royal Society A* 372 (2014): 20130259, doi:10.1098/rsta.2013.0259.

[764] Anand, M., et al., "Understanding the Origin and Evolution of Water in the Moon through Lunar Sample Studies," *Philosophical Transactions of the Royal Society A* 372 (2014): 20130254, doi:10.1098/rsta.2013.0254.

[765] Dauphas, N., et al., "Geochemical Arguments for an Earth-like Moon-forming Impactor," *Philosophical Transactions of the Royal Society A* 372 (2014): 20130244, doi:10.1098/rsta.2013.0244.

[766] Elliot, T., "Shadows Cast on Moon's Origin," *Nature* 504 (2013): 90–91.

[767] Elkins-Tanton, L., "Planetary Science: Occam's Origin of the Moon," *Nature Geoscience* 6 (2013): 996–98, doi:10.1038/ngeo2026.

[768] Canup, R., "Lunar Conspiracies," *Nature* 504 (2013): 27–29.

[769] Origin of the Moon: Scientific discussion meeting organised by Professor Alex Halliday FRS and Professor David Stevenson FRS, 9:00 a.m. on Monday September 23, 2013, to 5:00 p.m. on Tuesday September 24, 2013, at The Royal Society, London.

[770] Stevenson, D., and Halliday, A., "Origin of the Moon: Challenges and Prospects," *Philosophical Transactions of the Royal Society A* 372, 2024 (2014): 20140289, doi:10.1098/rsta.2014.0289.

[771] Lithgow-Bertelloni, C., and Silver, P., "Dynamic Topography, Plate Driving Forces and the African Superswell," *Nature* 395 (1998): 269–72.

[772] Gurnis, M., et al., "Constraining Mantle Density Structure Using Geological Evidence of Surface Uplift Rates: The Case of the African Superplume," *Geochemistry, Geophysics, Geosystems* 1 (2000): 1–44.

[773] The escape velocity from Earth is about 11.186 km/s (40,270 km/h; 25,020 mph) at the surface of our planet.

[774] Jacobs J., *Reversals of the Earth's Magnetic Field* (Cambridge: Cambridge University Press, 1994).

[775] Glanz, J., "Worlds around Other Stars Shake Planet Birth Theory," *Science* 276 (1997): 1336.

[776] AU means Astronomical Unit and is the average distance of Earth from the Sun = 149.6 million Kilometers.

[777] Tsiganis, K., "How the Solar-System Didn't Form," *Nature* 528 (2015): 202–3.

[778] Jakubik, M., et al., "Considerations on the Accretion of Uranus and Neptune by Mutual Collisions of Planetary Embryos in the Vicinity of Jupiter and Saturn," (2012) arXiv:1107.2235v2 [astro-ph.EP], doi:10.1051/0004-6361/201117687.

[779] Izidoro, A., et al., "Terrestrial Planet Formation Constrained by Mars and the Structure of the Asteroid Belt," *Monthly Notices of the Royal Astronomical Society* 453 (2015): 3619–34.

[780] Dormand, J. R. and Woolfson, M., *The Origin of the Solar-system, the Capture Theory* (Chichester: Ellis Horwood Ltd., 1989).

[781] Boss, A., "Companions to Young Stars," *Scientific American* October (1995): 38–43.

[782] Duquennoy, A., and Mayor, M., "Multiplicity among Solar-Type Stars in the Solar Neighborhood. II - Distribution of the Orbital Elements in an Unbiased Sample,"*Astronomy and Astrophysics* 248 (1991): 485–524. ISSN 0004-6361.

[783] Seeds, M., "Binary Stars," Chapter 10, part of *Foundations of Astronomy* (Belmont, CA: Wadsworth, 1997).

[784] Henbest, N., and Couper, H., *The Guide to the Galaxy* (Cambridge: Cambridge University Press, 1994).

[785] Burrows, A., "Colloquium: Perspectives on Core-Collapse Supernova Theory," *Reviews of Modern Physics* 85 (2013): 245–61.

[786] Joss, P., "Type II Supernovae in Binary Systems in 'Compact Stars in Binaries,'" *Proceedings from I AU symposium 165* (August 15–19, 1994): 141. Bibliographic Code: 1996 I AUS.Vol165.p141J.

[787] Van de Kamp, P., *Dark Companions of Stars* (Dordrecht & Boston, MA: D Reidel Publishing Company), ISBN: 978-94-010-8586-1 [Reprinted from *Space Science Reviews*, 43 (1986)].

[788] Moriya, T., "Revealing the Binary Origin of Type Ic Superluminous Supernovae Through Nebular Hydrogen Emission," *Astronomy & Astrophysics* 584 (2015): L5. http://dx.doi.org/10.1051/0004-6361/201527515.

[789] Hoyle, F., *The Nature of the Universe* (Oxford: Blackwell, 1950).

[790] Burrows, A., "Supernova Explosions in the Universe," *Nature* 403 (2000): 727–33, doi:10.1038/35001501.

[791] Laming, J., "Lopsided Stellar Death," *Nature* 506 (2014): 298–99.

[792] Henbest, N., and Couper, H., *The Guide to the Galaxy* (Cambridge: Cambridge University Press, 1994), ISBN: 0 521 30622 1.

[793] Kuntz, K., and Snowden, S., "Deconstructing the Spectrum of the Soft X-Ray Background," *The Astrophysical Journal* 543 (2000): 195–215.

[794] Breitschwerdt, D., et al., "The Local-Bubble: Origin and Evolution," *Space Science Reviews* 78 (1996): 183–98.

[795] Galeazzi, M., et al., "The Origin of the Local 1/4-keV X-ray Flux in Both Charge Exchange and a Hot Bubble," *Nature* 512 (2014): 171, doi:10.1038/nature13525.

[796] Maiz-Apellaniz, J., "The Origin of the Local-Bubble," *The Astrophysical Journal* 560 (2001): L83–L86. arXiv:astro-ph/0108472v1 August 29, 2001.

[797] Frisch, P., "The Local-Bubble, Local Fluff and Heliosphere," *Lecture Notes in Physics* 506 (1998): 269–78.

[798] Cox, D., and Anderson, P., "Extended Adiabatic Blast Waves and a Model of the Soft X-ray Back Ground," *The Astrophysical Journal* 253 (1982): 268–89.

[799] Barstow, M., et al., "Oxygen O^{VI} in the Local Interstellar Medium," *The Astrophysical Journal* 723 (2010): 935–49.

[800] Kuntz, K., and Snowden, S., "Deconstructing the Spectrum of the Soft X-Ray Background," *The Astrophysical Journal* 543, no. 195 (2000): E215.

[801] Henbest, N., and Couper, H., *The Guide to the Galaxy* (Cambridge: Cambridge University Press, 1994).

[802] Puspitarini, L. et al., "Local ISM 3D Distribution and Soft X-ray Background: Inferences on Nearby Hot Gas and the North Polar Spur," *Astronomy & Astrophysics* 566 (2014): Article A13 12 pages, doi:10.1051/0004-6361/201322942.

[803] Welsh, B., et al., "The Local Distribution of Na I Interstellar Gas," *The Astrophysical Journal* 437 (1994): 638–57.

[804] Lallement, R., et al., "3D Mapping of the Dense Interstellar Gas Around the Local-Bubble," *Astronomy & Astrophysics* 411 (2003): 447–64.

[805] New observation satellites such as EUVE, ORFEUS-SPAS, CHIPS, ROSAT, CHANDRA, and SUZAKU have been producing high-resolution UV-absorption spectroscopy with HST-GHRS, HSTSTIS, HST-COS, IMAPS and FUSE.

[806] Welsh, B., et al., "Detection of Highly Ionized Carbon C^{IV} Gas Within the Local Cavity," *The Astrophysical Journal Letters* 712 (2010): L199–L202, doi:10.1088/2041-8205/712/2/L199.

[807] Barstow, M., et al., "Oxygen O^{VI} in the Local Interstellar Medium," *The Astrophysical Journal* 723 (2010); 935–49. doi:10.1088/0004-637X/723/2/1762

[808] Breitschwerdt, D., et al., "The Local-Bubble: Origin and Evolution," *Space Science Reviews* 78 (1996): 183–98.

[809] Puspitarini, L., et al., "Local ISM 3D Distribution and Soft X-ray Background; Inferences for Nearby Hot Gas," *Astronomy & Astrophysics*, manuscript no. inversionextinctionvsxray_oct29 c ESO 2013. October 29, 2013.

[810] Farhang, A., et al., "Probing the Local Bubble with Diffuse Interstellar Bands. (II). The DIB Properties in the Northern Hemisphere," *The Astrophysical Journal* 800 (2015): 64–80, doi:10.1088/0004-637X/800/1/64.

[811] Vergely, J., et al., "Spatial Distribution of Interstellar Dust in the Sun's Vicinity: Comparison with Neutral Sodium-Bearing Gas," *Astronomy & Astrophysics* 518 (2010): A31, doi:10.1051/0004-6361/200913962.

[812] Welsh, B., et al., "EUV Mapping of the Local Interstellar Medium: The Local Chimney Revealed," *Astronomy & Astrophysics* 352 (1999): 308–16.

[813] Crawford, I., et al., "High Resolution Observations of Interstellar Na I and Ca II Towards the Southern Opening of the Local Insterstellar Chimney: Probing the Disc-halo Connection," *Monthly Notices of the Royal Astronomical Society* 337 (2002): 720–30.

[814] Welsh, B., "The Interstellar Tunnel of Neutral-Free Gas Towards β Canis Majoris," *The Astrophysical Journal* 373 (1991): 556–59.

[815] The precise direction of the Tunnel is located between the angular position to Mirzam (Beta Canis Major) at galactic longitude l=226° and the bright local star Sirius (Alpha Canis Majoris) at galactic longitude l=227°.

[816] Lallement, R., et al., "3D Mapping of the Dense Interstellar Gas Around the Local-Bubble," *Astronomy and Astrophysics* 411 (2003): 447–464, doi:10.1051/0004-6361:20031214, See fig 4, p. 452.

[817] Frisch, P., et al., "Dust in the Local Interstellar Wind," *Astrophysics Journal* 525 (1999): 492, doi:10.1086/307869.

[818] Altobelli, N., "Flux and Composition of Interstellar Dust at Saturn from Cassini's Cosmic Dust Analyzer," *Science* 352 (2016): 312–18.

[819] Lallement, R., "3D Maps of the Local Interstellar Medium; Searching for the Imprints of Past Events, 13th Annual International Astrophysics Conference: Voyager, IBEX, and the Interstellar Medium," IOP Publishing, *Journal of Physics: Conference Series* 577 (2015): 012016.

[820] Maiz-Apellaniz, J., "The Origin of the Local-Bubble," *The Astrophysical Journal* 560 (2001): L83–L86.

[821] Cox, D., and Helenius, L., "Flux-tube Dynamics and a Model for the Origin of the Local Fluff," *The Astronomy Journal* 583 (2003): 205–28.

822 Fuchs, B., et al., "The Search for the Origin of the Local-Bubble," *Monthly Notices of the Royal Astronomical Society* 373 (2006): 993–1003.

823 Benitez, N., et al., "Evidence for Nearby Supernova Explosions," *Physical Review Letters* 88 (2002): 081101, 1–4.

824 https://jantoniadis.wordpress.com/research/ns-masses/.

825 Crawford, I., et al., "High Resolution Observations of Interstellar Na I and Ca II Towards the Southern Opening of the Local Insterstellar Chimney: Probing the Disc-halo Connection," *Monthly Notices of the Royal Astronomical Society* 337 (2002): 720–30.

826 Welsh, B., et al., "EUV Mapping of the Local Interstellar Medium: The Local Chimney Revealed," *Astronomy & Astrophysics* 352 (1999): 308–16.

827 Frisch, P., "The Local-Bubble, Local Fluff and Heliosphere," *LNP* 506 (1998): 269–78.

828 Lallement, R., et al., "3D Mapping of the Dense Interstellar Gas around the Local-Bubble," *Astronomy and Astrophysics* 411 (2003): 447–64. doi:10.1051/0004-6361:20031214.

829 Cox, D., and Helenius, L., "Flux-tube Dynamics and a Model for the Origin of the Local Fluff," *The Astronomy Journal* 583 (2003): 205–28.

830 Santos, F., "Optical Polarization Mapping toward the Interface between the Local Cavity and Loop I," *The Astrophysical Journal* 728 (2010): 104. Xiv:1012.3394v1 [astro-ph.GA] December 15, 2010.

831 Frisch, P. C., and Slavin, J., "Interstellar Dust Close to the Sun," *Earth Planets Space* 65 (2013): 175–82.

[832] Bizzarro, M., "Probing the Solar-System's Prenatal History," *Science* 345 (2014): 620–21.

[833] Lugaro, M., et al., "Stellar Origin of the 182Hf Cosmochronometre and the Presolar History of the Solar-System Matter," *Science* 345 (2014): 650–53.

[834] Hester, J., et al., "The Cradle of the Solar-System," *Science* 304 (2004): 1116–17.

[835] Desai, K., et al., "Supernova Remnants and Star Formation in the Large Magellanic Cloud," 2010, arXiv:1006.3344v1 [astro-ph.GA].

[836] [ISOTOPES: All isotopes of an element, all have the same number of protons but they have different numbers of neutrons. Isotopes are identified by the name of the element and its mass number (= number of protons plus the number of neutrons in its atomic nucleus). Some isotopes are unstable and radioactive: they decay into more stable isotopes, usually of a different element. The more unstable an isotope, the shorter its 'half-life': the average time required for half of the amount of the isotope in a material to decay (By definition, during the half-life of a radioactive isotope, the probability of any atom decaying is fifty-percent).]

[837] Webster, C., et al., "Measuring Isotope Ratios Across Thesolar-System," *International Workshop on Instrumentation for Planetary Missions* (2012), https://ssed.gsfc.nasa.gov/IPM/IPM2012/PDF/Revised_Orals/Webster-1030.pdf.

[838] Wallerstein, G., et al., "Synthesis of the Elements," *Reviews of Modern Physics* 69 (1997): 995–1084.

[839] Marty, Bernard, Alexander, Conel M. O'D., and Raymond, Sean N., "Primordial Origins of Earth's Carbon," in *Reviews in Mineralogy and*

Geochemistry Volume on Carbon on Earth (2012), arXiv:1211.2814v1 [astro-ph.EP].

[840] Pignatari, M., et al., "Carbon-rich Presolar Grains from Massive Stars: Subsolar 12C/13C and 14N/15N Ratios and the Mystery of 15N," arXiv:1506.09056v1 [astro-ph.SR] 2015.

[841] Wimmer-Schweingruber, R., "13C/12C Isotopic Ratio in the Solar Wind," *45th Lunar and Planetary Science Conference* (2014), https://www.hou.usra.edu/meetings/lpsc2014/pdf/1114.pdf.

[842] Meyer, B., et al., "Nucleosynthesis and Chemical Evolution of Oxygen," doi:10.2138/rmg.2008.68.4; http://nucleo.ces.clemson.edu/home/publications/preprints/data/Meyer_et_al_RIMG.pdf.

[843] Franchi, I., et al., "The Oxygen-isotopic Composition of Earth and Mars," *Meteorics & Planetary Science* 34 (1999): 657–61.

[844] p://www.lanl.gov/science/1663/january2012/story7full.shtml.

[845] McKeegan, A., et al., "The Oxygen Isotopic Composition of the Sun Inferred from Captured Solar Wind," *Science* 332 (2011): 1528–32, doi:10.1126/science.1204636.

[846] Hand, E., "The Solar-system's First Breath," *Nature* 452 (2008): 259. Bibcode:2008Natur.452.259H; doi:10.1038/452259a; PMID 18354437.

[847] Meyer, B., et al., "Presolar Silicon Carbide X Grains, Explosive Hydrogen Burning, and the Evolution of Massive Stars," *Abstact 5457 of 74th Annual Meteoritical Society Meeting* (2011), regarding the origin of the isotopic abundance of Nitrogen-15.

[848] Marks, P., and Sarna, M., "The Chemical Evolution of the Secondary Stars in Close Binaries, Arising from Common-Envelope Evolution

and Nova Outbursts," *Monthly Notices of the Royal Astronomical Society* 301 (1998): 699–720.

[849] Nittler, L., "New Presolar Silicon Carbide Grains with Nova Isotope Signatures," *Lunar and Planetary Science* 35 (2004): 1598.

[850] Arnett, W., "Type I supernovae. I - Analytic Solutions for the Early Part of the Light Curve," *The Astrophysical Journal* 253 (1982): 785–97.

[851] Arnould, M., and Goriely, S., "The p-process of Stellar Nucleosynthesis: Astrophysics and Nuclear Physics Status," *Physics Reports* 384 (2003): 1–84.

[852] Marhas, K., et al., "Short-lived Nuclides in Hibonite Grains from Murchison: Evidence for Solar-System Evolution," *Science* 298 (2002): 2182–85.

[853] Yin, Q-Z., et al., "Diverse Supernova Sources of Pre-solar Material Inferred from Molybdenum Isotopes in Meteorites," *Nature* 415 (2002): 881.

[854] Meynet, G., and Maeder, A., "The origin of Primary Nitrogen in Galaxies," *Astronomy & Astrophysics* 381 (2002): L25–L28, doi:10.1051/0004-6361:20011554.

[855] Meyer, B., et al., "Presolar Silicon Carbide X grains, Explosive Hydrogen Burning, and the Evolution of Massive Stars." *Abstact 5457 of 74th Annual Meteoritical Society Meeting* (2011)

[856] Pignatari, M., et al., "Carbon-Rich Presolar Grains from Massive Stars. Subsolar 12C/13C and 14N/15N ratios and the mystery of 15N," (2015), arXiv.org > astro-ph > arXiv:1506.09056.

[857] [Venus, Earth and Mars have approximately the same N15/N14 ratio, around 3.7×10^{-3}. In contrast, the Genesis Solar Wind Concentrator target material shows that implanted solar wind nitrogen has a 15N/14N ratio of 2.2×10^{-3} (the Sun is approximately 40% poorer in 15N, relative to Venus, Earth and Mars).]

[858] Owen, T., et al., "Protosolar Nitrogen." *The Astrophysical Journal* 553 (2001): L77–L79. [15N/14N ratio in Jupiter's atmosphere is 2.3×10^{-3}. In constrast, the solar wind 15N/14N ratio is 2.2×10^{-3}].

[859] Marty, B., et al., "A 15N-Poor Isotopic Composition for Thesolar-System as Shown by Genesis Solar Wind Samples," *Science* 332 (2011): 1533–36, doi:10.1126/science.1204656.

[860] Huss, G., "The Isotopic Composition and Fluence of Solar-Wind Nitrogen in a Genesis B/C Array Collector," *Meteoritics & Planetary Science* 47 (2012): 1436–48, doi:10.1111/j.1945-5100.2012.01406.x.

[861] Pignatari, M. et al., "Carbon-Rich Presolar Grains from Massive Stars: subsolar 12C/ 13C and 14N/15N ratios and the mystery of 15N," arXiv:1506.09056v1 [astro-ph.SR] 30 Jun 2015

[862] Brownlee, D., et al., "Comet 81P/Wild 2 Under a Microscope," *Science* 314 (2006): 1711–16.

[863] Messenger, S., et al., "Supernova Olivine from Cometary Dust," *Science* 309 (2005): 737–41.

[864] Floss, C., "Anomalous Nitrogen Isotopic Compositions in the Stardust-Rich Antarctic Micrometeorite T98G8: Affinities To Primitive Cr Chondrites And Anhydrous IDPs," *40th Lunar and Planetary Science Conference* (2009), http://www.lpi.usra.edu/meetings/lpsc2009/pdf/1082.pdf.

[865] Pizzarello, S., and Holmes, W., "Nitrogen-Containing Compounds in two CR2 Meteorites: 15N Composition, Molecular Distribution and Precursor Molecules," *Geochimica et Cosmochimica Acta* 73 (2009): 2150–62.

[866] Severinghaus, J., et al., "Timing of Abrupt Climate Change at the End of the Younger Dryas Interval from Thermally Fractionated Gases in Polar Ice," *Nature* 391 (1998): 141–46. See Figure 2 on p. 142.

[867] Kobashi, T., et al., "Argon and Nitrogen Isotopes of Trapped Air in the GISP2 Ice-Core during the Holocene Epoch (0–11,500 B.P.): Methodology and Implications for Gas Loss Processes," *Geochimica et Cosmochimica Acta* 72 (2008): 4675–86.

[868] Praetorius, S., et al., "North Pacific Deglacial Hypoxic Events Linked to Abrupt Ocean Warming," *Nature* 527 (2015): 362–66.

[869] Eldridge, J., "Windy Stars That Go with a Bang," *Nature* 509 (2014): 431–32.

[870] Ohnaka, K., and Tsuji, T., "Quantitative Analysis of Carbon Isotopic Ratios in Carbon Stars. I. 62 N-Type and 15 SC-Type Carbon Stars," *Astronomy and Astrophysics* 310 (1996): 933–51.

[871] Arnett, D., and Bazan, G., "Nucleosynthesis in Stars: Recent Developments," *Science* 276 (1997): 1359–62.

[872] Nittler, L., "Presolar Stardust in Meteorites: Recent Advances and Scientific Frontiers," *Earth and Planetary Science Letters* 209 (2003): 259–73.

[873] Zinner, E., "An Isotopic View of the Early Solar-System," *Science* 300 (2003): 265–67.

[874] Janka, H., "Explosion Mechanisms of Core-Collapse Supernovae," *Annual Review of Nuclear and Particle Science* 62 (2012): 407–51.

[875] Hungerford, A., et al., "Gamma-Ray Lines from Asymmetric Supernovae," *The Astrophysical Journal* 594 (2003): 390–403.

[876] Blodin, J., et al., "Stability of Standing Accretion Shocks, with an Eye toward Core-Collapse Supernovae," *The Astrophysical Journal* 584 (2003): 971–80.

[877] Fryer, C., and Heger, A., "Core-Collapse Simulations of Rotating Stars," *The Astrophysical Journal* 541 (2000): 1033–50.

[878] Laming, J., "Astrophysics: Lopsided Stellar Death," *Nature* 506 (2014): 298–99, doi:10.1038/506298 [a spatial asymmetry is key to explaining the supernova explosion].

[879] Boggs, S., et al., "^{44}Ti Gamma-Ray Emission Lines from SN1987A Reveal an Asymmetric Explosion," *Science* 348 (2015): 670–71.

[880] Grefenstette, B., et al., "Asymmetries in Core-Collapse Supernovae from Maps of Radioactive 44Ti in Cassiopeia A," *Nature* 506 (2014): 339–42, doi:10.1038/nature12997.

[881] Ryle, M., and Smith, F., "A New Intense Source of Radio-Frequency Radiation in the Constellation of Cassiopeia," *Nature* 162 (1948): 462–63, doi:10.1038/162462a0.

[882] Milisavljevic, D., and Fesen, R., "The Bubble-Like Interior of the Core-Collapse Supernova Remnant Cassiopeia A," *Science* 347 (2015): 526–30.

[883] Kawka, A., "LP 400-22, a Very Low Mass and High-Velocity White Dwarf," *The Astrophysical Journal Letters* 643 (2006): L123–L126.

[884] Rest, A., et al., "On the Interpretation of Supernova Light Echo Profiles and Spectra," *The Astrophysical Journal* 732 (2011): 1–17, doi:10.1088/0004-637X/732/1/2.

[885] Li, H., et al., "Self-Similar Fragmentation Regulated by Magnetic Fields in a Region Forming Massive Stars," *Nature* 520 (2015): 518–21, doi:10.1038/nature14291.

[886] Stello, D., et al., "A Prevalence Of Dynamo-Generated Magnetic Fields in the Cores of Intermediate-Mass Stars," *Nature* 529 (2016): 364–67, doi:10.1038/nature16171.

[887] Fuller, J., "Asteroseismology Can Reveal Strong Internal Magnetic Fields in Red Giant Stars," *Science* 350 (2015): 423–26.

[888] *News* "Magnetic Energy of Supernova," *Nature* 498 (2013): 274.

[889] Khokhlov, A., et al. "Jet-induced Explosions of Core Collapse Supernovae," *The Astrophysical Journal Letters* 524 (1999): L107–L110.

[890] Janka, H. -T., "Explosion Mechanisms of Core-Collapse Supernovae," *Annual Review of Nuclear and Particle Science* 62 (2012): 407–51, doi:10.1146/annurev-nucl-102711-094901.

[891] Kasen, D., and Bildsten, L., "Supernova Light Curves Powered by Young Magnetars," *The Astrophysical Journal* 717 (2010): 245–49.

[892] Mauerhan, J., et al., "The Unprecedented 2012 Outburst of SN 2009ip: A Luminous Blue Variable Star Becomes a True Supernova," *Monthly Notices of the Royal Astronomical Society* 430 (2013): 1801–10.

[893] Witz, A., "Binary Star to Spill Celestial Secrets," *Nature* 512 (2014): 13–14.

[894] Lugmair G., and Shukolyukov, A., "Early Solar-System Events and Timescales," *Meteoritics & Planetary Science* 36 (2001): 1017–26.

[895] Gilmour, D., "The Extinct Radionuclide Timescale of the Early Solar-System," *Space Science Reviews* 92 (2000): 123–32.

[896] Lugmair, G., and Shukolyukov, A., "Early Solar-System Timescales According to 53Mn-53Cr Systematics," *Geochimica et Cosmochimica Acta* 62 (1998): 2863–86.

[897] Wasserburg, G., et al., "Abundances of Actinides and Short-Lived Non-Actinides in the Interstellar Medium: Diverse Supernova Sources for the r-Processes" *The Astrophysical Journal* 466 (1996): L109–L113.

[898] Mostefaoui, S., et al., "^{60}Fe: A Heat Source for Planetary Differentiation from a Nearby Supernova Explosion," *The Astrophysical Journal* 625 (2005): 271–77.

[899] Dauphas, N., et al., "Iron 60 Evidence for Early Injection and Efficient Mixing of Stellar Debris in the Protosolar Nebula," *The Astrophysical Journal*, 686 (2008): 560–569, doi:10.1086/589959.

[900] Tachibana, S., et al., "Iron-60 in Pyroxene-Rich Ferromagnesian Chondrules," *The Astrophysical Journal* 639 (2006): 87–90.

[901] The 75th Annual Meeting of the Meteoritical Society Cairns, Australia, August 12–17, 2012. *Meteoritics & Planetary Science* 47 (2012): A2–A34, doi:10.1111/j.1945-5100.2012.01401.x.

[902] Tachibana, S., and Huss, G., "The Initial Abundance of 60Fe in Thesolar-System," *The Astrophysical Journal* 588 (2003): L41.

[903] Wasserburg, G. et al.,"Test of the Supernova Trigger Hypothesis with ^{60}Fe and ^{26}Al," *The Astrophysical Journal* 500 (1998): L189–L193A.

[904] Boss, A., and Keiser, S., "Who Pulled the Trigger: A Supernova or an AGB Star?" *The Astrophysical Journal Letters* 717 (2010): L1–L5, doi:10.1088/2041-8205/717/1/L1.

[905] McCorkell, R., et al., "Radioactive Isotopes in Hoba West and Other Iron Meteorites," *Meteoritics* 4 (1968): 113–22.

[906] Glanz, J., "How the Hectic Young Sun Cooked Up Stony Meteorites," *Science* 276 (1997): 1789–90, doi:10.1126/science.276.5320.1789.

[907] Guan, Y., et al., "SIMS Analyses of Mg, Cr, and Ni Isotopes in Primitive Meteorites and Short-Lived Radionuclides in the Early Solar-System," *Applied Surface Science* 231/232 (2004): 899–902.

[908] Eriksson, P., et al., eds., "The Precambrian Earth: Tempos and Events," *Developments in Precambrian Geology* 12 (2004) (Amsterdam, Netherlands: Elsevier BV, 2004): 1–20.

[909] Cameron, A., et al., *Astrophysical Implications of the Laboratory Study of Presolar Materials*, eds. Bernatowicz, T. and Zinner, E. (New York: AIP, 1997), 665.

[910] Breitschwerdt, D., et al., "The Locations of Recent Supernovae Near the Sun from Modelling 60Fe Transport," *Nature* 532 (2016): 73–76, doi:10.1038/nature17424.

[911] Wallner, A., et al., "Recent near-Earth Supernovae Probed by Global Deposition of Interstellar Radioactive 60Fe," *Nature* 532 (2016): 69–72, doi:10.1038/nature17196.

[912] Melott, A., "Supernovae in the Neighborhood," *Nature* 532 (2016): 40–41.

[913] Papanastassiou, D., and Wasserburg, G., "Strontium Isotopic Anomalies in the Allende Meteorite," *Geophysical Research Letters* 5 (1978): 595–98, doi:10.1029/GL005i007p00595.

[914] McCulloch, M., and Wasserburg, G., "Barium and Neodynium Isotopic Anomalies in the Allende Meteorite," *The Astrophysical Journal* 220 (1978): L15–L19.

[915] Goswami, J., "Short-lived Nuclides in the Early Solar-System: The Stellar Connection," *New Astronomy Reviews* 48 (2004): 125–32.

[916] Tuniz, C. et al., "Beryllium-10 Contents of Core Samples from the St. Severin Meteorite," *Geochimica et Cosmochimica Acta* 48 (1984): 1867–72.

[917] Hevey, P., and Sanders, I., "A model for Planetesimal Meltdown by ^{26}Al and Its Implications for Meteorite Parent Bodies," *Meteoritics & Planetary Science* 41 (2006): 95–106.

[918] Barucci, M., et al., *The Solar-System Beyond Neptune* (Tucson, AZ: University of Arizona Press, 2008).

[919] Gounelle, M., and Meynet, G., "Solar System Genealogy Revealed by Extinct Short-Lived Radionuclides in Meteorites," *Astronomy & Astrophysics* 545 (2012): A4, doi:10.1051/0004-6361/201219031.

[920] Lee, T., et al., "Aluminum-26 in the Early Solar-System – Fossil or Fuel," *The Astrophysical Journal* 211 (1977): L107–L110.

[921] Bouvier, A., and Wadhwa, M., "The Age of Thesolar-System Redefined by the Oldest Pb-Pb Age of a Meteoritic Inclusion,"

Nature Geoscience 3 (2010): 637–641, doi:10.1038/NGEO941. [Ca-Al inclusions are 4568.22 ± 0.17 Mya old].

[922] Zinner, E., and Göpel, C., "Aluminum-26 in H4 Chondrites: Implications for Its Production and Its Usefulness as a Fine-Scale Chronometer for Early-Solar-System Events," *Meteoritics and Planetary Science* 37 (2002): 1001–13.

[923] Kuroda, P., and Myers, W., "Variation of the Isotopic Composition of Xenon in the Solar-System," *Journal of Radioanalytical and Nuclear Chemistry* 247 (2001): 249–83.

[924] Nittler, L., "Presolar Stardust in Meteorites: Recent Advances and Scientific Frontiers," *Earth and Planetary Science Letters* 209 (2003): 259–27.

[925] Haenecour, P., et al., "First Laboratory Observation of Silica Grains from Core Collapse Supernovae," *The Astrophysical Journal Letters* 768 (2013): L17 (5pp.), doi:10.1088/2041-8205/768/1/L17.

[926] Gilmour, J., "The Solar-System's First Clocks," *Science* 297 (2002): 1658–59.

[927] Taylor, G., "A New Type of Stardust," *Planetary Science Research Discoveries* (2003), http://www.psrd.hawaii.edu/Aug03/stardust.html.

[928] Taylor, G., "Silicate Stardust in Meteorites," *Planetary Science Research Discoveries* (2004), http://www.psrd.hawaii.edu/June04/silicatesMeteorites.html.

[929] Nittler, R., et al., "Silicon Nitride from Supernovae," *The Astrophysical Journal* 453 (2009): L25, doi:10.1086/309743.

[930] Arnett, D., and Grant Bazan, G., "Nucleosynthesis in Stars: Recent Developments," *Science* 276 (1997): 1359–62, doi:10.1126/science.276.5317.1359.

[931] Beatty, J., "Homegrown Diamond Dust?," *Sky & Telescope* 104 (2002): 25 [origin of nanodiamonds in the nebula that surrounded the infant Sun and planets].

[932] McKeegan K., et al., "Isotopic Compositions of Cometary Matter Returned by 'Stardust' " *Science* 314 (2006): 1724–28, doi:10.1126/science.1135992.

[933] Kuroda, P., and Myers, W.,"Variation of the Isotopic Composition of Xenon in the Solar-System," *Journal of Radioanalytical and Nuclear Chemistry* 247 (2001): 249–83.

[934] Brownlee, D., et al., "Comet 81P/Wild 2 Under a Microscope," *Science* 314 (2006): 1711–16.

[935] Cameron, A., and Truran, J., "The Supernova Trigger for Formation of the Solar-System," *Icarus* 30 (1977): 447–61.

[936] Hoppe, P., et al., "Type II Supernova Matter in a Silicon Carbide Grain from the Murchison Meteorite," *Science* 272 (1996): 1314–16.

[937] Clayton, D., "Moving Stars and Shifting Sands of Presolar History," *Planetary Science Research Discoveries* (1997), http://www.psrd.hawaii.edu/July97/Stardust.html.

[938] Martel, L., and Taylor, G., "Ion Microprobe," *Planetary Science Research Discoveries* (2006), http://www.psrd.hawaii.edu/Feb06/PSRD-ion_microprobe.html.

[939] Nittler, L., "Presolar Stardust in Meteorites: Recent Advances and Scientific Frontiers," *Earth and Planetary Science Letters* 209 (2003): 259–73.

[940] Fu, R., et al., "Solar Nebula Magnetic Fileds Recorded in the Semarkona Meteorite," *Science* 346 (2014): 1089.

[941] Glanz, J., "How the Hectic Young Sun Cooked Up Stony Meteorites," *Science* 276 (1997): 1789.

[942] "The Night Sky Really Was Studded with Diamonds," *New Scientist* 11/5 (2002):12–13.

[943] Becker, L., et al., "Fullerenes: An Extraterrestrial Carbon Carrier Phase for Noble Gases," *Proceedings of the National Academy of Sciences of the United States of America* 97 (2000): 2979–83.

[944] Huss, G., "Ubiquitous Interstellar Diamond and SiC in Primitive Chondrites: Abundances Reflect Metamorphism," *Nature* 347 (1990): 159–62.

[945] Clayton D., et al., "Carbon and Nitrogen Isotopes in Type-II Supernova Diamonds," *The Astrophysical Journal* 447 (1995): 894–905.

[946] [By calculating the relative-molar-abundance (the relative number of atoms), the top-ten elements in the Sun are: Hydrogen 91.2%, Helium 8.7%, Oxygen 0.09%, Carbon 0.04%, Iron 0.03%, Sulfur 0.01%, Nitrogen 0.009%, Silicon 0.004%, Magnesium 0.004% and Neon 0.003%. However, about thirty percent of the elements found on Earth have never been identified in the sprectum of the Sun.]

[947] Wang, H., "Lifetime of the Solar Nebula Constrained by Meteorite Paleomagnetism," *Science* 355 (2017): 623–27.

[948] Dietz, R. S., "Sudbury Structure as an Astrobleme," *The Journal of Geology* 72 (1964): 412–34.

[949] Montmerle, T., et al., "Solar System Formation and Early Evolution: The First 100 Million Years," *Earth, Moon, and Planets* 98 (2006): 299–312.

[950] Holland, G., et al., "Deep Fracture Fluids Isolated in the Crust since the Precambrian Era," *Nature* 497 (2013): 357.

[951] Kuroda, P., and Myers, W.,"Variation of the Isotopic Composition of Xenon in the Solar-System," *Journal of Radioanalytical and Nuclear Chemistry* 247 (2001): 249–83.

[952] Morbidelli, A., et al., "Building Terrestrial Planets," *Annual Review of Earth and Planetary Sciences* 40 (2012): 251–75A.

[953] Alexander, C., et al. "The Provenances of Asteroids, and Their Contributions to the Volatile Inventories of the Terrestrial Planets," *Science* 337 (2012): 721–23.

[954] Simonson, B., and Glass, B., "Spherule Layers—Records of Ancient Impacts," *Annual Review of Earth and Planetary Sciences* 32 (2004): 329–61, doi:10.1146/annurev.earth.32.101802.120458.

[955] "Formation of Earth," *Our Planet*, The Collection-New Scientist 2, no. 4 (2015): 7–9, ISSN 2054-6386.

[956] Lugmair, G., "Earlysolar-system Timescales According to 53Mn-53Cr Systematics," *Geochimica Et Cosmochimica Acta* 62 (1998): 2863–86, doi:10.1016/S0016-7037(98)00189-6.

[957] Shen, J., et al., "Chromium Isotope Signature during Continental Crust Subduction Recorded in Metamorphic Rocks," *Geochemistry Geophysics Geosystems* 16 (2015): 3840–54, doi:10.1002/2015GC005944.

[958] Messenger, S., et al., "Supernova Olivine from Cometary Dust," *Science* 309 (2005): 737–41.

[959] Zimmer, C., "The Oldest Rocks on Earth," *Scientific American* March (2014): 43–47.

[960] Elliot, T., "Speed Metal," *Science* 344 (2014): 1086–87.

[961] Heger, A., et al., "Nucleosynthesis of Heavy Elements in Massive Stars," *Nuclear Physics A* 718 (2003): 159–66.

[962] Heger, A., et al., "Massive Star Evolution: Nucleosynthesis and Nuclear Reaction Rate Uncertainties," *New Astronomy Reviews* 46 (2002): 463–68.

[963] Linsky, J., et al., "What Is the Total Deuterium Abundance in the Local Galactic Disk?," *The Astrophysical Journal* 647 (2006): 1106–24.

[964] Kinman, T. D., "An Attempt to Detect Deuterium in the Solar Atmosphere," *Monthly Notices of the Royal Astronomical Society*," 116 (1956): 77.

[965] Scherb, F., "The Abundance of Deuterium and He3 in the Solar Wind" (2009), arXiv:0909.1279 [astro-ph.IM].

[966] Brownlee, D., et al., "Comet 81P/Wild 2 under a Microscope," *Science* 314 (2006): 1711–16.

[967] Alexander, C., "The Provenances of Asteroids, and Their Contributions to the Volatile Inventories of the Terrestrial Planets," *Science* 337 (2012): 721–23, doi:10.1126/science.1223474.

[968] Robert, F., "The D/H Ratio in Chondrites," *Space Science Reviews* 106 (2003): 87–101.

[969] Altwegg, K., et al., "67P/Churyumov-Gerasimenko, a Jupiter Family Comet with a High D/H Ratio," *Science* 347 (2015), doi:10.1126/science.1261952.
[The D/H ratio for 67P/Churyumov-Gerasimenko was (5.3 ± 0.7) × 10–4]

[970] Niemann, H., et al., "The Galileo Probe Mass Spectrometer: Composition of Jupiter's Atmosphere," *Science* 272 (1996): 846–49.
[The measured ratio of deuterium to hydrogen (D/H) = (5 +/- 2) × 10(-5)
The measured the 3He/4He ratio of (1.1 +/- 0.2) × 10(-4)].

[971] Lellouch, E., et al., "The Deuterium Abundance in Jupiter and Saturn from ISO-SWS Observations," *Astronomy & Astrophysics* 670 (2001): 610–22, doi:10.1051/0004-6361:20010259.
[Observations with the Short Wavelength Spectrometer (SWS) onboard the Infrared Space Observatory (ISO) are used to determine the D/H ratio in Jupiter's and Saturn's atmospheres.
The D/H ratio in hydrogen: (D/H)H_2= (2.25+/- 0.35) 10-5 in Jupiter and (1.70+0.75-0.45) 10-5 on Saturn.]

[972] Colgate, S., "The Production of Deuterium in Supernova Shocks," *The Astrophysical Journal* 181 (1973): L53–L54.

[973] Rossmann, R., and Callender, E., "Manganese Nodules in Lake Michigan," *Science* 162 (1968): 1123.

[974] Wallner, A., et al., "Recent Near-Earth Supernovae Probed by Global Deposition of Interstellar Radioactive 60Fe," *Nature* 532 (2016): 69–72, doi:10.1038/nature17196.

[975] *News*, "Where does all Earth's gold come from? Precious metals the result of meteorite bombardment, rock analysis finds," September 9, 2011, University of Bristol. "Ultra high precision analyses of some of the

oldest rock samples on Earth provides clear evidence that the planet's accessible reserves of precious metals are the result of a bombardment of meteorites more than 200 million years after Earth was formed," https://www.sciencedaily.com/releases/2011/09/110907132044.htm.

[976] Taylor, F., *The Scientific Exploration of VENUS* (Cambridge: Cambridge University Press, 2014).

[977] http://nssdc.gsfc.nasa.gov/planetary/factsheet/venusfact.html.

[978] http://www.esa.int/Our_Activities/Space_Science/Venus_Express/Watching_Venus_glow_in_the_dark.

[979] Prather, M., and McElroy, M., "Helium on Venus: Implications for Uranium and Thorium," *Science* 220 (1983): 410–11.

[980] Vinogradov, A., "The Content of Uranium, Thorium, and Potassium in the Rocks of Venus as Measured by Venera 8," *Icarus* 20 (1973): 253–59.

[981] Crisp, D., et al., "The Dark Side of Venus: Near-Infrared Images and Spectra from the Anglo-Australian Observatory," *Science* 253 (1991): 1263–66.

[982] Glyn, A., et al., "The Electric Wind of Venus: A Global and Persistent 'Polar Wind'-Like Ambipolar Electric Field Sufficient for the Direct Escape of Heavy Ionospheric Ions," *Geophysical Research Letters* 43 (2016): 5926–34, doi:10.1002/2016GL068327.

[983] Velikovsky, *Worlds in Collision* (London, UK: Victor Gollancz Ltd., 1950).

[984] Jones, M., et al., H "Imaging of a Circumsolar Dust Ring Near the Orbit of Venus," *Science* 342 (2013): 960–63.

[985] North Pole Netcam # 1, Friday August 13 at 14.56.05 p.m., 2004 UTC NOAA/PMEL.

[986] Bertaux, J.-L., and Clarke, J., "Deuterium Content of the Venus Atmosphere," *Nature* 338 (1989): 567–68, doi:10.1038/338567a0.
[Venus has a D/H ratio of 2 to 5×10^{-3} atoms or 2000–5000 deuterium atoms per million-hydrogen-atoms. The Pioneer Venus Large Probe orginally detected sixteen thousand atoms per million-hydrogen-atoms which may indicate a significant variation in the venusian atmosphere or instrument error].

[987] McElroy, M., and Hunten, D. M., "The Ratio of Deuterium to Hydrogen in the Venus Atmosphere," *Journal of Geophysical Research (Space Physics)* 74 (1969): 1720–39, doi:10.1029/JA074i007p01720.

[988] Altwegg, K., et al., "67P/Churyumov-Gerasimenko, a Jupiter Family Comet with a High D/H Ratio." *Science* 347 (2015): DOI: 10.1126/science.1261952
[Deuterium atoms per million-hydrogen-atoms of 67P/Churyumov-Gerasimenko as measured by Rosetta is about three times that in Earth's oceans, in contrast to Comet 103P/Hartley (a former Kuiper belt object) where there were 161 deuterium atoms per million-hydrogen-atoms is about the same. Comet Hale Bopp and Halley's Comet have been measured to contain a little more deuterium (about 200 deuterium atoms per million-hydrogen-atoms)].

[989] Lellouch, E., et al., "The Deuterium Abundance in Jupiter and Saturn from ISO-SWS Observations," *Astronomy & Astrophysics* 670 (2001): 610–22. Bibcode:2001A&A...370..610L, doi:10.1051/0004-6361:20010259.
[The abundance of deuterium in the atmosphere of Jupiter was directly measured by the Galileo space probe as 26 atoms per-million-hydrogen-atoms. A simlar result was the ISO-SWS observations: 22 atoms per million-hydrogen-atoms in Jupiter. This is about 17% of

the Earth deuterium-to-hydrogen ratio of 156 deuterium atoms per-million-hydrogen-atoms. Cometary bodies such as Comet Hale Bopp and Halley's Comet have been measured to contain relatively more deuterium (about 200 atoms D per million hydrogens)].

[990] Hallis, L., "Evidence for Primordial Water in Earth's Deep Mantle," *Science* 350 (2015): 795–97.

[991] http://nssdc.gsfc.nasa.gov/planetary/factsheet/venusfact.html.

[992] http://www.esa.int/Our_Activities/Space_Science/Venus_Express/ Venus_has_potential_but_not_for_water.

[993] [Astronomer Carl Sagan had a personal vendetta against Immanuel Velikovsky because his book *Worlds in Collision* which contained revolutionary ideas about the origin of Venus. Carl Sagan denounced Velikovsky at: 1974 AAAS conference, *Velikovsky's Challenge to Science*, in the 1977 conference proceedings, *Scientists Confront Velikovsky*, and in 1979 in Carl Sagan's own book, *Broca's Brain* in the section "Venus and Dr. Velikovsky"].

[994] https://www.newscientist.com/article/dn11652-climate-myths-co2-isnt-the-most-important-greenhouse-gas/.

[995] http://www.nasa.gov/topics/earth/features/vapor_warming.html.

[996] Morgan, J., and Lovering, J., "Uranium and Thorium Abundances in Chondritic Meteorites," *Talanta* 15 (1968): 1079–95.

[997] Reed, G., and Turkevich, A., "Uranium Content of Two Iron Meteorites," *Nature* 176 (1955): 794–95, doi:10.1038/176794a0.

[998] Palmer, K., and Ragnarsdottier, K., "The Uranium-Thorium and Rare Earth Element Geochemistry of Reduction Nodules from

Budleigh Salterton, Devon," *Annual Conference of the Ussher Society*, January (1994), http://www.ussher.org.uk/journal/90s/1994/documents/Kemp_et_al_1994.pdf.

[999] Firestone, Richard., West, Allen., and Warwick-Smith, Simon, *The Cycle of Cosmic Catastrophes* (Rochester, Vermont, USA: Bear & Company 2006) ISBN-13:978-1-59143 www.cosmiccatastrophes.com.

[1000] [Black-mat in the USA and surface dust from the Moon contain similar amounts of cobalt, cerium, cesium, hafnium, iron, lanthanum, magnesium, manganese, nickel, scandium, strontium, vanadium, yttrium, zinc, and zirconium. The relative abundance compared to titanium for; neodymium (Nd/Ti), samarium (Sm/Ti), europium (Eu/Ti), gadolinium (Gd/Ti), thorium (Th/Ti), and uranium (U/Ti) were identical for black mat and surface dust from the moon.] From: Firestone, Richard, West, Allen., and Warwick-Smith, Simon, *The Cycle of Cosmic Catastrophes* (Rochester, VT: Bear & Company, 2006), ISBN-13: 978-1-59143, www.cosmiccatastrophes.com.

[1001] Wieczorek, M., et al., "The Crust of the Moon as Seen by GRAIL," *Science* 339(2013):671–75.

[1002] Yamashita, N., et al., "Uranium on the Moon: Global Distribution and U/Th Ratio," *Geophysical Research Letters* 37 (2010): L10201, doi:10.1029/2010GL043061.

[1003] Witze, A., "Detectors Zero in on Earth's Heat: Geoneutrinos Paint Picture of Deep-Mantle Processes," *Nature* 496, no. 17 (2013), doi:10.1038/496017a.

[1004] Bellini, G., et al., "Measurement of Geo-Neutrinos from 1353 Days of Borexino," arXiv.org > hep-ex > arXiv:1303.2571 (2013).

[1005] Perkins, S., "Earth Still Retains Much of Its Original Heat," http://www.sciencemag.org/news/2011/07/earth-still-retains-much-its-original-heat.

[1006] Brunini, A., "On the Unmodeled Perturbations in the Motion of Uranus," *Celestial Mechanics and Dynamical Astronomy* 53 (1991): 129–43.
[Between its discovery in 1781 and 1800, Uranus was moving away from the direction of Gemini, as it travelled on its anticlockwise orbital path around the Sun. It move unexpectedly slowly, with a deceleration expressed as a tangential perturbation of minus-20 AU.Days^{-2}. From 1810 to 1820, Uranus progressively moved behind the Sun (as viewed from Gemini) and its tangential perturbation mysteriously switched from minus-20 to plus-30. From 1820 to 1870 Uranus turned around back toward Gemini: it travelled faster than expected, with its tangential perturbation of plus-30.
Around 1870 when Uranus passed across the Gemini zone again, it started moving away from this region of the heavens and the tangential perturbation, again dropped steadily from plus-30 to minus-15. In 1900, when Uranus passed behind the Sun again (as viewed from Gemini) and the tangential perturbation decreased again.
From 1900 to almost 1950 the tangential perturbation remained at minus-15 and the radial perturbation was plus-10. At this time Uranus was moving further away from the Sun, revolving on its orbit back toward the angular position of Gemini. From 1950 to 1970 the tangential perturbation switched from minus-15 to plus-30.]

[1007] Hoyt, W., "W. H. Pickering's Planetary Predictions and the Discovery of Pluto," *Isis* 67 (1976): 551–64, doi:10.1086/351668.

[1008] Tombaugh, C., "The Search for the Ninth Planet, Pluto," *Astronomical Society of the Pacific Leaflets* 5 (1946): 73–80.

[1009] Littman, M., *Planets Beyond: Discovering the Outer Solar-System* (New York: Wiley, 1990), 70, ISBN: 0-471-51053-X.

[1010] Brunini, A., "On the Unmodeled Perturbations in the Motion of Uranus," *Celestial Mechanics and Dynamical Astronomy* 53 (1991): 129–43.

[1011] Daniel, P., et al., "Periodic Comet Showers and Planet X," *Nature* 313 (1985): 36–38, doi:10.1038/313036a0.

[1012] Murray, J., "Arguments for the Presence of a Distant Large Undiscoveredsolar-System Planet," *Monthly Notices of the Royal Astronomical Society* 309 (1999): 31–34.

[1013] [An AU is the average distance between the Earth and the Sun, approximately 149.6 million kilometers].

[1014] Tegler, S. and Romanishin, W., "Extremely Red Kuiper-belt Objects in Near-circular Orbits Beyond 40 AU," *Nature* 407 (2000): 979–81.

[1015] Kavelaars, J. J. et al., "The Orbital and Spatial Distribution of the Kuiper Belt" part of Barucci, M. et al., eds., *The Solar-System Beyond Neptune* (Tucson, AZ: University of Arizona Press, 2008), 59–69.

[1016] ['Aphelion' is the point on the orbit of an object, where it is farthest from the Sun. The word 'Aphelion' is derived from the Greek words, '*apo*' meaning 'away from,' and '*helios*,' which was the name of the Greek god of the Sun.]

[1017] Allen, R., et al., "The Edge of the Solar-System," *The Astrophysical Journal* 549 (2001): 1241–44.

[1018] http://www.scribd.com/doc/36389862/Theory-of-Precession-walter-Cruttenden.

[1019] Chadwick, A., et al., "Sedna-Like Body with a Perihelion of 80 Astronomical Units," *Nature* 507 (2014): 471, doi:10.1038/nature13156.

[1020] News "Giant Ninth Planet?," *New Scientist* 29 March (2014): 7.

[1021] Dickinson, D., "Retrograde Rock "Niku" Defies Orbital Trend," *Sky and Telescope* August 23 (2016), http://www.skyandtelescope.com/astronomy-blogs/astronomy-space-david-dickinson/retrograde-rock-niku-rebels-against-the-orbital-trend/.

[1022] Chen, Y. -T., et al., "Discovery of a New Retrograde Trans-Neptunian Object: Hint of a Common Orbital Plane for Low Semi-Major Axis, High Inclination TNOs and Centaurs," arXiv:1608.01808 [astro-ph. EP], doi:10.3847/2041-8205/827/2/L24.

[1023] Orbital elements of the star-core-zeus estimated from ancient astronomy observations:

Periodicity:	4001 years
Mean Distance:	251.98 AU in 2012
Eccentricity (e):	0.9969519
Inclination (i):	113.5 degrees
Ascending node:	82.00 degrees
Arg of pericenter:	138.00 degrees
Mean anomaly(L):	326.5755838 degrees
Epoch:	2452230 Julian Days

The author assumed an April 30, 1628 BC fly-by.

[1024] www.exoplanet.eu.

[1025] Lissauer, J., et al., "Advances in Exo-Planet Science from Kepler," *Nature* 513 (2014): 336–44.

[1026] Clery, D., "Forbidden Planets: How the Zoo of Exo-Planets Has Tunred Planet Formation Theory Upside Down," *Science* 353 (2016): 438–41.

[1027] Finkbeiner, A., "Planets in Chaos," *Nature* 511 (2014): 22–24.

[1028] Kordopatis, G., et al., "The Rich Are Different: Evidence from the RAVE Survey for Stellar Radial Migration," *Monthly Notices of the Royal Astronomical Society* 447 (2015): 3526–35, doi:https://doi.org/10.1093/mnras/stu2726.

[1029] www.exoplanet.eu.

[1030] Buchhave, L. et al., "Three Regimes of Extrasolar Planet Radius Inferred from Host Star Metallicities," *Nature* 509 (2014): 593–95, doi:10.1038/nature13254.

[1031] Pasquini, L., et al., "Evolved Stars Suggest an External Origin of the Enhance Metallicity in Planet Hosting Stars," *Astronomy and Astrophyisics* 473 (2007): 979–82.

[1032] Gonzalez, G., "The Stellar Metallicity-Giant Planet Connection," *Monthly Notices of the Royal Astronomical Society* 285 (1997): 403–12.

[1033] Grether, D., and Lineweaver, C., "The Metallicity of Stars with Close Companions," *The Astrophysical Journal* 669 (2007): 1220–34.

[1034] Cayrel-de-Strobel, G., et al., "Catalogue of [Fe/H] Determinations for FGK Stars: 2001 edition," *Astronomy & Astrophysics* 373 (2001): 159–63, doi:10.1051/0004-6361:20010525.

[1035] Adibekyan, V., et al., "Overabundance of Alpha-Elements in Exo-Planet Host Stars,"arXiv:1205.6670 [astro-ph.EP] DOI: 10.1051/0004-6361/201219564.

[1036] Buchhave, L. et al., "An Abundance of Small Exo-Planets Around Stars with a Wide Range of Metallicities," *Nature* 486 (2012): 375–77, doi:10.1038/nature11121.

[1037] Sousa, S., et al., "Spectroscopic Stellar Parameters for 582 FGK Stars in the HARPS Volume-Limited Sample," arXiv:1108.5279 [astro-ph. EP], doi:10.1051/0004-6361/201117699.

[1038] Sozzetti, A., "On the Possible Correlation Between the Orbital Periods of Extrasolar Planets and the Metallicity of the Host Stars," *Monthly Notices of the Royal Astronomical Society* 354 (2004): 1194–200.

[1039] Grether, D., and Lineweaver, C., "The Metallicity of Stars with Close Companions," *The Astrophysical Journal* 669 (2007): 1220–34.

[1040] Takeda, G., et al., "Planetary Systems in Binaries. I. Dynamical Classification," *The Astrophysical Journal* 683 (2008): 1063–75.

[1041] Welsh, W., "The Robustness of Planet Formation," *Nature* 499 (2013): 33.

[1042] http://www.astronomy.com/news/2014/09/half-of-all-exo-planet-host-stars-are-binaries.

[1043] Gould, A., et al., "A Terrestrial Planet in a 1-AU Orbit Around One Member of a ~15-AU Binary," *Science* 345 (2014): 46.

[1044] Meibom, S., "The Same Frequency of Planets Inside and Outside Open Clusters of Stars," *Nature* 499 (2013): 55.

[1045] Harrington, R., "Planetary Orbits in Binary Stars," *Astronomical Journal* 82 (1977): 753.

[1046] Graziani, F., and Black, D., "Orbital Stability Constraints on the Nature of Planetary Systems," *The Astrophysical Journal* 251 (1981): 337–41.

[1047] Black, D., "A Simple Criterion for Determining the Dynamical Stability of Three-Body Systems," *Astronomical Journal* 87 (1982): 1333–37.

[1048] Malmberg, D., et al., "The Instability of Planetary Systems in Binaries: How the Kozai Mechanism Leads to Strong Planet–Planet Interactions," *Monthly Notices of the Royal Astronomical Society* 377 (2007): L1–L4, doi:10.1111/j.1745-3933.2007.00291.x.

[1049] Touma, J., and Sridhar, S., "The Disruption of Multiplanet Systems Through Resonance with a Binary Orbit," *Nature* 524 (2015): 439, doi:10.1038/nature14873.

[1050] Jensen, E., and Akeson, R., "Misaligned Protoplanetary Disks in a Young Binary Star System," *Nature* 511 (2014): 567–69.

[1051] Stephen, I., "Spatially Resolved Magnetic Field Structure in the Disk of a T Tauri Star," *Nature* 514 (2014): 597–99, doi:10.1038/nature13850.

[1052] Laughlin, G., and Adams, F., "The Frozen Earth: Binary Scattering Events and the Fate Of Thesolar-System," *Icarus* 145 (2000): 614–27.

[1053] Trimble, V., "White Dwarfs in the 1990's." *Bulletin of the Astronomical Society of India* 27 (1999): 549–66.

[1054] [In my book *Cataclysms & Renewals*, I provided a rough estimate of the density of star-core-zeus Potolo (a cold white dwarf) based on Dieterlen and Griaule. "Un Système Soudanais de Sirius," page 287. Griaule reported the density of Potolo was 480 donkey loads, equivalent to about 35,000 kg, squeezed in a grain grinding morter (approximately1 liter)...or a cow-hide bag for carrying grain (about five to fifty liters). This gives rise to a wide range of Dogon density estimates, between 1,000 to 35,000 kg/liter, for Potolo star-core-zeus. Theoretical White Dwarf mass-to-radius curves suggest that this density range corresponds to a White Dwarf of mass between five to twenty percent of a solar mass.

In *Star-Core-Zeus*, I continue to use the estimate that star-core-zeus is about ten-percent the mass of the Sun. However, recent measurements of white dwarfs in binary systems, show that the theoretical curves for electron degenerate matter, do not accurately predict White Dwarf radius from mass data. The radius of a ten-per cent solar-mass star-core, could be between two and three Earth diameters, depending on theoretical assumptions.]

[1055] Parsons, S., "Precise Mass and Radius Values for the White Dwarf and Low Mass M Dwarf in the Pre-Cataclysmic Binary NN Serpentis," *Monthly Notices of the Royal Astronomical Society MNRAS* 402 (2010): 2591–608, doi:10.1111/j.1365-2966.2009.16072.x.

[1056] Bours, M., et al., "Precise Parameters for Both White Dwarfs in the Eclipsing Binary CSS41177," *Monthly Notices of the Royal Astronomical Society (MNRAS)* 438 (2014): 3399–408, doi:10.1093/mnras/stt2453.

[1057] Filippenko, A., et al., "Type IIb Supernova 1993J in M81: A Close Relative of Type Ib Supernovae," *Astrophysical Journal Letters* 415 (1993): L103.

[1058] Kruse, E., and Agol, E., "KOI-3278: A Self Lensing Binary Star System," *Science* 344 (2014): 275–77.

[1059] Kilic, M., et al., "The Lowest Mass White Dwarf," *The Astrophysical Journal* 660 (2007): 1451–61.

[1060] Holberg, J., et al., "A New Look at the Local White Dwarf Population," *The Astronomical Journal* 135 (2008): 1225–38.

[1061] Kepler, S., et al., "White Dwarf Mass Distribution in the SDSS," *Monthly Notices of the Royal Astronomical Society* 375 (2007): 1315–24.

[1062] Holberg, J., et al., "Where Are All the Sirius-Like Binary Systems," *Monthly Notices of Royal Astronomical Society, Monthly Notices of the Royal Astronomical Society* 435 (2013): 2077–91, doi:10.1093/mnras/stt1433 2013.

[1063] Harrison, R., "Had the Sun a Companion Star?," *Nature* 270 (1977): 324–26.
Henrichs, H. F. and Staller, R. F. A., "Had the Sun Really Got a Companion Star?," *Nature* 273 (1978): 132–34.

[1064] Pineault, P., "If the Sun Had a Companion..." *Nature* 275 (1978): 729–30.

[1065] Hodgkin, S., et al., "Infrared Spectrum of an Extremely Cool White-Dwarf Star," *Nature* 403 (2000): 57–59.

[1066] Benvenuto, O., and Althaus, L., "Grids of White Dwarf Evolutionary Models with Masses from M = 0.1 to 1.2 M_{solar}," *Monthly Notices of the Royal Astronomical Society* 303 (1999): 30–38.

[1067] Provencal, J., et al., "Testing the White Dwarf Mass-Radius Relation with *Hipparcos*," *The Astrophysical Journal* 494 (1998): 759–67.

[1068] Kilic, M., et al., "The Lowest Mass White Dwarf," *The Astrophysical Journal* 660 (2007): 1451–61.

[1069] Althaus, L., et al., "New Evolutionary Sequences for Extremely Low-Mass White Dwarfs; Homogenous Mass and Age Determinations and Asteroseismic Prospects," *Astronomy & Astrophysics* 557 (2013): A19, 1–12.

[1070] Kilic, M., et al., "The Discovery of a Companion to the Lowest Mass White Dwarf," *The Astrophysical Journal* 664 (2007): 1088–92, doi:10.1086/518735 arXiv:0704.1813.

[1071] Alcock, C., et al., "Baryonic Dark Matter: The Results from Microlensing Surveys," in *The Third Stromlo Symposium: The Galactic Halo*, eds. Gibson, B., et al., *ASP Conference Series* 165 (1999): 362, ISBN: 1-886733-86-4.

[1072] Glanz, J., "Worlds Around Other Stars Shake Planet Birth Theory," *Science* 276 (1997): 1336, doi:10.1126/science.276.5317.1336.

[1073] Duquennoy, A., and Mayor, M., "Multiplicity among Solar-Type Stars in the Solar Neighbourhood: Distribution of the Orbital Elements of an Unbiased Sample," *Astronomy & Astrophysics* 248 (1991): 485–524. See Table 4, p. 509.

[1074] Kaplan, D., "A 1.05 M Solar Companion to PSR J2222-0137: The Coolest Know White Dwarf," *The Astrophysical Journal* 789 (2014): 119–28, doi:10.1088/0004-637X/789/2/119.

[1075] Koerding, E., "A transient Radio Jet in an Erupting Dwarf Nova," *Science* 320 (2008): 1318, doi:10.1126/science.1155492 arXiv:0806.1002v2.

[1076] Schmidt, G., "The Magnetic White Dwarfs," *Memorie della Societa Astronomica Italiana* 58 (1987): 77–81.

[1077] Schmidt, G., et al., "Magnetic White Dwarfs from the Sloan Digital Sky Survey: The First Data Release1," *The Astrophysical Journal* 595 (2003): 1101–13.

[1078] Suh, I. -S., and Mathews, G., "Mass-Radius Relation for Magnetic White Dwarfs," *The Astrophysical Journal* 530 (2000): 949–54.

[1079] Mosta, P., et al., "A Large-Scale Dynamo and Magnetoturbulence in Rapidly Rotating Core Collapse Supernovae," *Nature* 528 (2015): 376–79, doi:10.1038/nature15755.

[1080] Wickramasinghe, D., and Ferrario, L., "Magnetism in Isolated and Binary White Dwarfs," *Publications of the Astronomical Society of the Pacific* 112 (2000): 873–924.

[1081] Ferrario, L., et al., "Magnetic White Dwarfs," arXiv.org > astro-ph > arXiv:1504.08072[astro-ph.SR] 2015, doi:10.1007/s11214-015-0152-0.

[1082] Barvainus, R., "Of Dusty Tori and Black Holes," *Nature* 373 (1995): 103–4.

[1083] Buckley, D., et al., "Polarimetric Evidence of a White Dwarf Pulsar in the Binary System AR Scorpii," *Nature Astronomy* 1 (2017): Article number: 0029, doi:10.1038/s41550-016-0029.

[1084] Bergeneron, P., et al., "Discovery of Two Cool Magnetic White Dwarfs," *The Astrophys Journal* 400 (1992): 315–20.

[1085] Farihi, J., et al., "Evidence of Rocky Planetesimals Orbiting Two Hyades Stars," *Monthly Notices of the Royal Astronomical Society* 432 (2013): 1955–60, doi:10.1093/mnras/stt432.

[1086] Gaensicke, B., et al., "The Chemical Diversity of Exo-Terrestrial Planetary Debris Around White Dwarfs," *Monthly Notices of the Royal Astronomical Society* 417 (2011): 1210.

[1087] Tauris, T., and Takens, R., "Runaway Velocities of Stellar Components Originating from Disrupted Binaries via Asymmetric Supernova Explosions," *Astronomy & Astrophysics* 330 (1998): 1047–59.

[1088] [From an imaginary view point above the North Pole of the Sun].

[1089] http://www-history.mcs.st-and.ac.uk/Biographies/Cassini.html.

[1090] Dr. Irv Bromberg, University of Toronto, Canada http://www.sym454.org/seasons.

[1091] https://geodesy.curtin.edu.au/local/images/Earth_surfacegravity_lge.jpg; https://geodesy.curtin.edu.au/research/models/.

[1092] [From 50.25 arc seconds in 1900 to 50.29 arc seconds in 2000. SEE The Handbook of the British Astronomical Association 2004].

[1093] Cruttenden, W., *Lost Star of Myth and Time* (Pittsburg, PA: St Lynn's Press, 2006), www.stlynnspress.com; www.binaryresearchinstitute.com.

[1094] http://www.scribd.com/doc/36389862/Theory-of-Precession-walter-Cruttenden.

[1095] [1 km s^{-2} = 0.21 AU/year].

[1096] [In 1905: Radial Velocity Sirius was **-7.36 km/s**].

[1097] Campbell, W., "The Variable Radial Velocity of SIRIUS," *The Astrophysical Journal* 21 (1905): 176–84. Campbell, W., "The Variable Radial Velocity of Sirius, and the Inclination of Its Orbit-Plane," *Publications of the Astronomical Society of the Pacific* 17 (1905): 66–69.

[1098] [In 1967 (or a few years before): Radial Velocity Sirius was **-7.6 km/s**]. SIMBAD, quoting Evans, D. S., *The Revision of the General Catalogue of Radial Velocities* by I AU Symp., held in Toronto, Canada. 30 (1967): 57–62 held on microfiche by "Centre de données Stellaires" Strasbourg.

[1099] [In 2005 (or a few years before): Radial Velocity Sirius was **-8.6 km/s**].

Barstow, M., et al., "Hubble Space Telescope Spectroscopy of the Balmer Lines in Sirius B," *Monthly Notices of the Royal Astronomical Society* 362 (2005): 1134–42, doi:10.1111/j.1365-2966.2005.09359.x arXiv:astro-ph/0506600.

[1100] Baloch, A. and Fisk, L., *The Century of Space Science* (Dordrecht, Netherlands: Kluwer Academic Publishes, 2001), 'The Heliosphere,' 1141–61.

[1101] Smith, E., "Observations of the Interplanetary Sector Structure Up to Heliographic Latitudes of 16 Degrees: Pioneer 11," *Journal of Geophysical Research* 83 (1978): 717.

[1102] Aleksashov, D., et al., "Effects of Charge Exchange in the Tail of the Heliosphere Advances in Space Research," 34 (2004): 109–14.

[1103] Walkey, O., "An Abstract on the Solar Apex," *Monthly Notices of the Royal Astronomical Society* 106 (1946): 274.
[40,720 star motions were used to calculate the position of the Solar Apex (the apparent direction of travel of the Sun) and its velocity relative to local stars. The direction to the Solar Apex was initially calculated as toward RA 270.2 degrees and Dec +28.7° and was confirmed as RA 18h 03m (270 degrees 45minutes of arc) and Dec +30° using on radio astronomy. The local speed of the Sun toward the solar apex was estimated about twenty kilometers per second, about ten per cent of the orbital speed of the Sun around the Galactic center.]

[1104] Anderson, J., et al., "Study of the Anomalous Acceleration of Pioneer 10 and 11," last revised March 10, 2005 (this version, v5) *Physical Review D* 65 (2002): 082004, doi:10.1103/PhysRevD.65.082004; LA-UR-00-5654arXiv:gr-qc/0104064.
[Radio Doppler and ranging data from the distant spacecraft in the solar-system indicated that an anomalous acceleration was acting

on Pioneer 10 and 11, with a magnitude of P ~ 8 × 10⁻⁸ cm/s²,
directed toward the Sun. Much effort has been expended looking
for possible systematic origins of the residuals, but none has been
found].

[1105] Nikolai V., et al., "Termination Shock Asymmetries as Seen by the
Voyager Spacecraft: The Role of the Interstellar Magnetic Field and
Neutral Hydrogen," *The Astrophysical Journal* 668 (2007): 611–24.

[1106] Gruntman, M., et al., "Imaging Three-Dimensional Heliosphere in
EUV," *Solar Physics and Space Weather Instrumentation*, Proceedings
of SPIE Vol. OEI133 (Bellingham, WA: SPIE, 2005), 0277-
786X/05/$15, doi:10.1117/12.614492.
[An All-Sky map of the sky brightness at 30.4 nm, shows peaks in the
upwind direction, due to the glow of the Local ISM plasma beyond
the heliopause: at longitude 252 degrees and latitude +7 degrees
(ecliptic coordinates). Pickup ions in the solar wind also peak in the
opposite downwind direction].

[1107] Florinski, V., et al., "On the Possibility of a Strong Magnetic Field in
the Local Interstellar Medium," *The Astrophysical Journal* 604 (2004):
700–706.

[1108] Katushkina, O., et al., "Direction of Interstellar Hydrogen Flow
into the Heliosphere: Theoretical Modelling and Comparison with
SOHO/SWAN Data," *MNRAS* 446 (2015) 2929–43, doi:10.1093/
mnras/stu2218 doi:10.1093/mnras/stu2218.

[1109] Zank, G., et al., "Heliospheric Structure: The Bow Wave And The
Hydrogen Wall," *The Astrophysical Journal* 763 (2013): 20 (13pp),
doi:10.1088/0004-637X/763/1/20.
[Recent IBEX observations the local interstellar medium (LISM) is
flowing at 23.2 km s-1 past the solar-system.]

[1110] Schwadron, N., "Global Anisotropies in the TeV Cosmic Rays Related to the Sun's Local Galactic Environment from IBEX," *Science* 343 (2014): 988–90.

[1111] Swaczyna, P. et al., "The Energy-Dependent Position of the IBEX Ribbon Due to the Solar Wind Structure Paweł," *The Astrophysical Journal* 827 (2016): 71.

[1112] McComas, D., et al., "The Heliosphere's Interstellar Interaction: No Bow Shock," *Science* 336 (2012): 1291.

[1113] Wood, B., et al., "A New Detection of Lyα Absorption From The Heliotail," *The Astrophysical Journal* 780 (2014): 108 (12pp.).

[1114] Desiati, P. and Lazarian, A., "Heliospheric Boundary and the TeV Cosmic Ray Anisotropy," Cosmic Ray Anisotropy Workshop 2013 (CRA2013) IOP Publishing *Journal of Physics: Conference Series* 531 (2014): 012011, doi:10.1088/1742-6596/531/1/012011.

[1115] Ferriere, K., "Interstellar Magnetic Fields: From Galactic Scales to the Edge of the Heliosphere," 13th Annual International Astrophysics Conference: Voyager, IBEX, and the Interstellar Medium IOP Publishing, *Journal of Physics: Conference Series* 577 (2015): 012008, doi:10.1088/1742-6596/577/1/012008.

[1116] [The absorption or emission of photons with the correct wavelength can tell us something about the presence of hydrogen and free electrons in space. If star light shines through a cloud of hydrogen, light with wavelength 1216 angstroms, will excite neutral hydrogen atoms from their ground state, and the atoms absorb light and boost the electron to a higher energy state. The more neutral hydrogen atoms in their ground state, they will absorb more and the more of the light at wavelength 1216 angstroms will be absorbed. The amount of light absorbed ('optical depth') is proportional to the probability that the hydrogen will absorb the photon (cross section) times the number of hydrogen atoms along its path.]

[1117] 3C-161: Pearson, T., 'Compact Radio Sources in the 3C Catalog," *The Astronomical Journal* 90 (1985): 738–55.

[1118] Lallement, R., "3D Maps of the Local Interstellar Medium; Searching for the Imprints of Past Events, 13th Annual International Astrophysics Conference: Voyager, IBEX, and the Interstellar Medium," IOP Publishing, *Journal of Physics: Conference Series* 577 (2015): 012016.

[1119] Wood, B., "A New Detection of Ly alpha Absorption from the Heliotail," *The Astrophysical Journal* 780 (2014), (12pp).

[1120] Katushkina, O., et al., 'Direction of Interstellar Hydrogen Flow in the Heliosphere: Theoretical Modelling and Comparison with SOHO/SWAN Data," *MNRAS* 446 (2015): 2929–43.

[1121] Zamaninasab, M., et al., "Dynamically Important Magnetic Fields Near Accreting Supermassive Black Holes," *Nature* 510 (2014): 126–28, doi:10.1038/nature13399.

[1122] Albertazzi, B., "Laboratory Formation of a Scaled Protostellar Jet by Coaligned Poloidal Magnetic Field," *Science* 346 (2014): 325–28.

[1123] News "Satellites Show Magnetic Field in Decline," *Nature* 510 (2014): 448.

[1124] http://www.ngdc.noaa.gov/geomag/GeomagneticPoles.shtml.

[1125] Newitt, L., et al., " Recent Acceleration of the North Magnetic Pole Linked to Magnetic Jerks," *EOS* 83 (2002): 381–88.

[1126] Guyodo, Y., and Valet, J., "Global Changes in Intensity of the Earth's Magnetic Field during the Past 800 kyr," *Nature* 399 (1999): 249–52.

[1127] Dergachev, V., et al. "Impact of the Geomagnetic Field and Solar Radiation on Climate Change," *Geomagnetism and Aeronomy* 52 (2012): 959–76, doi:10.1134/S0016793212080063.

[1128] Knudsen, M. and Riisager, P., "Is There a Link between Earth's Magnetic Field and Low-Latitude Precipitation?," *Geology* 37 (2009): 71–74.

[1129] Gallet, Y., et al., "Does Earth's Magnetic Field Secular Variation Control Centennial Climate Change?," *Earth and Planetary Science Letters* 236 (2005): 339–47.

[1130] Knudsen, M., et al., "Variations in the Geomagnetic Dipole Moment during the Holocene and the Past 50 kyr," *Earth and Planetary Science Letters* 272 (2008): 319–29.

[1131] Petrova, G., et al., "Relation between the Changes in the Geomagnetic Moment and Paleoclimate for the Past 12 kyr," *Geomagnetism and Aeronomy* 38 (1998): 141–50 [Geomagnetism and Aeronomy (Engl. transl.), 1998, vol. 38, pp. 652–58].

[1132] Scafetta, N., "Empirical Analysis of the Solar Contribution to Global Mean Air Surface Temperature Change," *Journal of Atmospheric and Solar-Terrestrial Physics* 71 (2009): 1916–23.

[1133] Centennial changes in the heliospheric magnetic field, www.agu.org/pubs/crossref/2011/2010JA016220.shtml.

[1134] Lockwood, M. et al., 'A Doubling of the Sun's Coronal Magnetic Field during the Last 100 Years," *Nature* 399 (1999): 437–39.

[Measurements of the near-Earth interplanetary magnetic field reveal that the total magnetic field leaving the sun has risen by a factor 1.4 since 1964. Using surrogate interplanetary measurements, we find that the rise since 1901 is by a factor of 2.3. The Sun's properties, such as its luminosity, are related to its magnetic field, though the connections are as yet not well understood. Moreover, changes in the heliospheric magnetic field have been linked with changes in total cloud cover over the Earth, which may influence global climate change.]

[1135] Lam, M., et al., "The Interplanetary Magnetic Field Influences Mid-Latitude Surface Atmospheric Pressure," *Environmental Research Letters* 8 (2013): 1–5, http://iopscience.iop.org/article/10.1088/1748-9326/8/4/045001/meta.

[1136] Vasiliev, S., et al., "Reconstruction of the Greenland Temperature for the Last Millennium, Solar Activity, and the North Atlantic Oscillations," *Geomagnetism and Aeronomy* 44 (2004): 123–28 [Geomagnetism and Aeronomy (Engl. transl.), 2004, vol. 44, pp. 110–14].

[1137] Bond, G., et al., "Persistent Solar Influence on North Atlantic Climate during the Holocene," *Science* 294 (2001): 2130–36.

[1138] Hoyt, D., and Schatten, K., "A Discussion of Plausible Solar Irradiance Variations, 1700–1992," *Journal of Geophysical Research* 98 (1993): 18895–906.

[1139] Scherer, K., et al., "Interstellar-Terrestrial Relations: Variable Cosmic Environments, the Dynamic Heliosphere, and Their Imprints on Terrestrial Archives and Climate," *Space Science Reviews* 127 (2006): 327–465.

[1140] Richardson, I., et al., "Long Term Trends in Interplanetary Magnetic Filed Strength and Solar Wind Structure during the Twentieth Century," *Journal of Geophysical Research* 107 (2002): A10, p. 1304.

1141 [The structure of the solar atmosphere is very strange. Above the photosphere there is a sequence of outer shells: the chromosphere, 'the transition region,' 'the corona,' and the 'heliosphere.' The temperature of the chromosphere increases with altitude, from 4000 K at the bottom to 100,000 K at the top. Above the chromosphere is the 'Transition Region,' where there is a steep increase in temperature from 100,000 K to one million kelvin. The corona is the extended outer atmosphere of the Sun and the temperature rises rapidly up to 5 million Kelvin. The source of this heating is a mystery.]

1142 Babcock, H., "The Topology of the Suns Magnetic Field and the 22-Year Cycle," *The Astrophysical Journal* 133 (1961): 572.

1143 Charbonneau, P., "Dynamo Models of the Solar Cycle," *Living Reviews in Solar Physics* 7 (2010): 3.

1144 Brandenburg, A., The Case for a Distributed Solar Dynamo Shaped by Near-Surface Shear," *The Astrophysical Journal* 625 (2005): 625, arXiv:astro-ph/0502275v1.

1145 Cole, T., "Periodicities in Solar Activities," *Solar Physics* 30 (1973): 103.

1146 https://www.sciencedaily.com/releases/2016/10/161004113753.htm. *News: Helmholtz-Zentrum Dresden-Rossendorf* October 4, 2016. [The Sun's activity is determined by the Sun's magnetic field. Two combined effects are responsible for the latter: The omega and the alpha effect. Exactly where and how the alpha effect originates is currently unknown. Researchers are now putting forward a new theory. Their calculations suggest that tidal forces from Venus, the Earth and Jupiter can directly influence the Sun's activity.]

1147 Bollinger, C., "A 44.77 year Jupiter–Venus–Earth Configuration Suntide Period in Solar-Climatic Cycles," *Proceedings of the Oklahoma Academy of Science* 33 (1952): 307.

[1148] Okhlopkov, V, The 11-Year Cycle of Solar Activity and Configurations of the Planets," *Moscow University Physics Bulletin* 69 (2014): 257.

[1149] Charvatova, I., "Solar-terrestrial and Climatic Phenomena in Relation to Solar Inertial Motion," *Surveys in Geophysics* 18 (1997): 131.

[1150] Gray, L., et al., "Solar Influences on Climate," *Reviews of Geophysics* 48 (2010): RG4001.

[1151] Scafetta, N., "Empirical Evidence for a Celestial Origin of the Climate Oscillations and Its Implications," *Journal of Atmospheric and Solar-Terrestrial Physics* 72 (2010): 951.

[1152] Dergachev, V., " Long-Term Processes on the Sun, Responsible for the Tendency toward a Change in the Solar Radiation and the Earth's Surface Temperature," *Geomagnetism and Aeronomy* [(Engl. transl.), 40 (2000): 9–14.]

[1153] Mishraa, M. P., "Solar Activity and Cosmic Ray Intensity Variation," *29th International Cosmic Ray Conference* Pune 2, (2005): 159–62.

[1154] Svensmark, H., and Friis-Christensen, E., "Variation of Cosmic Ray Flux and Global Cloud Coverage – A Missing Link in Solar-Climate Relationships," *Journal of Atmospheric and Solar-Terrestrial Physics* 59 (1997): 1225.

[1155] Shea, M., and Smart, D., "Preliminary Study of Cosmic Rays, Geomagnetic Field Changes and Possible Climate Changes," *Advances in Space Research* 34 (2004): 420–25.

[1156] Svensmark, H. and Calder, N. *The Chilling Stars: A Cosmic View of Climate Change* (Cambridge: Icon Books Ltd., 2007).

[1157] Dergachev, V., et al., "Cosmic Ray Flux Variations, Modulated by the Solar and Earth's Magnetic Fields, and Climate Changes. Part 1. Time Interval from the Present to 10–12 ka Ago (the Holocene Epoch)," *Geomagnetism and Aeronomy* 46 (2006): 123–44 [Geomagnetism and Aeronomy (Engl. transl.), 2006, vol. 46, pp. 118–28].

[1158] Dergachev, V., et al., "Cosmic Ray Flux Variations, Modulated by the Solar and Earth's Magnetic Fields, and Climate Changes. Part 2: Time Interval from ~10000 to ~100000 Years Ago," *Geomagnetism and Aeronomy* 47 (2007): 116–25. [Geomagnetism and Aeronomy (Engl. transl.), 2007, vol. 47, pp. 109–17].

[1159] Dergachev, V., et al., "Cosmic Ray Flux Variations, Modulated by the Solar and Earth's Magnetic Fields, and Climate Changes. Part 3: A Time Interval of 1.5 Myr, Including the Pleistocene," Geomagnetism and Aeronomy 49 (2009): 3–17 [Geomagnetism and Aeronomy (Engl. transl.), 2009, vol. 49, pp. 1–13].

[1160] Fitzka, M., et al., "Trends in Spectral UV Radiation from Long-Term Measurements at Hoher Sonnblick, Austria," *Theoretical and Applied Climatology* 110 (2012): 585, doi:10.1007/s00704-012-0684-0.

[1161] Fountoulakis, I., "Short- and Long-Term Variability of Spectral Solar UV Irradiance at Thessaloniki, Greece: Effects of Changes in Aerosols, Total Ozone and Clouds," *Atmospheric Chemistry and PHYSICS* 16 (2016): 2493–505, www.atmos-chem-phys.net/16/2493/2016/; doi:10.5194/acp-16-2493-2016.

[1162] Steinhilber, F., et al., "Total Solar Irradiance during the Holocene," *Geophysical Research Letters* 36 (2009) : L19704, doi:10.1029/2009GL040142.

[1163] Lean, J., "Solar Irradiance Reconstruction" 2004 IGBP PAGES/World Data Center for Paleoclimatology Data Contribution Series #

2004-035. NOAA/NGDC Paleoclimatogy Program, Boulder, CO, USA.

[1164] http://www.johnstonsarchive.net/environment/warmingplanets.html.

[1165] Fenton, L., et al., "Global Warming and Climate Forcing by Recent Albedo Changes on Mars," *Nature* 446 (2007): 646–49, doi:10.1038/nature05718.
(Length of Martian Year=687 Earth Days).

[1166] Fenton, L., et al., "Global Warming on Mars," *AGU Fall Meeting 2006* (2006), abstract #P23A-0047.

[1167] NASA News. Mars is Melting: The south polar ice cap of Mars is receding, revealing frosty mountains, rifts and curious dark spots.' http://science.nasa.gov/science-news/science-at-nasa/2003/07aug_southpole/.

[1168] Malin, M., et al., "Observational Evidence for an Active Surface Reservoir of Solid Carbon Dioxide on Mars," *Science* 294 (2001): 2146–49.

[1169] James, P., et al.,"MOC Observations of Four Mars Year Variations in the South Polar Residual Cap of Mars," *Icarus* 192 (2007): 318–26.

[1170] Benson, J., and James, P., "Yearly Comparisons of the Martian Polar Caps: 1999–2003 Mars Orbiter Camera Observations," *Icarus* 174 (2005): 513–23.

[1171] Geissler, P., "Three Decades of Martian Surface Changes," *Journal of Geophysical Research.* 110 (2005): E02001, doi:10.1029/2004JE002345.

[1172] Smith, I., et al., "An Ice Age Recorded in the Polar Deposits of Mars," *Science* 352 (2016): 1075–78.

[1173] Thomas, P., et al., "South Polar Residual Cap of Mars: Features, Stratigraphy, and Changes," *Icarus* 174 (2005): 535–59.

[1174] Elliot, J., et al., "Global Warming on Triton," *Nature* 393 (1998): 765–67.

[1175] Lorenz, R., et al., "Seasonal Change on Titan Observed with the Hubble Space Telescope WFPC-2," *Icarus* 142 (1999): 391–401.

[1176] Herbert, B., et al., "Photometric Evidence for Volatile Transport on Triton," *AGU Fall Meeting* (2003), abstract #P51B-0443.

[1177] MIT News, http://news.mit.edu/1998/triton, June 24, 1998.

[1178] Olkin, C., et al., "The Thermal Structure of Triton's Atmosphere: Results from the 1993 and 1995 Occultations," *Icarus* 129 (1997): 178–201.

[1179] Elliot, J., et al., "The Prediction and Observation of the 1997 July 18 Stellar Occulation by Triton: More Evidence for Increasing Pressure in Triton's Atmosphere," *Icarus* 148 (2000): 347–69.

[1180] Marcus, P., et al., "Velocities and Temperatures of Jupiter's Great Red Spot and the New Red Oval and Their Implications for Global Climate Change," *Bulletin of the American Astronomical Society* 38 (2006): 554.

[1181] Baines, K., et al., "Polar Lightning and Decadal-Scale Cloud Variability on Jupiter," *Science* 318 (2007): 226–29.

[1182] Lockwood, G., and Thompson, D., "Photometric Variability of Uranus, 1972–1996," *Icarus* 137 (1999): 2–12.

[1183] Lockwood, G., and Jerzykiewicz, M., "Photometric Variability of Uranus and Neptune, 1950–2004," *Icarus* 180 (2006): 442–52.

[1184] Hammel, H., and Lockwood, G., "Long-term Atmospheric Variability on Uranus and Neptune," *Icarus* 186 (2007): 291–301.

[1185] Hammel, H., and Lockwood, G., "Suggestive Correlations between the Brightness of Neptune, Solar Variability, and Earth's Temperature," *Geophysical Research Letters* 34 (2007): L08203.

[1186] Lockwood, G., and Thompson, D., "Photometric Variability of Neptune 1972–2000," *Icarus* 156 (2002): 37–51.

[1187] Sicardy, B., et al., "Large Changes in Pluto's Atmosphere as Revealed by Recent Stellar Occultations," *Nature* 424 (2003): 168–70.

[1188] Pasachoff, J., et al., "The Structure of Pluto's Atmosphere from the 2002 August 21 Stellar Occultation," *Astrophysical Journal* 129 (2005): 1718–23.

[1189] Hansen, C., and Paige, D., "Seasonal Nitrogen Cycles on Pluto," *Icarus* 120 (1996): 247–65.

[1190] Elliot, J., et al., "Changes in Pluto's Atmosphere: 1988–2006," *Astronomical Journal* 134 (2007): 1–13.

[1191] Elliot, J., et al., "The Recent Expansion of Pluto's Atmosphere," *Nature* 424 (2003): 165–68.

[1192] Brown, M., "Pluto and Charon: Formation, Seasons, Composition," *Annual Review of Earth and Planetary Science* 30 (2002): 307–45.

[1193] Montmerle, T., "A Stellar Merry-Go-Round," *Science* 293 (2001): 2409–10.

[1194] Banas, K., et al., "Supernova Remnant associated with Molecular Clouds in the Large Magellanic Cloud," *The Astrophysical Journal* 480 (1997): 607–17.

[1195] Dubner, G., "Radio Observations of Supernova Remants and the Surrounding Molecular Gas," *Meme Memorie della Societa Astronomica Italiana* 75 (2008): 282. arXiv:1111.1702v1[astro-ph.HE] November 7, 2011.

[1196] Meier, D., et al., "Magnetohydrodynamic Production of Relativistic Jets," *Science* 291 (2001): 84–92.

[1197] Lepenta, G., and Kronberg, P., "Simulation of Astrophysical Jets: Collimation and Expansion into Radio Lobes," *The Astrophysical Journal* 625 (2005): 37–50.

[1198] Sincell, M., "Microquasars Raised Megaquestions," *Science* 291 (2001): 66–68.

[1199] [Celestial Coordinates were developed by ancient astronomers, to mark the positions of stars, which was continuously moving above them, as the starry-sky travelled from East to West. The positions of stars are given with respect to the fixed path of the Sun across the sky (the ecliptic), which is determined by the path of Earth's orbit around the Sun.

Right Ascension (RA) is the hour-angle along the ecliptic, from the spring Vernal-Equinox-Point, in the direction of the movement of the Sun. RA is given in astronomical-angle-measurement units: the angle traversed due to Earth-rotation in time-units of hours, minutes and seconds. There are 24 hours in a day of one Earth-rotation, and there are 360 degrees of arc in a circle, so one hour-angle is equivalent to fifteen degrees of arc.

Declination (DEC) is the angle from the ecliptic-to-pole, given in geometric-angle-measurement in arc-units: degrees, minutes and seconds. Declination (DEC) is an angular position above or below the ecliptic: positive for points northward and negative for points southward of the path of the Sun. As celestial coordinates are by definition tied to the slowly moving Vernal-Equinox-Point, the epoch of the position also has to be stated. This book uses J2000; the locations at the beginning of the twenty-first century AD.

[1200] Starry Night Backyard by Space.com.

[1201] Orbital Elements of the Star Core in the Orbital Model
Periodicity: 4001 years

Mean Distance	:	251.98 AU in 2012
Eccentricity (e)	:	0.9969519
Inclination (i)	:	113.5 degrees
Ascending node:	:	82.00 degrees
Arg of pericenter:	:	138.00 degrees
Mean anomaly(L)	:	326.5755838 degrees

Epoch: 2452230 Julian Days
(The author assumed an April 30, 1628 BC fly-by.)

[1202] [Skyview is an internet virtual telescope service developed by NASA, under the auspices of the High Energy Astrophysics Science Archive research centre (HEASARC) at the GSFC Laboratory for High Energy Astrophysics.] http://skyview.gsfc.nasa.gov.

[1203] [In the Third Cambridge Survey 3C-catalogue, radio-source 3C-161 was recorded with the following radio-frequency-bands and output: at 178 MHz flux density 78 mJy, at 408 MHz flux density 44.7 mJy, at 1400 MHz flux density 18.5 mJy, at 2700 MHz flux density 11.3 mJy, at 5000 MHz flux density 6.6 mJy and a continuum flux density exceeding 0.1 Jy beam^{-1} over 1 arcsec^2. [Jy was a unit of flux, in Watts × 10^{-24}/ m^2/Hz for measuring the weak astronomical radio signals] Edge, D., et al., "3C Surveys," *Membership - Royal Astronomical Society* 68 (1959): 37.

[1204] Pearson, T., 'Compact Radio Sources in the 3C Catalog," *The Astronomical Journal* 90 (1985): 738–55.

[1205] [3C-161 is the 161st object in the third Cambridge catalog of radio sources. It is a very strong *radio galaxy* many thousand of times further away then any of the other objects you will see in the Tour of Orion. Thus, 3C-161 is not associated with the Orion stars or any of the nebulae you will see in the tour. *Radio galaxies* are some of the strongest sources of radio waves we know of, but to us they tend not to be very strong because of the distance between us and the object. Most astronomers believe that a black hole at the center of some galaxies is the ultimate energy source that powers the radio emission.] http://www.gb.nrao.edu/~rmaddale/Education/OrionTourCenter/3C-161.html.

[1206] [Amateur astronomer, Otto Piechowski, Lexington, KY, Posted March 31, 2015, 8:53 p.m.

« I was observing beta Monocerotis and chose to check out the area of the radio source 3C-161. I found a 10th-ish magnitude starlike point at, what seemed to be the correct position relative to the surrounding stars as indicated in my Uranometria. I was using a 4 inch refractor. Would one/some of you check out 3C-161 visually, just to make sure it is not having some type of unusual visual spike. I am sure it is not. Secondly, would those of you with better charts tell me if there is a bright star (i.e. 10th-ish magnitude) near to the position of 3C-161. »] http://www.cloudynights.com/topic/496111-3c-161/.

[1207] Dwarakanath, K., and Shankar, N., "A Synthesis Map of the Sky at 34.5 MHz," *Journal of Astrophysics & Astronomy* 11 (1990): 323–410.

[1208] Fomalont, E., et al., 'The VSOP 5 GHz Continuum Survey: The Prelaunch VLBA Observations," *The Astrophysical Journal Supplement Series* 131 (2000): 95–183. [The Radio source 3C-161, J0627-0553, a steep spectrum (= -0.87), symmetric double source, resolved with the VLA at 5 and 1.4 GHz by Ulvestad et al. 1981 and Pearson, Readhead & Perley 1985, but could not be detected at its expected location in The VSOP 5 GHz Continuum Survey].

1209 [Changing J2000 positions of 3C-161 in Right Ascension due to parallax:

408 Hz H1sky	RA06 26 17.46
33 GHz WMAP Q	RA06 27 07.64
74 MHz VLA	RA06 27 10.78
1.4 GHz VLA	RA06 27 12.47
33 GHz WMAP K	RA06 27 28.88
33 GHz WMAP Ka	RA06 27 55.90
1420 MHz survey	RA06 27 57.83

A parallax shift of 2 minutes of Right Ascension, gives a parallax angle of 0.25°. This implies the object producing the powerful 3C-161 radio-signals is only 1 / Tan 0.25 = 1 / 0.00436 = 229 AU away from Earth (Sun). The parallax shift of 3C 161 may be slightly less, implying a range of 250 AU, but only a dedicated parallax experiment will product an accurate distance measurement.

The location of 3C-161 at RA06 24 46.77 in the older 35 MHz all-sky radio survey (GTEE) shows a larger Right Ascension shift, but similar errors in the location of other radio-sources in this survey, suggests there is an systematic error in positioning.

1210 Goss, W., et al., "Galactic H1 on the 50 AU Scale in the Direction of Three Extragalactic Sources Observed with MERLIN," *Monthly Notices of the Royal Astronomical Society* 388 (2008): 165–75.

1211 Barkume, K., "Small Scale Structures in the Interstellar Medium," *Thesis, Division of Mathematics and Natural Sciences, Reed College, Oregon, USA* (2003).

1212 Bzowski, M., "Local Interstellar Wind Velocity from Doppler shifts of Interstellar Matter Lines, *Acta Astronomica* 38 (1988): 443–53.

1213 Matsumoto, T., "Infrared Telescope in Space: IRTS," *Journal Space Science Reviews* 74, no. 1–2 (1995): 73.

[Parallax detected when Second Digitized Sky Survey-Near Infrared centred on IRAS 06240-0559 J2000. This survey was generated by scanning Schmidt near-IR plates of the sky at 1" resolution. Scanning and compression was performed at the Space Telescope Science Institute. Provenance Data taken by ROE, AAO, and CalTech, Compression and distribution by Space Telescope Science Institute. Frequency 450–600 THz Coverage All-sky, PixelScale 1" Projection Schmidt Equinox 2000 Epoch 1984–1999.], www.ir.isas.ac.jp/irts/irts_E.html.

1214 [The temperature of a human body at thirty-seven degrees Celsius (310 K), radiates infrared radiation between 10–12 microns.]

1215 [WISE All-WISE includes all data taking during the WISE full cryogenic phase, from January 7, 2010 to August 6, 2010, that were processed with improved calibrations and reduction algorithms and combines this with the NEOWISE postcryogenic survey to form the most comprehensive view of the full mid-infrared sky.]

1216 www.cosmos.esa.int/web/gaia/science-performance.

1217 Clery, D., "The Next Big Eye," *Science* 351 (2016): 805–9.

1218 http://www.jwst.nasa.gov/.

1219 [The journey of the Earth over two months from April to June is one-sixth of the circumference of Earth's orbit. 2 × 3.142 × 150E6 /6, km = 157E6 km. Size of the cloud of *Tishtrya* must had been huge 157E6/0.4E6 × 3476, km = 1.4E6 km in diameter (0.4E6 km is the distance to the Moon). If Tishtrya itself was a star-core of two earth-diameters, but observed to had the same diameter as the Moon, then it was only 2.93 million km from Earth (25512 km /3476 km × 0.4E6, km = 2.93 million km from Earth).

[1220] Cambell, E., et al., "Laboratory Confirmation of C60+ as the Carrier of Two Diffuse Interstellar Bands," *Nature* 523 (2015): 322–23, doi:10.1038/nature14566.

[1221] Kuniholm, P., et al., "Anatolian Tree Rings and the Absolute Chronology of the Eastern Mediterranean, 2220BC to 718BC," *Nature* 381 (1996): 780–82.

[1222] For calendar dates of the Great Flood see: *Noah's Ark and the Ziusudra Epic*, by Robert Best, Enlil Press, Fort Myers, Florida USA 1999, p. 45 Citing: Berossos, who quoted by Syncellus, trans. G. P. Verbrugghe and J. M. Wickersham, *Berossos and Manetho* (University of Michigan Press, 1996), 49–50. 'The Flood of Xisuthros' occurred on the fifteenth of Daisios, the eight Macedonian month. *The Civil and Literary Chronology of Greece* by H. F. Clinton, Fasti Hellenici, Vol 3, copied as Monograph-119 in *Burt Franklin Research and Source Works Series* 1965, pp. 349–58. The month of Diasios also corresponded to Iyyar, the second month of the Babylonian calendar. *Atrahasis: The Babylonian Story of the Flood* (Oxford: Clarendon Press, 1969), 137. Berossus also wrote that the Flood happened in June (Daisios 15) and this was copied in Genesis 7:11 of the Bible.]

[1223] [All observations are publicly available through the NASA virtual telescope data base (http://skyview.gsfc.nasa.gov). Skyview was developed as the internet virtual telescope by NASA under the auspices of the High Energy Astrophysics Science Archive research centre (HEASARC) at the GSFC Laboratory for High Energy Astrophysics.]

[1224] Matsuura, M., et al., "Herschel Detects a Massive Dust Reservoir in Supernova 1987A," *Science* 333 (2011): 1258–61, doi:10.1126/science.1205983.

[1225] Koo, B., et al., "Phosphorus in the Young Supernova remnant Cassiopaeia A," *Science* 342 (2013): 1346–48.

[1226] Taylor, G., "Cosmochemistry from Nanometers to Light Years," *Planetary Science Research Discoveries* (2006), http://www.psrd.hawaii.edu/Jan06/protoplanetary.html.

[1227] Blake, G., and Bergin, A., "Prebiotic Chemistry on the Rocks," *Nature* 520 (2015): 161 and 198.

[1228] Busemann, H., et al., "Interstellar Chemistry Recorded in Organic Matter from Primitive Meteorites," *Science* 312 (2006): 727–30.

[1229] Zenobi, R., et al., "Spatially Resolved Organic Analysis of the Allende Meteorite," *Science* 24 (1989): 1026.

[1230] Busemann, H., et al., "Interstellar Chemistry Recorded in Organic Matter from Primitive Meteorites,"*Science* 312 (2006): 727–30.

[1231] Hoyle, F., *Frontiers in Astronomy* (London: William Heinmann Ltd, 1955), 376pp.

[1232] Kozlovsky, Y., ed., "The Superdeep Well of the Kola Peninsula," *Springer Science & Business Media* (Berlin Heidelberg: Springer-Verlag, December 6, 2012).

[1233] Zhao, X., et al., "New Vanadium Compounds in Venezuela Crude Oil Detected by Positive-Ion Electrospray Ionization Fourier Transform Ion Cyclotron Resonance Mass Spectometry," *Scientific Reports* 4 (2014): 2454–64.

[1234] Hodgson, G., and Baker, B., "Porphyrins in Meteorites: Metal Complexes in Orgueil, Murray, Cold Bokkeveld, and Mokoia

Carbonaceous Chondrites," *Geochimica et Cosmochimica Acta* 33 (1969): 943–58.

[1235] Treibs, A., "Chlorophyll- und Häminderivate in organischen Mineralstoffen," *Angewandte Chemie* 49 (1936): 682–86, doi:10.1002/ange.19360493803.

[1236] Speight, J., *The Chemistry and Technology of Petroleum, Fifth Edition* (Boca Raton, FL: CRC Press, 2014).

[1237] Robinson, R., "Duplex Origin of Petroleum," *Nature* 199 (1963): 113–14.

[1238] Robinson, R. "The Origins of Petroleum," *Nature* 212 (1966): 1291–95.

[1239] Speight, J., *The Chemistry and Technology of Petroleum* (New York: Marcel Dekker, 1999), ISBN: 0-8247-0217-4.

[1240] Kudryavstev, N., "Against the Organic Hypothesis of Petroleum Origins," *Petroleum Economy*, Moscow 9 (1951): 17.

[1241] Kudryavstev, N., *Oil Gas and Solid Bitumens in Igneous and Metamorphic Rocks* (Leningrad: State Technical Press, 1959), 230.

[1242] Levin, B., "Organic Compounds in Thesolar-System," in *Problems of the Origin of Petroleum* (Kiev, USSR: Scientific Thought Press, 1966), 174–222.

[1243] Kudryavstev, N., "The State of the Question on Genesis of Oil in the Year 1966," in *Genesis of Oil and Gas* (Moscow, USSR: Nedra Press, 1967), 262–91.

[1244] Ikorsky, S., Gigashvili, G. M., Lanyov, V. S., Narkotiev, V. D., and Petersilye, I. A., et al., "The Investigation of Gases during the

Kola Superdeep Borehole Drilling (to 11.6 km depth)," *Geologisches Jahrbuch Reihe*, eds. Whiticar, M. J. and Faber, E. (Hannover: D. E. Schweizerbart Science Publishers, 1999), D107, 145–52.

[1245] Silvermans, R., and Epstein, S., "Carbon Isotopic Compositions of Petroleums & Other Sedimentary Organic Materials," *Bulletin - American Association of Petroleum Geologists* 42 (1958): 998–1012.

[1246] Kerridge, F., "Carbon, Hydrogen and Nitrogen in Carbonaceous Chondrites: Abundances, and Isotopic Compositions in Bulk Samples," *Geochimica et Cosmochimica Acta* 49 (1985): 1707–14.

[1247] Craig, H., "Carbon 13 in Plants & The Relationships Between Carbon 13 & Carbon 14 Variations in Nature," *Journal of Geology* 62 (1954): 115–49.

[1248] Grady, M., et al., "The Carbon and Oxygen Isotopic Composition of Meteoritic Carbonates," *Geochimica et Cosmochimica Acta* 52 (1988): 2855–66.

[1249] Harris, J., and Vis, R., "High-resolution Transmission Electron Allende Meteorite Microscopy of Carbon and Nanocrystals in the Allende Meteorite," *Proceedings of the Royal Society of London A* 459 (2003): 2069–76.

[1250] Pizzarello, S. et al., 'The Nature and Distribution of the Organic Material in Carbonaceous Chondrites and Interplanetary Dust Particles," *Meteorites and the Early Solar-System II*, eds. Lauretta, D. and McSween-Jr, H., (Tucson, AZ: University of Arizona Press 2006), 625–51, ISBN-10: 0816525625 ISBN-13: 978-0816525621.

[1251] Sephton, M., "Multiple Cosmic Sources for Meteorite Macro-molecules?," *Astrobiology* 15 (2015): 779–86, doi: 10.1089/ast.2015.1331.

[1252] Alexander, C., et al., "The Origin and Evolution of Chondrites Recorded in the Elemental and Isotopic Compositions of Their Macromolecular Organic Matter," *Geochimica et Cosmochimica Acta* 71 (2007): 4380–403.

[1253] Busemann, H., et al., "Interstellar Chemistry Recorded in Organic Matter from Primitive Meteorites," *Science* 312 (2006): 727–30, doi:10.1126/science.1123878.

[1254] Sephton, M., "Organic Compounds in Carbonaceous Meteorites," *Natural Product Reports* 19 (2002): 292–311.

[1255] Schmitt-Kopplina, P., et al., "High Molecular Diversity of Extraterrestrial Organic Matter in Murchison Meteorite Revealed 40 Years after Its Fall," *PNAS* 107 (2010): 2763–68.

[1256] Cody, G., and Alexander, C., "NMR Studies of Chemical Structural Variation of Insoluble Organic Matter from Different Carbonaceous Chondrite Groups," *Geochimica et Cosmochimica Acta* 69 (2005): 1085–97.

[1257] Cody, G., et al., "Establishing a Molecular Relationship Between Chondritic and Cometary Organic Solids," *Proceedings of the National Academy of Sciences of the United States of America* 108 (2011): 19171–176.

[1258] Cody, G., et al., "Solid-state (1H and 13C) Nuclear Magnetic Resonance Spectroscopy of Insoluble Organic Residue in the Murchison Meteorite: A Self-Consistent Quantitative Analysis," *Geochimica et Cosmochimica Acta* 66 (2002): 1851–65.

[1259] Taylor, G., "Interstellar Organic Matter in Meteorites: Carbonaceous Chondrites Contain Organic Compounds with High Deuterium/ Hydrogen Ratios, Suggesting They Formed in Interstellar Space," *Hawaii Institute of Geophysics and Planetology (2006) Planetary Science*

Research Discoveries. http://www.psrd.hawaii.edu/May06/meteorite-Organics.html.

[1260] Nakamura-Messenger, K., et al., "Organic Globules in the Tagish Lake Meteorite: Remnants of the Protosolar Disk," *Science* 314 (2006): 1439–42.

[1261] Park, R., and Epstein, S., "Metabolic Fractionation of C13 & C12 in Plants," *Plant Physiology* 36 (1961): 133–38.

[1262] Sandford, S., "Organics in the Samples Returned from Comet 81P/Wild 2 by the Stardust Spacecraft," part of Kwok, S., and Sandford, S., (editors), *Organic Matter in Space*, Proceedings I AU Symposium, No. 251 (International Astronomical Union, 2008), doi:10.1017/S1743921308021777.

[1263] Sandford, S., et al., "Organics Captured from Comet 81P/Wild 2 by the Stardust Spacecraft," *Science* 314 (2006): 1720–24.

[1264] De Gregorio, B. et al., "Isotopic Anomalies in Organic Nanoglobules from Comet 81P/Wild 2: Comparison to Murchison Nanoglobules and Isotopic Anomalies Induced in Terrestrial Organics by Electron Irradiation," *Geochimica et Cosmochimica Acta* 74 (2010): 4454–70.

[1265] Glavin, D., et al., "Detection of Cometary Amines in Samples Returned by Stardust," *Meteoritics & Planetary Science* 43 (2008): 399–413.

[1266] Elsila, J., et al., "Cometary Glycine Detected in Samples Returned by Stardust," *Meteoritics & Planetary Science* 44 (2009): 1323–30.

[1267] Wirick, S., "Organic Matter from Comet 81P/Wild 2, IDPs, and Carbonaceous Meteorites; Similarities and Differences," *Meteoritics & Planetary Science* 44 (2009): 1611–26.

[1268] Sandra Pizzarell, S., and Shock, E., "The Organic Composition of Carbonaceous Meteorites: The Evolutionary Story Ahead of Biochemistry," *Cold Spring Harbor Perspectives in Biology* 2 (2010): a002105, doi: 10.1101/cshperspect.a002105.

[1269] Pizzarello, S., and Cooper, G., "Molecular and Chiral Analyses of Some Protein Amino Acid Derivatives in the Murchison and Murray Meteorites," *Meteoritics & Planetary Science* 36 (2001): 897–909.

[1270] Kvenvolden, K. et al., "Evidence for Extraterrestrial Amino-acids and Hydrocarbons in the Murchison Meteorite," *Nature* 228 (1970): 923–26.

[1271] Botta, O., and Bada, J., "Extraterrestrial Organic Compounds in Meteorites," *Surveys in Geophysics* 23 (2002): 411–67, doi:10.1023/a:1020139302770.

[1272] Botta, O., et al., "Relative Amino Acid Concentrations as a Signature for Parent Body Processes of Carbonaceous Chondrites," *Origins of Life and Evolution of Biospheres* 32 (2002) : 143–63, doi: 10.1023/a:1016019425995.

[1273] Botta, O., et al., "Strategies of Life Detection: Summary and Outlook," *Space Science Reviews* 135 (2008): 371–80, doi:10.1007/s11214-008-9357-9.

[1274] Shimoyama, A., and Ogasawara, R. "Dipeptides and Diketopiperazines in the Yamato-791198 and Murchison Carbonaceous Chondrites," *Origins of Life and Evolution of Biospheres* 32 (2002): 165–79.

[1275] Mautner M., et al., "Meteorite Organics in Planetary Environments: Hydrothermal Release, Surface Activity and Microbial Utilization," *Planetary and Space Science* 43 (1995): 139–47.

[1276] Hand, E., "Mars Rover Finds Long-Chain Organic Compounds," *Science* 347 (2015): 1402–3.

[1277] Glaser, R., et al., "Adenine Synthesis in Interstellar Space: Mechanisms of Prebiotic Pyrimidine-Ring Formation of Monocyclic HCN-Pentamers" *Astrobiology* 7 (2007) DOI: 10.1089/ast.2006.0112

[1278] Callahana, M., et al., "Carbonaceous Meteorites Contain a Wide Range of Extra-Terrestrial Nucleobases," *PNAS* 108 (2011): 13995–998, doi:10.1073/pnas.1106493108, www.pnas.org/cgi/doi/10.1073/pnas.1106493108. [There were two families of nucleobases: one-ring pyrimidines including uracil, thymine and cytosine; and two-ring purines including adenine and guanine. Adenine, guanine and cytosine were found in both DNA and RNA, but thymine was only found in DNA and uracil was only found in RNA.]

[1279] Meierhenrich, U., *Amino-acids and the Asymmetry of Life, Advances in Astrobiology and BioGeophysics* (New York: Springer, 2008), ISBN: 978-3-540-76885-2.

[1280] Joyce G., et al., "RNA Evolution and the Origins of Life," *Nature* 310 (1989): 602.

[1281] Albert Guijarro, A., and Miguel Yus, M., *The Origin of Chirality in the Molecules of Life: A Revision from Awareness to the Current Theories and Perspectives of This Unresolved Problem* (London: Royal Society of Chemistry, 2009), ISBN: 978-1-84755-875-6.

[1282] Cohen, B., and Chyba, C., "Racemization of Meteoritic Amino Acids," *Icarus* 145 (2000): 272–81, doi:10.1006/icar.1999.6328.

[1283] Botta, O. and Bada, J. "Extra-terrestrial Organic Compounds in Meteorites," *Geophysical Survey* 23 (2002): 411–67.

[1284] Sephton, M., and Botta, O., "Recognizing Life in the Solar-System: Guidance from Meteoritic Organic Matter," *International Journal of Astrobiology* 4 (2005): 269–76.

[1285] Cronin, J., and Pizzarrello, S., "Enantiomeric Excesses in Meteoritic Amino-Acids," *Science* 275 (1997): 951–55.

[1286] Pizzarello, S., et al., "Non Racemic Isovaline in the Murchison Meteorite: Chiral Distribution and Mineral Association," *Geochimica et Cosmochimica Acta* 67 (2003): 1589–95.

[1287] Engel, M., and Macko, S., "Isotopic Evidence for extra-terrestrial Non-racemic Amino-Acids in the Murchison Meteorite," *Nature* 389 (1997): 265–68.

[1288] Pizzarello, S., "Chemical Evolution and Meteorites: An Update," *Origins of Life and Evolution Of Biospheres* 34 (2004): 25–34.

[1289] Arteaga, O., et al., "Chiral Biases in Solids by Effect of Sheer Gradients: A Speculation on the Deterministic Origin of Biological Homochirality," *Origins of Life and Evolution of Biospheres* 40 (2010): 27–40.

[1290] Meinert, C., et al., "Photonenergy-Controlled Symmetry Breaking with Circular Polarized Light," *Angewandte Chemie International Edition* 53 (2014): 210–14, doi:10.1002/anie.201307855.

[1291] Griesbeck, A., and Meierhenrich, U., "Asymmetric Photochemistry and Photochirogenesis," *Angewandte Chemie International Edition* 41 (2002): 3147–54.
Cerf, C. and Jorissen, A., "Is Amino-Acid Homochirality Due to Asymmetric Photolysis in Space?," *Space Science Reviews* 92 (2000): 603–12.

[1292] Nahon, L., et al., "Advance Search for the Origin of Life's Homochirality: Asymmetric Photon Induced Processes on Chiral

Compounds with Far UV Circular Polarized Synchrotron Radiation," *Proceeding of SPIE* (2007): 6694–703, doi:10.1117/12.729474.

[1293] Nuevo, M., et al., "Enantiomeric Separation of Complex Organic Molecules Produced from Irradiation of Interstellar/Circumstellar Ice Analogues," *Advances in Space Research* 39 (2005): 400–404.

[1294] Meierhenrich, U., *Amino-acids and the Asymmetry of Life, Advances in Astrobiology and BioGeophysics*, (New York, NY:Springer, 2008) ISBN 978-3-540-76885-2.

[1295] Takano, Y. et al., "Asymmetric Synthesis of Amino Acid Precursors in Interstellar Complex Organics by Circular Polarized Light," *Earth and Planetary Science Letters* 254 (2007): 106–14.

[1296] de-Marcellu, P., et al., "Detection of Aldehydes and Sugars in Laboratory Simulated Astrophysical Ices: Astrochemical and Prebiotic Significance," *Interstellar Ices to Polycyclic Aromatic Hydrocarbons symposium to honor Lou Allamandola's Contributions to the Molecular Universe*. Annapolis, MD, USA, September 13–17, 2015.

[1297] Shanmugan, S., and Boyer, C., "Organic Photocataclysts for Cleaner Polymer Synthesis," *Science* 352 (2016): 1053.

[1298] Theroit, J., et al., "Organocatalyzed Atom Transfer Radical Polymerization Driven by Visible Light," *Science* 352 (2016): 1082–86.

[1299] McLaren, A., and Shugar, D., *Photochemistry of Proteins and Nucleic Acids* (New York: Pergamon Press, 1964).

[1300] McGeoch, J., and McGeoch, M., "Polymer Amide as an Early Topology," *PLoS One* 9, no. 7 (2014): e103036, doi:10.1371/journal. pone.0103036.

[1301] Lee, S., et al., "Controlled Formation of Peptide Bonds in the Gas Phase," *Journal of the American Chemical Society* 133 (2011): 15834–37, doi: 10.1021/ja205471n.

[1302] Johnson, W., 'Protein Secondary Structure and Circular Dichroism: A Practical Guide," *Proteins* 7 (1990): 205–14, doi:10.1002/prot.340070302.

[1303] Fox, S., and Dose, K., *Molecular Evolution and the Origin of Life* (New York: Marcel Dekker, Inc, 1977).

[1304] Fox, S., "The Proteinoid Theory of the Origin of Life and Competing Ideas," *American Biology Teacher* 36 (1974): 161–72, 181.

[1305] Leman., L., et al., "Carbonyl Sufide-Mediated Prebiotic Formation of Peptides," *Science* 306 (2004): 283–86.

[1306] Meierhenrich, U., and Thiemann, W., "Photochemical Concepts on the Origin of Biomolecular Asymmetry," *Origins of Life and Evolution of Biospheres* 34 (2004): 111–21.

[1307] Meinert, C., et al., "Ribose and Related Sugars from Ultraviolet Irradiation of Interstellar Ice Analogs," *Science* 352 (2016): 208–12, doi:10.1126/science.aad8137.

[1308] Pizzarello, S., and Weber, A., "Stereoselective Syntheses of Pentose Sugars Under Realistic Prebiotic Conditions," *Origins of Life and Evolution of Biospheres* 40 (2010): 3–10.

[1309] Pizzarello, S., and Weber, A., "Prebiotic Amino Acids as Asymmetric Catalysts," *Science* 303 (2004): 1151.

[1310] Pizzarello S., Weber A., "Stereoselective Syntheses of Pentose Sugars under Realistic Prebiotic Conditions," *Origins of Life and Evolution of Biospheres* 40 (2010): 3–10.

[1311] Pizzarello, S., et al., "Molecular Asymmetry in Extraterrestrial Chemistry: Insights from a Pristine Meteorite," *Proceedings of the National Academy of Sciences* 105 (2008): 3700–3704.

[1312] Kemp, J., et al., "Discovery of Circular Polarized Light from a White Dwarf," *The Astrophysical Journal* 161 (1970): L77–L79.

[1313] Bonner, W., and Rubenstein, E., "Supernovae, Neutron Stars and Biomolecular Chirality," *Biosystem* 20 (1987): 99–111.

[1314] Rubenstein, E., et al., "Supernovae and Life" *Nature* 306 (1983): 118.

[1315] Chyba, C., "Origins of Life: A Left-Handedsolar-System?," *Nature* 389 (1997): 234–35.

[1316] Cheung, C., "Detection of Optical Synchrotron Emission from the Radio Jet of 3C 279 C," *The Astrophysical Journal* 581 (2002): L15–L18.

[1317] Kemp, J., et al., "Discovery of Circular Polarized Light from a White Dwarf," L77–79.

[1318] Wickramasinghe, D. T., and Lilia Ferrario, L., "Magnetism in Isolated and Binary White Dwarfs," *Publications of the Astronomical Society of the Pacific* 112 (2000): 873–924.

[1319] Schmidt, G., et al., "Combined Ultraviolet-Optical Spectropolarimetry of the Magnetic White Dwarf CD 229," *Astrophysical Journal* 463 (1996): 320–25.

[1320] Greenstein, J., et al., "Spectra of White Dwarfs with Circular Polarization," *The Astrophysical Journal* 169 (1971): L63–L69.

[1321] Greenberg, J. M. et al. "Interstellar Dust, Chirality, Comets and the Origins of Life: Life from Dead Stars?," *Journal of Biological Physics* 20 (1994): 61.

[1322] Cronin, L., and Walker, S., "Beyond Prebiotic Chemistry:What Dynamic Properties Allow the Emergence of Life," *Science* 352 (2016): 1174–75.

[1323] Rietmeijer, F., and Nuth, J., "Collected Extraterrestrial Materials: Constraints on Meteor and Fireball Compositions," *Earth, Moon, and Planets* 82–83 (2000): 325–50.

[1324] Mojzsis, S., et al., "Oxygen-isotope Evidence from Ancient Zircons for Liquid Water at the Earth's Surface 4,300 Myr Ago," *Nature* 409 (2001): 178–81.

[1325] Wilde, S., et al., "Evidence from Detrital Zircons for the Existence of Continental Crust and Oceans on the Earth 4.4 Gyr Ago," *Nature* 409 (2001): 175–78.

[1326] Delsemme, A., "The Deuterium Enrichment Observed in Recent Comets Is Consistent with the Cometary Origin of Seawater," *Planetary and Space Science* 47 (1999): 125.

[1327] Morbidelli, A., et al., "Source Regions and Time Scales for the Delivery of Water to Earth," *Meteoritics & Planetary Science* 35 (2000): 1309–20.

[1328] Wilde S., et al., "Evidence from Detrital Zircons for the Existence of Continental Crust and Oceans on the Earth 4.4 Gyr Ago," *Nature* 409 (2001): 175–78.

[1329] Farquhar, J., et al., "The Atmosphere – History," in *Treatise in Geochemistry Vol. 6*, eds. Holland, H., and Turekian, K. (New York: Pergamon Press, 2014), 91–138.

[1330] Rasmussen, B. and Buick, R. "Redox State of the Archean Atmosphere: Evidence from Detrital Heavy Minerals in Ca. 3250–2750 Ma Sandstones from the Pilbara Craton, Australia," *Geology* 27 (1999): 115–18.

[1331] Zahnle, K., et al., "The Loss of Mass-Independent Fractionation in Sulfur due to a Palaeoproterozoic Collapse of Atmospheric Methane," *Geobiology* 4 (2006): 271–83.

[1332] Tomkins, A., et al., 'Ancient Micrometeorites Suggestive of an Oxygen-Rich Archaean Upper Atmosphere," *Nature* 533 (2016): 235, doi:10.1038/nature17678. [4.5 billion to 2.5 billion years ago, the Earth's early lower atmosphere contained less than 0.001 per cent of the present-day atmospheric oxygen (O2) level. There are multiple lines of evidence for low O2 concentrations on early Earth of the atmosphere in the Archaean era. There was also an anomalous sulfur isotope ($\Delta^{33}S$) signature of pyrite (FeS2) in seafloor sediments from this period. There is also evidence from fossil micrometeorites from limestone sedimentary rock that had accumulated slowly 2.7 billion years ago, now preserved in Australia's Pilbara region. Nickle-iron metal in these cosmic spherules were partly oxidized while molten, then quench-crystallized to form spheres of interlocking dendritic crystals primarily of magnetite (Fe_3O_4), with wüstite (FeO)+metal. This strange chemistry probably originally occurred in the super-nova explosion plume].

[1333] Rudraswami, N., et al., "Refractory Metal Nuggets in Different Types of Cosmic Spherules," *Geochimica et Cosmochimica Acta* 131 (2014): 247–66.

[1334] Whitby, J., et al., "Extinct ^{129}I in Halite from a Primitive Meteorite: Evidence for Evaporite Formation in the Early Solar-system," *Science* 288 (2000): 1819–21, doi:10.1126/science.288.5472.1819.

[Scientists at the University of Manchester and the Natural History Museum in London found 4.6 billion year old salt crystals and small amounts of water in the "Monahans" and "Zag" meteorites. The "Zag" meteorite, was named for having landed near Zag, Morocco in August 1998, originally weighed around 175 kg. The Monahans meteorite landed in Texas on March 22, 1998. Both are thought to have originated from the same, larger, parent body. Halite crystals from the Zag H3-6 chondrite contain essentially pure (monoisotopic) xenon-129 (^{129}Xe), which had been produced in the early history of the solar-system by the decay of short-lived iodine-129 (^{129}I) (half-life = 15.7 million years). Correlated release of ^{129}Xe and ^{128}Xe, produced artificially from ^{127}I by neutron irradiation, corresponded to an initial (^{129}I/^{127}I) ratio of $(1.35 \pm 0.05) \times 10^{-4}$, close to the most primitive early solar-system value. If the ^{129}Xe was produced by in situ decay, then the halite formed from an aqucous fluid within 2 million years of the oldest known solar-system minerals.]

[1335] O'Neil, J., et al., "Implications of the Nuvvuagittuq Greenstone Belt for the Formation of Earth's Early Crust," *Journal of Petrology* 52 (2011): 985–1009.

[1336] Schieber, J., and Baird, G., "On the Origin and Significance of Pyrite spheres in Devonian Black Shales of North America," *Journal of Sedimentary Research* 71 (2001): 155–66.

[1337] Orgel, L., "Self-organizing Biochemical Cycles" *PNAS* 97 (2000): 12503–507.

[1338] Pace, N., "The Universal Nature of Biochemistry," *PNAS* 98 (2001): 805–8.

[1339] Bell, E., et al., "Potentially Biogenic Carbon Preserved in a 4.1 Billion-Year-Old Zircon," *Proceedings of the National Academy of Sciences of the United States of America* 112 (2015): 14518–21, doi:10.1073/pnas.1517557112; ISSN 1091-6490.

[1340] Dodd, M. S., et al., "Evidence for Early Life in Earth's Oldest Hydrothermal Vent Precipitates," *Nature* 543 (2017): 60–65, doi:10.1038/nature21377.

[1341] Yoko, O., et al., "Evidence for Biogenic Graphite in Early Archaean Isua Metasedimentary Rocks," *Nature Geoscience* 7 (2014): 25–28, doi:10.1038/ngeo2025.

[1342] Mojzsis, S., et al., "Evidence for Life on Earth before 3800 Million Years Ago," *Nature* 384 (1996): 55–59.

[1343] Rosing, M., "13C-Depleted Carbon Microparticles in >3700-Ma Sea-Floor Sedimentary Rocks from West Greenland," *Science* 283 (1999): 674.

[1344] Fedo, C., et al., "Geological Constraints on Detecting the Earliest Life on Earth: Perspective from the Early Archaean (older than 3.7Gyr)," *Philosophical Transactions of the Royal Society B* 361 (2006): 851–68.

[1345] Borenstein, S., "Scientists Find 3.7 Billion-Year-Old Fossil, Oldest Yet," August 31, 2016, http://phys.org/news/2016-08-scientists-billion-year-old-fossil-oldest.html.

[1346] Nutman, A., et al. "Rapid Emergence of Life Shown by Discovery of 3,700-Million-Year-old Microbial Structures," *Nature* 537 (2016): 535–38, doi:10.1038/nature19355.

[1347] Noffke, N., et al., "Microbially Induced Sedimentary Structures Recording an Ancient Ecosystem in the ca. 3.48 Billion-Year-Old Dresser Formation, Pilbara, Western Australia," *Astrobiology* 13 (2013): 1103–24, doi:10.1089/ast.2013.1030.

[1348] Lazcano, A., et al., "How Long Did It Take for Life to Begin and Evolve to Cyanobacteria?," *Journal of Molecular Evolution* 39 (1994): 546–54.

[1349] Olson, J., "Photosynthesis in the Archean Era," *Photosynthesis Research* 88 (2006): 109–17.

[1350] Head, I., et al., "Biological Activity in the Deep Subsurface and the Origin of Heavy Oil," *Nature* 426 (2003): 344–52.

[1351] Lowman, P., *Exploring Space Exploring Earth: New Understanding of the Earth from Space Research* (Cambridge: Cambridge University Press, 2002), 210–14.

[1352] https://en.wikipedia.org/wiki/Deepwater_Horizon.

[1353] Gold, T., "The Deep, Hot Biosphere," *Proceedings of the National Academy of Sciences of the United States of America* 89 (1992): 6045–49.

[1354] Dolfing, J., et al., "Thermodynamic Constraints on Methanogenic Crude Oil Biodegradation," *The ISME Journal* 2 (2007): 442–52, doi:10.1038/ismej.2007.111.

[1355] Head, I. M., et al., "Biological Activity in the Deep Subsurface and the Origin of Heavy Oil," *Nature* 426 (2003): 344–52, doi:10.1038/nature02134.

[1356] Parkes, R., et al., "Deep Bacterial Biosphere in Pacific Ocean Sediments," *Nature* 371 (1994): 410–13.

[1357] Whitman, W., et al., "Prokaryotes: The Unseen Majority," *Proceedings of the National Academy of Sciences of the United States of America* 95 (1998): 6578–83.

[1358] Lawton, T., and Rosenzweig, A., "Methane Make It or Break It," *Science* 352 (2016): 892–93.

[1359] Inagaki, F., "Exploring Deep Microbial Life in Coal-Bearing Sediment Down to ~2.5 km Below the Ocean Floor," *Science* 349 (2015): 420–24.

[1360] Lane, N., and Martin, W., "The Origin of Membrane Bioenergetics," *Cell* 151 (2012): 1406–16.

[1361] [Generally present day cells have a specific sodium/potassium partion: potassium levels of 150 mM K+ inside cells, compared to 10 mM K+ outside cells, and sodium levels of 40 mM inside cells, compared to 400 mM Na+ outside. For comparison; Sea-water is 480mM Na+ and 10mM K+.]

[1362] Mulkidjaniana, A., et al., "Origin of First Cells at Terrestrial, Anoxic Geothermal Fields," *Proceedings of the National Academy of Sciences of the United States of America* 109 (2012): E821–E830, doi:10.1073. pnas.1117774109.

[1363] News: Russian hot springs point to rocky origins for life, https://www.newscientist.com/article/dn21471-russian-hot-springs-point-to-rocky-origins-for-life/.

[1364] Auchtung T., et al., "16S rRNA Phylogenetic Analysis and Quantification of Korarchaeota Indigenous to the Hot Springs of Kamchatka, Russia," *Extremophiles* 15 (2011): 105–16, doi:10.1007/s00792-010-0340-5.

[1365] Reigstad, L., et al., "Diversity and Abundance of Korarchaeota in Terrestrial Hot Springs of Iceland and Kamchatka," *ISME Journal* 4 (2010): 346–56, doi:10.1038/ismej.2009.126.

[1366] Barns, S., et al., "Perspectives on Archaeal Diversity, Thermophily and Monophyly from Environmental rRNA Sequences," *Proceedings of the National Academy of Sciences of the United States of America* 93 (1996): 9188–93. Bibcode:1996PNAS...93.9188B, doi:10.1073/pnas.93.17.9188.

[1367] Seitz, K., et al., "Genomic Reconstruction of a Novel, Deeply Branched Sediment Archaeal Phylum with Pathways for Acetogenesis and Sulfur Reduction," *ISME Journal* 10 (2016): 1696–705, doi:10.1038/ismej.2015.233.

[1368] Bloche, E., et al., "Reactions Depending on Iron Sulphide and Linking Geochemistry with Biochemistry," *PNAS* 89 (1992): 8117–20.

[1369] Russell, M., and Martin, W. "The Rocky Roots of the Acetyl-CoA Pathway," *Trends in Biochemical Sciences* 29, no. 7 (2004): 358–63.

[1370] Chen, I., and Walde, P., "From Self-Assembled Vesicles to Protocells," *Cold Spring Harbor Perspectives in Biology* 2 (2010): a002170, doi: 10.1101/cshperspect.a002170.

[1371] Deamer, D., et al., "The First Cell Membranes," *Astrobiology* 2 (2002): 371–82.

[1372] Pace, N., "The Universal Nature of Biochemistry," *PNAS* 98 (2001): 805–8.

[1373] Dodd, M. S., et al., "Evidence for Early Life in Earth's Oldest Hydrothermal Vent Precipitates," Nature 543 (2017): 60-65. doi:10.1038/nature21377

[1374] The basic pre-life chemical-reaction which transformed into metabolism had the following basic pathway:
$R1-C=C-R2 + H_2S + H_2O + H+$ (intracellular) $\rightarrow$ $H-S-CO-CH_3 + R1-H + H-R2$.

[1375] Haroon, M., "Anaerobic Oxidation of Methane Coupled to Nitrate Reduction in a Novel Archaeal Lineage," *Nature* 500 (2013): 567–70, doi:10:1038/nature12375.

[1376] Mayer, F., and Muller, V.,"Adaptations of Anaerobic Archaea to Life Under Extreme Energy Limitation," *FEMS Microbiology Reviews* 38 (2014): 449–72, doi:10.1111/1574-6976.12043.

[1377] Fuchs, G., "Alternative Pathways of Carbon Dioxide Fixation: Insights into the Early Evolution of Life?," *Annual Review of Microbiology* 65 (2011): 631–58, doi:10.1146/annurev-micro-090110-102801.

[1378] Knoll, A., et al., "Life: The First Two Billion Years," *Philosophical Transactions of the Royal Society B* 371 (2016): 20150493. http://dx.doi.org/10.1098/rstb.2015.0493.

[1379] Wongnate, T., "The Radical Mechanism of Biological Methane Syntheis by Methy-Coenzme M Reductase," *Science* 352 (2016): 953–58.

[1380] Eady, R., Robson, R., and Postgate, J., "Vanadium Puts Nitrogen in a Fix," *New Scientist* 114 (1987): 59.

[1381] Blochl, E., et al., "Reactions Depending on Iron Sulfide and Linking Geochemistry with Biochemistry," *PNAS* 89 (1992): 8117–120.

[1382] Gold, T., *The Deep Hot Biosphere* (New York: Copernicus, 1999).

[1383] Hall, A., "Pyrite-pyrrhotine Redox Reactions in Nature," *Mineralogical Magazine* 50 (1986): 223–29.

[1384] Pasek, M., "Rethinking Early Earth Phosphorus Geochemistry," *PNAS* 105 (2008): 853–58. La-Cruz, N., "The Evolution of the Surface of the Mineral Schreibersite in Prebiotic Chemistry," *Physical Chemistry Chemical Physics* 18 (2016): 20160–167, doi:10.1039/C6CP00836D.

[1385] La-Cruz, N., "The Evolution of the Surface of the Mineral Schreibersite in Prebiotic Chemistry," *Physical Chemistry Chemical Physics* 18 (2016): 20160–167, doi:10.1039/C6CP00836D.

[1386] Schwartz, A., "Phosphorus in Prebiotic Chemistry," *Philosophical Transactions of the Royal Society B* 361 (2006): 1743–49, doi:10.1098/rstb.2006.1901.

[1387] Jordan, I., et al., "A Universal Trend of Amino Acid Gain and Loss in Protein Evolution," *Nature* 433 (2005): 633–38.

[1388] Seitz, K., et al., "Genomic Reconstruction of a Novel, Deeply Branched Sediment Archaeal Phylum with Pathways for Acetogenesis and Sulfur Reduction," *ISME Journal* 10 (2016): 1696–705, doi:10.1038/ismej.2015.233.

[1389] News "Archaea Revealed from Genomes," *Nature* 530 (2016): 9.

[1390] Elkins, J., et al., "A Korarchaeal Genome Reveals Insights into the Evolution of the Archaea," *Proceedings of the National Academy of Sciences of the United States of America* 105 (2008): 8805–6, doi:10.1073/pnas.0801980105.

[1391] Ralser, M., "The RNA World and the Origin of Metabolic Enzymes," *Biochemical Society Transactions* 42 (2014): 985–88.

[1392] Fuchs, G., and Stupperich, E., "Evolution of Autotrophic CO_2 Fixation," *Evolution of Prokaryotes*, eds. Schleifer, K. and Stackebrandt,

E. FEMS Symposium No. 29 (London: Academic Press, 1985), 235–51.

[1393] Ljungdahl, L., "A Life with Acetogens, Thermophiles, and Cellulolytic Anaerobes," *Annual Review of Microbiology* 63 (2009): 1–25.

[1394] Ragsdale, S., and Pierce, E., "Acetogenesis and the Wood-Ljungdahl Pathway of CO2 Fixation," *Biochimica et Biophysica Acta* 1784 (2008): 1873–98.

[1395] [An ancient reaction step was Acetyl CoA + phosphate (P) → acetyl P, the forerunner of ATP].

[1396] Orgel, L. E. and Crick, F. H. "Anticipating an RNA World Some Past Speculations on the Origin of Life: Where Were They Today?," *The FASEB Journal* 7, no. 1 (1993): 238–39.

[1397] Leslie, E., Orgel, L., and Crick, F., "The RNA World on Ice: A New Scenario for the Emergence of RNA Information," *Journal of Molecular Evolution* 61 (2005): 264–73.

[1398] Nelson, K., et al., "Peptide Nucleic Acids Rather than RNA May Had Been the First Genetic Molecule," *PNAS* 97 (2000): 3868–71.

[1399] Zhaxybayea, O., and Gogarten, J., "Cladogenesis, Coalescence and the Evolution of the Three Domains of Life," *Trends in Genetics* 20 (2004): 182–87.

[1400] Lane, N., et al., "How Did LUCA Make a Living? Chemiosmosis in the Origin of Life," *BioEssays* 32 (2010): 271–80.

[1401] "Size Limits of Very Small Microorganisms" (*Proceedings of a Workshop Space Studies Board, Commission on Physical Sciences, Mathematics and*

Applications, National Research Council (Washington, DC: Natl. Acad. Press, 1999).

[1402] Weiss, M., et al., "The Physiology and Habitat of the Last Universal Common Ancestor," *Nature Microbiology* 1 (2016): Article number: 16116, doi:10.1038/nmicrobiol.2016.116.

[1403] Lane, N., *The Vital Question: Why Is Life the Way It Is?* (London: Profile Books Ltd., 2015).

[1404] Hand, E., "A New Giant Planet, Still Unseen, Appears to Be Shaping the Orbits of Objects Beyond Neptune," *Science* 351 (2016): 330–33.

[1405] Batygin, K., and Brown, M., "Evidence for a Distant Giant Planet in the Solar-system," *The Astronomical Journal* 151 (2016): 1–12, doi:10.3847/0004-6256/151/2/22.

[1406] www.findplanetnine.com/p/blog-page.html.

[1407] Relative angular momentum of 'planet-9':
Angular Momentum (L) = Mass × angular velocity × distance (from the Sun)
Angular momentum (L) of Earth revolution = 2.7×10^{40} kg m^2 s-1
Angular momentum (L) of the Sun rotation = 1.1×10^{42} kg m^2 s-1
Angular momentum (L) of 'planet-9' revolution (@ average radius 700 AU, 10 Earth masses)
= 1.9×10^{44} kg m^2 s-1

[1408] Mustill, A., et al., 'Is There an Exo-Planet in the Solar-System?," eprint arXiv:1603.07247 (2016).

[1409] [Niku, (2011 KT19) has since been assigned the code 471325 by the I AU's Minor Planet Center]

[1410] Chen, Y.-T., et al., "Discovery Of A New Retrograde Trans-Neptunian Object: Hint of a Common Orbital Plane for Low Semi-Major Axis, High Inclination TNOs and Centaurs," arXiv:1608.01808v1 [astro-ph.EP] August 5, 2016.

[1411] [Comparison of orbital elements of Niku and Star-Core-Zeus:
Niku: i=110, Star-Core-Zeus: i=113
Compare Niku to Star-Core
Mean distance = 26 AU, 262 AU
Semi-Major axis (a) = 36 AU, 250 AU
(Aphelion to Perhelion distance) = Approximately 72 AU, 500 AU
Eccentricity (e) = 0.3336, 0.9969
Inclination (i) = 110.3, 113.5
An inclination greater than 90° = retrograde
Ascending Node = 244, 82 (sum 326)
Arg of Pericentre = 322.6, 138
Mean Anolamaly (L) = 326.6]

[1412] Mann, A., "Hunt for Planet Nine Heats Up," *Science* 354 (2016): 399–400.

[1413] Sheppard, S., and Trujillo, C., "New Extreme Trans-Neptunian Objects: Towards a Super-Earth in the Outersolar-system," arXiv:1608.08772v5 [astro-ph.EP] September 12, 2016.

[1414] Batygin, K., and Brown, M., "Generation of Highly Inclined Trans-Neptunian Objects by Planet Nine," arXiv:1610.04992v1 [astro-ph.EP] October 17, 2016.

22473265R10310

Printed in Great Britain
by Amazon